The Bible and Constitution

Made America Great

By Providing Freedom and Liberty to Citizens

Scot Wolf

The Bible and Constitution Made America Great
By Providing Freedom and Liberty to Citizens.

Copyright © 2014 by Scot Wolf. All rights reserved. No part of this book may be used or reproduced in any manner whatsoever without written permission, except in the case of quotations embodied in critical articles and reviews.

SGW Book Partners

First edition

Produced in the United States of America

Library of Congress Control Number: 2015900235

ISBN: 978-0-9909237-1-8

Heavenly Father, Lord God Almighty, may the words in this book please You. May the citizens of America turn to You of their own free will which You have graciously given; recognizing Your power and righteousness. Amen.

Front Cover: America as a great nation is represented by its flag and a majestic eagle, its national symbol. The nation stands on its foundation of the Bible and the Constitution. The Bible shown is the Aitken Bible, the first to be printed in colonial America. The Constitution was written in 1787.

This book is dedicated to the brave men and women who have served in America's armed forces, from the Revolutionary War to today's War on Terror. They have fought and sacrificed so the rest of us may remain free to enjoy our liberties.

A special thanks to Kathy Pasco who assisted greatly in proofing and editing and Pastor Russ Bowder who checked scriptural content.

Chapters:
1. Introduction 1
2. Free Will from God, Liberty from Government 11
3. Creation and Evolution: Two Competing Theories 29
4. God's Death Penalty 79
5. The Bible on Holy War 93
6. The Old Testament Government Established by God 103
7. God's New Covenant 131
8. The Rich and The Poor 147
9. Taxation in the Bible 173
10. America's Religious Christian Heritage 183
11. Religion and Choice in Schools 215
12. US Constitution 235
13. Freedom of Religion - First Amendment 263
14. Judges and Senators 277
15. Abortion in the Bible and Constitution 301
16. Homosexuality and Marriage 311
17. Slavery in the Bible and America 343
18. Immigration and The American Ideal 367
19. The Federal Government's Financial Crisis 399
20. The Solution: Return to The Constitution 441
21. Health Care Cost Crisis and Solution 471
22. Social Security 491
23. Political Bias in the News Media 509
24. Christians No Longer Welcome in Democrat Party 543
25. Federal Elections: Return to the Constitution 565
26. Summary 589

Appendices:
Appendix 1: County and State Re-Alignment 603
Appendix 2: Kings of Judah 607
Appendix 3: Biblical Genealogies from Shem to Abram 609
Appendix 4: Biblical Genealogies from Noah to Adam 611
Appendix 5: Education Spending Per Student by State 613
Appendix 6: Senate Vote to Confirm Kagan to Supreme Court 614
Appendix 7: US Census Data on Immigrants 616
Appendix 8: Immigration Made California a Big Government
             Democrat Party State 618
Appendix 9: State Gasoline Taxes 621
Appendix 10: US Government Agencies 622
Appendix 11: Defunding Agencies and Government Shutdowns ... 632
Appendix 12: Federal Government Abuse of Freedoms 634

Bibliography – Resources – References 644

Introduction

Never has the world seen a nation as great as the United States of America. The nation has been home to numerous inventors and inventions that greatly increased the standard of living for the citizens of nation and the world. No longer do America's citizens spend most of their time working just to put food on the table. Salaries are spent on incredible electronic items, entertainment, amazing travel opportunities, or healthcare treatments that were unavailable to even the richest people on earth in previous centuries. America's poor often live better than the middle classes of other nations. The prosperity is the result of freedom for the citizens. Freedom is the secret to America's greatness and success.

The source of this freedom can be found in the two works that most shaped America: The Bible and The US Constitution. America's founders followed the God of the Bible and adhered to biblical teaching. They used many biblical principles in founding the nation and drafting its Constitution. As long as their principles are followed, America will continue to be successful. Look at the similarities between the Bible and the Constitution:

- Both recognize an Almighty God who created the universe.
- Both prescribe liberty and freedom for the people.
- Both call for a small central (national) government, with as many issues as possible being settled at the local level.
- Both recognize the societal need for a moral people that will help each other when in need while being willing to work to support themselves.

America's founders grasped one of the key biblical tenets – God-given free will. God made humans free to do whatever they desire. Unfortunately this results in both good and evil. This includes the choice to follow and worship God (or not), to love your neighbor (or not), and to respect your neighbors property (or not). These God-given freedoms can be taken away, for example when one man steals from, or murders another. The founders realized that the role of government was to prevent these types of infringements. To protect the God-given freedoms for all citizens. The freedom to pursue life, liberty, and happiness any way the citizen desires, as long as he does not interfere with another's freedom to do the same. When people have freedom, and are secure knowing that their lives and property are both protected, they will thrive. The result is the greatest nation the world has ever seen.

The founders distinguished between their faith and their government. America has never been a theocracy, a government with an official religion. This would take away freedom of the citizens to choose their religion and how they worshiped God. Both the Constitution and Bible should play important roles in society, but those roles differ.

Societal Roles for the Constitution and Bible
- The Bible - A guide for the life of the individual
- The Constitution - Rules for the national government established by the people

The Bible, being dictated by God, has shaped all humanity more than any other work. For a follower of God, the Bible is the guide for life and trumps all other ideologies. It forms the cornerstone of the Christian and Jewish (Old Testament) religions. The Bible explains how the Earth and man came to exist (created by God) and provides a narrative of human history from its inception. It details the plan God followed to redeem humanity from sin by sending a Savior. This is the main purpose of the Bible. Jesus rose from the dead in order to offer salvation to all mankind. People have free will to believe this miracle happened, or not believe it. Same with the other miracles described in the Bible.

Sidebar: Humans are free to dismiss the early chapters of Genesis, but in doing so they eliminate the reason for the rest of the Bible. Without the beginning of the story, the end won't make sense. There is no reason or need for Abraham, God's nation of ancient Israel, or even Christ, the Savior, if the first part of Genesis is removed.

The Bible shows God's Will for how humans should live (Love God...; Love your neighbor...). It is a governing document for the individuals, churches or other organizations who choose to follow it. God does not force humans to follow His desires as spelled out in

Introduction

the Bible. Nor should Christians try to force others to follow. It violates free will. *Use of force* is a key theme throughout this book. Anytime a person is forced to do something, their freedom is restricted. The Constitution was written to limit the use of force by the federal government.

The US Constitution follows many of the suggestions the Bible offers for society. Not surprising, since its authors were students of the Bible and knew it well. From the Pilgrims to the Founders, the Bible played an enormous role in American society. The Founders attempted to form a society where the government would use force only to protect the God-given rights of "life, liberty and the pursuit of happiness."

The Constitution is the governing document for the federal government. It is the rulebook the government must follow. The Founders were each representatives of one of the original thirteen colonies that won independence from England. State representatives wrote the Constitution, and the states ratified it to make it the governing document of the land. Today, it is sometimes glossed over that our nation is the United *States* of America. The states united to form a nation because they considered it beneficial to do so. They ceded certain powers to the federal government and kept others for themselves. New states pledged to uphold the Constitution upon being granted statehood. Elected representatives in the federal government swear to uphold the Constitution as do members of the military. The US Constitution is the supreme law of the land.

America has undergone a silent political revolution over the last 80 years. During this time the federal government began to ignore key components of the Constitution (and the Bible). The revolution has dramatically changed the country and removed a large degree of freedom from citizens. America now needs a peaceful counter-revolution, or reformation, to return to founding principles.

<u>Reformation of Government</u>
It is human nature for good worthy organizations to become corrupt over time and veer away from their intended purpose. The Bible presents numerous examples of the kings of Israel moving away

from the government God desired - and a few kings who repented and returned to governing according to God's plan. The Christian Church became corrupted by non-biblical teachings over time. A number of leaders (Luther, Calvin, Tyndale and many others) stepped forward to reform the church, and return it to a foundation of God's true teachings. The US Government now needs a similar reformation. It has abandoned many of the core principles of the Constitution – the rules it is supposed to govern by.

Foundational freedoms were built into the Constitution. They are best captured in the Bill of Rights. The first of which is freedom of religion and the press. This prevents the federal government from interfering in citizen's lives. The federal government has no more right to ban prayer at a public event, than it has the right to ban a newspaper or TV channel from the public. Prayer and other decisions are left up to the organizers of the event's itinerary. One person being offended by prayer is no different than one person being offended by the content of a media organization. The government simply cannot ban either.

Once the government ignores or violates one freedom, it becomes much easier to ignore others. Freedom of religion, freedom to own guns (bear arms), and freedom to conduct business as one desires (commerce) are the freedoms most often targeted for abuse. But if these can be abused, why not the right to a jury trial, or the right to not have police invade your home without a court warrant? The ignoring of one right can quickly lead to the ignoring of multiple rights. The metaphorical slippery slope.

States have lost the freedom to govern as they wish within the boundaries of the Constitution. Today's federal government tramples all over states. They collect much more money (40% maximum tax rate vs 13% top state tax rate) than the states. They use this money to manage areas that should be the domain of the states: Education, great quantities of land, housing programs, food programs, agriculture programs, and energy programs. The list goes on and on. These programs all have copious regulations that citizens and states must follow.

What difference does it make if the federal government runs these

Introduction

programs instead of states? First, it is a violation of the Constitution. Second, the federal government is notoriously inefficient and wasteful. Thirdly, and most importantly, not all citizens want every aspect of their lives regulated and controlled by government. If states perform the bulk of the government duties, citizens can chose the state government that best suites them. This freedom is especially needed in present times where the nation is deeply divided.

America Overcoming Crises
America did not become a great nation by chance. People fought to create the nation and to keep it strong. Several specific national crises greatly altered the course of the nation. Every time pro-freedom forces prevailed.

- The Revolutionary War determined whether America would become an independent nation of liberty or a vassal colony to England.
- The Civil War decided whether America would continue to exist as a single nation. It also finally abolished slavery, liberating an entire class of people.
- During World War II, America defeated two authoritarian imperialist nations, Germany and Japan. These nations had both initiated wars of conquest before declaring war on America. The victory cemented America's position as a world power, a pro-freedom power.

The book, *The Fourth Turning*, notes these crises happened approximately 80 years apart. It also predicts America will undergo a new crisis as it approaches the next 80 year mark. The next crisis will almost certainly involve the size, scope and power of the federal government. The federal government has assumed powers well beyond that authorized by the Constitutional, with the result of reduced freedom for its citizens. Both economic and religious freedom have been harmed.

In the case of the Civil War, the crisis resulted from unresolved issues from an earlier crisis. After the Revolution, the dominant objective became forming a national government from the thirteen independent colonies. A number of founders wanted to abolish slavery in the Constitution, but sadly some states rejected this. The issue of slavery was left to simmer until it erupted into the Civil War. Likewise the Great Depression just before World War II sowed the seeds for the next crisis. The economic distress during the Depression (arguably extended in America by government), led to a series of federal government programs to "fix" the economy. These programs were the first major attempt by the federal government to manage the free-market economy, and were not constitutional. The federal government attempted to dictate how much of certain items citizens could produce, regulate wages, and "stimulate" the economy with government spending. Of course, the government had to greatly increase taxes to pay for these programs and the bureaucratic administrators.

The level of federal government intrusiveness dropped significantly at the close of the War, but then resumed an increasing trend-line toward greater and greater control and intrusion. One can see the next crisis brewing as Americans attempt to regain their freedoms from an usurping federal government. This will hopefully be a peaceful political battle, as opposed to the other crises which became wars.

Look what is transpiring: Ranchers in western states oppose the federal government controlling land that belongs to their state. Tea Party movements, word-playing on the Boston Tea Party, have begun to rally against big-government. The IRS targets political groups it does not like. Libertarians have become angry and distressed at the government monitoring their phones and social media websites. Churches are finding it difficult to follow their religious beliefs with respect to abortion, as an increasingly secular federal government tries to force them to accept the practice. The federal government struggles to keep the multitude of promises it has made to citizens. As more and more citizens cease working and begin collecting benefits, the government will run low on funds.

America is increasingly dominated by two opposing belief systems. One system wants the government to provide jobs, healthcare, food and housing to the citizens. It also dictates how people live, what kind of cars can be driven, what kind of energy can be produced,

Introduction

how land can be used, and even the types of lightbulbs that can be bought. It also believes it "owns" the incomes of citizens and can take as much as it wants or needs. The other belief system wants the government to leave citizens alone to live their lives. The government should be used only to protect the nation and citizens from being attacked. These belief systems are not compatible with each other. A crisis is bound to occur as these systems clash.

This crisis will go to the very heart of what America is. What laws, if any will be followed, and who will follow them. What does law-following have to do with it? As was stated earlier, the Constitution is the supreme law of the nation. If its provisions are not followed, why should any law be followed? What if citizens decide to arbitrarily ignore laws they do not agree with like tax law? The nation cannot survive if citizens in-mass suddenly stop complying with tax law and paying their taxes. Anarchy will ensue. A strong nation needs fair laws that are willingly followed by the citizens.

A Constitutional Federal Government: Averting the Crisis for a Divided Nation

The way to avert this crisis is right in front of the nation. It is called the US Constitution. The Constitution gives each state the latitude to follow the belief system their citizens desire. Whether it be the big-government liberal belief, or the limited government conservative belief, or some new way yet to be tried.

There is no longer any need for conservatives and liberals to have endless back and forth arguments on which government policies are best for the economy: high or low tax rates; heavy or light regulation; business subsidies or no subsidies; welfare or workfare. States will be able to design government policy on each of these areas that best suit their citizens. It will be apparently easy to see which policies work best from examining the results in the states. It is entirely possible that different Americans will prefer different policies and consider theirs "more successful". Americans will have the freedom to vote with their feet and move to states having policies they prefer. Using the Constitution, and its state-centric approach, the arguments change. For example:

- Does high government taxation and spending/investment drive economic growth and prosperity? Becomes: Is it beneficial for my state to tax and invest in this business?
- Which energy sources (solar, wind, nuclear, oil, coal...) are best for both present and future needs? Becomes: Will my state be better off pushing one type of energy over another?
- Should abortion be legal? Becomes: Should the citizens of a state make abortion legal?
- Should the government provide healthcare?
  Becomes: Should the citizens of my state provide healthcare for its citizens.
- Is it wise to legalize marijuana? Becomes: Is it wise for a state to legalize marijuana in that state?

The answer is likely to vary state by state. In each of these areas, the Constitution places the governmental responsibility at the state or local level. Chapter 20 lays out a plan to more permanently return the federal government to its original limited role in America, by following the Constitution. Briefly, the federal government is prevented from performing many functions is does today if the 10th Amendment is followed. Move these functions down the government responsibility chain to the states.

This solution will require a massive transfer of authority, power, and resources from the federal government to the state governments. If the nation acts soon, there can be a several year period where those responsibilities, agencies and programs can be transferred, including initial funding, in an orderly manner. At present there is ample revenue for the federal government to help states during the transition. This may not be the case if the nation continues on its current course for too much longer.

This book is also an excellent reference book. It captures key teachings of the Bible and Constitution on a number of issues, beginning with the next chapter on free will. Chapter 3 examines creation and evolution. Chapter 4 explores the biblical view of death as a punishment from God. Chapter 5 contrasts the biblical holy war in the book of Joshua with jihad. The next 4 chapters

Introduction

review covenants between God and man, the poor, and taxes. Chapters 10 and 11 review America's religious heritage and religion in schools. The next two chapters focus on the Constitution and freedom of religion. Chapter 14 shows how Presidents and US Senators are responsible for the courts straying from the Constitution. The next 4 chapters cover the issues of abortion, homosexuality, slavery, and immigration. Chapters 19 and 20 go into detail on the financial crisis being caused by the federal government and the solution. Chapters 21 and 22 give special attention to healthcare and Social Security. Chapter 23 documents news bias in the media and its affect on elections. Chapter 24 explores the hostility of the Democrat party to Christians who follow the Bible. Chapter 25 details a voting strategy to return the nation to its constitutional foundation.

Free Will from God, Liberty from Government

> Freedom prospers when religion is vibrant and the rule of law under God is acknowledged.
> - President Ronald Reagan. March 8, 1983 Speech.

God gave each of us free will beginning with the first humans, Adam and Eve.

> *Genesis 2:16-17 And the LORD God commanded the man, "You are free to eat from any tree in the garden; but you must not eat from the tree of the knowledge of good and evil, for when you eat from it you will certainly die."*

Adam and Eve had a choice that God clearly explained. They had free will to eat from the tree or not eat from the tree, but with free will came consequences. Adam and Eve had to pay for their decision to eat the forbidden fruit – their decision led to their deaths.

Sidebar: While humans have the free will to believe events in *Genesis* never happened, these events represent key teachings from God, and place the rest of the Bible in proper context. The *Genesis* narrative explains a concept many humans struggle with: God's fairness. God, the Creator, made the rule that if humans sin, they die an earthly death. He never promised humans 70 years of life, in good health, before that death. Because of sin, every human is living on borrowed time while on earth. More on this in Chapter 4.

From Adam and Eve forward each human has had the God-given right to choose to be as evil as Adolf Hitler, as saintly as Mother Theresa, or anywhere in between. Not all humans follow God's teachings or desires for humanity, of course. Free will given by God also allows humans to enslave fellow humans or mistreat them in other ways. This is not the will of God, however, anymore than God wanted Adam to eat from the forbidden tree, or Cain to kill Abel. Free will allows humans to do things that greatly displease God. Slavery and abortion, perfect societal examples of this, are discussed in detail in later chapters.

Why would God give humans the ability to do evil, as part of their free will? Here is one example that pet owners can relate to: You want a pet and have a choice. You can buy a perfectly behaved dog who happens to be a stuffed animal, or you can buy a puppy from a breeder. The stuffed dog is so much easier! It will never chew on any of your favorite possessions, will never pee or poop on the rug, and will never bark. It perfectly obeys you. Unfortunately, it can never love you the way a real dog can. So you buy the real dog, try to teach it right from wrong, and forgive it when it disobeys you.

God has given each human free will. Even to the point of humans, His creations, being able to choose whether or not to believe in Him. Humans are free to claim there is no God. Many have done so now and in the past. Humans may decide to worship God, or to mock God. Jesus endured this torture personally during his trial. Soldiers mocked and hit Him.

> *Matthew 27:29-31 and then twisted together a crown of thorns and set it on His head. They put a staff in His right hand. Then they knelt in front of Him and mocked Him. "Hail, king of the Jews!" they said. They spit on Him, and took the staff and struck Him on the head again and again. After they had mocked Him, they took off the robe and put His own clothes on Him. Then they led Him away to crucify Him.*

How humiliating for an all-powerful God to put up with this. Forgetting the physical torture, how many humans would tolerate being verbally mocked when they could easily prove themselves to be correct. Yet God allows humans, His creations, to mock Him. He gives them free will to do so. Those who choose to mock God aren't hurting God; they are hurting themselves. One assumes that the mocking saddens God greatly, but it doesn't hurt Him.

Sidebar: This doesn't mean that a Christian should stand idly by and listen to modern-day mockers. Christians have the free will to verbally defend their God. Many chapters of this book attempt to do just that. Christians may choose to leave the presence of those who mock God. If a magazine or TV show mocks God, tune it out, cancel your subscription, or complain to the authors/producers/networks. Realize that mockers have the ability to stand on the proverbial street corner and mock God, just as a Christian can stand there and preach the Gospel. At least this is so in nations where the

Free Will from God, Liberty from Government

government protects citizens' free speech.

God teaches through the Bible that because of decisions to sin, all people face eternal damnation away from God's presence – the worst punishment possible. Very serious consequences indeed. God sent a Savior to prevent this. It is up to each person to accept God's offer or ignore it, using their free will. Every human determines their actions and decides their beliefs. If God wanted forced belief, He could have simply created humans as puppets. It is not God's will to force a person into belief. Humans have God-given free will and the ability to reject God and God's teachings, but God hopes all humans will learn the truth about God, follow His ways and be saved.

> *1 Timothy 2:3-6 This is good, and pleases God our Savior, who wants all people to be saved and to come to a knowledge of the truth. For there is one God and one mediator between God and mankind, the man Christ Jesus, who gave himself as a ransom for all people. This has now been witnessed to at the proper time.*

God gave free will and wants humans to live in freedom. Only government, or other humans, can take away this freedom. The following passages refer specifically to God's law for ancient Israel where citizen servants were to be given freedom after their time of service had expired.

> *Leviticus 25:10 Consecrate the fiftieth year and* **proclaim liberty** *throughout the land to all its inhabitants.*

> *Isaiah 61:1-2 The Spirit of the Sovereign LORD is on me, because the LORD has anointed me to proclaim good news to the poor. He has sent me to bind up the brokenhearted,* **to proclaim freedom** *for the captives and release from darkness for the prisoners, to proclaim the year of the LORD's favor.*

> *Jeremiah 34:17 Therefore, this is what the LORD says: You have not obeyed me; you have not* **proclaimed freedom** *for your fellow countrymen.*

David, recognized as the greatest king of ancient Israel, sums up what a follower of God should do and can achieve:

> *Psalm 119:43-47 Never take your word of truth from my mouth, for I have put my hope in your laws. I will always obey your law, for ever and ever. I will **walk about in freedom, for I have sought out your precepts.** I will speak of your statutes before kings and will not be put to shame, for I delight in your commands because I love them.*

David strove to obey God's commands. Following God's law and His will should lead to freedom. Notice how David proudly tells foreign rulers about God – he apparently was a very powerful witness for the Lord.

The tenants of free will and freedom continue in the New Testament. Jesus reads Isaiah 61 and claims he has fulfilled the promise.

> *Luke 4:16-21 [Jesus]went to Nazareth, where he had been brought up, and on the Sabbath day he went into the synagogue, as was his custom. He stood up to read, and the scroll of the prophet Isaiah was handed to him. Unrolling it, he found the place where it is written:*
>> *"The Spirit of the Lord is on me, because he has anointed me to proclaim good news to the poor. He has sent me to **proclaim freedom** for the prisoners and recovery of sight for the blind, to set the oppressed free, to proclaim the year of the Lord's favor."*
>
> *Then he rolled up the scroll, gave it back to the attendant and sat down. The eyes of everyone in the synagogue were fastened on him. He began by saying to them, "Today this scripture is fulfilled in your hearing."*

Jesus is talking about freedom from sin and death in addition to the healing miracles He performed. Earthly death will still come to us, but Jesus offers freedom through eternal life after our earthly death.

The Apostle Paul continues to proclaim freedom in several of his epistles.

> *Romans 8:20-21 For the creation was subjected to frustration, not by its own choice, but by the will of the one who subjected it, in hope that the creation itself will be liberated from its bondage to decay and **brought into the freedom** and glory of the children of God.*

> *2 Corinthians 3:17 Now the Lord is the Spirit, and where the Spirit of the Lord is, there is **freedom**.*

> *Ephesians 3:12 In Him [Jesus] and through faith in Him we may approach God with **freedom** and confidence.*

James, the brother of Jesus, and an early church leader in Jerusalem, also discusses freedom. James proclaims that God's law, if it is followed, leads to freedom for the follower. Confirming God's intent for followers to live in earthly freedom.

> *James 1:25 But whoever looks intently into the perfect law that gives **freedom**, and continues in it—not forgetting what they have heard, but doing it—they will be blessed in what they do.*

> *James 2:12 Speak and act as those who are going to be judged by the law that gives **freedom**,*

Peter, one of Jesus Apostles, and another early church leader reminds us that we should not use our earthly freedom to sin or commit evil. Responsibility comes with freedom.

> *1 Peter 2:16* **Live as free people**, *but do not use your freedom as a cover-up for evil; live as God's slaves.*

The Bible's historical narratives are full of human beings acting out their free will. Many following God's wishes – many choosing not to. God's teaching is for us to live in freedom while choosing to follow His guidelines for out lives.

Free Will to be a Christian
In America you have free will to choose whether to be a Christian or not. This right of free will is given by God, and not taken away by the government (unlike some totalitarian regimes around the world which dictate faith). In an ABC News poll, 83% of Americans claimed Christianity as their faith. If you are a Christian and attend a church you likely recite the Apostles Creed, dating back to the early church, which summarizes the Christian faith.

> Apostles Creed
> I believe in God, the Father Almighty, maker of heaven and earth.
>
> And in Jesus Christ, His only Son, our Lord, who was conceived by the Holy Spirit, born of the virgin Mary, suffered under Pontius Pilate, was crucified, died and was buried. He descended into hell. The third day He rose again from the dead. He ascended into heaven and sits at the right hand of God the Father Almighty. From thence He will come to judge the living and the dead.
>
> I believe in the Holy Spirit, the holy Christian Church, the communion of saints, the forgiveness of sins, the resurrection of the body, and the life everlasting. Amen.

Notice the creed uses "I". It is a declaration of what the individual believes. The creed is used by most if not all Christian denominations. The founders of America were also Christians who attended church and recited this creed. Chapter 10 reviews the religious heritage that the founders left America.

Notice, too, that the reciter states a belief that God created the heaven and earth and that God is all powerful. This powerful God also performs the miracle of resurrecting our bodies after death. In fact, you cannot be a Christian unless you believe in the miracle of Jesus Christ's resurrection after being crucified on the cross, which the Church celebrates as Easter every year. By definition a Christian believes in this miracle. The science of man cannot explain Jesus' resurrection or the creation of the earth.

> Sidebar: Historical Evidence
> Jesus' death and resurrection should not be taken on blind

faith. There is ample historical evidence to show that these events actually happened. The most compelling evidence is Jesus' empty tomb. The tomb had been guarded by Roman soldiers at the request of the Jewish leaders. The soldiers faced the death penalty for allowing Jesus' body to disappear, so it's not likely they were willing participants in a hoax or deception attempt.

Josh McDowell is just one of the people throughout history who have examined the factual foundation of the Christian religion. He lays out the evidence for and against Jesus' Resurrection in Chapter 9 of *More Than A Carpenter*.

"I was unable to explain away the fact that Jesus' Resurrection was a real event in history," states Professor McDowell. After spending more than 700 hours studying the subject and thoroughly investigating its foundation.... (p85).

More Than A Carpenter is a powerful book, but it won't take 700 hours to read. It can be read in an afternoon, and is a great way to begin to examine the facts regarding the foundation of the Christian religion. The author encourages readers to act like a judge, by examining the facts, then making their own personally informed decision. - the author.

Every human has the free will (from God) to choose to examine the factual foundation of the Bible or not. Same with Jesus' Resurrection, the biblical account of Creation (next chapter), the other miracles in the Bible, and modern day miracles such as the one told in *90 Minutes in Heaven*.

Should a Christian believe the Bible?
The Bible is the story of God and man: God's creation of the heavens, earth and humanity; man's fall into sin away from God; and God's plan to save or redeem mankind. A key element of that plan is Jesus the Messiah, who the Apostle John equates with Scripture (the Word).

> *John 1:1-2,14 In the beginning was the Word, and the Word was with God, and the Word was God. He was with God in the beginning.... The Word became flesh and made His dwelling among us. We have seen His glory, the glory of the*

> one and only Son, who came from the Father, full of grace and truth.
>
> *Romans 9:5* ...from [the patriarchs] is traced the human ancestry of the Messiah, who is God over all, forever praised! Amen.

Paul goes on to say that ALL Scripture is inspired by God. Not some scripture, but all of it.

> *2 Timothy 3:16-17* All Scripture is God-breathed and is useful for teaching, rebuking, correcting and training in righteousness, so that the servant of God may be thoroughly equipped for every good work.

Jesus speaks directly to Jews (God's people) who were ashamed of His teachings. It is a dire warning.

> *Mark 8:38* "If anyone is ashamed of me and my words in this adulterous and sinful generation, the Son of Man will be ashamed of them when he comes in his Father's glory with the holy angels."

When some Christians reject portions of the Bible, are they rejecting part of Christ? Are they acting ashamed of God and Jesus? Will Jesus then be ashamed of them in the final days? These are challenging questions, but ones that Christians should consider carefully before exercising their free will to dismiss portions of the Bible.

<u>Collective Salvation and Free Will</u>
The theological twist known as collective salvation isn't grounded in scripture, and conflicts with free will and consequences that is in scripture.

> Question: "What is collective salvation?"
>
> Answer: Basically, "collective salvation" means "unless we are all saved, none of us will be saved" or "we as individuals must cooperate and sacrifice for the good of the whole." Another way to state what collective salvation means is "I

can't be saved on my own. I have to do my part by cooperating with the group, even sacrificing, to ensure everyone else's salvation. It is then that we're all saved together." Scripture, however, is clear that salvation is a process by which God saves individuals through the sacrifice of Christ on the cross. Each person must come to Christ individually, not collectively. - Gotquestions.org.

*Matthew 16:26-27 What good will it be for **someone** to gain the whole world, yet forfeit their soul? Or what can anyone give in exchange for their soul? For the Son of Man is going to come in his Father's glory with his angels, and then he will reward **each** person according to what they have done.*

In addition to the this passage, there are numerous others that speak to individual judgment and salvation. How is it then that some preach there will be a collective salvation? This teaching has even influenced President Obama.

"Our collective service can shape the destiny of this generation," Obama said. "Individual salvation depends on collective salvation."
- Speech at Wesleyan University. Obama Wants You. Investors.com. 07/31/2008.

Collective salvation and two related topics, social justice and God's nation-judgments, will be discussed further in chapters 6, 7, and 8. For now the focus will be its effect on free will.

What does collective salvation have to do with freedom and free will? Very little until government force comes into play. If someone chooses to believe that their eternal life is tied to their nation's or their neighborhood's actions, rather than their own actions, that is their right. It's not biblical, but people are free to believe non-biblical things. However, when government officials decide to use government power to make the state or nation "pleasing" to God or some other deity, it takes away the freedom of citizens.

For example, it is pleasing to God if poor people are cared for by others in society. So a government seeking to please God may forcibly take from productive citizens and use the collected tax dollars to care for the poor. This is the foundation of social justice theology. Likewise a government seeking to please God may ban homosexual acts by its citizens since God considers these acts an abomination. In both of these cases the citizens' free will is taken away by the government.

Liberal Christians want the government to carry out God's desire that the helpless poor be cared for. But, God is very clear that loving Him and worshiping Him is more important than loving your neighbor. Jesus tells us this in Matthew, where He restates Old Testament scripture.

> <u>Matthew 22: 36-40</u>
> *"Teacher, which is the greatest commandment in the Law?"*
> *Jesus replied: "'Love the Lord your God with all your heart and with all your soul and with all your mind.' This is the first and greatest commandment. And the second is like it: 'Love your neighbor as yourself.' All the Law and the Prophets hang on these two commandments."*

The first commandment given by God, is that He alone is God – there are no others.

> *Exodus 20:3 "You shall have no other gods besides Me.*

So if liberal Christians are sincere about using government to carry out God's desire, they will surely want the government to remove any other gods form society, except for the God of the Bible. But they never propose this. They only focus on economic issues where the government force is used to redistribute wealth; Issues that God places second in importance to worshiping Him. Logically, *if government force is to be used, it should first be used to remove any other gods from society.*

As we began this chapter with Adam and Eve having free will to commit sin, God continues to give humans free will today. God doesn't want humans to be forced to worship Him, any more than He wants people to be forced to care for their neighbor in need.

Freedom and Government

The founders of America understood God's intentions for freedom. The founders followed Paul's teaching in Roman's 13 when they established the functions and roles of the government.

> *Romans 13:10 Love does no harm to a neighbor. Therefore love is the fulfillment of the law.*

America's laws were set up to insure one person did not harm another. The government stopped at that point. There were none of the modern day assumptions that a function of government was to care for large numbers of citizens. More on this in Chapter 12. Make no mistake though, there is a need for government force in society. But it should be used sparingly.

> "Government is not reason; it is not eloquent; it is force. Like fire, it is a dangerous servant and a fearful master."
> - George Washington.

Government force should be used to protect the citizens from those who would harm them. For example, robbers or thugs may attack or steal from citizens. Local government should stop this. A foreign government may attack the nation. National government should protect citizens from this. Both cases require government force and taxation to protect citizens' freedoms. When government begins using force to control innocent people, it has gone too far.

> "A government can't control the economy without controlling people. And they know when a government sets out to do that, it must use force and coercion to achieve its purpose. They also knew, those Founding Fathers, that outside of its legitimate functions, government does nothing as well or as economically as the private sector of the economy."
> - Ronald Reagan. A Time for Choosing Speech. 1964.

Use of government force with respect to domestic matters should be viewed on the following scale:

No Government Force
- Anarchy = No government resulting in gang rule (the strong take what they wish)
- Limited Government = Government force used only to protect one citizen from harming another citizen.
- Socialistic or Big Government = Government takes away large degrees of freedom in order to care for citizens and direct their actions.

Maximum Government Force

The center of the scale, with limited government, maximizes the freedom and liberty of the citizenry. The outer edges result in a greater loss of liberty for the citizens. America's founders knew this and established limited government for their nation. They believed strongly in freedom and liberty.

> "Good constitutions are formed upon a comparison of the liberty of the individual with the strength of government: If the tone of either be too high, the other will be weakened too much." - Alexander Hamilton. 1788. Founding Father Quotes.

Thomas Jefferson perhaps wrote most frequently on freedom and liberty. Probably not surprising as he also drafted the Declaration of Independence. Here are a few statements by Jefferson:

> "Almighty God hath created the mind free, and manifested His supreme will that free it shall remain by making it altogether insusceptible of restraint..." - TRTJ. P 603.

> "The God who gave us life gave us liberty at the same time; the hand of force may destroy, but cannot disjoin them."
> - (1774) TRTJ. P523.

> "Liberty... is the great parent of science and virtue... a nation will be great in both always in proportion as it is free."
> - (1789) TRTJ. P524.

Other founders also wrote about freedom and liberty. Here are just a few of their statements. Many more can be found if one examines

Free Will from God, Liberty from Government

their writings.

> "The liberty enjoyed by the people of these states of worshiping Almighty God agreeably to their consciences is not only among the choicest of their blessings but also of their rights."
> - George Washington. 1789. TRGW. p765.

> "They who can give up essential liberty to obtain a little temporary safety deserve neither liberty nor safety."
> - Benjamin Franklin. 1775. TRBF. P419.

> "The right to freedom being the gift of God Almighty,...."
> - Samuel Adams. 1772. Founding Father Quotes.

> "Every man who loves peace, every man who loves his country, every man who loves liberty ought to have it ever before his eyes that he may cherish in his heart a due attachment to the Union of America and be able to set a due value on the means of preserving it."
> - James Madison. Federalist No. 41, January 1788.

> "Interwoven as is the love of liberty with every ligament of your hearts, no recommendation of mine is necessary to fortify or confirm the attachment."
> - George Washington. Farewell Address. September 19, 1796

The Founders Created a Federal Government Maximizing Freedom
Seeing the founders' love of liberty, it is not surprising they focused on it when creating their government.

> We hold these truths to be self-evident, that all men are created equal, that they are endowed by their Creator with certain unalienable Rights, that among these are Life, Liberty and the pursuit of Happiness.--That to secure these rights, Governments are instituted among Men, deriving their just powers from the consent of the governed, --That whenever any Form of Government becomes destructive of these ends, it is the Right of the People to alter or to abolish it, and to institute new Government, laying its foundation on such

principles and organizing its powers in such form, as to them shall seem most likely to effect their Safety and Happiness.
- Declaration of Independence. July 4, 1776.

Thomas Jefferson, author of the Declaration (and future President), wrote very eloquently as to the purpose of government. Look at the key points in just this portion:

- People are given rights by God; including "Life, Liberty and the pursuit of Happiness."
- The purpose of government is to secure these rights for the citizens.
- Government has power only from the consent of the governed.
- When government fails to secure the citizens Liberty and Freedom, the people can move to a new government that *does* secure those key rights.

America's founders wrote free will into the Declaration of Independence. They referred to it as the right, "endowed by their Creator", of all people to "Life, Liberty, and the Pursuit of Happiness." The founders lived under the King of England, who had assumed dictatorial powers over England's colonies, including America. They wrote and ratified a constitution that limited the national government's powers to specific defined areas not covered by the states. In total the role of government was to protect the liberty of the citizens.

> In a dinner at Mt. Vernon, back in revolutionary times, Lafayette turned to his host and said "General Washington, you Americans, even in war & desperate times have a superb spirit. You are happy and you are confident. Why is it?" Washington answered, "**There is freedom**, there is space for a man to be alone and think, and there are friends who owe each other nothing but affection." So simple an answer and so true.
> - Ronald Reagan. Reagan in His Own Hand. 2001. P224.

Free Will from God, Liberty from Government

<u>The Trend to Big Government and Away from Freedom</u>
The federal government of America has traditionally supported its citizens' free will. Free will was defined as allowing citizens to live their lives with minimal interference from the national government. State governments were primarily concerned with only preventing one citizen from harming another. Murder, assault, theft, slander and other crimes were enforced to protect one citizen from another's transgressions. But few things in life are constant.

> "The natural progress of things is for liberty to yield and government to gain ground."
> - Thomas Jefferson. 1788. TRTJ p524.

Jefferson realized the nature of government to continually expand and grow its power. Jefferson was not clairvoyant. He had simply spent large amounts of time studying historical governments including the Democracy of Greece and the Republic of Rome.

The trend of growing government began in the 1930's when the federal government began to assume responsibilities of caring for some citizens. To do this the government must take away property from one citizen and give it to another, for all government revenue comes from taking wealth from the citizenry. The federal government continued to grow itself through a variety of programs like the New Deal, the War on Poverty, Social Security, Medicare, and Medicaid, with every program removing more free will from certain citizens by seizing their income and directing their lives. For free will is also the ability to do what one wishes with one's wealth, as long as one does not harm another.

In recent times, some Americans have become confused by what can be a "right" of citizens. There can be no right that violates another's free will. Some argue that all citizens have a right to eat, or a right to healthcare. It is not a "right" if exercising that right involves taking something from another citizen. If every citizen has a right to eat, then any citizen can go to any restaurant and demand free food; any citizen can go to any supermarket and take whatever food they want or need; any citizen can go to another citizens home and take whatever food is there. This isn't a right; it is theft. A citizen does not have the "right" to take the property of another.

But what about caring for those in need? (Full discussion in Chapter 8) Should the government use force to collect tax money for this noble goal? At the nation's founding, this societal goal was left to Christian charity. The wealthy, following God's desire and their God-given free will, helped those in need. But what if some of the wealthy have become Ayn Rand disciples (religion-free philosophy of taking from no one and giving to no one). Do these citizens have the freedom to live in this manner? Not if the government uses its force to perform the task.

The federal government has also interfered with the free practice of religion, despite the Constitution forbidding it to do so (Chapter 13). The federal government simply does not have the constitutional power to ban prayer or religious displays. This goes for all displays, including Nativity Scenes, Ten Commandment Monuments, Crosses, Stars of David, or symbols of any other religion that a local government chooses to display.

Today, the federal government has even assumed the power to ban certain light bulbs or mandate what kinds of insurance a citizen must buy. The Founders would be shocked to see how the citizens have allowed the government to take control of their lives, removing their free will to live in the manner they choose.

Appendix 12 details how the federal government has begun harassing political enemies and using military-style force against non-violent citizens. These are disturbing trends that go against the nation's founding principles.

Conclusion
Fortunately for freedom-loving citizens, federal government growth and power has not always increased in America. Two recent periods offer hope: The Presidency of Ronald Reagan in the 1980's, and the election of a conservative Congress in 1994, served as deviations to the trend of an ever increasing federal government. Reagan was a hero to lovers of limited government.

> "I hope we once again have reminded people that man is not free unless government is limited."
> - Ronald Reagan. Farewell Address. Jan 11, 1989.

Free Will from God, Liberty from Government

Citizens are most free when most government is local. Leave as many functions as possible to the neighborhoods, then the cities, then the counties, then the states. Citizens may maximize their freedom, by moving within the United States and choosing the government that best suits them. (Appendix 1 shows a path for counties to escape from overbearing state governments.) If maximum free will is to be re-achieved in America, the roles of state and federal government must be dramatically changed.

As a citizen, do you want freedom for yourself? Will you allow other citizens to have their freedom? A goal of this book is to make citizens realize the freedom they have lost, and encourage them to regain that freedom through the electoral process. In America, citizens have the responsibility to vote and elect national leaders every two years. As you exercise your free will, will you vote for politicians who use the federal government to increase your freedoms or those who use government force to remove your freedoms? Remember, a government that can take away one person's freedom may choose to take away your freedom next.

A consistent theme throughout this book is how both the Constitution and the Bible offer the freedom to choose what to believe and how to live. Therefore governments, especially the federal government courts, should not "force" a citizen to believe either creation or evolution, the two main theories as to the beginning of life on Earth. This is the focus of the next chapter.

Creation and Evolution: Two Competing Theories

This chapter will examine the two main theories on how human life and our planet came into existence. Each theory describes a radically different approach and expands into very different historical time lines. An outline of the chapter follows.

   I. Both Theories Require Faith
      A) Scientific Models and Consensus are not the same as Facts
      B) Neither Theory can be Proven via Scientific Method
  II. Darwin's Theory of Evolution and the Big-Bang Theory
      A) Problems with Evolution Theory
         1. Evolution contradicts survival of the fittest
         2. Dating models have given false and contradicting results
            a) Dating model validation
         3. Big-Bang Theory has several large unanswered questions
            a) Where did original matter come from?
            b) It violates the scientific Law of Entropy
         4. DNA has never become more complex over generations of species
         5. How did plants survive for millions of years without bees?
         6. Some dinosaur fossils contain tissue residue
         7. More questions Evolution Theory cannot answer.
 III. Creation Theory in the Bible
      A) Large parts of the Bible are Historical Narrative
         1. Historical accuracy of the Bible is very good
         2. Historical writings are sole sources of information on most ancient peoples
      B) Biblical Historical Account
         1. What is a day?
         2. Six day creation in scripture
         3. Biblical time line
  IV. Observations and explanations supporting Creation Theory
      A) Great Flood
         1. Geological model
         2. Hydroplate Theory
      B) Events Demonstrate Creation Theory Plausibility
         1. How do canyons form?

2. How long did it take coal to form?
3. Oil formed in minutes – not millions of years
C) Human DNA May Corroborate Biblical Timeline
D) The Ice Age
E) Questions in Creation Theory
 1. Where do dinosaurs fit?
V. Allow Debate of Theories
VI. Who Believes Creation Theory?
A) Christians
B) America's Founders
VII. Miracle Science Cannot Explain: *90 Minutes in Heaven*
A) Many other historical miracles

Everyone accepts as fact that the Earth, planets, stars, universe, humans, animals and plant life exist and therefore came to be. There are two main competing theories as to *how* these things came to be: 1) Big-Bang followed by Evolution (called simply Evolution for brevity); 2) Creation as taught in the Bible.

<u>I. Both Theories Require Faith</u>
Today it has become widely accepted in the scientific community that the Theory of Evolution is true and the age of the earth is billions of years. It all happened by chance. Some scientists do believe the world was created by God, though. Regardless of which theory one chooses to believe, faith is required.

- A follower of the Bible will believe that the Bible is the Word of God, and therefore true, including the Creation story. Faith is required to believe that the Bible accurately describes the Creation process, performed by an all-powerful God.

- A believer in Evolution will believe that this theory is true even though no one has ever witnessed a living cell being created from non-living matter (dirt) and no evidence has been found of the intermediate life forms (those between single cells and life forms we see today, like a fish, a dog or a cow). Faith is required to believe that the first cell came to be, then morphed into numerous lifeforms over millions or billions of years.

Creation and Evolution: Two Competing Theories

In both theories the actual act of life-formation and planet creation are super-natural, or unnatural events-events simply not seen in everyday life. Super-natural elements of the theories cannot be studied with science. That is why they are more accurately considered a matter of faith than one of science. Humans are limited to using geology, archaeology, and other scientific disciplines to gather clues about the history of the earth from our environment and then constructing the best theories possible. There simply is no scientific proof *how* the Earth and its inhabitants came to be.

If one is undecided about which theory to have faith in, Creation has existed for 6000 years, while Evolution has been around only 150 years. Creation has stood the test of time much longer.

A. Scientific models and consensus are not the same as facts
There is an established consensus in recent years in both the scientific community and the media that Evolution is the correct theory. Many in this group will claim Evolution is fact. Sometimes people confuse consensus with proven fact. The scientific community has in the past adopted theories that became the consensus of the day but have been proven false with time.

- An obvious example was the "consensus" that the Earth was flat. Once science progressed sufficiently, it was proven that the Earth is a sphere, not a flat disk.
- Another example is the medical science "consensus" treatment of bleeding a patient to help heal them. This treatment was prescribed for George Washington while he was on his deathbed. In fact bleeding just makes a person weaker and can hasten death if the patient is gravely ill (as happened with Washington).
- A third example occurred in the 1970's as scientific consensus determined that the Earth was cooling and possibly facing another Ice Age. Two articles from Time Magazine's website describe a popular scientific theory of that era:
    Another Ice Age? Time. June 24, 1974
    The Cooling of America. Time. Dec. 24, 1979

These ideas seem foolish today when the scientific consensus is now global warming. But they illustrate a point that "consensus" opinions of scientists can be wrong if there is not proven fact behind them.

Today some scientists will state that it is a "fact" that the Earth is 4.6 billion years old. *This is not a fact.* The fact is there are dating models that have been used by scientists to estimate dates of rocks to billions of years. But are these models any more accurate than the global cooling models of the 1970's? Rocks of known ages have been "dated" by the models as millions of years old when the rocks were known to be less than 100 years old.

It is of great scientific interest to develop dating models, but it is also necessary to prove the models can work accurately with known samples. Validation of the model is crucial.

B. Neither Theory can be Proven via Scientific Method
From a scientific viewpoint, both Creation and Evolution are theories. These theories deal with the question: How? How did the earth and humanity reach its current state of being. Neither theory can be scientifically proven, because no man was present to witness the creation or evolution of the first human. No experiment can be performed to recreate the conditions in a lab for study. Humans are left to examine the geological and fossil evidence and determine to the best of our ability which theory is most accurate.

A quick review of the scientific method follows. This method is used to expand the knowledge base and evaluate theories.

> The 4 Stages of the Scientific Method
> 1. State the question.
> 2. Form a hypothesis or theory (educated guess of the answer to the question).
> 3. Do experiments (to test whether the theory is right or not).
> 4. Interpret the data (results) and draw conclusions.

Stage 1: In this case the question is: How were the Earth, planets, stars, universe, humans, animals and plant life created?

Creation and Evolution: Two Competing Theories

Stage 2: There are two primary competing hypotheses (theories) about how these things came to be:

1) CREATION: God created the earth, planets, stars, universe, humans, animals and plant life and describes the creation process in Genesis.
2) EVOLUTION: The earth, planets, stars and universe happened by chance with no intelligent design or intervention. Human, animal, and plant life began as single cells and evolved into present day life forms over billions of years.

Stage 3: The formation of the Earth and the beginning of life cannot be studied in a lab as an experiment and there are no living human witnesses or surviving accounts of the event. (The Bible does give an account, but Adam was not present to witness the Creation - although Eve did come to him as an adult woman.) Therefore neither theory can be scientifically proven. The creation of the earth cannot be recreated by experiment. That is why each theory will almost assuredly remain a hypothesis from a scientific standpoint. The only experimentation possible is study of the earth as it is now, hoping to find clues about the past. It is possible to study rock strata and fossils to learn about the past, but this learning is limited.

Stage 4: Scientists are able to analyze data from our surroundings and apply the results to each theory and debate which is more valid.

As we move forward, it is important to realize neither "The Bible states so" nor "scientists say so" are valid scientific proof. Scientific facts can be proven. For example: In physics, gravitational force is 9.8 meters/second squared. This is an accepted fact and has been measured numerous times. Other things must remain as hypotheses or theories until they can be studied or measured, if this is even possible.

Let's examine the theories of Creation and Evolution in more detail.

II. Darwin's Theory of Evolution and the Big-Bang Theory
The Big-Bang Theory is a hypothesis to explain how the Earth as well as the other planets and stars came to exist. The theory is:

> Matter was once concentrated in an extremely hot and dense state that exploded. The planets and stars were created as the matter cooled and condensed into individual masses. This happened by chance.

The theory does not explain where the initial source of matter originated.

Darwin's Theory of Evolution assumes the Earth was already in existence (from the Big-Bang) and attempts to explain how the life forms came to be in their present state. It was proposed by Darwin in 1859 in his book: "On the Origin of Species by Means of Natural Selection, or the Preservation of Favoured Races in the Struggle for Life". Summarized it states:

> Human, animal, and plant life began as single cells and evolved into present day life forms over millions or billions of years. Again this happened by chance or random events in nature.

The theory does not explain where the first living cell came from that initiated the evolution process.

For evolution to occur many centuries are required. Therefore, according to evolutionary theory, the Earth is billions of years old. Current consensus in the theory has the Earth's age about 4.6 billion year old. The theory has also been filled in over this time with many eras and periods having been created. The chart on the following page summarizes the time line most evolutionists follow. Similar evolutionary time lines can be found on various websites.

This is the approximate time line you will see if you visit most science or historical museums that display dinosaurs or other fossils. Unfortunately, it is usually presented as fact rather than a scientific theory. The displays with dates should always contain language along the lines of: "dating models estimate…" if they want to be scientifically accurate.

Creation and Evolution: Two Competing Theories

Era	Period	Millions of years	Major Biological Events
Cenozoic Era	Quaternary	Today 1.5	Civilization arises late in period. Humans evolve. Large mammoths, saber-toothed cats evolve. Dominate until 10,000 years ago when many go extinct.
Cenozoic Era	Tertiary	23	Rise of the mammals and birds. Rodents, primates, pigs, cats, dogs, bears and whales evolve.
Mesozoic Era	Cretaceous	65	Period ends with the mass extinction of the dinosaurs. Marsupials, sharks, bees and butterflies evolve. Flowering plants.
Mesozoic Era	Jurassic	145	Dinosaurs dominate the land. Small Mammals and birds.
Mesozoic Era	Triassic	200	Mammals, dinosaurs and crocodiles evolve.
Paleozoic Era	Permian	251	Period ends with mass extinction of many marine and animal species. Amphibians dominate the land.
Paleozoic Era	Carboniferous	299	Swamps on land. Sponge reefs in oceans. Reptiles evolve. Cockroaches evolve.
Paleozoic Era	Devonian	354	Amphibians evolve. The first trees and land plants.
Paleozoic Era	Silurian	417	Spiders, scorpions and insects evolve. Freshwater fish evolve.
Paleozoic Era	Ordovician	443	First land plants appear. Primitive fungi and sea weed evolve. Corals, shelled organisms, and starfish evolve.
Paleozoic Era	Cambrian	488	First fish appear. No known life on land yet.
	Pre-Cambrian	543 4,600	First multi-celled organisms evolve. First single celled organisms evolve. Origin of Earth.

A. <u>Problems with Evolution Theory</u>
There are a number of problems with Evolution Theory. To begin with it contradicts itself and nature observation with respect to survival of the fittest.

1. <u>Evolution contradicts survival of fittest</u>
Part of Darwin's Theory is the strongest of a species survive. This is often called "Darwinian" or "survival of the fittest". It is broadly accepted by scientists as occurring in nature. It creates a major issue for Evolution. For example, the preceding chart shows

amphibians evolving from fish. So fish somehow start to grow legs for land maneuvering. However, the initial legs will be useless on the land and a hindrance to swimming in the water. A fish with partially evolved legs will be weaker swimmer than a fish without them. Nature predicts this partially evolved species of fish will not survive when competing with normal fish for food. A partially-evolved species is a weak mutant that nature routinely destroys under its survival of the fittest principle.

2. Dating models have given false and contradicting results

Rock and carbon dating models have been used to create the million-billion-of-years epochs. Some rock dating models claim the Earth is billions of years old. There may well be flaws in these models as they have given erroneous results and may never have been properly validated.

The dating models were likely designed to predict results matching the evolutionist's geologic time-scale listed earlier. Therefore models will date rocks, fossils, and other artifacts, placing them in the correct era. Except it is possible that the algorithms used are not accurate or even severely flawed. There are plenty of examples where the dating methods give incorrect or conflicting dates for items of known historical age. Often multiple scientific dating methods do not even agree.

- One example is rock from a dacite lava dome at Mount St. Helen's volcano. Although we know the rock was formed in 1986, the rock was 'dated' by the potassium-argon (K-Ar) method as 0.35 ± 0.05 million years old.
- Another example is K-Ar 'dating' of five andesite lava flows from Mt. Ngauruhoe in New Zealand. The 'dates' ranged from < 0.27 to 3.5 million years—but one lava flow occurred in 1949, three in 1954, and one in 1975!
- For example, in Australia, some wood was buried by a basalt lava flow, as can be seen from the charring. The wood was 'dated' by radiocarbon (^{14}C) analysis at about 45,000 years old, but the basalt was 'dated' by the K-Ar method at c. 45 million years old!
    - Refuting Evolution. Ch.8

- Fossil wood from a quarry near the town of Banbury, England, some 80 miles north-west of London, was dated using the carbon-14 method. The ages calculated ranged from 20.7 to 28.8 thousand years old. However, the limestone in which the wood was found was of Jurassic age, of 183 *million* years. Clearly the dating methods are in conflict.
  - Radioactive Dating Methods. CreationRevolution.com. March 15, 2012.

Most scientists assume that layers of earth strata were formed over millions of years. If true their varying dating models (argon, carbon...) must agree on ages of items taken from the same strata layer. Otherwise either the models are incorrect or the strata formation theory is false.

How does radioactive argon rock dating work?

> The K-Ar method is probably the most widely used radiometric dating technique available to geologists. It is based on the radioactivity of ^{40}K, which undergoes dual decay by electron capture to ^{40}Ar ..... ^{40}Ar, however, is an inert gas that escapes easily from rocks when they are heated but is trapped within the crystal structures of many minerals after a rock cools. Thus, in principle, while a rock is molten the ^{40}Ar formed by the decay of ^{40}K escapes from the liquid. After the rock has solidified and cooled, the radiogenic ^{40}Ar is trapped within the solid crystals and accumulates with the passage of time. If the rock is heated or melted at some later time, then some or all of the ^{40}Ar may be released and the clock partially or totally reset.
>   - How Old is the Earth? A Response to "Scientific" Creationism. www.talkorigins.org . G. Brent Dalrymple. 1984-2006

Also in the article, Dalrymple refutes rock-dating anomalies like those mentioned earlier. He attributes the erroneous results to poor lab techniques and uses a humorous allegorical story:

> The advocates of "scientific" creationism frequently point to apparent inconsistencies in radiometric dating results as evidence invalidating the techniques. This argument is specious and akin to concluding that all wristwatches do not

work because you happen to find one that does not keep accurate time.

Sidebar: Note the quotes around scientific in Dalrymple's response. The clear implication is that those scientists who think the dating models may be flawed aren't really scientists at all. The author truly wishes that *all* scientists would treat each other with the respect their degrees deserve. Heated debates on the flaws and weaknesses of theories improve science for all men. Attacks on character or intelligence of the debaters accomplishes little.

So who is correct? Can the models accurately determine the ages of rocks? Here is the author's perspective:

Scientific testing is very good at measuring exact amounts of Carbon-14 or radioactive Argon-40 isotopes in samples at the present time. However to use these methods to date materials, it must be **assumed** how much of the element was present at the formation of the material in order to **calculate** elapsed time. (Argon-40 for rock / Carbon-14 for wood). It is in these assumptions where there is a large potential for error.

Assuming Dalrymple is correct, and the earth is 4.5 billion years old, he is assuming he has a good understanding of the Earth's environment and the conditions under which the rocks were formed 4.5 billion years ago. He assumes he knows exactly how much potassium and argon-40 were in the rock initially. Are these valid scientific assumptions? Just what was the Earth's surface like 4.5 billion years ago? And more importantly: How does he know? Where is the proof required to substantiate this assumption as fact?

Sidebar: These questions apply to the Creation Theory as well. Even though it ages the Earth at thousands of years rather than millions, it contains a massive event called the Great Flood, which *may* have shifted continental plates, altered the rotation of the Earth on its axis, and changed the radioactivity of the planet (See: In the Beginning). The key word is may. We simply do not know what exactly happened during this planetary upheaval.

With respect to carbon-dating (*Creation Answers Book* has a good explanation of carbon dating model on p.68), scientists assume how much carbon-12 and carbon-14 were present in the atmosphere during the time the plant or animal lived. This initial ratio must be known, then compared to the present amounts in the sample, to calculate ages. Except both the amounts of carbon and the ratio of 12/14 carbon in the atmosphere are not constant. They change over time. Volcanic activity, industrial activity, level of forestation, and burning of coal/oil all change the levels of carbon in the atmosphere. In fact current global-warming theory is based on changes in carbon dioxide levels being responsible for the temperature change. So any time a scientist claims a bone or piece of buried wood is 20,000 years old, the first question to ask is: Where is your proof of the levels of carbon and carbon-14 in the atmosphere 20,000 years ago?

It also an accepted mathematical modeling principle that extrapolating beyond the data set is poor practice and is often inaccurate. For dating, the data set is limited to samples where the age is known. For example, a volcano erupts in 2005: Rocks taken from those lava streams are known to be 8 years old in 2013. A piece of wood furniture known to be constructed in 1890 can be safely assumed to have been built from a tree harvested near that date. So the age of the wood is known. Items with known ages form the data set for dating models. When scientists predict an item in millions of years old, they are extrapolating far beyond their data set of known ages.

None-the-less Dalrymple presents his conclusions in his books as facts rather than theories. And he will argue and debate his conclusions with unlimited vigor as he has staked his reputation on his theories being facts. While it might be interesting to some to see a scientific debate between two scientists regarding rock dating, it would likely become filled with scientific jargon not easily followed by most people. Another way is to assess the dating models' worth by validating them.

<u>a. Dating model validation</u>
It can be demonstrated whether current rock dating methods are accurate. Perform a scientific experiment to test the validity of the method. Its called a blind test. Collect 20 rock samples. Take some from fresh volcanic activity known to be less than 5 years old, some

from historic volcanic activity known to be around 100 years old, some from sites previously dated to be millions of years old, and some unknown ages from deep within the Earth's crust. The rocks must be similar in appearance. Label the rocks only by random letter (A-T) and submit them to the leading rock dating lab. The lab is blind – it has no idea where the samples were collected, which are of known age and which are not. If the lab provided dates match the known dates then the dating system works; if not then the system doesn't work. Validation proves the worthiness of the model.

If the earlier mentioned dating discrepancies are true, it is entirely possible that the algorithm used to calculate the rocks' ages will not be able to distinguish between a known five year old rock and one thought to be millions of years old. In this case the calculated ages are unreliable and the dating algorithm is useless from a scientific standpoint.

Going back to Dalrymple's wristwatch analogy: It is not that one watch doesn't keep accurate time. The question is do any of the watches ever tell the time to be 1:00 or 1:05? Or do the watches only give times between 10:00 and 12:00? Can the model distinguish between 10 year old rocks and supposed million year old rocks? Or do the dating models never give dates less than millions of years old? These are the questions that proper model valuation will answer.

3. The Big-Bang Theory has several large unanswered questions.
The theory states that a massive explosion scattered matter throughout the universe and the matter then formed planets and stars without any creative guidance being imposed.

To begin with, this theory does not explain where the initial matter or material originated. Science can explain how elements can be transformed but not how elements are created. For example water (H_2O) is comprised of the two elements hydrogen and oxygen. Science has developed numerous processes to make water from hydrogen and oxygen or vice verse. But science has no method for creating the elements hydrogen or oxygen without input matter.

The theory also violates Entropy, the Second Law of Thermodynamics. Entropy is simply explained by all things tend toward a state of disorder (chaos). For example, if red sugar and green sugar (staples for Christmas cookies!) are mixed together, they will remain mixed. No matter how long the granules are mixed the red and green will not separate from each other into their original red-green components. They are in a state of disorder. This will continue unless acted upon by another force to restore order. In other words you can take a tweezers and remove the red granules from the green granules (a lot of work!).

Another example of Entropy is explosions. Has the explosion of a building ever resulted in a house or car being formed? No. If a building is demolished by an explosion, all that results is a pile of rubble. No useful articles have ever been formed from an explosion, unless the explosion is used by a creator. So the theory that planets were formed by a chance massive explosion is contradictory to every known example seen by man. Explosions do not create objects; they destroy them.

In observing our environment it becomes obvious that to create complex objects there needs to be an intelligent designer or creator applying work. This concept is absent from the Big Bang Theory.

4. DNA has never become more complex over generations
Entropy is also a problem that arises with Evolution. DNA is the blueprint for all life forms. By its definition, Evolution assumes DNA becomes more complex over time, with more genetic information added. This must happen for the amoeba-to-man evolution to occur. The only problem is the addition of new DNA information, of increasing DNA complexity, is not observed in science.

> 'It doesn't matter if one population breaks into several subgroups, even to the extent of not reproducing with each other anymore. In fact, you would expect that to happen after the Flood, so coyotes, wolves, dingoes, and so on might have had a common ancestor, but the key is that there's no new information—that natural processes don't create any new DNA information. I've observed 40 generations of selection of fruit flies. I've seen lots of defective flies because of

mutations, but I've never seen new, additional genetic information appear which would give hope to evolutionists. The belief in amoeba-to-man evolution needs a huge amount of new genetic information.'
- Dr. James Allan, M.Sc.Agric. (Stellenbosch), Ph.D. In Six Days.

Dr. Allan touches on another great point. Because apes and humans have a percentage of common DNA does not mean that there was a common ancestor between humans and apes. That is an assumption. Another competing assumption is that a Creator made both humans and apes and used a similar DNA blueprint when creating them. Since humans and apes are similar in many physical characteristics (2 arms, 2 legs, 1 head, similar skeletal structure.....) it would be expected that the blueprint would have a lot in common.

Once a successful design has been created it is not surprising that it is reused by the creator. Consider a home builder. The builder may reproduce numerous homes using the same basic blueprint containing a living room, kitchen, dining room, two bathrooms, and several bedrooms. The builder likely tweaks the floor plan slightly for each home. He may add a sun porch, build some with stone or brick and others with siding. But the blueprints are largely the same from house to house. Is it surprising that God would do likewise? He created a basic DNA blueprint that was very good, so He reused it to make numerous species – each having tweaks to make them different.

5. How did plants survive for millions of years without bees?
Nature has many interdependent relationships that cannot be explained by the Theory of Evolution. One of these is the relationship between bees and plants. Plants need the pollination of bees to survive. Bees need the plant pollen to survive.

> If all of the bees in the world were to die today, that within a year there would be the worst famine in history and hundreds of millions of people would die of starvation. Many insects pollinate flowers, but not like bees do. Many farmers have bee hives near their fields to insure their crops get pollinated. Without the bees nearby, many crops would fail or not produce nearly as much as they do with bees.

Some plants rely entirely on bees to pollinate them. For one reason or another, very few other insects pollinate some of these flowers. Without bees, a number of plants would soon become extinct.

And this is why they pose a problem for evolution. According to most evolutionists, flowers evolved about 200 million years ago and bees evolved only 100 million years ago. So how did all of the evolving plants get pollinated for the first 100 million years without bees?

    - Bees: A Honey of a Problem for Evolution. Creationrevolution.com. July 2012.

6. Some dinosaur fossils contain tissue residue

Evolution theory states that dinosaurs became extinct about 65 million years ago. However recent archaeological work has uncovered tissue samples from dinosaurs. Soft tissue cannot have survived 65 million years.

> Scientists from 10 universities and institutions have verified that the collagen protein in dinosaur bone is primordial – i.e. from the dinosaur.... blood vessels, blood cells, tendons and medullary bone [have also been discovered.]
>
>   - Dinosaur Protein Is Primordial. Creation Evolution . July 26, 2011.

Dinosaur Bone Tissue Study Refutes Critics

Original dinosaur tissues in fossil bones are probably the most controversial finds in all of paleontology....The latest report on this subject characterized original dinosaur biochemicals found inside fossil bones, and it adds further proof of the chemicals' originality.

North Carolina State University's Mary Schweitzer and lead author of the study used an array of different techniques to analyze the apparent bone cells inside the dinosaur bone. One method used antibodies, which are chemicals that bind to specific targets. She and her co-authors found that antibodies known to bind chemicals that vertebrates, not bacteria, produce clearly indicated that original vertebrate proteins were in the dinosaur bones.... Schweitzer and her colleagues wrote, "Here, we present morphological, microscopic, and chemical evidence that these are indeed altered remnants of original cells."

    - icr.org. Brian Thomas, M.S. November 5, 2012. *Bone*. October 16, 2012.

Finding any residue of dinosaur flesh in fossils is impossible if dinosaurs became extinct millions of years ago. This scientific data just threw another major unanswered question into the standard Evolutionary Theory.

7. More questions Evolution Theory cannot answer:
   1) Where did the first single cell come from that started the evolution? How was it formed?

   Has it been duplicated in a lab or observed in nature?

   2) How did the first cell survive and reproduce?

   Even a simple cell is incredibly complex. A large number of DNA proteins are required.

   > One such clue is the minimum essentials required for growth and reproduction. If that number is small enough, then life might conceivably have formed by chance.
   >
   > A team of biologists at the Stanford University School of Medicine employed a new method to estimate the minimum genetic information *required for the survival of bacteria* called *Caulobacter crescentus*, which are commonly used in labs. The researchers found 480 essential protein-coding genes, plus 532 other essential regions, on the bacterial DNA, according to a Stanford press release.
   >
   > Thus, this experiment found that the number of DNA regions required for the basic life of this bacterium was 1,000.
   >
   > - First Cell's Survival Odds Not in Evolution's Favor

   It is suggested in the article that the odds of this happening by chance are 1 in 1 with 400,000 zeroes (1 in 1000 has 3 zeroes). So it is a miracle or supernatural event.

   3) Why and how did this first cell reproduce? Where are the two-celled organisms?

   4) Each component in a life form (eyes, ears, brain, nerves, skin,...) is itself composed of a number of components, which are themselves made up of large numbers of cells. Why would a group of cells begin developing into eye

components, when the eye is useless without a brain and nerves to connect to the brain?

5) Did the heart evolve first or the blood, arteries, and veins? Are there examples of organisms with blood flow and no heart?

6) Which evolved first: bones, ligaments, tendons, or muscles? Why would that component evolve when it would be useless without the others?

7) What parts of the basic mammal digestive system involved first: the mouth, stomach, or intestines?

8) Is there any record of a mammal with a partially evolved digestive system? (That is the components in the process of being formed but not yet functioning.)

9) In the systems discussed in Q4-8, what is the possibility of a creature with a partially-evolved system being able to survive for more than a very short time?

10) Where are the intermediate (partially-evolved) life forms today? (i.e an animal with evolved eyesight, but no evolved nerves.)

11) Where are the fossils of intermediate (partially evolved) life forms? (i.e stages between single cell and animal/human.)

12) How many stages of evolution are required to move from "a group of cells" to a minnow or small fish?

13) Where are the species able to breathe in both air and water? This is a critical step in moving from water to land.

14) If life was formed by cells evolving into living organisms, why did the life-forming process change from evolution into sexual reproduction?

15) Which came first, the chicken or the egg? Why and how did an evolved chicken begin laying eggs? Why is a rooster required?

With each of these questions: **The answers must come from solid study, research and hands-on observation to be scientific fact. Otherwise the answers are stories or more theory – and require faith.**

If one takes an honest look at the complexity of the human body, with the numerous organs and body components, all requiring each other to function, the idea of evolution begins to appear very impractical if not impossible. By Evolution definition each component/organ must evolve slowly over many years, yet the body cannot live at all without the component/organ functioning. Quite a dichotomy.

Even taking a simpler animal, how does one make the leap from from a multi-celled organism to a multi-organed animal? Take the stomach. Evolution dictates slow change over long time periods. So the first stomach must have taken multiple (hundreds of?) generations to evolve. But a partially-evolved stomach is useless, unable to accept raw food or pass out digested food. It is a drain on the organism taking resources from the other cells and giving nothing back in return. Now it is possible for a scientist to create a story of how the first stomach evolved. But without proof, belief in the story is mere faith.

There is no recorded evidence of cell-to-species evolution being observed in recorded history. (This is why the theory assumes millions of years.) What Darwin observed while creating his theory was micro-evolution. Micro-evolution is very real. An example is dog breeding. Breeders can develop, or micro-evolve, traits or characteristics in a breed. So over hundreds of years breeders can develop German Shepherds, Golden Retrievers, and Beagles. But the breeders began with a DOG, not a cell blob.

It is a huge leap of faith to go from micro-evolution to the Theory of Evolution.

> The irony is devastating. The main purpose of Darwinism was to drive every last trace of an incredible God from biology. But the theory replaces God with an even more incredible deity – omnipotent chance.
> - T. Rosazak, Unfinished Animal, 1975, p101

There is nothing wrong with a theory having unanswered questions. There is a lot wrong with presenting such a theory as scientific fact.

Creation and Evolution: Two Competing Theories

III. Creation Theory in the Bible

We'll now examine Creation Theory as given in the Bible. Understand that the Bible makes no attempt to scientifically prove the theory. It simply states what it states and leaves it up to readers to believe it or not. This does not mean blind faith because the Bible is not anti-science. Humans are supposed to understand God's Creation to the best of our ability, including scientific study.

> *Romans 1:20 For since the creation of the world God's invisible qualities—his eternal power and divine nature—have been clearly seen, being understood from what has been made, so that people are without excuse.*

A. Parts of the Bible are Historical Narrative

Those unfamiliar with the Bible may assume it is just a philosophical work. This is not true. Large parts of the Bible are historical narrative, basically a history book.

> In fact over 40% of the Old Testament is historical narrative... The following books are largely or entirely composed of narrative material: **Genesis**, Joshua, Judges, Ruth, 1 and 2 Samuel, 1 and 2 Kings, 1 and 2 Chronicles, Ezra, Nehemiah, Daniel, Jonah, and Haggai. Moreover, Exodus, Numbers, Jeremiah, Ezekiel, Isaiah, and Job also contain substantial narrative portions.
> - How to Read the Bible for All Its Worth. P89.

1. Historical accuracy of the Bible is very good

The Bible has proven to be a remarkably accurate narrative of history. The author does not know of one instance where the Bible has been proven to be historically or factually inaccurate.

Now, there have been plenty of instances where people have interpreted the Bible incorrectly. One example is the church in the Middle Ages insisting that the Earth is the center of the universe. They interpreted this from the Genesis creation story. But read the story carefully, and you will notice that the physical location of the Earth with respect to the universe is never specified. Man made an assumption that the Earth was at the center in physical location, because the Earth was at the center of the story. Science has shown that the Earth is not the center of the universe.

There is also rampant speculation that the early Bible history could not be accurate because it was passed down through the generations until Moses (or another scribe) put the stories in writing.

Most of us have played the grade school game where the children are placed in a circle and a sentence is told to the first child and passed around the circle being told from one child to the next. By the time the sentence returns to the originator, it has little resemblance to the original sentence. Everyone then laughs at how the sentence was distorted by the multiple retelling.

However, how many of us have listened to a grandparent tell a family story at weekly dinners or at holidays? The story has been told over and over until you could tell it yourself!

This is how the early history was passed down. Family units stayed close together. Creation, the earliest story, would have to have been told to Adam directly from God. Adam would have retold the story over and over again, maybe around the fire after dinner. At some point Adam's children would have taken over and told the story to their children. Adam was probably still around to verify the details of the story were accurate as he lived for centuries. Noah and his family continued the process after the flood.

2. Historical writings are sole sources of information on most ancient peoples

Can it be proven that Adam and Noah lived and were real people? There is simply no evidence as in marked graves or mummified bodies. However, the same can be said for most other ancient historical figures. Can we prove Alexander the Great actually lived, other than with historical writings? How about Julius Caesar? These men were emperors who lived centuries later than Adam and Noah, yet there is little if any physical evidence in the world to prove they lived. We rely on historical writings to inform us about these men and their lives.

B. Biblical Historical Account

Here is the Creation history recorded in the Bible in Genesis. God

Creation and Evolution: Two Competing Theories

would have told the account to Adam, who passed it down to his children.

<u>Genesis 1 - Genesis 2:2 The Beginning</u>
In the beginning God created the heavens and the earth.

Now the earth was formless and empty, darkness was over the surface of the deep, and the Spirit of God was hovering over the waters.

And God said, "Let there be light," and there was light. God saw that the light was good, and He separated the light from the darkness. God called the light "day," and the darkness he called "night." And there was evening, and there was morning—the first day.

And God said, "Let there be an expanse between the waters to separate water from water." So God made the expanse and separated the water under the expanse from the water above it. And it was so. God called the expanse "sky." And there was evening, and there was morning—the second day.

And God said, "Let the water under the sky be gathered to one place, and let dry ground appear." And it was so. God called the dry ground "land," and the gathered waters he called "seas." And God saw that it was good.

Then God said, "Let the land produce vegetation: seed-bearing plants and trees on the land that bear fruit with seed in it, according to their various kinds." And it was so. The land produced vegetation: plants bearing seed according to their kinds and trees bearing fruit with seed in it according to their kinds. And God saw that it was good. And there was evening, and there was morning—the third day.

> Sidebar: Some say that the above verse proves Creation did not occur in actual days. After all, plants do not grow and produce seeds in a single day. It is important to remember that an all-powerful God is directing the creation process. He may very well have accelerated normal plant life cycles. The Bible

offers additional testimony regarding this. In Jonah 4, God caused a shade plant to grow in one day, then die the following day. In Matthew 21, Jesus cursed a fig tree, and the tree immediately withered and died. God is not bound by normal plant life cycles.

And God said, "Let there be lights in the expanse of the sky to separate the day from the night, and let them serve as signs to mark seasons and days and years, and let them be lights in the expanse of the sky to give light on the earth." And it was so. God made two great lights—the greater light to govern the day and the lesser light to govern the night. He also made the stars. God set them in the expanse of the sky to give light on the earth, to govern the day and the night, and to separate light from darkness. And God saw that it was good. And there was evening, and there was morning—the fourth day.

And God said, "Let the water teem with living creatures, and let birds fly above the earth across the expanse of the sky." So God created the great creatures of the sea and every living and moving thing with which the water teems, according to their kinds, and every winged bird according to its kind. And God saw that it was good. God blessed them and said, "Be fruitful and increase in number and fill the water in the seas, and let the birds increase on the earth." And there was evening, and there was morning—the fifth day.

And God said, "Let the land produce living creatures according to their kinds: livestock, creatures that move along the ground, and wild animals, each according to its kind." And it was so. God made the wild animals according to their kinds, the livestock according to their kinds, and all the creatures that move along the ground according to their kinds. And God saw that it was good.

Then God said, "Let us make man in our image, in our likeness, and let them rule over the fish of the sea and the birds of the air, over the livestock, over all the earth, and over all the creatures that move along the ground."

So God created man in his own image, in the image of God

> he created him; male and female he created them.
>
> God blessed them and said to them, "Be fruitful and increase in number; fill the earth and subdue it. Rule over the fish of the sea and the birds of the air and over every living creature that moves on the ground."
>
> Then God said, "I give you every seed-bearing plant on the face of the whole earth and every tree that has fruit with seed in it. They will be yours for food. And to all the beasts of the earth and all the birds of the air and all the creatures that move on the ground—everything that has the breath of life in it—I give every green plant for food." And it was so.
>
> God saw all that he had made, and it was very good. And there was evening, and there was morning—the sixth day.
>
> Thus the heavens and the earth were completed in all their vast array.
>
> By the seventh day God had finished the work he had been doing; so on the seventh day he rested from all his work. And God blessed the seventh day and made it holy, because on it he rested from all the work of creating that he had done.

Genesis 2 goes on to describe day six of the Creation in greater detail, focusing on how Eve was created from Adam.

> Gen 2:7 Then the Lord God formed a man from the dust of the ground and breathed into his nostrils the breath of life, and the man became a living being.
>
> Gen 2:18-22 The Lord God said, "It is not good for the man to be alone. I will make a helper suitable for him."
> ... So the Lord God caused the man to fall into a deep sleep; and while he was sleeping, he took one of the man's ribs and then closed up the place with flesh. Then the Lord God made a woman from the rib he had taken out of the man, and he brought her to the man.

The Genesis account had to be told to Adam and Eve by God because they were not created until day six and, therefore, could not know it. Adam and Eve thought the narrative important enough that they passed it down to their offspring. The story continued to be passed down from generation to generation either orally or on clay tablets, until it was written down in current form, likely by Moses.

1. What is a day?
Genesis uses the words "day" and "night" as literal words, meaning a 24 hour Earth period. Hebrew scholars will confirm the literal intent of the words. One Hebrew Scholar, Dr. Robert V. McCabe, gives several reasons why readers should understand it this way:

- The Hebrew noun יוֹם *yôm*, "day," is used in this context 14 times, 13 times in the singular and once in the plural (v. 14) (it is used in Genesis 1:5 [twice], 8, 13, 14 [twice], 16, 18, 19, 23, 31; 2:2 [twice] and 2:3). The reason why this is significant is that *yôm* always refers to a normal literal day when it is used as a singular noun and is not found in a compound grammatical construction.

- Genesis 1:5 defines a day as a period of light separated from darkness.

- Each creation day has a numeric qualifier—"one day," v. 5, "second day," v. 8, etc. When *yôm* is used with a numerical qualifier in the Old Testament, it is not used in an extended, non-literal sense.

- The word 'day' in this context is qualified by 'evening' and 'morning'. Each numbered creation day is associated with 'and there was evening and there was morning' (1:5, 8, 13, 19, 23, 31). Whether 'evening' and 'morning' are used together in a context with 'day' (19 times beyond the 6 uses in Genesis 1) or they are used without 'day' (38 times), they are used consistently in the Old Testament as a reference to literal days.
  - www.creation.com/robert-mccabe-old-testament-scholar-genesis

This meaning is very difficult to grasp for many who read the Bible, because it requires the reader to believe that an all-powerful God exists who is capable of creating the universe in a six-day period. For purposes of Creation Theory, the Bible should be interpreted as it was written. This means a six day Creation. The Bible is the

Creation and Evolution: Two Competing Theories

authority for this theory.

A possibility does exist that God's days were not 24 hour periods. God could have simply used "day" to mean an equal period of time as He told the Creation story to Adam in order to illustrate the work week he was to follow: six days of work then one day of rest. The only reason to consider this is if data is uncovered that indicates the days in the Creation narrative were actually longer periods of time. Some readers of the Bible even try to combine Creation Theory with Evolution Theory in an attempt to have both be true. Anyone is free to propose any theory they wish, of course. But these hybrid theories (where a day = millions or billions of years, and Adam evolved from an ape) are stand-alone theories. Proponents are creating their own creation story, not using the one found in the Bible.

In any case, the most important element of the theory is that **God created** the Earth, stars, planets, man, animals, and plants. Not *how long* it took.

2. Six Day Creation in Scripture
Scripture offers additional testimony to the six day Creation.

> *Exodus 20:11 For in six days the LORD made the heavens and the earth, the sea, and all that is in them, but he rested on the seventh day. Therefore the LORD blessed the Sabbath day and made it holy.*
>
> *Exodus 31:17 It will be a sign between me and the Israelites forever, for in six days the LORD made the heavens and the earth, and on the seventh day he rested and was refreshed.'"*
>
> *Nehemiah 9:6 You alone are the LORD. You made the heavens, even the highest heavens, and all their starry host, the earth and all that is on it, the seas and all that is in them. You give life to everything.*

Jesus Himself states that God made man and woman at the beginning of creation.

> *Mark 10:6 "But at the beginning of creation God 'made them male and female' (Gen. 1:27)*

As often is the case Jesus quotes earlier scripture, in this case from Genesis. The Bible is consistent throughout. Jesus doesn't alter the creation narrative.

3. Biblical Timeline

So when did Creation occur according to the Bible? Day one through six, in year one. However, this doesn't help us with our current dating system, which is based on the Roman calendar and the birth of Christ (BC means before Christ). Scripture does not provide an exact date, but does provide enough historical information to generally place it.

Historical Bible Timeline

Historical Event	Years
Multiple historical sources place the **destruction of Jerusalem by the Babylonians** in 586 BC (Before Christ). From 2014 AD, this was 2600 years ago. 2 Kings 25:1-2 *Nebuchadnezzar king of Babylon marched against Jerusalem.....The city was kept under siege until the eleventh year of King Zedekiah.*	2,600
1 and 2 Kings records the reigns of Kings in Judah, the Southern Kingdom of Ancient Israel. 433 years are recorded beginning with King Solomon and ending with King Zedekiah. See Appendix for Scripture.	433
*1 Kings 6:1 In the 480th year after the Israelites came out of Egypt, in the fourth year of **Solomon's reign** over Israel, in the month of Ziv, the second month, he began to build the temple of the LORD.* (476 years from start of Solomon's reign to leaving Egypt)	476
Exodus 12:40 Now the length of time the Israelite people lived in Egypt was 430 years.	430
*Genesis 47:28 **Jacob** lived in Egypt 17 years, and the years of his life were 147.* (Jacob was born 130 years before Israel entered Egypt)	130
*Genesis 25:26 **Isaac** was 60 years old when Rebekah gave birth to Jacob and Esau.* (Time from Isaac birth to Jacob birth)	60
*Genesis 21:5 Abraham was 100 years old when his son **Isaac** was born to him.* (Time from **Abraham** birth to Isaac birth)	100
Shem to Abraham Genealogy and birth-spans from Genesis 11. See Appendix for Scripture.	390
Adam to Noah Geneaology and birth-spans from Genesis 5. See Appendix for Scripture.	1,556
Biblical Age of the Earth (Approximate)	**6,175**

The table approximates the age of the earth for purposes of the Creation Theory. The Bible indicates the Earth is roughly 6-7000 years old.

Creation and Evolution: Two Competing Theories

The Bible historically documents the human genealogy from Adam to Christ. It also lists the ages and births of the people in the earliest portions of the genealogical line. There are two main genealogies in Genesis, one in Genesis 5, which covers the period from Adam to Noah, and one in Genesis 11 which covers the period from Shem to Abraham. There is also extensive detail covering the reign of kings of both Judah (South Kingdom) and Israel (North Kingdom). The kings of Judah are used in this example. (See Appendices 2-4)

The 6000+ year age is an interpretation of the Bible and as such also offers insight into the use of the Bible for purposes beyond the actual text. For example, concluding that 433 years passed from Solomon to the fall of Jerusalem is an interpretation or analysis. The 433 years is calculated by summing the individual kings' tenures provided in Scripture. While the Bible accurately states the length of each rule and the succession of rulers, it does not mention co-regency, where there is overlapping rule between the father and son. The analysis assumes each rule is independent and the reigns can be stacked to calculate the overall length of the Judean Kingdom. In fact a good study Bible will also contain information from other sources that show several Judean kings had periods of co-regency. For example, Hezekiah ruled for 29 years and his son Manasseh ruled for 55 years. A good study Bible will inform the reader that Manesseh and Hezekiah co-ruled for 10 of those years. So the entire time passing is only 74 years, not 84 years as used in the above analysis. Therefore the above time line is known to only approximate the age of the Earth for purposes of the theory. It is not assumed to be accurate to the year.

There are other interpretations for the Genesis genealogies, that assume the genealogies are "telescoped", meaning some generations were omitted. If true, this could allow additional hundreds or thousands of years to be added, but not millions. This interpretation does not accurately represent the text in the author's opinion. For example: *"Seth had lived **105 years**, he became the father of Enosh"* seems to clearly state Seth is Enosh's father – not a great-great-grandfather.

The Bible does NOT place a priority on giving the reader the exact age of the Earth. *The Bible does place a priority on telling about an all-powerful God, who did the creating.* Debates regarding young vs. old earth are interesting, but much less important than recognizing the Creator, and His majestic work.

This historical account leads to the following Creation Theory or hypothesis:

> God created the earth, planets, stars, universe, humans, animals and plant-life as described in Genesis.

IV. Observations and Explanations Supporting Creation Theory

The account answers who did the creating, but says very little about the processes God used in Creation. The account does explain how the seven day week came to be a standard measure of time. It requires belief that there is a God with infinitely more power and intellect than any human possesses.

The next sections will explain how these events may have happened. Explaining how life came to be is beyond scientific ability. But other parts of the Bible such as the Great Flood can be explained - again with theories that match observations that have been seen.

The Biblical account of a great worldwide flood described in Genesis is told in Chapter 4: God's Death Penalty.

A. Scientific support for the Great Flood

There is scientific evidence indicating a worldwide flood occurred.

> What evidence would one expect from a global watery cataclysm that drowned the animals, birds and people not on the Ark? All around the world, in rock layer after rock layer, we find billions of dead things that have been buried in water-carried mud and sand. Their state of preservation frequently tells of rapid burial and fossilization, just like one would expect in such a flood.
>
> There is abundant evidence that many of the rock strata were laid down quickly, one after the other, without significant time breaks between them. Preservation of animal tracks, ripple marks and even raindrop marks, testifies to rapid covering of these features to enable their preservation.

Polystrate fossils (ones which traverse many strata) speak of very quick deposition of the strata. The scarcity of erosion, soil formation, animal burrows and roots between layers also shows they must have been deposited in quick succession....

The world-wide distribution of many geological features and rock types is also consistent with a global Flood. The Morrison Formation is a layer of sedimentary rock that extends from Texas to Canada... The limited geographic extent of unconformities (clear breaks in the sequence of deposition with different tilting of layers, etc.) is also consistent with the reality of the global Flood. And there are many other evidences for the Flood.

The problem is not the evidence but the mind-set of those looking at the evidence. One geologist testified how he never saw any evidence for the Flood—until, as a Christian, he was convinced from the Bible that the Flood must have been a global cataclysm. Now he sees the evidence everywhere.

- Creation Answers Book. P159.

There is striking evidence that all peoples on Earth have come from Noah, found in the Flood stories from many cultures around the world — North and South America, South Sea Islands, Australia, Papua New Guinea, Japan, China, India, the Middle East, Europe and Africa. Hundreds of such stories have been gathered. (Frazer, J.G. 1918. Folklore in the Old Testament: studies in comparative religion, Vol. 1, Macmillan, London, pp. 105–361)

- Creation Answers Book. P155.

1. Geological model

Dr. Tas Walker, along with Creation Ministries International, has created a geological model based on the biblical record. A model explains the rock layers of the Earth and how they would have been formed according to Creation Theory. The model assumes a catastrophic flood in which volcanic activity plus large amounts of flood sediment created the bulk of the rock layers seen today. The model is shown on the next page.

Dr. Walker's Biblical Geological Model

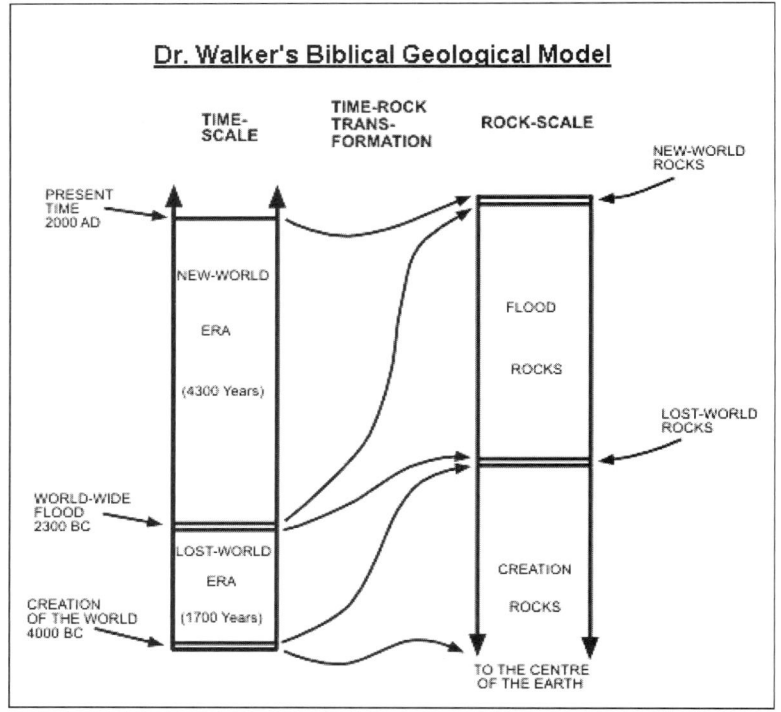

The scale is divided into four parts, each clearly identified with the biblical record. Two events are shown, the Creation event having a duration of six days and the Flood event lasting about one year. The 1700 year period between the Creation event and the Flood event is called the Lost-World era while the 4300 year period from the Flood event to the present time is called the New-World era.
More detailed models are available on Dr. Walker's website.

A key scientific advantage of this Creation Theory is it's use of Noah's worldwide biblical flood, which accounts for the large number of fossils. Fossils are essentially animals buried alive in mud. A worldwide catastrophe like the flood, in which most of the planet's life was destroyed, would have produced a large number of carcasses trapped beneath the sediment of receding flood waters.

2. Hydroplate Theory
The Flood was catastrophic and may have radically changed the landscape of the earth. One theory suggests the flood transformed the Earth from a single landmass with few mountains into our current continental structure with large mountain ranges and oceans. One of the best sources of scientific information supporting a massive flood comes from Dr. Walt Brown. Dr. Brown heads The

Creation and Evolution: Two Competing Theories

Center for Scientific Creation, and has written a book (available on-line at the website) *In the Beginning: Compelling Evidence for Creation and the Flood.* The book has three main parts, the second dealing with a theory of how the flood occurred and evidence supporting the theory.

> The Hydroplate theory [was] developed during more than 35 years of study by Dr. Walt Brown, a former evolutionist. This theory explains a catastrophic event in earth's history and solves a host of recognized problems.
> - www.creationscience.com

> [The Hydroplate Theory] will show, in ways an interested layman can understand,... that a global flood, with vast and unique consequences, did occur. For example, coal, oil, and methane did not form over hundreds of millions of years; they formed in months. Fossils and layered strata did not form over a billion years; they formed in months. The Grand Canyon did not form in millions of years; it formed in weeks. Major mountain ranges did not form over hundreds of millions of years; each formed in hours. These statements may appear shocking, until one has examined the evidence...
> - In the Beginning. P109.

The Center for Scientific Creation website has a short video explaining the Hydroplate Theory and the dramatic continental shifting and other changes that it proposes occurred during the flood. It is well worth watching.

> *Genesis 7:11-12 ... all the springs of the great deep burst forth, and the floodgates of the heavens were opened. And rain fell on the earth forty days and forty nights.*

One interesting part of the theory is that the springs of the great deep bursting may have shot tons of muddy water into the atmosphere which returned to the surface as torrential muddy rain and hail. The hail may have trapped and frozen numerous animals alive in the northern latitudes where they have been discovered thousands of years later. Frozen woolly mammoth carcasses could be a result of the flood.

Another interesting part of the theory explains how kangaroos and other animals got to Australia: The sea levels were dramatically lower, and the newly shifted continents much higher immediately after the flood ended. This lasted until Peleg's time, when sea levels rose to submerge land routes between continents.

> *Gen 10:25, 1 Chron 1:19 Two sons were born to Eber: One was named Peleg, [Peleg means division.] because in his time the earth was divided; his brother was named Joktan.*

Rising water divided the continents in Peleg's day
In English, we have the words archipelago (a sea having, or dividing, many islands) and pelagic (relating to or living in the sea). Pelagic sediments or deposits are sediments on the ocean floor. Pelagic frequently refers to life forms found in the sea. Bathypelagic means relating to or living in the deep sea. Also, the prefix pelag means sea.

Dr. Bernard Northrup, a Hebrew professor, has shown that peleg originally meant division by water. That meaning is embedded in all three language families of Noah's offspring, so its meaning probably preceded the multiplication of languages at Babel.

Therefore, the earth was probably divided by water in Peleg's day. The Hydroplate Theory explains how and why.... Although it is difficult for many of us to see how waters that covered all earth's preflood mountains could drain to below today's sea level, three lines of evidence show that sea level was once almost three miles lower....

[The continents had risen high above the flood waters] Then, in the centuries after the flood, the crushed, thickened, buckled, and sediment-laden continents sank into the mantle and the earth regained a more spherical shape; sea level had to rise in compensation. Eventually, sea level approached today's level.

With sea level much lower for a few centuries after the flood, imagine how many migration paths existed for animals and man to populate today's continents and islands. God's commands (Genesis 9:1, 11:4–9) for humans and animals to populate the "whole earth" after the flood must have been doable. If, after the flood, sea level was where it is today, repopulating the "whole earth" would have been difficult, if not impossible, for those first receiving God's command. The wisdom and urgency of God's command are apparent when we realize that sea level was steadily rising. The "window of opportunity" for global migration was disappearing in Peleg's day.

[Strong linguistic and scientific arguments] point to an earth being divided by rising water in the days of Peleg and suggest that our ancestors knew, a few centuries after the flood, of rising sea levels that would separate, or had separated, continents.

- In the Beginning. FAQ.

B. Recent Geological Events Illustrate Creation Theory

Below are two examples of the Mount St. Helen's volcanic eruption allowing scientific observation to occur. It is not often that humans can view the kind of disruptive geologic activity that could have occurred at the Earth's Creation or in the Flood.

1. How do canyons form?

Evolutionists believe that canyons are formed by rivers over millions of years. They teach that rivers and streams gradually cut away at the rock walls and carry the loose rocks and pebbles downstream.

At one time, they claimed the Grand Canyon in Arizona was carved out by the Colorado River over more than 100 million years. Then they changed it to less than 50 million years, and the last I heard from a friend who spends a lot of time rafting in the Grand Canyon, they now are saying that it was carved in only 5-10 million years.

In 1980, Mount St. Helens erupted sending a mudflow down through the Toutle River. In a matter of a few hours, the mud and debris carved a canyon up to 100 feet deep. Not only did the mudflow carve out this canyon, but it also carved out numerous side canyons as well. The result was a landscape that looked like the Grand Canyon, only $1/40^{th}$ the size. Researchers named the new canyon the Little Grand Canyon.

Since the time of Mount St. Helens, there have been other examples of canyons 20-40 feet deep cut into river channels by local floods. One example occurred in the Texas Hill Country in 2002 when flood waters overflowed the dam at Canyon Lake. The flood waters carved deep, steep walled canyons out of the rock layers downstream from the dam. The area is now referred to as the Canyon Lake Gorge.

A number of geologists that believe in biblical creation believe that the Grand Canyon was carved out when a large lake left over from the Genesis Flood broke through its shores, causing a massive flood that flowed down the Colorado River pathway. Occurring so soon after the Flood, the layers of sediment laid down by the Flood would not have completely hardened into solid rock. When the flood waters started to cut through, it quickly carved out the mighty canyon that would later attract millions of visitors today.

Observational science has demonstrated that canyons like the Grand Canyon, the Little Grand Canyon and Canyon Lake Canyon can be formed in the matter of days instead of millions of years. This is causing any evolutionary geologists to re-think the formation of the Grand Canyon and how long it took to carve.
- Posted on July 29, 2011 by R.L. David Jolly @ CreationRevolution.com

There is an entire chapter in the book, *In the Beginning: Compelling Evidence for Creation and the Flood* giving a detailed theory explaining the many geological features of the Grand Canyon. The theory examines modern terrain and postulates that two massive lakes breached their walls which led to the forming of the Grand Canyon and the Colorado River. The book can be read in its entirety at The Center for Scientific Creation website: www.creationscience.com.

2. How long does it take coal to form?
When we examine swamps and peat bogs today, we do not find the same things happening as the evolutionists teach. Instead of the flat top and bottom layers we see in most coal beds, modern swamps and bogs have irregular layers along with many plant and tree roots passing through the thin layers of peat found along the bottom. These roots break up

the layers of peat and mud, making them very irregular.

Another problem with the evolutionary theory of coal formation is the very slow processes we see happening today in the swamps and bogs. It takes approximately 10 feet of plant material to form 1 foot of coal and we just don't see thick layers (many feet thick) of peat forming in today's swamps and bogs.

If swamps and bogs are not responsible for the formation of the vast coal deposits we see on every continent, is there any modern evidence to explain how they could have formed?

After Mount St Helens erupted in the early 1980's, geologist Dr. Steve Austin was studying the thousands of logs floating on Spirit Lake near the base of the volcano. The force of the eruption blew trees down for miles around the mountain. Several thousand of these trees ended up in Spirit Lake. Dr. Austin noticed that a number of the trees were floating in various stages. Some were floating upright as one end of the log became more waterlogged than the other end. As these logs became completely full of water, they sunk to the bottom of the lake.

Dr. Austin also observed that many of the floating logs would rub against each other, causing the bark to peel off. As the bark became water logged it also sank to the bottom of the lake. Using scuba gear, he dove down to the bottom of Spirit Lake to examine what was happening. Dr. Austin found a layer of bark measuring over three feet thick on the bottom of the lake. This layer of bark was also being mixed with silt, appearing to be the perfect scenario for the formation of peat. He also noticed that a number of logs that had been vertically floating had sunk to the bottom and were still upright in positions. Since various logs sank at different times, the ends that sank first were buried at various depths in the layer of bark peat.

Based upon his observations at Spirit Lake, Dr. Austin instantly thought about the billions of trees that would have been uprooted and washed away by the Genesis Flood. Some plants would be buried in place. Some would be ground up and destroyed. Most, however, probably floated atop the floodwaters, until they became waterlogged and sank to the bottom....

The Flood provides an explanation for the origin of coal consistent with an earth only thousands of years old. The enormous coal reserves on our planet are a reminder and tribute to a beautiful and bountiful world now lost.
- Creation Revolution. Posted on August 26, 2011 by R.L. David Jolly

Another consensus is that oil and gas take millions of years to form. They are called fossil fuels because they had to have been formed from plant life from the dinosaur era millions of years ago. But what if it *didn't* take millions of years to form oil? What if the oil formed much more quickly.

3. Oil formed in minutes – not millions of years

A new scientific discovery that takes algae and turns it into crude oil in minutes rather than millions of years could be the end of constant worries over "peak oil."

Engineers at the Department of Energy's Pacific Northwest National Laboratory (PNNL) announced that they have created a process that takes an enriched stew of algae and turns it into crude oil which, in turn, can be made into a usable bio-fuel. The development was announced in a recent issue of the journal Algal Research.

In a press release, PNNL described, "In the PNNL process, a slurry of wet algae is pumped into the front end of a chemical reactor. Once the system is up and running, out comes crude oil in less than an hour, along with water and a byproduct stream of material containing phosphorus that can be recycled to grow more algae."

"It's a bit like using a pressure cooker, only the pressures and temperatures we use are much higher," Elliott said. "In a sense, we are duplicating the process in the Earth that converted algae into oil over the course of millions of years. We're just doing it much, much faster."
- Geek Oil: Scientists Manufacture Biofuel from Algae in Minutes. www.breitbart.com. Warner Todd Huston. Dec. 18, 2013.

Notice the standard conventional thinking on display "the process in the Earth that converted algae into oil over the course of millions of years." There is no thought that this could also mean it didn't take the earth millions of years to produce oil. If Creation Theory is correct there would have been a large amount of vegetation trapped under sediment and rock from the Flood.

The key element of Creation Theory is that **God created the Earth**. The Bible is definitive on that. The exact age of the earth is open to different interpretations. The Bible simply does not deem it important enough to provide a chronology beginning with year one and progressing forward.

C. Human DNA patterns may corroborate biblical time line
A recent scientific study on human DNA pointed to a remarkable event approximately 5000 years ago where human DNA suddenly began to diversify. This time frame is consistent with the biblical historical time line where a worldwide flood reduced the human population to eight people: Noah, his wife, Noah's three sons and their wives.

> Human DNA Variation Linked to Biblical Event Timeline
> A new study reported in the journal Science has advanced our knowledge of rare DNA variation associated with gene regions in the human genome. By applying a demographics-based model to the data, researchers discovered that the human genome began to rapidly diversify about 5,000 years ago. Remarkably, this data coincides closely with biblical models of rapid diversification of humans after the global flood.
>
> Typically, evolutionary scientists incorporate hypothetical deep time scales taken from paleontology or just borrowed from other authors to develop and calibrate models of genetic change over time. In contrast this Science study used demographic models of human populations over known historical time and known geographical space. The resulting data showed a very recent, massive burst of human genetic diversification.
>
> The authors [of this study]wrote, "The maximum likelihood time for accelerated growth was 5,115 years ago." Old-earth proponents now have a new challenge: to explain why—after

millions of years of hardly any genetic variation among modern humans—human genomic diversity exploded only within the last five thousand years?

- Jeffrey Tomkins, Ph.D. www.icr.org. July 23, 2012.

Recall the Bible time line would have this initial genetic start twice. Once when God created Adam and Eve. The second being Noah and family after the Flood. Scientists should go where the data leads them. It may well be the case here that it leads them to an anomaly explained by the Bible history.

The *Creation Answers Book* is another resource that has four chapters dealing with the Flood.

D. Ice Age

The Ice Age fits into the biblical history soon after the Flood. Most creation scientists believe the Flood triggered the Ice Age. The volcanic and tectonic plate activity caused oceans to warm, water to evaporate, at high rates, leading to high snow levels in cold areas. Massive snowfalls triggered the Ice Age.

> Sliding hydroplates generated frictional heat, as did movements within the earth resulting from the rising of the Atlantic floor and subsiding of the Pacific Ocean floor. Floods of lava spilling out, especially onto the Pacific floor, became vast reservoirs of heat that maintained elevated temperatures in certain ocean regions for centuries—the ultimate and first "El Niño." Warm oceans produced high evaporation rates and heavy cloud cover.
>
> Temperatures drop as elevation increases. For example, for every mile one climbs up a mountain, the air becomes about 28°F colder. Therefore, after the flood, the elevated continents were colder than today. Conversely, lowered sea levels meant warmer oceans. Also, volcanic debris in the air and heavy cloud cover shielded the earth's surface from much of the Sun's rays.
>
> At higher latitudes and elevations, such as the newly elevated and extremely high mountains, this combination of high precipitation and low temperatures produced immense snow falls—perhaps 100 times those of today. Large temperature

Creation and Evolution: Two Competing Theories

> differences between the cold land and warm oceans generated high winds that rapidly transported moist air up onto the elevated, cool continents where heavy snowfall occurred, especially over glaciated areas. As snow depths increased, glaciers moved in periodic spurts, much like an avalanche. During summer months, rain caused some glaciers to melt partially and retreat, marking the end of that year's "ice age."
> - In the Beginning: Compelling Evidence for Creation and the Flood. Hydroplate Theory: Ice Age. creationscience.com.

> To develop an ice age, where ice accumulates on the land, the oceans need to be warm at mid- and high latitude, and the land masses need to be cold, especially in the summer. Warm oceans evaporate lots of water, which then moves over the land. Cold continents result in the water precipitating as snow rather than rain, and also prevent the snow from thawing during summer. The ice thus accumulates quickly.
>
> However, the global Flood described in the Bible provides a simple mechanism for an ice age. We would expect warm oceans at the end of the global Flood, due to the addition of hot subterranean water to the pre-Flood ocean and heat energy released through volcanic activity.
> - The Creation Answers Book. P 205-206.

It is very possible that the following verses refer to the Ice Age that Job may have lived through. But this is far from certain.

> *Job 37: 6, 9-10 He says to the snow, 'Fall on the earth,' and to the rain shower, 'Be a mighty downpour.'...*
> *The tempest comes out from its chamber, the cold from the driving winds. The breath of God produces ice, and the broad waters become frozen.*
>
> *Job 38:29-30 From whose womb comes the ice? Who gives birth to the frost from the heavens when the waters become hard as stone, when the surface of the deep is frozen?*

Creation Theory, based on the Biblical time line, has the Earth being thousands of years old rather than billions. It explains how both a Great Flood and an Ice Age occurred during those thousands of years. It can place Creation to within hundreds of years on our modern calendar system. The key to the theory is that God is responsible for all. God doesn't always reveal as much as humans would like to know, however.

E. Questions in Creation Theory
There are many questions in Creation Theory for which the answers cannot be proven. That's why it is a theory. The simple answer to every question is: That's how God did it. But that does not satisfy the curiosity of human nature. Creation Theory requires belief in an almighty God and His miracle of Creation. The Bible is full of miracles performed by God that are beyond current human scientific understanding. Creation Theory assumes that God has power and ability that humans cannot understand.

However, just because humans cannot explain something does not mean it did not happen. Examples of this occur every time a mother conceives a baby in her womb or every time a cat has kittens or a dog has a litter of puppies. It is a miracle that male sperm and female eggs can unite and grow into a a full-grown human being. Science cannot reproduce this. It cannot create a sperm or an egg, much less an entire being. Yet humans often do not consider these things miracles because they are seen often as part of everyday life.

It is also important to remember that the starting point of this chapter is that there are two competing theories that require faith. When scientists or non-believers say that evolution is fact, they raise the bar from an explanation of how things could have happened, to needing scientific proof of how things happened. They give themselves a much harder standard to meet.

Let's examine one question that jumps out if Creation Theory can be true: What about the dinosaurs?

1. Where do Dinosaurs Fit in the Creation Theory?
Creation Theory would consider dinosaurs to be animals that would have been created by God at the same time as other animals. They would have lived at the same time as man. Before assuming this is a far-fetched part of the theory, consider the Book of Job may describe two dinosaurs.

Creation and Evolution: Two Competing Theories

Several chapters in the book of Job consist of God "putting Job in his place". God is so much superior to Job that Job has no right to question the Almighty God. Several verses in this section refer to great animals that God created. These are mighty animals that God can easily approach, but a single human would not dare to approach. Behemoth and Leviathan may very well refer to dinosaurs.

> *Job 40: 15-19 "Look at Behemoth, which I made along with you and which feeds on grass like an ox. What strength it has in its loins, what power in the muscles of its belly! Its tail sways like a cedar; the sinews of its thighs are close-knit. Its bones are tubes of bronze, its limbs like rods of iron. It ranks first among the works of God, yet its Maker can approach it with his sword.*
>
> *Job 41: 12-14 "I will not fail to speak of Leviathan's limbs, its strength and its graceful form. Who can strip off its outer coat? Who can penetrate its double coat of armor? Who dares open the doors of its mouth, ringed about with fearsome teeth?*

The Behemoth with a tail like a cedar tree (Lebanon cedars are very large and were used in the construction of temples and palaces) could be describing what paleontologists today would call a Brontosaurus. The Leviathan could well well be describing a Stegosaurus based on pictorial renderings from fossils.

For the words in these passages to mean anything to Job, Job must have known animals by these names, so would have understood what God was talking about. God would not use words that meant nothing to Job.

The dinosaur fossils found today were likely created by the flood. Thousands if not millions of animals would have been buried before their carcasses decayed by the mass amount of sediment generated by the flood waters.

One sub-hypothesis is that dinosaurs became extinct with the flood. Another is that the dinosaurs were on the ark and hunted to extinction by man post-flood. How could a massive dinosaur fit on the ark? Chapter 13 of *The Creation Answers Book* provides a simple answer. The dinosaur would have been a newly hatched one that was still very small. It is likely that all the animals on the ark were very young from a simple matter of logistics and space. Is it easier to feed a full grown lion or a freshly weaned lion cub? Is it easier to feed a calf or a 2000 lb. cow? The miracle of the ark is not in the storage and feeding of the animals; it is in God bringing newborn pairs of every animal to Noah.

Regardless of whether dinosaurs survived the Flood, Creation Theory still requires their co-existence with man. Is this possible? Yes. Primitive man has hunted and killed grizzly bears, polar bears, lions, tigers, and elephants with spears and bows and arrows. Men were definitely capable of hunting, or protecting themselves from, dinosaurs. Man is the most feared predator the world has ever seen. God gave man the ability to subdue and dominate the other animals in the land.

An interesting observation is that the Bible historical narrative has lions present in Israel. Judges 14 records Samson killing a young lion, and later eating honey from a hive bees had made in the lion carcass. Of course there are no wild lions in Israel today. Why not? Man killed them and destroyed their habitat over time. Something similar may have happened with dinosaurs. We do not know whether the dinosaurs became extinct as a result of the flood, the following ice age, man's activities, or a combination.

As noted earlier in this chapter, the existence of dinosaur flesh in fossils points to a recent extinction as would have happened in Creation Theory.

V. Allow full debate of theories
Shouldn't every American citizen have the free will to believe in or have faith in theories they think are most true? Isn't that part of God-given free will that a good government will protect? It's not always true in America today.

Many in academia refuse to allow free will and freedom of discussion. In *Expelled: No Intelligence Allowed* (2008), Ben Stein examines the issue of suppression of academic freedom with respect to the theories of the origination of the world. Stein interviews expelled academics and other supporters of Intelligent Design, as well as scientists who support Darwinism. The conclusion: Professors in the United States are being fired from their jobs for promoting, or even exploring the possibility of, Intelligent Design as an alternative to Darwinism.

This type of behavior is not acceptable, especially in university settings that claim to be beacons of free thought and speech. Scientific understanding and learning only flourish when there is a full and open debate of the leading hypotheses. The scientific process is first and foremost about debate and discussion. Anyone trying to stifle or stop debate is thwarting the scientific process. In the Middle Ages some church leaders stifled scientific debate. Today, on the Creation-Evolution issue, it seems to be the secular evolution-believers that wish to prevent debate and discussion from occurring. How is that being scientific? It's the opposite of scientific method.
In school, students should not be forced to accept Evolution as a fact when it is not. Just as they should not be forced to accept Creation as a fact. They should be taught both as widely accepted theories along with the strengths and weaknesses of each theory.

In America today, Creation has been removed from the classrooms by order of the federal courts. There is no constitutional authority for the federal government to dictate education curriculum.

VI. Who Believes Creation Theory?
A number of people both today and in the past have believed in Creation Theory. In fact, Evolution Theory was not even around for much of recorded history.

A. Christians
Christians believe that God created the world because it is taught in the Bible. In most churches around the world, today as well as in the early church, Christians proclaim their faith in the words of the Apostles Creed. The Creed summarizes key tenets of the Christian faith. It begins:

"I believe in God the Father Almighty, Maker of heaven and earth....."

Every Christian is proclaiming that they, as an individual, believe God is all powerful, and did indeed create the earth and the lifeforms on the earth.

<u>Romans 1:18-22, 24-25</u>
The wrath of God is being revealed from heaven against all the godlessness and wickedness of people, who suppress the truth by their wickedness, since what may be known about God is plain to them, because God has made it plain to them. **For since the creation of the world God's invisible qualities—his eternal power and divine nature—have been clearly seen, being understood from what has been made, so that people are without excuse.**
For although they knew God, they neither glorified him as God nor gave thanks to him, but their thinking became futile and their foolish hearts were darkened. Although they claimed to be wise, they became fools.

There is a biblical contradiction to evolution too.

Romans 5:12 Therefore, just as sin entered the world through one man, and death through sin, and in this way death came to all people, because all sinned—

If death came about because of sin, then there was no death before sin. So how did animals supposedly die for millions of years before Adam sinned? Either the Bible is wrong, or the evolutionary time line is wrong.

Creation is a logical requirement for salvation taught in the Bible. The birth, life, death and resurrection of Jesus Christ only mean something if the accounts in Genesis about God's creation of a perfect world and man's sin that ruined that world are true. If Adam wasn't a real person, then death would not be a penalty for sin. If death was not a penalty for sin, then why did Jesus have to die for humanity to cleanse it of that sin? Jesus is the Savior - he saved humanity from its own sin.

Creation and Evolution: Two Competing Theories

If you are a Christian and doubt Creation, read Mark 10:6 again and ask yourself if Jesus is lying or are your beliefs incorrect? Because Jesus says God created man and woman. The Bible also acknowledges that many non-believers will consider Jesus' resurrection (and Creation?) foolishness according to human wisdom.

> *1 Corinthians 1:23,25 but we preach Christ crucified: a stumbling block to Jews and foolishness to Gentiles.... For the foolishness of God is wiser than human wisdom, and the weakness of God is stronger than human strength.*

B. America's Founders believed in Creation and the God of the Bible
There is an entire chapter (10) in this book detailing the deeply religious nature and beliefs of America's founders. Here we will add one more strong piece of evidence: The Declaration of Independence. This major document of American history was drafted by future President Thomas Jefferson, and signed by 56 statesmen from the 13 colonies. Below are three key excerpts that illustrate the importance God has in the document. God is referenced in the first two paragraphs and in the closing paragraph of the Declaration.

> Declaration of Independence
> When in the Course of human events, it becomes necessary for one people to dissolve the political bands which have connected them with another, and to assume among the powers of the earth, the separate and equal station to which the **Laws of Nature and of Nature's God** entitle them, a decent respect to the opinions of mankind requires that they should declare the causes which impel them to the separation.
>
>> The Laws of Nature and (of) Nature's God, is a somewhat shorthand way of saying "the law of nature and the law of nature's God." ... The concepts embodied in the phrase didn't originate with Jefferson. The *law of nature* was a common term used by historic legal writers such as Grotius, Burlamaqui, Blackstone and others. The *law of*

> *nature's God*, a lesser used term, was more commonly called *the divine law*, or *the revealed law*, meaning the laws of God revealed in verbal form.
> - www.lonang.com

We hold these truths to be self-evident, that all men are created equal, that they are endowed by their **Creator** with certain unalienable Rights, that among these are Life, Liberty and the pursuit of Happiness......

> *Genesis 1:1 In the beginning God created the heavens and the earth.*
> *Genesis 1:27 So God created mankind in his own image...*
> *Genesis 14:22 .... the LORD, God Most High, Creator of heaven and earth....*
>
> Genesis 14 is one of 13 times in Scripture where God is referred to as Creator. This terminology is common to those who study the Bible.

And for the support of this Declaration, with a firm reliance on the protection of **Divine Providence**, we mutually pledge to each other our Lives, our Fortunes and our sacred Honor.

> Traditional theism holds that God is the Creator of heaven and earth, and that all that occurs in the universe takes place under ***Divine Providence*** — that is, under God's sovereign guidance and control.
> - Stanford Encyclopedia of Philosophy
> (plato.stanford.edu/entries/providence-divine/)

VII. A Miracle Science Cannot Explain: *90 Minutes in Heaven*

This chapter began with the thought that people should be free to believe what they want. This includes the right to believe that the miracles in the Bible, like people rising from the dead, or a six day Creation, are folklore or fairy tales. Although this belief contradicts recorded eyewitness testimony:

Creation and Evolution: Two Competing Theories

> Our Saviors deeds were always there to see, for they were true: those who were cured or those who rose from the dead were seen not only when they were cured or raised, but were constantly there to see, not only while the Savior was living among us, but also for some time after His departure. Some of them in fact survived right up to our own time.
> - Eusebius: The Church History. p.136.

The idea of an all powerful God capable of raising His Son from the dead after three days, or raising others like Lazarus (John 11) from the dead (also after three days, a perfect example of foreshadowing), can be difficult to grasp for many.

If you have this viewpoint, how do you explain what happened to Don Piper? His story is told in the book: *90 Minutes in Heaven: A True Story of Death and Life.* As Piper is driving across a bridge, he collides with a semi-truck that crosses into his lane. He is pronounced dead at the scene by emergency responders. For 90 minutes, Piper's mangled body lay in his crumpled car against the side of the bridge. A passing minister is led to pray for Don even though he knows the man is dead. Piper miraculously comes back to life. Piper is pried from the car and rushed to the hospital where he begins a long arduous recovery from his severe physical injuries.

Later, Piper will recount first to friends, then to millions of readers in the book, that while dead he received a taste of heaven. Piper recalls being greeted by those who had influenced him spiritually, hearing beautiful music and feeling true peace and heavenly bliss.

Now, one can dismiss Piper's recounting of his time in heaven as simply being a dream. But there is no disputing the fact that Piper was pronounced dead, yet 90 minutes later awoke. How does one scientifically explain this? The temperatures were not sub-zero, where a body can be clinically dead for a short time then be revived. Yet, there are numerous eye-witnesses to the accident that confirm Piper's dead body and revival. Don Piper is also "constantly there for us to see" and will be as long as he lives on this Earth.

A Christian's explanation is that God performed a miracle. He brought Piper back to life without any brain damage (his body was very badly damaged in the accident), and used him to witness to God's existence and power, plus the existence of life after death in heaven. God will restore life to a dead body according to the Bible.

One hundred years from now, all the eye-witnesses to the miracle of Don Piper's return from death will be gone from this earth. And many will scoff that the event ever happened. Just as they did after the eyewitnesses to the resurrections that took place during Jesus' time.

A. Many Other Historical Miracles
The Bible is full of similar acts of God. Christianity should be belief in factual, not fictional stories. That is what scripture is meant to be.

- When God told Adam the story of Creation, he believed it as fact.
- When Adam fell asleep and woke to find a fully grown woman beside him, he knew it happened.
- When Noah built an ark that saved his family from a great flood, he knew it to be a fact. His family and their immediate heirs knew it as fact too.
- When Abraham was told to sacrifice his only son, then was given a ram to take Isaac's place, he passed the story to his heirs as fact.
- When Joseph was sold into slavery, then rose to Pharaoh's second-in-command, his father and brothers witnessed it and believed it as fact.
- When Moses was placed in a basket in the Nile, to be found and adopted by Pharaoh's daughter, his mother knew it as fact.
- When the Israelites lived through the 10 plagues in Egypt, they knew it to be true.
- When the Israelites crossed a parted sea, then watched the sea swallow the pursuing army, they knew it really happened.
- When Joshua was directed by God to march around Jericho with trumpets blasting, and witnessed the city walls collapse, he saw it happen.

Creation and Evolution: Two Competing Theories

- When David, as a young boy, slew a great warrior named Goliath, the Israelite army witnessed it.
- When Jesus raised Lazarus to life after three days in the grave, people witnessed it and believed it as fact.
- When Jesus, Himself, was crucified and raised from the dead after three days, His followers saw and believed it.
- When Saul, the main persecutor of Christians, sees a vision of Jesus, then becomes Paul, the greatest evangelist the world has ever seen, it was known to be a true story.

Every human has free will whether to believe the miracles in the Bible or not, to believe whether the stories contained in the Bible are factual or fictional. However belief does not equal fact, and non-belief does not equal fiction.

Conclusion
In conclusion, as you, the reader, ponders whether to believe Creation or Evolution, be sure to consider all the facts that are available, and realize that science cannot explain all that happens.

Bible-believing Christians need to realize that non-believers view the Bible as the equivalent to Aesop's Fables – a series of fictional stories. So telling a non-believer that the Bible-says-so is the equivalent of someone telling you Aesop says so. It doesn't carry much weight. But there is scientific data that supports Bible-based theories, especially with respect to the flood.

Non-believers need to realize that scientists-say-so, is no more valid than the Bible-says-so. (It could be argued that scientific theories are less valid, because they have changed over time, while the Bible has remained constant.) There are many elements of the Evolution and Big-Bang Theories that are also fable-like, in that they run counter to any scientific observations. Therefore, recognize that these are theories, not facts.

If both sides will agree to distinguish between facts that are proven, and theories which are not proven, it is possible to have reasonable discussions. With respect to theories, **respect everyone's free will. Do not force an evolution believer to accept creationism. Do not force a creation believer to accept**

evolutionism. If the subject of 'how man came to be' is to be discussed in schools or in the political arena, make sure both theories, with their respective strengths and weaknesses are fully discussed.

God's Death Penalty

The last chapter dealt with Creation and the biblical time line. Prominent in that time line is a great worldwide flood that eradicated most humans and animals. Why did God do this? Or more generally: How can a loving God allow people to die?

This question is often asked by Christians struggling to deal with the death of a loved one or by non-believers mocking God. The answer to this question is in scripture. All of us will die. Period. God has given every human a death sentence. Why? Because humans sinned and earned earthly death. Recall this passage from Chapter 2:

> *Genesis 2:16-17 And the LORD God commanded the man, "You are free to eat from any tree in the garden; but you must not eat from the tree of the knowledge of good and evil, for when you eat from it you will certainly die."*

God, as Creator, had every right to make this rule and any other rule. A problem some humans have understanding this is they believe Genesis to be made up rather than a true history of man. Humans have a God-given free will to believe in this way. But in so doing, they just discarded a key passage explaining the reason for earthly death. If God answers a question in Scripture, and humans refuse to believe the answer, who is to blame?

Some Christians desire to create their own God. They read the passages where Jesus shows love, and they make up their own God consisting of only love. If anyone wants to know and seek God, they must seek to know all facets of God – not just the "love" part that makes humans feel good. There is also a jealous component to God, and a righteous component that He uses to judge us.

Since God created the world and humans and animals, God can do with them as He pleases. God is all powerful and in control. That is hard for many humans to accept. Paul explains in his Epistle to the Romans:

> *Romans 9:14-15 What then shall we say? Is God unjust? Not at all! For He says to Moses,*
> > *"I will have mercy on whom I have mercy, and I will have compassion on whom I have compassion." (Exodus 33:19)*

> Romans 9: 20-21 But who are you, a human being, to talk back to God?
> "Shall what is formed say to the one who formed it, 'Why did you make me like this?'" (Isaiah 29:16; 45:9)
> Does not the potter have the right to make out of the same lump of clay some pottery for special purposes and some for common use?

Maybe a human example will make understanding easier. Let's use an example of a woman buying a dog. She loves the dog. Unfortunately, the dog escapes the fenced yard and bites a child. Witnesses say the child did nothing to provoke the dog. So the woman decides she must have the dog put to sleep because it has shown itself to be dangerous to others. She still loves the dog, but she gives it the death penalty. The woman owns the dog. She has the right to euthanize the dog, especially since the dog has "sinned" by biting a child. This analogy falls a little short, because God made humans instead of buying them so He has even more authority.

There are numerous passages in the Bible recording God's love for His human creations. But, once man disobeyed God, sin and death became part of life on Earth. God did not introduce sin; man did. Man reaps the consequences.

> Romans 5:12 Therefore, just as sin entered the world through one man, and death through sin, and in this way death came to all people, because all sinned—

Once humans had fouled God's perfect creation by choosing to sin, death on earth became a reality. Adam and Eve were told they would die. It appears that the first animals were immediately slain for their skin to create clothing for the sinful humans. An illustration of sin leading to death.

> Genesis 3:21 "By the sweat of your brow you will eat your food until you return to the ground, since from it you were taken; for dust you are and to dust you will return."

> Genesis 3:21 The LORD God made garments of skin for Adam and his wife and clothed them.

God's Death Penalty

In addition to earthly death, the Bible teaches all humans will be judged by God at their death as the following passages by Paul and Isaiah indicate.

> *Romans 14:10-12   For we will all stand before God's judgment seat. It is written:*
>> *"'As surely as I live,' says the Lord, 'every knee will bow before me; every tongue will acknowledge God.'"[Isaiah 45:23]*
>
> *So then, each of us will give an account of ourselves to God.*

Sin has consequences. "The wages of sin is death," writes the Apostle Paul. Fortunately for us, God loved man enough to redeem humanity and offer eternal life through Christ.

> *Romans 6:23 For the wages of sin is death, but the gift of God is eternal life in Christ Jesus our Lord.*

Although God sentenced humans to earthly death as a consequence for humans' sin, God longs for all humans to come to Him, and repent of their sin and receive eternal life.

> *2 Peter 3:9 The Lord is not slow in keeping his promise, as some understand slowness. Instead he is patient with you, not wanting anyone to perish, but everyone to come to repentance.*

Even though humans would now face earthly death and judgment by God, they did not stop sinning. Instead, the amount and magnitude of sin escalated. Bible history continues with Cain murdering his younger brother Abel.

> <u>Genesis 4: 8-15</u>
> Now Cain said to his brother Abel, "Let's go out to the field." While they were in the field, Cain attacked his brother Abel and killed him.
>
> Then the LORD said to Cain, "Where is your brother Abel?"
>
> "I don't know," he replied. "Am I my brother's keeper?"

> *The LORD said, "What have you done? Listen! Your brother's blood cries out to me from the ground. Now you are under a curse and driven from the ground, which opened its mouth to receive your brother's blood from your hand. When you work the ground, it will no longer yield its crops for you. You will be a restless wanderer on the earth."*
>
> *Cain said to the LORD, "My punishment is more than I can bear. Today you are driving me from the land, and I will be hidden from your presence; I will be a restless wanderer on the earth, and whoever finds me will kill me."*
>
> *But the LORD said to him, "Not so; anyone who kills Cain will suffer vengeance seven times over." Then the LORD put a mark on Cain so that no one who found him would kill him.*

God punished Cain by driving him from his fellow man, but forbade anybody to kill Cain, promising vengeance on the one who would do so.

The history implies that sin continued to escalate. One of Cain's descendants, Lamech, kills a man and proudly boasts that God will protect him from any seeking his death in retribution.

> *Genesis 4:23-24 Lamech said to his wives, "Adah and Zillah, listen to me; wives of Lamech, hear my words. I have killed a man for wounding me, a young man for injuring me. If Cain is avenged seven times, then Lamech seventy-seven times."*

There appears to be no remorse or repentance to God by Lamech for killing another man. Instead, Lamech seems to have no fear of punishment and seems to mock God. God had protected Cain by declaring seven-times vengeance on anyone seeking to avenge Abel's death by killing Cain. Lamech boasted that no one dare try to kill him or God will seek 77-times vengeance. This behavior is a prime example as to why God eventually did institute the death penalty for murder.

Bible history continues the story of man's early history with sin escalating further. It gets so bad that God finally proclaims the death penalty to the world. He gives His reasoning below.

> *Genesis 6: 5-7 The LORD saw how great the wickedness of the human race had become on the earth, and that every inclination of the thoughts of the human heart was only evil all the time. The LORD regretted that he had made human beings on the earth, and his heart was deeply troubled. So the LORD said, "I will wipe from the face of the earth the human race I have created—and with them the animals, the birds and the creatures that move along the ground—for I regret that I have made them."*

Only Noah and his family were seen by God as being righteous.

> *Genesis 6: 8, 9 But Noah found favor in the eyes of the LORD. Noah was a righteous man, blameless among the people of his time, and he walked faithfully with God.*

The Ultimate Death Penalty: The Great Flood.

> *Genesis 6:11-22*
> *Now the earth was corrupt in God's sight and was full of violence. God saw how corrupt the earth had become, for all the people on earth had corrupted their ways. So God said to Noah, "I am going to put an end to all people, for the earth is filled with violence because of them. I am surely going to destroy both them and the earth. So make yourself an ark of cypress wood; make rooms in it and coat it with pitch inside and out. This is how you are to build it: The ark is to be three hundred cubits [450 ft.] long, fifty cubits [75 ft.] wide and thirty cubits [45 ft.] high. Make a roof for it, leaving below the roof an opening one cubit[18 in.] high all around. Put a door in the side of the ark and make lower, middle and upper decks. I am going to bring floodwaters on the earth to destroy all life under the heavens, every creature that has the breath of life in it. Everything on earth will perish. But I will establish my covenant with you, and you will enter the ark—you and your sons and your wife and your sons' wives with you. You are to bring into the*

ark two of all living creatures, male and female, to keep them alive with you. Two of every kind of bird, of every kind of animal and of every kind of creature that moves along the ground will come to you to be kept alive. You are to take every kind of food that is to be eaten and store it away as food for you and for them."

Noah did everything just as God commanded him.

<u>Genesis 7:11-24</u>
In the six hundredth year of Noah's life, on the seventeenth day of the second month—on that day all the springs of the great deep burst forth, and the floodgates of the heavens were opened. And rain fell on the earth forty days and forty nights.

On that very day Noah and his sons, Shem, Ham and Japheth, together with his wife and the wives of his three sons, entered the ark. They had with them every wild animal according to its kind, all livestock according to their kinds, every creature that moves along the ground according to its kind and every bird according to its kind, everything with wings. Pairs of all creatures that have the breath of life in them came to Noah and entered the ark. The animals going in were male and female of every living thing, as God had commanded Noah. Then the LORD shut him in.

For forty days the flood kept coming on the earth, and as the waters increased they lifted the ark high above the earth. The waters rose and increased greatly on the earth, and the ark floated on the surface of the water. They rose greatly on the earth, and all the high mountains under the entire heavens were covered. The waters rose and covered the mountains to a depth of more than fifteen cubits [23 ft.]. Every living thing that moved on land perished—birds, livestock, wild animals, all the creatures that swarm over the earth, and all mankind. Everything on dry land that had the breath of life in its nostrils died. Every living thing on the face of the earth was wiped out; people and animals and the creatures that move along the ground and the birds were wiped from the earth. Only Noah was left, and those with him in the ark.

God's Death Penalty

The waters flooded the earth for a hundred and fifty days.

Notice scripture stating *"the LORD shut him in."* When God's judgment of the Flood began, it was final. Noah would have been unable to open the ark and save any more people. There were probably people pleading and screaming to be let in as the water rose. Noah and his family could likely hear their screams. Noah's father, who was still alive according to the genealogies, likely perished in the Flood as well. Imagine Noah's father living near the ark, but Noah not able to save him. Most likely a very sad day for Noah, despite he and his children being saved.

It is also likely that quite a large number of humans and animals survived for a while by clinging to floating debris, or maybe they even got into small boats. But after 150 days of flooding they all would have died, having no food to eat. The Flood was definitely a horrible, tragic event.

The previous chapter shared an excellent website with a short video of how the flood may have occurred. It explains where the water may have came from and where it may have went after the Flood. (www.creationscience.com.)

God promised to never send another flood and sealed the covenant with a rainbow.

> *Genesis 8:20-22*
> *Then Noah built an altar to the LORD and, taking some of all the clean animals and clean birds, he sacrificed burnt offerings on it. The LORD smelled the pleasing aroma and said in his heart: "Never again will I curse the ground because of humans, even though every inclination of the human heart is evil from childhood. And never again will I destroy all living creatures, as I have done.*
>
> *"As long as the earth endures, seedtime and harvest, cold and heat, summer and winter, day and night will never cease."*
>
> *Genesis 9:11-13*
> *I establish my covenant with you: Never again will all life be destroyed by the waters of a flood; never again will there be a flood to destroy the earth."*

> *And God said, "This is the sign of the covenant I am making between me and you and every living creature with you, a covenant for all generations to come: I have set my rainbow in the clouds, and it will be the sign of the covenant between me and the earth.*

Some use their free will to mock the Flood as a "story" that never happened. This, of course, is their right to do so. As is their right to mock God, and mock God's final judgment. The Bible says this is not a wise course for a human to follow.

> *2 Peter 3: 3-7 Above all, you must understand that in the last days scoffers will come, scoffing and following their own evil desires. They will say, "Where is this 'coming' He [Jesus] promised? Ever since our ancestors died, everything goes on as it has since the beginning of creation." But they deliberately forget that long ago by God's word the heavens came into being and the earth was formed out of water and by water. By these waters also the world of that time was deluged and destroyed. By the same word the present heavens and earth are reserved for fire, being kept for the day of judgment and destruction of the ungodly.*

There are additional New Testament passages referencing the Flood that both reinforce it as an actual event, and further explain it.

> *Hebrews 11:7 By faith Noah, when warned about things not yet seen, in holy fear built an ark to save his family. By his faith he condemned the world and became heir of the righteousness that is in keeping with faith.*

> *1 Peter 3: 19-21 After being made alive, [Jesus] went and made proclamation to the imprisoned spirits — to those who were disobedient long ago when God waited patiently in the days of Noah while the ark was being built. In it only a few people, eight in all, were saved through water, and this water symbolizes baptism that now saves you also—not the removal of dirt from the body but the pledge of a clear conscience toward God. It saves you by the resurrection of Jesus Christ*

God's Death Penalty

God changed the law and instituted <u>the death penalty for murder</u> in an attempt to prevent post-flood violence.

> *Genesis 9:6 "Whoever sheds human blood, by humans shall their blood be shed; for in the image of God has God made mankind.*

<u>More Examples of Mass Death from Godly Judgment</u>
The flood is not the only time God displays His righteous wrath by causing mass death. Scripture records an example of His destroying two entire cities for their evil behavior. It also illustrates God's mercy as He sends angels to rescue Lot, the only righteous man living there, and his family. The rest of the evil townsmen tried to rape the angels, who had appeared as men.

> <u>*Sodom and Gomorrah Destroyed*</u>
> *Genesis 18:20-21 Then the LORD said, "The outcry against Sodom and Gomorrah is so great and their sin so grievous that I will go down and see if what they have done is as bad as the outcry that has reached me. If not, I will know."*
>
> *Genesis 19:24-25 Then the LORD rained down burning sulfur on Sodom and Gomorrah—from the LORD out of the heavens. Thus he overthrew those cities and the entire plain, destroying all those living in the cities—and also the vegetation in the land.*

In addition to Sodom and Gomorrah, there are other instances of God punishing large groups of people for disobedience or evilness.

> *Exodus 12:29 At midnight the LORD struck down all the firstborn in Egypt, from the firstborn of Pharaoh, who sat on the throne, to the firstborn of the prisoner, who was in the dungeon, and the firstborn of all the livestock as well.*
>
> <u>*Numbers 16:1-2, 31-33, 35*</u>
> *Korah son of Izhar, the son of Kohath, the son of Levi, and certain Reubenites—Dathan and Abiram, sons of Eliab, and On son of Peleth—became insolent and rose up against Moses. With them were 250 Israelite men, well-known community leaders who had been appointed members of*

> the council.
>
> As soon as [Moses] finished saying all this, the ground under them split apart and the earth opened its mouth and swallowed them and their households, and all those associated with Korah, together with their possessions. They went down alive into the realm of the dead, with everything they owned; the earth closed over them, and they perished and were gone from the community.
>
> And fire came out from the LORD and consumed the 250 men who were offering the incense.

> 1 Samuel 6:19 But God struck down some of the inhabitants of Beth Shemesh, putting seventy of them to death because they looked into the ark of the LORD. The people mourned because of the heavy blow the LORD had dealt them.

> 2 Kings 19:35 That night the angel of the LORD went out and put to death a hundred and eighty-five thousand in the Assyrian camp. When the people got up the next morning— there were all the dead bodies!

This event is recorded in Chronicles and Isaiah as well. Being quoted in three separate places marks it as a major event of great significance. Only some events from Jesus' life are recorded more often – four times in the Gospels. It was a miracle performed by God to save the His people from the invading Assyrians.

Jesus, Himself, validates the Great Flood, and the destruction of Sodom and Gomorrah as actual events by speaking of them. He also refers to His second coming in a similar fashion.

> <u>Luke 17: 26-30</u> (also Matthew 24: 37-39)
> "Just as it was in the days of Noah, so also will it be in the days of the Son of Man. People were eating, drinking, marrying and being given in marriage up to the day Noah entered the ark. Then the flood came and destroyed them all.
>
> "It was the same in the days of Lot. People were eating and drinking, buying and selling, planting and building. But

the day Lot left Sodom, fire and sulfur rained down from heaven and destroyed them all.

"It will be just like this on the day the Son of Man is revealed.

This is a strong prophecy by God of a final judgment day that will also be a dramatic real event.

Individuals God Put to Death
There are also examples in the Bible of God directly putting people to death if it served God's purposes. In these examples, the people who died, had broken one of God's commands, or were evil, and God made an example of them.

Genesis 38:7 But Er, Judah's firstborn, was wicked in the LORD's sight; so the LORD put him to death.

Genesis 38:10 What he [Onan] did was wicked in the LORD's sight; so the LORD put him to death also.

Leviticus 10:1-2 Aaron's sons Nadab and Abihu took their censers, put fire in them and added incense; and they offered unauthorized fire before the LORD, contrary to his command. So fire came out from the presence of the LORD and consumed them, and they died before the LORD.

2 Samuel 6:7 The LORD's anger burned against Uzzah because of his irreverent act; therefore God struck him down, and he died there beside the ark of God.

Acts 5:5 When Ananias heard this, he fell down and died. And great fear seized all who heard what had happened.

These examples are rare considering the thousands of years scripture covers, but are examples of God issuing the death penalty when it serves His overall plans.

While God has issued death penalties both in mass and for small groups, Peter tells us that God only punishes the unrighteous and the unrepentant.

2 Peter 2:4-9   For if God did not spare angels when they sinned, but sent them to hell, putting them in chains of darkness to be held for judgment; if He did not spare the ancient world when He brought the flood on its ungodly people, but protected Noah, a preacher of righteousness, and seven others; if He condemned the cities of Sodom and Gomorrah by burning them to ashes, and made them an example of what is going to happen to the ungodly; and if He rescued Lot, a righteous man, who was distressed by the depraved conduct of the lawless (for that righteous man, living among them day after day, was tormented in his righteous soul by the lawless deeds he saw and heard)— if this is so, then the Lord knows how to rescue the godly from trials and to hold the unrighteous for punishment on the day of judgment.

There is a biblical narrative where God appears to issue an unjust death penalty. Abraham had long waited for a son, and finally God blessed him with Isaac, his only son with his wife Sarah. Then God tells Abraham to sacrifice Isaac – kill him for God. Isaac had done nothing evil. He hadn't killed anybody. Why was God doing this? God was testing Abraham's faithfulness.

<u>Genesis 22:2-13 Abraham's Faith Tested</u>
Then God said, "Take your son, your only son, whom you love—Isaac—and go to the region of Moriah. Sacrifice him there as a burnt offering on a mountain I will show you."

Early the next morning Abraham got up and loaded his donkey. He took with him two of his servants and his son Isaac. When he had cut enough wood for the burnt offering, he set out for the place God had told him about. On the third day Abraham looked up and saw the place in the distance. He said to his servants, "Stay here with the donkey while I and the boy go over there. We will worship and then we will come back to you."

Abraham took the wood for the burnt offering and placed it on his son Isaac, and he himself carried the fire and the knife. As the two of them went on together, Isaac spoke up and said to his father Abraham, "Father?"

"Yes, my son?" Abraham replied.

> *"The fire and wood are here,"* Isaac said, *"but where is the lamb for the burnt offering?"*
>
> *Abraham answered, "God himself will provide the lamb for the burnt offering, my son." And the two of them went on together.*
>
> *When they reached the place God had told him about, Abraham built an altar there and arranged the wood on it. He bound his son Isaac and laid him on the altar, on top of the wood. Then he reached out his hand and took the knife to slay his son. But the angel of the LORD called out to him from heaven, "Abraham! Abraham!"*
>
> *"Here I am," he replied.*
>
> *"Do not lay a hand on the boy," He said. "Do not do anything to him. Now I know that you fear God, because you have not withheld from Me your son, your only son."*
>
> *Abraham looked up and there in a thicket he saw a ram caught by its horns. He went over and took the ram and sacrificed it as a burnt offering instead of his son.*

It is impossible to read this story without seeing the foreshadowing. An innocent only son is being sacrificed for God's purposes. It is the role Jesus would play some two thousand years later when God ordered His only Son to die on the cross for humanity.

It also shows the nature of God. He tested Abraham, but did not take an innocent life. God does not want human sacrifice. It is not pleasing to God. Some will say it was cruel of God to put Abraham to such a test. There is a saying that applies: To whom much is given, much is expected. God had chosen Abraham to be the father God's chosen people; those who would be responsible for recording God's Scripture, and producing the Messiah for the entire world. Abraham, because of his faith, played a key role in God's redemptive plan.

The chapter opened with the question: How could a loving God allow death? Humans brought it on themselves with sin and evil behavior. God is a loving God. But, He is also a righteous God. Humans earned the earthly death penalty. In His righteousness, God has sometimes intervened to directly deal out the punishment –

but only to those who deserved it.

It doesn't have to end with death though. Every human accepting Jesus as Savior will receive eternal life. That is God's love trumping all.

> *John 3:16-18 For God so loved the world that he gave his one and only Son, that whoever believes in him shall not perish but have eternal life. For God did not send his Son into the world to condemn the world, but to save the world through him. Whoever believes in him is not condemned, but whoever does not believe stands condemned already because they have not believed in the name of God's one and only Son.*

The Bible on Holy War

One of the issues facing the world today is the threat of Jihad, of Holy War, conducted by some in the Muslim faith. Jihad has been expressed through terrorist activities, the best known in America being the tragic attacks of 9/11/2001 on the World Trade Center and the Pentagon. The author is not an expert on the Koran, and therefore unable to say whether that book instructs its followers to spread their faith by war or whether extremists have misinterpreted it for their terrorist acts.

The author is very familiar with the Bible and can safely say it does not support Holy War. Anyone reading the Old Testament and concluding that it does, simply has not read the entire book and placed it in context. Bible history does show occasions where God uses war to achieve His will. The most obvious example being the conquest of Canaan (Israel on modern maps) described in the book of Joshua.

> Sidebar: The difference between Christ and Muhammad.
> The differences are easily seen in the approaches the two leaders of their religions used. Jesus never used force to spread the religion which came to be named after Him. This is easily seen at Jesus' arrest. Jesus rebukes his followers when they attempt to use force to protect Him.
>
> *Matthew 26:50-56*
> *Then the men [armed with swords and clubs, sent by the chief priests] stepped forward, seized Jesus and arrested him. With that, one of Jesus' companions reached for his sword, drew it out and struck the servant of the high priest, cutting off his ear.*
>
> *"Put your sword back in its place," Jesus said to him, "for all who draw the sword will die by the sword. Do you think I cannot call on my Father, and he will at once put at my disposal more than twelve legions of angels? But how then would the Scriptures be fulfilled that say it must happen in this way?"*
>
> *In that hour Jesus said to the crowd, "Am I leading a rebellion, that you have come out with swords and clubs to capture me? Every day I sat in the temple courts teaching, and you did not arrest me. But this has all taken place that*

the writings of the prophets might be fulfilled." Then all the disciples deserted him and fled.

In contrast to Christ, Muhammad was a warrior. He spread Islam by forcibly uniting the tribes of Arabia and conquering Mecca (630 AD). The leaders of Islam continued conquering lands until they controlled large portions of the old Persian and Roman Empires by the early 700's. Muhammad used Islam to become a powerful ruler; Christ pointedly refused to establish earthly power.

As we examine the Bible's account of war and the resulting deaths it causes, we must remember the proper biblical perspective. God made the earth and humans that inhabit it. This is Bible history recorded in Genesis and reprinted in Chapter 3.

Since God created the Earth and humans, He can do whatever He wishes with His creation. Much like if a child builds a sandcastle he can knock it over if he chooses. A creator has the right to do what he wants with his creations. This logic applies to man and to God.

God reminds us of His authority and power in His discussion with Job.

> *Job 38: 4-6 (God speaking to Job)*
> *"Where were you when I laid the earth's foundation? Tell me, if you understand. Who marked off its dimensions? Surely you know! Who stretched a measuring line across it? On what were its footings set, or who laid its cornerstone?"*
>
> *Job 40: 4-5 (Job answering the Lord)*
> *"I am unworthy—how can I reply to you? I put my hand over my mouth. I spoke once, but I have no answer— twice, but I will say no more."*

God did destroy human civilization once because sin had become too great (The Flood in Genesis covered in the Chapter 4). God says He was so saddened by the destruction that He promised to never send another flood.

With that perspective, we can examine God's use of war to achieve His will of establishing Israel. God promised an area of land to Abraham's descendants. This was part of God's plan to redeem all humanity.

> *Genesis 15:18-21 On that day the LORD made a covenant with Abram and said, "To your descendants I give this land, from the Wadi of Egypt to the great river, the Euphrates—the land of the Kenites, Kenizzites, Kadmonites, Hittites, Perizzites, Rephaites, Amorites, Canaanites, Girgashites and Jebusites."*

God foretold that Abraham's offspring would go to a foreign land, become slaves, leave slavery, and return to the land. He states the current inhabitants will be punished at their return. Why did God punish the inhabitants? One huge reason: They sacrificed their children to the false god Molech. God clearly instructs His followers to eliminate this evil practice.

> *Leviticus 18:21 Do not give any of your children to be sacrificed to Molech, for you must not profane the name of your God. I am the LORD.*

> *Leviticus 20: 2-5 "Say to the Israelites: 'Any Israelite or any alien living in Israel who gives any of his children to Molech must be put to death. The people of the community are to stone him. I will set my face against that man and I will cut him off from his people; for by giving his children to Molech, he has defiled my sanctuary and profaned my holy name. If the people of the community close their eyes when that man gives one of his children to Molech and they fail to put him to death, I will set my face against that man and his family and will cut off from their people both him and all who follow him in prostituting themselves to Molech.*

For punishment, God declared the inhabitants of the land should die and be destroyed by Joshua and Israel. See what happens when God declares war.

Joshua 1 : The LORD Commands Joshua
After the death of Moses the servant of the LORD, the LORD said to Joshua son of Nun, Moses' aide: "Moses my servant is dead. Now then, you and all these people, get ready to cross the Jordan River into the land I am about to give to them—to the Israelites. I will give you every place where you set your foot, as I promised Moses. Your territory will extend from the desert to Lebanon, and from the great river, the Euphrates—all the Hittite country—to the Great Sea on the west. No one will be able to stand up against you all the days of your life. As I was with Moses, so I will be with you; I will never leave you nor forsake you. "Be strong and courageous, because you will lead these people to inherit the land I swore to their forefathers to give them. Be strong and very courageous. Be careful to obey all the law my servant Moses gave you; do not turn from it to the right or to the left, that you may be successful wherever you go. Do not let this Book of the Law depart from your mouth; meditate on it day and night, so that you may be careful to do everything written in it. Then you will be prosperous and successful. Have I not commanded you? Be strong and courageous. Do not be terrified; do not be discouraged, for the LORD your God will be with you wherever you go."

So Joshua ordered the officers of the people: "Go through the camp and tell the people, 'Get your supplies ready. Three days from now you will cross the Jordan here to go in and take possession of the land the LORD your God is giving you for your own.' "

Joshua 6: 1-5
Now Jericho was tightly shut up because of the Israelites. No one went out and no one came in.

Then the LORD said to Joshua, "See, I have delivered Jericho into your hands, along with its king and its fighting men. March around the city once with all the armed men. Do this for six days. Have seven priests carry trumpets of rams' horns in front of the ark. On the seventh day, march around the city seven times, with the priests blowing the trumpets. When you hear them sound a long blast on the trumpets, have all the people give a loud shout; then the wall of the city will collapse and the people will go up, every man straight in."

Joshua 6:20-21
When the trumpets sounded, the people shouted, and at the sound of the trumpet, when the people gave a loud shout, the wall collapsed; so every man charged straight in, and they took the city. They devoted the city to the LORD and destroyed with the sword every living thing in it—men and women, young and old, cattle, sheep and donkeys.

The Snare of False gods

Why would God destroy the people of that land? God gives the reason for this harsh punishment: The inhabitants of the promised land and their false-god worship would lead Israel away from God's true teachings and cause them to sin. The inhabitants if left alive would be a snare or trap the people could succumb to.

Exodus 23:32-33 "Do not make a covenant with them or with their gods. Do not let them live in your land, or they will cause you to sin against me, because the worship of their gods will certainly be a snare to you."

Exodus 34: 11-13 Obey what I command you today. I will drive out before you the Amorites, Canaanites, Hittites, Perizzites, Hivites and Jebusites. Be careful not to make a treaty with those who live in the land where you are going, or they will be a snare among you. Break down their altars, smash their sacred stones and cut down their Asherah poles.

Deuteronomy 7:16 You must destroy all the peoples the LORD your God gives over to you. Do not look on them with pity and do not serve their gods, for that will be a snare to you.

Judges 2: 1-4 The angel of the LORD went up from Gilgal to Bokim and said, "I brought you up out of Egypt and led you into the land that I swore to give to your forefathers. I said, 'I will never break my covenant with you, and <u>you shall not make a covenant with the people of this land, but</u>

> *<u>you shall break down their altars.</u>' Yet you have disobeyed me. Why have you done this? Now therefore I tell you that I will not drive them out before you; they will be thorns in your sides and their gods will be a snare to you." When the angel of the LORD had spoken these things to all the Israelites, the people wept aloud.*

Scripture lists multiple occasions where the tribes failed to fulfill God's wishes and fully conquer the land (Joshua 13:13, 16:10, 17:11, Judges 1:21-2:5).

God was proven correct. The following examples in scripture show how the people began following the evil and barbaric practices of child sacrifice to Molech that God found detestable.

> *2 Kings 23:10 [King Josiah] desecrated Topheth, which was in the Valley of Ben Hinnom, so no one could use it to sacrifice his son or daughter in the fire to Molech.*

> *Jeremiah 32:35 [The people of Israel and Judah built high places for Baal in the Valley of Ben Hinnom to sacrifice their sons and daughters to Molech, <u>though I never commanded, nor did it enter my mind, that they should do such a detestable thing</u> and so make Judah sin.*

Sidebar: It is possible that if the tribes of Israel had had stronger faith, they would have been immune to the snares of Molech from the conquered inhabitants. In that case, God may very well have spared their lives with the possibility of them being converted to follow the One True God. But we already know from the earlier history of the golden calf in Exodus that the Israelites were quick to abandon God. Or God may have simply decided that the inhabitants deserved the punishment of a death sentence for their evil actions. In any case, God is God.

In summary, God promised an area of land to Abraham and his descendants. God chose war as a means of carrying out this promise. God gave additional reason and justification for His divine action: The inhabitants of the land were practicing child sacrifice and worshiping false gods. This event qualifies as a Holy War, but it was a one-time action by God, not the standard means for His followers to spread their faith.

An example of mercy: Also in the Old Testament we see God's grace and mercy on display as He sends a prophet to preach to Nineveh. Nineveh was one of the largest cities in the ancient world, the capitol city of the Assyrian Empire which bordered ancient Israel. The Assyrians were enemies of the Israelites. (The Assyrians would later conquer the northern Kingdom of Israel – as God carried out a covenant curse on His people). Despite this God sent a prophet to minister to the people of Nineveh, calling them back to God.

> *Jonah 3: 1-5, 10*
> *Then the word of the Lord came to Jonah a second time: "Go to the great city of Nineveh and proclaim to it the message I give you."*
>
> *Jonah obeyed the word of the Lord and went to Nineveh. Now Nineveh was a very large city; it took three days to go through it. Jonah began by going a day's journey into the city, proclaiming, "Forty more days and Nineveh will be overthrown." The Ninevites believed God. A fast was proclaimed, and all of them, from the greatest to the least, put on sackcloth.*
>
> *When God saw what they did and how they turned from their evil ways, he relented and did not bring on them the destruction he had threatened.*

Jonah was greatly upset that God spared Nineveh from punishment. He wished God would destroy the enemy of his nation. Instead God chastised Jonah:

> *Jonah 4:11 "And should I not have concern for the great city of Nineveh, in which there are more than a hundred and twenty thousand people who cannot tell their right hand from their left—and also many animals?"*

This is consistent behavior on God's part seen throughout the Bible: God always cares about all humans. This does not mean God does not punish humans when God deems it necessary.

Just as God didn't tell His people the Israelites to go and crush the city of Nineveh, God doesn't want his modern-day followers to engage in war to convert people. In fact He teaches that the opposite will occur for his followers – they will be victims of attacks. Jesus prophesies about the coming Jewish attack on the early Christian Church (told in Acts)

> *John 16:2-3 They will put you out of the synagogue; in fact, the time is coming when anyone who kills you will think they are offering a service to God. They will do such things because they have not known the Father or me.*

Jesus says the Jews will kill because "They have not known the Father or me." Implied is that any person truly knowing God would never kill another human in God's Name.

At the end of Matthew Jesus issues the Great Commission to his disciples.

> *Matthew 28:19-20 Therefore go and make disciples of all nations, baptizing them in the name of the Father and of the Son and of the Holy Spirit, and teaching them to obey everything I have commanded you. And surely I am with you always, to the very end of the age."*

Jesus is talking directly to His disciples, and through scripture directly to His followers today. Anyone trying to read forced conversion of people to Christianity into this passage need look no further than what Jesus did and what His disciples did after receiving this mission. Throughout the book of Acts, the disciples taught and preached and with the Holy Spirit converted thousands of Jews and Gentiles to followers of Christ by peaceful means. Throughout the book of Acts the violence and protests come from Jews who refuse to accept Christ and turn to rioting to stop the disciples from preaching. The decision to accept Christ and follow God should be made with a person's free will, not because others are forcing the person.

Evangelism, the spreading of God's Word, is a mission directed to individual followers and to groups of followers known as the church (churches today, as there are many). Also realize that once again

The Bible on Holy War

God is giving people the free will to choose whether to follow Christ or not and free will whether to work toward this mission.

To further illustrate how God doesn't intend "Holy War" to be used to spread His message, one need look no further that the story of Stephen. Stephen was one of seven disciples chosen to administer the distribution of food within the early church. Stephen was "known to be full of the Spirit and wisdom."

A group of Jews brought false witnesses against Stephen and accused him of blasphemy, the punishment for which was death by stoning.

> <u>Acts 7:54-60 The Stoning of Stephen</u>
> *When the members of the Sanhedrin heard this, they were furious and gnashed their teeth at him. But Stephen, full of the Holy Spirit, looked up to heaven and saw the glory of God, and Jesus standing at the right hand of God. "Look," he said, "I see heaven open and the Son of Man standing at the right hand of God."*
>
> *At this they covered their ears and, yelling at the top of their voices, they all rushed at him, dragged him out of the city and began to stone him. Meanwhile, the witnesses laid their coats at the feet of a young man named Saul. While they were stoning him, Stephen prayed, "Lord Jesus, receive my spirit." Then he fell on his knees and cried out, "Lord, do not hold this sin against them." When he had said this, he fell asleep.*

God let one of His strongest believers perish even though he was innocent. Had Jesus wanted "Holy War" He could have sent a few lightning bolts down to stop the stoning. He could have appeared in His glory and left the mob blind at the sight of Him. Jesus did none of those things. He could have commanded Stephen and the other disciples to take up arms and overthrow the corrupt Sanhedrin in the name of Jesus. That is not God's Way. The message of Jesus was and is to be spread by peaceful teaching, not brute force.

When the Bible is taken in full context it can easily be seen that God does not tell His followers to spread their faith by force or by use of holy war. Rather God wants people to come to Him via their own free will which He has given them.

The Bible and Constitution Made America Great

The Founders of America realized this, especially with respect to the national government. Therefore, in America, there is freedom of religion that is guaranteed by our constitution. This means free will to follow whichever religion a citizen chooses and their means of worship. As with all constitutional rights, it ends when one person begins to threaten another. There is no right for any religion to preach Holy War, just as there is no right to yell "fire" in a crowded theater.

The Old Testament Government Established by God

We can gain insight into God and how He wants humans to live by studying the laws of the nation of Israel in the Old Testament. Their law came directly from God, not from men. God established the laws that the government and the people should follow. God's law gives humans freedom and dictates that other humans not take the freedom away. It also dictates that citizens live in a God-pleasing manner.

It is important to realize that the laws were directed at individuals in ancient Israel and were enforced at the city level by town elders. Modern governments often chose portions of this law as a basis for their modern law. This is the case in the United States. Many if not all of the colonial states enforced a good portion of the Old Testament laws. Some are commonly accepted and still enforced today (laws against robbery, stealing, perjury....).

The government established by God in the Bible for the His chosen people was a theocracy. In a theocracy, there is a single state religion. God installed Himself as the ultimate leader of the people.

> *Exodus 6:7 I will take you as my own people, and I will be your God. Then you will know that I am the LORD your God, who brought you out from under the yoke of the Egyptians.*

This is the basis for the Old Testament covenant between God and the ancient nation of Israel. Under this covenant God established a government and gave the law.

Free Will and the Law
God continued His practice of allowing the people free will to follow God's plan. The people chose to follow Moses (and God) and leave Egypt. The people were always free to leave Israel (That is how *Ruth* begins, with her family leaving Israel). It is important to remember that even if one chose to move to a neighboring land, one would be subject to the ' laws of that land.

An example of the free will and choices the people were able to make is found in Joshua. Joshua was the general who led the Israelites in battle. The following passage comes after the armies have completed the initial conquest of the promised land.

> *Joshua 24: 14-15 "Now fear the Lord and serve him with all faithfulness. Throw away the gods your ancestors worshiped beyond the Euphrates River and in Egypt, and serve the Lord. But if serving the Lord seems undesirable to you, then **choose for yourselves** this day whom you will serve, whether the gods your ancestors served beyond the Euphrates, or the gods of the Amorites, in whose land you are living. But as for me and my household, we will serve the Lord."*

Notice how Joshua tells the people to choose whether to follow God or not. Joshua, as the leader of the army, could have commanded the people worship God. But he did not. He told the people to choose. That was God's way then, and always has been.

Throughout the Old Testament, God continued to give people free will. The people were always free to follow God's commands or reject them. There are many instances where God directly punished the people for disobedience, but the people always had the choice. Even in the area of worship, there are examples of the government removing false gods and their temples, but no examples of the government forcing the people to worship God. God wants His people to willingly follow Him.

<u>Difference between Old and New Covenants</u>
Specific details of the covenant relationship between God and His followers has changed over time. God made a covenant agreement with Abraham long before the law was given in Leviticus and Deuteronomy. The main sign of that covenant was circumcision. Later the laws of Moses were added. One element is always present: Paul states in Romans that faithfulness to God is the underlying power of any covenant agreement.

> *Romans 4:9-10 Is this blessedness only for the circumcised, or also for the uncircumcised? We have been saying that Abraham's faith was credited to him as righteousness. Under what circumstances was it credited? Was it after he was circumcised, or before? It was not after, but before!*

The Old Testament Government Established by God

The New Testament covenant instituted by Christ is between God and those who are His followers. There is not a single nation, rather followers in many nations. The government of ancient Israel is replaced by the church(es) with respect to carrying out God's will on Earth. Modern governments are not bound by the laws of the Old Testament. Although many nations have adopted the portion of laws respecting mans interaction with man (murder, stealing...). This includes America which inherited its basic common law from England which took sections from scripture.

Old Covenant Background
As we look back at the government God established for ancient Israel (around 1500 BC), it is important to place the events in the proper context and timing of God's plan. God had already wiped out the world once for its wickedness – saving only Noah, his family, and animals to repopulate the earth. Abraham had emerged as a man of great faith in God, and God had promised to bless him with with numerous descendants and give them the land of Canaan as a homeland. Jacob, Abraham's grandson, had moved to Egypt to escape famine, and stayed there for 400-some years. The clan had the favor of Pharaoh (through Joseph) and grew many-fold. Eventually a new Pharaoh seized the Israelis and made them slaves. God would rescue the people and with Moses as their leader deliver them from bondage into their new homeland.

Moses himself may have known very little about God or Abraham, Isaac, and Jacob, since he was raised in Pharaoh's court from infancy. However after fleeing Egypt, God led Moses to Jethro, a priest of Midian (named for descendants of Midian, a son of Abraham – Gen 25:1). Moses would marry Jethro's daughter.

> *Exodus 18:1 Now Jethro, the priest of Midian and father-in-law of Moses, heard of everything God had done for Moses and for his people Israel, and how the LORD had brought Israel out of Egypt.*

Jethro was evidently a strong believer in God who had maintained the worship practices of Abraham. Jethro also would have been able to provide Moses with the word-of-mouth heritage that Moses would turn into the book of Genesis.

> *Exodus 18:11-12 Now I know that the LORD is greater than all other gods, for he did this to those who had treated Israel arrogantly." Then Jethro, Moses' father-in-law, brought a burnt offering and other sacrifices to God, and Aaron came with all the elders of Israel to eat a meal with Moses' father-in-law in the presence of God.*

The Bible doesn't specifically say, but it appears that the people during their stay in Egypt had forgotten most of their knowledge about God except for the fact that there was a God of Abraham, Isaac, and Jacob. This would explain why the people were so quick to grumble at every sign of trouble despite the miracles God was performing all around them. It would also explain why the Israelites quickly made and worshiped a golden calf, similar to the idol worship of the Egyptians.

> <u>Exodus 32:1,3-4</u>
> When the people saw that Moses was so long in coming down from the mountain, they gathered around Aaron and said, "Come, make us gods who will go before us. As for this fellow Moses who brought us up out of Egypt, we don't know what has happened to him."
>
> So all the people took off their earrings and brought them to Aaron. He took what they handed him and made it into an idol cast in the shape of a calf, fashioning it with a tool. Then they said, "These are your gods, Israel, who brought you up out of Egypt."

The Lord was very angry, and threatened to destroy the people but Moses intervened and begged God not to do so.

> *Exodus 32:9-10 "I have seen these people," the LORD said to Moses, "and they are a stiff-necked people. Now leave me alone so that my anger may burn against them and that I may destroy them. Then I will make you into a great nation."*

God listened to Moses, and spared the people; but the anger can be seen in the tone God uses with the people. It may very well have been necessary for God to treat them like a slave driver would treat slaves, since this was what the people were accustomed to in Egypt.

Note the free will: The people chose to make a golden calf and worship it (Exodus 32). God allowed them to worship what they wanted. But, God could chose to punish transgressions as He did in this case by sending a plague on the people (32:35). There are consequences for sin.

Here is the outline for the government created by God for Israel:

I. Government Structure in the Wilderness
II. Peacetime Government in the Promised Land
   A) Unique Small Government – No King
   B) Israel Requests a King
III. Laws of the Nation
   A) Ten Commandments
   B) Death Penalty Offenses
   C) Economic and Property Laws
     1. Tithing
     2. Gleaning
     3. Property ownership
     4. Indentured servants
IV. Examples of Government Enforcement of the Law
V. Old Testament Nation-Government Judgments
VI. Interpreting the Law for Individuals vs Government

I. Government Structure in the Wilderness

As God was leading Israel through the wilderness into the promised land, a centralized militaristic government was needed. The government was a theocracy. God, Himself was the leader and commanded loyalty and worship from His people. Moses, a strong prophet-king was second in command to God.

> *Exodus 13:21-22 By day the LORD went ahead of them in a pillar of cloud to guide them on their way and by night in a pillar of fire to give them light, so that they could travel by day or night. Neither the pillar of cloud by day nor the pillar of fire by night left its place in front of the people.*

Even in this centralized government there was a strong reliance on tribal leaders (local government) to solve issues. Problems were solved to the greatest possible extent at the local level where they originated. The hard cases they brought to Moses (national government), but every small matter they judged themselves.

> *Exodus 18:13-26*
> *The next day Moses took his seat to serve as judge for the people, and they stood around him from morning till evening. When his father-in-law saw all that Moses was doing for the people, he said, "What is this you are doing for the people? Why do you alone sit as judge, while all these people stand around you from morning till evening?"*
>
> *Moses answered him, "Because the people come to me to seek God's will. Whenever they have a dispute, it is brought to me, and I decide between the parties and inform them of God's decrees and instructions."*
>
> *Moses' father-in-law replied, "What you are doing is not good. You and these people who come to you will only wear yourselves out. The work is too heavy for you; you cannot handle it alone. Listen now to me and I will give you some advice, and may God be with you. You must be the people's representative before God and bring their disputes to him. Teach them his decrees and instructions, and show them the way they are to live and how they are to behave. But select capable men from all the people—men who fear God, trustworthy men who hate dishonest gain—and appoint them as officials over thousands, hundreds, fifties and tens. Have them serve as judges for the people at all times, but have them bring every difficult case to you; the simple cases they can decide themselves. That will make your load lighter, because they will share it with you. If you do this and God so commands, you will be able to stand the strain, and all these people will go home satisfied."*
>
> *Moses listened to his father-in-law and did everything he said. He chose capable men from all Israel and made them leaders of the people, officials over thousands, hundreds, fifties and tens. They served as judges for the people at all times. The difficult cases they brought to Moses, but the simple ones they decided themselves.*

The Old Testament Government Established by God

> <u>Deuteronomy 1:13-16 (Moses speaking to the people)</u>
> *Choose some wise, understanding and respected men from each of your tribes, and I will set them over you."*
> *You answered me, "What you propose to do is good."*
>
> *So I took the leading men of your tribes, wise and respected men, and appointed them to have authority over you—as commanders of thousands, of hundreds, of fifties and of tens and as tribal officials.*
>
> *And I charged your judges at that time, "Hear the disputes between your people and judge fairly, whether the case is between two Israelites or between an Israelite and a foreigner residing among you.*

Here is the militaristic government structure God established to lead Israel to the Promised Land. Israel was organized by twelve tribes which came from the sons of Jacob. The officials within the tribes were to act as judges to resolve matters within their units of review.

<u>Government Structure of Israel in the Wilderness:</u>
God
Moses
Aaron and Joshua (advisers to Moses)
12 Tribes
1 official for every 1000 families by tribe
1 official for every 100 families by tribe
1 official for every 50 families by tribe
1 official for every 10 families by tribe
Male Head of the Family
Women and Children of Family

Each issue was to be handled at the lowest level possible. Local government handling local problems keeps larger government units from becoming overwhelmed.

<u>II. Peacetime Government in the Promised Land</u>
After Moses died and Joshua led the Israelite army to defeat the inhabitants of the Promised Land, a new government was formed. The central government dissolved in that there was no strong national leader, and control reverted to the twelve tribes. Each

tribal town probably chose its own leaders and judges to implement God's laws for the town. God was still present as the overall leader of the nation, but was no longer as visible as during the military campaign.

God promised the people blessings or curses for the nation, depending on their obedience to God's directions.

> *Deuteronomy 28:2,7 All these blessings will come on you and accompany you if you obey the LORD your God:... The LORD will grant that the enemies who rise up against you will be defeated before you. They will come at you from one direction but flee from you in seven.*
>
> *Deuteronomy 28:15,25 However, if you do not obey the LORD your God and do not carefully follow all his commands and decrees I am giving you today, all these curses will come on you and overtake you: .... The LORD will cause you to be defeated before your enemies. You will come at them from one direction but flee from them in seven,....*

God gave the people free will similar to His directions to Adam and Eve in the Garden of Eden. God told what He wanted, and listed the expected outcomes of compliance or non-compliance. It's free will because God was not physically present on a daily basis enforcing the law, like an earthly king would. The people had a choice whether to follow God's wishes or not. Scriptural narrative tells the Israelite people went through cycles of obeying and disobeying throughout their history. Thereby confirming the freedom to disobey.

Note: This is like present times. God is not present in a physical form making humans follow His will. It is up to the individual to follow or not. (The national scope of the Mosaic covenant differs with the individual focus present in the rest of the Bible)

A. Unique Small Government – No King
Scripture describes the government that God gave the Israelites as they settled into their new homeland. The peacetime government was very small and local, consisting of town elders or leaders. There

was no central government – no king. The national church and national religion, the priests, existed as before.

> *Deuteronomy 16:18-20 Appoint judges and officials for each of your tribes in every town the LORD your God is giving you, and they shall judge the people fairly. Do not pervert justice or show partiality. Do not accept a bribe, for a bribe blinds the eyes of the wise and twists the words of the innocent. Follow justice and justice alone, so that you may live and possess the land the LORD your God is giving you.*
>
> *Deuteronomy 25:1 When people have a dispute, they are to take it to court and the judges will decide the case, acquitting the innocent and condemning the guilty.*

The town leaders served as judges and court officials, continuing the pattern established under Moses. There are no government taxes mentioned in scripture to support the judges or court officials. They likely worked on their land or in their jobs to support themselves (as Saul did; described later in chapter).

This government may have been one of the most economically free ever created. There was no central government other than God. God did expect tithes (10% giving) and this was law, but there were no government agents to enforce it. Town elders served as part-time judges to resolve disputes but there is no evidence these judges could levy taxes. It seems as individuals made their own decisions whether to follow the tithing law – just as with today's followers of God.

It is remarkable that God did not establish a king or a powerful central government. All the other nations in the area had kings. The Israelites had left Egypt where a powerful Pharaoh ruled the land. During the journey to the promised land and the military campaign, the people had been ruled by Moses, then Joshua, both powerful leaders. The natural progression would have been to appoint a king to lead the nation. But God opted for no central government, no king. Only local city/town government was established to enforce the laws of the land. The main function of a strong central government – keeping the people of the nation safe from foreign invaders – was a function God promised to do Himself.

<u>B. Israel Requests a King</u>
Eventually, the people of Israel rejected God's ideal, king-less small government. They decided they wanted a king, the ancient day equivalent of today's national government. God warned them against a king, telling them a king will make them slaves and take (tax) 10% of the goods the people produce.

> *1 Samuel 8: 9-18 Samuel told all the words of the LORD to the people who were asking him for a king. He said, "This is what the king who will reign over you will do: He will take your sons and make them serve with his chariots and horses, and they will run in front of his chariots. Some he will assign to be commanders of thousands and commanders of fifties, and others to plow his ground and reap his harvest, and still others to make weapons of war and equipment for his chariots. He will take your daughters to be perfumers and cooks and bakers. He will take the best of your fields and vineyards and olive groves and give them to his attendants. He will take a tenth of your grain and of your vintage and give it to his officials and attendants. Your menservants and maidservants and the best of your cattle and donkeys he will take for his own use. He will take a tenth of your flocks, and you yourselves will become his slaves. When that day comes, you will cry out for relief from the king you have chosen, and the LORD will not answer you in that day."*

It took a while before God's predictions about the king came to pass. In 1 Samuel 9, Saul is anointed the first king of Israel. Initially, King Saul acted very much like a common man still supporting himself and working his fields.

> *1 Samuel 11:5 Just then Saul was returning from the fields, behind his oxen...*

If the king was still working his fields, it strongly implies the town leaders and judges were also supporting themselves through their work. There apparently was no salaried class of government officials in that society. The priests, the church class, were to be supported by the community (tithes) according to God's direction.

Scripture tells us that later kings of Israel built a palace, used servants to tend to themselves, and officials to carry out their orders, as well as a forming standing army. They taxed the people pay for these things, just as God had predicted. Although, it doesn't take great skill to predict the Israelite government would grow itself, just like other governments throughout history.

The kings continued the practice of appointing judges at the city level (local) to resolve disputes among the people originally initiated by Moses.

> *2 Chronicles 19:5-6 [King Jehoshaphat] appointed judges in the land, in each of the fortified cities of Judah. He told them, "Consider carefully what you do, because you are not judging for mere mortals but for the LORD, who is with you whenever you give a verdict.*

By today's standards the king governments were still small and unobtrusive. The tax burden was low compared with current times. There is no indication of excessive regulation expanding on the law, as the Pharisees had done in Jesus day. Laws were primarily enforced at the local level. If a citizen was harmed in some way, the citizen would bring his case before a judge and receive justice according to the law. *(Note: This is very similar to the principle in our Constitution where states are chartered to do the bulk of the governing.)*

III. Laws of the Nation
The Old Testament that God's people were to follow covered both man's relationship to God (common in a theocracy) and man's relationship to other men. Some laws are considered more important than others. Jesus listed these two laws as the most important:

> *Deuteronomy 6:5 Love the Lord your God with all your heart and with all your soul and with all your strength.*

> *Leviticus 19:18 Do not seek revenge or bear a grudge against anyone among your people, but love your neighbor as yourself. I am the Lord.*

There are 613 laws in all by most counts listed in the Old Testament. The Ten Commandments are probably the best known of the laws. The law also contained the death penalty for numerous serious offenses. Additional laws covered: animal sacrifices to God, health-hygiene and diet, those in poverty, treatment of servants, property use, agriculture, marriage-divorce and family life, fighting of wars, treatment of non-citizens (aliens) and the physical appearance of citizens. The next sections will explore the Ten Commandments, the death penalty crimes, and laws dealing with economic matters.

A. Ten Commandments
The main laws of the nation of Israel are summed up in what is commonly referred to as the Ten Commandments. These formed the foundation of the covenant relationship between God and His people. (They still provide a guide for a god-pleasing life today). God followed the format of a suzerain-vassal treaty which was commonly used by ruling kings in that era. It would have not been unusual for the suzerain to order the vassal's copy to be kept on public display in that nation's capitol. God had used a similar treaty (minus the stone tablets) with Abraham in Genesis 17.

> Suzerain-vassal : A covenant regulating the relationship between a great king and one of his subject kings. The great king claimed absolute right of sovereignty, demanded total loyalty and service (the vassal must "love" his suzerain) and pledged protection of the subject's realm and dynasty, conditional on the vassal's faithfulness and loyalty to him. The vassal pledged absolute to his suzerain – whatever the suzerain demanded – and exclusive reliance on the suzerain's protection. Participants called each other "lord" and "servant" or "father" and "son".
>
> Commitments made in these covenants were accompanied by self-maledictory oaths [made by the vassal]. The gods were called upon to witness the covenants and implement the curses of the oaths if the covenants were violated.
> - Concordia Self Study Bible, P18.

The Old Testament Government Established by God

The Ten Commandments as given in the Bible (Exodus 20:1-17) :

And God spoke all these words: "I am the LORD your God, who brought you out of Egypt, out of the land of slavery.

"You shall have no other gods before Me. You shall not make for yourself an image in the form of anything in heaven above or on the earth beneath or in the waters below. You shall not bow down to them or worship them; for I, the LORD your God, am a jealous God, punishing the children for the sin of the parents to the third and fourth generation of those who hate me, but showing love to a thousand generations of those who love me and keep my commandments.

"You shall not misuse the name of the LORD your God, for the LORD will not hold anyone guiltless who misuses his name.

"Remember the Sabbath day by keeping it holy. Six days you shall labor and do all your work, but the seventh day is a sabbath to the LORD your God. On it you shall not do any work, neither you, nor your son or daughter, nor your male or female servant, nor your animals, nor any foreigner residing in your towns. For in six days the LORD made the heavens and the earth, the sea, and all that is in them, but he rested on the seventh day. Therefore the LORD blessed the Sabbath day and made it holy.

"Honor your father and your mother, so that you may live long in the land the LORD your God is giving you.

"You shall not murder.

"You shall not commit adultery.

"You shall not steal.

"You shall not give false testimony against your neighbor.

"You shall not covet (look at with envy) your neighbor's house. You shall not covet your neighbor's wife, or his male or female servant, his ox or donkey, or anything that belongs to your neighbor."

Exodus 31:18 When the LORD finished speaking to Moses on Mount Sinai, he gave him the two tablets of the covenant law, the tablets of stone inscribed by the finger of God.

> In keeping with ancient Near East practice, these were duplicates of the covenant document, not two sections of the Ten Commandments. One copy belonged to each party of the covenant. Since Israel's copy was to be laid up in the presence of her God (according to custom) both covenant tablets (God's and Israel's) were to be placed in the Ark (Ex. 25:21).
> - Concordia Self Study Bible, Notation on Ex. 31:18, P132.

Assuming God continued to follow the customs of the day, only the main terms of the covenant agreement would have been written on the stone tablets meant for public display. The rest of the covenant terms (the details and other laws) would have been written on paper. The Book of the Law referred to in 2 Kings 22:11 is likely the written portion of the covenant.

The government was a theocracy per the First Commandment. *"You shall have no other gods before Me."* God commands total obedience from the nation of Israel. Worshiping another god or gods was not acceptable. Other gods or idols were to be destroyed. There was no freedom of religion in the law as the following verses testify to:

Exodus 34:13-14 Break down their altars, smash their sacred stones and cut down their Asherah poles. Do not worship any other god, for the LORD, whose name is Jealous, is a jealous God.

> Asherah Poles: Asherah was the name of the wife of El, the chief Canaanite god. Wooden poles, perhaps carved in her image, were often set up in her honor and placed near other pagan objects of worship.
> -Concordia Self Study Bible, Notation on Ex. 34:13, P136.

Deuteronomy 7:5 This is what you are to do to them: Break down their altars, smash their sacred stones, cut down their Asherah poles and burn their idols in the fire.

> *Deuteronomy 12:3 Break down their altars, smash their sacred stones and burn their Asherah poles in the fire; cut down the idols of their gods and wipe out their names from those places.*

Worshiping a false god was a death penalty offense in the law.

> *Deuteronomy 17: 2-5 If a man or woman living among you in one of the towns the Lord gives you is found doing evil in the eyes of the Lord your God in violation of his covenant, and **contrary to my command has worshiped other gods,** bowing down to them or to the sun or the moon or the stars in the sky, and this has been brought to your attention, then you must investigate it thoroughly. If it is true and it has been proved that this detestable thing has been done in Israel, **take the man or woman who has done this evil deed to your city gate and stone that person to death.***

B. Death Penalty Offenses

Worshiping a false god was not the only death penalty crime. There were many others (see below). Local town government would have been responsible for enforcing these laws. Notice the specific language referenced above is "stone that person to death." Other laws use "is to be put to death" or similar language.

Capital Crimes
- Worshiping other gods (Deuteronomy 17:5)
- For killing another (Exodus 21:12-14)
- Attacking a parent (Exodus 21:15)
- Kidnapping (Exodus 21:16)
- Cursing a parent (Exodus 21:17)
- Not controlling an animal that kills a person (Exodus 21:29)
- Bestiality (Exodus 21:19)
- Desecrating the Sabbath (Exodus 31:14)
- Sacrificing children to gods (Leviticus 20:2)
- Adultery (Leviticus 20:10)
- Homosexual sex (Leviticus 20:13)
- Being a medium with the dead (Leviticus 20:27)

- Blasphemy (Leviticus 24:16)
- Non-priests approaching the tabernacle/temple sanctuary (Numbers 1:51, 3:10)
- Inciting rebellion against the LORD (Deuteronomy 13:5)

These were harsh laws by today's standards. It is safe to assume that there is not a single American who would want to live under these onerous punishments.

C. Economic and Property Laws

This section will examine the laws from an economic perspective. The laws seem to have been designed to create opportunity for as many in society as possible. It is important to note what God did NOT do with respect to the economic law. He did not establish a communal system where the resources were owned by the state or tribe, nor a central government tasked with the responsibility of caring for the poor. Both of these themes have been discussed in modern America as 'biblical', but they are not in the law. God didn't put that responsibility in the government He established for His people. Instead, followers were expected to share their harvests (income) with the priests (church) and the poor.

Notice the contrast with the death penalty laws. While God's intentions are clear and the economic laws contain specific commands, there is no defined punishment in the law for perpetrators. There is no government enforcement specified in the law. No "put to death", "pay a tax", "shall be punished" or other penalty language is present.

1. Tithing

People were expected to give 10% to the Lord to support priests (Levites) who were to maintain the state religion and fulfill the duties God demanded and an additional 10% once every third year for the poor. Notice "tithe" is used rather than "tax". Giving is consistent with I Corinthians in the New Testament which states that followers of God should be cheerful givers.

> *Leviticus 27:30, 32 A tithe of everything from the land, whether grain from the soil or fruit from the trees, belongs to the LORD; it is holy to the LORD. Every tithe of the herd*

and flock—every tenth animal that passes under the shepherd's rod—will be holy to the LORD.

Deuteronomy 14:28-29 At the end of every three years, bring all the tithes of that year's produce and store it in your towns, so that the Levites (who have no allotment or inheritance of their own) and the foreigners, the fatherless and the widows who live in your towns may come and eat and be satisfied, and so that the LORD your God may bless you in all the work of your hands.

Deuteronomy 26:12 When you have finished setting aside a tenth of all your produce in the third year, the year of the tithe, you shall give it to the Levite, the foreigner, the fatherless and the widow, so that they may eat in your towns and be satisfied.

Levites were priests or modern day church workers.
Deuteronomy 18:1,5 The Levitical priests—indeed, the whole tribe of Levi—are to have no allotment or inheritance with Israel. They shall live on the food offerings presented to the LORD, for that is their inheritance. For the LORD your God has chosen them and their descendants out of all your tribes to stand and minister in the LORD's name always.

2. Gleaning
Gleaning was another method of citizens caring for the needy. Farmers were instructed to leave crops in the field that would be a source of food for the needy. Note how God also protects aliens (those people from other cultures immigrating into Jewish society). People could then glean, or collect remaining crops, from the field post-harvest.

Leviticus 19:9-10 When you reap the harvest of your land, do not reap to the very edges of your field or gather the gleanings of your harvest. Do not go over your vineyard a second time or pick up the grapes that have fallen. Leave them for the poor and the alien. I am the LORD your God.

This is what Jesus and his disciples were doing as recorded in

Matthew:

> *Matthew 12:1 At that time Jesus went through the grainfields on the Sabbath. His disciples were hungry and began to pick some heads of grain and eat them.*

Matthew goes on to record the Pharisees challenging Jesus about picking grain on the Sabbath day claiming this "work" was unlawful. Jesus corrects them and teaches the true meaning of the Sabbath law. It was understood by both Jesus and the Pharisees that picking grain from the edge of the farmers' field was lawful (Jesus and the disciples were poor monetarily).

Several points can be drawn from gleaning that will be helpful in comparing it to modern programs in America. First the farmer did have free will to ignore God's instruction and harvest every last morsel from his field (seen in *Ruth*). Second, the law only applied to the edge of the field, which is a small percentage of the total crop. The law did not allow the poor to harvest the center of the field. Thirdly, the law did not give the poor the right to enter the farmers barn and help themselves to harvested grain (or baked bread). This would be stealing, a violation of the Ten Commandments. Once harvested the grain belonged to the farmer. This did not prevent the farmer from being generous with his grain as Boaz did with Ruth (Ruth 3:15).

Some liberal Christians have concluded that the federal government Food Stamp program in the US is the equivalent of gleaning in the Old Testament law. They miss a key point: There were no government (king) agents forcibly taking grain from the farmers. Also, with gleaning, the poor had to work to obtain their food. With Food Stamps the food is given with no effort on the part of the poor person. This goes against biblical teaching, best seen in this New Testament verse:

> *2 Thessalonians 3:10 We gave you this rule: "If a man will not work, he shall not eat."*

An interesting observation is that even with the emergence of a king and a centralized government, God could have put the responsibility of caring for the poor onto the king. God does not. He leaves this responsibility to the citizens and the priests.

3. Property Ownership

All property ultimately belonged to God since He created it. The land that had been conquered to form the new nation was divided and given to families establishing individual property ownership (rather than a communal or socialistic system of ownership). Joshua (chapters 13-19) describes the land being "deeded" to the tribes and clans (citizens) of Israel. The land was divided among the tribes and property markers were placed.

> *Deuteronomy 19:14 Do not move your neighbor's boundary stone set up by your predecessors in the inheritance you receive in the land the LORD your God is giving you to possess.*

The laws were designed to keep property ownership in the family where it originated. Under the Jubilee law, a citizen couldn't really "buy" a property from another citizen, only "rent" it for the period until the next Jubilee year, when the property would be returned to the original owner's family. The "renter-owner" would harvest the crops or fruits from the property for the years until it was returned.

> *Leviticus 25: 13, 28*
> *"In this Year of Jubilee everyone is to return to their own property."*
> *But if they do not acquire the means to repay, what was sold will remain in the possession of the buyer until the Year of Jubilee. It will be returned in the Jubilee, and they can then go back to their property.*

God wanted His people to live free and remain free, not be forced into serfdom or into slavery as the Egyptians had been when Pharaoh bought all the Egyptians' property in Genesis. This provision guaranteed that every generation of families would have an opportunity to make a living from the land.

Land equaled opportunity in an agrarian society, so those with land had more opportunity than those without. It wasn't perfect as the firstborn usually inherited the land, leaving younger brothers landless. But there would be more opportunity for more people than if the land was owned by only a few.

The system did not guarantee equal outcome. Many had land and, wealth could most easily be obtained by successfully using the land. Wealth was an outcome and was not guaranteed. Whether a family became wealthy, depended on their skill, their ambition, and blessings from God. God has often used wealth as a blessing and continues to do so to this day. If a family struggled and was forced to sell their land, the land was to be returned to the family once every 50 years in a Jubilee Year, giving the next generation a chance to be successful.

4. Indentured-Servants

God favored His people being free. However, not everyone would succeed (as described above with the Jubilee law). So God made additional provisions in the law. If a citizen was forced, out of economic necessity, to sell themselves as an indentured servant, it was to be only a limited-term contract. The servant was to be freed after a maximum of six years.

> *Deut. 15:12-15 If any of your people—Hebrew men or women—sell themselves to you and serve you six years, in the seventh year you must let them go free. And when you release them, do not send them away empty-handed. Supply them liberally from your flock, your threshing floor and your winepress. Give to them as the LORD your God has blessed you. Remember that you were slaves in Egypt and the LORD your God redeemed you. That is why I give you this command today.*

IV. Examples of Enforcement of the Law

There are some scriptural examples of the Old Testament law being enforced. As could be expected from a theocratic government, many of the enforcement examples are for citizens not being loyal to God.

Numbers 15:36 describes a man being stoned to death for breaking the sabbath law (Third Commandment). God decided the man's fate and authorized the punishment. Later in *Numbers* many citizens are given the death penalty for worshiping the false god Baal (First

Commandment violation).

> Numbers 25:4-5   The LORD said to Moses, "Take all the leaders of these people, kill them and expose them in broad daylight before the LORD, so that the LORD's fierce anger may turn away from Israel." So Moses said to Israel's judges, "Each of you must put to death those of your people who have yoked themselves to the Baal of Peor."

There are several examples of national leaders enforcing the command from God to have "no other god's before Me" (First Commandment).

> Judges 6:25 That same night the LORD said to [Gideon], "Take the second bull from your father's herd, the one seven years old. **Tear down your father's altar to Baal and cut down the Asherah pole beside it.** Then build a proper kind of altar to the LORD your God on the top of this height. Using the wood of the Asherah pole that you cut down, offer the second bull as a burnt offering." So Gideon took ten of his servants and did as the LORD told him. But because he was afraid of his family and the townspeople, he did it at night rather than in the daytime.

> 2 Kings 18:3-5 He (Hezekiah) did what was right in the eyes of the LORD, just as his father David had done. **He removed the high places, smashed the sacred stones and cut down the Asherah poles.** He broke into pieces the bronze snake Moses had made, for up to that time the Israelites had been burning incense to it. Hezekiah trusted in the LORD, the God of Israel. There was no one like him among all the kings of Judah, either before him or after him.

> 2 Kings 23:13-14 The king also desecrated the high places that were east of Jerusalem on the south of the Hill of Corruption—the ones Solomon king of Israel had built for **Ashtoreth the vile goddess of the Sidonians, for Chemosh the vile god of Moab, and for Molek the detestable god of the people of Ammon.** Josiah

smashed the sacred stones and cut down the Asherah poles and covered the sites with human bones.

> *2 Chronicles 14:2-3 Asa King of Judah did what was good and right in the eyes of the LORD his God. He **removed the foreign altars and the high places**, smashed the sacred stones and cut down the Asherah poles.*

> *2 Chronicles 17:6 His (Jehoshaphat) heart was devoted to the ways of the LORD; furthermore, he removed the **high places and the Asherah poles** from Judah.*

Look back to 2 Kings 23. King Solomon led the people astray by promoting idol worship. King Ahab in Israel is also listed in 1 Kings 21 as building temples to Baal and Asherah poles. So there is a pattern in the Jewish kingdoms of kings alternating back and forth between idol worship and worshiping only the true God. Probably a reason God opposed the creation of a king.

Jewish leaders (following the Old Testament Law) tried to stone Jesus because he committed blasphemy (Second Commandment), claiming to be God.

> *John 10:33 "We are not stoning you for any good work," they replied, "but for blasphemy, because you, a mere man, claim to be God."*

There are few, if any, examples of the lesser Old Testament laws being enforced. It is a reasonable assumption that judges (local government) would have enforced the criminal law including all the non-death penalty offenses where one citizen was harmed by another. As stated earlier, it appears that this was a passive enforcement. A wronged citizen would bring a case against another citizen to a town judge in an attempt to correct that wrong.

There is one example of gleaning laws being followed, though not enforced. Ruth asked permission to glean (Ruth 2:7). In theory, Ruth should have been able to glean without asking permission, and take a case to court if she had been refused permission. This narrative implies a lack of town agents or Levites actively visiting properties and enforcing the law.

Unfortunately, Jeremiah indicates the citizens didn't follow the indentured servant - slavery laws either.

> *Jeremiah 34:14 'Every seventh year each of you must free any fellow Hebrews who have sold themselves to you. After they have served you six years, you must let them go free.' Your ancestors, however, did not listen to me or pay attention to me.*

People of the day didn't always follow God's intentions or laws. This is not God's fault however. Humans have always abused our God-given free will. God tells us what is best. We decide whether to listen or not.

Despite the implications of these two examples, some have argued that the theocratic government enforced tithing to care for the poor. There is no scriptural evidence to support this. In theory, a Levite priest could have brought a case against a farmer claiming the farmer had not tithed to the church. It is much more likely that the action of tithing was another example of free will. God called on His people to tithe and support the Levites (church), but it was up to the people to obey. Of course, the king would have employed tax collectors to make sure income from taxes was collected throughout the nation.

V. Old Testament Nation-Government Judgments

There are many times in the Old Testament where God pronounces or prophesies judgment on one of Israel's neighboring nation-states such as Egypt, Edom, Ammon or Damascus. As part of His covenant with the nation of ancient Israel, curses were promised to the nation when the people disobeyed God.

> *<u>Deuteronomy 28: 15-29</u>*
> *However, if you do not obey the Lord your God and do not carefully follow all his commands and decrees I am giving you today, all these curses will come on you and overtake you:*
> *.... The fruit of your womb will be cursed, and the crops of*

> *your land, and the calves of your herds and the lambs of your flocks.....*
>
> *The Lord will send on you curses, confusion and rebuke in everything you put your hand to, until you are destroyed and come to sudden ruin... The Lord will strike you with wasting disease, with fever and inflammation, with scorching heat and drought, with blight and mildew, which will plague you until you perish.... The Lord will turn the rain of your country into dust and powder...*
>
> *The Lord will cause you to be defeated before your enemies... Your carcasses will be food for all the birds and the wild animals... The Lord will afflict you with the boils of Egypt and with tumors, festering sores and the itch, from which you cannot be cured. The Lord will afflict you with madness, blindness and confusion of mind... You will be unsuccessful in everything you do; day after day you will be oppressed and robbed, with no one to rescue you.*

It is unclear if God continues to judge nation-states in modern times. It is possible that God does bring earthly judgment (famines, floods, defeats in wars...) on nations today. The author doesn't see clear evidence that those nations *not* following God face more of these difficulties than nations that *do*. The belief that God judges nations has led to a modern teaching called collective salvation. This is not consistent with many other Bible passages which teach individual salvation. More on this in the next chapter.

In the new covenant begun by Jesus, there are no no examples of nations being judged, or government force being used, to achieve any of the God-pleasing objectives present in Old Testament covenants. An implication that nation-judgements may have ended with Jesus.

VI. Interpreting the Law for Individuals and Government Today
The author believes a sound interpretation of God's will for His followers today is to encourage fellow citizens to worship God; refrain from sinful acts like abortion, adultery, or homosexuality; and help those truly in need. There is no question that a Christian can use the Mosaic Testament Law to assist in leading a God-

pleasing life. A totally different question is: **Should the government use force to make its citizens lead a God-pleasing life?** There is no question that the laws in ancient Israel were designed to make the people pleasing to God. And God used that nation as part of His plan to bring forth the Messiah to redeem the entire world. But does God want governments today to force citizens into God-pleasing lifestyles? As will be seen in the next chapter, the answer is "No".

Why is government force against God's wishes? Look no further that Genesis 3 which predates the Mosaic Law. Cain and Abel burned grain and animal flesh as a sacrifice offering to God. God made grain and animals to begin with - and could easily create more. Therefore, the physical burnt grain and flesh were useless to God. What God wants is for us to willingly give up something for Him to show our love and respect for Him, our Creator. That is what is pleasing to God: the willingness to give up part of the fruits of our labor to use for God's purposes rather than ours. This can't be achieved if a government tax man is forcibly confiscating the labor efforts of the citizens. There is no willingness if the person has no choice. Therefore, money taken by forced taxation will neither please nor displease God. God wanted Cain and Abel to willingly give, just as He states in the New Testament.

> *2 Cor 9:7 Each of you should give what you have decided in your heart to give, not reluctantly or under compulsion, for God loves a cheerful giver.*

Yet, despite scripture stating "not under compulsion", use of government force is exactly what some modern liberal churches preach with respect to caring for the poor. This modern church preaching, often called social justice, is often traced back to the anti-poverty laws found in the Mosaic Covenant listed earlier. Technically, the social justice doctrine doesn't even apply the Old Testament poverty laws correctly. The laws actually specify people give their offerings for the poor to the priests, not the king. The churches of the day administered the aid for the poor, not the national government.

Curiously, these liberal churches only advocate government force for social justice anti-poverty measures – not for anything else. They tend to be silent on government force to stop abortions or homosexual acts, both of which were death penalty offenses in the Mosaic Law. These liberals also fail to preach that the US government should remove mosques, as the ancient Israelite kings removed the Asherah poles and Baal shrines. Are these churches really interested a biblical God-pleasing society?

For discussion's sake, let's assume that a modern government should force citizens to lead God-pleasing lives, either to avoid a nation-judgment by God or simply because "It's the right thing to do". Old Testament Law, as given by God, must be used to define God-pleasing. Therefore, a good God-pleasing government should:

- Establish and promote religious activity dedicated to the one true God.
- Ban other religions.
- Outlaw blasphemy.
- Ban homosexual activity.
- Outlaw adultery in marriages.
- Ban abortion and implement the death penalty for those killing an unborn child.
- Mandate that citizens give 10% of their income to a church.

Each of these regulations (plus many others) is in the Mosaic Law. So a government following God's will as defined in the Old Testament would have to do these things. Which Christian in America would want to see *all* of these regulations implemented by government? There probably isn't one. Those claiming the current welfare programs in America, which force the rich to care for the poor through forced government taxation, have no desire for the government to enforce the other laws that are God-pleasing. This is hypocritical to say the least. There is further discussion of social justice in Chapter 8: The Rich and the Poor.

Really, this theological question is trumped by the fact that America has her own constitutional laws to govern by. As will be seen in Chapters 12 and 13, the Constitution forbids the **federal**

The Old Testament Government Established by God

government from using force to do any of these things. The Constitution does not allow state governments to ban any religious activity either. However, it does allow states to use force to regulate many things, including adultery, homosexuality, abortion, or poverty-reduction programs. Close reading of history shows that several states did regulate some of these areas at the time the Constitution was ratified. Whether states choose to do so today is up to the citizens and elected leaders of that state.

In conclusion, the study of God's laws and government can indeed offer a follower of God insight into how God wishes humans to live and interact with each other. It is important to remember that the Bible applies to the lives of individual followers of God – not to governments. The God-given laws of ancient Israel do not apply as government enforced laws in America. America has its own Constitution that applies. And it is very much in agreement with the Bible, not surprisingly, since the writers all followed the God of the Bible.

God's New Covenant

The Old Testament covenant between God and Abraham centered on God's promise to create a nation of Abraham's descendants (Israel) that would fulfill God's promise to bless the world with a savior. The covenant and laws given to Moses created a nation for the Messiah. Jesus Christ fulfilled the promise to Abraham and ushered in God's newest covenant with the world. By dying on the cross, Jesus assumed the burden of all sin for those who believe in Him. The New Testament focuses on an individual's relationship with God. The followers of God now live in many different nations, with many different governments, sometimes surrounded by non-followers. This new covenant was given to individuals, not to governing authorities. In fact, the Jewish government actively opposed the new Christian movement.

Some of the multitude of laws were directly removed in the New Testament. For example, the animal sacrifices were no longer needed after Christ became the ultimate sacrificial lamb. Also, dietary laws were repealed through God speaking to Peter. The other laws became rules for individuals to follow if they chose. Their government may or may not adopt a portion of the rules as its law.

One can easily see the difference in covenants if Moses and Jesus are compared. Moses was selected to build a nation; Jesus to form a church. Jesus had infinitely more power, since He is God, while Moses was only a prophet-king. Yet Jesus limited His miracles to smaller groups or individuals. Moses stood before Pharaoh and brought plagues on Egypt when Pharaoh refused to let God's people go. Moses channeled God's power to open the sea, let the entire nation of Israel pass, then close it on top of Pharaoh's pursuing army. Jesus did no miracles on a nation-wide basis. Jesus did not march into Caesar's Palace in Rome and demand independence for Israel. It would have been a magnificent site, Jesus in His robes, glowing like during the transfiguration, with the disciples in tow, walking to Rome, raining down lightning bolts on any Roman army that dared try to stop Him. Upon reaching the palace, Jesus could have shook the earth until Caesar fell to his knees pleading with Jesus to stop and save the city. Jesus could have sat on the throne while Caesar begged forgiveness for having dared to call himself a god. Or Jesus could have told Caesar that he would now report to the new government in Jerusalem, which would be headed by the committee of the twelve disciples. Jesus could then have and given the disciples new stone tablets and laws for the government of the second kingdom based out of Jerusalem. It would have been the talk of the world! It would have been even bigger than the defeat of Pharaoh that Moses performed. But it did not happen that way.

This is what the Jewish people expected from the long-promised Messiah. Why wouldn't they? They grew up celebrating Passover like we celebrate Christmas today. Passover marked God's final plague against Pharaoh's Egypt where an angel killed the firstborn sons unless there was the blood of a lamb on the door frame of the house. If there was blood, the angel of death would "pass over" that house, not bringing death. After the Passover, Moses led the people of Israel out of bondage and out of Egypt. Why wouldn't the people of Jesus' day expect even more powerful acts when the Messiah appeared? The Messiah was always to be greater than Moses!

Except that was not God's plan. Jesus never assumed a position of earthly governmental power. Jesus didn't set up a government. He focused His ministry on individuals. It is individual faith that is the cornerstone of the new covenant. No longer is there one temple and one nation for God's people. There are many churches and many nations for God's people – those who follow Christ. Individual believers and churches are called on to carry out God's will on earth.

This is summarized in the Great Commission, where Jesus speaks to His disciples and through scripture to His modern day believers.

> *Matthew 28:19-20 Therefore go and make disciples of all nations, baptizing them in the name of the Father and of the Son and of the Holy Spirit, and teaching them to obey everything I have commanded you. And surely I am with you always, to the very end of the age."*

This is the basis for the evangelism that Christians and churches practice where they try to convert non-believers. They are following instructions from God.

Sidebar: The author's belief is that some Christians take this too far, and preach to people who are aware of the message of Christ, but choose not to follow. This just irritates the person being preached to. Respect their choice and free will. Focus on reaching people who are open to hearing the message. Jesus, as He was sending His disciples out to teach, told them to leave those unwilling to listen.

> *Matthew 10:14 If anyone will not welcome you or listen to your words, leave that home or town and shake the dust off your feet.*

The new covenant is further explained by Paul in Romans. Followers of God are expected to honor the government of the nation in which they live. No longer is one nation the home of all God's people. Many different nations are now the home of the followers.

> *Romans 13:1-7 Submission to Governing Authorities*
> *Let everyone be subject to the governing authorities, for there is no authority except that which God has established. The authorities that exist have been established by God. Consequently, whoever rebels against the authority is rebelling against what God has instituted, and those who do so will bring judgment on themselves. For rulers hold no terror for those who do right, but for those who do wrong. Do you want to be free from fear of the one in authority? Then do what is right and you will be commended. For the one in authority is God's servant for your good. But if you do wrong, be afraid, for rulers do not bear the sword for no reason. They are God's servants, agents of wrath to bring punishment on the wrongdoer. Therefore, it is necessary to submit to the authorities, not only because of possible punishment but also as a matter of conscience. This is also why you pay taxes, for the authorities are God's servants, who give their full time to governing. Give to everyone what you owe them: If you owe taxes, pay taxes; if revenue, then revenue; if respect, then respect; if honor, then honor.*

The above passage does not mean a follower of God should blindly follow their government if it contradicts God's will. The Apostles demonstrated this shortly after Jesus' death. As you read, remember the Apostles are contradicting their local government, the Jewish Sanhedrin.

> <u>Acts 5:27-42</u>
> The apostles were brought in and made to appear before the Sanhedrin to be questioned by the high priest.
>
> "We gave you strict orders not to teach in this name," he said. "Yet you have filled Jerusalem with your teaching and are determined to make us guilty of this man's blood."
>
> Peter and the other apostles replied: "We must obey God rather than human beings! The God of our ancestors raised Jesus from the dead —whom you killed by hanging him on a cross. God exalted him to his own right hand as Prince and Savior that he might bring Israel to repentance and forgive their sins. We are witnesses of these things, and so is the Holy Spirit, whom God has given to those who obey him."
>
> When they heard this, they were furious and wanted to put them to death.....
>
> They called the apostles in and had them flogged. Then they ordered them not to speak in the name of Jesus, and let them go.
>
> The apostles left the Sanhedrin, rejoicing because they had been counted worthy of suffering disgrace for the Name. Day after day, in the temple courts and from house to house, they never stopped teaching and proclaiming the good news that Jesus is the Messiah.

The Jewish government forbade the disciples from teaching about Jesus. The disciples ignored the government decree, which was counter to God's will. They refused to obey the government. But notice how they did it. They did not rebel with force. They just continued to stand and preach God's truth despite government objections. (In America we are truly blessed to have a constitution that prevents the government from controlling our speech.)

One of Jesus' disciples, Peter, sums up the new covenant's many believers, many different nations' reality in the following passage. In context, Peter had been led by the Spirit to Cornelius, a Roman Centurion, who was a believer of God. Peter goes on to preach to and baptize the crowd at Cornelius' house.

God's New Covenant

> *Acts 10:34-35 Then Peter began to speak: "I now realize how true it is that God does not show favoritism but accepts from every nation the one who fears Him and does what is right.*

Notice it is the "one (an individual) who fears" God that is accepted, from any nation not just Israel (Jew or descendant of Abraham). God doesn't save nations. He saves individuals.

> *Roman's 14:12 So then, each of us will give an account of ourselves to God.*

Read any Gospel or New Testament book and it is full of passages directed to the individual. How the individual should live to please God, individual behavior that is sinful, and individual faith in Jesus that will save the individual are the focus.

<u>Collective Salvation is a False Teaching.</u>
This is in contradiction to the theology taught by some liberal pastors who teach "collective salvation" where our eternal fates are linked together with the nation or group we happen to live in. The biblical narrative simply does not support this teaching. Looking back to the chapter on God's Death Penalty, we see an example of God saving eight righteous people from the Flood. God had judged the world to be evil and requiring destruction, so collective salvation would require Noah to perish as well. Likewise God saves Lot and his family when Sodom and Gomorrah are slated for destruction. Both are examples of God acting to save righteous individuals when the collective group has been judged, found guilty, and scheduled for the death penalty. Were collective salvation theology to be true, then Dietrich Bonhoeffer, a Lutheran pastor who opposed the Nazi reign in Germany, and was executed by them, would be doomed eternally because he happened to live in Germany at the time it was ruled by evil men. Clearly, an individual is not doomed or saved by the actions of those around them. They are saved by their faith and the grace of God.

Politicians sometimes use collective salvation to justify government action to force people to behave as the politician wishes. Our fates are all tied together. Our neighbor's actions can drag us down and cause us to lose eternal life, therefore we must control their actions. If a society is to be judged as a whole, then all kinds of busy-body actions become acceptable where the government controls people "for the greater good" as defined by the government.

If there is any doubt remaining about the incorrectness of collective salvation, the Apostle Peter clarifies it for us.

> *1 Peter 1:17-19 Since you call on a Father who **judges each person's work impartially**, live out your time as foreigners here in reverent fear. For you know that it was not with perishable things such as silver or gold that you were redeemed from the empty way of life handed down to you from your ancestors, but with the precious blood of Christ, a lamb without blemish or defect.*

When determining eternal salvation, God the Father, will judge each person based on his or her faith and life.

<u>God gives Law and Gospel</u>
Followers of God have historically also worshiped false gods. The Israelite's god of choice was a golden calf (Aaron in the wilderness, Jeroboam in the northern kingdom). Christians today don't make golden calves. They have progressed to making God into a god that pleases them. For example, when a Christian says God is Love and it is alright to do anything we please, that Christian just created an idol in his mind that he is worshiping. God gave humans Law and Gospel. When humans ignore the Law, they just created a new god-idol to worship. A god with no rules, or definitions of sin, that humans may disagree with. In reality, God is who God is, and God gets to make the rules. Jesus himself stated that keeping the Law would be an act of love towards God.

> *John 14:15 If you love Me, keep my commands.*

Is the reverse true? By dismissing the Law does one show hate to God? As sinners, many Christians fall into the trap of remaking God to suit themselves. Church leaders should take special care not to preach only Gospel and no Law, lest they lead their followers into idol worship.

Salvation and Tolerance
There is a misunderstanding unbelievers often have about Christians. Christians are called intolerant because they believe that only Christians will go to heaven and receive eternal life. This is sometimes expressed as: "Person XYZ is a good, moral person; it's ridiculous to think he or she will not get eternal life." Or "I won't worship a God who would condemn so many good people to eternal death."

First, understand that Christians do not decide who receives eternal life. It is strictly up to God, who created us. It is God's decision. God does say that His decision will not be arbitrary, though. Jesus Himself tells us that those not accepting His words will be condemned at their death – their last day.

> John 12:47-48 "As for the person who hears my words but does not keep them, I do not judge him. **For I did not come to judge the world, but to save it. There is a judge for the one who rejects me and does not accept my words**; that very word which I spoke will condemn him at the last day."

These words are very heartening to a Christian. Jesus is telling us He came to save us, not judge us. Christians are thankful indeed to Christ their Savior. God will judge according to the Law for those who do not accept Jesus. No human can keep the law, especially after Jesus restated it in Matthew to include bad thoughts as sin as well as actions. So the judgment will lead to condemnation. Is this fair? Well, God created us, so God has the right to make whatever rules He wishes. Likewise, God can save or condemn whoever He wishes by whatever criteria He chooses. If a person struggles with this, take it up with God and pray for understanding.

It is this teaching from Jesus, that causes the "intolerant" label. Christians should accept and tolerate other religions. Christians should not violate others free will by forcing Christianity onto them. Look no further than Paul, the greatest evangelist, and author of many books in the New Testament. Paul preached the Good News of Jesus and left it up to the people whether they chose to receive and accept the message or not. Paul never forced anyone to accept

Christianity. Christians are tolerant of other religions. This can be seen in early America, where Christianity was the common religion, but other religions views were tolerated. A key tenant of the Christian religion will always be that humans are saved through Christ, not by any other means.

So, Christians are tolerant of other religions. Other religions need to also tolerate Christianity. There is going to be disagreement. It is unavoidable. Judaism teaches salvation through keeping the law of Moses in the Torah. Islam teaches salvation through works and belief in Allah. Other religions teach salvation through other beliefs or good works. What makes Christianity correct, in the author's opinion, is the Bible, which tells the history of man, including the creation of the world, man's sin, and God's redemptive plan culminating with Christ. Others are free to believe in the religion of their choice. But if Christ is truly God, then He has stated there are eternal consequences for rejecting Him as Savior.

Economic Systems in the New Covenant.
As discussed in the previous chapter, in the Old Testament God established an economic system and government for His people in ancient Israel that was based on private property. In the new covenant, there is an example of a communal type living arrangement: the early Christian Church. Some have called this socialism. But this is inaccurate, since those joining the early church community did so voluntarily, whereas socialism uses government force.

In the early Christian church (soon after Jesus' ascension and the Holy Spirit revealing Itself at Pentecost) many people came to believe in Jesus. Some of these new church members shared their resources in a type of commune. Participation was voluntary. Members had free will to share their possessions with the group or not. A believer's possessions were not taken from them by force, rather it was out of God inspired fellowship.

> *Acts 4:32 - All the believers were one in heart and mind. No one claimed that any of his possessions was his own, but they shared everything they had.*

The story of Ananias and Sapphira tells us some important details about the commune. The most important is that God was leading the Church, evidently in a very active manner.

> *Ananias and Sapphira Acts 5:1-11*
> *Now a man named Ananias, together with his wife Sapphira, also sold a piece of property. With his wife's full knowledge he kept back part of the money for himself, but brought the rest and put it at the apostles' feet.*
>
> *Then Peter said, "Ananias, how is it that Satan has so filled your heart that you have lied to the Holy Spirit and have kept for yourself some of the money you received for the land? Didn't it belong to you before it was sold? And after it was sold, wasn't the money at your disposal? What made you think of doing such a thing? You have not lied just to human beings but to God."*
>
> *When Ananias heard this, he fell down and died. And great fear seized all who heard what had happened. Then some young men came forward, wrapped up his body, and carried him out and buried him.*
>
> *About three hours later his wife came in, not knowing what had happened. Peter asked her, "Tell me, is this the price you and Ananias got for the land?"*
>
> *"Yes," she said, "that is the price."*
>
> *Peter said to her, "How could you conspire to test the Spirit of the Lord? Listen! The feet of the men who buried your husband are at the door, and they will carry you out also."*
>
> *At that moment she fell down at his feet and died. Then the young men came in and, finding her dead, carried her out and buried her beside her husband.*
>
> *Great fear seized the whole church and all who heard about these events.*

A husband and wife sold their property and claimed to give the entire proceeds to the church, while keeping a portion for themselves. The couple owned the land and was free to do with it what they wanted. Peter says, *"Didn't it belong to you before it was sold? And after it was sold, wasn't the money at your disposal?"* Keeping a portion of the sales price was perfectly fine, but lying

The Bible and Constitution Made America Great

(probably in order to be recognized and praised for donating their entire worth) to the Apostles and to God was not. God struck the couple dead on the spot. Harsh justice indeed.

So the early Church had many commune-type properties. All members wanted to join, all recognized God as their leader, all had the same mindset, and all were willing to give their effort to God and to others. Freeloaders were dealt with by a simple rule:

> 2 Thessalonians 3:10 We gave you this rule: "If a man will not work, he shall not eat."

Without rules like this, there surely would have been some people who joined the church only to receive free meals – that came from the work and donations of other members. It is immoral to be able to work, choose not to, and expect your neighbors to take care of you. This is a key difference between biblical church care and government care. More in chapter 8.

Some Christians advocate for communal living today. Often though, they really want the government to force others to live under a socialistic government that distributes wealth. Forcing people is a gross violation of free will. Any group can voluntarily choose to form a commune today if they wish. It may even be successful if all members are willing to put in their best effort. After all, a family unit is basically a small commune where the parents provide for the children (and possibly the grandparents). Everything is shared.

The Pilgrims tried to copy the early church model in Plymouth when they came to America. Rush Limbaugh reads an account of the first Thanksgiving on his radio show every year on the Wednesday before Thanksgiving. Regardless of what you may think of Rush, (the author likes his show) the story is historically factual. Largely from William Bradford's diary, the story begins with the Pilgrims setting up their society with ideas drawn from the Bible. They failed horribly.

The First Thanksgiving
On August 1, 1620, the Mayflower set sail. It carried a total of 102 passengers, including forty Pilgrims led by William

God's New Covenant

Bradford. On the journey, Bradford set up an agreement, a contract, that established just and equal laws for all members of the new community, irrespective of their religious beliefs. Where did the revolutionary ideas expressed in the Mayflower Compact come from? From the Bible. The Pilgrims were a people completely steeped in the lessons of the Old and New Testaments. They looked to the ancient Israelites for their example. And, because of the biblical precedents set forth in scripture, they never doubted that their experiment would work.

The journey to the New World was a long and arduous one. And when the Pilgrims landed in New England in November, they found, according to Bradford's detailed journal, a cold, barren, desolate wilderness. He wrote that there were no friends to greet them. There were no houses to shelter them. There were no inns where they could refresh themselves. And the sacrifice they had made for freedom was just beginning. During the first winter, half the Pilgrims — including Bradford's own wife — died of either starvation, sickness or exposure.

"When spring finally came, Indians taught the settlers how to plant corn, fish for cod and skin beavers for coats." Yes, it was Indians who taught the white man how to skin beasts. "Life improved for the Pilgrims, but they did not yet prosper! This is important to understand because this is where modern American history lessons often end." Thanksgiving is actually explained in some textbooks as a holiday for which the Pilgrims gave thanks to the Indians for saving their lives, rather than as a devout expression of gratitude grounded in the tradition of both the Old and New Testaments.

Here is the part [of Thanksgiving] that has been omitted: The original contract the Pilgrims had entered into with their merchant-sponsors in London called for everything they produced to go into a common store, and each member of the community was entitled to one common share.

"All of the land they cleared and the houses they built belong to the community as well. They were going to distribute it equally. Nobody owned anything. They just had a share in it.

Bradford, who had become the new governor of the colony, recognized that this form of collectivism was as costly and destructive to the Pilgrims as that first harsh winter, which had taken so many lives. He decided to take bold action. Bradford assigned a plot of land to each family to work and manage, thus turning loose the power of the marketplace.

That's right. Long before Karl Marx was even born, the Pilgrims had discovered and experimented with what could only be described as socialism. And what happened? It didn't work! Surprise, surprise, huh?"

What Bradford and his community found was that the most creative and industrious people had no incentive to work any harder than anyone else, unless they could utilize the power of personal motivation! But while most of the rest of the world has been experimenting with socialism for well over a hundred years – trying to refine it, perfect it, and re-invent it – the Pilgrims decided early on to scrap it permanently. What Bradford wrote about this social experiment should be in every school child's history lesson. If it were, we might prevent much needless suffering in the future.

"'The experience that we had in this common course and condition, tried sundry years...that by taking away property, and bringing community into a common wealth, would make them happy and flourishing – as if they were wiser than God,' Bradford wrote. 'For this community [so far as it was] was found to breed much confusion and discontent, and retard much employment that would have been to their benefit and comfort. For young men that were most able and fit for labor and service did repine that they should spend their time and strength to work for other men's wives and children without any recompense...that was thought injustice.

Why should you work for other people when you can't work for yourself? What's the point?

The Pilgrims found that people could not be expected to do their best work without incentive. So what did Bradford's community try next? They unharnessed the power of good old free enterprise by invoking the undergirding capitalistic principle of private property. Every family was assigned its own plot of land to work and permitted to market its own crops and products. And what was the result? 'This had very good success,' wrote Bradford, 'for it made all hands industrious, so as much more corn was planted than otherwise would have been.'

... In no time, the Pilgrims found they had more food than they could eat themselves.... So they set up trading posts and exchanged goods with the Indians. The profits allowed them to pay off their debts to the merchants in London. And the success and prosperity of the Plymouth settlement attracted more Europeans and began what came to be known as the 'Great Puritan Migration.'"

Can you think of a more important lesson one could derive from the pilgrim experience? So in essence there was thanks to the Indians, because they taught us how to skin beavers and how to plant corn when we arrived, but the real Thanksgiving was thanking the Lord for guidance and plenty -- and once they reformed their system and got rid of the communal bottle and started what was essentially free market capitalism, they produced more than they could possibly consume, and they invited the Indians to dinner, and voila, we got Thanksgiving, and that's what it was: inviting the Indians to dinner and giving thanks for all the plenty is the true story of Thanksgiving. The last two-thirds of this story simply are not told.
  - *See I Told You So* - Rush Limbaugh. P70-71

This story was troubling to the author for quite a while. "Is the Bible wrong? Does the 'Christian Way' not work?" I gave the account to a Christian friend who was more religious than I to read. She gave it back, refusing to even discuss it. It was as if I had given her something that was a threat to her faith, rather than an account from colonial American history. After all, these were Christians trying to follow the teachings of the Bible. (Note: The Bible does explain God and humanity very well, once humans understand and interpret it correctly.)

The Pilgrims had tried to set up a society based on God's will, but failed. It was actually study of the Old Testament law that helped the author out of the dilemma. It finally became clear, that while trying to follow God's will, the Pilgrims had misinterpreted scripture. They based their model entirely on the New Testament early church. They ignored the Old Testament society that God had set up for Israel, which had private property.

The Pilgrims even failed to interpret the early Christian church model correctly. Members of that church took their money and their possessions and *voluntarily* chose to donate them to the church community. The Pilgrims commune formed a government that *mandated* every person's production (vegetables, hunted game, firewood...) be given to the central store where everyone could take what they needed. The collectivist colony failed. Colony members simply did not work very hard when they personally would not reap the rewards of their labor. The Pilgrims soon went to the Old Testament model of land ownership and became successful. This model was copied by the founders of America.

Thomas Jefferson, a student of history, agreed that large scale communistic communities were impractical.

> "That on the principle of a communion of property, small societies may exist.... But I do not feel ... an extended society like that of the United States, or of an individual state, could be governed happily on the same principle."
> - Thomas Jefferson. 1822. (TRTJ. p373)

A hundred-some years later Karl Marx would sum up this government-mandated sharing philosophy, "From each according to his abilities, to each according to his needs." This philosophy of a government mandating that people share resources in a common pool has never worked and never will. Human nature is self-serving rather than community serving, so people tend to work harder to benefit themselves than their community. Many will decide not to work if food, housing, and healthcare are provided to them for free and viewed as entitlements. I think God knows this and that is why He set up the type of government He did in ancient Israel.

There are some in America who really want a socialistic system in spite of its repeated failures in history. Of course these people are free to start their own commune any time they choose. But typically they are not content with directing their own life. They want to control other peoples lives as well. They opine for a government that will force all citizens to live as they want everyone to live. Thankfully America has a constitution that, when followed, gives citizens the freedom to direct their own lives, and prevents the national government from having the power to control their lives.

In summation, the covenant that Jesus gave us is very similar to the older covenant in many areas. Law and Gospel are present, and the bulk of the Law did not change with respect to unlawful activities. The New Testament was written for individuals to follow, and assumes that Christians may be living in countries with many different types of government.

The next chapter will concentrate on biblical teaching with respect to the poor. Caring for the poor, is the reason given for a huge number of government programs. Christians should follow God's teachings in this and all other areas.

The Rich and the Poor

Rich and poor have this in common: The Lord is the Maker of them all. Proverbs 22:2

The two previous chapters focused on the Old and New Testaments and their teachings on government. This chapter will go into more detail on wealth, the poor, what the Bible says on these issues, and what the government role should be.

There are often misconceptions about wealth in modern American society. Wealth is not evil; it is a blessing according to scripture. God does not hate wealth as He has often blessed His people with this gift. He does ask that you remember Him who has given you blessings.

Genesis 13:2 [Abraham] had become very wealthy in livestock and in silver and gold.

Genesis 26:12-13 Isaac planted crops in that land and the same year reaped a hundredfold, because the LORD blessed him. The man became rich, and his wealth continued to grow until he became very wealthy.

1 Chronicles 29:28 [King David] died at a good old age, having enjoyed long life, wealth and honor.

Deuteronomy 8:18 But remember the LORD your God, for it is he who gives you the ability to produce wealth, and so confirms his covenant, which he swore to your forefathers, as it is today.

There is an entire chapter in the Bible, 1 Kings 4, mostly devoted to describing King Solomon's wealth and his wisdom, with which God had blessed him.

Scripture also teaches that while money or wealth is not a problem, *love* of money and wealth can be. Loving money can easily lead people to do evil things.

1 Timothy 6:10 For the love of money is a root of all kinds of evil. Some people, eager for money, have wandered from the faith and pierced themselves with many griefs.

The Bible also teaches that there will always be poor in society:

> *Deuteronomy 15:11 There will always be poor people in the land. Therefore I command you to be openhanded toward your fellow Israelites who are poor and needy in your land.*

Jesus echoes Deuteronomy when He says that there will always be poor people on earth.

> *Matthew 26:11 The poor you will always have with you, but you will not always have me [Jesus].*
>
> *Mark 14:7 The poor you will always have with you, and you can help them any time you want. But you will not always have me[Jesus].*
>
> *John 12:8 You will always have the poor among you, but you will not always have me [Jesus].*

Why will there always be poor people? There are multiple reasons.

- Some people are born with handicaps that prevent them from caring for themselves or being productive members of society.
- Some people are simply lazy and prefer to beg others for food (or live off government programs). Some may have alcohol or drug addiction problems.
- Some people may have become sick and unable to work. Maybe expensive medical problems have arisen and the person did not insure properly.
- Still others are temporarily poor. Maybe they lost a job through no fault of their own. Or maybe they took a business risk that didn't pay off.

God cares about the poor as He cares about all humans. He commands his followers to "be openhanded " or generous toward the poor and needy in Deuteronomy 15. God often speaks with concern for the poor in scripture.

> *Isaiah 61:1-2 The Spirit of the Sovereign LORD is on me, because the LORD has anointed me to proclaim good news to the poor. He has sent me to bind up the brokenhearted, to*

> *proclaim freedom for the captives and release from darkness for the prisoners, to proclaim the year of the LORD's favor.*
>
> *Luke 4:16-21 [Jesus]went to Nazareth, where he had been brought up, and on the Sabbath day he went into the synagogue, as was his custom. He stood up to read, and the scroll of the prophet Isaiah was handed to him. Unrolling it, he found the place where it is written:*
>
>> *"The Spirit of the Lord is on me, because he has anointed me to proclaim good news to the poor. He has sent me to proclaim freedom for the prisoners and recovery of sight for the blind, to set the oppressed free, to proclaim the year of the Lord's favor."*
>
> *Then he rolled up the scroll, gave it back to the attendant and sat down. The eyes of everyone in the synagogue were fastened on him. He began by saying to them, "Today this scripture is fulfilled in your hearing."*

Jesus claimed it as part of His mission to proclaim good news to the poor. Jesus being "The Word", as John tells us in his Gospel account, often quotes Old Testament scripture.

What do followers of God do about the poor? Help them and assist them by using their personal wealth. The Bible is clear that helping the poor is the will of God, and there are numerous passages and parables instructing followers of God to help the needy. Some Christians of a liberal persuasion believe that government is tasked by the Bible to care for the poor (social justice). This teaching is really not present in the Bible and will be discussed later. It does point to the importance of scriptural examples when claiming biblical teaching. If there aren't any, one should be highly skeptical.

The next part of the chapter will provide biblical teaching with respect to wealth and poverty. Some basic tenets that will be shown are:

- People are to help the poor with their own resources as this pleases God.

- There is a distinction between the helpless and the lazy. Those unable to work are to be supported. Those able to work are to support themselves.
- Widows and orphans are singled out as being not able to support themselves in Old Testament society. Today that would be the handicapped, the elderly, or those physically unable to work.

What is missing in the Bible is any call for massive government-run assistance programs as currently exist in America.

Teachings from Psalms and Proverbs further clarify God's message that His followers should willingly help the needy with their wealth.

> *Proverbs 22:9 A generous man will himself be blessed, for he shares his food with the poor.*
>
> *Proverbs 28:27 He who gives to the poor will lack nothing, but he who closes his eyes to them receives many curses.*
>
> *Proverbs 29:7 The righteous care about justice for the poor, but the wicked have no such concern.*
>
> *Psalm 112:9 They have freely scattered their gifts to the poor, their righteousness endures forever;*

Gleaning, allowed the poor to harvest grain from the edges of fields, was discussed in Chapter 6. As was pointed out, this is a law from God to followers. There is no penalty in the law for noncompliance, therefore no government involvement is required. Other laws specifically stated a punishment for violation, which local town elders (government) would enforce.

> *Leviticus 19:9-10 When you reap the harvest of your land, do not reap to the very edges of your field or gather the gleanings of your harvest. Do not go over your vineyard a second time or pick up the grapes that have fallen. Leave them for the poor and the alien. I am the LORD your God.*

The Rich and the Poor

Jesus' Parables

Jesus, being God, is of course the greatest teacher who ever lived. Jesus often taught by using parables – stories that illustrated the points He was making. Following are some of the parables that relate to the rich and the poor.

During His ministry, Jesus showed that giving to the poor is a way to "have treasure in heaven." He also chided the wealthy man for not giving to the poor. A key point to remember is that the poor in Jesus' time were not like the poor in America, where some even battle obesity. The poor were much more like the poor in Haiti where starvation is the concern. The following is not truly a parable, because it is an actual person approaching Jesus. Jesus does turn it into a teaching moment, though.

> *The Rich and the Kingdom of God Mark 10: 17-27*
>
> *As Jesus started on his way, a man ran up to him and fell on his knees before him. "Good teacher," he asked, "what must I do to inherit eternal life?"*
>
> *"Why do you call me good?" Jesus answered. "No one is good—except God alone. You know the commandments: 'You shall not murder, you shall not commit adultery, you shall not steal, you shall not give false testimony, you shall not defraud, honor your father and mother.'"*
>
> *"Teacher," he declared, "all these I have kept since I was a boy."*
>
> *Jesus looked at him and loved him. "One thing you lack," he said. "Go, sell everything you have and give to the poor, and you will have treasure in heaven. Then come, follow me."*
>
> *At this the man's face fell. He went away sad, because he had great wealth.*
>
> *Jesus looked around and said to his disciples, "How hard it is for the rich to enter the kingdom of God!"*
>
> *The disciples were amazed at his words. But Jesus said again, "Children, how hard it is to enter the kingdom of God! It is easier for a camel to go through the eye of a needle than for someone who is rich to enter the kingdom of God."*

The disciples were even more amazed, and said to each other, "Who then can be saved?"

Jesus looked at them and said, "With man this is impossible, but not with God; all things are possible with God."

Jesus, being able to see into the hearts of men, likely responded the way He did because He saw a love of wealth in the man. The good news for the rich man and for all of us is that even though we fail to live up to God's expectations for us, we can still be saved because "all things are possible with God."

Jesus spoke several more parables regarding the rich and wealthy. In the next parable, the premise is a man who has been greatly blessed by God with wealth through an abundant harvest. Jesus finished by telling us to be rich toward God. In other words use the blessing of wealth as God intended, by helping the needy and supporting the church with a portion of your wealth. The parable also reminds us that life on this earth is finite and will end at a time we do not know. Notice that the rich man has free will to choose what to do with his riches.

<u>Luke 12: 16-21 The Parable of the Rich Fool</u>
And he told them this parable: "The ground of a certain rich man yielded an abundant harvest.

He thought to himself, 'What shall I do? I have no place to store my crops.'

"Then he said, 'This is what I'll do. I will tear down my barns and build bigger ones, and there I will store my surplus grain. And I'll say to myself, "You have plenty of grain laid up for many years. Take life easy; eat, drink and be merry."'

"But God said to him, 'You fool! This very night your life will be demanded from you. Then who will get what you have prepared for yourself?'

"This is how it will be with whoever stores up things for themselves but is not rich toward God."

Notice too that Jesus' parable is about the individual's decision, not

The Rich and the Poor

government action. This is worth noting because many Christians in America have come to believe that God's directives for helping the needy should be enforced by government. In the parable Jesus doesn't scold the Sanhedrin (Jewish government of the day) and say: "Fools! Why do you let the rich man keep all that wealth! Go and take it and distribute it to the poor!" Jesus never taught that government force was the solution. According to scripture, it is up to the individual to willingly do good works that please God.

A Biblical example of willing good works occurs later in Luke when a wealthy person finds salvation. Notice how Zacchaeus willingly gives his wealth to the poor. He willingly atones for sins by repaying those he cheated. He chooses to respond to God's desires for His followers to help those in need.

> <u>Luke19:2, 8-10</u>
> *A man was there by the name of Zacchaeus; he was a chief tax collector and was wealthy.*
>
> *But Zacchaeus stood up and said to the Lord, "Look, Lord! Here and now I give half of my possessions to the poor, and if I have cheated anybody out of anything, I will pay back four times the amount."*
>
> *Jesus said to him, "Today salvation has come to this house, because this man, too, is a son of Abraham. For the Son of Man came to seek and to save the lost."*

Another parable, "The Rich Man and Lazarus", shows the consequences of not caring enough to help those truly in need. In this parable, Jesus portrays a rich man who won't even share table scraps with a *helpless crippled* man laid at his doorstep. Careful reading shows Lazarus was laid there. He was unable to walk or care for himself. How heartless and cruel the rich man was. The dogs are described as being more compassionate.

> <u>Parable told by Jesus in Luke 16:19-31</u>
> *"There was a rich man who was dressed in purple and fine linen and lived in luxury every day. At his gate was laid a beggar named Lazarus, covered with sores and longing to eat what fell from the rich man's table. Even the dogs came and licked his sores.*

> "The time came when the beggar died and the angels carried him to Abraham's side. The rich man also died and was buried. In hell, where he was in torment, he looked up and saw Abraham far away, with Lazarus by his side. So he called to him, 'Father Abraham, have pity on me and send Lazarus to dip the tip of his finger in water and cool my tongue, because I am in agony in this fire.'
>
> "But Abraham replied, 'Son, remember that in your lifetime you received your good things, while Lazarus received bad things, but now he is comforted here and you are in agony. And besides all this, between us and you a great chasm has been fixed, so that those who want to go
>
> from here to you cannot, nor can anyone cross over from there to us.'
>
> "He answered, 'Then I beg you, father, send Lazarus to my father's house, for I have five brothers. Let him warn them, so that they will not also come to this place of torment.'
>
> "Abraham replied, 'They have Moses and the Prophets; let them listen to them.'
>
> " 'No, father Abraham,' he said, 'but if someone from the dead goes to them, they will repent.'
>
> "He said to him, 'If they do not listen to Moses and the Prophets, they will not be convinced even if someone rises from the dead.' "

Why does Jesus condemn the rich man in the parable? Because he ignored God's law (the constitutional law for Israel) to help those in need. Two passages from The Old Testament illustrate God's expectations and instructions for the ancient Jewish society.

> Leviticus 25:35 If one of your countrymen becomes poor and is unable to support himself among you, help him as you would an alien or a temporary resident, so he can continue to live among you.
>
> Deuteronomy 15:7 If there is a poor man among your brothers in any of the towns of the land that the LORD your God is giving you, do not be hardhearted or tightfisted toward your poor brother.

The Rich and the Poor

As discussed in Chapter 6, notice how the language of these laws was directed at individuals. There is no government role specified, nor any societal punishment of perpetrators listed that would be carried out by government.

Back to the parable, the wealthy man did not follow God's will and scriptural teachings on caring for a neighbor in need. The rich man had free will to do what he wanted with his wealth. But with free will comes consequences. His consequence was eternal damnation in hell.

Notice what Jesus *didn't say* in the parable. He does not call on the Jewish government to seize food from the rich man and give it to Lazarus. Jesus doesn't call on the Roman governor, Pontius Pilate, to tax the rich man and give money to Lazarus. He doesn't even scold the temple priests for not intervening in the situation. The teaching is for individuals to assist the needy with their own resources.

Another parable Jesus uses to teach is "The Good Samaritan". It also illustrates the use of one's own resources to help those in need.

> *The Parable of the Good Samaritan (Luke 10: 25-37)*
> *On one occasion an expert in the law stood up to test Jesus. "Teacher," he asked, "what must I do to inherit eternal life?"*
> *"What is written in the Law?" he replied. "How do you read it?"*
> *He answered, "'Love the Lord your God with all your heart and with all your soul and with all your strength and with all your mind; and, 'Love your neighbor as yourself.'"*
> *"You have answered correctly," Jesus replied. "Do this and you will live."*
> *But he wanted to justify himself, so he asked Jesus, "And who is my neighbor?"*
> *In reply Jesus said: "A man was going down from Jerusalem to Jericho, when he was attacked by robbers. They stripped him of his clothes, beat him and went away, leaving him half dead. A priest happened to be going down the same road, and when he saw the man, he passed by on*

> *the other side. So too, a Levite, when he came to the place and saw him, passed by on the other side. But a Samaritan, as he traveled, came where the man was; and when he saw him, he took pity on him. He went to him and bandaged his wounds, pouring on oil and wine. Then he put the man on his own donkey, brought him to an inn and took care of him. The next day he took out two denarii [a days wages] and gave them to the innkeeper. 'Look after him,' he said, 'and when I return, I will reimburse you for any extra expense you may have.'*
>
> *"Which of these three do you think was a neighbor to the man who fell into the hands of robbers?"*
>
> *The expert in the law replied, "The one who had mercy on him."*
>
> *Jesus told him, "Go and do likewise."*

In the parable, the Samaritan uses his own time and money to help out the man in need. He doesn't just drop off the man at the next available town; he arranges for his care. Again there is no mention of government being responsible for the needy man's care. No mention of punishment for the priest or Levite who failed to follow God's wishes as spelled out in numerous Old Testament economic laws. Recall from Chapter 6 that societal or government punishment only was called for in the law where harm was actively done to another.

The New Testament continues teaching followers of God to assist the poor: Notice how the passages speak to the action of individuals, not of governments. There is no instruction to *take* your neighbor's wealth and give it to the poor. Followers are instructed to use their own possessions to please God. It should be noted that at the time these passages were written, the poor were much worse off than the typical American poor person.

> *Luke 12:33 Sell your possessions and give to the poor. Provide purses for yourselves that will not wear out, a treasure in heaven that will not be exhausted, where no thief comes near and no moth destroys.*

The Rich and the Poor

> *Acts 10:31 Cornelius, God has heard your prayer and remembered your gifts to the poor.*

> *Romans 15:26 For Macedonia and Achaia were pleased to make a contribution for the poor among the saints in Jerusalem.*

> *James 2:14-17 What good is it, my brothers and sisters, if someone claims to have faith but has no deeds? Can such faith save them? Suppose a brother or a sister is without clothes and daily food. If one of you says to them, "Go in peace; keep warm and well fed," but does nothing about their physical needs, what good is it? In the same way, faith by itself, if it is not accompanied by action, is dead.*

> *1 John 3: 17-18 If anyone has material possessions and sees a brother or sister in need but has no pity on them, how can the love of God be in that person? Dear children, let us not love with words or speech but with actions and in truth.*

<u>Orphans and Widows</u>
Orphans and widows are often singled out in the Bible to be helped, as they were most helpless. In Old Testament society there were few ways for a single woman or orphaned child to make a living. They were dependent on the charity and good deeds of others. These passages specifically refer to justice, giving equal treatment under the law. A just society should protect the poor and the rich, the powerful and the helpless, equally under the law. This is the biblical definition of justice for which America should strive.

> *Isaiah 10:2 to deprive the poor of their rights and withhold justice from the oppressed of my people, making widows their prey and robbing the fatherless.*

> *Psalm 82:3 Defend the cause of the weak and fatherless; maintain the rights of the poor and oppressed.*

> *Exodus 21:22 Do not take advantage of a widow or an orphan.*

Zechariah 7:10 Do not oppress the widow or the fatherless, the foreigner or the poor. Do not plot evil against each other.'

James 1:27 Religion that God our Father accepts as pure and faultless is this: to look after orphans and widows in their distress and to keep oneself from being polluted by the world.

1 Timothy 5:3-5 Give proper recognition to those widows who are really in need. But if a widow has children or grandchildren, these should learn first of all to put their religion into practice by caring for their own family and so repaying their parents and grandparents, for this is pleasing to God. The widow who is really in need and left all alone puts her hope in God and continues night and day to pray and to ask God for help.

1 Timothy 5:8-10 Anyone who does not provide for their relatives, and especially for their own household, has denied the faith and is worse than an unbeliever. No widow may be put on the list of widows [to be cared for by the church] unless she is over sixty, has been faithful to her husband, and is well known for her good deeds, such as bringing up children, showing hospitality, washing the feet of the Lord's people, helping those in trouble and devoting herself to all kinds of good deeds.

1 Timothy 5:16 If any woman who is a believer has widows in her care, she should continue to help them and not let the church be burdened with them, so that the church can help those widows who are really in need.

Notice the emphasis in Timothy for the widows having real need and the criteria for how a widow should lead her life in order to receive aid. Also it is the responsibility of believers - first the family, then the church body - to care for those in need.

<u>Lazy vs Truly Needy</u>
While there are numerous passages with respect to helping the needy, the Bible also teaches able-bodied people should support

The Rich and the Poor

themselves and work. Only the truly needy should be assisted.

> *Genesis 2: 15 The LORD God took the man and put him in the Garden of Eden to work it and take care of it.*
>
> *Ecclesiastes 2:24 A man can do nothing better than to eat and drink and find satisfaction in his work. This too, I see, is from the hand of God.*
>
> *Proverbs 10:4 Lazy hands make a man poor, but diligent hands bring wealth.*
>
> *Proverbs 12:27 The lazy do not roast any game, but the diligent feed on the riches of the hunt.*
>
> *Proverbs 14:23 All hard work brings a profit, but mere talk leads to poverty.*
>
> *Proverbs 28:19 Those who work their land will have abundant food, but those who chase fantasies will have their fill of poverty.*
>
> *Proverbs 30:9 ...I may become poor and steal, and so dishonor the name of my God.*
>
> *Ephesians 4:28 Anyone who has been stealing must steal no longer, but must work, doing something useful with their own hands, that they may have something to share with those in need.*
>
> *1 Thessalonians 4:11 You should mind your own business and work with your hands, just as we told you.*
>
> *2 Thessalonians 3:10 We gave you this rule: "If a man will not work, he shall not eat."*

This is the main failure of the federal government's entitlement programs. They ignore the wise teaching in the Bible that people who are able to work should work. By not distinguishing the able-bodied from the helpless, the government has created a class of freeloaders expecting to perpetually live off the work of others.

The Social Justice Approach to the Poor

> Thou shalt force thy neighbor to care for the poor.
> - The commandment that isn't.

Social justice was discussed to some degree in Chapters 6 and 7. Its focus is using the government to care for the poor. It justifies this approach either by quoting poverty laws of ancient Israel (with the assumption that these laws were enforced by government) or by using the Old Testament nation-judgments as reason to make our nation God-pleasing in order to avoid God's judgment (a version of collective salvation). There are two fallacies in social justice. First, it focuses only on the giving of money to the poor and ignores all other biblical teaching about behaviors that please God. Second, it calls on the government to forcibly take the money from "the rich", rather than encouraging charitable giving which is often stated in the Bible.

One of the biggest proponents of social justice for the poor is Jim Wallis and his group Sojourners.

> Jim Wallis, CEO of Sojourners, is a bestselling author, public theologian, speaker, and international commentator on ethics and public life. "Sojourners mission is to articulate the biblical call to social justice, inspiring hope and building a movement to transform individuals, communities, the church and the world."
> - Sojourners website. sojo.net

> In a January 13, 2006 radio interview with Interfaith Voices, Wallis was asked, "Are you then calling for the redistribution of wealth in society?"
> He replied, "Absolutely, without any hesitation. That's what the gospel is all about."
> -www.newsrealblog.com/2010/10/25/8-biblical-verses-that-leftists-have-gotten- completely-wrong

The Gospel is all about the redistribution of wealth in society. Interesting take on the Gospel by Wallis. He would be closer to the truth *if* government force were not involved. It truly does please

The Rich and the Poor

God when His followers choose to use their wealth to help others. But the government redistribution of wealth is not the same, as there is nothing voluntary about government taxes.

The author, as well as most Christians, would consider the Gospel to be primarily about Jesus' resurrection and God's redemption of humanity. John 3:16 is often referred to as the "Gospel in a nutshell".

> *John 3:16 For God so loved the world that he gave his one and only Son, that whoever believes in him shall not perish but have eternal life.*

There is no mention of redistribution of wealth in the passage. If we dig a little deeper in the Gospels, we can find Jesus telling us what He believes to be most the important parts of scripture.

> *Matthew 22:37-40 Jesus replied: "'Love the Lord your God with all your heart and with all your soul and with all your mind.' This is the first and greatest commandment. And the second is like it: 'Love your neighbor as yourself.' All the Law and the Prophets hang on these two commandments."*

> Jesus quotes earlier Scripture here as is often the case:
> *Deuteronomy 6:5 Love the Lord your God with all your heart and with all your soul and with all your strength.*
> *Leviticus 19:18 Do not seek revenge or bear a grudge against anyone among your people, but love your neighbor as yourself. I am the Lord.*

Maybe Jim Wallis is assuming that "loving your neighbor" is fulfilled by government forcefully redistributing wealth. But if that is the case, shouldn't the government also force people to worship God to show their love for Him? Loving God *is* more important than loving your neighbor according to Jesus. Yet, Sojourners does not advocate forced worship like they advocate forced wealth redistribution.

Why does Jim Wallis ignore the first and greatest commandment, as well as the other Ten Commandments? The Gospel in a nutshell according to Jim Wallis is: Live however you want, ignoring God's wishes for your lifestyle, but the government will force you to "share" large portions of your wealth. A quick review of the website confirms this summary. Sojournary openly supports or silently approves of homosexual marriage and abortion, two other key religious-political issues in our nation today. The author suspects it is because Wallis is driven more by a political agenda than a biblical one.

Social justice supporters want government to take from the rich and give to the poor. Jim Wallis claims the Gospels, the new covenant between God and His followers, support this philosophy. Yet, Jesus' parables and the many passages quoted previously all call for individuals to choose to help the poor, not be forced to by their government. Where are the Bible passages calling for government to care for the poor on the Sojourners' website? Where are the passages that state "take your neighbors wealth and give it to the poor"? Wallis provides none (there aren't any). It is not hard to conclude that Wallis is a false teacher – teaching what is not in the Bible, yet claiming that it is there, as well as, ignoring large parts of biblical teaching that he doesn't like.

Sojourners is not the only group that has fallen into this trap of thinking. Other Christians have as well. Those believing the Bible endorses government force to care for the poor need to point to a parable of Jesus where He tells followers to "go and take from the rich man and give to the needy." There isn't one. Both "The Good Samaritan" and "The Rich Man and Lazarus" parables teach followers of God to use their own resources to care for the needy.

A more accurate interpretation of the Bible than the social justice view is that God's commands are directed at the individual believer. This is especially true in the New Testament. Jesus took this approach in both the parables of "The Rich Man and Lazarus" and "The Good Samaritan". The Apostle Paul also follows this approach.

> *2 Corinthians 8:8 ...see that you also excel in this grace of giving. I am not commanding you, but I want to test the sincerity of your love.*

The Rich and the Poor

> *2 Corinthians 8:12 For if the willingness is there, the gift is acceptable according to what one has, not according to what one does not have.*
>
> *2 Corinthians 9:7-8 Each of you should give what you have decided in your heart to give, not reluctantly or under compulsion, for God loves a cheerful giver. And God is able to bless you abundantly, so that in all things at all times, having all that you need, you will abound in every good work.*

Notice the theme of willing, cheerful giving to those in need. If Godly love is in one's heart, generosity will be there too.

God prefers his followers to cheerfully and willingly carry out all of His commands.

> *Titus 2:13-14 ...our great God and Savior, Jesus Christ, who gave himself for us to redeem us from all wickedness and to purify for himself a people that are his very own, eager to do what is good.*
>
> *Colossians 1:10 ...so that you may live a life worthy of the Lord and please him in every way: bearing fruit in every good work,*

But wait. In Timothy the rich are commanded to give:

> *1 Timothy 6:17-19 Command those who are rich in this present world not to be arrogant nor to put their hope in wealth, which is so uncertain, but to put their hope in God, who richly provides us with everything for our enjoyment. Command them to do good, to be rich in good deeds, and to be generous and willing to share. In this way they will lay up treasure for themselves as a firm foundation for the coming age, so that they may take hold of the life that is truly life.*

This command by God through Paul is still meant to be taken personally by the individual. Timothy, assuming he acted on Paul's words, is issuing the commands as a pastor of a church, to individuals who are rich. Timothy had no ability (as a government does) to use force to take the wealth from a rich person who chose not to give or be generous. In a free society, the rich have free will from God to follow God's commands or not.

Do notice the difference between Timothy and Corinthians with respect to "command". In one verse Paul states that he is not "commanding" believers to give; in the other he "commands" the rich to be generous. It could be concluded that the rich are held to a higher standard than believers of more modest means. More is expected of them with respect to using their wealth in a God-pleasing manner. This would be consistent with teaching in "The Parable of the Talents" told by Jesus in Matthew 25 and Luke 19.

Doing good works is pleasing to God. A good work is an action that a person does, of their own accord, to help another. Government actions cannot be considered a good work because they are funded by taxation which is not voluntary for the individual taxed. Citizens not paying their taxes are subject to fines, having their assets seized, or even imprisonment.

The Bible does not endorse *forced* redistribution of wealth from one person to another (although Karl Marx did). Forced wealth redistribution violates the tenet of God-given free will. In fact, taking money from one person by force and giving it to another could be considered stealing, a violation of one of God's other commandments. The Bible doesn't list caring for the poor as a responsibility of government. It puts that responsibility onto individuals, family, and the church or charities. Should the government set up a program to help people that is funded exclusively by voluntary contributions, then contributing to that program would be a charitable good work.

Those who want to try to use the 1 Timothy 6 "command" to justify government taxation of the rich, need to explain how this command differs from the First Commandment – "You will have no other gods before Me". How many Christians also want the government to enforce God's other commands? Abortion would be illegal and would result in the death penalty for the abortionist. Homosexuality would be illegal with homosexual acts resulting in the death penalty. 10% of every citizen's income would be collected and sent to the church. Sunday (the Sabbath day) would be holy, requiring church attendance, and no work be done on that day. All of these Old Testament commands from God are also in the Bible. To be consistent, a Christian advocating government enforcement of one of these commands should advocate for all of them.

Constitutional Law
The founders of America based their laws on the Bible. They realized that the Mosaic Law was given by God to the theocratic Jewish nation in ancient Israel. So rather than copy the law directly and make America a theocracy, they took the new covenant approach (Chapter 7). Laws with respect to God were not incorporated into the Constitution. Laws to punish a citizen who harmed another were left primarily to the states. There was no government involvement in caring for the poor. They followed the New Testament where these tasks were left to individuals and the charities they formed. The U.S. Constitution does not authorize the federal government to run programs for the poor. (Of course, the nation hasn't followed its Constitution closely in recent times.)

As was stated in Chapter 7, Christians should follow their Constitution and government as described in Romans. Those Christians truly believing that government is needed to care for the poor have several options. They can amend the Constitution to give the federal government that authority. Or they can use state, county, or city governments to run programs to help the poor. The Constitution gives states tremendous freedom to govern their citizens. Readers will also see in Chapter 12 that the U.S. Constitution clearly does not grant the federal government the power to do this task. **The U.S. Constitution prevents the federal government from forcing the rich to help the poor, just as it prevents the federal government from forcing the unfaithful to worship God.**

Sidebar: Some U.S. Catholic Church bishops have supported the federal government's welfare programs done in the name of helping the poor (social justice). They misread the Bible's intentions that charity be used rather than force of government. But the bishops are now learning a valuable lesson: A federal government powerful enough to ignore the Constitution and force "the rich" to care for "the poor", is powerful enough to ignore the Constitution and force the Catholic Church to provide abortion services and birth control (violating its religious beliefs) to its employees, as it has with ObamaCare.

As we will see in the next portion of the chapter, the federal government has proved itself to be quite the failure in its attempts to care for the poor. In America today, overall tax rates are more than double what God recommended in the Old Testament (Chapter 9). Yet we still have poor people and uneducated people in society. The next sections will examine the federal government's failed efforts to manage poverty in America.

<u>The Failures of the Federal Government</u>
The fact that the federal government has failed to prevent poverty is not surprising. For one thing: How can anyone reasonably expect an organization based in a single city – Washington DC - to care for 300+ million people over 3.79 million square miles? It's not very practical.

It's also a problem of effectiveness when government anti-poverty programs become known as entitlements. If a person is entitled to receive a government check every week, there is no incentive to work. It has become widely known that there are jobs that Americans just won't do. Of course not! Why would anyone want to clean toilets or work in the hot fields picking vegetables when they can sit at home in air conditioning watching TV?

The biblical system is superior. Each follower of God is to help out his neighbor in need. People know if their neighbor is down on his luck and needs short term help or is just chronically lazy. Most poor people will not go to their neighbor every week and ask for money, but they will expect a check from the government. Politicians have conditioned them to believe this.

Beginning in the 1930s with President Franklin Roosevelt, and escalating in the 1960s with President Lyndon Johnson, the federal government has fought a "war on poverty". This effort has done little to reduce the number of Americans in poverty.

> Putting the best possible face on the War on Poverty, we should note that in 1959 and 1960, before the War on Poverty began, poverty was measured at approximately 22 percent of the population, some 39 million Americans. ...39 million Americans were counted as poor in 1959, nearly the same number as the nearly 37 million Americans counted as poor in 2004. Despite all the money and effort expended by government, a core group of poor persists, resistant to any and all efforts to remove them from the poverty rolls. It is this core group of "underclass" Americans that the War on Poverty and the political Left has failed. If the War on Poverty was meant to eliminate poverty,... then a new strategy is needed.
> - Democrats' War on Poverty Has Failed, Jerome R. Corsi and Kenneth Blackwell, 09/06/2006

President Ronald Reagan discussed the government's efforts in his 1988 State of the Union Address. Even then there were a massive number of different programs in place and billions of dollars being spent. Reagan hit on a key reason for this failure: Government programs have broken-up the stable family unit.

> Today the Federal Government has 59 major welfare programs and spends more than $100 billion a year on them. What has all this money done? Well, too often it has only made poverty harder to escape. Federal welfare programs have created a massive social problem. With the best of intentions, government created a poverty trap that wreaks havoc on the very support system the poor need most to lift themselves out of poverty: the family. Dependency has become the one enduring heirloom, passed from one generation to the next, of too many fragmented families.
> - President Ronald Reagan, State of the Union Address, 1988

Government has not changed its approach since the 1980s, just increased the spending levels. In 2011, there were 70 federal government poverty programs with total spending of $953 billion dollars. Assuming 40 million people in poverty, this equals almost $24,000 per person in poverty.

It is clear that President Obama is intent on not only continuing the failed war on poverty but expanding and growing the size of the welfare state. President Obama's 2011 budget will increase spending on welfare programs by 42 percent over President Bush's last year in office. Total spending on the welfare state (including state spending) will rise to $953 billion in 2011.

Means-tested welfare spending or aid to the poor consists of government programs that provide assistance deliberately and exclusively to poor and lower-income people—for example, food stamps, public housing, Medicaid, and Temporary Assistance for Needy Families. There are currently over 70 different federal means-tested programs on the books.

Nearly all state welfare expenditures are matching contributions that the federal government requires of its welfare programs, a "welfare tax" that the federal government imposes on the states.

- Heritage Foundation, Expanding the Failed War on Poverty: Obama's 2011 Budget Increases Welfare Spending to Historic Levels, Published on March 21, 2010 by Kiki Bradley

The federal government approach to caring for the poor seems to be create numerous overlapping programs that spend billions of dollars. When these fail to eliminate poverty, add more programs and spend even more money. Albert Einstein reportedly defined insanity as: "Doing the same thing over and over again and expecting different results." The federal government will never be able to end poverty.

Context is also required when examining the poor in America. America is such a rich country that in many instances the poor are quite well off by standards in other countries, or standards present in biblical times.

Heritage Foundation Study on Poverty in America.
The poorest Americans today live a better life than all but the richest persons a hundred years ago. The typical household defined as poor by the government had:
- A car and air conditioning.

- For entertainment, the household had two color televisions, cable or satellite TV, a DVD player, and a VCR. If there were children, especially boys, in the home, the family had a game system, such as an Xbox or a PlayStation.
- In the kitchen, the household had a refrigerator, an oven and stove, a microwave, and a coffee maker.
- Other household conveniences included a clothes washer, clothes dryer, ceiling fans, and a cordless phone.

Poor families certainly struggle to make ends meet, but in most cases, they are struggling to pay for air conditioning and the cable TV bill as well as to put food on the table. Their living standards are far different from the images of dire deprivation promoted by activists and the mainstream media.

    - Article: Air Conditioning, Cable TV, and an Xbox: What Is Poverty in the United States Today?

The study shows that most of the poor in America have a lot of luxury items. The mom watching cable TV while the kid plays on the XBOX is not quite the picture that some want to paint to show the poor are starving and don't know where their next meal is coming from.

This has led to an entitlement culture among many of the poor in America. It's not their fault. They are told by politicians that they are entitled to live their current lifestyle even if it is funded by tax dollars – which are taken from other people. It is really easy for these people to accept this lifestyle where there is no need to educate yourself, support yourself or better yourself.

Oprah Winfrey has experienced this firsthand in her interactions with poor inner city schools across America.

"Say what you will about the American educational system -- it does work," Oprah tells Newsweek. "If you are a child in the United States, you can get an education." And she doesn't think that American students -- who, unlike Africans, go to school free of charge -- appreciate what they have. "I

became so frustrated with visiting inner-city schools that I just stopped going. The sense that you need to learn just isn't there," she says. "If you ask the kids what they want or need, they will say an iPod or some sneakers. In South Africa, they don't ask for money or toys. They ask for uniforms so they can go to school."
- Newsweek interview with Oprah Winfrey January 8, 2007

Oprah is a very successful and wealthy woman. She is to be commended for using some of her wealth to find truly needy people and help them. She is following the biblical model. Oprah also is a solid Democrat. She sees the problem with inner city American kids, but she doesn't realize that the very government anti-poverty programs championed by the politicians she endorses cause the attitude she doesn't like in the inner city kids.

Many poor Americans have become comfortable in their poverty. They are content to receive government food and housing and ignore education which is the best avenue for becoming self-sufficient and leaving poverty. This is not a new phenomenon. Benjamin Franklin, one of America's founders and frequent ambassador to Europe, noted in 1772:

> "I am for doing good to the poor, but...I think the best way of doing good to the poor, is not making them easy in poverty, but leading or driving them out of it. I observed...that the more public provisions were made for the poor, the less they provided for themselves, and of course became poorer. And, on the contrary, the less was done for them, the more they did for themselves, and became richer."
> - TRBF. P453.

Note the failure of the current federal government's "War on Poverty." The federal government has taken on this issue, spent billions of dollars, and failed. Largely because they have allowed millions of people to remain on the poverty roles even though they are poor only due to their idleness. America's poor are able to live very comfortably while not working and in poverty. The government ignores the harsh biblical New Testament teaching of not working means not eating. By the way, the author does not believe anyone in America should starve. A method of feeding the poor while encouraging them to become self-sufficient is described in Chapter 20.

Dr. Walter Williams, a widely known professor and economist notes the difference between noble charitable actions and (immoral) government actions that forcibly redistribute money among people.

> There are people in need of help. Charity is one of the nobler human motivations. The act of reaching into one's own pockets to help a fellow man in need is praiseworthy and laudable. Reaching into someone else's pocket is despicable and worthy of condemnation.
> - Walter Williams . www.quotationcollection.com

We've explored the biblical teaching, and the liberal social justice teaching with respect to the poor. One of the politicians best known for his views on social justice is President Barack Obama. For years, Obama attended a church where one of the main tenets taught was social justice.

Why Doesn't Obama Help His Brother?
It has been well reported that President Obama has a brother living in a hut in Kenya in poverty. (If this is news to the reader, you are probably getting news only from liberal sources. See Chapter 23 on News Bias. To be fair, George Hussein Onyango Obama, is only Barack's half-brother, sharing the same father but a different mother. George told a British newspaper, *The Telegraph*, that first found him that "I live here on less than a dollar a month." So it is true poverty, not the American poverty where many poor have nice apartments, TV's and air conditioning.

George Obama appears to be a case where someone following God's teachings in the Bible would step up and help this person. Especially if they were a family member. However, President Obama has never helped George. Even $10 a month would greatly increase George's income.

Why hasn't Obama helped his brother? No one can know for sure except Obama, and he isn't talking. However, it would be consistent with social justice teaching that the government is responsible for George's well being, not individuals. So Obama would expect the

Kenyan government to offer the assistance. This view of social justice absolves the individual from any responsibility outside of paying taxes to the government. This also explains why many prominent liberal politicians donate so little to charities. They view taxes as their sole responsibility to society.

This chapter will close with a well known fictional story of a champion of the poor: Robin Hood.

Robin Hood
Many, especially on the left, have quoted the story of Robin Hood as the first champion of social justice. After all Robin Hood stole from the rich and gave to the poor. The devil is in the details though. Here's a brief synopsis of the story:

> Sir Robin of Locksley, a Saxon Lord, rebels against Prince John who has raised the *tax rates* on the people. Declared an outlaw, he flees to Sherwood forest and assumes the name Robin Hood. He begins to *rob the rich tax collectors* and give back to the poor, the townspeople that are heavily-taxed by the Sheriff of Nottingham and Prince John.

Notice a key portion of the story that the social justice crowd conveniently ignores. Robin Hood was rebelling against corrupt government. The rich in the story are two government leaders, who have gotten rich through high taxation of the people. Set in modern day America, the equivalent plot would be Robin Hood stealing from the IRS agents, who following their orders from the President, have unfairly taxed the people at too high a level. Robin Hood returns the money to the rightful owners – the taxpayers! *Robin Hood was a Conservative TEA (Taxed Enough Already) Party Vigilante,* not a social justice government agent.

Taxation in the Bible

Taxes have been around as long as governments. There are numerous times in the Bible when taxes are mentioned. Many are just a reference to paying taxes to a king with no other detail.

In 1 Samuel 17:25, King Saul offers a tax exemption to anyone who could defeat Goliath. *"The king will ... exempt his family from taxes in Israel."* This might be the first historical example of a government using the tax code to reward (or punish) behavior.

Amos refers to kings unfairly taxing the people for personal benefit.

> *Amos 5:11-12 You levy a straw tax on the poor and impose a tax on their grain. Therefore, though you have built stone mansions, you will not live in them; though you have planted lush vineyards, you will not drink their wine. For I know how many are your offenses and how great your sins.*

Daniel 11 prophesies about a Persian king collecting taxes. Nehemiah 5 states there was a king's tax on the restored nation of Israel. The book of Ezra also mentions taxes paid to to the kings of Persia.

Matthew 9 tells us that Matthew was a tax collector for Rome when Jesus called him to be an apostle. The people of Israel had a very low view of tax collectors. (Similar to Americans' view of the IRS?)

> *Matthew 9:9-11 As Jesus went on from there, he saw a man named Matthew sitting at the tax collector's booth. "Follow me," he told him, and Matthew got up and followed him. While Jesus was having dinner at Matthew's house, many tax collectors and sinners came and ate with him and his disciples. When the Pharisees saw this, they asked his disciples, "Why does your teacher eat with tax collectors and sinners?"*

Luke 19 tells the story of Zacchaeus, the tax collector, finding salvation. It seems Zacchaeus had cheated the people and was not well liked.

> *Luke 19:2,5-10 A man was there by the name of Zacchaeus; he was a chief tax collector and was wealthy... When Jesus*

> reached the spot, he looked up and said to him, "Zacchaeus, come ..... I must stay at your house today." So he came down at once and welcomed Him gladly. All the people saw this and began to mutter, "He has gone to be the guest of a sinner."
>
> But Zacchaeus stood up and said to the Lord, "Look, Lord! Here and now I give half of my possessions to the poor, and if I have cheated anybody out of anything, I will pay back four times the amount."
>
> Jesus said to him, "Today salvation has come to this house, because this man, too, is a son of Abraham. For the Son of Man came to seek and to save the lost."

Temple Tax
The Bible also states that Jewish society had a tax that went to the temple rather than the government. God told Moses to make each Jewish citizen pay an atonement fee as an offering to the Lord that was to be used to support the Tent of Meeting (their temple while in in the wilderness; equivalent to their church building). This could be considered a tax since it was a specified amount that must be paid. Numbers 1 tells us that those counted in the census were men, over the age of 20, who could serve in the army.

> *Exodus 30: 11-16* Then the LORD said to Moses, "When you take a census of the Israelites to count them, each one must pay the LORD a ransom for his life at the time he is counted. Then no plague will come on them when you number them. Each one who crosses over to those already counted is to give a half shekel, according to the sanctuary shekel, which weighs twenty gerahs. This half shekel is an offering to the LORD. All who cross over, those twenty years old or more, are to give an offering to the LORD. The rich are not to give more than a half shekel and the poor are not to give less when you make the offering to the LORD to atone for your lives. Receive the atonement money from the Israelites and use it for the service of the tent of meeting. It will be a memorial for the Israelites before the LORD, making atonement for your lives."

Taxation in the Bible

The tax applied to rich and poor alike. Every man owed the same amount.

King Joash (King of Judah, 835-796 BC) re-instituted this policy to pay for temple upkeep.

> *2 Chronicles 24: 8-9 At the king's command, a chest was made and placed outside, at the gate of the temple of the LORD. A proclamation was then issued in Judah and Jerusalem that they should bring to the LORD the tax that Moses the servant of God had required of Israel in the wilderness.*

Evidently this policy became the temple tax which was collected annually in Jesus' time.

> <u>Matthew 17: 24-27 The Temple Tax</u>
> *After Jesus and his disciples arrived in Capernaum, the collectors of the two-drachma temple tax came to Peter and asked, "Doesn't your teacher pay the temple tax?"*
>
> *"Yes, he does," he replied.*
>
> *When Peter came into the house, Jesus was the first to speak. "What do you think, Simon?" he asked. "From whom do the kings of the earth collect duty and taxes—from their own children or from others?"*
>
> *"From others," Peter answered.*
>
> *"Then the children are exempt," Jesus said to him. "But so that we may not cause offense, go to the lake and throw out your line. Take the first fish you catch; open its mouth and you will find a four-drachma coin. Take it and give it to them for my tax and yours."*
>
> The annual temple tax was required of every male 20 years of age and older. It was worth half a shekel (approximately two days wages) and was used for the upkeep of the temple.
> - Concordia Study Bible. P1475

Notice the distinction between the temple tax, which was collected, and tithing, which seemed to be left to the individual rather than mandated.

There are also several instances in the Bible that give more insight into government taxation. In the narrative of Genesis, there is the account of Joseph levying a 20% income tax for Pharaoh in Egypt.

One liberal Christian friend actually pointed to the story of Joseph and Pharaoh in Egypt and the famine as an example of the government taking care of the people with tax revenue. She obviously didn't read the story all the way to completion. Pharaoh ended up owning the peoples' land, homes and possessions in exchange for "taking care of them". The people were serfs to Pharaoh once the famine ended.

First realize that this story is a part of God's larger plan and promise to build a nation from Abraham's descendants. God intended to take the children of Jacob (Israel) to Egypt where He could grow them into a nation. God carried out this plan by taking Joseph to Egypt as a slave, miraculously raising him to Pharaoh's second in command (Genesis 41:39), then giving the Israelis a section of Egypt as their home (Genesis 47:5). In part of the plan, God created seven years of abundance followed by seven years of famine. Joseph (for Pharaoh) collected (taxed) 20% of the grain during the years of abundance. When the famine hit, Joseph sold the grain back to the people and to neighboring countries (including the Israelis). By the time the famine was over the people of Egypt had traded all their money, livestock, and land for food to eat. They had become serfs to Pharaoh.

> *Joseph and the Famine - Genesis 47: 13-27*
> *There was no food, however, in the whole region because the famine was severe; both Egypt and Canaan wasted away because of the famine. Joseph collected all the money that was to be found in Egypt and Canaan in payment for the grain they were buying, and he brought it to Pharaoh's palace. When the money of the people of Egypt and Canaan was gone, all Egypt came to Joseph and said, "Give us food. Why should we die before your eyes? Our money is all gone."*
>
> *"Then bring your livestock," said Joseph. "I will sell you food in exchange for your livestock, since your money is gone." So they brought their livestock to Joseph, and he*

gave them food in exchange for their horses, their sheep and goats, their cattle and donkeys. And he brought them through that year with food in exchange for all their livestock.

When that year was over, they came to him the following year and said, "We cannot hide from our lord the fact that since our money is gone and our livestock belongs to you, there is nothing left for our lord except our bodies and our land. Why should we perish before your eyes—we and our land as well? Buy us and our land in exchange for food, and we with our land will be in bondage to Pharaoh. Give us seed so that we may live and not die, and that the land may not become desolate."

*So Joseph **bought all the land in Egypt for Pharaoh**. The Egyptians, one and all, sold their fields, because the famine was too severe for them. The land became Pharaoh's, and Joseph **reduced the people to servitude**, from one end of Egypt to the other. However, he did not buy the land of the priests, because they received a regular allotment from Pharaoh and had food enough from the allotment Pharaoh gave them. That is why they did not sell their land.*

Joseph said to the people, "Now that I have bought you and your land today for Pharaoh, here is seed for you so you can plant the ground. But when the crop comes in, give a fifth of it to Pharaoh. The other four-fifths you may keep as seed for the fields and as food for yourselves and your households and your children."

"You have saved our lives," they said. "May we find favor in the eyes of our lord; we will be in bondage to Pharaoh."

*So Joseph established it as a law concerning land in Egypt —still in force today—that **a fifth of the produce belongs to Pharaoh**. It was only the land of the priests that did not become Pharaoh's.*

Now the Israelites settled in Egypt in the region of Goshen. They acquired property there and were fruitful and increased greatly in number.

The abundance, taxes, and famine seem to be one-time occurrences used by God to achieve His plan to make Israel a nation. The story by itself should not be interpreted as support for high (if 20% is high) taxes, since the people ended up as slaves to Pharaoh (government). God clearly is opposed to the people becoming slaves as stated by laws in Deuteronomy and Leviticus.

The King's Tax in Israel
More relevant is 1 Samuel 8: 9-18, which describes how a king (government) will take 10% of the peoples' crops and animals as a tax – an income tax. This passage is written as a warning to the Israelites as part of the *bad things a king will do*. See Chapter 6 on God's government in the Old Testament to review the discussion.

One of the things Jesus did was to transition from the old covenant – one nation of God's people, to the new covenant – many nations with God's people. One example of Jesus legitimizing a non- Israeli government in the new covenant occurs when He was asked about paying taxes to Caesar, the Roman ruler. Jesus responds in the affirmative, but to quote Paul Harvey, there is a "rest of the story".

Is Jesus endorsing paying taxes to Caesar?
(Luke 20:20-26, also Matthew 22, Mark 12)

> *Keeping a close watch on him, they sent spies, who pretended to be sincere. They hoped to catch Jesus in something he said, so that they might hand him over to the power and authority of the governor. So the spies questioned him: "Teacher, we know that you speak and teach what is right, and that you do not show partiality but teach the way of God in accordance with the truth. Is it right for us to pay taxes to Caesar or not?"*
>
> *He saw through their duplicity and said to them, "Show me a denarius. Whose image and inscription are on it?"*
>
> *"Caesar's," they replied.*
>
> *He said to them, "Then give back to Caesar what is Caesar's, and to God what is God's."*
>
> *They were unable to trap him in what he had said there in public. And astonished by his answer, they became silent.*

Taxation in the Bible

To answer the question: Yes. Jesus' mission was not to establish an earthly kingdom. God had already shown his power when He toppled Pharaoh and mighty Egypt (Exodus). Yet Jesus did not attempt to institute a new independent government for Israel. Rather, the new covenant Jesus was instituting called for followers to live under many nations rather than a single nation (Israel) and pay taxes to those governments. However, there is more to the story. Roman coin inscriptions listed Caesar as God. Would Jesus endorse a government where the leader claimed divinity? Probably not.

By saying "Give to Caesar what is Caesar's, and to God what is God's", Jesus is once again mocking and condemning those who sought to trap Him. By using the Roman coins the Pharisees were tacitly acknowledging Caesar's divinity. Surely this embarrassed them as they were proud of their "superiority" in following the law, which starts with "Thou shall have no other gods before Me."

Roman silver *denarius* bearing image of Tiberius. The Latin inscription reads [clockwise from left of emperor's ear]: ***Augustus Ti****(berius)* ***Caesar Divi Aug****(usti)* ***F****(ilius)* ["Augustus Tiberius, son of the Divine Augustus"]. According to the synoptic gospels, it was a coin like this that prompted Jesus to say: "Caesar's things give back to Caesar and God's things to God" [Mark 12:15-17 & parallels]. This denarius' inscription identifying Tiberius *Caesar* as son of the *divine* Augustus magnifies the rhetorical irony of that saying.
- www.virtualreligion.net

The coins were also a reminder that Israel was a conquered nation subservient to Roman rule. At its founding, God had intended Israel to worship and trust in Him for protection. God promised to defend the nation against all enemies. However, failing to follow God's law would bring about the nation's downfall.

God's covenant with Israel called for blessings to follow faithfulness and curses to follow unfaithfulness. The **ultimate curse** was to be conquered by another nation, described in Deuteronomy.

Deuteronomy 28:15 However, if you do not obey the LORD your God and do not carefully follow all his commands and decrees I am giving you today, all these curses will come upon you and overtake you....

Deuteronomy 28:49-52 The LORD will bring a nation against you.... They will lay siege to all the cities throughout your land until the high fortified walls in which you trust fall down. They will besiege all the cities throughout the land the LORD your God is giving you.

Israel repeatedly did not follow God's desires for the nation. Israel's continued disobedience finally resulted in the nation's downfall as God had said. These sanctions were fulfilled when Assyria conquered Israel (northern kingdom – 2 Kings 17) and Babylon conquered Judah (southern kingdom – 2 Kings 24). God did not do this lightly. He sent numerous prophets (Elijah, Elisha, Joel, Hosea, Amos, Micah and Isaiah) to urge Israel to turn back to Him and follow His will. As was said in Chapter 2, humans have free will, but it comes with consequences.

In the period between the Old and New Testaments, Israel repeated this cycle. 1 Maccabees tells the story of how a Jewish priest and his family lead the Jewish nation back to independent status in 163 BC. Evidently, the leaders again did not follow God's law during this period as there was infighting between the rulers and treaties were again made with Rome, the emerging power of the day. Finally, a civil war started between pro-Pharisee and anti-Pharisee coalitions. Rome settled the dispute when they came and conquered Jerusalem in 63 BC.

So with one simple statement, Jesus had reminded the Pharisees of Israel's failures to keep the law God had given them, and the fact that Roman rule was a resulting sanction or curse from the law the Pharisees often "boasted" of upholding.

As a side note: Contrast the Roman coin calling Caesar a god, with U.S. currency which has "In God We Trust" proudly inscribed.

Taxation in the Bible

Apostle Paul on Taxes in the New Covenant
Paul confirms the New Testament – new covenant between God and His followers. Followers are to live under many nations and governments, paying taxes to those governments.

> *Romans 13:1, 6-7*
> *Everyone must submit himself to the governing authorities, for there is no authority except that which God has established. The authorities that exist have been established by God. .... This is also why you pay taxes, for the authorities are God's servants, who give their full time to governing. Give everyone what you owe him: If you owe taxes, pay taxes; if revenue, then revenue; if respect, then respect; if honor, then honor.*

Paul acknowledges the government's ability to collect taxes. There is no mention or endorsement for the government to take from one person and give to another. Other Bible passages leave that responsibility to the individual or church (Chapter 8).

What can a society learn about tax policy from scripture?
There really aren't strong statements in scripture on tax policy – that is not the focus of the Bible. If a society wants to draw guidelines, it can do so. Here are a few guidelines that can be drawn.

Everyone Paid the Tax
As discussed above, a temple tax was used where every person, both poor and rich, paid a fixed fee. While not a tax, the Widows Offering (Mark 12:41-44) describes a poor person giving a huge portion of her income to God. Jesus praises her. He doesn't scold her and tell her to let the "rich" carry the burden of supporting the temple. Those attempting to use scripture as a guide in creating a tax system should not exempt the poor from paying taxes either. The other taxes or tithes discussed below, apply to all those with income.

The Amount of Tax
10% For the national government: The king, according to 1 Samuel, levied a 10% tax on crops and herds – the income of that day. Again it can be assumed that all having income paid the 10% income tax.

The Tax was Applied at a Single Rate
Every portion of income was taxed at the given tax rate. This would be called a flat-rate tax today. Notice how there is nothing in the Bible that endorses or even discusses the "progressive" income tax rates used in modern countries where the different income levels are taxed at different rates.

Other Societal Responsibilities
In the Bible, there is a difference between taxes and tithes. Taxes were collected by men. There are many examples of governments collecting taxes. There is also the example of the temple tax. Tithes were obligations from the individual to God or society. There is no mention of these being enforced by earthly tax collectors.

<u>4% to Care for the Poor</u>: Deuteronomy 14:28-29 and 26:12 describe another tithe to be given to the priests and poor every third year. These passages imply a 3-4% annual giving rate from all income earners. Today this would be a charitable donation to support the poor.

<u>10% For the Church</u>: As stated in God's Government chapter, Leviticus 27:30-32 describes a 10% offering to the Lord that everyone was to pay. Also known as tithing, this was an instruction by God to support the priests and temple (pastors and church workers of that day).

Overall Societal Burden: 25%
Were all the Old Testament taxes and tithes summed, a top rate of approximately 25% can be calculated. Remember, that in Israel, this amount paid all government worker salaries, all church worker salaries, all anti-poverty programs, and national defense.

Note that the tax burden is much higher in America, with a top national tax rate of around 40%, plus additional state and local income taxes that may also be imposed.

America's Religious Christian Heritage

No one can deny that many of the founding fathers of the United States of America were men of deep religious convictions based in the Bible and their Christian faith in Jesus Christ. Of the 56 men who signed the Declaration of Independence, nearly half (24) held seminary or Bible school degrees.
- Christian Quotes of the Founding Fathers. Mary Fairchild. www.Christianity.About.com

The Christian nature of the Founders is referenced in the Constitution:

"done in Convention by the Unanimous Consent of the States present the Seventeenth Day of September in the **Year of our Lord** one thousand seven hundred and Eighty seven and of the Independence of the United States of America"
- US Constitution. Article VII.

"Year of our Lord" is direct reference to Jesus Christ and the date is the years after His birth. The God of the Bible is present in the US Constitution. No state opposed the inclusion of God in the governing document of the nation. In fact most thought as Washington did:

"It is impossible to rightly govern a nation without God and the Bible."
- 1st President George Washington. www.foundingfatherquotes.com

God gives all humans free will and wants them to live in freedom. Only government, or other humans, can take away this freedom. This was a basis of the American Declaration of Independence, and US Constitution. The founders were Christians. It is evident by their actions and their writings. There were, however, many different views on Christianity, just as there are today. The founders referred to them as religious societies or sects. Today they are called denominations or church bodies. So in order to come together and form a nation, it was imperative that the new national government not select one of these sects and make it a state religion. This is the meaning of the 1st Amendment and its purpose for being added to the Constitution. Note the alignment with God-given free will for men.

Many secularists today will insist America is not a Christian nation. What they really mean is America is not a theocracy, where worship is prescribed for the people. This is true. The federal government has never tried to enforce religious practices (until the last 50 years when it began banning religion). America has always been predominantly Christian and was founded by Christians. Any analysis of the founding documents of the original colonies makes this clear.

> Now there will probably be found few persons **in this or any other Christian country** who would deliberately contend that it was unreasonable or unjust to **foster and encourage the Christian religion generally as a matter of sound policy as well as of revealed truth.**
> - Commentaries on the Constitution of the United States. Volume 3. 1833. Supreme Court Justice Joseph Story. P723. Google.com/books.

"It cannot be emphasized too strongly or too often that this great nation was founded, not by religionists, but by **Christians**; not on religions, but on the **Gospel of Jesus Christ**. For this very reason peoples of other faiths have been afforded asylum, prosperity, and freedom of worship here."
- Patrick Henry, 1st Governor of Virginia

Although the Constitution prevents the federal government from setting up a national religion, some of the states did have state-sponsored religions. Procon.org has researched religion in the original 13 colonies, and and concluded: "All 13 American colonies had some form of state-supported religion. This support varied from tax benefits to religious requirements for voting or serving in the legislature." All colonies were predominantly Christian. Eight of the colonies had state-sponsored churches. Five did not.

Official Church of Colony at Founding
Anglican/Church of England: Maryland, New York, North Carolina, South Carolina, Virginia

Puritan/Congregational Church: Connecticut, Massachusetts, New Hampshire

No Official Church: Delaware, Georgia, New Jersey, Pennsylvania, Rhode Island

Even those colonies without a state church were Christian by charter. Some examples of the colonies mandating religious activity in their charters:

- The colonial governor of Virginia in 1617 declared it a **crime not to go to church** on Sundays and holidays.

- Connecticut Colony Charter in 1662 called for all residents to have "the knowledge and obedience of the onely true God and Saviour of mankind, and the **Christian faith**."

- Charter of Rhode Island, 1663: Called for residents to pursue "the holy **Christian faith** and worship".

- New York's Charter of Liberties and Privileges in 1683 dictated that anyone professing "faith in God by **Jesus Christ**" will not be punished for any difference of opinion. In other words all Christian denominations were free to practice in New York.

- Charter of Delaware, 1701: "All Persons who also profess to believe in **Jesus Christ**, the Saviour of the World, shall be capable (notwithstanding their other Persuasions and Practices in Point of Conscience and Religion) to serve this Government in any Capacity, both legislatively and executively..."

Sidebar: Referring back to Chapters 2, 6 and 7, government laws mandating Christianity are not following God's will. God gives humans choice on whether to follow Him and His God-given laws.

The Constitution had written provisions to guarantee the new national government would not "infringe on" a citizens right to practice religion. **The Freedom of Religion offered by the First Amendment, which actually states "Congress shall make no law", did not apply to the states,** which would have still been free to prescribe religion for its citizens.

The majority of the 13 colonies did write religious restrictions into their state's constitutions. Most restrictions applied to office holders in the state governments, requiring a belief in Protestant Christianity. All states by this time allowed freedom for each citizen to practice any denomination of Christianity:

- Maryland State Constitution, Article XXXIII, in 1776 stated: "That, as it is the duty of every man to worship God in such manner as he thinks most acceptable to him; all persons, **professing the Christian religion**, are equally entitled to protection in their religious liberty..."
- Delaware State Constitution Oath of Office, 1776: "I _____, do **profess faith in God the Father, and in Jesus Christ His only Son, and in the Holy Ghost, One God, blessed for evermore; and I do acknowledge the holy scriptures of the Old Testament and New Testament to be given by Divine Inspiration.**"
- North Carolina Constitution, 1776: "That no person, who shall deny the being of **God or the truth of the Protestant religion, or the divine authority of the Old or New Testaments** ...., shall be capable of holding any office or place of trust or profit in the civil department within this State."
- Pennsylvania Constitution in 1776 required oath for elected representatives: "I do believe in **one God, the Creator and Governor of the Universe**, the rewarder of the good and punisher of the wicked. And I do acknowledge the **Scriptures of the Old and New Testament to be given by Divine inspiration.**"
- New Jersey Constitution (1776): "That there shall be no establishment of any one religious sect in this Province, in preference to another; and that **no Protestant inhabitant of this Colony shall be denied the enjoyment of any civil right**, merely on account of his religious principles...."
- Georgia Constitution in 1777 allowed for citizens to have free exercise of their religion, but also required that Representatives be of the **Protestant religion.**
- South Carolina Constitution, 1778, requirements for a state authorized church: "That there is one eternal God, and a future state of rewards and punishments. That God is publicly to be worshiped. That the **Christian religion is the true religion.** That the **holy scriptures of the Old and New Testaments are of divine inspiration**, and

are the rule of faith and practice".

- The Massachusetts Constitution in 1780 mandated that all elected officials take an oath of office that included their professing the **Christian faith**.
- New Hampshire Constitution in 1784 required all elected officials to be of the **Protestant (Christian)** religion.
- Connecticut Constitution (1818). Article I. Section 4.: "No preference shall be given by law to any **Christian sect or mode of worship**."

  - Procon.org. Religion in the Original 13 Colonies.

In fact, every American colony from its foundation down to the revolution, with the exception of Rhode Island, (if indeed that state be an exception,) **did openly** by the whole course of its laws and institutions, **support and sustain in some form the Christian religion**, and almost invariably gave a peculiar sanction to some of its fundamental doctrines. And this has **continued to be the case in some of the states down to the present period without the slightest suspicion that it was against the principles of public law or republican liberty.**

  - Commentaries on the Constitution of the United States. Volume 3. 1833. Supreme Court Justice Joseph Story. P724. Google.com/books.

Constitutional Sidebar: Amendment 14, ratified in 1868, states in part: "No State shall make or enforce any law which shall abridge the privileges or immunities of citizens of the United States...". While written to protect newly freed slaves, most interpret this as also applying to religion. So per the 1st Amendment, states "shall make no law respecting an establishment of religion, or prohibiting the free exercise thereof...". Of course the states are then also bound by the 2nd Amendment, "the right of the people to keep and bear Arms, shall not be infringed." So any state or city gun banning law is as unconstitutional as a city mandating worship in a particular church.

The Declaration of Independence is the precursor to the Constitution. It contains key clauses concerning God: "the separate and equal station to which... Nature's **God entitle them**"; "men are **endowed by their Creator** with certain unalienable Rights, that among these are Life, Liberty and the pursuit of Happiness."; "a firm reliance on the protection of **Divine Providence.**"

God is recognized as the source of all rights, and it is recognized that God created all people equally with respect to having those rights.

Sidebar: Some Christians criticize the founders of America for fighting a war to achieve independence from Britain. If one reviews the events leading up to the Revolutionary War, it was the King of England who sent his army to America in order to enforce his will on the colony. This included British soldiers entering any colonist's home at the soldiers' pleasure. The Declaration of Independence simply stated that the Americans wanted to end the colonial relationship and become an independent nation. The King of England responded by declaring war. It is analogous to a woman (the colonies) in an abusive marriage who declares she wants a divorce. The man (England) resents her action, so attempts to use force to make her remain in the relationship. What Christian will tell the woman that she must stay with the man in an abusive relationship?

George Washington, The first President, leader of the Revolutionary Army, and convener of the US Constitutional Convention typifies the prevailing Christian religious views of the nation's founders. Washington speaks of prayers to an all-powerful God that God may bless the nation's people with happiness and liberty.

> President George Washington's 1st Inaugural Address.
> It would be peculiarly improper to omit in this first official act my fervent supplications to that **Almighty Being** who rules over the universe, who presides in the councils of nations... that His benediction may consecrate to the liberties and happiness of the people of the United States a Government instituted by themselves for these essential purposes, and may enable every instrument employed in its administration to execute with success the functions allotted to his charge.... No people can be bound to acknowledge and adore the invisible hand which conducts the affairs of men more than the people of the United States.
>   - TRGW. P522-523.

In an open letter to the states, Washington acknowledges the common faith of the nation, as well as, his thoughts that national happiness would occur if the citizens imitated the characteristics of Jesus.

> I now make it my earnest prayer that God would have you, and the state in which you preside, in his holy protection;...that He would most graciously be pleased to dispose us all to do justice, to love mercy, and to demean ourselves with that charity, humility, and pacific temper of mind which were the characteristics of **the Divine Author of our blessed religion**, and without an humble imitation of whose example in these things, we can never hope to be a happy nation.
> - 1783. TRGW. p.723.

There are numerous other writings and speeches by Washington dealing with his, and the nation's, faith in God; there are enough to make a book only of Washington's words. A few examples are listed below:

> That great and glorious **Being**....is the beneficent **Author** of all the good that was is or ever will be.
>
> It is the duty of all nations to acknowledge the providence of **Almighty God**, to obey His will, to be grateful for His benefits, and humbly to implore His protection and favor.
> - 1789 Thanksgiving Proclamation by Washington. TRGW. P699.

> "The will of Heaven is not to be controverted or scrutinized by the children of this world. It therefore becomes the creatures of it to submit with patience and resignation to the **will of the Creator**,..."
> - Washington 1793 letter. TRGW. P699

> "While just government protects all in their religious rights, true religion affords to government its surest support."
> - Washington to Dutch Reformed Church in 1789. TRGW. P702.

> "While all men... are protected in worshiping the **Deity** according to the dictates of their consciences,... no man who is profligate in his morals, or a bad amber of the civil

community, can possibly be a true **Christian** or a credit to his own religious society."
> - Washington 1789. TRGW. P654.

"The liberty enjoyed by the people of these states of worshiping Almighty God agreeably to their conscience, is not only among the choicest of their blessings, but also of their rights."
> - Washington. Addressing the Quakers. 1789. foundingfatherquotes.com

Washington, while being the most famous of America's founders, was far from alone in his expressions and actions of faith in God. A few examples of other founders:

"In the supposed state of nature, **all men are equally bound by** the laws of nature, or to speak more properly, **the laws of the Creator**. "
> - Samuel Adams letter to the Legislature of Massachusetts, January 17, 1794, www.westillholdthesetruths.org

"Our Constitution was made only for a **moral and religious people**. It is wholly inadequate to the government of any other."
> - John Adams Address to First Brigade of the Third Division of the Militia of Massachusetts, October 11, 1798, www.westillholdthesetruths.org

"I often note with equal pleasure that **God gave this one connected country to one united people** – a people descended from the same language, **professing the same religion**, attached to the same principles of government, very similar in manners and customs, who by their joint counsels, arms, and efforts, fighting side by side through a long bloody war, have nobly established general liberty and independence. "
> - John Jay, The Federalist Papers Federalist No. 2

"If we abide by the principles taught in the Bible, our country will go on prospering."
> - Daniel Webster. (1782-1852), US Senator. quotes.liberty-tree.

Further proof of America's religious heritage is found in the state constitutions. All 50 thank or offer praise to God in the text.

America's Religious Christian Heritage

Every State praised God at their founding
Alabama 1901, Preamble. We the people of the State of Alabama, invoking the favor and guidance of **Almighty God**, do ordain and establish the following Constitution ...

Alaska 1956, Preamble. We, the people of Alaska, grateful to **God** and to those who founded our nation and pioneered this great land......

Arizona 1911, Preamble. We, the people of the State of Arizona, grateful to **Almighty God** for our liberties, do ordain this Constitution...

Arkansas 1874, Preamble. We, the people of the State of Arkansas, grateful to **Almighty God** for the privilege of choosing our own form of government...

California 1879, Preamble. We, the People of the State of California, grateful to **Almighty God** for our freedom.....

Colorado 1876, Preamble. We, the people of Colorado, with profound reverence for the **Supreme Ruler of Universe**....

Connecticut 1818, Preamble. The People of Connecticut, acknowledging with gratitude the good Providence of **God** in permitting them to enjoy ...

Delaware 1897, Preamble. Through Divine Goodness all men have, by nature, the rights of worshiping and serving their **Creator** according to the dictates of their consciences ...

Florida 1885, Preamble. We, the people of the State of Florida, grateful to **Almighty God** for our constitutional liberty, establish this Constitution...

Georgia 1777, Preamble. We, the people of Georgia, relying upon protection and guidance of **Almighty God**, do ordain and establish this Constitution...

The Bible and Constitution Made America Great

Hawaii 1959, Preamble. We, the people of Hawaii, Grateful for **Divine Guidance** ... establish this Constitution.

Idaho 1889, Preamble. We, the people of the State of Idaho, grateful to **Almighty God** for our freedom, to secure its blessings...

Illinois 1870, Preamble. We, the people of the State of Illinois, grateful to **Almighty God** for the civil, political and religious liberty which He hath so long permitted us to enjoy and looking to Him for a blessing on our endeavors...

Indiana 1851, Preamble. We, the People of the State of Indiana, grateful to **Almighty God** for the free exercise of the right to chose our form of government...

Iowa 1857, Preamble. We, the People of the State of Iowa, grateful to the **Supreme Being** for the blessings hitherto enjoyed, and feeling our dependence on Him for a continuation of these blessings ... establish this Constitution.

Kansas 1859, Preamble. We, the people of Kansas, grateful to **Almighty God** for our civil and religious privileges, establish this Constitution.

Kentucky 1891, Preamble. We, the people of the Commonwealth of Kentucky grateful to **Almighty God** for the civil, political and religious liberties...

Louisiana 1921, Preamble. We, the people of the State of Louisiana, grateful to **Almighty God** for the civil, political and religious liberties we enjoy...

Maine 1820, Preamble. We the People of Maine, acknowledging with grateful hearts the goodness of the **Sovereign Ruler of the Universe** in affording us an opportunity ... and imploring His aid and direction.

Maryland 1776, Preamble. We, the people of the state of Maryland, grateful to **Almighty God** for our civil and religious liberty...

Massachusetts 1780, Preamble. We, therefore, the people of Massachusetts, acknowledging, with grateful hearts, the goodness of the **Great Legislator of the Universe**, in affording us, in the course of His providence...

Michigan 1908, Preamble. We, the people of the State of Michigan, grateful to **Almighty God** for the blessings of freedom....

Minnesota, 1857, Preamble. We, the people of the State of Minnesota, grateful to **God** for our civil and religious liberty.....

Mississippi 1890, Preamble. We, the people of Mississippi in convention assembled, grateful to **Almighty God**, and invoking His blessing on our work.....

Missouri 1845, Preamble. We, the people of Missouri, with profound reverence for the **Supreme Ruler of the Universe**, and grateful for His goodness, establish this Constitution.

Montana 1889, Preamble. We, the people of Montana, grateful to **Almighty God** for the blessings of liberty. establish this Constitution.

Nebraska 1875, Preamble. We, the people, grateful to **Almighty God** for our freedom...

Nevada 1864, Preamble. We the people of the State of Nevada, grateful to **Almighty God** for our freedom establish this Constitution,.....

New Hampshire 1792, Part I. Art. I. Sec. V. Every individual has a natural and unalienable right to worship **God** according to the dictates of his own conscience....

New Jersey 1844, Preamble. We, the people of the State of

New Jersey, grateful to **Almighty God** for civil and religious liberty which He hath so long permitted us to enjoy, and looking to Him for a blessing on our endeavors....

New Mexico 1911, Preamble. We, the People of New Mexico, grateful to **Almighty God** for the blessings of Liberty.....

New York 1846, Preamble. We, the people of the State of New York, grateful to **Almighty God** for our freedom, in order to secure its blessings....

North Carolina 1868, Preamble. "We, the people of the State of North Carolina, grateful to **Almighty God, the Sovereign Ruler of Nations**, for the preservation of the American Union and the existence of our civil, political and religious liberties, and acknowledging our dependence upon Him for the continuance of those blessings to us and our posterity...

North Dakota 1889, Preamble. We, the people of North Dakota , grateful to **Almighty God** for the blessings of civil and religious liberty, do ordain...

Ohio 1852, Preamble. We the people of the state of Ohio, grateful to **Almighty God** for our freedom, to secure its blessings and to promote our common.

Oklahoma 1907, Preamble. Invoking the guidance of **Almighty God**, in order to secure and perpetuate the blessings of liberty ...

Oregon 1857, Bill of Rights, Article I. Section 2. All men shall be secure in the Natural right, to worship **Almighty God** according to the dictates of their consciences...

Pennsylvania 1776, Preamble. We, the people of Pennsylvania, grateful to **Almighty God** for the blessings of civil and religious liberty, and humbly invoking His guidance....

Rhode Island 1842, Preamble. We the People of the State of Rhode Island grateful to **Almighty God** for the civil and religious liberty which He hath so long permitted us to enjoy, and looking to Him for a blessing....

South Carolina, 1778, Preamble. We, the people of the State of South Carolina, in Convention assembled, grateful to **God** for our liberties, do ordain and establish this Constitution for the preservation and perpetuation of the same.

South Dakota 1889, Preamble. We, the people of South Dakota, grateful to **Almighty God** for our civil and religious liberties ... establish this constitution.

Tennessee 1796, Art. XI.III. That all men have a natural and indefensible right to worship **Almighty God** according to the dictates of their conscience...

Texas 1845, Preamble. We the People of the Republic of Texas, acknowledging, with gratitude, the grace and beneficence of **God**...

Utah 1896, Preamble. Grateful to **Almighty God** for life and liberty, we establish this Constitution...

Vermont 1777, Preamble. Whereas, all government ought to be instituted and supported, for the security and protection of the community, as such, and to enable the individuals who compose it, to enjoy their natural rights, and the other blessings which the **Author of Existence** has bestowed upon man....

Virginia 1776, Bill of Rights, XVI. That religion, or the duty which we owe to our **Creator**, and the manner of discharging it, can be directed only by reason and conviction, not by force or violence; and therefore all men are equally entitled to the free exercise of religion, according to the dictates of conscience; and that it is the mutual duty of all to practice **Christian forbearance, love, and charity** towards each other.

Washington 1889, Preamble. We the People of the State of Washington, grateful to the **Supreme Ruler of the Universe** for our liberties, do ordain this Constitution...

West Virginia 1872, Preamble. Since through **Divine Providence** we enjoy the blessings of civil, political and religious liberty, we, the people of West Virginia reaffirm our faith in and constant reliance upon **God**.

Wisconsin 1848, Preamble. We, the people of Wisconsin, grateful to **Almighty God** for our freedom, domestic tranquility.

Wyoming 1890, Preamble. We, the people of the State of Wyoming, grateful to **God** for our civil, political and religious liberties, and desiring to secure them to ourselves and perpetuate them to our posterity, do ordain and establish this Constitution.

- Procon.org. References to "God" in State Constitutions.

Not all of the founding fathers fit into current Christian denominational definitions. Some defined their own faith. But the important point to remember is all used the Christian Bible as the basis for their faith.

Jefferson and Franklin were Independent-Minded Christians - NOT Deists

A myth often prevalent today is that the founders were deists. Deism is the belief that God created the world, but takes no action that affects it post creation. Benjamin Franklin and Thomas Jefferson are the two founders most often cited as being deists. Their lives and writings contradict that assertion, though.

The most obvious rebuttal of Jefferson and Franklin being deists is the first national seal that they proposed. Benjamin Franklin and Thomas Jefferson served on the First Great Seal Committee in 1776 to design a seal for the new nation.

Benjamin Franklin's proposal is preserved in a note of his own handwriting: "Moses standing on the Shore, and extending his Hand over the Sea, thereby causing the same to overwhelm Pharaoh who is sitting in an open Chariot, a Crown on his Head and a Sword in his Hand. Rays from a Pillar of Fire in the Clouds reaching to Moses, to express that he acts by Command of the Deity.

Thomas Jefferson also suggested allegorical scenes. For the front of the seal: children of Israel in the wilderness, led by a cloud by day and a pillar of fire by night.
- www.greatseal.com

A sketch of the committee's proposal is shown below:

Proposed First Seal of the United States of America (back side)

"Pharaoh sitting in an open Chariot, a Crown on his head and a Sword in his hand, passing through the divided Waters of the Red Sea in Pursuit of the Israelites.

Rays from a Pillar of Fire in the Cloud, expressive of the divine Presence and Command, beaming on Moses who stands on the shore and extending his hand over the Sea causes it to overwhelm Pharaoh."

"Motto: Rebellion to Tyrants is Obedience to God."

- www.greatseal.com

Note how they propose a scene from the Bible to place on the seal. A scene where God is performing a miracle by parting the sea and leading the Israelites out of Egypt. This is God at His most active. Not a god of deism that takes no part in the world. It is impossible for a deist to propose such an outlandish design. After all a deist, by definition, cannot believe the book of Exodus in which God performed miracle after miracle against Pharaoh, then appeared in the form of a cloud pillar by day, and fire pillar by night, to lead His people out of bondage.

Were Jefferson and Franklin Christians?

There is an old saying. If it walks like a duck, looks like a duck, and quacks like a duck, it is a duck! Apply this logic to determine whether or not a person should be called a Christian. Now this aspect only covers outward appearances. It is impossible to see into another person's heart. Only God can do that. No human can know whether another human is a sincere Christian in his heart and will be saved by God. With this being the case, society then and now will consider a person to be a Christian if they call themselves Christian, attend a Christian church, and act like a Christian. There are Christians in America today who do not believe parts of the Bible (their free will). Society still considers them Christians. This is the standard being applied, not whether there is theological accuracy in all of their beliefs and writings.

Thomas Jefferson
Private faith:
Jefferson's faith is a complex subject. There is no doubt that he studied the Bible seriously and was a firm believer in an Almighty God. He considered himself a Christian, but may have doubted that Jesus was part of the God Trinity (Father – Son – Holy Spirit) that is a tenet of standard Christian theology. The following quotes from Jefferson describe his faith.

> " My views of [the Christian religion]... are the result of a life of inquiry and reflection and very different from the anti-Christian system imputed to me by those who know nothing of my opinions. To the corruptions of Christianity, I am indeed opposed; but not to the precepts of Jesus himself. I am a Christian, in only the sense in which he wished anyone to be - sincerely attached to his doctrines in preference to all others; ascribing to himself every human excellence and believing he never claimed any other."
> - 1803 Letter. TRTJ p364.

Jefferson may have truly questioned Jesus' divinity, believing that Jesus only considered himself human. Or he may have meant that Jesus was a perfect man (without sin), having every human excellence. Jefferson thought the church had unnecessarily complicated religion.

America's Religious Christian Heritage

"When we shall have done away the incomprehensible jargon of the Trinitarian arithmetic that three is one and one is three;.... When we have unlearned everything which has been taught since His day, and got back to the pure and simple doctrines He inculcated, we shall then be truly and worthily His disciples." - 1821 Letter. TRTJ. P 365-366.

Jefferson was particularly fond of Jesus' teachings. In an 1822 letter Jefferson summarized the teachings of Jesus as he believed them, taken straight out of the Bible.

"The Doctrines of Jesus are simple, and tend all to the happiness of man:
1. That there is only 1 God and He is all perfect.
2. That there is a future state of rewards and punishments.
3. That to love God with all thy heart and thy neighbor as thyself is the sum of religion."
- Thomas Jefferson. TRTJ p. 366.

Jefferson considered Jesus the ultimate teacher. He created a book, *The Morals of Jesus*, in which he re-wrote the teachings of Jesus from the four Gospels, each verse written side by side in *four Languages* – Greek, Latin, French and English. This is referred to as the "Jefferson Bible". It omits Jesus' resurrection and miracles. Some conclude that Jefferson therefore did not believe in either. This may be true, or Jefferson may have just wanted a synopsis of Jesus' actual teachings and life on earth.

We also do not know how Jefferson's faith evolved later in his life. He may have fully accepted Jesus as God and Savior.

"Toward the end of his life, Jefferson apparently changed his mind about the divinity of Jesus. The letters Jefferson wrote during his final years contain references to 'our Savior'."
- TRTJ Editor comment. P364

Calling Jesus "Savior" strongly implies that Jefferson did recognize Jesus as the Son of God who died for our sins. It is hard to believe that a man studying the Bible to the degree that Jefferson did could not conclude Jesus was God as well as man. Jesus' words from Scripture that Jefferson studied:

> *John 10:30 I and the Father are one.*
>
> *John 10:38 ...the Father is in Me, and I in the Father."*

Regardless of Jefferson's views on Jesus' divinity, there is no doubt he studied the Bible and followed the God of the Bible.
Eyewitness accounts tell us Thomas Jefferson was a religious individual who attended church. Jefferson's grandson stated that Jefferson was a very active member of a Christian congregation:

> "He [Jefferson] was regular in attendance at church taking his prayer book with him. He drew the plan of the Episcopal church in Charlottesville, was one of the largest contributors to its erection, and contributed regularly to the support of its minister." - TRTJ p302.

> "I never heard from him the expression of one thought, feeling or sentiment inconsistent with the highest moral standard or the purest Christian charity... His moral character was of the highest order, founded upon the purest and sternest models of antiquity, but softened, chastened, and developed by the influences of the all-pervading benevolence of the doctrines of Christ – which he had intensely and admiringly studied." - TRTJ p 320.

Jefferson is also on the record as telling a visitors who did not believe the Bible to be true, "Then sir, you have studied it to little purpose." (TRTJ p321).

Jefferson's faith continued as he neared the end of his earthly life.

> Jefferson stated from his deathbed, "... I now resign my soul, without fear, to my God." He had long believed that he would live on in another existence. -TRTJ p314.

By today's societal definitions, Jefferson would be called a Christian. He claimed to be a Christian and attended a Christian church. From a theological viewpoint, a pastor or priest may very well express concern for Jefferson's salvation, as Jefferson at times expressed a lack of belief in Jesus also being God, as well as man.

> Sidebar: By societal definition, Barack Obama is a Christian. He claims Christianity as his faith and attended a "christian" church. In theological terms, Obama's Christianity is debatable. Obama's church, headed by Jeremiah Wright, mixes Christian teachings with socialism and black liberation theology. Wright is recorded as cursing America using God's name in vain during a sermon. (How many Christian pastors violate one of God's Ten Commandments while giving a sermon?) So many Christian clergy may very well question whether Obama is truly saved. The societal definition of Christianity is much broader than the theological definition.

That sums up the complexity of Jefferson's personal religious beliefs. What is not in question is his public support of God and the Bible.

Public faith:
Jefferson was, of course, a national leader both pre- and post-revolution, drafting the Declaration of Independence, and later serving as 3rd President. Jefferson would no doubt have drafted the U.S. Constitution as well, had he not been ambassador to France at the time. That being the case, Jefferson's close political follower and fellow Virginian, James Madison wrote the Constitution.

Jefferson considered God supreme and all-powerful and knew the nation needed to turn to God. In addition to the Declaration of Independence, Jefferson wrote the following"

> "We are not in a world ungoverned by the laws and the power of a Superior Agent. Our efforts are in His hand, and directed by it, and He will give them their effect in His own time."
>   - TRTJ p404.

> "And can the liberties of a nation be thought secure when we have removed their only firm basis, a conviction in the minds of the people that these liberties are the gift of God? That

they are not to be violated but with his wrath? Indeed I tremble for my country when I reflect that God is just: that his justice cannot sleep for ever."
- Thomas Jefferson Notes on the State of Virginia, Query 18. 1781

In a Bill for Establishing Religious Freedom in 1779, Jefferson referred to God as "Almighty God", "the Holy Author of our religion" and "Lord of both body and mind". Jefferson's use of "our religion" implies that he recognized a common theme among the first Americans: the religion taught in the Bible.

Here Jefferson refers to God as that Being, and a Superior Agent responsible for blessings of the nation. Note Jefferson's use of God - even in an official address to Congress. Hardly the words of an atheist, deist, or one wanting God removed from government.

> "When we assemble together... to consider the state of our beloved country, our just attentions are first drawn to those pleasing circumstances which mark the goodness of that Being from whose favor they flow, and the large measure of thankfulness we owe for His bounty."
> - Jefferson's Second Annual Message to Congress in 1802. TRTJ. P404.

> "We are not in a world ungoverned by the laws and power of a Superior Agent. Our efforts are in His hand, and directed by it, and He will give them their effect in His own time.
> – Thomas Jefferson 1815 Letter. TRTJ. p. 404.

Jefferson believed religion was an important factor in creating the government and that liberty or free will to worship God as one sees fit is a fundamental right.

> "Religion, as well as reason, confirms the soundness of those principles on which our government has been founded and its rights asserted."
> --Thomas Jefferson to P. H. Wendover, 1815. ME 14:283

> "Among the most inestimable of our blessings, also, is that... of liberty to worship our Creator in the way we think most agreeable to His will; a liberty deemed in other countries

incompatible with good government and yet proved by our experience to be its best support."
--Thomas Jefferson: Reply to John Thomas et al., 1807. ME 16:291

Jefferson also often used prayer publicly. A few examples:

In 1774, Jefferson and Virginia's other elected leaders called for "a day of fasting, humiliation and prayer, to implore heaven to avert us from the evils of civil war.... and to turn the hearts of the King and Parliament to moderation and justice."
- TRTJ p428.

"May that Infinite Power [God] which rules the destinies of the universe lead our councils to what is best and give then a favorable issue for your peace and prosperity."
- 1st Inaugural Address. TRTJ p403.

"I offer my sincere prayers to the Supreme Ruler of the Universe, that He may long preserve our country in freedom and prosperity."
- TRTJ p 403.

"I join in addressing Him whose Kingdom ruleth overall to direct the administration of [our citizens] affairs to their own greatest good."
- TRTJ p 403.

"When we assemble together... to consider the state of our beloved country, our just attentions are first drawn to those pleasing circumstances which mark the goodness of that Being [God] from whose favor they flow, and the large measure of thankfulness we owe for His bounty."
- 2nd Annual Message to Congress. TRTJ p404.

"I pray God, that these principles [of the Declaration of Independence] may be eternal."
- Jefferson letter to James Madison. TRTJ p 312.

Benjamin Franklin

> "A **Bible** and a newspaper in every house, a good school in every district - all studied and appreciated as they merit - are the principal support of virtue, morality, and civil liberty."
> - Benjamin Franklin. Letter dated March 1778 to the Ministry of France.
> quotes.liberty-tree.ca

And some consider Benjamin Franklin an atheist? Hardly. In his early teens, Franklin did adopt deism for a short time. He writes: "I soon became a thorough deist." However several years later Franklin rethinks this belief, writing: "I began to suspect that this doctrine [of deism] though it might be true, was not very useful." (TRBF. P 40-41)

Deists believe in God, but question God's involvement in the world. Franklin's dabbling in deism was evidently not very deep as he later writes of his spiritual views and beliefs:

- I never doubted the existence of the Deity.
- He made the world and governs it by his providence.
- The most acceptable service of God was the doing of good to man.
- Our souls are immortal.
- All crime will be punished and virtue rewarded, either here or hereafter.
  - TRBF. P62.

A deist does not believe God takes an active role in the world, which is of course contrary to "governing" it.

In 1728 Franklin wrote a pamphlet, "Articles of Belief and Acts of Religion." Readers of the Bible will see many similarities. Some excerpts:

> [God] has given us reason, whereby we are capable of observing his wisdom in the creation, he is not above caring for us, being pleased with our praise, and offended when we slight him or neglect his glory.
>
> I love him, therefore for his goodness, and I adore him for

his wisdom.

Let me then not fail to praise my God continually, for it is his due, and it is all I can return for his many favors and great goodness to me.
- Reprinted in TRBF. p41-42

The *Real Benjamin Franklin* further details the man's religious activity in a section, Franklin and the Philadelphia Churches, on pages 61-63.

Franklin was a religious man, raised as a Presbyterian, but seldom attended church services. Franklin wrote that he found the minister's sermons "very dry, uninteresting and unedifying'. Instead he worshiped privately on Sundays using his own liturgy.

Nonetheless Franklin contributed annually to help support the Presbyterian minister and even contributed to the building of churches of different denominations.

Further example of Franklin's religious beliefs occurred in 1748 when he proposed the first day of fasting in Pennsylvania.

"It is the duty of mankind on all suitable occasions to acknowledge their dependence on the Divine Being." Franklin expressed in prayer "that He would take this province under His protection ... and unite our hearts and strengthen our hands in every undertaking that may be for the public good." - TRBF. P73.

Benjamin Franklin was an elder statesman during the Constitutional Convention and was instrumental in bringing the attendees of many different denominations together in prayer.

I have lived, Sir, a long time; and the longer I live, the more convincing proofs I see of this Truth, that God governs in the Affairs of Men. And if a Sparrow cannot fall to the Ground without his Notice, is it probable that an Empire can rise without his aid?
-Benjamin Franklin, Motion for Prayers, Constitutional Convention. June 28, 1787

Again, a deist would have the belief that God would have no interest in the affairs of man and surely would not assist in the new nation's rise. Franklin's words and life are not consistent with deism.

Leaving Jefferson and Franklin, how did others view America's religious views? American Christianity was summarized by French historian Alex deTocqueville as follows:

> The early American colonists brought with them into the new world a form of **Christianity** which I cannot better describe than by styling it a democratic and republic religion.
>
> All the sects (religious groups) of the United States are comprised within the great unity of **Christianity**, and **Christian morality** is everywhere the same.
>
> There is no country in the world where the **Christian religion retains a greater influence over the souls of man than America**.
> - deTocqueville, Democracy in America, p311,314

America's First English Bible
How many Americans today realize that the first Bible printed in America was paid for with tax dollars by Congress? The Bible was very important to early Americans.

Called "The Bible of the Revolution", Robert Aitken's little Bible was called for by an act of the United States Congress. The Bible was small enough to fit into the coat pocket of the Revolutionary War soldiers. (www.greatsite.com)

The war with Britain cut off the supply of Bibles to the American colonies with the result that Congress instructed its Committee of Commerce to import 20,000 Bibles from "Scotland, Holland, or elsewhere." However on January 21, 1781, Philadelphia printer Robert Aitken (1734–1802) petitioned Congress to officially sanction a publication of the Old and New Testament that he was preparing at his own expense. Congress passed a resolution endorsing Aitken's Bible. (www.myloc.gov)

The Bible is preserved today in the Library of Congress:

America's Religious Christian Heritage

The Holy Bible, Containing the Old and New Testaments: Newly translated out of the Original Tongues.... Philadelphia: Robert Aitken, 1782. Rare Book and Special Collections Division, Library of Congress. Call number: BS185 1782 .P5

<u>Prayer and Chaplains in Congress</u>
Congress has always begun its daily sessions with prayer. The first prayer of the Continental Congress occurred in 1774. The Continental Congress was of course made up of the colonies who would not declare independence from Britain until 1776.

<u>The Prayer in the First Congress, A.D. 1774</u>
O Lord our Heavenly Father, high and mighty King of kings, and Lord of lords, who dost from thy throne behold all the dwellers on earth and reignest with power supreme and uncontrolled over all the Kingdoms, Empires and Governments; look down in mercy, we beseech Thee, on these our American States, who have fled to Thee from the rod of the oppressor and thrown themselves on Thy gracious protection, desiring to be henceforth dependent only on Thee. To Thee have they appealed for the righteousness of their cause; to Thee do they now look up for that countenance and support, which Thou alone canst give. Take them, therefore, Heavenly Father, under Thy nurturing care; give them wisdom in Council and valor in the field; defeat the malicious designs of our cruel adversaries; convince them of the unrighteousness of their Cause and if they persist in their sanguinary purposes, of own unerring justice, sounding in their hearts, constrain them to drop the weapons of war from their unnerved hands in the day of battle!

Be Thou present, O God of wisdom, and direct the councils of this honorable assembly; enable them to settle things on the best and surest foundation. That the scene of blood may be speedily closed; that order, harmony and peace may be effectually restored, and truth and justice, religion and piety, prevail and flourish amongst the people. Preserve the health of their bodies and vigor of their minds; shower down on them and the millions they here represent, such temporal blessings as Thou seest expedient for them in this world and crown them with everlasting glory in the world to come. All this we ask in the name and through the merits of Jesus Christ, Thy Son and our Savior. Amen.

> - Reverend Jacob Duché, Rector of Christ Church of Philadelphia, Pennsylvania. September 7, 1774, 9 o'clock a.m.

The election of the Rev. William Linn as Chaplain of the House on May 1, 1789, continued the tradition established by the Continental Congresses of each day's proceedings opening with a prayer by a chaplain. The early chaplains alternated duties with their Senate counterparts on a weekly basis. The two conducted Sunday services for the Washington community in the House Chamber every other week.

Since the election of Rev. Linn in 1789, the House has been served by chaplains of various religious denominations, including Baptist (7), Christian (1), Congregationalist (2), Disciples of Christ (1), Episcopalian (4), Lutheran (1), Methodist (16), Presbyterian (15), Roman Catholic (1), Unitarian (2), and Universalist (1). The current chaplain is Reverend Daniel P. Coughlin, a Roman Catholic.

> — Office of the Chaplain, US House of Representatives. www.chaplain.house.gov

From its beginnings in the 1770's, Congress has begun its sessions with a prayer from a Christian chaplain. The first prayer specifically used the name of "Jesus Christ, Thy Son and our Savior"-- another example of the Christian faith present in America. Christian prayer was common in early American government.

The counterpart to the House of Representatives in Congress is the Senate. They have their own chaplain.

Office of the Senate Chaplain
When the Senate first convened in New York City on April 6, 1789, one of its first orders of business was to appoint a committee to recommend a candidate for chaplain. On April 25, the Senate elected the Right Reverend Samuel Provoost, Episcopal Bishop of New York, as its first chaplain. Since

America's Religious Christian Heritage

that time, the Senate has been served by chaplains of various religious denominations, including Episcopalians (19), Methodists (17), Presbyterians (14), Baptists (6), Unitarians (2), Congregationalists (1), Lutherans (1), Roman Catholic (1), and Seventh-day Adventist (1).
- senate.gov/artandhistory/history/common/briefing/Senate_Chaplain.htm#2

The Senate Chaplain also opens the Senate session each day with a prayer.

Bibles for Presidential Oaths of Office
Another example of the Bibles role in American society can be seen each time a president is sworn into office. A Bible is used, and in many cases a particular passage is selected and has been recorded. The table below lists the inaugural Bible information.

PRESIDENT	DATE	EDITION
George Washington	1789	Genesis 49:13
George Washington	1793	Passage not known
John Adams	1797	Passage not known
Thomas Jefferson	1801, 1805	Passage not known
James Madison	1809, 1813	Passage not known
James Monroe	1817, 1821	Passage not known
John Q. Adams	1825	Passage not known
Andrew Jackson	1829, 1833	Passage not known
Martin Van Buren	1837	Proverbs 3:17
William H. Harrison	1841	Passage not known
John Tyler	1841	Passage not known
James K. Polk	1845	Passage not known
Zachary Taylor	1849	Passage not known
Millard Fillmore	1850	Passage not known
Franklin Pierce	1853	Affirmed the oath
James Buchanan	1857	Passage not known
Abraham Lincoln	1861, 1865	Matthew 7:1; 18:7; Revelations 16:7
Andrew Johnson	1865	Proverbs 21
Ulysses S. Grant	1869, 1873	Passage not known, Isaiah 11:1-3
Rutherford B. Hayes	1877	Psalm 118:11-13
James A. Garfield	1881	Proverbs 21:1
Chester A. Arthur	1881	Psalm 31:1-3
Grover Cleveland	1885	Psalm 112:4-10; Random

The Bible and Constitution Made America Great

Benjamin Harrison	1889	Psalm 121:1-6
Grover Cleveland	1893	Psalm 91:12-16
William McKinley	1897, 1901	II Chron. 1:10, Proverbs 16
Theodore Roosevelt	1901, 1905	No Bible, James 1:22-23
William Howard Taft	1909	I Kings 3:9-11
Woodrow Wilson	1913, 1917	Psalm 119, Psalm 46
Warren G. Harding	1921	Micah 6:8
Calvin Coolidge	1923	Passage not known
Calvin Coolidge	1925	John 1
Herbert C. Hoover	1929	Proverbs 29:18
Franklin D. Roosevelt	1933, 1937, 1941, 1945	I Corinthians 13
Harry S. Truman	1945, 1949	Closed, Mat. 5:3-11 & Ex. 20:3-17
Dwight D. Eisenhower	1953, 1957	Ps 127:1 & II Chron 7:14; Ps 33:12
John F. Kennedy	1961	Closed Bible
Lyndon B. Johnson	1963, 1965	Missal, Closed family Bible
Richard M. Nixon	1969, 1973	Isaiah 2:4
Gerald R. Ford	1974	Proverbs 3:5-6
James E. Carter	1977	Family Bible open to Micah 6:8
Ronald W. Reagan	1981, 1985	II Chronicles 7:14
George H. W. Bush	1989	Matthew 5
William J. Clinton	1993, 1997	Galatians 6:8, Isaiah 58:12
George W. Bush	2001, 2005	Closed Bible, Open Bible
Barack Obama	2009	Closed Bible

The information is courtesy of the Architect of the Capitol. It has been compiled by the Office of the Curator from contemporary accounts and other sources in the files of the Architect of the Capitol.

National Monuments Showing America's Religious Heritage

Finally, the major monuments in the nation's capitol contain numerous references to God and the national faith. This begins with the rising sun in the East that first shines on the Washington Monument lighting up the words "Praise be to God." inscribed on the panel at the very top of the obelisk.

Washington Monument

"At its topmost point, inscribed on the aluminum tip of the capstone, is the Latin phrase Laus Deo -- **"Praise be to God."** Along the stairway to that height are 190 carved tributes donated by

states, cities, individuals, associations, and foreign governments. The blocks resound with quotations from Scripture -- "**Holiness to the Lord**" (Exodus 28), "**Search the Scriptures**" (John 5:39), "The memory of the just is blessed" (Proverbs 10:7) -- and such invocations as, "May Heaven to this Union continue its Benefice."
- www.religiousliberty.com

Jefferson Memorial
Inscribed around the chamber on the interior of the dome:
"I have sworn upon the **altar of God** eternal hostility against every form of tyranny over the mind of man."

On one panel are excerpts from the Declaration of Independence:
"We hold these truths to be self-evident: that all men are created equal, that they are **endowed by their Creator** with certain inalienable rights, among these are life, liberty, and the pursuit of happiness, that to secure these rights governments are instituted among men...."

On a second panel is an excerpt from "A Bill for Establishing Religious Freedom, 1777", written for the Virginia Assembly:
"**Almighty God hath created the mind free**...All attempts to influence it by temporal punishments or burthens...are a departure from the plan of the **Holy Author of our religion**...No man shall be compelled to frequent or support any religious worship or ministry or shall otherwise suffer on account of his religious opinions or belief, but all men shall be free to profess and by argument to maintain, their opinions in matters of religion. I know but one code of morality for men whether acting singly or collectively."

On the third panel:
"**God who gave us life gave us liberty. Can the liberties of a nation be secure when we have removed a conviction that these liberties are the gift of God?** Indeed I tremble for my country when I reflect that God is just, that his justice cannot sleep forever. Commerce between master and slave is despotism. Nothing is more certainly written in the book of fate than these people are to be free."
- Rediscovering God in America. P43-46.

Lincoln Memorial

Inscribed into the wall are the words of Lincoln's famous Gettysburg Address:

"Four score and seven years ago our fathers brought forth, on this continent, a new nation, conceived in Liberty, and dedicated to the proposition that all men are created equal. ....that **this nation, under God**, shall have a new birth of freedom—and that government of the people, by the people, for the people, shall not perish from the earth."

"The words of Lincoln's Second Inaugural Address, carved in granite, thunder from inside the Memorial that bears his name, praying that the "mighty scourge of war may speedily pass away" but recalling that "the **judgments of the Lord** are true and righteous altogether."

- www.religiousliberty.com

Lincoln's second inaugural address, considered by some to be his greatest speech,... is a mere 700 words in length, but it **mentions God fourteen times and quotes the Bible twice**.

- Rediscovering God in America. P52.

Arlington National Cemetery - Tomb of the Unknown Soldier

"in honored glory an American soldier **known but to God.**"

US Capitol Building

The U.S. Capitol also bears public witness to the legacy of biblically inspired faith that Americans have passed on from generation to generation. New England statesman and orator Daniel Webster was voted by the United States Senate in the 1980s as one of the five greatest senators ever to serve in that chamber. In 1851, when the new House and Senate wings of the Capitol were begun, Webster gave a speech that was deposited in the cornerstone. Its final words are these:

"...be it then known, that on this day the Union of the United States of America stands firm, that their constitution still exists unimpaired, and with all of its original usefulness and glory, growing every day stronger and stronger in the affection of the great body of the American people, and attracting more and more the admiration of the world. And all here assembled, whether belonging to public life or to private life, with **hearts devotedly thankful to Almighty God** for the preservation of the liberty and happiness of the country, unite in sincere and fervent prayers that this deposit, and the walls and arches, the domes and towers, the columns and the entablatures, now to be erected over it, may endure forever."

- www.religiousliberty.com

Liberty Bell
And last but not least, do not forget the Liberty Bell, another historic monument residing in Philadelphia. Made in 1752, the bell is inscribed with a Bible passage. Leviticus 25:10: "Proclaim Liberty throughout all the land unto all the inhabitants thereof"

> "Tradition tells of a chime that changed the world on July 8, 1776, with the Liberty Bell ringing out from the tower of Independence Hall summoning the citizens of Philadelphia to hear the first public reading of the Declaration of Independence by Colonel John Nixon."
>
> - www.ushistory.org/libertybell

There is overwhelming evidence that America was founded as a Christian nation. The evidence is seen in the founding documents, inscribed on national memorials, preserved in the Library of Congress, and seen in the prayers and statements of the early national leaders. Americans wanted to express their faith and belief in God.

Religion and Choice in Schools

"By removing the Bible from schools we would be wasting so much time and money in punishing criminals and so little pains to prevent crime. Take the Bible out of our schools and there would be an explosion in crime."
- Benjamin Rush. www.foundingfatherquotes.com.

Education of children should be primarily determined by parents. Schools should be able to choose their curriculum with input by parents, and parents should be able to choose the schools their children attend. This is basic free will. This is how education used to be in America before the federal government became involved. Note: The federal government has no authority to be involved in education. See Chapter 12 on the Constitution.

The federal government did become involved with education, though. Just as it ignored the Constitution's limitations on its involvement in education, it ignored the First Amendment restrictions on banning religious activity. The federal government has succeeded in banning God from schools, at least when it comes to the Bible and prayer. However, this is really very silly because if God were to be completely banned from schools, then much of American history must be banned as well.

- The Declaration of Independence, which birthed our Country on July 4th, 1776, must be banned as it recognizes human rights come from our "Creator".
- The US Constitution must be banned because it contains "Year of our Lord" which is Christ, the God of the Bible.
- The constitutions of the 50 states cannot be taught as all reference God.
- No presidential inauguration can be watched as a Bible is used to swear in the new president.
- There can be no field trips to the national monuments in Washington, DC, as "God" is inscribed on them in numerous places.
- Many speeches of presidents cannot be studied as they contain "God" or cite scripture. This includes Washington's Inaugural Address, Lincoln's Gettysburg Address, Franklin Roosevelt's D-Day prayer in World War II, and George W. Bush's address to the nation after the 9-11 attacks.

The Bible and Constitution Made America Great

- Sessions of the Unites States Senate or the United States House of Representatives cannot be watched as they both open with prayer to God.

It is simply impossible to teach or study American History while banning God from the curriculum. Given America's religious heritage and reliance on the Bible (Chapter 10), it is not surprising to find God, religion and the Bible were often prominent in the teaching of the early schools in America.

Religion in Schools
Let's examine the religious curriculum of schools at the time America's Constitution was written and ratified.

Benjamin Franklin described the **5 Fundamental Points to be taught in schools:**

1. There exists a **Creator** who made all things, and mankind should recognize and worship HIM.
2. The **Creator** has revealed a moral code of behavior for happy living which distinguishes right from wrong.
3. The **Creator** holds mankind responsible for the way they treat each other.
4. All mankind live beyond this life.
5. In the next life mankind are judged for their conduct in this one.

All five of these tenets run through practically all of the founders writings. These are the beliefs which the founders sometimes referred to as "the religion of America" and they felt these fundamentals were so important in providing "good government and the happiness of mankind" that they wanted them taught in public schools along with morality and knowledge. (5000 Year Leap, p. 61. Skousen)

Congress passed the Northwest Ordinance in 1787. **The law specified religion and morality be taught** in territories, which were under control of Congress until statehood was established.

<u>Northwest Ordinance Article 3</u>
Religion, morality, and knowledge, being necessary to good government and the happiness of mankind, schools and the means of education shall forever be encouraged. The utmost good faith shall always be observed towards the Indians; their lands and property shall never be taken from them without their consent; and, in their property, rights, and liberty, they shall never be invaded or disturbed, unless in just and lawful wars authorized by Congress; but laws founded in justice and humanity, shall from time to time be made for preventing wrongs being done to them, and for preserving peace and friendship with them.

The first education laws in the American colonies were passed in Massachusetts in the mid 1600's. The colonial laws required the teaching of religion to students. The law states that knowledge of scripture is important to thwart Satan, who desires people to be ignorant of what the Bible says. How many citizens today are ignorant of what the Bible says?

<u>The Massachusetts Law of 1642</u>
It is therefore ordered that .... all masters of families doe once a week (at the least) catechize their children and servants **in the grounds & principles of Religion**, ...

<u>The Massachusetts Law of 1647</u>
It being one chief point of that old deluder, Satan, to keep men from **the knowledge of Scriptures**, as in former times, by keeping them in an unknown tongue, so in these latter times, by persuading them from the use of tongues that so at last the true sense and meaning of the original might be clouded by false glosses of saint-seeming deceivers, that learning might not be buried in the graves of our fathers, in church and commonwealth, the Lord assisting our endeavours,—it is therefore ordered.... [The law goes on to require every community of 50 or more residents hire a teacher for children.]

The New England Primer, first published about 1690, combined lessons in spelling with a short catechism and versified injunctions to piety and faith in Calvinistic fundamentals. .. The primer fulfilled the purposes of Education in New England, where Puritan colonists stressed literacy as conducive to scriptural study. For about fifty years, this eighty-page booklet, four and a half by three inches in size, was the only elementary textbook in America, and for a century more it held a central place in primary education. - Gale Encyclopedia of US History.

The Primer contained morning and evening prayers, The Lord's Prayer, and The Apostles Creed.

THE NEW ENGLAND PRIMER 1777 edition
(reprints can be purchased at amazon.com)

Who was the first man? *Adam.*

Who was the first woman? *Eve.*

Who was the first Murderer? *Cain.*

Who was the first Martyr? *Abel.*

Who was the oldest Man? *Methuselah.*

Who built the Ark? *Noah.*

Who was the Patientest Man? *Job.*

Who led *Israel* into *Canaan*? *Joshua.*

Who was the strongest Man? *Sampson.*

Who killed *Goliath*? *David.*

Who was the wisest Man? *Solomon.*

Who was in the Whale's Belly? *Jonah.*

Who saves lost Men? *Jesus Christ.*

Who is *Jesus Christ*? *The Son of God.*

Who was the Mother of Christ? *Mary.*

Who betrayed his Master? *Judas.*

Who denied his Master? *Peter.*

Who was the first Christian Martyr? *Stephen.*

Who was chief Apostle of the *Gentiles*? *Saul.*

A sample of the 107 questions from the short catechism contained in the Primer.

Q. 5. Are there more Gods then one ?
A. There is but ONE only, the living and true GOD.

Q. 6. How many persons are there in the God-head ?
A. There are three persons in the God-head, the Father, the Son, and the Holy Ghost, and these three are one GOD, the same in substance, equal in power and glory.

Q. 9. What is the work of creation ?
A. The work of creation is God's making all things of nothing by the word of his power, in the space of six days, and all very good.

Q. 23. What offices doth Christ execute as our Redeemer ?
A. Christ as our Redeemer executes the office of a prophet, of a priest, & of a king, both in his estate of humiliation and exaltation.

Q. 24. How doth Christ execute the office of a prophet ?
A. Christ executeth the office of a prophet in revealing to us by his word and spirit, the will of God for our salvation.

Q. 25. How doth Christ execute the office of a priest ?
A. Christ executeth the office of a priest in his once offering up himself a sacrifice to satisfy divine justice, and reconcile us to God, and in making continual intercession for us.

Q. 26. How doth Christ execute the office of a king ?
A. Christ executeth the office of a king in subduing us to himself, in ruling and defending us, and in restraining and conquering all his and our enemies.

Q. 42. What is the sum of the ten commandments ?
A. The sum of the ten commandments is, to love the Lord our God with all our heart, with all our soul, with all our strength, and with all our mind, and our neighbour as ourselves.

Q. 85. What doth God require of us that we may escape his wrath and due due to us for sin?
A. To escape the wrath and curse of God due to us for sin, God requireth of us faith in Jesus Christ, repentance unto

life, with the diligent use of all outward means whereby Christ communicateth to us the benefits of redemption.

Colonial Education in Virginia

The primary education of upper class children in colonial days included reading, writing, simple math, poems, and prayers. Paper and textbooks were scarce so boys and girls recited their lessons until they memorized them. The three most commonly used books were the Bible, a primer, and a hornbook.

Colonial Hornbook

This hornbook has
the cross,
the alphabet in small letters,
the vowels, and
then the capitals.
Below these are combinations of the consonants and vowels,
then the trinity phrase given by a resurrected Jesus in Matthew 28,
and **the Lord's Prayer**.

American Antiquarian Society (1916): "The Hornbook and Its Use in America." by George A. Plimpton.

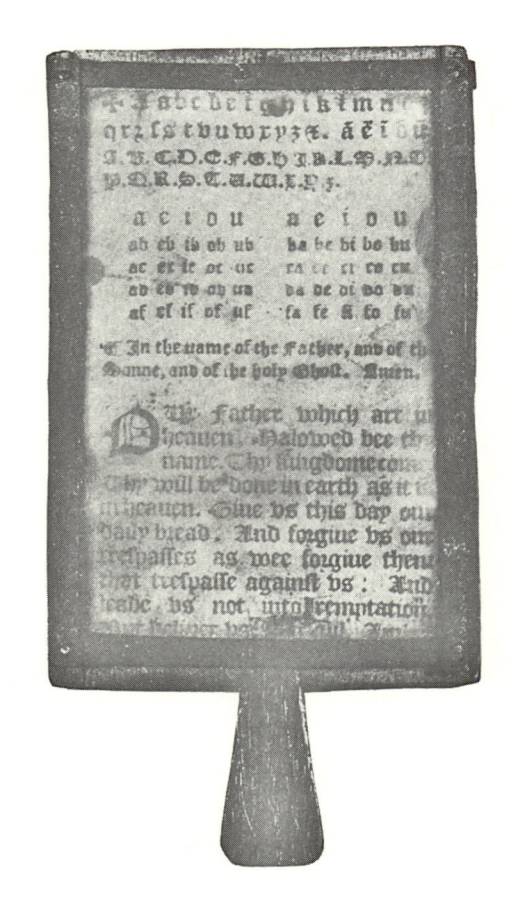

Dr. Benjamin Rush wrote a tract arguing for the Bible to be used in public schools.

Benjamin Rush's 1830 tract

A DEFENCE OF THE USE OF THE BIBLE IN SCHOOLS

Penned By Dr. Benjamin Rush (1745-1813), signer of the Declaration of Independence.

This tract, The Bible in Schools, is taken from an early collection of tracts published by the American Tract Society around 1830.

American Tract Society - Box 462008 - Garland, TX 75046 - USA

It is now several months since I promised to give you my reasons for preferring the Bible as a schoolbook to all other compositions. Before I state my arguments, I shall assume the five following propositions:

1. That Christianity is the only true and perfect religion; and that in proportion as mankind adopt its principles and obey its precepts they will be wise and happy.

2. That a better knowledge of this religion is to be acquired by reading the Bible than in any other way.

3. That the Bible contains more knowledge necessary to man in his present state than any other book in the world.

4. That knowledge is most durable, and religious instruction most useful, when imparted in early life.

5. That the Bible, when not read in schools, is seldom read in any subsequent period of life.

My arguments in favor of the use of the **Bible as a schoolbook** are founded.......

As the previous examples show, religion was a staple curriculum in the schools in America as it became a nation; and the religion was biblically based.

Chapter 13 will discuss how Supreme Court decisions beginning in the mid 1900s ignored the 1st Amendment, which forbids the federal government from banning religion.

<u>Public Schools not Serving the Majority</u>
With the courts now banning religious activity in the public school system, parents have little or no choice in how their tax dollars are spent on education. Christian parents can either send their children to secular schools, where God, prayer, the Ten Commandments, and the Bible are banned, or pay tuition and send their children to a private school. In this case the parents are forced to pay twice for their children's education. They pay once through taxes that go to the secular public schools and again for the tuition for the private or parochial school. The atheistic or secular parent is perfectly happy with the secular school system as it is. Why is a minority rewarded at the expense of the majority? A poll by ABC news shows 83% of Americans identify themselves as Christian while only 13% respond as having no faith (agnostic/atheistic/secular). The remaining 4% are other religions. Why are we accommodating the 13% at the expense of the 83%? The majority of parents should be able to choose the education their children receive.

The current federally controlled system is the opposite of how America, a representative republic, was established to work. Whether religion and prayer is present in a school's curriculum should be the decision of the elected school board. The school board is elected by the community and therefore represents the community's decision. This is majority rule. So if a school board elects to teach religion classes in public school, that is their right under the Constitution. Secular believers will not like this, but they have a choice. They can try to convince the community to change its views and elect pro-secular members to the school board. Or they can choose to home-school their children. This is the same choice that religious parents will face if they live in a majority secular community.

Choice in Schools with Tax Credits

Even if the federal government ceases its interference in public school curriculum, a public school is still a monopoly. The government dictates the curriculum and controls the tax dollar financing. An even better solution transfers school control to parents by giving them the power of consumers. Let all parents choose the education their children receive. Simply take the total budget a community spends on K-12 education, divide by the number of K-12 children, and give parents that amount with a tax credit. The parent will decide which school best meets the parent's needs and values. Then the parent will pay the school the parent chooses, or the parent may chose to home-school.

This solution does the most to make all parents happy by giving them the ultimate choice. A Christian parent won't be forced to send their child to a school where they are taught a morality differing from the parent's beliefs. Likewise a secular parent won't be forced to send their child to a school following biblical teachings. A simple method is to issue education tax credits, just like today's earned income tax credits. Here is how it can work:

1. Transfer all spending on K-12 education into tax credits.
2. The size of the credit is the entire education budget divided by the number of students. Let's assume $10,000.
3. The parent pays tuition at the school of their choosing. Most schools will set tuition at the tax credit amount. ($10,000)
4. When the parents file their tax return, they receive a tax credit for tuition (up to $10,000) to reimburse them.
5. Parents receive a check for the amount of the credit over their tax burden.

The same amount of money is spent on education, but the parents control which school gets the money. So the parents can choose the school that has a curriculum and overall school service they prefer. Any parent not finding a school to their liking is still free to home-school their children.

The Supreme Court has already ruled that school tax credits are constitutional.

Supreme Court's Decision Favors Arizona School Choice

The Supreme Court's decision to throw out the challenge to Arizona's tuition tax credit plan gives needed breathing room to that state's emerging and innovative school-choice system.

Arizona's tuition tax credit program is just one part of the state's bold school-choice plan to empower parents with the opportunity to select the best schools for their children. Arizona families can send their children to a vast array of charter schools that specialize in everything from drama to the classics to math and science. Home schooling flourishes with minimal state regulation, and home-school students can participate in extracurricular offerings, such as band or sports, at nearby public schools.

Arizona helps parents who believe private schools are best for their children by offering a state income tax credit to individuals who voluntarily donate to school tuition organizations that award scholarships to students attending private schools.

Lawmakers in Arizona believe that school choice improves education, so they studied the relevant Supreme Court decisions and fashioned a tuition tax credit plan that complies with the Constitution.

- Human Events. Jordan Lorence. 4/21/2011.

There is also the side benefit of competition. Every time an American goes to the store to purchase a product, they have multiple choices available so they can select the product they prefer. Companies offering these products must compete for sales dollars. Only companies producing products best meeting a consumer need will be able to make sales and stay in business. If schools are made to compete, only those offering the best in teaching, curriculum, and services will prosper. The parents get to choose what they consider to be the best school product for their children.

Government run organizations are notoriously bloated and incompetent. Government run schools are no different. John Stossel has done a number of great stories detailing the incompetence on ABC's 20/20 and the Fox Business Channel. Stossel writes:

Religion and Choice in Schools

<u>School Competition Rescues Kids</u>
For years, American education from kindergarten through high school has been a virtual government monopoly.
Conventional wisdom is that government must run the schools. But government monopolies don't do anything well. They fail because they have no real competition. Yet competition is what gives us better phones, movies, cars -- everything that's good.

If governments produced cars, we'd have terrible cars. Actually, governments once did produce cars. The Soviet bloc puts its best engineers to work and came up with the Yugo, the Volga and the Trabant. The Trabant was the best -- the pride of the Eastern Bloc. It was produced by actual German engineers -- known for their brilliance. Yet even the Trabant was a terrible car. Drivers had to put the oil and gas in separately and then shake the car to mix them. Trabants broke down and spewed pollution. When government runs things, consumers suffer.

Our school system is like the Trabant. Economist Milton Friedman understood this before the rest of us did. In 1955, he proposed school vouchers. His plan didn't call for separating school and state -- unfortunately -- but instead sought a second-best fix: Give a voucher to the family, and let it choose which school -- government-run or private -- their child will attend. Schools would compete for that voucher money. Today, it would be worth $13,000 per child. (That's what America spends per student today.) Competition would then improve all schools.

Friedman's idea was ignored for decades, but now there are voucher experiments in many states.

Do vouchers work? You bet they do. Just ask the low-income kids in Washington, D.C., who have participated in the D.C. Opportunity Scholarship Program. The U.S. Department of Education found that the voucher kids read better than their government-school counterparts.
- John Stossel. Townhall.com. Oct 26, 2011.

Education tax credits will let parents choose the schools that best reflect the values they wish their children to have. It will also give parents control rather than government bureaucrats. Always trust the parents over a bureaucrat with no stake in the game. Partial vouchers, which most states have experimented with, should become full tuition tax credits. Divide the money spent on education by the number of students. Give every parent an education tax credit for the *full* amount spent on education. Parents then control the education system, not bureaucrats.

Education Spending Example
The author believes most Americans have no idea how much is spent on public school education in America. Likely because much of the current spending does not get to the children. Much of it goes to government bureaucracy or teachers' unions. For example, in 2011, New York state spent over $19,000 per student in K-12. (See Appendix 5: Education Spending Per Student by State in 2011) Can you imagine how schools would compete to draw students to their schools if each new student was worth $19,000 per year in voucher funding? The parents would have the power to reward good schools and punish poor schools.

In New York for example, 25 students in a classroom with $19,000 per student, should be receiving $475,000 in education spending from the state of New York. And this is just one class! Where is that money going? Is the teacher paid $150,000? That leaves $325,000 for the classroom space, books and education supplies per year. There should be millionaire teachers and education palaces all over New York with this kind of spending. This quick example shows how much education funding is squandered on government bureaucracy. With a tax credit system, each parent would receive $19,000 to spend at the school the parent selects for their child.

So where does the education spending go? Much of it to bureaucrats who do not teach. While governor of Minnesota, Tim Pawlenty proposed that 75% of education funding in that state must be spent in the classroom. There was outrage expressed by the MN Teachers' Union. Is 25% overhead not enough for government run education? What private sector business exists with 25% overhead?

Religion and Choice in Schools

<u>Let Parents Choose Curriculum: Homosexuality Example</u>
Another reason for school choice is that states often do a poor job in selecting curriculum. For example, why is sex education taught to young children? Why is homosexuality taught when it applies to very small ,percentage of the population (Chapter 16)? Parents may very well decide that older students need to be taught basic human reproduction in a health class as part of the curriculum. But, there are many Christian parents who will not want their children taught about homosexuality in schools.

With school choice vouchers, parents can evaluate different schools and decide if they want their children in a school featuring homosexual education. Everybody wins: except those who wish to force parents to accept an agenda the parent doesn't want.

While there are many government workers who sincerely seek to do a good job for the public, there are some who are really out of step with mainstream America. The latter seem to be establishing the curriculum for schools. As in sex education for 5 and 6 year-old children.

> <u>Sex Education for Kindergarteners</u>
> "Ideally, comprehensive sexuality education should start in kindergarten and continue through 12th grade," says the "National Sexuality Education Standards" report, drawn up by a range of advocates, academics and public education officials.
>
> The 45-page report determines "age-appropriate" guidelines for comprehensive sexuality education in the areas of anatomy, identity, pregnancy, sexually-transmitted diseases (STDs) and others.
> - CNSNews.com. Elizabeth Harrington. January 17, 2012

The report was heavily influenced by homosexual-lesbian activist groups, working with bureaucrats to author it. The stated goal of the report: "to create a strategic plan for sexuality education policy and implementation."

National standards become a joke if this is the focus (author's opinion, but let parents decide). With all the problems schools have teaching kids to read, write, and solve math problems, why are the education bureaucrats focused on early age sex education? The parents should decide when and how to educate their children with respect to sex.

Also from the report:
> Standards to be introduced in kindergarten and be met by the second grade include: "Identify different kinds of family structures" and "Demonstrate ways to show respect for different types of families."

This is politically-correct speak for homosexual families with two-mommies, or two-daddies. The goal is to teach that these must be respected and are perfectly OK. Sorry, but that decision is up to the parents. Homosexual parents are free to teach their kids that homosexuality is fine. Christian parents are free to teach their kids that homosexuality is sinful behavior. Why should schools teach anything about such a controversial subject?

This report illustrates how the federal government wastes money spent on education. Take federal funding away from education, and let the states decide how it should best be spent. Many "brilliant" studies and reports such as sex education for kindergarteners will likely disappear. Or maybe not. California or other liberal states may well decide to continue funding them – that is their choice. And the residents have the choice to decide whether to continue voting for these politicians.

<u>California Curriculum</u>
Here is an example of state government *promoting* homosexuality in schools. Why are children being force fed a pro-homosexual agenda? This moral question should be left to the parents.

> <u>California Gov Signs Landmark Law to Teach Gay History</u>
> California has become the first state in the nation to require public schools to add lessons about gay history to social studies classes,...
>
> The bill has drawn criticism from some churches and conservative groups that argue such instruction would expose students to a subject that some parents find

objectionable.

Democratic state Sen. Mark Leno of San Francisco, the bill's author, has said that teaching gay history in public schools will teach students to be more accepting of gays and lesbians.

Supporters suggest slain San Francisco politician Harvey Milk would be an appropriate choice. Leno contends Milk's fight for civil rights is as worthy of class study as Dr. Martin Luther King, Jr.'s. He adds this kind of "inclusive curriculum" will help protect students who may look, or act, differently.

But critics don't buy the anti-bullying argument, and say SB 48 hijacks history class to promote a gay agenda.

"In the past, history taught about what people did, what they accomplished," says Brad Dacus, head of the Pacific Justice Institute. "It didn't focus on their sexuality and what they did in the bedroom. Yet that is what this legislation will impose on every public school in the state of California dealing with heterosexuality, homosexual role models, transgender role models, all the way down to the kindergarten level."

Dacus adds, "It's California tax dollars from parents who are paying for this kind of indoctrination that's being put into public schools. That demeans them, their family, and their relationships."

Leno says it's the same criticism voiced years ago when schools embraced ethnic and women's studies.

"We should not be afraid to teach our children of the broad diversity of human experience," he says. "It's not going away, it's always been with us. We have different kinds of people, who are, under law, to be treated equally. Why would we not want to teach our children this?"

He says inclusive education is as important as the 3R's. "This all goes together."

But critics worry parents who object to this curriculum will be labeled intolerant, and that kids will start thinking about sexuality and gender identity at a very young age.

- Published July 14, 2011, FoxNews.com

Should sexual preference really be a focus of history classes?

Slavery, the Civil War to end slavery, and the push to give black people equal treatment are all legitimate historical subjects in American history. A person is born with a certain skin color and has no choice in the matter. People choose their sexual behavior patterns.

Minnesota

California is not the only state to begin pushing pro-homosexual agendas in schools. Here is an example from Minnesota, another Democrat controlled state.

> ### The real agenda behind antibullying campaign
> The campaign for antibullying legislation is driven not by a dramatic escalation in bullying but by a crusade to use the power of the state to shape your 10-year-old's attitudes and beliefs about sexuality and family structure. The drive is being led by OutFront Minnesota -- the state's most prominent LGBT group, whose legal director was a member of the governor's task force and whose executive director also directs the "Safe Schools for All Coalition."
>
> The governor's task force gives the green light to activist groups like OutFront to move into public and private schools. It calls for "actively enlisting ... community-based advocacy groups" to "change peer and community norms" and develop bullying-intervention strategies.
>
> Not surprisingly, the task force's proposed new antibullying regime would not treat all children equally, despite lip service to this goal. Instead, it focuses on students in "protected classes," including sexual orientation and "gender identity or expression."
>
> Under the task force's vague and overbroad definitions of bullying and harassment, students could be punished for "direct or indirect interactions" that other students --especially those in protected groups -- claim to find "humiliating" or "offensive," that have a "detrimental effect" on their "social or emotional health," or even that promote a "perceived imbalance of power."
>
> By this standard, a student who voices reservations about same-sex marriage could be accused of bullying LGBT

students.

[A similar program in Minneapolis] had little to do with bullying, and much to do with ensuring that kids as young as age 5 submit to the group's orthodoxy on sexuality and family structure.

The curriculum advised teachers not to call students "boys and girls," on grounds this can create "internal dissonance" in some children. It called for students to read books like "Sissy Duckling," and to be evaluated on "whether or not [they] feel comfortable making choices outside gender expectations." Kids in grades three to five "acted out" being members of nontraditional families, including same-sex-headed families.

In lesson after lesson, teachers were instructed to urge their students -- ages 5 to 11 -- to reject traditional views on sexuality and family structure as hurtful "stereotypes," and to use group exercises and classic indoctrination techniques to pressure them to adopt the curriculum designers' attitudes and beliefs.

- Startribune.com. Katherine Kersten. January 12, 2013

This program isn't an anti-bullying program, its a *pro-homosexual indoctrination program*. An anti-bullying program would simply teach kids not to make fun of each other and not intimidate fellow students. The goal of this program is to indoctrinate young children with views that are against the religious teachings of Christianity, the religion of a large majority of Americans.

This example reinforces why parents should be given the choice about schools. A Christian parent should not be forced to send their child to a school where they are taught a morality differing from the parent's beliefs. Likewise, if a homosexual parent wishes their child to learn all about homosexuality in the classroom, let them send their child to such a school. The teaching of homosexuality is offensive to Christian parents and children. What business does a school have teaching Christian children that what they learn in the Bible is wrong? A bigger question is: Why are schools teaching anything about sexual preferences? Don't they have more important subjects to teach--like economics, reading, mathematics, geography, and US history?

Organizing for Parental Choice in School

It will be up to parents to form groups and network with other parents to achieve the ability to choose schools for their children. Parents must lobby their state legislators to get tax credit legislation passed. As a group parents will have power, both in pressing their agenda with legislators, and voting for legislators who share their views.

Teachers' unions in each state are a powerful political force. They donate heavily to politicians, and oftentimes will use union workers to phonebank or drop campaign literature on behalf of their favored politicians. To counter this force parents must be a counterbalancing political force. There is one thing politicians value more then donations: Votes! If concerned citizens form groups and begin issue-voting for their representatives, they can become a powerful political force for school choice. Groups will be able to reward state politicians by voting for them or against them based on their performance.

If you are a Christian, Jewish, or Muslim parent in California, are you going to let your child be indoctrinated by their public school, being taught something against your religion? Why not form a group within your church, synagogue or mosque that pressures your state representative to give all parents a tax credit to send their child to a school matching the values of the parent?

This tactic also should be adopted by inner city parents. Inner city public school quality is notoriously bad. For example:

> ### Only 7% of Detroit Public-School 8th Graders Proficient in Reading
> In the public schools in Detroit, Mich., according to the U.S. Department of Education, only 7 percent of the eighth graders are grade-level proficient or better in reading.
> .... eighth graders do even worse in math than they do in reading..., only 4 percent scored highly enough to be rated "proficient" or better in math.
> - CNSNews.com.Terence P. Jeffrey. December 11, 2012.

Isn't it time to free the children from schools that do not or cannot teach them basic knowledge? Parents of children in Detroit public schools should form a group and demand a tax credit that will allow them to enroll their kids in a school that will teach them what they need to be successful in life. Find and vote for representatives that will give you the ability to control your children's education.

Parents currently sending children to a private school, should also form political groups to request tax credits. Why are you paying taxes for public education that your child cannot use?

Parochial school principals or teachers, how much better could the children be educated if the school's parents had access to thousands of dollars in tax credits to pay for education? There is money available *if* you organize.

Summary
In conclusion, considering the large amount of religious content in early American schools, it is ludicrous as well as unconstitutional for the federal government to ban religion from school or school activities. It is up to the states and local communities to determine what religious content, if any, is present in their schools. The ultimate way to allow each parent to have religious liberty is to give parents tax credits and let them choose the schools their children attend. This also has the benefit of allowing parents with poorly performing public schools to find better options. It will also introduce competition, which improves the product while lowering costs in every industry where it exists.

US Constitution

"The Constitution... approaches nearer to perfection than any government hitherto instituted among men. The Constitution is the guide which I will never abandon."
- George Washington, 1st President and General of the Revolutionary Army. TRGW. P662, 664.

"The Constitution on which our Union rests, **shall be administered by me [as President] according to the safe and honest meaning contemplated by the plain understanding of the people of the United States at the time of its adoption....**"
- Thomas Jefferson letter. March 27, 1801. www.quotationcollection.com

"The Constitution is the sole source and guaranty of national freedom."
- President Calvin Coolidge. Nomination acceptance speech. August 4, 1924.

Why is the US Constitution important? It is a contract between the American citizens and their government. The contract specifies the rules the government must follow when using government power. As discussed in Chapter 2, the US Constitution was designed to maximize freedom for the citizens.

In our future commentaries upon the constitution we shall treat it then, as it is denominated in the instrument itself, as **a constitution of government ordained and established by the people of the United States** for themselves and their posterity. **They have declared it the supreme law of the land. They have made it a limited government. They have defined its authority. They have restrained it to the exercise of certain powers and reserved all others to the states or to the people.** It is a popular government. Those who administer it are responsible to the people. It is as popular and just as much emanating from the people as the state governments. **It is created for one purpose, the state governments for another. It may be altered and amended and abolished at the will of the people.** In short it was made by the people, made for the people, and is responsible to the people.
- Commentaries on the Constitution of the United States. Volume 1. P382

Notice the understanding in early America that the state governments and the federal government were separate and each had defined responsibilities to perform. That distinction has been lost in recent times. To often today, everything is lumped into "government" with no thought as to which level of government is being referenced.

The Constitution represents the national interest. Newly elected presidents, senators, representatives and Supreme Court justices swear to uphold it. Military officers swear to defend it. America was unique at its founding in that its leaders swore to defend a document of liberty rather than a king or group of men.

> Presidential Oath:
> (Article II, Section I of the U.S. Constitution)
> "I do solemnly swear (or affirm) that I will faithfully execute the office of President of the United States, and will to the best of my ability, preserve, protect and defend the Constitution of the United States."
>
> Congressional Oath (US Senators and Representatives):
> I do solemnly swear (or affirm) that I will support and defend the Constitution of the United States against all enemies, foreign and domestic; that I will bear true faith and allegiance to the same; that I take this obligation freely, without any mental reservation or purpose of evasion; and that I will well and faithfully discharge the duties of the office on which I am about to enter: So help me God.
>
> Supreme Court Justice Oath:
> "I, do solemnly swear that I will administer justice without respect to persons, and do equal right to the poor and to the rich, and that I will faithfully and impartially discharge and perform all the duties incumbent upon me as [TITLE] under the Constitution and laws of the United States. So help me God."
>
> Commissioned Military Officers Oath:
> "I do solemnly swear that I will support and defend the Constitution of the United States against all enemies, foreign and domestic; that I will bear true faith and allegiance to the

same; and that I will obey the orders of the President of the United States and the orders of the officers appointed over me, according to regulations and the Uniform Code of Military Justice. So help me God." (Title 10, US Code)

The Constitution also requires <u>national and state leaders</u> to uphold the Constitution:

> The Senators and Representatives before mentioned, and the Members of the several State Legislatures, and all executive and judicial Officers, both of the United States and of the several States, shall be bound by Oath or Affirmation, to support this Constitution;... (Article. VI.)

Note that the language calls for support of the Constitution, not the rulings of judges. This is especially true if those rulings violate the actual words and meaning of the Constitution.

Why should the average citizen care if the Constitution is followed? The Constitution guarantees humanity's God-given basic rights: life, liberty and freedom. It protects citizens from excessive use of force by government. It spells out the specific roles that the federal government should perform, and limits it to those roles.

<u>The Difference between a Constitutional Republic and a Democracy</u>
There is an old joke: What happens when three wolves and two sheep form a democracy and decide what to have for dinner? They vote and one of the sheep loses and becomes dinner.

Or with a slightly different take: What happens when three wolves and two sheep form a republic? They elect a wolf as president and the wolf decides that a sheep should be served for dinner.

Only a properly written and enforced Constitution protects the minority sheep from abuse of power of the government or its fellow "citizens".

America's constitution protects the minority from a majority vote democracy. For example, let's say there is a certain Hollywood star or starlet of liberal persuasion who is arguing for redistribution of wealth in a debate before a live audience. Why not let all those in attendance vote on a proposal to take $10 million from the star and distribute it to the audience with each audience member receiving $100,000? After all, Forbes recently showed the actor had a net worth of almost $55 million, so definitely wouldn't miss the money. And the "working families" in the audience are probably more deserving of the money than the actor is. The vote will be by secret ballot with everyone, including the actor, able to vote. So the democratic vote will be totally legitimate for this group. The proposal to redistribute the actor's money might very well pass by a large margin, maybe even a 90+ % landslide. This is the danger of mob-rule democracy and the welfare state mentality.

If this rule was in effect, there would be few if any actors (or any other wealthy people) going before live audiences! The example shows why it is important to have a Constitution with well-written rule-of-law and a government in place to protect the minority from "popular" democratic votes. It is the Constitution which provides the rules that contain the government's power and keeps it from abusing its power to harm citizens.

Sidebar: A republic is a form of government where the people elect leaders to represent them, as opposed to a true democracy where the people vote on each and every issue. America's founders thought a republic to be superior, as it would allow wise men to represent the people, and decide the issues for the nation.

Religion in the Constitution
As discussed in Chapter 10, the United States was founded by religious men who followed the tenets of the Bible. Following the Revolutionary War, the former colonies came together as states to create a nation and national government.

Principles used to form the government came directly from the Declaration of Independence that had begun the war eleven years earlier.

> We hold these truths to be self-evident, that all men are created equal, that they are endowed by their Creator with certain unalienable Rights, that among these are Life, Liberty

US Constitution

and the pursuit of Happiness.--That to secure these rights, Governments are instituted among Men, deriving their just powers from the consent of the governed.
- Declaration of Independence

What a powerful opening statement that forms the basis for a Godly government:
- All men are created by God and are equal.
- All men have the rights given by God to life, to liberty (free will to make choices), and to pursue happiness.
- The job of government is to secure these rights for men.
- Powers to the government come only with the agreement of those who are governed.

Founding Father, and 3rd President of the United States, Thomas Jefferson, summed up his view on the general role of government in his Inaugural Address in 1801:

"What is necessary to make us a happy and prosperous people? A wise and frugal government which shall restrain men from injuring one another, which shall leave them otherwise free to regulate their own pursuits of industry and improvement, and shall not take from the mouth of labor the bread it has earned. That is the sum of good government."
- TRTJ p432.

Federal Government Powers
The US Constitution authorizes specific powers to Congress and the national / federal government. The powers fall into four general areas: monetary, military, interstate commerce, and law enforcement. Powers not listed were intended to remain with the state governments or local communities.

Powers specified to Congress by the Constitution
Monetary
- To collect taxes or duties.
- To borrow money on the credit of the United States.
- To coin money and regulate its value.

- To provide for the punishment of counterfeiting the currency of the United States.

Military
- To declare war or authorize other actions against foreign nations.
- To raise and support armed forces.

Interstate Commerce
- To regulate commerce with foreign nations and among the states.
- To establish a uniform rule of naturalization and immigration laws.
- To establish uniform bankruptcy law throughout the United States.
- To establish a postal system and roads to support it.
- To issue patents to inventors and maintain a patent office.
- Fix the standard of weights and measures (English, Metric...).

Law Enforcement
- To constitute federal courts below the Supreme Court.
- To define and punish piracy and felonies committed on the high seas.
- To define and punish offenses against the law of nations (ambassadors, embassies...).
- To exercise exclusive law-making for the District of Columbia (seat of government).
- The Senate shall have the sole power to try all impeachments for removing a federal official (including judges, senators, representatives, and president).

These powers were meant by the writers to be specific and well-defined. They were approved and ratified by the states as being specific and well-defined.

Thomas Jefferson clearly expressed his view that federal government actions must be among those specifically listed in the Constitution, or should not be performed.

> Resolved, That the several States composing, the United States of America, are not united on the principle of unlimited submission to their general government; but that, by a compact they... delegated to that government certain definite powers, reserving, each State to itself, the residuary mass of right to their own self-government; and that **whensoever the [federal] government assumes undelegated powers, its acts are unauthoritative, void, and of no force.**
>
> ... one of the amendments to the Constitution having also declared, that "the powers not delegated to the United States by the Constitution, not prohibited by it to the States, are reserved to the States respectively, or to the people," ... **therefore all [Congress] acts which assume to create, define, or punish crimes, other than those so enumerated in the Constitution, are altogether void, and of no force**; and that the power to create, define, and punish such other crimes is reserved, and, of right, appertains solely and exclusively to the respective States, each within its own territory.
>
> - Thomas Jefferson. Kentucky Resolution of 1798.

The writers of the Constitution realized that as the country grew and changed over time the Constitution would need to be changed as well. Therefore they included the process for changing or amending the Constitution.

> US Constitution - Article. V
> The Congress, whenever two thirds of both Houses shall deem it necessary, shall propose Amendments to this Constitution, or, on the Application of the Legislatures of two thirds of the several States, shall call a Convention for proposing Amendments, which, in either Case, shall be valid to all Intents and Purposes, as Part of this Constitution, when ratified by the Legislatures of three fourths of the several States, or by Conventions in three fourths thereof, as

the one or the other Mode of Ratification may be proposed by the Congress.

There are two methods specified to amend the Constitution. In both methods an amendment must be proposed in step 1 and ratified in step 2.

Method 1:
1) 2/3 Senate (67 Senators) and 2/3 of the House (290 Representatives) pass an Amendment.
2) ¾ of the state legislatures (38 states) ratify the amendment.

Method 2:
1) 2/3 of the states legislatures (34 states) call a convention to propose amendments.
2) ¾ of the state legislatures (38 states) ratify the amendment (or ¾ of the state conventions ratify).

George Washington fully supported changing the Constitution only by amendment.

> If in the opinion of the people, the distribution or modification of the constitutional powers be in any particular wrong, let it be corrected by an amendment in the way in which the Constitution designates. But let there be no change by usurpation; for though this, in one instance may be the instrument of good, it is the customary weapon by which free governments are destroyed.
> - Farewell Address in 1796. TRGW. P 665

Washington would have been appalled at the arguments some judges make today that the Constitution is a "living document" meant to be interpreted however they please; this is how "free governments are destroyed." More on this in Chapter 14.

The national leaders and many citizens were concerned that the Constitution as ratified gave the new federal government too much power. So the Bill of Rights was created and added to the Constitution soon after its ratification.

US Constitution

<u>The Bill of Rights</u>
The newly formed Congress, in one of its first acts, followed the amendment process (method 1) to add 10 amendments to the Constitution. These came to be known as The Bill of Rights. The sole purpose was to more clearly define the limits and restrictions on the power the federal government possessed. The amendments made crystal clear the specific rights citizens had that **the government could not take away.**

> Bind [government leaders] down from mischief by the chains of the Constitution.
> - Thomas Jefferson, 1798, Kentucky Resolutions. TRTJ p382.

Each of the amendments specified a limitation on the federal government's use of power so that it could not take away that freedom from the citizen. The Bill of Rights is summarized below.

Amendment 1: Congress will not prevent the free exercise of religion for citizens, free speech of citizens, the right of citizens to assemble and address the government, and freedom of the press.

Amendment 2: The right of a citizen to have and use weapons will not be taken away by the federal government.

Amendment 3: The federal government cannot make citizens house soldiers in their home.

Amendment 4: The federal government cannot search a citizen's possessions without a warrant and probable cause of crime.

Amendment 5: The federal government may not try a person for a death penalty crime without the person first being indicted by a grand jury.

Amendment 6: The federal government must give those accused of a crime a speedy and public trial. The government must provide the accused a lawyer and the ability to call defense witnesses.

Amendment 7: The federal government must offer a citizen a trial by a jury, and the case may only be tried once.

Amendment 8: The federal government may not require excessive bail nor inflict cruel and unusual punishment.

Amendment 9: The listing of specific rights of the people in the Constitution, against federal government infringement, is only a partial list, other rights of the people also exist.

Amendment 10: The federal government possesses only those powers and responsibilities given to it by the Constitution.

The Bill of Rights further clarified where federal government power was to be used. The first eight amendments list specific citizen rights that the federal government may not take away, thus limiting its power. The 9th Amendment states that there are other rights citizens possess which have not been specifically listed. This amendment implies any ambiguity should be decided in favor of limiting federal government power and recognizing the freedom of the citizen. The 10th Amendment clearly states any power not specified for the federal government belongs to the state or local government or to the citizens.

> The powers not delegated to the United States by the Constitution, nor prohibited by it to the States, are reserved to the States respectively, or to the people.
> - 10th Amendment, ratified 1791.

Jefferson quoted the 10th Amendment often:

> "I consider the foundation of the Constitution as laid on this ground: All "the powers not delegated to the United States by the Constitution, nor prohibited by it to the States, are reserved to the States respectively, or to the people." To take a single step beyond the *boundaries specifically drawn around the powers of Congress* is to take possession of a boundless field of power, no longer susceptible to any definition."
> - Thomas Jefferson 1791. TRTJ p380.

Many of the problems facing the United States today are directly because the 10th Amendment has been ignored by most politicians and citizens for the last 80-90 years. Government at the local level is much more responsive to the citizens than a national government can ever hope to be. This wisdom comes directly from Moses in the Bible (*Exodus 18:13-26* in Chapter 6).

The Federalist Papers were written and published during the years 1787 and 1788 to educate voters and persuade them to ratify the proposed Constitution. The Papers consist of 85 essays outlining how the new government would operate and why this type of government was the best choice for the United States of America. The essays were written by James Madison (father of the Constitution and 4th President of the United States), John Jay (1st Chief Justice of the Supreme Court) and Alexander Hamilton (1st Secretary of the Treasury). Below are some key excerpts from the Federalist Papers that shed light and understanding on the thoughts of the country's founders regarding division of government power.

> The powers delegated by the proposed Constitution to the **federal government are few and defined.** Those which are to remain in the **State governments are numerous and indefinite**. The former will be exercised principally on external objects, as war, peace, negotiation, and foreign commerce; with which last the power of taxation will, for the most part, be connected. **The powers reserved to the several States will extend to all the objects which, in the ordinary course of affairs, concern the lives, liberties, and properties of the people, and the internal order, improvement, and prosperity of the State.**
> - FEDERALIST No. 45, James Madison

> The principal purposes to be answered by union are these the common defense of the members; the preservation of the public peace as well against internal convulsions as external attacks; the regulation of commerce with other nations and between the States; the superintendence of our intercourse, political and commercial, with foreign countries.
> - FEDERALIST No. 23, Alexander Hamilton

When the Bill of Rights (of citizens) were passed, they only applied to the federal government. The restrictions on government actions were also applied to the state governments with the 14th

Amendment. This amendment was ratified in 1868, and was intended to prevent state governments from discriminating against citizens of color. It reads in part:

> "No State shall make or enforce any law which shall abridge the privileges or immunities of citizenship of the United States."
> - 14th Amendment

> ... the view that the 14th Amendment's Due Process Clause literally incorporates the text of the various provisions of the Bill of Rights.... the "incorporation doctrine" was complete. ...provisions of the Bill of Rights are deemed applicable to the states in precisely the same manner that they are applicable to the federal government.
> - Heritage Guide to the Constitution. P397.

Some of the privileges of citizenship now protected by the US Constitution with passage of the 14th Amendment:

- States will make no laws establishing a state religion.
- States will not prevent the free exercise of religion for citizens.
- States will not prevent the free speech of citizens.
- States will not prevent the the right of citizens to assemble and address the government.
- States will not prevent the freedom of the press.
- States will not prevent a citizen from having and using weapons.
- States cannot make citizens house soldiers in their homes.
- States cannot search a citizen's possessions without a warrant and probable cause of crime.
- States must give those accused of a crime a speedy and public trial.
- States must provide the accused a lawyer and the ability to call defense witnesses.

It should be noted that most of these citizen rights were already established in the constitutions of the various states. But now the rights were guaranteed to apply by the force of the US Constitution.

When did America Partially Abandon the Constitution?
Thankfully, the American people have not fully abandoned the Constitution. In fact it can be argued that the people haven't abandoned it at all. They still support the Constitution; they just are no longer taught in schools what the document states and means. Instead they are taught that judges have the final say and "case law " trumps the written words in the Constitution. Case law is nothing more than a judicial decision in a past case that sets a "legal precedent". Case law pales in importance when compared to the actual words of the Constitution or, at least, it should.

The abandonment effort began around 1900. Rather than attack the still popular Constitution, progressive politicians used like-minded judges to re-interpret it. Presidents and senators seeking more power began putting judges on the Supreme Court who didn't respect the words, meaning, or intent of the Constitution.

> "We are under a Constitution, but the Constitution is what the judges say it is."
> - Charles Evan Hughes, Chief Justice of the U.S. Supreme Court. 1907.

Remember that the Constitution is a contract between the people and the government. Let's assume a farmer signs a contract to sell the grain he harvests to a company for $3 a bushel. It turns out that there is a record harvest that year and the market price for grain drops to $2 a bushel. The farmer is very happy indeed that he "locked in" his price with the company, except the company reinterprets the contract. "The contract assumed the market price would be $3 or higher." say the company lawyers, therefore "the $3 price is really $2 since the market price dropped." The farmer is outraged. There were no clauses in the contract about market pricing at all! He will lose hundreds of thousands of dollars. So the farmer takes his contract to court. The farmer had better hope an originalist judge hears his case, one who will take the contract to mean what it states, rather than an activist judge, who may very well "interpret" the contract to mean something else entirely. When one hears the term "Rule of Law," this is exactly what is meant: Laws, contracts, and constitutions are followed as intended.

Here's another example using poker: You, the reader, are challenged to a game of poker, but your opponent appoints a judge to "interpret the rules" of the game, and have the final say. It soon becomes obvious to you, the reader, that the judge isn't following the rules at all! You have a flush, but the judge rules that the opponents full house beats a flush for this hand. You complain bitterly because the judge ruled several hands ago that the opponents flush did beat your full house. Are you, the reader, happy playing this game when a judge can arbitrarily change the rules with no input from the players? No. For it to be an honest game the judge MUST enforce the written rules that both players agreed to. It is the same with the Constitution. The nation needs honest judges on the federal courts who will follow the Constitution's rules for government as written - not as the judges want the rules to be.

Judges believing and saying "the Constitution is what the judges say it is" is a recipe for despotism. It is five unelected judges on the Supreme Court feeling they have the power to arbitrarily make or void national laws at their whim, with no regard to the written wording of the Constitution. This is much more like the old Soviet Union Politburo than the nation of freedom and liberty envisioned by the founders. The Politburo was free to make up rules and interpret them in ways that benefited themselves. The Politburo was the law. America has always been every man being accountable to the law, including leaders.

In the 1930s a tragedy occurred that greatly accelerated the abandonment of the Constitution. The nation was in the middle of the Great Depression, the longest economic downturn in America's history. Recessions happen. They are part of the boom and bust cycles that occur in a free-market economy. What should have been a recession followed by a recovery, instead turned into a depression. Why? Largely because a big-government Republican, Herbert Hoover, raised tariffs which resulted in a trade war with Europe, and a big-government Democrat, Franklin Roosevelt (FDR), spent the next eight years interfering with the economy. An excellent book on the matter is: *New Deal or Raw Deal?: How FDR's Economic Legacy Has Damaged America*.

US Constitution

No attempt will be made here to argue whether FDR's economic programs were successful. The fact that the period is called the Great Depression, and lasted throughout his terms in office, proves lack of success. The important point is that most of FDR's programs **were not Constitutional responsibilities for the federal government.** FDR seized power from the states, where the Constitution placed it, and moved it to the federal government.

Was the Constitution amended? No. In fact, the justices followed the Constitution and ruled against FDR and the New Deal at first. But in the 1930s the court was divided between originalists and liberal-activists (see Chapter. 14 – Judges and Senators), like it is today. FDR seized on that and applied political pressure against the opposing justices, including IRS audits and threats to "pack the court" with justices who would rule in his favor.

> President Roosevelt's strong suit was politics, not economics. He played the political game both cleverly and ruthlessly, including using both the FBI and the Internal Revenue Service to harass and intimidate his critics and opponents.
> - Thomas Sowell. Senior fellow at the Hoover Institution. November 2, 2010.

There were four originalist judges (dubbed the Four Horsemen) trying to preserve the actual meaning of the Constitution. FDR and his allies in the media attacked and badgered these men until they gave up the fight, then finally retired from the court.

> Franklin Delano Roosevelt viciously attacked and tried to control the Supreme Court in order to secure his New Deal agenda. In 1935 the Court struck down as unconstitutional certain parts of FDR's New Deal.... FDR did not like that, because his New Deal depended on creating a massive federal regulatory bureaucracy within his executive branch control.
>
> So, on February 5, 1937, FDR announced his infamous "Court-Packing Plan," directly attacked the Supreme Court, and planned to stuff the Court with his loyalist lackeys. FDR followed up with a March 9, 1937 Fireside Chat where he said that America needed his Court-Packing Plan and "must take action to save the Constitution from the Court, and the Court

from itself."

On March 29, 1937, the Supreme Court bowed to FDR's unprecedented political attacks and decided three cases in favor of the New Deal. By 1941 the Supreme Court's "Four Horsemen," Justices Butler, McReynolds, Sutherland and Van Devanter, were gone,.... Thus, the New Deal Juggernaut rolled full-steam ahead with no one left to protect the American people from the huge federal regulatory bureaucracy that still pervades every aspect of American life...
- Court-Packing, Chicago-Style. John Shu. May 8, 2010.

Ironic that FDR called on the court to "save the Constitution" by ruling in favor of programs that were unconstitutional according to the written meaning. FDR must be ranked as one of the most anti-Constitution presidents in US history. Recall that the Constitution is the rules for governing for the nation. FDR forced changes in those rules he did not like without going through the amendment process, which requires broad public support. The jokes from the chapter's beginning have new meaning: The wolf doesn't like the rule protecting the sheep, so the wolf just ignores that rule. It is no surprise that FDR would later round up citizens of Japanese and German ancestry and put them in prison camps during World War II. FDR ignored rules he did not like, as long as he could convince a majority that he was "correct". In FDR's worldview, the Constitution was not about to restrain him from doing whatever he wished.

Also notice the political skill of FDR. America then, as now, supports the Constitution. So FDR didn't condemn the Constitution – he praised it. He just "redefined it" to mean whatever he wanted it to mean. "The Constitution is what the judges say it is." That behavior leads to tyranny, where those in power, make up the rules that they like and enforce them as they like.

Constitutional Clauses Most Abused
One of the most egregious examples of abuse is the 1st Amendments Freedom of Religion clause. The whole next chapter is devoted to that topic.

Here are a few other clauses of the Constitution that have been misinterpreted or taken out of context. As with any document or book, a single clause must be considered as part of the entire document. All the clauses together make up the entire work. Therefore they must be interpreted within the context of the whole document.

2nd Amendment
Entire Books have been written on the 2nd Amendment, but here is a brief discussion.

> Amendment II,
> (Bill of Rights, Ratified December 15, 1791)
> A well regulated Militia, being necessary to the security of a free State, the right of the people to keep and bear Arms, shall not be infringed.

"The right of the people to keep and bear arms shall not be infringed." How much clearer can this amendment be? The federal government cannot restrict a citizen's right to own guns. Why was this added? The founding fathers had just fought a war against their former government headed by the King of England. They fully realized that their heirs might one day have to resist their government again. The citizens do not have the ability to defend themselves if the government has disarmed them. The Second Amendment helps insure that government doesn't exceed its Constitutional limits and trample on the citizens. It also allows citizens the right to protect themselves from criminals.

Spending and General Welfare Clause
This spending clause is one of the greatest powers given to Congress.

> Article 1. Section 8. Clause 1.
> The Congress shall have Power To lay and collect Taxes, Duties, Imposts and Excises, to pay the Debts and provide for the common Defense and general Welfare of the United States;

Taken within the framework of the Constitution, two areas are given where Congress should spend money: common defense and general welfare.

- Common defense is easy to understand as it refers to the armed forces and military Congress deems necessary to defend the nation from attack.
- General welfare has become more difficult to understand as the term "welfare" was applied to wealth transfer programs in the 1930s – in an attempt to make the programs seem constitutional.

The original welfare definition is as follows:

> welfare *noun*: The state of doing well especially in respect to good fortune, happiness, well-being, or prosperity.
> - www.merriam-webster.com

So general welfare meant the overall good fortune and well-being of the nation. The criteria used by early congresses and presidents was the entire nation must benefit from the expenditure.

> Article 1. Section 8. Clause 1. does contain its own limitation, namely that spending under the clause be for the "general" (that is national) welfare.... President Monroe contended that Congress's power to spend was restricted "to purposes of common defense and of general, national, not local or state benefit." ...the interpretation held by Jefferson, Madison, and Monroe is the one that prevailed for most of the first 70 years after the adoption of the Constitution.
> - Heritage Guide to the Constitution. P93-94.

The Guide goes on to give examples of proposed spending that was rejected because it did not meet the national, general criteria in the Constitution. The Congress refused to make a loan to a glass manufacturer. The Congress did not provide aid to citizens of Savannah, GA after the city was destroyed by a fire. The Congress did authorize spending for a lighthouse because it would benefit the coastal trade of the entire nation and therefore interstate commerce.

> President Buchanan (1857-1861) took it as a given that the funds raised by Congress from taxation were "confined to the

execution of the enumerated powers as delegated to Congress." The idea that the resources of the federal government... could be diverted to carry into effect any measure of state domestic policy Congress saw fit to support **"would be to confer upon Congress a vast and irresponsible authority**, utterly at war with the well known jealousy of Federal power which prevailed at the formation of the Constitution."
- *Heritage Guide to the Constitution. P94.*

The interstate highway system built in the 1950s would be constitutional as it benefits the commerce of the entire nation by allowing goods to be transported in a timely manner. The second, newer definition of welfare programs, where taxes are collected and payments are given to *individuals* would never have passed the original constitutional criteria, and would not be allowed under the Constitution today.

Progressive politicians have made the phrase "general welfare" one of the most abused clauses in the Constitution by claiming it allows them to spend on anything they please. The founders repeatedly dismissed this as illogical. General welfare must be understood within the framework of the full language of the Constitution. President Thomas Jefferson interpreted the clause correctly for us:

General Welfare Clause Interpretation
[The Constitution authorizes Congress] To lay taxes to provide for the general welfare of the United States, that is to say, "to lay taxes for the purpose of providing for the general welfare." For the laying of taxes is the power, and the general welfare the purpose for which the power is to be exercised. **They are not to lay taxes ad libitum for any purpose they please**; but only to pay the debts or provide for the welfare of the Union. In like manner, **they are not to do anything they please to provide for the general welfare,** but only to lay taxes for that purpose.

To consider the latter phrase, not as describing the purpose of the first, but as giving a distinct and independent power to do any act they please, which might be for the good of the Union, would render all the preceding and subsequent enumerations of power completely useless. It would reduce the whole instrument to a single phrase, that of instituting a Congress with power to do whatever would be for the good of the United States; and, as they would be the sole judges of the good or evil, it would be also a power to do whatever evil they please.

It is an established rule of construction where a phrase will bear either of two meanings, to give it that which will allow some meaning to the other parts of the instrument, and not that which would render all the others useless. Certainly no such universal power was meant to be given them. It was intended to lace them up strictly within the enumerated powers, and those without which, as means, these powers could not be carried into effect.
- Thomas Jefferson. 1791. TRTJ p452.

Jefferson further elaborates in the Kentucky Resolution in 1798. A phrase like general welfare cannot be taken out of context. It must be interpreted within the framework of the Constitution which specifies the role of Congress and the federal government.

> Words meant by the [Constitution] to be subsidiary only to the execution of limited powers ought not be construed as themselves to give unlimited powers, nor a part to be taken to as to destroy the whole residue of the [Constitution].
> - TRTJ p453.

James Madison, drafter of the Constitution, and the 4th President of the United States, wrote in Federalist 41 in 1788:

> Some.... have grounded a very fierce attack against the Constitution, on the language in which it is defined. It has been urged and echoed, that the power "to lay and collect taxes, duties, imposts, and excises, to pay the debts, and provide for the common defense and general welfare of the United States," **amounts to an unlimited commission to exercise every power which may be alleged to be necessary for the common defense or general welfare.** No stronger proof could be given of the distress

under which these writers labor for objections, than their stooping to such a **misconstruction**.
- FEDERALIST No. 41, James Madison

To restate Madison: To say that the spending clause allows Congress to spend on anything allegedly tied to common defense or general welfare is a gross misconstruction of the meaning of the clause. Madison unequivocally states that the phrase "general welfare" does *not* give Congress unlimited power to spend money on whatever it wishes. Madison calls such arguments a "fierce attack against the Constitution."

Jefferson and Madison both tell us that "general welfare" does not override the other provisions of the Constitution. In light of this, the power of Congress to spend money has been greatly abused in recent times.

Justice Joseph Story confirms this view of "general welfare" in his writings. In the 1830s, the nation was still following the Constitution as written and intended.

> **The constitution was from its very origin, contemplated to be the frame of a national government of special and enumerated powers, and not of general and unlimited powers.** This is apparent as will be presently seen from the history of the proceedings of the convention which framed it; and it has formed the admitted basis of all legislative and judicial reasoning upon it, ever since it was put into operation, by all who have been its open friends and advocates as well as by all who have been its enemies and opponents. **If the clause to pay the debts and provide for the common defense and general welfare of the United States is construed to be an independent and substantive grant of power**, it not only renders wholly unimportant and unnecessary the subsequent enumeration of specific powers, but it plainly extends far beyond them and creates a general authority in congress to pass all laws which they may deem for the common defense or general welfare. **Under such circumstances the constitution would practically create an unlimited national government.**
> - Commentaries on the Constitution of the United States. Vol. 2. 1833. P.369.

It is clear that "promoting the general welfare" does not give Congress the power to do whatever it pleases. Congress is bound by the 10th Amendment, which specifically grants all non-specified powers to the states or people. Those who think the 10th Amendment does not apply should be asked if the 1st Amendment also does not apply. Congress may very well decide that it can "promote general welfare" by censoring the press and controlling content of newspapers and TV news. After all, it harms the nation when the press criticizes national leaders in Congress! Congress would be free to do so if not bound by the 1st Amendment.

Remember that the spending clause in the Constitution limits only Congress and the federal government. **State governments are perfectly free under the Constitution to tax their citizens and spend money as the state sees fit.**

Interstate Commerce
The Constitution gives Congress the power to regulate the trade of goods between states and control any goods being imported or exported into the nation. This includes duties, tariffs, or outright bans on goods.

> Article 1. Section 8. Clause 3.
> Congress Shall have the power to regulate Commerce with foreign Nations, and among the several States, and with the Indian Tribes.

Congress does not have the power to regulate commerce within a state. States are individual governing bodies with their own ability to regulate commerce within their borders if they choose. Congress stepping in and regulating trade within a state is an abuse of power.

This is best seen with the arguments made by Madison in Federalist #42 where he explains the purpose of the clause is to prevent states from imposing tariffs on goods from another state.

> FEDERALIST No. 42, James Madison
> The defect of power in the existing Confederacy to regulate the commerce between its several members, ... A very material object of this power was the relief of the States

which import and export through other States, from the improper contributions levied on them by the latter.... Were these at liberty to regulate the trade between State and State, it must be foreseen that ways would be found out to load the articles of import and export, during the passage through their jurisdiction....

(Summary: Giving the Interstate Commerce power to Congress will prevent states from levying tariffs and duties on goods moving between the states. Madison goes on in the paper to give two examples of European nations, Switzerland and Germany, that ensure free trade between their internal political units.)

Judge Andrew Napolitano, a constitutional scholar, explains the meaning the founders intended with the Commerce Clause.

> James Madison, who argued that to regulate meant to keep regular, would have shuddered at such circular reasoning [employed by modern courts]. Madison's understanding was the commonly held one in 1789, since the principle reason for the Constitutional Convention was to establish a central government that would prevent ruinous state-imposed tariffs that favored in-state businesses. It would do so by assuring that commerce between the states was kept "regular."
>
> - Wall Street Journal Online. SEPTEMBER 15, 2009

Dr. Walter Williams is a long known champion of liberty and proper interpretation of the US Constitution. He writes on the abuse of the Interstate Commerce Clause:

> A key failing of the Articles of Confederation was the propensity of states to erect protectionist trade barriers. When the Framers met in Philadelphia in 1787 and wrote the constitution that governs us today, **they addressed that failure and through the commerce and the privileges and immunities clauses that created a national free-trade zone. Thus, the original purpose of the commerce clause was primarily a means to eliminate trade barriers among the states.** They didn't intend for the commerce clause to govern so much of our

lives.
> - Dr. Walter Williams. George Mason University. October 30, 2003.

Dr. Williams goes on to illustrate a severe example of abuse of the commerce regulation power where a small farmer was fined for harvesting twelve acres of wheat on his land for his use, because he violated a wheat production law set during the New Deal era by the national government. This abuse of power is totally inconsistent with the rest of the Constitution.

Nancy Pelosi (Democrat-CA) does not understand the clause or else chooses to misinterpret it. She claims the Interstate Commerce clause gives Congress the power to mandate a citizen purchase a product – health insurance in this case.

> When CNSNews.com asked House Speaker Nancy Pelosi (D-Calif.) on Thursday where the Constitution authorized Congress to order Americans to buy health insurance--a mandate included in both the House and Senate versions of the health care bill--Pelosi dismissed the question by saying: "Are you serious? Are you serious?"
>
> Pelosi's press secretary later responded to written follow-up questions from CNSNews.com by emailing CNSNews.com a press release on the "Constitutionality of Health Insurance Reform," that argues that Congress derives the authority to mandate that people purchase health insurance from its constitutional power to regulate interstate commerce.
> - CNSNews.com. Matt Cover. October 22, 2009

Nancy Pelosi, as Speaker, is the leader of Democrats in the House. It has to be assumed that she speaks for the majority of Democrats in the House since they voted to make her their leader. So this statement represents the thinking of a large majority of Democrat politicians in Washington, D.C. Scary!

Think about it. Does Congress have the power to tell a citizen, by force of law, what products he must buy, what he can produce, how much he can produce, and how much he can make from his labor? If so, Congress can come to you and say, "Joe, you are a plumber. But there are too many plumbers in your city, so you must find another profession." Are you now happy if you are Joe? Do you like the federal government being able to tell you when, where, and how to work?

If the federal government has this much power, the US is basically a dictatorship. The nation needs to return to the proper meaning of this clause: to do nothing more than prevent states from setting up duties to tax goods coming across the state line from a neighboring state.

It is up to citizens and voters to know the correct constitutional meaning of these clauses and make sure their politicians do, as well.

It is easily seen that recent politicians have distorted the meanings of constitutional clauses on general welfare, interstate commerce, and federal spending. These clauses should be interpreted as written and in the context in which they were intended. Thomas Jefferson wrote about the proper interpretation and understanding of the Constitution:

> On every question of construction carry ourselves back to the time when the Constitution was adopted, recollect the spirit manifested in the debates and instead of trying what meaning may be squeezed out of the text or invented against it, conform to the probable one in which it was passed.
>
> Laws are made for men of ordinary understanding and should, therefore, be construed by the ordinary rules of common sense. Their meaning is not to be sought for in metaphysical subtleties which may make anything mean everything or nothing at pleasure.
>   - Thomas Jefferson letter to William Johnson, June 12, 1823. www.quotationcollection.com

Distorting the Constitution or taking it out of context wasn't always the normal way in America. Our representatives used to realize that the Constitution meant what it stated. The national prohibition of alcohol experiment is an excellent example.

Prohibition – an example of Federal and State Powers

The limited powers the Constitution places on the federal government can be seen by the fact that the nation passed the 18th Amendment, ratified in 1919. It banned the manufacture, sale or transportation of intoxicating liquors (alcohol). The Constitution did not give the federal government the power to ban or regulate alcohol, because, per the 10th Amendment, the power is left to state/local governments. Americans realized in 1919 that the federal government could only exercise power that was specifically stated in the Constitution. So Congress needed to pass an amendment, and the states needed to ratify it, to give the federal government that power. In 1933, Congress and the states repealed the amendment removing the power of the federal government to ban alcohol. Again, the country amended the Constitution to change the powers of the federal government.

Article I of the Constitution does give Congress the power to regulate commerce with foreign nations, therefore it has the power to ban the importation of alcohol from outside the country. The Constitution specifies the powers Congress and the federal government have. Local governments could and can ban the sale and manufacture of alcohol in their jurisdictions if they wish. Some counties do.

Note how things have changed today. By what authority does the federal government pursue its "War on Drugs"? The Constitution does not mention drugs, legal or illegal. Congress has every power to control importation, and therefore, stop any drug from entering the country, but no power to make possession illegal. The federal government simply claimed this power for itself. This power clearly belongs to states or counties to exercise if they wish.

Here are a pair of quotes of wisdom from Dr. Williams regarding the proper scope of constitutional rights:

> A right, such as a right to free speech, imposes no obligation on another, except that of non-interference. The so-called right to health care, food or housing, whether a person can afford it or not, is something entirely different; it does impose an obligation on another. If one person has a right to

something he didn't produce, simultaneously and of necessity it means that some other person does not have right to something he did produce. That's because, since there's no Santa Clause or Tooth Fairy, in order for government to give one American a dollar, it must, through intimidation, threats and coercion, confiscate that dollar from some other American.
- Dr. Walter Williams www.quotationcollection.com

Government is necessary, but the only rights we can delegate to government are the ones we possess. For example, we all have a natural right to defend ourselves against predators. Since we possess that right, we can delegate authority to government to defend us. By contrast, we don't have a natural right to take the property of one person to give to another; therefore, we cannot legitimately delegate such authority to government.
- Dr. Walter Williams www.quotationcollection.com

Constitutional Compromise: The States Decide

How many times have you heard a pollster or news commentator say "The American people want compromise, they want their politicians to come together and get things done." It is very difficult to do this when an issue is polarizing and people feel strongly on both sides. The founders of America faced a similar dilemma when they dealt with slavery (discussed in Chapter 17). Their solution: Keep the issue at the state level. Let each state decide the issue for that state. That was the only way to bring the states together and form a union. That is the approach that needs to be taken with the controversial political issues today, such as abortion and homosexual marriage.

Important point: States cannot decide issues that are in the Constitution, only those that the Constitution does not address. The Constitution trumps state law. For example, a state could not legalize slavery today. There are amendments that forbid a state from doing so. There are also amendments that protect numerous citizen rights by preventing the government from taking those rights away. The Constitution has no amendments dealing with beginning of life or abortion or marriage. So these should be left to each state to decide until the Constitution is amended to reflect those issues.

By following the actual words of the Constitution, America can return to a nation where the federal government again maximizes freedom for its citizens by focusing only on those tasks the people have given it.

Freedom of Religion - First Amendment

"Almighty God hath created the mind free, and manifested His supreme will that free it shall remain by making it altogether insusceptible of restraint... the Holy Author of our religion, who being Lord of both body and mind, yet chose not to propagate it by coercions on either, as was in His almighty power to do, but extend it by its influence on reason alone." - TRTJ. P 603.

So wrote Thomas Jefferson about a bill for establishing religious freedom in Virginia in 1779. Jefferson was the Governor of Virginia at the time, and believed God created mankind with the "free mind" to worship God as each man should choose. This belief would carry into the Constitution's First Amendment.

Any discussion of freedom of religion in America must begin with the First Amendment of the Constitution which protects this important liberty. The First Amendment was part of the Bill of Rights, which was passed to further strengthen the limits on the federal government already contained in the Constitution.

> Amendment 1 - Freedom of Religion, Press, Expression.
> (Ratified 12/15/1791)
> **Congress shall make no law respecting an establishment of religion, or prohibiting the free exercise thereof**; or abridging the freedom of speech, or of the press; or the right of the people peaceably to assemble, and to petition the Government for a redress of grievances.

The amendment is clear and has two components.
1) The federal government shall not establish or mandate a national religion (Catholic, Lutheran, Baptist, Methodist....)
2) The federal government must not prohibit the free practice of religion.

Supreme Court Justice Joseph Story confirms the intent in his Commentaries on the Constitution:

> **The real object of the amendment** was not to countenance much less to advance Mahometanism or Judaism or infidelity by prostrating Christianity but **to exclude all rivalry among Christian sects and to**

prevent any national ecclesiastical establishment which should give to an hierarchy the **exclusive patronage** of the national government. It thus cut off the means of religious persecution the vice and pest of former ages and of the subversion of the rights of conscience in matters of religion which had been trampled upon almost from the days of the Apostles to the present age.
- Commentaries on the Constitution of the United States. Volume 3. 1833. Supreme Court Justice Joseph Story. P728. Google.com/books.

So at the time of its ratification, the 1st Amendment was understood to prevent the national government from exclusively supporting a particular Christian denominational church. The amendment also prevented the federal government from persecuting any denomination or non-Christian religion. The religions of Islam and Judaism (as well as any other) were to be tolerated, and followers of those minority religions were free to practice them.

This was the widely understood meaning at the time the amendment was adopted and the meaning attributed to it by the Supreme Court. In fact early commentaries on the Constitution discussed the role of government in fostering Christianity in general among the population.

And at all events it is impossible for those who believe in the truth of Christianity as a divine revelation to doubt that it is **the especial duty of government to foster and encourage it** among all the citizens and subjects. **This is a point wholly distinct from that of the right of private judgment in matters of religion and of the freedom of public worship according to the dictates of one's conscience.**
- Commentaries on the Constitution of the United States. Volume 3. 1833. Supreme Court Justice Joseph Story. P723. Google.com/books.

Notice the distinction between the federal government encouraging Christianity and the freedom of private worship. Many today have muddied this distinction – some purposefully. It was perfectly fine, and even the duty, of the federal government to have prayer sessions or church services in Congress, as well as doing other things to promote Christianity among the general population. It was not permissible to dictate the general population worship a specific way or mandate attendance at church services. This is a perfect example of government protecting the free will from God, discussed in Chapter 2. A citizen living in Washington, DC has free will to attend or not attend a church service held in the Capitol Building. The citizen does not have the right to demand the service be canceled because it offends him or her.

An important point: The Constitution does not <u>require</u> the federal government to promote religion. This is left to the majority of the population to decide, through their elected representatives. In early America the Congress was supportive of the Christian religion. Whether current leaders are supportive is largely dependent on whether the citizens want them to be.

Also to be noted, it is not a constitutional responsibility of the federal government to support a specific church organization. Therefore subsidies should not be given to a church organization, any more than the government should give money to an individual.

There is nothing in the amendment to prevent religion in the government. In fact religion has historically been present in the government. For example:

- The Bible is and has been used to swear in every president during the inauguration. It is the Christian Bible used, not the Jewish Torah (First 5 books of the Old Testament), not the Koran, not any other religious book.
- The US Congress has, from its inception, begun with daily prayer from a Christian pastor or reverend.
- Congress passed the Northwest Ordinance in 1787, which specified religion and morality be taught in territories which were under control of Congress (until statehood was established).
- In 1781, Congress passed a resolution endorsing the Old and New Testament (Aitken's Bible). This was the first Bible published in the United States.

President Thomas Jefferson reiterated the constitutional view concerning religion in his second inaugural address:

> In matters of religion I have considered that its free exercise is placed by the Constitution independent of the powers of the General Government. I have therefore undertaken on no occasion to prescribe the religious exercises suited to it, but have left them, as the Constitution found them, under the direction and discipline of the church or state authorities acknowledged by the several religious societies.
> - Thomas Jefferson, March 4, 1805.

In America today there are many who detest religion and Christianity in particular. It is within their free will to do so. However they are not satisfied with practicing their own views in private. They wish to transform society to mimic their non-religious views. The logic used by liberal-secular groups and judges to achieve their goal is the separation of church and state.

The Establishment (Separation) Clause:
Separation of Church and State Myth
Thanks to an activist Supreme Court (detailed in the next chapter), there is seldom a discussion on religion in America without the phrase "Separation of Church and State" coming to the forefront. Surely this phrase plays a prominent role in the US Constitution. Well, not exactly. The phrase is **not** present in the Constitution at all, much less in the First Amendment which deals with religion.

The Establishment of Religion Clause was *created* by the Supreme Court in 1947, referring back to a letter written by Thomas Jefferson in 1802 for its basis. There is not a credible explanation as to how the Court did not discover the "meaning" of Jefferson's letter for 145 years, except that early justices actually turned to the Constitution's words when ruling on cases.

> The modern view of the Establishment of Religion Clause began with *Everson v Board of Education of Ewing* in 1947, where the Court initiated the current separationist approach....
>
> The Supreme Court chose to base its understanding of the clause on its interpretation of a letter by Thomas Jefferson to the Danbury Baptist Association of Connecticut in 1802....

Freedom of Religion - First Amendment

> Jefferson's metaphor of a "wall of separation" was interpreted by the Court as the authoritative statement of a "high and impregnable" barrier between the church and state even though this was itself an expansion beyond Jefferson's own meaning and practice.
> – Heritage Guide to the Constitution. p304

The Establishment Clause is a perfect example of justices on the court creating law by inventing meanings and "new interpretations" of the Constitution. Jefferson's many other statements on religion and government listed earlier in the chapter ought to make clear he did not support the establishment clause's "separation of church from state" interpretation. Jefferson's actions confirm it.

> While serving as 3rd President of the United States, Thomas Jefferson chaired the school board for the District of Columbia. In that capacity, he wrote the first plan of education adopted by the city of Washington. His plan directs teachers to use the *Bible* and *Isaac Watts' Hymnal* as the primary books by which to teach reading.
> - One Nation Under Man. P37.

> Thomas Jefferson allowed public buildings, including the US Capitol, to be used for church services. He also used the Bible as text for teaching reading in the District of Columbia.
> -- God in America p46.

Jefferson's actions while President indicate he believed in the government fostering Christianity in the nation, while not endorsing a specific denomination (sect) over another.

Interpretation Fallacies
Judges supporting the "separation myth" of the Establishment Clause believe that it is good practice to take one phrase from one letter written by Thomas Jefferson and use it to determine constitutional law. They must believe Jefferson to be the ultimate authority on the constitution for this to be so. What else does Jefferson say about our Constitution?

> "You seem to consider the judges as the ultimate arbiters of all Constitutional questions; a very dangerous doctrine

indeed, and one which would place us under the despotism of an oligarchy.... but the constitution in keeping three departments distinct and independent, restrains the authority of the judges to judiciary organs..."
- Jefferson to William Jarvis (1820). TRTJ. p.498.

So judges having sole authority to determine constitutional issues leads to *despotism* and *tyranny*. Surely these activist judges realize their ruling on "separation" in 1947 was tyrannical, and they had no authority to force the President or Congress to do anything. To be consistent, Establishment Clause supporters must also support these words of Jefferson, "judges as the ultimate arbiters of all Constitutional questions [is] a very dangerous doctrine indeed' . Jefferson gives judges no authority to change the Constitution.

Another Jefferson comment on government is:

"We do not mean that our people shall be burdened with oppressive taxes to provide sinecures for the idle or the wicked under color of providing for a civil list."
- Jefferson, 1775. (TRTJ. p. 641.)

"We do not mean that our people shall be burdened with oppressive taxes to provide sinecures for the idle..." Jefferson's words are clear; no oppressive taxes are to be used by government to give money to the idle. Since welfare recipients are idle, and paying for the programs causes oppressive taxation, isn't it obvious that all welfare programs are illegal? By logic, every judge using the Establishment Clause to rule on religion must surely also rule that all government welfare programs are unconstitutional. Another constitutional issue has been determined because Jefferson has penned the answer. How silly the logic is of taking a phrase in a letter and trying to use it to make constitutional law. The whole judicial logic behind the Establishment Clause quickly falls apart.

Jefferson's writings should be analyzed and given considerable weight as he was an important founder of America and a drafter of our Declaration of Independence; however, he is not the final arbiter of the meaning of the Constitution. The author is simply pointing out the inconsistency of selectively pulling words from Jefferson's writings.

Freedom of Religion - First Amendment

Jefferson also wrote clearly on his view of the 1st Amendment to the US Constitution:

> The Constitution, which expressly declares, that "Congress shall make no law respecting an establishment of religion, or prohibiting the free exercise thereof, or abridging the freedom of speech or of the press": thereby guarding in the same sentence, and under the same words, the **freedom of religion, of speech, and of the press**: .... libels, falsehood, and defamation, equally with heresy and false religion, are **withheld from the [jurisdiction] of federal tribunals**.
> - Thomas Jefferson, Kentucky Resolution of 1798

Jefferson really links religion, speech, and press in this writing. What if in the future a judge decided to treat the press the same way it has treated religion? They are, after all, in the same amendment.

Separation of News Media (Press) and State
Out of the blue, activist-judges have now "ruled" that there should be a "Separation of News Media and State." A wall should exist between the two. To comply, any newspaper would be banned from government. It would be "unconstitutional" to have The New York Times or The Washington Post in any federal government office building. These papers, and all other papers, are offensive to somebody, therefore cannot be tolerated in government. Private citizens may have newspapers, but government cannot.

Likewise, could someone not decide they want to be news-free? They no longer believe in news. This new group of "atheistic news-haters" sues to prevent any news company content from being in public. This includes public schools and libraries. News media must be removed from the public square because they are offended. Trying to take news out of today's government and culture is just as idiotic and incorrect as trying to remove every trace of religion from government and the public square.

Religion at Local Events
A perfect example of religious displays at a local venue is captured in the following story regarding a stone monument with the 10

Commandments of the Bible displayed.

> ### ACLU Sues to Remove 10 Commandments Display From NM Courthouse Lawn
> It isn't uncommon for religious displays to serve as primary targets for atheists and church-state separatist groups. Case in point: last week, the American Civil Liberties Union New Mexico (ACLU) filed a lawsuit on behalf of Jane Felix and B.N. Coone, residents who are offended by the presence of a Ten Commandments display that is on the front lawn of the Bloomfield, New Mexico City Hall.
>
> The residents who oppose the display, which was privately donated to the government and placed on the lawn back in July 2011, believe that it is a violation of the separation of church and state. In the filing with the U.S. District Court of New Mexico, the ACLU called the display "an excessive government entanglement with religion" and ordered the monument to be "immediately removed from the real property owned by the City of Bloomfield, New Mexico."
>
> ACLU of New Mexico Executive Director Peter Simonson says that he and his organization have no opposition to private citizens and organizations posting the Ten Commandments. But he contends that the government's endorsement (i.e. the location) of the religious monument is unacceptable.
>   - TheBlaze.com. February 14, 2012.

Now the 1st Amendment clearly states that the federal government may NOT ban religious activity like the display of the Ten Commandments. In fact, it would be perfectly constitutional if the local government of New Mexico had paid for the monument.

But we have a number of judges on the courts who have made up law that suits their personal beliefs. Since Justice Ruth Bader Ginsburg, a Democrat appointee, served as General Council to the ACLU before taking her seat on the Supreme Court, it is pretty obvious she will side with the ACLU in this case. Ginsburg helped shape the political-legal philosophy of the ACLU. Ginsburg will ignore the written words of the Constitution and insert what she wishes the Constitution stated.

Freedom of Religion - First Amendment

It is a simple matter to resolve what, if any, religion takes place in public places. It is up to the caretaker of the public place, since every public place has a caretaker. For example, the White House belongs to the people. But the president makes the rules for who can visit the White House and what they can do while the visitors are there. Think not? Try getting 20-30 people together and going into the White House to have a protest or a meeting. You will not get into the building, and will be arrested if you do not have the president's permission. This despite the fact that every American has the constitutional right to address or protest their government. It is the same with all public buildings.

This was understood in early America. Going back to the church services Jefferson allowed in public buildings: Most federal buildings fall under the Executive branch, so it was up to Jefferson to decide which if any services could be held in them. Likewise, Congress decides which if any services occur in the Capitol building. It is not "establishing a religion" to allow a religious service to be held. Establishing a religion would mean using government force to make citizens attend a service. This has never been done. Citizens have the free will to attend or not attend the church service. The service can be multi-denominational Christian, single-denominational Christian, or non-Christian. In all likelihood the type of service will be dictated by the majority of the citizens, in order to please most of the citizens.

The same principle applies to state or federal parks. There is an agency, appointed by elected officials to be park caretakers, that decides what activities or displays can be on the land. State governors decide what activities occur in governors' mansions. State government representatives decide what activities can occur in their state capitol buildings. The mayor and city council decide which activities or displays can take place on city land and in city parks and buildings.

In each of these instances, the ultimate decision makers are elected representatives. Citizens can vote them out of office if they do not like the decisions being made.

Judges have ruled that prayer by a minister at a public event such as a school football game or graduation ceremony is unconstitutional. First, put aside the fact that prayer at public events *was* considered constitutional for almost 200 years. Does prayer at a public event interfere with a citizen's right to practice religion? No. Since America is predominantly Christian, most prayers will be Christian. So what is a minority atheist, Jew, or Muslim to do? They can stand in tolerant, respectful silence, honoring the desires of the majority. They do not have to participate or pray along. But there are also neighborhoods in America where Jews or Muslims are the majority. It is likely that prayer here will be to God (God the Father for Christians) or to Allah. What is a Christian to do? Stand in tolerant, respectful silence, honoring the desires of the majority. The school board will have to decide which, if any, prayers to allow. A school board may even allow multiple prayers, as professional baseball teams do with national anthems and a visiting Canadian team.

Should there be prayer at a public school event? Who owns the school? The people - It is their decision. The people elect city leaders or school boards to carry out their will. The school board or school principal will decide whether there will be a prayer and who to invite to lead the prayer. The school will probably go with the majority. A 90% Catholic community will likely have prayer lead by a local priest or father. A 90% Lutheran community will likely have prayer lead by a Lutheran pastor. A 90% Jewish community will likely have prayer lead by a rabbi. A mixed denomination community could rotate between the denominations. The founding fathers used public prayer often, recognizing the God who created each citizen and the nation. They thought it strengthened society to pray.

Freedom to practice religion has not been interfered with by any of these public prayers. But, the federal courts **banning prayer** does interfere with the free practice of religion. The act of banning a religious activity by the federal government violates the First Amendment.

Do minorities have the right to have prayer to their deity included as well? No. As was stated earlier, public property is owned by the local citizens. They elect caretakers in local government that control use of the property. Those caretakers make the rules. The people can change caretakers through elections. Let's assume a group of several hundred people get together in a community and decide to worship Satan and pray to him (an extreme example, selected on purpose). This minority has the right to worship privately as they choose as long as they do not advocate violence or perform violent acts against others. They also have the right to petition local government for their prayers to be included in community events. However, they have no right to demand one of their leaders lead a prayer at a public event. The courts have no power to force the school board to accept a prayer leader from this minority group. The decision is up to the local officials.

Likewise is true with other forms of public displays of religion, such as nativity scenes around Christmas-time.

>School Replaces Baby Jesus with Frosty the Snowman
>Principal Brenda Jones told television station WJHG the decision to keep Baby Jesus in the closet came after an official with the Dept. of Education dropped by to discuss the separation of church and state.
>
>"The Dept. of Education [federal government] came in and talked to us about the legalities of religion in the school systems and the separation of the two," Jones told the television station.
>
>....former board member Betty Duffee told the Jackson County Floridan that she believes the principal had no choice.
>
>"There are people in the community that are threatening to sue the school board (over separation of church and state issues), and it costs a tremendous amount of money to defend something you know you will lose," she said. "It's not that we're against it; it's just that the federal law prohibits it."
>
>Duffee told the newspaper that the decision not to display the Nativity is a "tragic thing."
>
>"I know it's hard to see this happen, because it feels like we're losing a freedom, but this is the state of affairs in this nation," she said.
>
>- Fox News Radio. Todd Starnes. Nov. 30, 2012.

This squashing of religious freedom is exactly what happens when federal judges misinterpret the Constitution's First Amendment. The principle and the school board have the right to display Baby Jesus at Christmas if they so desire. They have been entrusted to manage the property, so are able to display any religious items they choose to display. The federal government apparently applied pressure to "encourage" the school to remove Jesus from the display. This is clearly a move by the federal government to stop religious expression. While not a clear-cut violation of the First Amendment (the display was not banned) it is against the spirit of the amendment.

The citizens should hold their senators responsible for this type of federal government interference. It is senators who confirm judges to the Supreme Court who have made rulings banning Nativity Scenes, which are unconstitutional. More on this in the next chapter.

Atheists' and secularists' goal is to banish all forms and symbols of Christianity from public view in America. They want Christianity locked into private churches and never allowed out. But that is not the America that was founded. Look no further than the following case. The city seal includes a cross, the symbol of Christianity. The city seal was adopted in the 1880s. No federal court or citizen had any issues with it for 130 years because Americans for most of that period understood the true meaning of the Constitution.

> <u>Atheists want cross removed from 131-year-old city seal in Florida</u>
> The atheist group Americans United complains that the seal used by DeLand, Florida, happens to contain a cross. Liberty Counsel founder Mat Staver tells OneNewsNow the complaint really illustrates the absurdity of groups like Americans United.
>
> Staver, Mat (Liberty Counsel)"This seal is part of the very founding seal of the city of DeLand. It's 131 years old. No one has ever complained for 131 years until the Americans United for Separation of Church and State filed this letter."
> - OneNewsNow.com. Charlie Butts. September 10, 2013.

Freedom of Religion - First Amendment

The chapter closes with another example of the federal courts removing religious symbols. In Utah, memorial crosses were placed along highways were Utah State troopers had been killed. A group of atheists filed a lawsuit claiming their rights were violated under the "Separation Clause".

> <u>Supreme Court Turns Down Utah Crosses Case</u>
> The case landed at the Supreme Court after the 10th U.S. Circuit Court of Appeals ruled in 2010 that the crosses — found by roadsides and in remote canyons where the troopers lost their lives — are an unconstitutional government endorsement of religion, even though the nonprofit Utah Highway Patrol Association, which erected them, is not a religious organization, and no public funds were used to set them up.
> - Citizenlink.com. October 31, 2011. Karla Dial.

The atheists won the case at the Appeals Court level and the Supreme Court refused to hear it. So this is now the law of the land in the 10th Circuit, covering Utah as well as Colorado, Kansas, New Mexico, Oklahoma and Wyoming.

Recall, the words of the Constitution state Congress shall not make laws "prohibiting the free exercise thereof" with respect to religion and "abridging the freedom of" with respect to the press. So how is it unconstitutional for a patrolmen's group to put a cross next to a federal highway but fine to allow newscasts to be broadcast over federal airwaves? The courts have no constitutional authority to prohibit either. "Freedom to practice" does not mean "freedom from being exposed to". Citizens can be exposed to religion just as they can be exposed to newscasts. The federal government cannot ban either one according to the Constitution – if the words in the document are actually read and used.

Note: The caretaker could decide to remove crosses from roads. This is likely the state of Utah or the county governments.

Pagan Society vs Christian Society

> *1 Peter 2:11-12 Living Godly Lives in a Pagan Society*
> *Dear friends, I urge you, as foreigners and exiles, to abstain from sinful desires, which wage war against your soul. Live such good lives among the pagans that, though they accuse you of doing wrong, they may see your good deeds and glorify God on the day he visits us.*

The audience Peter addresses lived among a majority of pagans (or non-believing Jews). They were a Christian minority. While, all Christians could be considered foreigners in the earthly world until they go to their true home in heaven, America was founded as a super-majority Christian nation. Christians in America have always been free to express their faith in God. But this is changing. For the last 80 years the federal government has been pushing the nation toward atheistic paganism, banning God and Christian symbols from all public areas – despite the First Amendment expressly preventing this. American Christians must decide whether they value living in a Christian nation, or are content to live as if surrounded by pagans. After reading and understanding their constitutional rights, Americans must decide if they will use the voting booth to protect their rights from a power-seeking federal government. This is discussed in the next chapter and in Chapter 25.

> To those who cite the First Amendment as reason for excluding God from more and more of our institutions and everyday life, may I just point out, the First Amendment of the Constitution was not written to protect the people of this country from religious values; it was written to protect religious values from government tyranny.
> - Ronald Reagan. US Chamber of Commerce. 1982. creationrevolution.com.

Judges and Senators

> If in the opinion of the people, [there is any wrong in the Constitution] let it be corrected by amendment in the way in which the Constitution designates. But let there be no changes by usurpation; for though this, in one instance may be the instrument of good, it is the customary weapon by which free governments are destroyed.
> - George Washington Farewell Address in 1796. TRGW. P666.

Over the last 80-90 years there has indeed been a great usurpation of the Constitution. As President Washington predicted, it has lead to a great loss of freedom. Nowhere is this more evident than in the examination of religious freedom in the nation. It is long past time to hold judges and senators responsible for upholding the religious liberty promised in America's Constitution. Judges directly usurp the Constitution when they issue rulings contrary to the text of the document. Senators are responsible for confirming (or rejecting) those judges and giving them the power to usurp.

Many judges on the court today rule on cases based on their political beliefs rather than the text and meaning of the laws and the Constitution. Deciding cases based on political beliefs is referred to as judicial activism. Deciding cases on the constitutional text is called original intent.

Justice Scalia represents a classic originalist (or textualists to use his term) judge on the court:

> Scalia says abortion, gay rights are easy cases
>
> Justice Antonin Scalia says his method of interpreting the Constitution makes some of the most hotly disputed issues that come before the Supreme Court among the easiest to resolve.
>
> Scalia calls himself a "textualist" .... that means he applies the words in the Constitution as they were understood by the people who wrote and adopted them.
>
> So Scalia parts company with former colleagues who have come to believe capital punishment is unconstitutional. The framers of the Constitution didn't think so and neither does he.
>
> "The death penalty? Give me a break. It's easy. Abortion? Absolutely easy. Nobody ever thought the Constitution prevented restrictions on abortion. Homosexual sodomy?

Come on. For 200 years, it was criminal in every state," Scalia said at the American Enterprise Institute.
- MARK SHERMAN, Associated Press. October 5, 2012

Consider the possible judicial rulings on abortion as an illustrative example to see the differences between activism and originalism:

- A federal judge following the <u>original intent</u> of the Constitution would decline to rule on abortion. The Constitution does not contain language on the practice of abortion or stating whether a baby in the womb is a life and entitled to the protections of a citizen. Therefore abortion is left to state law per the 10th Amendment.

- <u>Liberal activist judges,</u> as the ones who created current abortion rulings, beginning with the Roe v Wade case, have ruled that abortion is a constitutionally protected right and access to abortion must be allowed by state and federal law.

- A <u>conservative activist judge,</u> could very well rule that since the Declaration of Independence specifies that life is a right, a baby living in the womb is definitely alive and abortion kills the baby. Therefore abortion is murder and any abortion provider must be tried according to applicable murder laws. (See the Establishment Clause in the previous chapter. Liberal activist judges took one phrase from a single letter Jefferson wrote and used it to make law.)

The nation is far better off without activist judges, whether their political beliefs are conservative or liberal. All judges should rule according to the original intent, meaning, and language of the Constitution.

Should the NFL have activist referees?
What if an officiating crew in the National Football League acted like activist judges? They could. In any given game the officiating crew has complete control to enforce the rules of the game. Let's say a crew decided that the game is too violent especially with respect to quarterbacks. So the officials "interpret" the rules that *any* tackle of

the quarterback by a defender is roughing the passer, a 15 yard penalty on the defense. The most a defender can do is hold the quarterback until the official blows the whistle, ending the play. Throwing the QB to the ground is a penalty. The likely result? The game would be dramatically altered. The score would be inflated (77-73 perhaps? higher?) as the defenses would be crippled in their efforts to stop passing plays.

What would happen after the game? The NFL would certainly remove the officials from their duties. The league would not let a group of rogue officials change the way the game is played using only their beliefs. The game day officials are tasked with enforcing the rules, not creating them. Americans should do the same with rogue activist judges. Those federal judges refusing to follow the rules the Constitution provides should be removed from their duties (impeached) by their bosses (the US Senate).

Established Case Law
Many, including most politicians in the Democrat Party, will proclaim *Stare Decisis* - established case law should not be overturned. The author has noticed that these politicians only claim this in respect to judicial rulings with which they agree. One of the problems with lawyers is they are trained to argue both sides of every case in law school. This is needed, as our legal system requires legal representation for both plaintiff and defendant. But it often leads to hypocrisy in legislative leaders who will cite *Stare Decisis* for decisions they like, but openly condemn court decisions they do not like. It is better to use the written text of the Constitution as the guiding Northstar.

It is incredibly ironic that Roe v Wade, the case that established abortion law and made it legal in the entire United States, was a gross violation of *Stare Decisis*. There was no case law to support the judges' decision in Roe. The judges made up law, changed the Constitution, and overturned existing law in all 50 states. And Democrats cheered.

Stare Decisis is indeed good practice, unless the case law violates the written text and meaning of the Constitution. The courts have been wrong and ruled against the Constitution many times. For example, in the 1850s the Supreme Court ruled in *Dred Scott v. Sandford* that people of African descent held as slaves were not protected by the Constitution and could never be U.S. citizens despite the Constitution clearly giving Congress the power to determine citizenship. (Congress had determined that some states were "free states" and some were "slave states" at this time.) The court overrode Congress AND the Constitution in this case. See Chapter 18 for a more detailed discussion on slavery and the Constitution.

The next focus will be on the courts and their incorrect unconstitutional rulings regarding religion. These are examples of both liberal judicial activism and violation of *Stare Decisis* as the judges overturned existing case law.

The Courts Battle against Religion
Beginning in the 1940s, the Supreme Court began removing God from the public square, based on the judges' personal preferences rather than constitutional text. The court has repeatedly banned religious activity. Some examples:

- Ruled that States could not offer voluntary or elective religious courses (1948).
- Ruled that it was unconstitutional for the students to recite a long-standing prayer (1962).
- Ruled that public school children can not read the Bible at school (1963).
- Ruled that states can not require that creationism be taught in the public schools (1968).
- Ruled that states can not post the Ten Commandments in their public school classrooms (1980).
- Made it illegal for a pastor, priest or member of the clergy to offer an invocation or benediction at a public school graduation ceremony (1992).
- Declared it unconstitutional for students to pray over the loud speaker system before a football game (2000).

- Sourced from Brannon Howse. www.worldviewweekend.com.

Judges and Senators

How could all of these religious actions have been constitutional for the first 150+ years of America, but now are not? There were no amendments or changes made to the constitution regarding religion during this period. The First Amendment still states: "Congress shall make no law respecting an establishment of religion, or prohibiting the free exercise thereof." If the US Congress cannot ban religion, it is for sure that US courts do not have the constitutional authority to do so. As discussed in the previous chapter, the federal government should neither ban nor mandate religious activity according to the amendment. Judges should use the written text of the Constitution to form the basis of their rulings.

Removing Crosses from Public Land
The next step in the liberal activist court's battle against religion is attempting to remove crosses from public lands. In the Mojave War Memorial Cross Case, four judges ruled that a cross must be removed after being erected 75 years ago after World War I by the Veterans of Foreign Wars (VFW).

In a 5-4 decision, the majority ruled that the lower federal court was wrong in ruling that the cross must be removed. The usual swing vote on the court, Justice Anthony Kennedy, wrote the plurality opinion in the case. Kennedy wrote, "Here one Latin cross in the desert evokes far more than religion. It evokes thousands of small crosses in foreign fields marking the graves of Americans who fell in battles, battles whose tragedies are compounded if the fallen are forgotten." It is a shame that all Americans cannot agree with this simple historical fact.

Who should decide whether a cross can be displayed on public land? The owners of the land. In this case the owner is the federal government, so ownership decisions fall to the president and Congress as they control all federal land and set the rules. Our elected representatives decide what can be displayed on the land or constructed on the land. In this case, in an attempt to avoid controversy, Congress transferred the land to the Veterans of Foreign Wars, a private group. Still four justices voted to order a private land owner remove the cross. The court has truly turned into a despotic oligarchy as President Thomas Jefferson warned.

The courts should only intervene if constitutional rights were violated. In this case the First Amendment applies. The government was not establishing a religion by allowing a cross to be displayed, nor was anyone's freedom to practice religion taken away. Freedom to practice does not mean freedom from exposure to symbols of other religions. The court has no authority to order a cross (or a building or any other structure) erected or removed.

The Mojave Cross is not the only example of atheist activists attempting to ban crosses. There are several more in their pipeline. Another cross case example is occurring at the 911 memorial.

> Atheists Attack the Ground Zero Cross
> An atheist group has filed a lawsuit to have the Ground Zero Cross removed from the 9/11 museum in New York. Their claim? The existence of the Cross has brought on headaches, indigestion, even mental pain. These claims are ridiculous. So is the lawsuit.
>
> The Ground Zero Cross is two intersecting steel beams that survived the Twin Towers' collapse on 9/11. It is a powerful remembrance and is a symbol of hope to many. The cross is a constitutionally sound memorial, and should continue to stand at The National September 11 Memorial and Museum.
> - ACLJ.org/american-heritage. August 20, 2012.

Still another cross case in Rhode Island.

> Atheists Threaten Lawsuit Over 'Unconstitutional' RI Firehouse Cross & WWI Monument
> Atheist activists are at it again. This time, the target of secular angst is a cross that appears in front of a firehouse in Woonsocket, Rhode Island. The Freedom From Religion Foundation (FFRF), a well-known atheist group, is threatening to sue the city if the religious symbol isn't removed.
>
> The Christian cross, part of a World War I memorial that was built in Woonsocket back in 1921, is causing a great deal of angst among secularists who stand firmly opposed to its presence on public property. Taking on even more significance beyond WWI, the monument was re-dedicated back in 1952 to honor three fallen WWII soldiers who lived

> in the area and has since been a public statement of remembrance.
>
> In a April 13 letter sent from the FFRF to Leo Fontaine, the city's mayor, FFRF staff attorney Rebecca Markert called the presence of the cross "unconstitutional" and claimed that a concerned citizen made the group aware of its presence.
>
> - TheBlaze.com. Billy Hallowell. April 25, 2012

Activist judges on the court, have established the precedent for atheists to scour the country, removing crosses wherever they find them. It starts with a letter like this. The city will often cave and remove the cross at the threat of litigation. If the city stands firm, FRFF will file a lawsuit. The city then faces legal costs from the lawsuit. If there are activist judges in the lower federal court, the city will lose the early rounds of the case. The city will likely be successful at the Supreme Court - IF they pay the legal costs to go that far – and IF no more activist judges are appointed before the case reaches the highest court.

Of course all Christian religious symbols are being targeted for removal, not just crosses. A war memorial constructed by soldiers following World War II is being targeted as well. The memorial happens to be a statue of Jesus with his arms opened in welcome.

> Court Must Reject Atheist Suit Targeting Jesus Statue in Montana
>
> It's a troubling pattern that we see often. An atheist group is "offended" by a statue or memorial that they consider to be offensive. They file a federal lawsuit to try to get it removed.
>
> This time, it's happened in Montana - a case we have been involved in for more than a year. As you'll recall, a statue of Jesus was put in place on Big Mountain at the Whitefish Mountain Resort in Montana in the 1950's by WW II veterans who were also members of the Knights of Columbus. The veterans were inspired by monuments they saw in the mountains of Europe during the war. The statue of Jesus, they said, was put in place to commemorate the service of local WW II veterans - a war memorial.
>
> .....the FFRF filed a federal lawsuit earlier this year in an effort to have the memorial removed.
>
> - ACLJ.org/american-heritage. Aug. 28, 2012

This time the lawsuit failed, and the Jesus statue remains in place. However, with enough liberal-activist judges on the courts, the statue will be ordered removed or destroyed. Of course as will be examined later in the chapter, many of the senators who confirmed those liberal-activist judges on the court will "disagree" with the ruling, but make a statement something like "the Constitution must be upheld" (believing that the Constitution is whatever their judges say it is). **The Senators will never mention that they are responsible for those judges, and therefore responsible for the distorted ruling.**

The Supreme Court Battle
Justices on the Supreme Court, and other federal courts, are appointed by presidents and confirmed by senators. Justices appointed in the last 30 years decided the Mojave Cross case. Analysis reveals that:

- **The four Justices appointed by Democrat Presidents (Clinton, Obama) voted to remove the cross.**

- **The five Justices appointed by Republican Presidents (Reagan, Bush, Bush) voted to allow the cross to remain.**

During this time period, there has been a huge difference in political philosophy of the judges appointed by each party. Justices appointed by Democrats are of left leaning/activist persuasion (the Constitution means whatever the judges want it to mean). Justices appointed by Republicans have been of original intent (the Constitution means what was written) persuasion. All judges appointed by Democrat presidents voted to remove the cross, effectively banning crosses from the public square. Voting to ban a cross is clearly a violation of the written text of the First Amendment. The ruling is consistent with liberal judicial activism.

The chart on the next page illustrates the difference between the political parties. Democrat presidents and senators are firmly in the liberal/activist camp which favors the banning of religion in public. Republicans are clearly in the original-intent camp.

US Supreme Court Justices in 2014

Justice	Appointed By	Senate Control	Persuasion	Age	Year Appointed
Antonin Scalia	Reagan (R)	D	O	77	1986
Clarence Thomas	G. H.W. Bush (R)	D	O	65	1991
John Roberts Chief Justice	G. W. Bush (R)	R	O	58	2005
Samuel Alito	G. W. Bush (R)	R	O	62	2006
Anthony Kennedy	Reagan (R)	D	S	77	1988
Sonia Sotomayor	Obama (D)	D	L/A	59	2009
Elena Kagan	Obama (D)	D	L/A	53	2010
Stephen Breyer	Clinton (D)	D	L/A	75	1994
Ruth Bader Ginsburg	Clinton (D)	D	L/A	80	1993

R = Republican, D = Democrat
O = Original Intent, S = Swing, L/A = Left / Activist

It is a safe prediction that were a new case to come before the court dealing with religion (allowing prayer to be said in schools, allowing posting of the 10 Commandments, allowing the Bible to be read in schools) the four activist justices would vote to ban the religious practice, while the four originalist justices would vote to allow the practice. The case would be decided by Justice Kennedy who is more of an unpredictable swing vote.

Economic Freedom in Jeopardy as well
Religious freedom is not the only area where activist judges are disregarding the US Constitution. The Constitution greatly limits the federal government, and they wish the government to have great power. Judges are also changing the rules for eminent domain. Eminent domain allows a government to seize a citizen's private property without the owner's consent as long as compensation is given. It is allowed in the Constitution (Amendment V "...nor shall private property be taken for public use, without just compensation.").

The key wording is "for public use". This was long understood to mean for direct government use, for example, construction of a road, or building a military base. Recent activist judges have expanded the clause to give the government much greater power. In their mind, public use is anything that benefits the government, including taking private property from one owner and giving it to a new owner.

> In *Kelo v. City of New London* (2005), the city of New London planned to use eminent domain to acquire property for a redevelopment project that would replace exiting private homes in good condition with private office space and parking lots. The property owners argued that the taking was not "for public use", and thus violated the 5th Amendment. In a 5-4 Opinion, the Court upheld the taking, holding that where a government presents a "comprehensive development plan", with "public benefits".... the taking satisfies the public use requirement.
>   - The Heritage Guide to the Constitution. P344.

Justice Stevens, a liberal-activist, wrote the majority opinion for the Kelo case. Justice Kennedy, the court's swing vote, this time voted with the activist block of judges, allowing them to win the decision.
One of the activist justices, David Souter, received more than he bargained for after the Kelo Decision. A private developer proposed using the Kelo ruling to take Souter's house and build a hotel.

> Press Release – Lost Liberty Hotel
> Could a hotel be built on the land owned by Supreme Court Justice David H. Souter? A new ruling by the Supreme Court which was supported by Justice Souter himself itself might allow it. A private developer is seeking to use this very law to build a hotel on Souter's land.
>
> Justice Souter's vote in the "Kelo vs. City of New London" decision allows city governments to take land from one private owner and give it to another if the government will generate greater tax revenue or other economic benefits when the land is developed by the new owner.
>
> On Monday June 27, Logan Darrow Clements, faxed a request to Chip Meany the code enforcement officer of the

Judges and Senators

> Towne of Weare, New Hampshire seeking to start the application process to build a hotel on 34 Cilley Hill Road. This is the present location of Mr. Souter's home.
>
> Clements, CEO of Freestar Media, LLC, points out that the City of Weare will certainly gain greater tax revenue and economic benefits with a hotel on 34 Cilley Hill Road than allowing Mr. Souter to own the land.
>
> The proposed development, called "The Lost Liberty Hotel" will feature the "Just Desserts Café" and include a museum, open to the public, featuring a permanent exhibit on the loss of freedom in America. Instead of a Gideon's Bible each guest will receive a free copy of Ayn Rand's novel "Atlas Shrugged."
>
> Clements indicated that the hotel must be built on this particular piece of land because it is a unique site being the home of someone largely responsible for destroying property rights for all Americans.
>
> The Towne of Weare has five people on the Board of Selectmen. If three of them vote to use the power of eminent domain to take this land from Mr. Souter we can begin our hotel development."
>
> - www.freestarmedia.com. hotellostliberty2.

The Lost Liberty Hotel was never built, as the town did not vote to seize the judges home, but the point was made. The government should not have the power to take private land or property from one owner and give it to another. No one's property is truly safe with the government having this power. It also invites "crony capitalism", where businessmen make donations to politicians, in exchange for "favors" such as eminent domain land transfers.

Again: It is up to citizens to punish the politicians who place judges on the courts that take away citizens' freedoms. Do you want the government to be able to take your house and give it to a developer? If you voted for a president who places activist-judges on the Court, your answer is "Yes".

Sidebar: Justice Souter results from Bork Nomination
Justice Souter was on the Supreme Court from 1990 through 2009. He was appointed by President George H. W. Bush, a Republican.

How did a Republican end up appointing a moderate-to-liberal activist judge? The answer is the Robert Bork Supreme Court nomination battle of 1987. Judge Bork was nominated by President Ronald Reagan. Bork was an outspoken originalist judge. This greatly threatened many liberals who depended on the courts to force their preferred policies on America; policies which they could not implement by legislation. During the nomination battle, the national Democrat Party and its liberal allied interest groups attacked Judge Bork from every conceivable angle, including personal. The attack process became known as "Borking", and resulted in the Democrat- controlled Senate voting to reject the judge mostly along party lines (Republican senators voting to confirm, Democrat senators voting to reject).

When the next opening on the Supreme Court emerged, George Bush opted for Souter, a stealth candidate rather than fight the Democrat Party to place an outspoken originalist judge on the court. Conservatives were told that Souter was an originalist judge, but did not have a record that could allow him to be "Borked". Souter ended up being a moderate-to-liberal judge rather than an originalist. Conservatives in the Republican Party learned from that and succeeded in getting Clarence Thomas confirmed to the Supreme Court in 1991, despite Democrat and liberals attempt to "Bork" him, as well. From Clarence Thomas forward, the political parties have been consistent: Republican appointed judges have been originalist, Democrat appointed judges have been liberal-activist.

ObamaCare Decision
A major decision was handed down in June, 2012, on a healthcare law known by many as ObamaCare. This law was 2700 pages in length and gave the federal government unprecedented power over the states and citizens. For the first time the federal government could mandate that a citizen must buy health insurance. The court was expected to strike down the law 5-4 with Justice Kennedy swinging to the originalist block. In a surprise decision, the law was upheld 5-4, only it was Chief Justice Roberts who joined the liberal-activist block to form the majority. Roberts used convoluted logic that stated Congress wasn't really passing a mandate; it was just using its taxing power. So Congress can't make a citizen buy health

insurance, but it can "tax" a citizen who doesn't buy it. The tax can be any amount Congress chooses, so set high enough could serve as a ban for most people.

A popular debate/discussion on ObamaCare focused on whether Congress could now force citizens to buy broccoli once a week because it was healthy for them. Five justices just decided that while Congress can't mandate the purchase of broccoli, it can tax a citizen who does not purchase it. So in the future citizens may face a choice of buying their broccoli or paying a tax ($5? $50? Any amount Congress chooses). Wait till the broccoli farmers begin to lobby Congress!

It doesn't stop there. What if Congress decides that the best way to fight crime is for every citizen to own a handgun? It can now pass a law that taxes citizens, say $1500 per year, if they do not own a handgun for crime prevention purposes. How can the citizens be "free" if the government has this amount of power to manage citizens' lives?

Why did Roberts rule this way? No one knows but Roberts himself. Roberts may have just wanted Congress to repeal this major piece of legislation rather than the court overturning it. (By being a "tax" it can be repealed by a simply majority in the Senate.) Roberts may have also been worried about his image in the dominate media (Chapter 23). The media would have harshly criticized him for overturning a law that the media strongly favored. It is also possible that Roberts feared the kind of political pressure/threats that Obama could have used, as FDR did, to intimidate the court (Chapter 12). Whatever reason, Roberts clearly broke from his normal originalist-leaning rulings in this case. Roberts' decision would have had no impact if there had not been four liberal-activist judges for him to join.

Constitution Held in Disdain by Activist Judges
Liberal activist judges tend to hold much of the Constitution in disdain. It is disturbing to see a sitting Supreme Court Justice, speaking to a world-wide audience, telling that audience NOT to follow the US constitutional principles, which assume God-given rights that the government cannot take away. It is a safe

assumption that Ginsburg, a Democrat appointed justice, reflects the views of the other three Democrat appointed justices, as well as the leadership of the Democrat Party.

> Ginsburg: I wouldn't use U.S. Constitution as a Model
> "I would not look to the U.S. Constitution, if I were drafting a constitution in the year 2012," Ginsburg said in an interview on Al Hayat television last Wednesday. "I might look at the constitution of South Africa. That was a deliberate attempt to have a fundamental instrument of government that embraced basic human rights, have an independent judiciary. It really is, I think, a great piece of work that was done."   - FoxNews.com. February 06, 2012.

The difference between Justice Ginsburg's views on the Constitution and President George Washington's views stated at the beginning of this chapter are striking indeed.

In reality, it doesn't matter if a Supreme Court Justice respects or admires the Constitution or not, as long as they fulfill their duty and rule on cases according to the Constitution. But as we have seen, these judges do not like the rule-of-law framework provided by the Constitution, so they often ignore constitutional text whenever it suits their political views.

Justices Scalia (originalist) and Breyer (liberal-activist) had a debate in 2005 on whether foreign law should be used to interpret the US Constitution. Scalia sums up the originalist view:

> JUSTICE SCALIA: You have to ask yourselves, Why is it that foreign law would be relevant to what an American judge does when he interprets -- interprets, not writes -- I mean, the Founders used a lot of foreign law. If you read the Federalist Papers, it's full of discussions of the Swiss system, German system. It's full of that. It is very useful in devising a constitution. But why is it useful in interpreting one?
>
> Now, my theory of what I do when I interpret the American Constitution is I try to understand what it meant, what was understood by the society to mean when it was adopted. And I don't think it changes since then.
>   - www.freerepublic.com. Focus.news.

Rules should be Rules

Let's say a family often plays a favorite card game. Pinochle, for example. Part of the scoring in that game is called "meld", and there are many different ways to score it. So the daughter in our family visits friends who use different rules for meld. She likes her friends' rules better. So she comes back home and proposes her family adopt her friends' meld rules. In essence she is proposing an amendment to her family's Pinochle meld rules. The family discusses the proposed rule change, and they may adopt or reject the changes. But the daughter cannot arbitrarily use her preferred rules in the family game unless the family adopts the rule change.

It is the same with foreign government laws. No matter how much an individual justice admires a particular law passed by a foreign court or government, it is irrelevant with respect to the rules established by the US Constitution, unless the law is adopted by amending the Constitution.

What is happening in America is that a number of politicians do not like the constitutional rules, and want to change them, but cannot convince a majority of Americans to support the changes. Therefore, they cannot pass amendments that would legally change the rules. Rather than respecting the rules and abiding by them, they resort to judges making up new rules as they go with no input from the American people.

Democrat Party Plan's for Judge-Rule

It is not accidental that Democrat presidents appoint judges who *make* law rather that *judge* law. It is their policy, widely known and expected among their party activists.

> First Lady Michelle Obama told two audiences at Democratic fundraising events on Tuesday that the justices her husband appointed to the Supreme Court will protect the right to "love whomever we choose."
>
> She also said these justices would protect "privacy"— presumably an allusion to the "right to privacy" the court invoked in the 1973 Roe v. Wade decision that legalized abortion in the United States.
>
> - CNSNews.com. Fred Lucas. October 26, 2011

The First Lady must be confusing *love* and *marriage*. More importantly, she just told her supporters *the next law* activist Supreme Court judges will make if Democrats have their way. Homosexual marriage will become a "constitutional" right and the courts will force all states to perform them, just like the court did with abortion in the 1970s. The agenda of the Democrat Party is to put their agenda in place via judicial fiat when they cannot enact it by the legislature. The difference is citizens can toss out a legislator who makes poor decisions, while a judge sits on the federal court for life – never having been elected by citizens. The only recourse a citizen has (excluding civil disobedience) is to hold their president and senators accountable for every judicial decision by an activist judge that goes against the written Constitution. Despotic, originally used by Jefferson, is an accurate descriptor because unelected judges are assuming power that belongs in the hands of the peoples' elected representatives.

US Senators
The party in control of the US Senate also has a significant impact, as the Senate must confirm all judicial appointments made by the president. Examining the senate confirmation votes of the last four justices illustrates the Democrat senators tend to vote for liberal-activist judges, and against originalist judges. The Republican senators are the opposite. They tend vote for originalist judges and against activist judges.

The Senate Confirmation Votes:

Kagan (Activist):	Democrat Senators	98% voted For;
	Republican Senators	12% voted For
Sotomayor (Activist):	Democrat Senators	100% voted For;
	Republican Senators	23% voted For
Roberts (Originalist):	Democrat Senators	50% voted For;
	Republican Senators	100% voted For
Alito (Originalist):	Democrat Senators	9% voted For;
	Republican Senators	98% voted For

The most recent Supreme Court Justice is Elena Kagan. She was widely thought to be a liberal-activist judge, and confirmed this suspicion with her vote on the Mojave Memorial Cross Case. The Senate vote to confirm Justice Kagan in 2010 was largely along party lines again: 63-37. The individual votes are shown in appendix 6.

A senator's voting record on judges needs to become a campaign issue for concerned citizens.

- **A senator voting to confirm a judge who bans religion, is the same as a senator voting to ban religion themselves.**

- **A senator voting to confirm a judge who takes away a citizen's economic freedom, is the same as a senator voting to remove the freedom themselves.**

The Senate has a constitutional role to confirm only qualified judges who will uphold the Constitution. Any senator who simply believes the Senate is a "rubber stamp" to confirm any judge the president appoints does not understand the Constitution.

Why has the Democrat Party, through the judiciary, adopted this despotic, religion-hostile position? Remember, Democrat presidents and senators who give these activist judges power are responsible for the resulting rulings. Banning religious activity is definitely hostile (as well as unconstitutional if the original intent is used). Are party grassroots members in favor of the position? Or is it a vocal minority lobby in Washington, DC pushing the position? Regardless, combining the Kagan confirmation vote with the Mojave Cross case, informs us that 98% of Democrat senators in essence voted to ban religion (a cross in this case).

Impeach Unlawful Judges
It is true that judicial nominees sometimes refuse to answer questions from senators that will allow them to judge the activist-originalist persuasion of the nominee. There is a remedy for this. Any federal judge who refuses to uphold the written text of the Constitution may be impeached. In an impeachment trial the Senate will vote whether the judge should be removed from office. It is a high bar as 2/3 of the Senate must vote to remove, but it is a way to hold the judges accountable once they are on the bench. In

turn, voters must hold their senators accountable.

Sidebar: While Republicans overall tend to place Constitution-honoring judges on the courts there are exceptions. Establishment Republican senator Mitch McConnell succeeded in placing a friend on the federal courts who happened to be a liberal activist judge.

> ### McConnell's Liberal Judge Forced Kentucky to Recognize Gay Marriages
>
> President George H. W. Bush nominated Judge G. Heyburn II in 1992 on Senator McConnell's recommendation. McConnell testified on behalf of Heyburn and called him an "excellent judicial appointment."
>
> However, Senator McConnell knew Heyburn was not a conservative. During his confirmation, McConnell called Heyburn a "progressive Republican."
>
> Senator McConnell recommended Heyburn because he was a friend and political supporter, not because he was committed to protecting the Constitution. Prior to his nomination, Heyburn worked as McConnell's general counsel and served as a county chairman for McConnell's campaign. Heyburn also donated to McConnell's campaign and helped stopped the rise of a potential Democratic challenger to McConnell.
>
> Last week's gay marriage decision is not the first time Judge Heyburn has trampled on the Constitution in order to impose his views on Kentucky. In 1998, Heyburn overturned the state's law banning partial-birth abortion.
>
> - www.senateconservatives.com. March 04, 2014.

Since McConnell evidently knew of the judges progressive leanings before nominating him, the voters of Kentucky should hold him accountable. In essence Mitch McConnell himself mandated Kentucky recognize gay marriages from other states, and overturned the state law on partial birth abortion.

The Pryor Example

An illustrative example of a Senator's personal views being irrelevant when voting as a Senator follows:

Judges and Senators

Embattled Pryor Invokes God, Bible in New Ad
Mark Pryor, the incumbent Democratic senator from Arkansas up for reelection next year, is releasing a new TV ad Wednesday in which he invokes his belief in God. The ad first aired on the news broadcast on ABC affiliate KATV in Little Rock Tuesday evening.

"I'm not ashamed to say that I believe in God and I believe in His word," says a bespectacled Pryor, who is holding an open Bible. "The Bible teaches us no one has all the answers--only God does. And neither political party's always right."

- www.weeklystandard.com. MICHAEL WARREN. Dec 4, 2013.

Let's assume Senator Pryor is sincere in his ad and truly does believe in God. The author certainly hopes that he does. As Christians, we want all people to know God and be saved by His Son. But, as voters, Christians are not voting for Pryor as a person. They are voting for him as a senator. Pryor's voting record indicates he does not follow his faith nor the Constitution when voting in the Senate. Senator Pryor is embattled because he voted for ObamaCare. This program is designed to give control of the entire medical industry to the federal government – an obvious violation of the 9th and 10th Amendments. Appendix 6 shows us that Senator Pryor also voted to confirm Elena Kagan to the Supreme Court. He also voted to confirm Sotomayor to the highest court. We have documented that these two are solid liberal activist judges greatly desired by the Democrat Party elites. As Senator, Mark Pryor voted for justices that will seek to ban God, and all symbols of Christianity from their positions on the court. While Mark Pryor may indeed be religious in his personal life, in his official duties as Senator, he ignores the Constitution and seeks to remove God from the public. Christians should wish Senator Pryor well, but vote to remove him from the Senate in the next election.

Democrat Senators Follow Party Line
The Democrat Party has become very good at getting the votes it needs from its members in the Senate, as seen in the vote tally on Supreme Court judicial nominees. This holds true for other areas as well. The two main legislative pushes of the Obama presidency were the $800+ billion dollar stimulus package in 2008 and the Affordable Care Act (ObamaCare) in 2009. In each of these, the

Democrats had 60 Senators and needed 60 votes to break a filibuster and pass the legislation. They got the votes they needed. Regardless of what the individual senators might have believed as individuals, or what they campaigned on. If there is ever a key vote that the liberal Democrat Party leadership needs for a judicial confirmation, or to pass a bill, the "moderate" senators fall into line and vote with the party.

A TV campaign commercial could be produced:

> Commercial: The Democrat Army Way
> Announcer: Some Democrat senators say they are liberal. Video: A close-up of a suited senator wearing a blue T-shirt with LIBERAL written on it.
>
> Announcer: Some Democrat senators say they are conservative. Video: A close-up of a suited senator wearing a red T-shirt with Conservative written on it.
>
> Announcer: Regardless of what they say or believe, the Democrat senators WILL vote the way they are told. Video: A group of senators standing in lines 3-4 deep as in an army inspection formation, mostly wearing liberal-blue shirts with a few conservative-red shirts present.
>
> Announcer: The Democrat senators always fall in line to do their duty to their party. Video: A look-a-like of Senate Majority Leader Harry Reid emerges dressed as a drill sergeant, wearing a blue beret.
>
> Reid addressing his "troops": We will pull together to pass this next bill.
>
> Senators in line-up, shouting in unison: Yes! Sir!
>
> Reid addressing his "troops": Just like we passed the Stimulus Bill
>
> Senators in line-up, shouting in unison: Yes! Sir!
>
> Reid addressing his "troops": Just like we passed ObamaCare
>
> Senators in line-up, shouting in unison: Yes! Sir!
>
> Reid addressing his "troops": I and President Obama need everyone of your votes again.

Judges and Senators

>Senators in line-up, shouting in unison: Yes! Sir!
>
>Video: President Obama look-a-like walks into view behind Reid.
>
>Obama: Sergeant, Are the senate troops ready?
>
>Reid, looking at Obama: Yes Sir! They are ready Sir!
>
>Obama: I'll need the troops to jump high to get my latest judge confirmed.
>
>Reid, addressing the troops: Hear the commander? Jump!
>
>Senate Troops: How! High! Sir!
>
>Reid: As high as you can! Jump!
>
>Video: The senate troops all jump in unison.
>
>Announcer: Regardless of what your Democrat senators say back home, when they go to Washington they become part of the Obama-Reid army, moving in lock-step with no dissent to pass ObamaCare, stimulus bills, bailout bills, and confirming activist judges that make their own law rather than following the Constitution.

This commercial is meant to be funny and mocking, but there is much underlying truth in it. Very few if any senators will go against the Democrat Party leadership wishes. Both parties pressure their senate members to "tow-the-party-line". Democrats just tend to be much more effective at this than Republicans.

It's time to hold elected senators accountable for their judicial confirmation votes as well as their other votes. No longer should politicians be able to place activist judges on courts and hide behind these judges' robes as religious activity is banned from society. As shown with Mark Pryor, it doesn't matter what the politician's personal beliefs are with respect to religion. What matters is the judges they place on courts. Senators confirming judges who ban religion are in effect voting to ban religion themselves.

<u>Christians Voting for the Banning of Christianity</u>
Most Christians attending a church service will pray the Lord's Prayer, taught to us by Jesus Himself. One of the petitions in this prayer is "Your Will be done on Earth as it is in Heaven." The

Christian is praying to God that God's will be done. God's will includes everyone knowing God and willingly worshiping Him. How can it then be God's will that God is banned from schools and other public places? Yet many of the same people praying this prayer will vote for federal politicians who place judges on the courts that use government power to ban God's Word.

The evidence has been presented in this chapter: **Christians voting for Democrat presidents, and Democrat senators, have voted to ban Christianity from the public forum.**

If you are a follower of God and a Democrat, are you going to do something about this? Will you work to change your party's position? Your senator's position? Or should you consider becoming independent and leaving a party that advocates the banning of religious activity? You have free will, so the choice is yours but wouldn't a person of faith either work to change the party position or leave the party? There is no reason for any party's leaders to reject religion in America, yet Democrats seem to have done so (More in Chapter 24).

Unless a Democrat senator specifically promises not to confirm activist judges, a vote for them is a vote to remove crosses and war memorials from public land and continued use of federal power to ban prayer and other religious activity. It is truly a shame that religious freedom and expression has become an issue where a major political party favors banning it. It does not have to be so. Both parties historically recognized the true meaning of the First Amendment. It could be this way again, if people of faith care enough to act. The author sincerely hopes all politicians will once again embrace constitutional religious freedom.

Christian Government Workers
Maybe you are reading this book and vote Democrat because you work for the government and consider your vote a "paycheck" issue. Voting Democrat means greater chances of future salary increases. It is your right as an American to vote for that reason (and any other reason). The question for you is: Are you going to let your party continue to ban religion?

Black Christians
A special message to Black Pastors and Black Christians (The author avoids using hyphenated-American terminology such as African-American; we are all American): Election polling has shown repeatedly that approximately 90% of Blacks vote for Democrat candidates. It also shows that most national Democrat politicians *cannot* be elected if they get only 50% of the black vote. This gives you tremendous power! If you simply tell your Democrat senators that you will not vote for them if they put religion-banning judges on the court, the senator will have to comply with your wishes – or lose their next election. Will you exercise this power?

Republicans Too
There are a few Republican senators who believe in confirming most judges that come before them for confirmation. They have a low standard for confirmation. If the reader has a Republican senator, do they rubber stamp every judge, both activist and originalist? Will you contact them and ask them to do their duty and uphold the Constitution by only confirming originalist judges?

It is up to the American people to understand the Constitution and vote for leaders who respect it. More will be covered on how to use voting strategy to secure constitutional freedoms in Chapter 25.

Abortion in the Bible and Constitution

"Abortion is advocated only by persons who have themselves been born." - Ronald Reagan

A Baby's Beating Heart Begins Early:
- Only 3 weeks and 1 day after fertilization, the heart begins to beat.
- By 4 weeks, the heart typically beats between 105 and 121 times per minute.
      - The Endowment for Human Development. www.ehd.org

A Baby - 20 Weeks After Conception

Stop abortions from being allowed after 20 weeks when a child feels pain. Stop the War on Children.

)•(heroic MEDIA

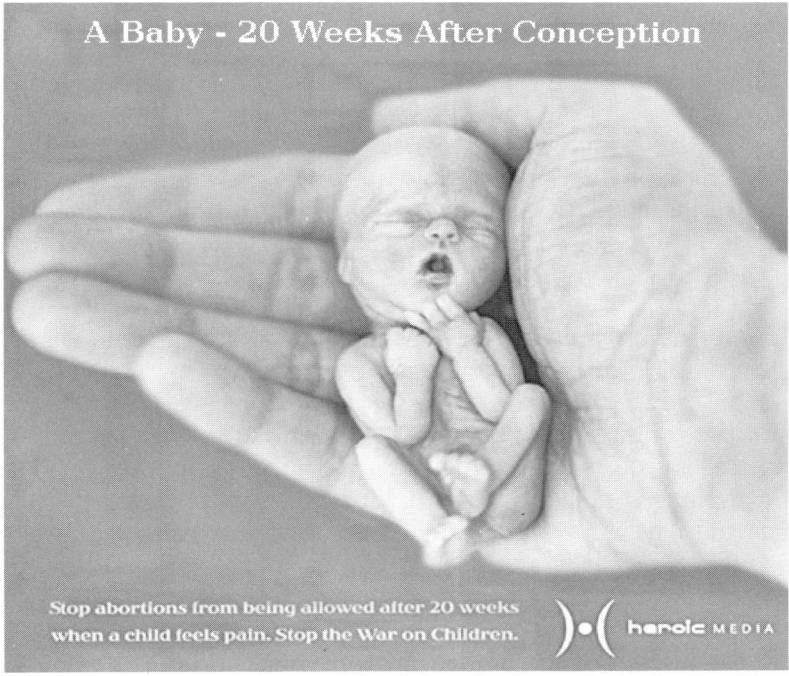

Photo of an unborn baby -- at 20 to 24 weeks (5 months in the womb).
- www.heroicmedia.org

From a human perspective, should all human life be valued and protected? Or just life that is convenient? A society that ceases to value all human life, and only values certain human life, can turn ugly very quickly. For example, those homeless people living on the streets – why not abort them? No one cares about them enough to provide them a home. They are not valuable. Just kill them. An elderly woman with no family left and confined to a bed may not be considered valuable to society. Should society abort them? Especially if the woman's money is gone and she is using healthcare resources that could go to another human being. Killing the woman is in society's best interest *if* there is no value placed on every life.

Most consider the previous two cases human life that should be protected by society. But what about an unborn baby? Is the baby in the womb a life and when does it become a life? Looking at the above picture, there can be little doubt that the baby in the womb IS a life. It's not a kidney, or a liver, or an eye. If one of these organs is removed from the body, it can never live on its own, and can never reproduce to form little organs. A baby in the womb, on the other hand, will be able to live on its own and reproduce. So should society protect this human life?

It is hard to recognize human life at conception, when there is only the tiny organism formed by the sperm and egg, so some could argue that this could indeed be killed. But within a few weeks there is a beating heart and blood flowing in the growing baby – not the mother's blood, but the baby's own blood that it has produced itself. At this point there is no question that it is a life, *a life distinct and distinguishable from the mother's.*

But, shouldn't a woman be free to have an abortion? Isn't it her free will to do so? An individual's free will always is restricted to not allow doing harm to another. A person has free will to make a fist but not the free will to punch another in the nose with it. State laws call this assault and will punish this harming of another individual. In the same manner, a woman having an abortion harms the baby, so her free will can be restricted. The woman still has free will to choose whether to have sexual relations and whether to use birth control devices. Unless the woman was raped.

Late-term abortion is an especially barbaric practice. What else would you call a procedure where a vacuum tube is inserted into a woman's womb and a baby (or fetus if you wish to dehumanize it) is sucked out through the tube?

Biblical Perspective
From a biblical perspective, the Bible clearly teaches against abortion and other forms of child sacrifice. Scripture teaches us that life begins in the womb.

Abortion in the Bible and Constitution

The Old Testament Law prescribes the same penalty for killing an unborn baby (fetus) as for killing a person.

Exodus 21:22 But if there is serious injury [to the fetus], you are to take life for life...

God repeatedly tells us life begins in the womb:

Psalm 22:10 From birth I was cast upon you; from my mother's womb you have been my God.

Psalm 139:13 For you created my inmost being; you knit me together in my mother's womb.

Isaiah 44:2 This is what the LORD says— he who made you, who formed you in the womb, and who will help you: Do not be afraid, O Jacob, my servant, Jeshurun, whom I have chosen.

Isaiah 44:24 "This is what the LORD says— your Redeemer, who formed you in the womb: I am the LORD, who has made all things, who alone stretched out the heavens, who spread out the earth by myself.

Isaiah 49:5 And now the LORD says— he who formed me in the womb to be his servant to bring Jacob back to him and gather Israel to himself, for I am honored in the eyes of the LORD and my God has been my strength.

Jeremiah 1:5 "Before I formed you in the womb I knew you, before you were born I set you apart; I appointed you as a prophet to the nations."
(This is a very strong passage to support life beginning at conception)

Hosea 12:3 In the womb he grasped his brother's heel; as a man he struggled with God.

Luke 1:41 When Elizabeth heard Mary's greeting, the baby leaped in her womb, and Elizabeth was filled with the Holy Spirit.

Luke 1:44 As soon as the sound of your greeting reached my ears, the baby in my womb leaped for joy.

Ecclesiastes 11:5 As you do not know the path of the wind, or how the body is formed in a mother's womb, so you cannot understand the work of God, the Maker of all things.

Once blood flows and a heart beats in a being, it is a life. Babies in the womb have beating hearts and their own blood flowing in their vessels.

Leviticus 17:14 because the **life of every creature is its blood.**

God also condemns child sacrifice to false gods, which was practiced by some cultures in the Old Testament. Molech was the false god that is most often mentioned.

Leviticus 18:21 Do not give any of your children to be sacrificed to Molech, for you must not profane the name of your God. I am the LORD.

Leviticus 20: 2-5 "Say to the Israelites: 'Any Israelite or any alien living in Israel who gives any of his children to Molech must be put to death. The people of the community are to stone him. I will set my face against that man and I will cut him off from his people; for by giving his children to Molech, he has defiled my sanctuary and profaned my holy name. If the people of the community close their eyes when that man gives one of his children to Molech and they fail to put him to death, I will set my face against that man and his family and will cut off from their people both him and all who follow him in prostituting themselves to Molech.

2 Kings 23:10 [Josiah] desecrated Topheth, which was in the Valley of Ben Hinnom, so no one could use it to sacrifice his son or daughter in the fire to Molech.

Jeremiah 32:35 [The people of Israel and Judah] built high places for Baal in the Valley of Ben Hinnom to sacrifice their sons and daughters to Molech, **though I never**

Abortion in the Bible and Constitution

commanded, nor did it enter my mind, that they should do such a detestable thing *and so make Judah sin.*

Remember that child sacrifice was a main reason God gave for ordering the death penalty for the people in the land of Canaan (See Chapter 5 God's Holy War) when the Israelites invaded. Is there any doubt that God would condemn today's practice of sacrificing children to the god of convenience through abortion?

In America today popular opinion on abortion is diametrically opposed to biblical teaching. Jesus did not eliminate the Law, He fulfilled the Law.

> *Matthew 5: 17-19 The Fulfillment of the Law*
> *"Do not think that I have come to abolish the Law or the Prophets; I have not come to abolish them but to fulfill them. For truly I tell you, until heaven and earth disappear, not the smallest letter, not the least stroke of a pen, will by any means disappear from the Law until everything is accomplished. Therefore anyone who sets aside one of the least of these commands and teaches others accordingly will be called least in the kingdom of heaven, but whoever practices and teaches these commands will be called great in the kingdom of heaven.*

Churches who have taught abortion is acceptable and not a sin are "least in the kingdom of heaven" according to Jesus. They are teaching a different law than the one God gave. They are restating God's Law, on their own, to suit there purposes. Some Christian politicians have also taught that abortion is OK, ignoring biblical teaching.

Sidebar: All humans break the Law and sin, hence the need for a Savior. If you are a woman who has had an abortion, or if you are a man who has encouraged a woman to have an abortion, it is clear you have sinned. God's Law convicts you. But as with other sins, if you repent, God will forgive you. God's Bible contains both Law and Gospel.

Constitutional Perspective

It is straightforward to believe that America's founders would have opposed abortion as they opposed slavery had it been an issue in their day. Abortion is not consistent with the overarching theme of "Life, Liberty, and the Pursuit of Happiness" that runs through the founding documents.

Since it wasn't an issue at the time of its writing, the Constitution does not speak to it. The country recognized this for many years, and it was left to state governments to make abortion law. All 50 states considered abortion to be illegal until the Supreme Court overstepped its authority and created a constitutional right to abortion.

Since abortion is not written into the Constitution, judges have no authority to declare it legal or illegal. As discussed in the previous chapter, a judge ruling on abortion is practicing judicial activism and is exceeding his or her authority. If the Constitution is amended to include abortion, then judges should rule on it. Until then, it is up to our elected representatives at the state level to make abortion law. That is where the Constitution places the responsibility. That is exactly where it was done until the Supreme Court usurped its role and interfered with state responsibility with its Roe v Wade decision in 1973. A state should decide whether abortion is legal or whether an abortion provider is committing murder just as a state government determines other laws in the state. The federal government should only make laws in the areas where it is constitutionally enabled.

Note the difference between abortion and slavery. The Supreme Court knew its proper role in the 1800s. It knew it did not have the power to ban slavery. It took constitutional amendments to ban slavery. But in the 1970s the Supreme Court arbitrarily changed the Constitution. There were no amendments banning or legalizing abortion. The justices just acted with no constitutional authority.

Politics of Abortion

Abortion frequently becomes an important issue in elections. It often arises because a journalist or debate moderator will question the candidates about the issue. The way the issue/question is posed makes it readily apparent whether the journalist has a liberal or conservative bias (See Chapter 23 for discussion on media bias).

A conservative biased journalist will question the candidate about partial birth abortion. This is a procedure where the baby is delivered from the womb, except for the head. The head is punctured while still in the womb causing the baby to die. Then the dead fetus is removed entirely from the womb. The Democrat Party platform calls for this and any other abortion procedure to be legal. It is a very difficult question for a pro-abortion-choice politician to handle. Many Democrat Party activists want this practice to remain legal, but large majorities of the population prefer the procedure be made illegal.

A liberal biased journalist (dominant in today's political journalism world) will question candidates about early term abortions where the woman was raped (or incest when a young woman is raped by her father). This is an especially tough question for a Republican politician to deal with. There are anti-abortion-choice Republican Party activists who believe all abortion should be illegal, and some will vote exclusively on this issue. Everyone can sympathize with an innocent woman being raped and having to deal with an unwanted pregnancy from her rapist, on top of the rape. Majorities of the population prefer abortion to be legal in these circumstances.

Two examples of the liberal bias version of the abortion question were prominent in the 2012 elections. Two conservative senate candidates, Todd Akin in Missouri and Richard Mourdock in Indiana, were asked rape-abortion questions and botched their answers. In fact their answers were so bad they are thought to have cost them their elections. Akin said in his answer, "If it's a legitimate rape, the female body has ways to try to shut that whole thing down." Mourdock said, "even when life begins in that horrible situation of rape, that is something that God intended to happen." There is no excuse for a politician, or anybody for that matter, saying something so offensive. While the author believes both candidates were struggling to enunciate a pro-life position, even if rape occurred the comments can be taken (or twisted) to minimize rape, a traumatic experience for both the woman and those who love her.

These rape questions and comments were also part of the strategy by the Democrat Party to create a media narrative that there was a "Republican War on Women". The author doesn't understand how so many political strategists can be so inept at dealing with such an accusation. That same election cycle, Bill Clinton was the keynote speaker at the Democrat Party National Convention. This is the same Bill Clinton who was publicly accused of *raping* a woman, Juanita Broderick. The allegation was credible enough to be aired on national television. It would seem to be easy to suggest that Bill Clinton waged a much more damaging "war on women" than any Republican. Or is a *comment* about rape more damaging to women than an *actual* rape?

Candidates Akin and Mourdock should have apologized for their offensive comments, then when the liberal-biased media continued to make an issue of them, they should have played the Clinton card, by stating something like: "My comment was offensive, I misspoke, and have apologized, but my comment pales in comparison to Bill Clinton, who allegedly raped a woman. I have never been accused of rape." With Bill Clinton being in the public eye, prominently on display at the Democrat Convention, there is no way he would not have responded. Clinton would probably claim he never raped anybody. In which case, the candidate's spokesmen could ask journalists whether they believe Clinton now since he was previously convicted of perjury (lying under oath) about sex. Now Bill Clinton is the bigger story, and the candidate comment is likely off the table for the remainder of the race. If either candidate's Democrat opponent tried to keep the issue alive, make them first condemn Bill Clinton, a Democrat icon.

In the future conservative political candidates for federal office can deal with abortion questions simply by stating that abortion, per the Constitution, is a matter left to the states. Since the candidate is running for federal office, abortion is not a campaign issue, so the question is irrelevant. The candidate can go on to pronounce support for judges who will recognize and rule that the Constitution leaves abortion law to the states. Unless the candidate is proposing a constitutional amendment to legalize or make abortion illegal, the abortion question is moot.

Voting

There are a number of Christians who are single issue voters on abortion. The author believes these voters should consider expanding this issue to focus on the broader issue of activist federal courts. If Christians had not let the courts ban prayer and the Bible from schools with activist judicial rulings, the courts would likely not have been able to intervene in abortion law either. Therefore focus on returning federal courts to their proper constitutional role. The way to do that is to hold your senators accountable. It is their votes which confirm every federal judge (Chapter 14). Those senators not vowing to vote down every activist judge coming before them do not deserve your vote.

US Senators' and US Representatives' personal beliefs and positions on abortion should be much less important than their views on the Constitution. Voters should expect their representatives to vote against federal spending on abortion, on the grounds that there is no constitutional authority for this type of expenditure. Likewise there isn't authority for representatives to pass a federal abortion law, which would be unconstitutional per the 10th Amendment (if the constitution is strictly interpreted). It will be governors and state legislators who will determine abortion law for their state, as was the case before the federal courts intervened. See more on voting strategy in Chapter 25.

Homosexuality and Marriage

> <u>Americans Have No Idea How Few Gay People There Are</u>
> Surveys show a shockingly high fraction think a quarter of the country is gay or lesbian, when the reality is that it's probably less than 2 percent.
>
> The Williams Institute at UCLA School of Law, a gay and lesbian think tank, released a study in April 2011 estimating based on its research that just 1.7 percent of Americans between 18 and 44 identify as gay or lesbian.....
> - The Atlantic. Garance Franke-Ruta. May 31, 2012.

This chapter will explore both homosexuality and homosexual marriage with respect to the Bible and the Constitution.

Homosexuality
 I. Biblical View of Homosexuality
    A) Jesus' Teaching
    B) Christians and Churches
    C) Defending the Bible Using a Savage Example
 II. Constitution and Government on Homosexuality
    A) Constitutional Rights
    B) Civil Rights Laws for Homosexuals
        1. Homosexuals as a Protected Class
        2. State Laws

A current topic in today's society is homosexual behavior. This chapter's focus is not about an individual's lifestyle choice. The author subscribes to the libertarian view that what two people willingly choose to do in private is their own concern. This view is also consistent with God-given free will. Ultimately, a homosexual will answer to God at death (as all humans will) where God will judge each of us. It is not up to Christians to judge others.

> *James 4:12 There is only one Lawgiver and Judge, the one who is able to save and destroy. But you—who are you to judge your neighbor?*

That does not mean that a follower of God, or a church, must accept or approve of homosexual behavior. They have free will as well. One of the duties of the church is to inform people of their sins and encourage them to repent and ask God for forgiveness. This is the reason why many mainstream churches will not allow open homosexuality in their membership. It's a sin, but the sinner refuses to repent. A responsible church would also take the same position for a perpetual liar, who refuses to admit lying is a sin and refuses to repent.

So if a person chooses to pursue a homosexual lifestyle, that is their right to do so. But they also have no right to force others to accept it. Isn't the best course of action to "live and let live"? In the author's opinion it really does no good for a Christian to preach at a committed homosexual. Likewise it does no good for a homosexual person to demand a Christian accept the homosexual lifestyle as normal (not sinful) which is contrary to biblical teaching.

Some have made the argument that homosexuality is OK because Jesus did not condemn it. That is a very misleading argument. The Old Testament laws were the constitution for Israel's society at Jesus' time (Chapter 6). As will be covered later in this chapter, these laws made homosexuality a death penalty offense. So homosexuals were not openly present in the society. Jesus was never asked about homosexuality. He would have no need to address sinful behavior that was not present. Several books of the New Testament targeted to non-Jewish societies do address homosexuality and label it as sinful behavior. As discussed in Chapter 7, the New Testament does not prescribe laws for government; rather it provides guidelines for individuals to lead a God-pleasing life. So homosexuality is no longer a death penalty offense, just a sinful behavior.

I. Biblical View of Homosexuality

> *If you keep my commands, you will remain in my love, just as I have kept my Father's commands and remain in His love. - Jesus speaking in John 15:10*

The biblical view of homosexuality is that it is sinful and results from temptation.

> *James 1:13-15 When tempted, no one should say, "God is tempting me." For God cannot be tempted by evil, nor does he tempt anyone; but each person is tempted when they are*

dragged away by their own evil desire and enticed. Then, after desire has conceived, it gives birth to sin; and sin, when it is full-grown, gives birth to death.

This passage speaks to sin and temptation in general. Every human is tempted by different things. Some covet or wish to steal the possessions of others, some love money or wealth in general, some are tempted by sexual relations outside of marriage. Still others are tempted by homosexual activity. There are endless temptations, and each person is unique in what will be most tempting to themselves. Without a doubt, there are some people that are very tempted by homosexual relationships.

Homosexual behavior is clearly identified as sinful in both Old and New Testaments. God has consistently condemned homosexuality. This practice is far from the only sin present in the world as Paul states below in Corinthians, but it is definitely a sin.

> *1 Corinthians 6:9-10, 18 Or do you not know that wrongdoers will not inherit the kingdom of God? Do not be deceived: Neither the sexually immoral nor idolaters nor adulterers* **nor men who have sex with men**, *nor thieves nor the greedy nor drunkards nor slanderers nor swindlers will inherit the kingdom of God..... Flee from sexual immorality. All other sins a person commits are outside the body, but whoever sins sexually, sins against their own body.*

In Romans, Paul links homosexual desires with punishment for abandoning belief in God. The Bible does not regard homosexuality as an acceptable lifestyle choice.

> *Romans 1:21-27 God's Wrath Against Sinful Humanity*
> *For although they knew God, they neither glorified him as God nor gave thanks to him, but their thinking became futile and their foolish hearts were darkened. Although they claimed to be wise, they became fools .....*
> *Therefore God gave them over in the sinful desires of their hearts to sexual impurity for the degrading of their bodies with one another. They exchanged the truth about God for*

a lie, and worshiped and served created things rather than the Creator—who is forever praised. Amen.
Because of this, God gave them over to shameful lusts. Even their women exchanged natural sexual relations for unnatural ones. **In the same way the men also abandoned natural relations with women and were inflamed with lust for one another. Men committed shameful acts with other men,** and received in themselves the due penalty for their error.

Other Bible passages condemning homosexuality and sexual impurity:

Galatians 5:19-21 The acts of the sinful nature are obvious: sexual immorality, impurity and debauchery; idolatry and witchcraft; hatred, discord, jealousy, fits of rage, selfish ambition, dissensions, factions and envy; drunkenness, orgies, and the like. I warn you, as I did before, that those who live like this will not inherit the kingdom of God.

Leviticus 18:22 Do not lie with a man as one lies with a woman; that is detestable.

Leviticus 20:13 If a man lies with a man as one lies with a woman, both of them have done what is detestable. They must be put to death; their blood will be on their own heads.

(As stated previously, this was one of the Old Testament laws that applied to ancient Israel. Homosexuality was a death penalty offense. See Chapter 6 for more detail.)

Genesis 19:4-7 Before they had gone to bed, all the men from every part of the city of Sodom - both young and old - surrounded the house. They called to Lot, "Where are the men who came to you tonight? Bring them out to us so that we can have sex with them." Lot went outside to meet them and shut the door behind him and said, "No, my friends. Don't do this wicked thing."

> *Jude 1:7 In a similar way, Sodom and Gomorrah and the surrounding towns gave themselves up to sexual immorality and perversion. They serve as an example of those who suffer the punishment of eternal fire.*

The biblical narrative tells us the men of Sodom and Gomorrah attempted to rape two visiting men who had come to save Lot - homosexual gang-rape.

These next passages refer to a proverbial term of reproach applied to those who practiced sodomy (ritual homosexuality).

> *Deuteronomy 23:17 No Israelite man or woman is to become a shrine prostitute.*
>
> *1 Kings 14:24 There were even male shrine prostitutes in the land; the people engaged in all the detestable practices of the nations the LORD had driven out before the Israelites.*
>
> *1 Kings 15:12 He expelled the male shrine prostitutes from the land and got rid of all the idols his fathers had made.*
>
> *1 Kings 22:46 He rid the land of the rest of the male shrine prostitutes who remained there even after the reign of his father Asa.*

Who can state after reading these passages, that God is accommodating toward homosexual activity?

A. Jesus' Teaching
The following story describes Jesus dealing with a woman who had committed adultery. It is highly applicable to homosexual behavior as well. In both cases the Old Testament law called for death of the lawbreaker, but Jesus introduced new treatment. This is one of many changes between the old covenant and the new covenant.

> *John 8:3-11 Jesus Treatment of an Adultering Woman*
> *The teachers of the law and the Pharisees brought in a woman caught in adultery. They made her stand before the*

> *group and said to Jesus, "Teacher, this woman was caught in the act of adultery. In the Law Moses commanded us to stone such women. Now what do you say?" They were using this question as a trap, in order to have a basis for accusing him.*
>
> *But Jesus bent down and started to write on the ground with his finger. When they kept on questioning him, he straightened up and said to them, "Let any one of you who is without sin be the first to throw a stone at her." Again he stooped down and wrote on the ground.*
>
> *At this, those who heard began to go away one at a time, the older ones first, until only Jesus was left, with the woman still standing there. Jesus straightened up and asked her, "Woman, where are they? Has no one condemned you?"*
>
> *"No one, sir," she said.*
>
> *"Then neither do I condemn you," Jesus declared. "Go now and leave your life of sin."*

Notice Jesus' teaching from the New Testament. He doesn't say adultery is no longer a sin. It still is. But there is no longer a death penalty for the offense. Jesus tells the woman to stop the sin, to not keep committing adultery. It is the same with homosexual behavior.

Sidebar: This is another example of God giving a law (no adultery) and a punishment (stoning) then changing part of the law – the punishment in this case. God can change His laws as He pleases. Humans cannot.

Jesus also makes God's view of homosexual activity and other immorality clear in Revelation. In these verses, Jesus dictates letters to Christian churches. (Those Bibles placing Jesus' words in red have these verses in red. They are Jesus' words.) Two verses speak of the Nicolaitans, a church group that taught it was acceptable to practice immorality, like homosexuality. Jesus strongly refutes this teaching and states that He hates the practice.

> *Revelation 2:6 But you have this in your favor: You hate the practices of the Nicolaitans, which I also hate.*

Homosexuality and Marriage

Revelation 2:15 Likewise, you also have those who hold to the teaching of the Nicolaitans. Repent therefore!

> Nicolaitans: A heretical sect within the church that had worked out a compromise with the pagan society. They apparently taught that spiritual liberty gave them sufficient leeway to practice idolatry and immorality.
> – Concordia Self Study Bible. p.1948.

Jesus is not hating the people. He is hating their immoral actions. Note Jesus' words: "hates the practices". In addition to hating immoral behavior, the verses can be interpreted to mean God hates the practices of approving or accommodating sinful actions. God's followers are not to teach activities which God defines as sinful to be acceptable.

Those churches that today seek to accommodate homosexual activity, or any other immoral activity, among their members, should study these verses. How is their attitude different from the Nicolaitans attitude of biblical times? It doesn't seem to be.

B. Christians and Churches

Christians practicing homosexuality and claiming it is not a sin are approaching dangerous territory. It is similar to the culture present late in John's (one of the 12 Disciples of Jesus) life. John addressed a culture under the influence of Gnosticism, which encouraged practicing sexual immorality. John's words are likely very applicable to today's culture where homosexuality and adultery have become common.

> This philosophy [Gnosticism] has led not only to flagrant immorality in exercise of fleshly desires, but also to the conclusion that God could not possibly have become flesh.
> – The Narrated Bible. F. LaGard Smith. P1656.

1 John 2: 4-5 Whoever says, "I know Him," but does not do what He commands is a liar, and the truth is not in that person. But if anyone obeys His word, love for God is truly made complete in them.

1 John 3: 4-6 Everyone who sins breaks the law; in fact, sin is lawlessness. But you know that He appeared so that He might take away our sins. And in Him is no sin. No one who lives in Him keeps on sinning. No one who continues to sin has either seen Him or known Him.

Christians sin. But Christians acknowledge their sin and go to Jesus to repent and ask for forgiveness. The danger territory for homosexuals is that they are not acknowledging their sin, nor asking for forgiveness.

Based on the numerous passages above it is clear that homosexual acts are sinful. So any Christian saying otherwise is not doing what God commands, and according to John, is a liar.

A church body that follows the Bible must also condemn homosexuality as a sin - if it wishes to follow God's teachings - in the same way it would condemn murder, theft, or adultery. Of course, a church has free will to adopt any position(s) it wishes on spiritual or political issues. But a church that doesn't follow the Bible's teaching is little more than a social group. Likewise, humans can use their God-given free will to practice homosexuality, just as humans have the free will to commit other sins.

Sidebar: How many times have you heard someone condemn Christianity or the Bible for being anti-homosexual? Yet these same people never seem to condemn the Muslim Sharia Law which contains the death penalty for homosexual behavior *in the present day*. Homosexuals are stoned to death in many Muslim countries. Shouldn't the *stoning to death* of a homosexual be condemned more severely than *calling them sinners*?

C. Defending the Bible Using a Savage Example
Followers of God should be able to defend the Bible and their faith from attacks. Defending often mean simply telling the truth about what the Bible states when taken in its entirety. For example, the following quotes came from Dan Savage, speaking at a supposed "anti-bullying" conference.

"People often point out that they can't help it, they can't help with the anti-gay bullying, because it says right there in Leviticus, it says right there in Timothy, it says right there in Romans that being gay is wrong. We can learn to ignore the bullshit in the Bible about gay people. The same way we have learned to ignore the bullshit in the Bible about shellfish, about slavery, about dinner, about farming, about menstruation, about virginity, about masturbation. We ignore bullshit in the Bible about all sorts of things. The Bible is a radically pro-slavery document."

"You can tell the Bible guys in the hall they can come back now because I'm done beating up the Bible. It's funny to someone who is on the receiving end of beatings that are justified by the Bible how pansy-ass people react when you push back."
- Dan Savage, at an "anti-bullying"conference. Mediaite.com. April 30. 2012

It seems from his comments that Dan Savage is a very angry individual. Dan is a homosexual and is angry that the Bible condemns his actions as a sin. But his issues are with God, not Christians. God gave us the Bible, and God defines homosexuality as sinful behavior. Dan is free to say whatever he wishes, but if he would read this book he would actually have a better understanding of what the Bible states. Let's analyze his comments, as an example of how to respond to people like Dan, assuming they want to have a conversation, and not just rant.

First of all, as a Christian, the author wants Dan to be saved. Christians want all humans to be saved rather than face eternal damnation. Christians are called to reach out to humans and teach them how to be saved by accepting Jesus as their Savior and recognizing God as He reveals Himself in the Bible. The author also respects Dan's free will to reject God and His teachings.

Dan talks of "bullying". Anyone "bullying" a fellow human being is not following the Bible's teachings and God's will, assuming that the "bullying" consists of physical assaults or verbal insults which are defined as sins. However, if Dan considers the Christian theology as stated in the Bible (homosexuality is a sin) as "bullying", then he needs to recognize everyone's right to free speech, including Christians.

The Bible and Constitution Made America Great

Dan correctly states that both Leviticus and Romans identify homosexuality as sinful behavior. What Dan fails to understand is the difference between the Old and New Testaments (covenants between God and His people). The Levitical laws in the Old Testament were given by God and were the law of the land (their constitution) for the people of ancient Israel (eating shellfish was also illegal). With the coming of Jesus and the sacking of Jerusalem in 70 AD by the Romans, the nation and those laws ceased to exist. The New Testament assumes God's followers now live among many nations. God's law still exists (with modifications) but it applies to the individual now (all foods, including shellfish, are acceptable for humans to eat). The individual chooses to follow God's Law, His recommendations for a healthy lifestyle, or not. This is God-given free will. Dan is free to ignore biblical teaching on homosexuality if he chooses. Much more detail was discussed in Chapters 6 and 7.

Tolerance should cut both ways. Dan and other homosexuals should respect lifestyle *choices* of Christians, and Christians should respect lifestyle *choices* of homosexuals. Tolerance does not equal approval. As stated earlier, it is curious that so many condemn Christianity for being intolerant, when the Muslim faith (at least how it is practiced in countries like Iran and Saudi Arabia) executes homosexuals. There is no tolerance in Islamic ruled countries for such activities. That is why it is so puzzling that Dan is very critical of the Bible, but not the Muslim faith. Sharia Law would be-head Dan for being a practicing homosexual. The author is unaware of any Christian nation that has a death penalty for homosexual acts.

Community laws are a different matter. Communities outlaw things all the time. Most communities will not allow a woman or a man to walk down the street naked. They will be arrested. Likewise a community could ban homosexual kisses (or even heterosexual kisses). What is legal and illegal is a discussion to be had between the community and its lawmakers.

Dan also states "The Bible is a radically pro-slavery document." Chapter 15 demonstrates the Bible is anti-slavery, not pro-slavery. Timothy clearly lists slave trading as an immoral, sinful behavior right along with homosexuality.

1 Timothy 1:10 for the sexually immoral, **for those practicing homosexuality, for slave traders** *and liars and perjurers—and for whatever else is contrary to the sound doctrine*

How does Dan see "homosexuality", but not "slave traders" when reading this passage? In all likelihood, Dan has never read the passage. He is just parroting what others have told him (incorrectly) the Bible says.

In summary, the Bible and Bible-following churches oppose homosexuality because it is a sin. With God-given free will, humans can make a life choice of homosexuality, but God states the choice is wrong. Since all are sinners, Christians should take care to condemn the sinful acts, rather than the sinner.

II. Constitution and Government on Homosexuality
The author has a libertarian view of government action with respect to homosexuality. As long as both participants are willing adults, they should be free to do what they wish with their bodies as long as they do not harm another. The Founding Fathers of America created the Constitution to be a very libertarian document as well. There is no authority for the federal government to become involved with homosexuality laws or regulations. However, American history shows that most, if not all states, did use their lawmaking authority to ban or restrict homosexual activity.

A. Constitutional Rights
It is humorous for some modern day liberal activist judges to "find" homosexual rights in the Constitution. Those judges just declared that all thirteen original states were in violation of the very document they ratified!

The Constitution leaves this area of law to the states. The states were far from accepting of homosexuality at the nations founding.

> The Founders on Homosexuality
> **Homosexuality was treated as a criminal offense in all of the original thirteen colonies**, and eventually

every one of the fifty states (see Robinson, 2003; "Sodomy Laws...," 2003). Severe penalties were invoked for those who engaged in homosexuality. In fact, few Americans know that the penalty for homosexuality in several states was death— including New York, Vermont, Connecticut, and South Carolina (Barton, 2000, pp. 306,482). Most people nowadays would be shocked to learn that Thomas Jefferson advocated "dismemberment" as the penalty for homosexuality in his home state of Virginia, and even authored a bill to that effect (1781, Query 14; cf. 1903, 1:226-227).
- www.apologeticspress.org. Dave Miller, Ph.D. May 23,2012.

So obviously there is nothing in the original constitutional text that forbids a state from banning homosexuality, and no amendments have been passed addressing homosexuality, States are free to regulate the practice as they wish. This doesn't mean that states should. The author's view is that what people do in their homes, that affects only themselves, should not be subject to state regulation.

According to the Constitution, states are allowed to regulate homosexual behavior if they so choose. Today, states do not actively regulate homosexual behavior, so a citizen in America can therefore freely choose to be a homosexual.

B. Civil Rights Laws for Homosexuals
Homosexual activists and some of their allies in the Democrat Party want to deem the civil rights laws in America to apply to homosexuals. The laws were not written to include homosexuals; they were written to prevent discrimination based on skin color. There is a key difference; the act of entering into a homosexual relationship is a choice. One can choose to have homosexual sex or not. The color of one's skin is not a choice. Humans are born with their skin pigment, just as they are born with their hair or eye color.

The Bible makes no judgment of humans based on skin color. In fact the Bible often mentions God seeing into one's heart and using that basis (personality) when evaluating humans. However, the Bible does list homosexual acts as sinful – not pleasing to God.

1. Homosexuals as a Protected Class

When a government gives homosexuals civil rights, a next logical step is to prevent homosexual activity from being criticized. That is the path Canada is following. It is truly sad to see a government promote and protect sinful behavior with the use of government force.

'Bible as Hate Speech' Signed into Law

Canadian measure said to 'chill' opposition to homosexual behavior.

Canada's governor general, the representative of Queen Elizabeth II, signed into law yesterday a controversial measure opposed by religious believers and free-speech advocates who say it will criminalize public expression against homosexual behavior.

The bill, passed 59-11 by the Senate on Wednesday, adds sexual orientation as a protected category in Canada's genocide and hate-crimes legislation, which carries a penalty of up to five years in prison.

As WorldNetDaily reported, opponents have feared if it becomes law, the Bible will be deemed "hate literature" under the criminal code in certain instances, as evidenced by the case of a Saskatchewan man fined by a provincial human-rights tribunal for taking out a newspaper ad with Scripture references to verses about homosexuality.

- WorldNetDaily.com. 04/30/2004

Canadian Pastor Fined and Gagged over Gay Comments

A Christian pastor in Canada has been fined $7,000 and told he must stop expressing his views on homosexuality in public.

The ruling orders Stephen Boissoin to "cease publishing in newspapers, by email, on the radio, in public speeches, or on the internet, in future, disparaging remarks about gays and homosexuals."

The scope of the ruling, which was delivered on Friday, has alarmed observers who are concerned about its impact on free speech and religious liberty.

- The Christian Institute. Tue, 10 Jun 2008.

The Bible and Constitution Made America Great

These examples occurred in Canada, where there is no strong First Amendment protecting citizens' speech and religion. However, do not be shocked if activist judges in America begin to ban the biblical teachings that they consider "hate speech". After all, by their warped reasoning, condemning homosexuality could be considered the same as "yelling fire" in a crowded theater, which is prohibited speech.

2. State Laws
States have the constitutional authority to make laws regulating homosexuality. In today's culture, many states are adopting pro-homosexual positions. This is especially prevalent in states with a large majority of Democrats. Chapter 11 details examples of states (California and Minnesota) developing and implementing pro-homosexual school curriculum for young children in grade schools. States have the authority to do this, but parents and Christians living in those states need to be on the alert to protect their faith and beliefs. It is truly sad in the opinion of the author, that some states are now choosing to teach children that homosexuality, a clearly-defined sinful behavior, is morally correct. Realize the difference between moral correctness and tolerance. Schools can teach tolerance without teaching sinful behavior is correct.

Homosexual Marriage
    I. Marriage and the Bible
    II. Definition of Marriage
    III. Madness of Changing Historic Societal Definitions
        A) Man-Woman
            1. Sports
            2. Bathroom Dilemma
            3. California Does It
        B) Products
    IV. Consequences of Redefining Marriage
        A) Traditional Terms Obsolete
        B) Homosexual Couples as a Protected Class
        C) State Benefits for Couples
    V. US Constitution on Marriage
        A) Defense of Marriage Act
        B) Traditional Marriage States
        C) Federal Government Forces Homosexual Marriage

Homosexuality and Marriage

I. Marriage and the Bible
Marriage is defined in the Bible as between a man and a woman. The word marriage appears in the Bible 47 times. In all instances it refers to a male-female union. Jesus Himself states plainly what constitutes a God-Pleasing marriage:

> *Matthew 19:4-6 "Haven't you read," he replied, "that at the beginning the Creator 'made them male and female,' and said, 'For this reason a man will leave his father and mother and be united to his wife, and the two will become one flesh'? So they are no longer two, but one flesh. Therefore what God has joined together, let no one separate."*

A few additional passages are quoted below. There are an additional 324 times the word wife is used, in reference to a woman's role as being married to a man.

> *Gen 2:24 That is why a man leaves his father and mother and is united to his wife, and they become one flesh.*
>
> *Jeremiah 29:6 Marry and have sons and daughters; find wives for your sons and give your daughters in marriage, so that they too may have sons and daughters.*
>
> *Hebrews 13:4 Marriage should be honored by all, and the marriage bed kept pure, for God will judge the adulterer and all the sexually immoral.*
>
> *1 Corinthians 7:3 The husband should fulfill his marital duty to his wife....*
>
> *Ephesians 5:33 However, each one of you also must love his wife as he loves himself...*

The Timothy and Titus letters describe how a church leader must be faithful to his wife.

> *1 Timothy 3:12 A deacon must be faithful to his wife and must manage his children and his household well.*
>
> *Titus 1:6 An elder must be blameless, faithful to his wife,....*

Anyone who follows the teachings of God in the Bible cannot accept homosexual marriage as "normal". It is sinful just as homosexuality is sinful. From a biblical perspective there is ample narrative of men having multiple wives. The most notorious was King Solomon who had numerous wives and concubines. It must be remembered that Bible narrative tells only the facts of what happened, both good and bad. It is necessary to go back to Genesis to learn that God intended one man and one wife for marriage.

> Sidebar: Those knowing their Bible history will know that the kings of ancient Israel often had multiple wives. This is not an endorsement by God of polygamy. Rather it is an historical account of followers of God not following His plan and intentions. Humans have always sinned from the time of Adam, and will continue to sin. It is interesting to note that there are historical examples of polygamous marriage, but no historical examples of homosexual marriage.

II. Definition of Marriage

> **Marriage: Legal union of a man and a woman.**
> - Oxford American Desk Dictionary and Thesaurus. Second Edition. July 2001.

Dictionaries have historically defined marriage as between a man and a woman. **This has been the societal definition of marriage for thousands of years.** Some are now trying to *alter* the definition by adding a homosexual variant. A recent definition is listed below. Note the wording "opposite sex" is now necessary for the first definition and "like a traditional marriage" for the second definition. Look how complicated things get as people attempt to change the historical definition of the word "marriage".

> New Modified Definition of *MARRIAGE*
> 1 The state of being united to a person of the opposite sex as husband or wife in a consensual and contractual relationship recognized by law.
> 2 The state of being united to a person of the same sex in a relationship like that of a traditional marriage.
> – www.merriam-webster.com. 2012.

<u>Further Modified Definition of *MARRIAGE*</u>
3 The state of being united to multiple persons in a relationship like that of a traditional marriage.
4 The state of being united to a sibling or child in a relationship like that of a traditional marriage.
5 The state of being united to a favorite pet in a loving relationship.

Definitions 3 - 5 were added by the author, and are not present in the dictionary (at least for now). But if a society is going to redefine words, how much longer will it be before these definitions are included as well? If the second definition can be added, why not definitions 3 - 5? States should have a lengthy public debate before going down the road of legal redefinitions.

There is no "traditional" and "non-traditional" marriage. Homosexual activists are trying to redefine marriage to include man-man and woman-woman homosexual relationships. They should not be allowed to do so. By redefining the definition of marriage, they hope to "normalize" homosexuality in society. A homosexual relationship is not a marriage and never will be. Call it a "civil union", a "love-pact", a "domestic-partnership" or whatever you want. But let the historical definition of marriage stand.

The historical definition of marriage does not discriminate against homosexuals. A homosexual man may choose to marry a woman if he chooses. He may also choose to enter a sexual partnership agreement with another man. Homosexuals have free will from God to pursue any type of sexual partnership they desire, including sinful ones. But if a person wants to enter a "marriage" it means an opposite sex relationship. These are societal and legal definitions that have always applied.

<u>III. Madness of Changing Historic Societal Definitions</u>
There is usually a good reason when societies throughout history have defined behaviors in a certain manner. One of these just discussed is marriage being between a man and a woman. A man-woman bond is important to society, because that is the only way to produce children, the next generation for the society. No children, and the society dies. Lets look at another crucial societal definition,

for man and woman.

A. Man and Woman
This is even more fundamental than marriage, and obviously is determined at birth. Society needs both men and women in equal numbers to be healthy.

> MAN: an individual human; an adult male human.
> WOMAN: an adult female person
> - www.merriam-webster.com

But what if a man wants to be considered a woman? Is the man free to add a second definition? What are the societal effects? Let's assume society allows woman to be redefined as it is proposed for marriage to be defined.

> WOMAN : (2) an individual human that wishes to be considered a woman like that of a traditional female.

1. Sports
This redefinition could be very advantageous for some men. Say a male basketball player isn't good enough to receive a scholarship at a major college, but is capable of starring were he to play on the women's team. By creating this new definition, the basketball player can compete and earn a scholarship on the women's team. Why should this male be punished by a societal definition? The student could also join the women's basketball team and if he had average athletic ability for a male, would likely become a dominant force competing against "traditional" females. The student might enjoy being the star of the women's team, rather than a bench-warmer for the men's team. There are many good female athletes, but in a standard population the top women cannot play hoops as well as the top men.

Or take it to the next level. Here's a potential real world example that would be rocking the professional sports world in California were the societal definition to change.

Candace Parker plays for the WNBA's Los Angeles Sparks where she reportedly makes around $100,000 a year. A pittance compared to the NBA, but still a nice salary. Candace is listed on the roster as a center/forward and is 6' 4" tall. She is also one of the few women who have dunked the basketball in games. In the NBA, forwards are usually a 6' 8" and up. 6' 4" is a good size for a guard. Anyone watching an NBA game or even an NCAA college game will realize men of that size *routinely* dunk the ball. They tend to be extremely athletic.

So here's the opportunity for a male basketball player to be a star, and make $100,000 per year. Just claim to be a woman inside and try-out for the Sparks. A male 6' 7" small forward who is not good enough to play in the NBA, is capable of being a dominating center in the WNBA – easily dunking against the smaller women. Maybe the man sells it buy growing "her" hair out a little and wearing lip gloss.

2. Bathroom Dilemma
A simple reason society defines man and woman is for privacy reasons while using the bathroom or lockerroom. What if a high school male begins wearing pink shirts and declares his gender preference is to be female? The student might enjoy entering women's restrooms and locker rooms. Heck, the student could even date another woman, if the student claimed to have the identity of a *lesbian* woman.

In a short time, the words man and woman will cease to mean anything at all in a society foolish enough to alter the meanings of words.

3. California Does It
The author thought these examples would illustrate the stupidity of changing and merging the definitions of man and woman. However, the author was shocked to learn that there is a bill in the state of California that would make this absurdity law!

> California Bill Would Allow Students to Use Bathrooms 'Consistent with His or Her Gender Identity'
> Assembly Bill 1266, introduced by Democratic Assemblyman Tom Ammiano, who represents a section of the city of San Francisco would:

"...require that a pupil be permitted to participate in sex-segregated school programs and activities, including athletic teams and competitions, and use facilities consistent with his or her gender identity, irrespective of the gender listed on the pupil's record."

California Gov. Brown Signs Transgender Student Bill
California has become the first state to enshrine certain rights for transgender K-12 students in state law, requiring public schools to allow those students access to whichever restroom and locker room they want.
- Newsmax.com. Aug12, 2013.

How long will it be before a man tries out for the WNBA Sparks? California law will not let the Sparks discriminate against the man for not being an actual woman. As long as the man claims to be a woman inside.

B. Products
Another example of words having meanings occurs in everyday life as products are used. If a person wants to drive a car, they are free to buy a car and drive it. If a person wants to drive a truck, they may buy a truck and drive it. But by definition, a person cannot buy a truck and claim to be driving a car.

If a person buys a computer, there are two main types: Macs or PC's. The definitional history goes back to the early days of the industry, where Apple made Macs, and IBM and others manufacturers made PC's. People have the choice to buy a Mac or a PC. They should chose the type that best meets their needs. However, a person cannot buy a PC and claim to have bought a Mac. It is not discrimination against the buyer, who had the option of buying a Mac.

Substitute relationship for computer. A marriage is a type of relationship, just like a Mac is a type of computer. If one wants a marriage, marry. If one wants a same-sex relationship, have one. Both are relationships, but they are not the same.

IV. Consequences of Redefining Marriage

Once marriage is redefined according to activists to be nothing more than a mutual, consenting, loving relationship, the door is open for siblings to marry, for men to marry multiple women, for women to marry multiple men, for parents to marry their children, and for men or women to marry their pets. Why not allow a woman to marry her Border Collie dog? Who is to place *any* restrictions on marriage. Everyone should have the freedom to marry according to activists. Marriage no longer means anything.

A. Traditional Terms Obsolete

Once a society begins to redefine terms such as marriage it cannot not stop there. Other logical changes will also happen. For example: France is eliminating "Mother" and "Father" as legal terms and replacing them with "parents" to accommodate homosexuals who have "married".

> France set to ban the words 'mother' and 'father' from official documents
> France is set to ban the words "mother" and "father" from all official documents under controversial plans to legalize gay marriage. The move, which has outraged Catholics, means only the word "parents" would be used in identical marriage ceremonies for all heterosexual and same-sex couples.
> - The Telegraph. September 24, 2012.

Ontario, Canada already took this action as soon as homosexual "marriage" became law. If marriage is no longer one man and one woman, terms like husband and wife must be eliminated as well.

> "Man and Woman", "Wife", "Husband", "Widow", "Widower" Banished From all Ontario Law
> TORONTO, February 25, 2005 (LifeSiteNews.com) – With the obscenely rapid, three-day introduction and passage of its same-sex "marriage" Bill 171, the Ontario government has advanced a revolutionary change in the way all laws and government programs and institutions refer to marriage and married persons. Everything referring to spouses must now be gender neutral. No longer can a married couple be referred to as "husband and wife" or "man and woman".

States in the America redefining marriage for homosexuals will likely follow-up with this change as well. The state of Washington is leading the way after passing its same-sex marriage law.

> <u>State to Eliminate "Bride" & "Groom" on Marriage Certificates</u>
> The words "bride" and "groom" – along with "husband" and "wife" are about to become archaic language in Washington state as officials prepare to remove the terms from marriage and divorce certificates...... the changes are necessary in response to the same-sex marriage law...
> - Foxnews.com. Todd Starnes. Nov 28, 2012.

This illustrates perfectly that once marriage has been redefined, terms like "bride", "groom", "husband" and "wife" can no longer be used. They are obsolete, and may be offensive to the small minority of homosexuals who insisted on changing the definition of marriage to begin with. Why are historically common societal words being changed to accommodate less than 2% of the population?

<u>B. Homosexual Couples as a Protected Class</u>
Similar pro-homosexual laws recently passed in Oregon make it illegal to discriminate against homosexuals. A baker, who is a Christian follower of God, politely refused to make a wedding cake for a homosexual couple. The baker should have the right to follow his religious beliefs, and the free will to choose who he wants to serve with his business. But maybe not in Oregon.

> <u>Did a baker break the law when he denied service to same-sex couple?</u>
> GRESHAM, Ore. -- A Gresham baker is the subject of a state investigation after he refused to make a wedding cake for a same-sex couple... That's what Oregon Attorney General's civil enforcement officers are looking into after one of the brides-to-be filed a complaint on Jan. 28.
>
> The woman who filed the complaint said she had previously bought a cake from Sweet Cakes for her mother's wedding. It was fine. But when her partner went back for their wedding cake on Jan. 17, the owner refused....
>
> "I apologized for wasting their time and said we don't do

same-sex marriages," he said. I "honestly did not mean to hurt anybody, didn't mean to make anybody upset, (it's) just something I believe in very strongly."

But beliefs aren't enough to cover him under state law. The Oregon Equality Act of 2007 prohibits discrimination against people based on their sexual orientation and gender identity. The statute includes public accommodations, such as businesses.
- Erica Nochlin, KATU News and KATU.com. Staff Published: Feb 1, 2013

The homosexual woman has the free will to chose another baker to make her wedding cake. There are plenty who will gladly accept her business. But instead, she attempts to use *government force* to make the baker make her a cake. This case is not Christians and homosexuals living in harmony; it is homosexuals forcing their lifestyle onto others.

The baker, because he chose to live according to his religious beliefs, will now face a state investigation. Of course he can always go to the Supreme Court and demand his constitutional rights be protected. But which judges are on the Court when his case gets there? Will there be a majority made up of liberal-activist judges appointed by Democrat presidents (Chapter 14)? They will likely decide that "homosexual rights" trump "religious rights" and there are no "constitutional issues" with government force being used to dictate how a citizen runs his business. Remember, activist judges twist the Constitution to mean whatever they want it to mean.

This story has a sad ending as the family finally gave up and closed their bakery store.

> Bakers Who Refused to Make Gay Couple's Wedding Cake Shut Down their Shop Following Threats, Anger
> Aaron and Melissa Klein, owners of Sweet Cakes by Melissa, an Oregon-based bakery that has fallen under intense scrutiny. Throughout 2013, the Christian couple and their business have been in the midst of a media firestorm after refusing to make a wedding cake for a lesbian couple. From threats to vicious phone calls and e-mails, the Klein family has been inundated with angry responses. Now, Aaron and

Melissa have announced that they are shutting down their shop.

From proclamations that Aaron should be shot to one apparent threat that he be raped, the hate and angst being thrown the Klein family's way is certainly serious in nature. Some have even wished for the couple's five children to be stricken with illness.
- TheBlaze.com. 09/02/2013.

Is there a better example of intolerance than this: death and rape threats against small business owners because they decided their religious beliefs did not allow them to participate in a homosexual marriage ceremony? The pro-homosexual activists lobby the people for acceptance and tolerance, but they seem unwilling to return the favor. Homosexual marriage is not about live-and-let-live. It is about forcing the population at large to accept homosexuality as a normal, mainstream behavior. Meanwhile, God has told us homosexuality is a sin and detestable behavior.

Another example of a state trying to force certain moral behaviors on their citizens is occurring in Washington. The state is attempting to force a Christian business to service a homosexual wedding ceremony.

State sues florist over refusing service for gay wedding
The state attorney general has filed suit against a florist in Eastern Washington, claiming her refusal to provide floral arrangements for a gay couple's wedding amounted to discrimination.

"Under the Consumer Protection Act, it is unlawful to discriminate against customers on the basis of sexual orientation," Attorney General Bob Ferguson said in a statement. "If a business provides a product or service to opposite-sex couples for their weddings, then it must provide same-sex couples the same product or service."
- Seattle Times. Lornet Turnbull. April 9, 2013.

Surely though a judge would never force a religious institution to violate its faith teachings. Wrong. An activist judge has already ruled that religious freedom can be reduced for "important societal goals" like homosexual marriages.

> <u>Judge Rules Christian facility cannot ban same-sex civil union ceremony on its own premises</u>
> A New Jersey judge ruled against a Christian retreat house that refused to allow a same-sex civil union ceremony to be conducted on its premises, ruling the Constitution allows "some intrusion into religious freedom to balance other important societal goals."...
>
> In March 2007, Ocean Grove Camp Meeting Association declined Harriet Bernstein and Luisa Paster's request to rent its Boardwalk Pavilion for the ceremony. The couple sued, claiming they had been discriminated against on the basis of their sexual orientation. In December 2008, the state Division on Civil Rights found the Christian campground had likely violated the state Law Against Discrimination (LAD) and joined the case.
>
> The United Methodist Church teaches, "The practice of homosexuality is incompatible with Christian teaching," and that "ceremonies that celebrate homosexual unions shall not be conducted by our ministers and shall not be conducted in our churches."
>
> - Lifesitenews.com. Ben Johnson. Jan 13, 2012.

How long will it be before a judge rules a Christian minister must marry a homosexual couple? It's coming if Christians do not engage politically by voting only for representatives who will protect their constitutional rights. Those politicians who freely trample (or let judges trample) your rights should never receive your vote. If Christians want religious freedom for themselves and for their fellow Christians, they must become engaged politically by voting for candidates who will protect those freedoms.

<u>C. State Benefits for Couples</u>
States have always imposed restrictions on marriage. Which state will let a man have multiple wives, or a woman multiple husbands? None. Polygamy is illegal. These consenting adults may indulge in these relationships, but they cannot be legal marriages under state laws. The same applies to a man wishing to marry his sister or a woman wishing to marry her brother. It will not be a recognized

marriage under state law. Likewise it is illegal for a person to marry their father or mother. It is also illegal to marry a pet. There are numerous relationships that are not recognized as legal marriages. Marriage is a privilege and not a right. A person simply cannot legally marry anyone or anything they choose. States define what is and is not a legal marriage.

The law has traditionally offered advantages to married couples. However, states are free to pass laws allowing any contractual relationship they choose. If a state wished to expand these advantages to non-married partners, that is up to the representatives and legislature of that state. However the state should probably then expand the advantages to all heterosexual or homosexual partnerships.

For example, if a man has a job with great insurance benefits and wishes to add an unemployed male friend as a roommate and temporary partner for the purposes of including him on his insurance plan, that should also be allowed. If two female sisters living together wish to enter a into a partnership for tax benefits, that should also be allowed.

V. US Constitution on Marriage

The actions by states detailed earlier forcing citizens to do business with homosexuals are likely unconstitutional on the grounds of a violation of religious beliefs. In the Bible, homosexuality is clearly listed as a sin and marriage is defined as one man and one woman.

> 1st Amendment: Congress shall make no law respecting an establishment of religion, or prohibiting the free exercise thereof; ....

> 14th Amendment: No State shall make or enforce any law which shall abridge the privileges or immunities of citizenship of the United States.

An even stronger case is made using the 9th Amendment.

> 9th Amendment   The enumeration in the Constitution, of certain rights, shall not be construed to deny or disparage others retained by the people.

In other words, the listing of only a few specific rights does not deny the other rights people have. What right is more fundamental to freedom than the right to choose who a citizen does business with? A citizen cannot be considered free when government force is used to dictate which customers they must serve or where they must shop.

The Constitution does not speak to marriage directly, leaving that area of law to the states. So if states want to go down the path of redefining marriage, they are free to do so. It does address the need for states to honor other states' laws for the betterment of the nation.

> <u>Article. IV. Section. 1.</u>
> Full Faith and Credit shall be given in each State to the public Acts, Records, and Judicial Proceedings of every other State. And the Congress may by general Laws prescribe the Manner in which such Acts, Records and Proceedings shall be proved, and the Effect thereof.
>> [The clause] was an essential mechanism for creating a "union" out of multiple sovereigns.... [James Madison] listed the clause as one of several that "provide for the harmony and proper intercourse among the states."
>> - Heritage Guide to the Constitution. P267.

The Constitution, with this clause and support by Congress, allows marriages in one state to be recognized by other states. For example, a married couple that moves from California to Arizona will not need to remarry in Arizona. Their marriage is already recognized and legal.

A. Defense of Marriage Act
Recognition of state marriages is very straightforward and simple *as long as states keep to the widely accepted legal definition of marriage as between a man and a woman.* But some states have not done so – a few have sought to also legally recognize man-man and woman-woman homosexual marriage. Congress has used its constitutional power to regulate these outlying states.

Congress responded with the Defense of Marriage Act.

> DOMA enables each state to refuse to recognize other states' acts, records, and judicial proceedings purporting to validate same-sex marriages.
> - Heritage Guide to the Constitution. P268.

Therefore, by constitutional definition, a homosexual marriage may, or may not, be legally recognized by other states. It is left up to each state to decide.

President Obama has decided not to enforce the Defense of Marriage Act.

> Seeking the real Obama on marriage
> On Feb. 23, Attorney General Eric Holder announced that President Obama and he had concluded that the Defense of Marriage Act's definition of marriage was discriminatory and unconstitutional.
>
> Holder further announced that the Department of Justice would not defend the statute in two district courts, and he released a letter he had sent to congressional leaders informing them of this decision.
> -WashingtonExaminer.com. Chris Gacek. 03/30/11

The president and his attorney general are hoping a liberal activist judge will have an easier time ruling against DOMA if they do not do their constitutionally required duty to defend the law. Obama swore to uphold laws like this when he became president. Congress makes federal law, and presidents enforce that law.

DOMA does not prevent states from changing the legal definition of marriage for their state if they choose to. They do have the legal right to do this. But why not create man-man or woman-woman civil unions or other contractual relationships for their states instead? It avoids the legal confusion and commotion that is occurring because of the attempts to change marriage. Wouldn't it be simpler to leave the age-old definition of marriage as being between a man and a woman? As stated earlier, this is not discriminatory to homosexuals. Homosexual men have the right to marry women; homosexual women have the right to marry men.

Homosexuality and Marriage

B. Traditional Marriage States
While some states are embracing pro-homosexual marriages, the voters in other states are not. These states are countering the problems caused by homosexual activists by defining marriage in their state constitutions.

> North Carolina voters approved a constitutional amendment on Tuesday defining marriage solely as a union between a man and a woman, making it the 30th U.S. state to adopt such a [definition].   - AP. 05/08/2012.

Sidebar: Some libertarian-minded people say "Get the government out of marriage entirely. I don't care who my neighbor marries." What these people really mean is "I don't care who my neighbor has a relationship with." That is respecting the neighbor's free will. However, as covered earlier marriage is a specific, historic, legally defined term, that cannot be altered without consequences. Homosexual activists do not stop at marriage. Remember the instances of government force being used to make citizens do business with homosexuals. Pro-homosexual agendas are being pushed into schools as well (See Chapter 11 for details). Recognition of homosexual marriage is often followed by "educating" children that some families have two mommies or two daddies, and these are good, wholesome families. This teaching violates the religious freedom of the majority of parents who are Christian.

C. Federal Government Forces Homosexual Marriage
Some are not content to let states define marriage for themselves. They wish to force homosexual marriage upon every state. This effort is led by homosexual activists and many in the Democrat Party, as discussed earlier with the actions of President Obama and Attorney General Holder. The main thrust is carried out by judges appointed and confirmed by Democrats.

> Federal judge strikes down Texas gay marriage ban
> A federal judge, saying he was complying with the U.S. Constitution and not trying to defy the people of Texas, struck down Texas' ban on gay marriage, but left it in place Wednesday pending a ruling by an appeals court later this year.

Judge Orlando Garcia issued his ruling in Austin in response to a challenge by two gay couples of the state's 2005 constitutional amendment, which had been approved by 76 percent of voters, and a 2003 law banning gay marriage.

Garcia's decision, however, rejected the argument by the office of Texas Attorney General said each state has the right to define marriage as best fits the traditions of its citizens. Texas also argued that traditional marriage best supports the state's interest in the area of procreation and child rearing.

"After careful consideration, and applying the law as it must, this Court holds that Texas' prohibition on same-sex marriage conflicts with the United States Constitution's guarantees of equal protection and due process," Garcia wrote in a 48-page opinion. "Texas' current marriage laws deny homosexual couples the right to marry, and in doing so, demean their dignity for no legitimate reason."

He continued that regulation of marriage "has traditionally been the province of the states and remains so today," but that "any state law involving marriage or any other protected interest must comply with the United States Constitution."

... Garcia, who was nominated to the federal bench by President Bill Clinton in 1994.
 - USA TODAY. Doug Stanglin and Michael Winter. February 26, 2014.

Did you vote for Bill Clinton? Did you realize you were also voting for a federal judge, appointed by Clinton, to override state laws and state constitutions and create a "right" for homosexual marriage? Chapter 14 discusses how Democrats and activists use federal judges to implement their agendas.

Some have proposed a constitutional amendment to define marriage. This is an effort to reign in liberal-activist judges. These judges imposed liberal morality on the states in forcing them to allow abortion. The fear is liberal-activist judges will do the same with marriage, forcing all 50 states to accept homosexual marriage. An amendment defining marriage treats the symptom, not the problem. The problem is activist judges forcing their political views on the country with their rulings. Judges should use the words and meaning of the constitution, including respecting those rights left to the states. Judges not willing to do this should face *impeachment and removal from office*. This is a more logical course of action than pursuing an amendment.

Who cares if American society follows biblical teaching if not Christians? It will fall on Christians and the Church to make federal judges an issue in presidential and senatorial elections.

Slavery in the Bible and America

The Bible teaches that all humans are creations of God and are all related. Genesis begin with Adam and Eve, the first humans. It later describes Noah and his three sons (and their wives) as the only survivors of a great worldwide flood. If records were perfect, every human could trace ancestral lineage to Noah. God instructed the survivors to "Be fruitful and increase in number and fill the Earth." But, instead of filling the Earth, the people clustered and began building a great tower (Tower of Babel). So God scattered them by confusing their language. The Bible doesn't give more detail, but if the intent is to divide and scatter the people, the most effective way would be to use physical appearance (genetics) as well as language. With people looking different and speaking different languages, they migrated apart from each other – to what is now Europe, Asia, Africa and the Americas. **The Bible teaches EVERY human is related by common ancestry.**

Unfortunately, being sinful, humans also began to think their own groups were superior, and other groups were inferior. The extreme of this behavior resulted in slavery in early America. The Bible speaks against the practice of forcing one human to work for another as a slave.

As has been written in earlier chapters, the Bible must be taken in its entirety. Passages about issues such as slavery cannot be examined in isolation if proper understanding is to be obtained. The passages below are all-encompassing, and indicate a follower of God is to show love toward everyone (neighbors and enemies, as well as, servants).

> *Leviticus 19:18 Do not seek revenge or bear a grudge against anyone among your people, but love your neighbor as yourself. I am the LORD.*
>
> *Matthew 5:43-44 "You have heard that it was said, 'Love your neighbor and hate your enemy.' But I tell you, love your enemies and pray for those who persecute you.*

Obviously, forcing a person to work as a slave is not consistent with these general directives from God telling humans to love one another. But, the Bible also directly and strongly condemns the practice of kidnapping people and forcing them into slavery.

Slavery is described as evil and the death penalty is prescribed for such action in the Old Testament.

> *Exodus 21:16 Anyone who kidnaps someone is to be put to death, whether the victim has been sold or is still in the kidnapper's possession.*
>
> *Deuteronomy 24:7 If someone is caught kidnapping a fellow Israelite and treating or selling them as a slave, the kidnapper must die. You must purge the evil from among you.*

Similarly, in the New Testament, slave trading is condemned. The action is listed as ungodly and sinful along with murder, perjury and homosexuality. These practices are clearly against God's Law.

> *1 Timothy 1:8-11 We know that the law is good if one uses it properly. We also know that the law is made not for the righteous but for lawbreakers and rebels, the ungodly and sinful, the unholy and irreligious, for those who kill their fathers or mothers, for murderers, for the sexually immoral, for those practicing homosexuality,* ***for slave traders*** *and liars and perjurers— and for whatever else is contrary to the sound doctrine that conforms to the gospel concerning the glory of the blessed God, which he entrusted to me.*

Both Old and New Testaments condemn slavery and regard it as against the will of God.

Old Testament
So why do some Old Testament laws regulate slaves? The slaves described in the Bible would be called indentured servants using today's definitions. The slaves among ancient Hebrews were poor people who willingly sold their services for a period of time. It was a way to make a living. So the Bible gives the following rules for citizens who sold themselves as slaves.

> *Exodus 21:2-3 "If you buy a Hebrew servant, he is to serve you for six years. But in the seventh year, he shall go free, without paying anything. If he comes*

alone, he is to go free alone; but if he has a wife when he comes, she is to go with him.

Leviticus 25:39-40 "'If any of your fellow Israelites become poor and sell themselves to you, do not make them work as slaves. They are to be treated as hired workers or temporary residents among you; they are to work for you until the Year of Jubilee.

Deuteronomy 15:12 If any of your people — Hebrew men or women — sell themselves to you and serve you six years, in the seventh year you must let them go free.

The Bible goes on to state a slave (servant) should be treated generously and given provision to begin their new life of freedom after their period of serving is over.

Deuteronomy 15:13-15, 18 And when you release them, do not send them away empty-handed. Supply them liberally from your flock, your threshing floor and your winepress. Give to them as the LORD your God has blessed you. Remember that you were slaves in Egypt and the LORD your God redeemed you. That is why I give you this command today. Do not consider it a hardship to set your servant free, because their service to you these six years has been worth twice as much as that of a hired hand. And the LORD your God will bless you in everything you do.

There is also provision for a citizen servant who chooses to remain a permanent slave rather than have his freedom.

Deuteronomy 15:16-17 But if your servant says to you, "I do not want to leave you," because he loves you and your family and is well off with you, then take an awl and push it through his earlobe into the door, and he will become your servant for life. Do the same for your female servant.

Did the Hebrew people obey God's commands regarding slavery? Scripture written by the prophet Jeremiah says no. This isn't the fault of God; however, it is the fault of the sinful humans. Read Jeremiah's account of scripture condemning forced slavery.

> *Jeremiah 34:8-17*
> *The word came to Jeremiah from the LORD after King Zedekiah had made a covenant with all the people in Jerusalem to proclaim freedom for the slaves. Everyone was to free their Hebrew slaves, both male and female; no one was to hold a fellow Hebrew in bondage. So all the officials and people who entered into this covenant agreed that they would free their male and female slaves and no longer hold them in bondage. They agreed, and set them free. But afterward they changed their minds and took back the slaves they had freed and enslaved them again.*
>
> *Then the word of the LORD came to Jeremiah: "This is what the LORD, the God of Israel, says: I made a covenant with your ancestors when I brought them out of Egypt, out of the land of slavery. I said, 'Every seventh year each of you must free any fellow Hebrews who have sold themselves to you. After they have served you six years, you must let them go free.' Your ancestors, however, did not listen to me or pay attention to me. Recently you repented and did what is right in my sight: Each of you proclaimed freedom to your own people. You even made a covenant before me in the house that bears my Name. But now you have turned around and profaned my name; each of you has taken back the male and female slaves you had set free to go where they wished. You have forced them to become your slaves again.*
>
> *"Therefore this is what the LORD says: You have not obeyed me; you have not proclaimed freedom to your own people. So I now proclaim 'freedom' for you, declares the LORD —'freedom' to fall by the sword, plague and famine. I will make you abhorrent to all the kingdoms of the earth.*

God promised to punish the sinful people with death, plague and famine. Not only had the people not freed their slaves from bondage, as was God's desire, they had promised God to do so, then broke their promise. God's prophecy was quickly fulfilled as the Babylonians sacked Jerusalem and the remaining cities of Judah in

586 BC. The Jewish people would be in exile under foreign rule for the next 50-some years.

Non-Hebrew People
The Bible does make an exception in ancient Israel for a non-Hebrew (non citizens) to become a slave. Remember in this era, Israel followed God, while the other nations did not. These nations may have practiced child sacrifice as the inhabitants on Canaan did (See Chapter 4 on God's Death Penalty).

> *Leviticus 25:44-46 "'Your male and female slaves are to come from the nations around you; from them you may buy slaves. You may also buy some of the temporary residents living among you and members of their clans born in your country, and they will become your property. You can bequeath them to your children as inherited property and can make them slaves for life, but you must not rule over your fellow Israelites ruthlessly.*

Why did God allow this? To start, the text says "you may buy", implying that slaves were for sale in neighboring countries. Since these nations did not follow God, they had no reason to follow the Exodus 21:16 law banning forced slavery. It isn't specified whether the slaves in the surrounding nations had sold themselves or were forced into slavery. Some citizens of those nations may very well have been slave traders. Remember free will from God allows humans to sin against other humans.

Secondly, Israel was God's chosen people and they followed God. Surrounding nations did not follow God, as they had their own gods and religions. So a slave entering service to a Hebrew was entering service to a follower of God. The slave would be exposed to God and might choose to accept God and become a follower. Thus the slave might find the path to eternal life.

If Hebrews of that era followed God's directive to Abraham in Genesis, slaves were to be circumcised, just as Hebrews.

> *Genesis 17:13 Whether born in your household or bought with your money, they must be circumcised. My covenant in your flesh is to be an everlasting covenant.*

With circumcision, a slave had joined the covenant and was able to follow God. This was a blessing!

How could being sold as a slave be a blessing? Remember that the Bible deals with earthly life as well as eternal life. The opportunity to achieve eternal life by following God was a small price to pay for becoming a slave. The foreign slave also would be protected by the laws listed above. A follower of God, if sincere in his faith, would not abuse either his slaves or animals. If one was going to be a slave, one would have a better life living under a follower of God, rather than a godless master. See the abuse and hardship the Israelite slaves endured while living under Pharaoh in Egypt (Exodus).

God reminds the Hebrews that they were once slaves as well, so they should treat their slaves well and allow them to participate in the Jewish festivals.

> *Deuteronomy 16:11-12 And rejoice before the LORD your God at the place he will choose as a dwelling for his Name — you, your sons and daughters, your male and female servants, the Levites in your towns, and the foreigners, the fatherless and the widows living among you. Remember that you were slaves in Egypt, and follow carefully these decrees.*

Sidebar: Since the Old Testament deals with Israel and her neighbors, we know that Israel descended from Abraham through Isaac and Jacob. We also know that neighboring countries were populated by Esau's descendants. Esau was Jacob's brother, so their race and skin color were very similar. There was no black-white skin racism as happened in America.

New Testament
What about the New Testament passages on slavery? The New Testament brought about a covenant change (see Chapter 7). No longer was there a nation (Israel) set aside to follow God. God's plan was not to overthrow the Roman Empire and create an earthly kingdom or return Israel to a world power. Instead, the church was now to be present in many nations and subject to many laws. Some

of those nations would allow slavery. Slavery was present in the Roman Empire which governed much of the world in New Testament times. But slavery was different then from the slavery practiced in early America.

> What many fail to understand is that slavery in biblical times was very different from the slavery that was practiced in the past few centuries in many parts of the world. The slavery in the Bible was not based exclusively on race. People were not enslaved because of their nationality or the color of their skin. In Bible times, slavery was more a matter of social status. People sold themselves as slaves when they could not pay their debts or provide for their families. In New Testament times, sometimes doctors, lawyers, and even politicians were slaves of someone else. Some people actually chose to be slaves so as to have all their needs provided for by their masters.
> - www.gotquestions.org/bible-slavery

As was stated earlier, the Bible speaks against forced slavery (1 Timothy 1:8-11), listing it as a sin. So a believer in Christ would free personal slaves that had been forced into service (bondage) by a slave trader, if he wished to avoid sin.

The following passages are speaking to master-slave relationships in Roman society that resulted from a mutually agreed upon contract. Notice how scripture reminds that we are all subject to a heavenly Master, and a master's voluntary-contract slaves should be treated well. In modern society, master-slave could be replaced by boss-worker for understanding these passages.

> *1 Corinthians 7:21-24 Were you a slave when you were called? Don't let it trouble you — although if you can gain your freedom, do so. For the one who was a slave when called to faith in the Lord is the Lord's freed person; similarly, the one who was free when called is Christ's slave. You were bought at a price; do not become slaves of human beings. Brothers and sisters, each person, as responsible to God, should remain in the situation they were in when God called them.*

Ephesians 6:5-9   Slaves, obey your earthly masters with respect and fear, and with sincerity of heart, just as you would obey Christ. Obey them not only to win their favor when their eye is on you, but as slaves of Christ, doing the will of God from your heart. Serve wholeheartedly, as if you were serving the Lord, not people, because you know that the Lord will reward each one for whatever good they do, whether they are slave or free. And masters, treat your slaves in the same way. Do not threaten them, since you know that he who is both their Master and yours is in heaven, and there is no favoritism with him.

Colossians 3:22 - 4:1 Slaves, obey your earthly masters in everything; and do it, not only when their eye is on you and to curry their favor, but with sincerity of heart and reverence for the Lord. Whatever you do, work at it with all your heart, as working for the Lord, not for human masters, since you know that you will receive an inheritance from the Lord as a reward. It is the Lord Christ you are serving. Anyone who does wrong will be repaid for their wrongs, and there is no favoritism. Masters, provide your slaves with what is right and fair, because you know that you also have a Master in heaven.

1 Peter 2:18-21   Slaves, in reverent fear of God submit yourselves to your masters, not only to those who are good and considerate, but also to those who are harsh. For it is commendable if someone bears up under the pain of unjust suffering because they are conscious of God. But how is it to your credit if you receive a beating for doing wrong and endure it? But if you suffer for doing good and you endure it, this is commendable before God. To this you were called, because Christ suffered for you, leaving you an example, that you should follow in his steps.

Because Paul refers to slave trading in Timothy, we can assume that it did exist along with contract slavery. Those following God's teachings should have allowed their bondage slaves to earn their freedom. The Bible did not intend to immediately overthrow forced slavery by open rebellion against a government that allowed it,

Slavery in the Bible and America

anymore than the Bible intended to overthrow the Roman Empire. A work with-in method was used instead to eliminate the practice over time. This method employed by God proved successful as the Roman Empire was converted to Christianity, and today followers of Christ do not practice bondage slavery.

> Another crucial point is that the purpose of the Bible is to point the way to salvation, not to reform society. The Bible often approaches issues from the inside out. If a person experiences the love, mercy, and grace of God by receiving His salvation, God will reform his soul, changing the way he thinks and acts. A person who has experienced God's gift of salvation and freedom from the slavery of sin, as God reforms his soul, will realize that enslaving another human being is wrong. A person who has truly experienced God's grace will in turn be gracious towards others. That would be the Bible's prescription for ending slavery.
> - www.gotquestions.org/bible-slavery

Slavery in America
The following background on slavery in America can be found in on-line encyclopedias. It began early in colonial history as indentured servitude and morphed into forced slavery.

> Slavery in the United States existed as a legal institution in North America for more than a century before the founding of the United States in 1776, and continued mostly in the South until the passage of the Thirteenth Amendment to the United States Constitution in 1865. The first English colony in North America, Virginia, acquired its first Africans in 1619, after a ship arrived, unsolicited, carrying a cargo of about 20 Africans. Thus, a practice established in the Spanish colonies as early as the 1560s was expanded into English North America.

> Slavery spread to the areas where there was good-quality soil for large plantations of high-value cash crops, such as tobacco, cotton, sugar, and coffee. The slaves did the manual labor involved in raising and harvesting these crops. By the

early decades of the 19th century, the majority of slaveholders and slaves were in the southern United States, where most slaves were engaged in a work-gang system of agriculture on large plantations.

Before the widespread establishment of [forced] slavery (outright ownership of a human being, and of his/her descendants), much labor was organized under a system of bonded labor known as indentured servitude. This typically lasted for several years for white and black alike. People paid with their labor for the costs of transport to the colonies. They contracted for such arrangements because of poor economies in their home countries. Between 1680 and 1700, slave labor began to supplant indentured servitude in much of colonial America. .... By the 18th century, colonial courts and legislatures had racialized slavery, essentially creating a caste system in which slavery applied nearly exclusively to Black Africans and people of African descent, and occasionally to Native Americans.
  - Wikipedia: Slavery in the United States

A "triangle of trade" emerged, linking the continents of Europe, Africa, and the Americas. Slave traders from Portugal, the Netherlands, England, and France brought raw and manufactured materials (such as iron, glass, guns, cloth, and horses) to African traders. African rulers profited from this trade, waging war on neighbors or requiring tribute in the form of slaves, which they, in turn, bartered to Europeans for the exotic luxury items they supplied. European traders packed slaves into sailing ships for the notorious Middle Passage, which averaged two to three months in the sixteenth century but could be completed in as little as 20 to 40 days by the nineteenth century. Survivors of the transatlantic voyage were sold to slaveholders for sugar, gold, tobacco, and rum, which in turn were sold in Europe.
  - www.encyclopedia.com/topic/SlaveTrade

Black Africans were captured and made slaves by black African rulers, were sold to slave traders, and were finally sold to white plantation owners in colonial America. They were treated as property. This is the sad state of slavery in colonial America. Free will concepts such as contracted indentured servitude were replaced with forced-labor slavery. As discussed earlier in the chapter, forced labor is very much anti-biblical, and not consistent with God's plan of each human having free will and choice to lead his life. This background shows the environment the founders of America were born into and the environment that existed when the Constitution was written.

The plague of legalizing forced-slavery must be born mostly by the white colonists. However a black colonist plays the key role as the first man to permanently own a slave. Wikipedia reports that the first forced slave was a black man named John Casor. He began as an indentured servant of another black man, landowner Anthony Johnson. Johnson refused to free Casor after his period of service expired. Casor sued for his freedom, but in 1654 a Virginia court ruled against him, making him a slave for life. He was the first permanent forced slave in colonial America. The story of John Casor was reported on the Glenn Beck Show that aired on the Fox News Channel.

While white Americans should bear the brunt of the blame for slavery in America, a black man was actually the first to own a bondage slave. Also, black tribal leaders of Africa were willing participants in the slave trade. Slavery ended in America with white Americans defeating other white Americans in a bloody Civil War. Slavery is much more complex than the simple racial argument sometimes used today that all whites are "guilty" and all blacks are "innocent". Also remember that both the slaves and the masters of that era are no longer alive today.

America's Founders Opposed Slavery

> The abolition of domestic slavery is the great object of desire in those colonies, where it was unhappily introduced in their infant state.
> - Thomas Jefferson , A Summary View of the Rights of British America 1774.

> Every measure of prudence, therefore, ought to be assumed for the eventual total extirpation of slavery from the United States....I have, throughout my whole life, held the practice of slavery in...abhorrence.
> - John Adams letter, June 8, 1819. www.westillholdthesetruths.org

We have seen the mere distinction of color made in the most enlightened period of time, a ground of the most oppressive dominion ever exercised by man over man.
- James Madison speech referencing slavery at the Constitutional Convention, June 6, 1787. www.westillholdthesetruths.org

This abomination [slavery] must have an end. And there is a superior bench reserved in heaven for those who hasten it.
- Thomas Jefferson. 1787. TRTJ. P 631.

Slavery is such an atrocious debasement of human nature, that its very extirpation, if not performed with solicitous care, may sometimes open a source of serious evils.
- Benjamin Franklin Address to the Public, November, 1789. www.westillholdthesetruths.org

I believe a time will come when an opportunity will be offered to abolish this lamentable evil. Everything we do is to improve it, if it happens in our day; if not, let us transmit to our descendants, together with our slaves, a pity for their unhappy lot and an abhorrence of slavery.
- Patrick Henry letter to Robert Pleasants, January 18, 1773. www.westillholdthesetruths.org

"I wish from my soul that the legislature of this State could see a policy of a gradual Abolition of Slavery. "
- George Washington. August 4, 1797 letter. www.foundingfatherquotes.com

"The scheme, my dear Marqs. which you propose as a precedent, to encourage the emancipation of the black people of this Country from that state of Bondage in which they are held, is a striking evidence of the benevolence of your Heart. I shall be happy to join you in so laudable a work."
- George Washington letter to Marquis de Lafayette, April 5, 1785. www.westillholdthesetruths.org

There must doubtless be an unhappy influence on the manners of our people produced by the existence of slavery among us. The whole commerce between master and slave is a perpetual exercise of the most boisterous passions, the most unremitting despotism on the one part, and degrading

submissions on the other. Our children see this, and learn to imitate it; for man is an imitative animal.
- Thomas Jefferson, Notes on the State of Virginia, Query 18. 1781. TRTJ. P 628

So why did the founding fathers not end slavery or at least free their own slaves? State laws at the time promoted slavery and prevented slaves from being easily freed. Virginia, home state of Washington, Jefferson, Madison, and Henry, was a slave state. State laws promoted slave holding and made it difficult, if not impossible, for a citizen of the state to free their slaves.

Let's examine Thomas Jefferson for some insight. Jefferson has many other writings against slavery in addition to those written here, yet Jefferson had slaves working at Monticello. Jefferson first tried to change state law.

> In 1769, I became a member of the [Virginia] legislature.... I made one effort in that body for the permission of the emancipation of slaves, which was rejected; and indeed during the regal government nothing liberal could expect success.
> - Jefferson's autobiography. 1821. TRTJ. P 630.

Jefferson was thwarted in his attempt to free slaves in Virginia. The other legislators would not go along with his proposal. Jefferson supported later attempts to ban slavery as well. Though retired for quite some time, Jefferson publicly "expressed unqualified approval when his son-in-law, Thomas Mann Randolph, then Governor of Virginia, proposed a 'plan of general emancipation' to the state legislature." (TRTJ, P289)

Jefferson further wrote in 1825 on the abolition of slavery:

> The march of events has not been as such to render its completion practicable within the limits of time allotted to me; and I leave its accomplishment as the work of another generation.... The abolition of the evil is not impossible; it ought therefore not to be despaired of.

Jefferson was not able to free slaves in Virginia, but he evidently treated his slaves very well and his slaves liked him greatly. During one of Jefferson's trips back to Monticello, his slaves were down the road waiting for Jefferson's arrival. They joined the carriage for the final distance to Monticello and once the carriage stopped, carried Jefferson into the house; some slaves even kissing Jefferson's hands along the way. (TRTJ. P. 151)

Jefferson could have freed his own slaves (a process called manumission), but this process was extremely difficult and expensive under Virginia law.

> In 1691, the General Assembly passed a law aimed at making masters think twice before freeing any of their slaves. While manumission by deed or will was legal under this law, it required a newly freed slave to leave the colony within six months and the former master to pay for the trip.
> Manumission became much more difficult in 1723. Paragraph 17 of the *1723 Act Directing the Trial of Slaves, Committing Capital Crimes; and for the More Effectual Punishing Conspiracies and Insurrection of Them; and for the Better Government of Negros, Mulattos, and Indians, Bond or Free* stated that "No negro, mullatto, or Indian slaves, shall be set free, upon any pretense whatsoever, except for some meritorious services, to be adjudged and allowed by the governor and council, for the time being."
> The act permitted manumission only upon approval of the governor and council and then only as a reward for public service. Should a slave be set free in any other manner (by will or deed, for example), the act required churchwardens to return the person so freed to slavery by sale at public outcry.
> - Manumission Takes Careful Planning and Plenty of Savvy

In Virginia, anyone seeking to free their slaves would have had to petition the governor and council, obtain approval (not often granted as 20 were granted over a 50 year window), then pay for the slaves' transportation out of Virginia.

In the case of Jefferson, his slaves seemed to be relatively happy. Would they have wanted freedom to live in Virginia and work instead of being slaves? Almost assuredly so. But that was not an option under state law of that day. Their alternative was being uprooted and transported to a northern state that did not have slavery. Not being able to read or write (state laws prevented slaves being taught these things), it is very uncertain that the former slaves would have been better off trying to obtain work in unfamiliar surroundings. Assuming Jefferson could have gotten approval from the government to free a slave, he may very well have decided the slave would be better off in the current situation.

Fellow Virginian George Washington, also inherited slaves. David Barton has researched and written an excellent article on Washington and slavery in Virginia. Washington refused to sell his slaves even though he had more than he needed to efficiently run Mount Vernon, and could have enriched himself by selling unneeded slaves that were property under Virginia law. Instead Washington cared for the slaves, recognized their marriages and kept their families together.

> Hired labor was almost impossible to find in Virginia. Given the economic system at the time the only way Washington could discontinue his use of slaves would be to abandon his plantation altogether.
>
> His humane policies toward [slaves] nearly ruined him financially. As his slaves had children his slave holdings expanded and grew far beyond his need. Many ate his goods without being able to contribute to the well being of the plantation. "One good field hand was worth as much as a small city lot," one historian has observed. "By selling a single slave Washington could have paid for two years the taxes he so complained about. But he stood firm on his moral principles, refusing to sell any of his slaves. He could not bring himself to "traffic in the human species."
> -TRGW. P446.

Those today who accuse Jefferson or Washington of being a hypocrite for not freeing their slaves need to be fully aware of the social, political and economic environment in which they lived, and the options available to them.

So how did a Christian nation not only allow but practice slavery? The simple answer is Christians are sinners as are all humans.

Humans have often not followed God's plans for us. Add in the fact that those colonists who were pro-slavery changed the definition of the word. Slavery had never before been defined as subjecting an entire race of people to permanent property status. Using this new meaning, it was possible to justify the practice by taking scripture out of context: forgetting or not realizing the master-slave discussed in the New Testament was describing voluntary indentured servitude over a period of time. Thankfully many Christian pastors and leaders recognized that colonial American slavery was not consistent with the overall themes of scripture and spoke out against it. Founders like Jefferson and Washington should be praised as they fought against an immoral practice, even though the practice benefited them financially.

On a side note, today many want to silence Christian pastors and keep them from discussing social or political topics that scripture speaks to. How much longer would America have allowed slavery if Christian pastors hadn't opposed it from the pulpit? Christian pastors have a duty to preach on topics where society has gone astray from God's teachings just as Dr. Martin Luther King Jr. did when, as a Christian minister, he fought for equal rights for Americans of color.

The author understands how some black people are angry at white people for the injustice of slavery against their ancestors. Sadly this anger is fostered in some college level black-study programs. The author would encourage black people who feel this way to remember that there were also white people who fought to free slaves in America, in addition to the evil ones who practiced slavery. Black slaves did not rise up and free themselves. White men fought white men in the Civil War to end slavery in America. So if you still feel anger, also add some kind and thankful feelings for those white men who fought on your ancestors' behalf.

<u>Slavery vs Abortion</u>
"How could anyone think slavery was acceptable or something to be tolerated, ?" we ask from today's vantage point. The equivalent moral issue for the country today is abortion. "How can anyone tolerate the killing of babies?", the anti-abortion groups ask. "How can anyone prevent a mother from doing whatever she wishes with

Slavery in the Bible and America

her body?", the pro-abortion groups ask, even if this means destroying a baby inside her womb.

"The fetuses aren't really human and therefore do not deserve protections in the law accorded to humans", the pro-choice proponents of abortion proclaim, just as pro-slavery advocates in colonial America proclaimed that blacks were not fully human and deserving of equal protection under the law.

"I'm personally against abortion, but it is a woman's right to chose" some politicians will claim as they support abortion being legal. This is the same as stating "I'm personally against slavery, but it is an owner's right to chose". How many colonists personally were against slavery, but were fine if others chose to practice it? Thankfully, many did choose to fight to end slavery. A white person in colonial America had no reason to oppose slavery except on moral grounds. From an economic standpoint they benefited from slavery. Yet many white people did take up the cause of abolition, because they correctly interpreted their Bibles and knew that forced slavery was wrong in the eyes of God.

Abortion and slavery are both morally reprehensible practices that are stains on American history. Both practices are against the teachings in the Bible.

Groups critical of the founders for not abolishing slavery, better examine themselves for not abolishing abortion. For example, most polls show black citizens vote 90% for the Democrat Party. This is their right to do so. They likely vote this way because they believe that Democrat politicians provide them with welfare benefits or government jobs and give then other economic advantages such as affirmative action. Yet the Democrat Party is clearly the party voting to keep abortion fully legal in America. (See the chapter on Judges and Senators.) They phrase it as pro-choice for women, but the effect is legalized abortion on demand, any time a woman wants. Black Americans who vote Democrat are enabling abortion to remain legal. How does this differ from those colonists in colonial America who voted for politicians who made laws to keep slavery legal?

Why haven't more black Christians, especially black pastors, taken up the cause to abolish abortion? Where are the black leaders, the Jeffersons and Washingtons, that vocally oppose the practice and fight to make it illegal? Black leaders may very well decide that their main cause is promoting racial harmony and promoting equal rights, and they do not want to dilute their efforts by opposing abortion. This is their free will choice to do so. But, can they then condemn colonial white Americans for not doing more to abolish slavery?

It has become politically popular among some circles today to criticize or condemn colonial America for slavery. This criticism is justified. However, do the critics also condemn abortion in modern society?

> *How can you say to your brother, 'Brother, let me take the speck out of your eye,' when you yourself fail to see the plank in your own eye? You hypocrite, first take the plank out of your eye, and then you will see clearly to remove the speck from your brother's eye.*
> *- Jesus in Luke 6:42*

Jesus is telling us not to be quick to condemn another sinner, when we have sinned ourselves. Here, the concept applies politically. The hypocrisy is condemning one group for allowing a morally detestable practice in their day, when your group is allowing an equally detestable practice today. Those condemning the legalization of slavery in colonial America should be condemning the legalization of abortion in today's America if they wish to avoid the charge of hypocrisy.

<u>The Constitution on Slavery</u>
Some will try to discredit the Constitution as it exists today because it allowed slavery to continue at the time of its ratification. This is silly, as the Constitution is simply the rules and law the federal government must follow. The Constitution can be amended and was, regarding slavery, so the current Constitution does not permit the evil of slavery.

To achieve the original ratification of all states a political compromise was required. Many in the North wanted slavery abolished. Many in the South insisted on slavery remaining legal as the plantation economy in the South depended on it.

Imagine you are trying to put together a union of states to form a new nation in modern America, each with differing views on abortion. If abortion is outlawed, there is no way liberal states like California or New York are going to join. Legalize abortion and conservative states like Utah and Oklahoma may very well not join. So a theoretical compromise is reached. In this case assume it is to let states decide on whether abortion should be legal. No one is happy, but the political obstacle is removed.

Going back to colonial America, a similar compromise was needed to get every state to sign on.

> The real difference of interests, lay not between large and small, but between the Northern and Southern states. The institution of slavery and its consequences formed a line of discrimination.
> -James Madison, Convention Debates. April 14, 1787. www.westillholdthesetruths.org

The writers of the Constitution crafted a much tougher slavery compromise than simply letting member states decide the issue. Here are the details of the slavery compromise they constructed.

The first part was the counting of slaves as 3/5 of a man. The Constitutional language is listed below. Notice how the word "slave" does not appear. 'All other persons' are used instead. The writers intended for slavery to disappear over time.

> <u>Article I - The Legislative Branch, Section 2 – The House</u>
> Representatives and direct Taxes shall be apportioned among the several States which may be included within this Union, according to their respective Numbers, which shall be determined by adding to the whole Number of free Persons, including those bound to Service for a Term of Years, and excluding Indians not taxed, **three fifths of all other Persons.**

Explaining the 3/5 Count of Slaves in the Census

The census is called for in the Constitution for the specific purpose of determining a state's number of representatives in the Congress. Each state's number of representatives is determined by the population of that state. Whether slaves were counted as persons for representation purposes or not would have a major impact on the number of representatives. Therefore, the 3/5 Rule was about control of the House of Representatives.

In this simple example, assume a state receives 1 representative for every 500 persons in the state.

	Free State	**Slave State**
Persons	3000	3000
Citizens	3000	1000
Slaves	0	2000
Representatives (0 slaves counted)	6	2
Representatives (3/5 slaves counted)	6	4
Representatives (all slaves counted)	6	6

Persons in Slave State under 3/5 rule = 1000 + 2000 * 3/5 = 2200.
2200/500 = 4.4 or 4 Representatives

The slave state receives 2 representatives if slaves are NOT counted, but 6 representatives if slaves are fully counted. **Slave states wanted slaves to be fully counted** so they could match the free states in number of representatives and balance control of the House of Representatives in Congress. If slaves were NOT counted, free states would have a much larger number of representatives and would control Congress, enabling them to pass anti-slavery legislation if they chose.

Provision for Banning the Slave Trade

The second part of the compromise was the provision to end the slave trade in the near future.

> Article 1, Section 9, 1ˢᵗ Clause
> The Migration or Importation of such Persons as any of the States now existing shall think proper to admit, shall not be prohibited by the Congress prior to the Year one thousand eight hundred and eight, but a tax or duty may be imposed on such Importation, not exceeding ten dollars for each Person.

This portion of the constitution restricted Congress from banning states from importing slaves immediately at the demand of the slave states. Congress was restricted from enacting such legislation for 20 years until 1808. The 20 years was another compromise. Slave states feared Congress would immediately ban the slave trade.

> Delegates from Georgia and South Carolina announced that they would not support the constitution without the restriction [on Congressional action to ban importation of slaves].
> - Heritage Guide to the Constitution, p150.

Again compromise was needed or the constitution would not have been approved by every state.

James Madison wrote that while the immediate banning of slavery would have been preferred, it was still "a great point gained in favor of humanity" that slave trafficking, a "barbarism of modern policy", would be terminated in 20 years time.

> It were doubtless to be wished, that the power of prohibiting the importation of slaves had not been postponed until the year 1808, or rather that it had been suffered to have immediate operation. But it is not difficult to account, either for this restriction on the general government, or for the manner in which the whole clause is expressed. It ought to be considered as a great point gained in favor of humanity, that a period of twenty years may terminate forever, that within that period, it will receive a considerable discouragement from the federal government, and may be totally abolished, by a concurrence of the few States which continue the unnatural traffic, in the prohibitory example which has been given by so great a majority of the Union. Happy would it be

> for the unfortunate Africans, if an equal prospect lay before them of being redeemed from the oppressions of their European brethren!
> - James Madison, Federalist #42

Congress did act to ban the import of slaves immediately after the 20 year compromise-restriction ended.

> Congress passed, and President Thomas Jefferson signed into law, a federal prohibition of the slave trade, effective January 1, 1808, the first day that Article 1, Section 9, Clause 1 allowed such a law to go into effect.
> - Heritage Guide to the Constitution, p151.

It is not just "old white men" who view the constitution as an anti-slavery document. Frederick Douglas was a black man and former slave. He described the US Constitution as anti-slavery and a "glorious liberty document".

> Frederick Douglass (February 1818 – February 20, 1895) was born a slave in Talbot County, Maryland. Douglas was an American social reformer, orator, writer and statesman. After escaping from slavery, he became a leader of the abolitionist movement, known for his dazzling oratory and incisive antislavery writing. He stood as a living counter-example to slaveholders' arguments that slaves did not have the intellectual capacity to function as independent American citizens. He became a major speaker for the cause of abolition. Douglass came to agree that the United States Constitution was an anti-slavery document.
> - Excerpts From Wikipedia, the free encyclopedia

> "Take the Constitution according to its plain reading," he challenged the Rochester Ladies Anti-Slavery Society on July 5, 1852, in Rochester, New York. "I defy the presentation of a single pro-slavery clause in it." In fact, Douglass told the crowd gathered to hear his Independence Day address, "Interpreted as it ought to be interpreted, the Constitution is a glorious liberty document."
> - Frederick Douglass and the Fourth of July. James A. Colaiaco. reason.com/archives/2006/10/01

Slavery in the Bible and America

Despite the slave trade being stopped in 1808, the despicable practice of slavery continued until the nation finally fought a four year Civil War (1861-1865), largely over the issue of slavery. Finally, at the conclusion of the war, slavery was abolished and the Constitution amended. Three key amendments abolished slavery, granted citizenship, and guaranteed the right to vote.

> Amendment 13 - Slavery Abolished.
> (Ratified 12/6/1865)
> 1. Neither slavery nor involuntary servitude, except as a punishment for crime whereof the party shall have been duly convicted, shall exist within the United States, or any place subject to their jurisdiction.
> 2. Congress shall have power to enforce this article by appropriate legislation.
>
> Amendment 14 - Citizenship Rights.
> (Ratified 7/9/1868)
> 1. All persons born or naturalized in the United States, and subject to the jurisdiction thereof, are citizens of the United States and of the State wherein they reside. No State shall make or enforce any law which shall abridge the privileges or immunities of citizens of the United States; nor shall any State deprive any person of life, liberty, or property, without due process of law; nor deny to any person within its jurisdiction the equal protection of the laws.
> 2. Representatives shall be apportioned among the several States according to their respective numbers, counting the whole number of persons in each State, excluding Indians not taxed.
> 5. Congress shall have power to enforce this article by appropriate legislation.

This guaranteed citizenship for all former slaves and removed the 3/5 compromise from the Constitution.

Amendment 15 - Race No Bar to Vote.
(Ratified 2/3/1870)
1. The right of citizens of the United States to vote shall not be denied or abridged by the United States or by any State on account of race, color, or previous condition of servitude.

2. Congress shall have power to enforce this article by appropriate legislation.

The Constitution, once amended, is permanently changed. So our present day Constitution bans slavery and protects all citizens' rights. It is the final law of the land.

Immigration and The American Ideal

> American institutions rest solely on good citizenship. They were created by people who had a background of self-government. New arrivals should be limited to our capacity to absorb them into the ranks of good citizenship.
> - President Calvin Coolidge. First Annual Message. December 6, 1923.

America's Immigration situation is often looked at in a vacuum, as if it was a snapshot in time with no history. It is impossible to have an honest discussion on immigration without the facts. Appendix 7 lists some important census data on immigrants. **In 2010 40 million people were foreign-born**, that is born outside of the US. These people composed **13% of the entire US population**. This enormous number of immigrants exceeds "our capacity to absorb them into the ranks of good citizenship."

Chapter Outline
I. Biblical View
II. Constitutional View
III. Legal Immigration
IV. Illegal Immigration, Sanctuary, and Lawlessness
V. Political Dynamic
VI. Economic Impact of Immigration
VII. Terrorism and Crime
VIII. The American Ideal and Immigrant Assimilation
IX. Solution

I. Biblical View
There are a few lessons to be learned from the Bible applicable to our nation's immigration policy. The Old Testament taught citizens in ancient Israel to treat immigrants well, as part of God's plan to bring the immigrants to God, so they could know and follow God, too. There are also parts of the Old Testament where the Israelis are warned not to let aliens or non-believers become a snare that could lure the citizens away from God. It is safe to assume that immigrants were expected to assimilate into the Jewish culture and obey the laws of God and the nation. It is important to remember that these laws had several harsh aspects, including the death penalty for many acts that God considers sinful.

One Biblical expert clarifies that in Hebrew (the language of the

Israelites), there were separate words to distinguish between legal immigrants seeking to join the Old Testament Jewish nation and foreigners who merely wished to work in Israel. Going back to Chapter 6, ancient Israel lived under laws (their constitution) given them by God. Immigrants were expected to follow those laws, just as the citizens were.

Misquoting Bible to Push for Amnesty
Dr. James Hoffmeier challenged [some in] the evangelical community's use of Scripture to push amnesty for illegal aliens .... Hoffmeier is on the staff of Trinity Evangelical Divinity School and an expert in how to understand the context of the Bible. ...
Hoffmeier detailed for the audience how the Bible actually has three different [Hebrew] words for what are commonly translated now into English as one word: "foreigner." Those three words are "ger," "nekhar" and "zar."

"What has happened, I regret, in the recent [immigration] discussion is that two different ideas have been blurred and the distinction between categories of foreigners has been lost," Hoffmeier said. ".... I think it's fair to say that the 'ger,' I would call them the legal immigrant... but you abide by the laws of the land. And that's precisely what Biblical law is advocating. It clearly demarcates between these two categories of people. ...the people who are advocating using Scripture for the undocumented illegal immigrant or whatever the last catch word is that we can use are trying to credit the non-legal resident with the same rights that Biblical law calls for with the legal foreign resident. There, I think, lies the problem."

The two other words, "nekhar" and "zar," Hoffmeier noted, were clearly distinguished from the legal immigrants, or "ger," in Biblical times. "There are two other words used in Hebrew that are translated as 'foreigner,'—'nekhar' and 'zar,'" Hoffmeier said. "Both of these words mean foreigners. And in Biblical law, you can see all of the protections go to the 'ger,' what I call the legal immigrant. They get the social benefits, and to join in the community worship and they have to observe Kosher dietary laws. Now, the foreigner, you can charge them interest. They can eat non-Kosher food. They're not a part of the community. The Biblical law clearly makes a distinction."

Hoffmeier has written a book on the topic, *The Immigration Crisis: Immigrants, Aliens, and the Bible*....
  - www.breitbart.com. Matthew Boyle. Nov 19, 2013.

There is a clear distinction made among the foreigners in the Israelite government. A similar distinction can be made in America. There are legal immigrants who seek to legally join the American culture. These are different from those merely seeking to work and send money back to their families in their nation of origin. They are also different from those who migrate seeking to receive welfare.

Chapters 7 and 8 showed scripturally how Christians and their churches are to use their own resources to perform good deeds by helping the poor. Most churches that want open borders or amnesty also expect the federal government to care for these foreigners. That violates the free will of other taxpaying citizens. It also violates our Constitution.

Chapters 13 and 14 showed how liberal big-government advocates have turned the Constitution upside down, using federal government power to ban religious activity - a practice expressly forbidden by the Constitution. Is it the will of God to have Christianity banned from the public areas? No. Are these potential immigrants helping those big federal government politicians get elected? Yes. (See the later section on the political dynamics.) Should churches be aligned with these forces if they truly seek God's will on Earth?

The Bible teaches its followers to obey the laws of the government in power, including immigration law. Obviously, those immigrants here illegally have broken these laws and are not obeying them. So church leaders who try to hide illegal aliens, or lobby for amnesty, are not following biblical teaching. The proper thing to do is to help the person if hungry or thirsty, then turn the illegal over to the authorities. Churches do not make law nor get to decide who is a citizen of the nation.

Another story in the Bible is relative to immigration: The Tower of

Babel. In this story, the people were divided once they didn't have a common language.

> ### Genesis 11 - The Tower of Babel
> *Now the whole world had one language and a common speech.... [The people] said, "Come, let us build ourselves a city, with a tower that reaches to the heavens, so that we may make a name for ourselves; otherwise we will be scattered over the face of the whole earth."*
>
> *But the Lord came down to see the city and the tower the people were building. The Lord said, "If as one people speaking the same language they have begun to do this, then nothing they plan to do will be impossible for them. Come, let us go down and confuse their language so they will not understand each other."*
>
> *So the Lord scattered them from there over all the earth, and they stopped building the city. That is why it was called Babel — because there the Lord confused the language of the whole world. From there the Lord scattered them over the face of the whole earth.*

The relevance of the story is the importance of common speech. Once the people did not share a common language they separated and divided. A common language is therefore essential for people to achieve a common goal or form a strong nation. In the US, that language is English. It is the language in which our founding documents were written. For two centuries, immigrants came to America and adopted English as their main language. Any person seeking to join a new nation as a citizen should learn the native language of that nation. A nation without a common language cannot be strong.

The lessons of the Bible are to encourage immigrants who will follow the constitution and laws of the nation while adopting the culture and language of the host nation – if the nation wants to remain united and strong. While instructive and informative, the Bible is not the law of the land in America, the Constitution is.

II. Constitutional View

> **US Constitution. Article I. Section. 8.**
> The Congress shall have Power....To establish a uniform Rule of Naturalization,....
>> Few powers are more fundamental to sovereignty than the control over immigration and the vesting of citizenship in aliens (naturalization).
>> - Heritage Guide to the US Constitution. P109.

According to the Constitution, immigration law is fully the responsibility of Congress and the federal government.

> It is of the deepest interest to the whole Union to know who are entitled to enjoy rights of citizens in each state since they thereby in effect become entitled to the rights of citizens in all the states. **If aliens might be admitted indiscriminately to enjoy all the rights of citizens... the Union might itself be endangered by an influx of foreigners hostile to its institutions, ignorant of its powers, and incapable of a due estimate of its privileges.**
> - Commentaries on the Constitution of the United States. Volume 3. 1833. Supreme Court Justice Joseph Story. P2. Google.com/books.

It was clearly understood in early America that for those seeking to emigrate to America, citizenship was a privilege and not a right. It was recognized that for the nation's founding principles to survive, only those people sharing the nation's principles should be allowed to join the nation as citizens.

> James Madison seemed to speak the sentiment of most when at the [Constitutional] Convention he expressed his wish "to invite foreigners of merit and republican principles among us. America was indebted to emigration, for her settlement and prosperity."
> - Heritage Guide to the US Constitution. P109.

Wise immigration policy gave citizenship privileges only to those aliens who understood and respected America's democratic republican government: aliens who understood and sought to live under a government designed to offer citizens "the right to life, liberty, and the pursuit of happiness."

III. Legal Immigration
US immigration policy radically changed in the 1960s. It moved away from the bringing in of immigrants from Europe, who were a closer cultural fit with existing Americans, toward immigrants from other third world nations.

> ### Kennedy Shaped Modern-Day Immigration System
> In 1965, [Ted] Kennedy sponsored the Immigration and Nationality Act, which lifted national quotas on immigrants entering the country.... Before 1965, it was nearly impossible for immigrants from anywhere besides Western Europe to come to the United States.
>
> The law made family reunification the basis for immigration. This ushered in a flood of immigrants from Latin America and Asia. The foreign-born population went from 10 million to nearly 30 million in 40 years. The system that Kennedy created has vexed people who favor strict restrictions on immigration.
>
> "They created these immigration chains," said Mark Krikorian, from the Center for Immigration Studies, "where one person comes here and then brings his brother, who brings his wife and so on, creating the mass immigration that we have today."
> - www.WBUR.org. Bianca Vázquez Toness. Aug. 27, 2009.

How are *40 million foreign-born people* (Appendix 7 - 2010 census), not even speaking English as a native language, going to become part of the American culture, following the melting pot model? They didn't and haven't.

> ### The 1965 Immigration Act: Anatomy of a Disaster
> America's current mass immigration mess is the result of a change in the laws in 1965. Prior to 1965, despite some changes in the 50's, America was a low-immigration country basically living under immigration laws written in 1924. Thanks to low immigration, the swamp of cheap labor was

372

largely drained during this period, America became a fundamentally middle-class society, and our many European ethnic groups were brought **together into a common national culture**.
- FrontPageMagazine.com. Ben Johnson. December 10, 2002

The 1965 Immigration Act was not alone in creating the problems in America. While it increased legal immigration, millions more entered into the nation illegally. The federal government solved this problem with the 1986 Immigration Reform and Control Act. They granted amnesty to millions of illegal trespassers and promised to secure the border to dtop future illegal entry.

Immigration reform's flaws revealed in the 1986 amnesty
The three main components [of the 1986 Immigration Reform and Control Act] were a big amnesty for the estimated million or so aliens who were illegally in the U.S., strengthened border controls to keep more aliens from entering the U.S., and sanctions on employers to prevent the future employment of illegal aliens. The idea was that the amnesty would not attract more illegal immigrants to the U.S. because they would be deterred by stronger border controls and employer sanctions.
- www.newsworks.org. Jan Ting. November 3, 2013.

So why are there millions of illegal-aliens in America today if the problem was solved with amnesty in 1986? The federal government did not secure the border and the promise of amnesty encouraged still more foreigners to come into America illegally. Appendix 7 census data shows the number of foreign- born rising from 9.6 million in 1970, to 19.8 million in 1990. The 1986 amnesty made million of illegals legal, but did nothing to stop illegal immigration. One can expect any future amnesty laws to have the same effect.

Despite the 1986 amnesty and the considerable loosening of US immigration law since 1965, some still claim the laws are too restrictive and preventative. National leaders of Mexico have criticized US immigration law in this manner. But Mexico's own immigration laws are much tougher than US immigration law. In fact until Mexico softened their immigration law in 2011, Mexico had the toughest stance on immigration in the Americas. Even the reformed law is tougher than US law.

Mexico's Immigration Laws: The Untold Story

The Law Library of Congress released a report in April 2006 ... [which] observed how Mexican law considers "[i]llegal entry a federal crime ... penalized with imprisonment for up to two years, a fine from three hundred to five thousand Mexican Pesos, and deportation." Repeat offenders receive even harsher sanctions of 10-year imprisonment and a fine of up to five thousand pesos and deportation.

Although Mexico reformed [their immigration law] in January 2011, our neighbors to the south continue the policy of maintaining fines at the current level of five thousand pesos, or $418.10 in March 2011, for those who don't follow deportation orders (Chapter 8, Article 117).

Among the other findings of the Library of Congress, through its "enforcing arm, the National Institute of Migration – INAMI" (the equivalent of ICE here in the USA), the Mexican Police Force, may carry out the following:" (Chapter 10, Article 151)

- Perform verification visits

- Cause a foreigner to appear before immigration authorities

- Perform migration inspection operations on routes or at temporary points different from established inspection locations

- Obtain such other elements of proof as may be necessary for the application of the Act, its regulation, and additional administrative provisions

Lastly, "the authorities of the country, whether federal, local, or municipal, and the notaries public and commercial brokers are required to request that the foreigners whom they deal with prove their legal presence in the country" and illegal immigrants who wish to get married to Mexican citizens "must request authorization from the Secretariat of the Interior."

- Heritage.org. Andres Celedon. April 4, 2011

Mexico strictly enforces their immigration law, which is designed to prevent immigrants from poorer southern neighboring nations from freely coming to Mexico. Enforcement includes imprisonment, fines and deportation for those breaking the law. It is *extremely hypocritical* for Mexico to criticize America with respect to immigration policy.

Sidebar: Why do the Mexican politicians want an open border with America? It serves their interests. Workers not able to find work in Mexico can cross the border and find work. Some will cross the border and obtain generous welfare payments in America. In both cases people who were a burden to Mexico are now not. Also do not forget the Mexicans who cross into America and send money back home to support relatives and families still in Mexico. This infusion of cash helps the nation of Mexico.

If America is to save her identity and founding principles, she must return to earlier successful immigration policies, dramatically reducing the number of new immigrants until the current foreign-born population declines and assimilates.

IV. Illegal Immigration, Sanctuary, and Lawlessness
In addition to the huge numbers of foreign-born citizens, there are also huge numbers of people who have crossed the border and entered the country illegally. When a person breaks a law, they commit an illegal act. This is widely understood in almost every other area of law, but many liberals seek to use "undocumented" instead of "illegal" when discussing immigrants.

In addition to altering the language, these people also prefer to ignore immigration law that they do not agree with. Immigration law is one of the areas in America today where large segments of the population simply wish to ignore the national law. This is very poor precedent, as it soon leads to all laws as being viewed as arbitrary. The founders recognized this.

> Laws or ordinances unobserved or partially attended to, had better never have been made...
> - George Washington. 1787. TRGW. P726.

> If the laws are to be so trampled upon with impunity.... there is an end to republican government, and nothing but anarchy and confusion is to be expected thereafter; for some other man or [group] may dislike another law and oppose it with equal propriety until all laws are prostrate (completely overcome)...
> - George Washington. 1794. TRGW. P726.

In America today, some politicians and government officials are ignoring federal laws they disagree with. This is unfortunately occurring even in the federal government itself. The Executive Branch (President) is in charge of the IRS, and apparently has been encouraging or allowing the IRS bureaucracy to violate citizenship laws passed by Congress. Why is the IRS interacting with lawbreakers? It's issuing identification numbers and checks to people who have broken the law, and continue to break it. If the IRS can send a check, it can forward the address to immigration enforcement officials.

> IRS Sent $7,319,518 in Refunds to One Bank Account Used by 2,706 Aliens
> Since 1996, the IRS has issued what it calls Individual Taxpayer Identification Numbers (ITINs) to two classes of persons: 1) non-resident aliens who have a tax liability in the United States, and 2) **aliens living in the United States who are "not authorized to work in the United States."** - CNSnews.com. Terence P. Jeffrey. June 24, 2013

> The Obama Administration Pays Illegal Aliens to Come Here
> A basic premise of immigration law is that immigrants to the U.S. are expected to be self-supporting. We obviously don't want to attract people who have no intention of working, but simply want to benefit from our generous welfare system. This principle is incorporated into the *Immigration and Nationality Act*, which provides:
>
>> An alien who, in the opinion of the consular officer at the time of application for a visa, or in the opinion of the Attorney General at the time of application for admission or adjustment of status, is likely at any time to become a public charge is inadmissible.

(The post then gives examples of how the Obama administration is subverting this aspect of the immigration laws including an advertisement encouraging illegal aliens to apply for food stamps.)

Barack Obama's mania to make everyone a dependent of the federal government extends even to illegal aliens. The Treasury Inspector General for Tax Administration has uncovered the astonishing fact that the Obama administration pays billions of dollars in child tax credits to illegal aliens:

A few tidbits from the IG's report:

> * In one instance, four illegal aliens fraudulently claimed that 20 children lived with them in the same trailer and received from the IRS $29,608 in ACTC refunds. The children claimed did not even live in the U.S.
>
> * The Inspector General recommended that, "Legislation should be considered to require a Social Security Number in order to be eligible for the ACTC, consistent with the requirements for the Earned Income Tax Credit... As it now stands, the payment of Federal funds through this tax benefit appears to provide an additional incentive for aliens to enter, reside, and work in the U.S. without authorization, which contradicts Federal law and policy to remove such incentives."

(The article then shows a chart with government data: $5.6 Billion was sent was sent to illegal aliens in 2011 with the number expected to grow to $7.4 Billion in 2012.)

Republican Senators proposed [legislation to end the fraud, but Democrat Majority Leader] Harry Reid refused to allow it to come to the Senate floor for a vote. So at the same time that the United States is going broke, with $16 trillion in debt, we are bribing people from all over the world, illegally as well as legally, to enjoy federal benefits at taxpayer expense. And Barack Obama and Harry Reid refuse to permit anything to be done, even to the extent of limiting blatant fraud.

- Powerline.com. John Hinderaker. August 7, 2012

One would think that if the federal government could mail checks to illegal aliens they could find them to deport them. Obviously, the federal government does not want to. This may be just another example of the federal government being so big and complicated that it is impossible for Congress or the President to manage it. Another explanation is a number of politicians and bureaucrats want to violate federal laws by importing poor people into the country. It lends credence to the political dynamic that many politicians, especially Democrats, want the immigrants (illegal or legal) for support at election time.

Some cities are also flaunting federal authority to determine citizenship status, by openly declaring themselves sanctuary cities where lawbreakers are welcome and will not be punished.

> Sanctuary Cities are Illegal
> Sanctuary policies directly violate Federal law. Section 642 of the Illegal Immigration Reform and Immigrant Responsibility Act of 1996 (IIRIRA) provides that:
> "Federal, State, or local government entity or official may not prohibit, or in any way restrict, any government entity or official from sending to, or receiving from, the Immigration and Naturalization Service information regarding the citizenship or immigration status, lawful or unlawful, of any individual."
> However, neither DHS [Department of Homeland Security] nor the Department of Justice (DOJ) has ever challenged a sanctuary policy.
> - www.numbersusa.com/content/learn/illegal-immigration/sanctuary-cities

It is also entirely possible that the politicians sponsoring sanctuary cities for immigrants are perfectly happy keeping them on the welfare roles in exchange for their votes which help the politicians stay in power. Illegal immigrants likely *are* voting unless the state enforces a photo ID requirement at the polling place and is not giving ID's to illegals.

If ignoring federal immigration laws were not enough, some cities are now even trying to get illegals the ability to legally vote. (It is a safe assumption that many illegal immigrants already vote illegally in states where there is same day voter registration requiring no voter identification.)

> NEW HAVEN, CT (WCBS 880) - One Connecticut mayor is asking the legislature to allow illegal immigrants to vote in local elections. Mayor John DeStefano argues that illegal immigrants who live in New Haven pay local taxes and their kids go to school in the city. That's why he believes these city residents deserve the right to vote on local issues.

Now these cities' leaders want to enable illegal aliens to vote legally. The bigger question is: If the person is KNOWN to be residing in a city ILLEGALLY, why aren't the proper authorities notified and the illegal person fined or deported? The answer: city mayors and councilmen have figured out how to use illegal immigrants as a source of political power for themselves. The illegals are given safe haven in exchange for their votes. Since the federal government pays for welfare benefits, the illegals cost the city government nothing. More on immigration political dynamics is discussed later.

If city officials do not obey federal law, why should anyone follow the local laws these officials pass?No city will look at a tax cheat and allow them to get by with no fines or incarceration. Many cities are very anxious to pass numerous laws controlling peoples lives. Everything from smoking bans, to banning plastic bags in grocery stores, to regulating property appearance has been enacted as law. Can citizens simply ignore the laws they do not agree with? Can the illegal immigrants ignore these laws, too, as they ignore federal laws? The city administrators will certainly say "NO". They want their laws followed and enforced but will flagrantly not enforce the laws of the nation.

Surely Congress is outraged that so many local officials are ignoring federal law passed by Congress, duly authorized by the Constitution. Well, not exactly. Some members of Congress actively encourage law-breaking with respect to immigration laws. One would think a member of Congress would be especially sensitive to law-breaking, as they make the laws. If they do not take their own laws seriously, can they expect any other citizen to?

<u>Congressional representatives urge Brown to sign [sanctuary] bill</u>
Twenty-eight of California's congressional representatives are throwing their weight behind state legislation that would make it harder to deport immigrants who are in the country illegally.

The representatives -- all Democrats, including House Minority Leader Nancy Pelosi of San Francisco -- sent a letter to Gov. Jerry Brown urging him to sign the bill if it reaches his desk.

The bill, known as the Trust Act, "establishes a bright line standard between local law enforcement and federal immigration enforcement".... [It] would limit local law enforcement's role in working with federal authorities to begin deportation proceedings.
- www.latimes.com. Chris Megerian. August 14, 2013.

These Congresspeople are teaching and instructing states and cities to ignore federal law. They think this behavior will only apply to immigration law. But once started, it could easily spread to other areas of the law. Actions like this lead the nation toward all laws being ignored as President Washington warned. Can anyone pick laws they do not want to follow and ignore them? Can a rich person ignore the income tax laws that Congress makes? Can a banker ignore the banking laws that Congress passes? Who gets to choose which laws are enforced and which are not?

Some politicians propose amnesty for illegal aliens who broke the immigration laws. Will they also propose tax amnesty for tax cheaters who break the tax laws? After all small businessmen struggling to make a living should be given a pass for not paying their taxes, shouldn't they? The tax laws are onerous and unfair to many, so no person should be attacked for not following them. Right? Here's betting you will see immigration-amnesty loving politicians strenuously opposed to tax amnesty or any other moves to weaken enforcement of the tax laws. Taxes are a main source of power for politicians – especially big government ones.

Immigration and The American Ideal

VIII. Political Dynamic

There is a political element to immigration that cannot be ignored. Conservatives have accused Democrats for years of favoring immigration solely for increasing their political power. A ranking Democrat, in charge of border security no less, has now confirmed this accusation.

> ### Janet Napolitano: Immigrants will change Arizona from red to blue
> Homeland Security Secretary Janet Napolitano says the influx of immigrants into Arizona will put this conservative stronghold into the hands of the Democratic Party.
> The former Arizona governor predicted her state would turn blue in coming elections — just like Nevada, New Mexico and Colorado has gained in Democratic popularity...
> – The Washington Times. Cheryl K. Chumley. March 27, 2013

> ### Immigration reform could be bonanza for Democrats
> The immigration proposal pending in Congress would transform the nation's political landscape for a generation or more — pumping as many as 11 million new Hispanic voters into the electorate... that, if current trends hold, would produce an electoral bonanza for Democrats and cripple Republican prospects in many states they now win easily.
>
> Beneath the philosophical debates about amnesty and border security, there are brass-tacks partisan calculations driving the thinking of lawmakers in both parties over comprehensive immigration reform, which in its current form offers a pathway to citizenship — and full voting rights — for a group of undocumented residents that roughly equals the population of Ohio, the nation's seventh-largest state.
>
> If these people had been on the voting rolls in 2012 and voted along the same lines as other Hispanic voters did last fall, President Barack Obama's relatively narrow victory last fall would have been considerably wider, a POLITICO analysis showed.
> - politico.com. EMILY SCHULTHEIS. 4/22/13.

The Democrat Party buys votes and power by giving poor voters government benefits that are paid for by taking money from other productive citizens. They are pleased if immigrants are coming to the nation to go on welfare and vote for them. If the sole concern was to help foreigners find work and "do jobs Americans won't do" a work visa program would fill the need just fine. But workers on visas won't give them new voters.

As covered in Chapter 12, using the federal government to pay welfare benefits ignores key parts of the Constitution which leave these tasks to the states or the people. It also harms the citizens already living in America, as their taxes increase to provide the welfare benefits for new welfare-receiving citizens.

The poll of Hispanics in America supports the political element of the immigration issue. 80% of Hispanic immigrants favor big government policies. These are natural Democrat voters since Democrats have become the party of big government. Let us not forget that the policies these immigrants favor are the use of government force to take from other citizens in order to give the immigrants the welfare assistance they crave.

> Bigger Government or Smaller Government?
> When it comes to the size of government, Hispanics are more likely than the general public to say they would rather have a bigger government providing more services than a smaller government with fewer services. Some 75% of Hispanics say this, while 19% say they would rather have a smaller government with fewer services.
>
> Support for a larger government is greatest among immigrant Latinos. More than eight-in-ten (81%) say they would rather have a bigger government with more services than a smaller government with fewer services.
> - Pew Research. Hispanics and Their Views of Identity. April 4, 2012

These new immigrants cannot be expected to know that the Constitution, if followed, places these tasks at the state level of government. Those tasks are left to the states to perform, if performed at all, according to the Constitution.

<u>What Conservatives and the GOP Dare Not Say about Immigration</u>
The fact is that upon being naturalized, our modern-day immigrants generally vote Democrat by wide margins – irrespective of whether upon arrival they were labeled legal or illegal.

And the reality is this: Most of today's immigrants' native lands have socialist-type governments because their peoples support socialist politicians. This is why Democrats import them: so these new arrivals can support socialist politicians here. They're casting the votes Americans won't cast.
- www.newswithviews.com. Selwyn Duke. January 6, 2012.

Using California as an example (Appendix 8: Immigration Made California a Big Government Democrat Party State), Democrats (and some Republicans) want to use immigration to import big-government voters and turn Texas and other states into a solid-Democrat states as well. If they succeed they will own the presidency and control the Senate for the next 40 years. With control of these bodies comes control of the Supreme Court. And the US Constitution will become what liberal justices say it is (Chapter 14).

A few things to expect if America becomes like California:

- Balkanized sections will develop where either English or Spanish is the dominant language.
- Green energy (wind, solar) will be forced on the nation. This energy is considerably more expensive than traditional energy. The rich will not care; the poor will receive subsidies, the middle class' energy bills will soar.
- ObamaCare to morph into a federal government healthcare monopoly. (No worries – the rich will travel overseas to specialized clinics to obtain their care.)
- The nation's economy to resemble California's – A few very wealthy, a shrinking middle class, and a large welfare class.

California's model (the state has 12% of the country's population and one third of its welfare recipients) only works because the federal government tax dollars from other states subsidize California's welfare rolls. This could not exist if their own taxpayers had to pay the bill. If America copies California, taxes will rise sharply, benefits will be cut, or both will occur. Lower standards of living will likely exist for all but the very wealthy.

It is not just welfare that is the problem. The Democrat Party today is openly anti-Christian (Chapter 24), which mat not matter, except it believes in using government force to impose its views on the rest of America. Democrats don't want the Bible or prayer in local schools and use the federal government to ban it (Chapter 11). Democrats want homosexual marriage and use the federal courts to mandate it and require that Christians accept it (Chapter 16). Democrats want abortion and use ObamaCare to require abortion in every insurance plan (Chapter 21). Democrats consistently use government to force people to do what they want people to do. This is another key reason why so many conservatives oppose amnesty. By voting Democrat, illegal immigrants will take away the rights and freedoms of those conservative citizens. If enough immigrants (ignorant of America's Constitution and founding principles) begin voting in elections, they may very well tip the scales away from freedom towards a big-government state.

Sidebar: The author firmly supports immigrants in the mold of Ted Cruz, a Senator who understands and champions the US Constitution and Rafael Cruz, his father. These men recognize America as the land of liberty and opportunity. The Cruz's are of Hispanic decent. Democrats will not want immigrants like these men to enter the nation.

V. Economic Cost of Immigration
Immigration should be an important topic for every citizen of America because it affects each of them.

Take Mexico for example. Many Mexicans want to come to the US for work. But historically, why are there jobs in the US and not in Mexico? Because the Mexican government does not do a good job of creating an environment where job creators and entrepreneurs will flourish. The US government has historically done this quite well.

Immigration and The American Ideal

How? By providing a rule of law, rights to protect property, and low levels of taxation, to let the productive keep the bulk of their earnings. Immigrants, if allowed to vote for big government in the US, will just succeed in making America look more like Mexico, a land with not enough jobs for the people.

Current Immigration Policy Hurting Economic Growth
America is also paying the price of reduced growth and national prosperity with the current immigration policy.

> If the U.S. were to design an immigration policy from scratch that would most hurt growth, it would look much like our current one. It would favor the uneducated, unskilled and undocumented over the educated and skilled. It would make no demands for language assimilation. It would grant easy access to welfare. At the same time it would send ambitious college graduates back to their native lands.
> - The 4% Solution. Rich Karlgaard. Forbes. May 7, 2012.

Immigrants (Legal and Illegal) On Welfare for Years
It is not hard to see that millions of new immigrants, all expecting generous welfare benefits, will soon become a huge burden to the economy. The author fully respects the free will of states to follow the foolish policy of recruiting poor immigrants and giving them welfare. If the big government policies were carried out at the state level, it will only wreck a state's economy, not the entire nation's economy. If you as a reader disagree with the author, please prove your point. Move the policies to the state level and show the entire nation how well the policies work. Let a liberal state like California bring in poor legal immigrants and pay their welfare benefits using only taxes from other Californians.

Put another way, most conservatives will gladly embrace increased legal immigration numbers, in exchange for eliminating all of the federal welfare programs that are draining the wealth of the nation. In earlier immigration surges in America, these welfare programs did not exist.

> On Immigration, Pay Attention To Milton Friedman
> Free-market economist Milton Friedman once warned that **open borders are incompatible with a welfare state**.

> The $6.3 trillion cost of amnesty [in 2013] forecast by the Heritage Foundation illustrates it in spades.
>> - Investor's Business Daily. Editorials. 05/08/2013.

Today's immigrants aren't like the immigrants from the Ellis Island days in early America. Those immigrants received no welfare or government subsidies. Sure, some of them did receive 40 acres of frontier land, but it was 40 acres of wilderness that they had to turn into a farm with their own labor. America benefited as the frontier was settled. America receives no benefits from immigrants who come to America and use welfare benefits for 20 years. These immigrants are just a drain on the taxpayers who *are* working.

> ### Slow Path to Progress for U.S. Immigrants
> The study [from the Center for Immigration Studies], which covers all immigrants, legal and illegal, and their U.S.-born children younger than 18, found that immigrants..... lag well behind native-born Americans on factors such as poverty, health insurance coverage and home ownership.
> The study, based on 2010 and 2011 census data, found that 43% of immigrants who have been in the U.S. at least 20 years were using welfare benefits, a rate that is nearly twice as high as native-born Americans.....
>> - The Washington Times. Stephen Dinan. Aug. 8, 2012

It is no surprise that immigrants using welfare for multiple years never leave the poverty roles. Government-run welfare programs can be used as a mattress that the lazy can sleep comfortably on for as long as they wish.

VI. Illegal Immigration Tied to Crime

The following is part of an excellent article documenting the huge problem that illegal aliens and gangs are causing with respect to crime in America. Many illegal immigrants come to America to work, but it cannot be denied that there are large numbers who come to lead a life of crime.

> ### Criminal Illegal Immigrant Gangs Infest U.S.
> Today the Southern U.S. border is an open highway for those seeking to enter the United States without inspection.

Hispanic gangs are now the most powerful criminal operatives in the United States and in much of the world. The U.S. Department of Justice (DOJ) National Gang Intelligence Center (NGIC) and the Federal Bureau of Investigation (FBI) estimate that **80 percent of U.S. crime is committed by gangs,** including murder, rape, kidnapping, violent assaults, torture, robbery, and identity theft.

Criminal gangs are multiplying and successfully recruiting Hispanics born in the United States and abroad. Islamist terrorists have reached an accord with gangs for assistance in entering the United States without inspection...... Islamist terrorists are adopting Hispanic personas. Several gangs now specialize in serving as mentors to Islamist terrorists.

The DOJ estimates that **a million gang members operate in the United States** in gangs such as MS-13, the Bloods, the Crips, Sur-13, Mexican Mafia, Latin Kings, Surenos, Kurdish Pride, and Mexican Posse. Among gang members are illegal aliens and those born in the United States of illegal alien parents. The United States is infested with these gangs, many of them interlocked and many international in scope.

[A few state-specific crime incidents from the article]

Arizona. Before passing the SB 1070 bill (Support Our Law Enforcement and Safe Neighborhoods Act), the Arizona state legislature heard testimony from many of its citizens, among them ranchers whose land abuts the U.S-Mexico border. The hearings showed that the Arizona border with Mexico is out of control and that illegal aliens, drug smugglers, and gang members cross the border at will.

California. In April 2010, the La Habra police arrested a Hispanic gang member for the 2006 shooting of an African-American college student. The police advised that the Hispanic gang disliked African-Americans and that the shooting was without provocation. In Los Angeles, the County District Attorney and Superior Courts decline immigration enforcement actions involving gang members as a matter of policy. Los Angeles is a sanctuary city, where a spokesperson proudly states, "We treat all undocumented persons no differently than anyone else."

<u>Illinois</u>. In President Obama's hometown of Chicago, two Democrat state representatives have called for the governor to activate the National Guard to safeguard city streets. As of April of this year, 113 people have been killed in Chicago, where gang violence is out of control. Chicago's most famous gang member, Jose Padilla, is serving a 17-year sentence for his part in an al-Qaida dirty bomb plot. Padilla, a Latin King member, was serving time for kicking a rival gang member to death, when he converted to Islam. His prison conversion reflects a growing phenomenon of Hispanics becoming Islamists.

<u>Maryland.</u> The State Attorney's office estimates that 40 gangs with 1,150 members are currently active in the state. In Montgomery County, a bedroom-suburb of Washington, D.C., in November 2009, a member of MS-13 shot up a bus, killing a 14-year-old student and wounding two other children. The police chief excused the violence by saying that gang members were really just targeting each other. He could not say how many of them were illegal aliens. Officials refuse to acknowledge that being a "sanctuary community" has any bearing on the violence. Sanctuary communities, by refusing to ask the immigration status of those apprehended for crimes, become free zones for criminal alien gangs.

<u>Washington.</u> State Sen. Margarita Prentice, D-Renton, takes credit for "killing" anti-gang legislation. Saying that the legislation would have unfairly labeled "Latino" children, she ignores the link between illegal immigration and "Latino" gangs. In her state, 18 of the 26 "Most Wanted" criminals are illegal aliens.

<u>Wisconsin.</u> Madison had a gang killing on April 28. City police estimate that 40 gangs (at least 12 of them "Latino") have 1,100 gang members active in Madison. A police official noted that the city is experiencing an influx of West Coast-based "Latino" gangs.

- Newsmax.com. James Walsh. June 7, 2010.

How many illegal aliens are living a life of crime is impossible to know precisely. Especially when local law enforcement is forbidden from documenting illegal-alien crime by sanctuary laws passed by city leaders. One would think that even sanctuary cities would be interested in deporting illegal alien criminals. But many choose not to.

VII. The Terrorism Threat

After the World Trade Center Towers fell on 9/11, there were no shortage of politicians going on the record blaming intelligence agencies for not "connecting the dots" and stopping the terrorist attack before it happened. Yet some of these same politicians have no problem with illegal aliens moving about the country freely. How it is possible to "connect the dots" when so many in the government do not want to track illegals? The following example shows the TSA not bothering to check a visitor's immigration status before they attend flight school. Remember, this is the method the 9/11-terrorists learned to fly.

> ### TSA Let 25 Illegal Aliens Attend Flight School Owned by Illegal Alien
>
> The Transportation Security Administration (TSA) approved flight training for 25 illegal aliens at a Boston-area flight school that was owned by yet another illegal alien, according to the Government Accountability Office.
>
> The illegal-alien flight-school attendees included eight who had entered the country illegally and 17 who had overstayed their allowed period of admission into the United States, according to an audit by the GAO. Three of the illegal aliens were actually able to get pilot's licenses.
>
> Discovery of the trouble at the flight school began when local police--not federal authorities--pulled over the owner of the school on a traffic violation and were able to determine that he was an illegal alien.
>
> Rep. Mike Rogers (R.-Ala.), chairman of the House Homeland Security Subcommittee on Transportation Security, said he found the GAO's findings "amazing."
>
> "We have cancer patients, Iraq War veterans and Nobel Prize winners all forced to undergo rigorous security checks before getting on an airplane," said Rogers, "and at the same time,

ten years after 9/11, there are foreign nationals in the United States trained to fly just like Mohammed Atta and the other 9/11 hijackers did, and not all of them are necessarily getting a security background check."

Although the illegal alien who owned the Massachusetts flight school had not undergone a required TSA security threat assessment and had not been approved for flight training by the agency, he nonetheless held two Federal Aviation Administration (FAA) pilot licenses, also known as FAA certificates.

According to the 911 Commission Report, four of the Sept. 11 hijackers who entered the United States with legal visas had overstayed their authorized period of admission.
- CNSNews.com. Edwin Mora. July 18, 2012.

One of the primary functions of the government is to protect its citizens from attack. While most illegal immigrants are not terrorists, it only takes several trained pilots to steal a small airplane, fill it with explosives and fly it into a shopping mall filled with shoppers. The government cannot prevent this if they do not know the immigrant's documented legal status.

Boston Marathon Bombing: More Immigrant Terrorism
The final tragic example of America's national immigration policy gone amok is the bombing at the Boston Marathon which occurred on April 15, 2013. Several bombs were detonated at the finish line of the marathon, killing three and injuring over 100 innocent bystanders. The bombers, Tamerlan and Dzhokhar Tsarnaev were immigrants from Chechnya. Dzhokhar received his citizenship in 2012, Tamerlan's request was under review. The Tsarnaev family apparently was on welfare from the time they arrived in America.

Tsarnaev family received $100G in benefits
The Tsarnaev family, including the suspected terrorists and their parents, benefited from more than $100,000 in taxpayer-funded assistance — a bonanza ranging from cash and food stamps to Section 8 housing from 2002 to 2012, the Herald has learned.

"The breadth of the benefits the family was receiving was stunning," said a person with knowledge of documents

handed over to a legislative committee today.
- Bostonherald.com. Chris Cassidy. April 29, 2013.

In addition to admitting people that needed welfare and were, therefore, a burden to society, the Tsarnaev's were of Muslim heritage. Muslims have a long history of carrying out terrorist attacks against America and her citizens. The most famous attack being 9-11 when Muslim terrorists brought down the World Trade Center with hijacked airplanes. Why would the government allow more potential terrorists to enter the country? Most Muslims are not terrorists. But why take the chance? The federal government is partly to blame for the Boston Marathon bombing because it allowed the Tsarnaev's to enter America. The federal government did not allow German's to immigrate during World War I and II. At the time it considered the risk of new German immigrants being hostile was too great, even though most Germans would have become peace-loving citizens. Neither should the government allow pro-Jihad, or pro-terrorism Muslims to immigrate to America either. It is common national-security sense not to allow this.

VIII. The American Ideal and Immigrant Assimilation

We should insist that if the immigrant who comes here does in good faith become an American and assimilates himself to us he shall be treated on an exact equality with every one else, for it is an outrage to discriminate against any such man because of creed or birth-place or origin.

But this is predicated upon the man's becoming in very fact an American and nothing but an American. If he tries to keep segregated with men of his own origin and separated from the rest of America, then he isn't doing his part as an American. There can be no divided allegiance here. . . We have room for but one language here, and that is the English language, for we intend to see that the crucible turns our people out as Americans, of American nationality, and not as dwellers in a polyglot boarding-house; and we have room for but one soul loyalty, and that is loyalty to the American people.
- President Theodore Roosevelt. 1919 letter to the American Defense Society.

The American ideal has little to do with race or skin color. It has much to do with freedom. America's founding documents proclaim the God-given right for every person to have "Life, Liberty, and the Pursuit of Happiness". These freedoms include the right to worship in the way one wants; the right to say whatever you please as long as you do not slander a fellow citizen; the right to have commerce with and associate with anyone you choose to – or choose not to; the freedom to choose the level of government and taxation one desires.

Another part of the ideal is helping those in need with Christian charity. America is often referred to as the most charitable nation the world has ever known. Christian charity involves identifying and helping those in need, while encouraging those able to help themselves to take responsibility for their actions. Early America recognized this was best accomplished by individuals or charitable organizations operating at the local level. It was clearly shown in earlier chapters that government welfare programs funded by forced taxation are not charitable. These programs were not recommended by Jesus in the Bible and were not used by the nation's founders.

Assumed in the ideal was a common language in addition to the common principles. How can citizens possibly interact and choose representatives if all do not speak and understand a common language?

Those immigrating to America were expected to learn these principles and in turn were welcomed to America, which became known as the world's "melting pot", many nationalities forming one great culture. Their old culture was to become subordinate to the American culture.

Some recent immigrants allowed into America by the federal government do not seem to share the desire to become "American". An example of the failure of recent immigrants to assimilate:

> Message from Mogadishu
> Minnesota is home to the largest Somali community in the United States, numbering at least 32,000....We know they are mostly Muslim — we can see the hijabs, we are familiar

with the many local controversies to which their faith has given rise over the past 10 years — but are they loyal residents or citizens of the United States? In the conflict between the United States and the Islamist forces with which are contending, whose side are they on?

(The article describes two women convicted of providing support to a an affiliate of al Qaeda.)

[One convict] was not exactly remorseful after the jury returned its guilty verdicts. ...she stood before the judge and stated through an interpreter: "I am very happy." She added that she knew she was going to heaven.... As for the rest of us, she advised: "You will go to hell."

.... Members of the local Somali community materialized at the federal courthouse in Minneapolis to support the two Minnesota women convicted of supporting al Shabab. The [Somalis] appearing at the courthouse were apparently untroubled by the defendants' guilt of the crimes charged. On the contrary, they were troubled by the defendants' convictions — and not because of any evidence of innocence. The issue was beside the point. No voice expressly spoke up on behalf of law-abidingness or loyalty to the United States.
- Powerline. November 1, 2011. Scott Johnson

Did these women and their supporters not have to swear an oath to support the US Constitution before becoming citizens? Did they violate that oath with their actions? Should their citizenship be revoked? The country cannot stand strong if its citizens do not support the nation and the nation's culture.

During WWI and WW II Lutheran Churches with GERMAN ancestry proudly put American flags in the front of the churches, along with the Christian flag. Many still do to this day. This showed the church and its members supported America, not Germany.

Will Islamic mosques do the same thing – display the American flag - considering the nation is at war with Islamic terrorism? Or are the "citizens" loyal to the countries from which they came? At least in Minneapolis, the immigrants' loyalty seems to be with their previous country of residence.

Another example of recent immigrants not being loyal to their new country:

> CNN : Flying Mexican Flag Over US Flag Is OK
> A Mexican bar owner in Reno, Nevada flew the Mexican flag above that of the United States. Only problem is that this is specifically illegal under United States Code Section 7, Title Four, which states,
>
> (c) No other flag or pennant should be placed above or, if on the same level, to the right of the flag of the United States of America, except during church services conducted by naval chaplains at sea, when the church pennant may be flown above the flag during church services for the personnel of the Navy. No person shall display the flag of the United Nations or any other national or international flag equal, above, or in a position of superior prominence or honor to, or in place of, the flag of the United States at any place within the United States or any Territory or possession thereof......
>
> The brazen effrontery of the bar prompted an American veteran to cut down both flags. But when CNN reported on the event, they managed to significantly skew the perception. The CNN report simply states that the veteran was angry that the Mexican flag was placed above that of the US- no mention was made that it was in fact illegal under US law. CNN compounded their offense by showing in their video clip, not the actual words of the relevant US code that outlaws this action, but instead 'flag rules' taken from USHistory.org, thus downplaying the actual offense, by suggesting that the law is in fact merely recommended behavior. As in so much relating to the illegal alien lobby, apparently it is OK with CNN for immigrants to disrespect and/or disobey the laws of our country....
>
> -Newsbusters.org. Richard Newcomb. October 03, 2007

There is nothing wrong with Mexicans having pride in their home country. But if you put Mexico above the United States in your heart and your actions, then you should be a Mexican citizen, not a US citizen.

Germans who came to America in earlier times speak English, not

German. They studied the principles of America's founders, not the German Kaisers. They celebrate the Fourth of July as Independence Day for America, and Thanksgiving Day in November, not the German national holidays. They do not believe that large sections of the American Midwest, settled by German immigrants, should owe allegiance to Germany or the German culture. The Germans who came to America wanted to become Americans. They wanted to embrace the freedoms of America. There is a price to be paid for allowing new immigrants who do not know or care for the American culture into the country in large numbers. The nation will lose its cultural identity.

People of different cultures almost always choose to live with other people sharing their culture. It is human nature. So if a nation has large numbers of new immigrants with a dramatically different culture, it is natural for them to voluntarily segregate according to culture - very much like oil and water. This problem is even more severe in European nations than in America. Many European nations have seen rioting or other trouble with Islamic immigrants. In Sweden's case, the immigrants have a different faith (Islam vs secular or Christian), language (Arabic or Somali vs Swedish), political background (authoritarian vs democratic government) and skin color (olive vs white).

> Stockholm riots leave Sweden's dreams of perfect society up in smoke
> Like the millions of other ordinary Swedes whom he now sees himself as one of, Mohammed Abbas fears his dream society is now under threat. When he first arrived in Stockholm as refugee from Iran in 1994, the vast Husby council estate where he settled was a mixture of locals and foreigners, a melting pot for what was supposed to be a harmonious, multi-racial paradise.
> Two decades on, though, "white flight" has left only one in five of Husby's flats occupied by ethnic Swedes, and many of their immigrant replacements do not seem to share his view that a new life in Sweden is a dream come true. Last week, the neighborhood erupted into rioting, sparking some of the fiercest urban unrest that Sweden has seen in decades, and a new debate about the success of racial integration.

> "In the old days, the neighborhood was more Swedish and life felt like a dream, but now there are **just too many foreigners, and a new generation that has grown up here with just their own culture,**" he said, gesturing towards the hooded youths milling around in Husby's pedestrianised shopping precinct....
>
> Many Swedes were left asking why a country that prides itself on a generous welfare state, liberal social attitudes and a welcoming attitude towards immigrants should ever have race riots in the first place.
> - telegraph.co.uk. Colin Freeman. 25 May 2013.

Obviously, Mr. Abbas is the good kind of immigrant for a nation. He has adopted the nation's culture and considers himself Swedish, the nation he migrated to. But he, as an immigrant, realizes the problems caused by those who come to a nation but seek to maintain their old culture as the dominant culture in their lives, their failure to assimilate into the national culture. This is true for Sweden, America and any nation. It would be wise for nations to deport immigrants who are causing trouble and have no interest in assimilating into the national culture.

The chapter began with a quote from Calvin Coolidge on immigration in the 1920's. Here are some more thoughts from Coolidge that are relevant today.

> People, Not Lobbies: Immigration And The 1920s
> What Coolidge did believe in was "Americanism." By this he meant assimilation in one's public life, such as using English at work or in school and serving the country in war. Coolidge thought that if a newcomer wanted to be American, he deserved to be. "Whether one traces his Americanism back three centuries to the Mayflower, or three years to the steerage, is not half so important as whether his Americanism of today is real and genuine," the President said.
> Although Coolidge admired immigrants, he feared the establishment of national political interest groups based on ethnicity that could force new laws and government expansion at the national level. His theory was that a smaller

federal government would, eventually, benefit all, including new immigrants. This seems to have been accurate. In the 1920s charities grew and unemployment remained low under Coolidge's minimalist government. And some who landed jobs were immigrants.
-AMITY SHLAES. Forbes. April 13, 2013.

IX. The Solution
So what does America do now with the millions of illegal aliens currently living here?

Deport them? NO – unless they are committing crimes or causing other problems.

Give them amnesty and make them citizens? NO.

Cut off their federal welfare benefits? Yes.

Give them the ability to work legally in America? Yes.

Allow illegal aliens to apply for short term work visas. For the first round of visas, allow foreign workers currently in the US to apply. After that "grace period" the foreign worker must return to their home country to re-apply. The visa should be part of a comprehensive foreign worker program developed between the federal government and the states. Congress will regulate the number of visas given and the types of workers allowed into the program based on job demand. Companies could be fined that hire workers not in the visa system, with no proof of citizenship.

Any illegal aliens came here either to work or to collect welfare benefits. Had they wanted to be citizens, they would likely have applied for citizenship through the proper channels. So let each state decide on what type of worker program they want to set up, or even what type of state welfare benefits they want to hand out. But citizenship should be earned by going through proper legal channels.

Immigration Summary
- Return to pre-1965 US immigration laws. This will protect the culture and national identity of America. Only grant citizenship status to those who want to become part of the American culture and arrive legally.
- Require states, counties and cities to obey federal immigration law (like is done in Mexico).
- All immigrants must be tracked until they become citizens in order for the government to protect the population as a whole from crime and terrorism.
- The states and federal government should cooperate to implement a foreign worker program for areas where labor is needed.

Losing the American culture expressed in the Bible, the Declaration of Independence, and the Constitution will be tragic indeed. The American culture will prevail only if we, as a nation, manage our immigration process successfully.

"E pluribus unum" appears on the Seal of the United States. It is a Latin phrase meaning "Out of many, one". It was an unofficial motto of the United States and was a principle the Founders believed in. The United States must return to this principle, forming a singular nation and culture from many people, if it is to continue to be a strong nation.

The Federal Government's Financial Crisis

> If it moves, tax it. If it keeps moving, regulate it. And if it stops moving, subsidize it.
> - Ronald Reagan describing the federal government.

> The nation's founders would be horrified by today's congressional spending that consumes 25 percent of our GDP. Contrast that to the years 1787 to the 1920s when federal government spending never exceeded 4 percent of our GDP except in wartime.
> - Dr. Walter Williams, Professor of Economics.

This chapter discusses the financial problems of the federal government. It provides a sampling of news stories continually produced that document the unsustainable spending, inefficiency and waste of the federal government. Over decades, politicians have created a government that spends much more than it takes in, and is so massive in scope that it cannot be effectively managed. The biggest examples:

- Social Security: The program has serious demographic design flaws. Current law dictates it will pay billions more in benefits than it receives in taxes in the coming years. (Chapter 22)
- Medicare and Medicaid: The government programs to provide healthcare for the old and poor are projected to spend much much more that they collect in future years. (Chapter 21)
- ObamaCare: The government intrusion into the health insurance marketplace has already exceeded its cost expectations. Expect massive subsidy / spending requirements as long as the program exists.
- Baseline budgeting: Implemented in the 1970s, this gimmick automatically increases government department budgets each new fiscal year.
- Bloated defense budget: Often spending money on programs the military does not want, and liberally spreading money in as many congressional districts as possible so representatives can "bring home the bacon".

The end result is the federal government spending more than it takes in every year. Eventually this leads to a crisis. Governments, unlike other institutions or people, can create money to pay their bills in addition to taxing their citizens. So governments seldom go bankrupt. But high debt and poor economic policies eventually lead to economic malaise.

America is an economic superpower, so her economy can take a lot of punishment before weakening and failing. The US dollar is close to a world currency, being used as a medium of exchange for many transactions outside America, including the purchase and pricing of barrels of crude oil. Many doomsday forecasters overlook these facts when predicting the quick demise of America. The more likely analysis is that America is indeed approaching a financial crisis, but one that can be avoided if the present course of the government is changed. This chapter will examine the causes of the financial problems.

Outline:
    I.   Federal Government Spending and Debt
        A)   The Future US Debt Bomb
        B)   Inflation
        C)   If the US Government were a Family
        D)   How Did the Nation get here? An example
    II. Size of Federal Government Continues to Grow Despite Massive Debt
    III. Federal Workers Overpaid and Hard to Fire
    IV. The 2008 Mortgage Meltdown: Government Incompetence
    V. Federal Government: Waste, Excess and Incompetence
        A)   Redundancy and Duplicate Programs
        B)   Paying the Dead, Illegal, and Fictitious
        C)   The Fed: An Example of Congressional Oversight Failure
        D)   DEA Almost Kills Man Through Neglect
        E)   US Post Office: Inefficient Government Management
        F)   Federal Income Tax Code: More Incompetence
        G)   Silly Federal Regulations – Bad for Business
        H)   Government Creates New Agency With No Oversight
        I)   ObamaCare Website Fails to Work
    VI. Federal Government and Crony Capitalism
        A)   Auto Manufacturers : Bailing-Out Failing Companies

The Federal Government's Financial Crisis

      B)   Solyndra: Another example of the Failure of Government
      C)   Many More Solyndras (Failed Government Investments)
VII.   Final Example of Federal Government Excess: Transportation and the Federal Gas Tax
VIII.   Summary

I. Federal Government Spending and Debt.

The book, *The Fourth Turning*, predicts a crisis for America beginning around 2020. The book documents cycles of history that America has gone through. It proposes that the cycles are a result of human nature and generational differences. Every 80 years or so the country has faced a crisis that threatened the national survival. The three crises from history are: the American Revolution in 1776, the Civil War in 1860, and World War II in 1940. Each crisis took a full mobilization of the nation to overcome and prevail. The next crisis is due around 2020. It will likely involve US debt and the scope of the federal government.

Each of the previous crises has been a war, although World War II was immediately preceded by the Great Depression, that arguably was part of that crisis. Let us hope that with the advent of nuclear weapons, a war is not part of the next crisis. America will have enough on its plate dealing with the looming financial crisis brought on by the federal government spending well beyond its means.

A. The Future US Debt Bomb

Every year the federal government spends more than it takes in, it adds the difference to the national debt. From 2009-2012 the federal government spent $1 trillion more than it took in every year. Lately the federal government has been spending around $7 trillion a year. If deficit spending led to a robust economy, America should be having record growth.

The Bible and Constitution Made America Great

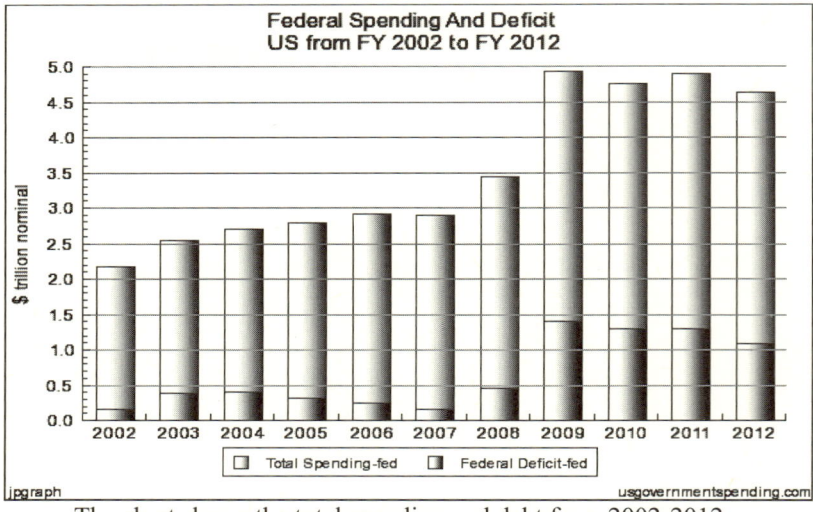

Federal Spending And Deficit US from FY 2002 to FY 2012

The chart shows the total spending and debt from 2002-2012.
The deficits are shown at the bottom of the bars.

The massive deficit spending every year has created a huge national debt. In 2013, the debt was around $17 trillion, or about $54,000 per US citizen.

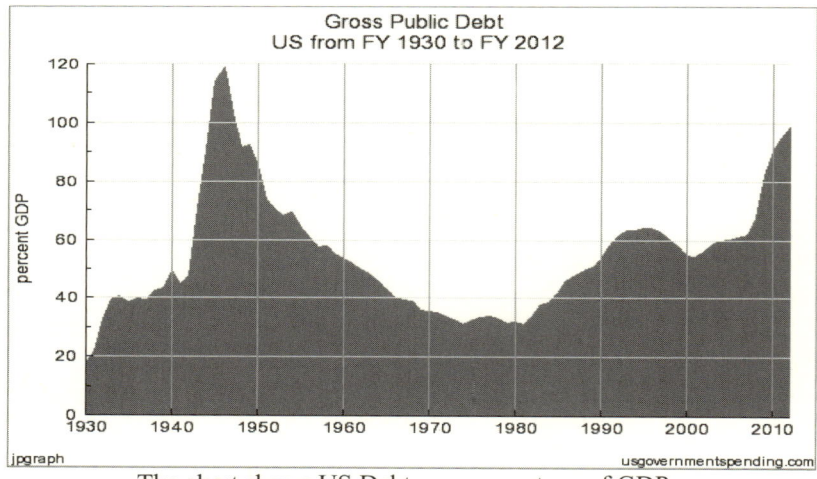

Gross Public Debt US from FY 1930 to FY 2012

The chart shows US Debt as a percentage of GDP.
Basically this is the size of debt compared to the size of the economy.

The debt is a serious problem, but is manageable at this moment in time. America had a debt record ratio of 120% during World War II in the 1940s. The country was fully mobilized to defeat Nazi Germany and Imperialist Japan. This level of debt was of course unsustainable were the spending to be maintained at those levels, but the war ended in 1945 and government spending dramatically decreased as the US went back to peacetime.

However, currently the federal government is getting ready to dramatically increase its spending, not decrease it. Politicians have made promises to subsidize senior citizens' retirement (Social Security) and healthcare (Medicare). These promises now require payment as baby boomers begin retiring.

ObamaCare may very well serve as a catalyst. It provides massive government control of the people (mandating that they buy a product) and heavily regulates the health insurance and medical providers. Expect economic growth to be reduced. ObamaCare was so shoddily implemented that the federal government has little idea of how many people enrolled, how many paid, and how many are owed a promised subsidy from the government. The cost estimates and spending projections used to pass the law are now meaningless. The one constant with government programs has been they cost more than estimated. If this holds true, expect ObamaCare spending to be much higher than thought beginning in 2014, the year it starts.

The US is heading toward a financial crisis if steps are not taken to reduce federal government spending and control the debt. So what will the crisis look like? Here are three possibilities:

1) A Collapse. Peter Schiff describes what could happen in a full-blown collapse. He makes the case in *The Real Crash* that the government's continuous borrowing and money printing is no longer tenable. The dollar could collapse as other nations lose faith in it, interest rates and consumer prices could soar and the US economy could implode. At this point, the Federal Reserve creating more money just leads to hyperinflation. The US dollar becomes Monopoly money in the most extreme case.

2) A Carter Malaise. This is describing an economic malaise similar

to what occurred during the Carter years in the late 1970s. Inflation reached 15% a year, and 30-year mortgage rates hit 18%. This is the prime example of stagflation in the US. The Misery Index, inflation rate plus unemployment rate, topped 21% under Carter. The US economic weakness was a key factor in Carter losing his re-election campaign.

3) The Japanese Lost Decades. The "lost decades" are the roughly 30 year period from the early 1990s through the present. Japan's economy contracted and its stock market remains well below its 1989 peak. The Japanese government created too much money that led to a bubble in both its stock and housing markets. The bubbles burst in1989. A liquidity trap followed, in which government stimulus efforts failed to spark economic growth. The Japanese economy remains in stagnation mode with low inflation or even deflation and falling wages.

B. Inflation
Inflation is the result of the government creating too much money, causing the value of the money to decrease and the price of goods and services to increase. Inflation erodes the ability of the citizen to purchase items.

> Inflation is taxation without legislation.
> - Milton Friedman, Nobel Award Economist

One of the ways weak inefficient governments try to cover up economic problems (usually from their own policies) is by creating excess money to pay its bills. The problems are usually seen in dictatorships in Africa or South America where the leader of the country just prints loads of paper money, which ultimately becomes worthless. The economic definition of money is a store of value. Paper currency is worthless unless it is backed by a government dedicated to supporting its worth.

An ideal currency will hold its value indefinitely. If this isn't the case, it hurts the citizens who depend on their national currency in order to buy and sell goods and services. Barring changes in production costs or changes in product performance, a product price shouldn't change over the years. But this is not true in the US. For example a man's suit that costs $450 today, cost only $20 in 1913.

If in 1913, an item cost $20, in 2011 it cost $454.
- www.usinflationcalculator.com

This is further demonstrated by the price of gold. The following chart shows the yearly average for the number of dollars needed to buy 1 ounce of gold. It was essentially held constant from the nation's founding until until the early 1970s, when the federal government removed the dollar's gold backing.

The chart shows two periods, 1970-1980, and 2000- present, where the federal government is creating much more money than is economically optimal. The result is inflation.

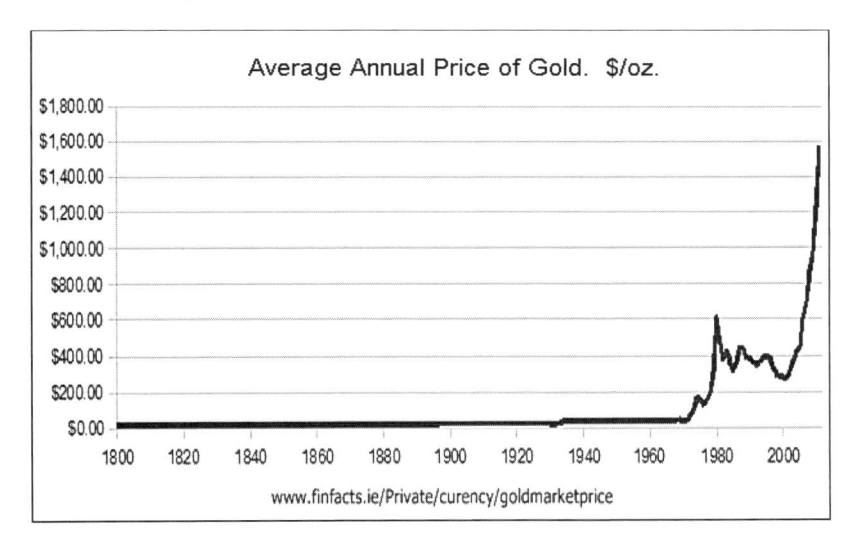

Average Annual Price of Gold. $/oz.

www.finfacts.ie/Private/curency/goldmarketprice

The official U.S. Government gold price has changed only four times from 1792 to the present. Starting at $19.75 per troy ounce, raised to $20.67 in 1834, and $35 in 1934. In 1972, the price was raised to $38 and then to $42.22 in 1973. A two-tiered pricing system was created in 1968, and the market price for gold has been free to fluctuate since then.

The US Constitution gives Congress the power to produce the nation's money and regulate its value.

<u>US Constitution: Article. I. Section. 8.</u>
The Congress shall have Power..... To coin Money, regulate the Value thereof,...

> (States are forbidden from issuing state currencies in Article I. Section 10.)

Congress has delegated this power to the Federal Reserve (The Fed). Unfortunately, Congress has given the Fed a dual mandate of low inflation and low unemployment. The second mandate should NOT be the focus of monetary policy and Congress should rescind the employment mandate. Leaving only low inflation or sound money as the Fed's concern.

The US government for most of its life has respected the value of money and tied it to gold so the money would retain value. This began to change in the 1930s, and fully collapsed in the early 1970s when the government abandoned the gold standard. Not surprisingly the nation has faced inflation ever since. Inflation erodes the value of the currency over time. Inflation can show up in various asset classes. Sometimes it is gold, silver or precious metals. It can also be land prices, house prices, food prices, stock prices, or any other item purchased with dollars.

Sidebar: Normally, the high levels of debt the US has compiled would lead to high interest rates. Financing the debt means a large number of bonds must be sold, and interest rates rise to make the bonds attractive to investors. But the federal government is cheating. The Federal Reserve is keeping interest rates low by buying the bonds itself with created money. If the Fed creates too many dollars, inflation will result at some point.

As the federal government has gotten larger, and made commitments it cannot easily pay for, it has resorted to the inflationary policies of poor governments around the world. This harms the citizenry, which is obligated to use the dollar to build savings and wealth.

<u>C. If the US Government were a Family</u>
It can be difficult to grasp the size of millions, billions, and trillions of dollars. Put in household terms though, it becomes

understandable. The numbers are taken from usgovernment-spending.com over the period from 1990-2010, but adjusted to household size.

Assume the US government is an upper-middle class family spending $125,000 per year in 1990. This covers all the family expenses including food, clothing, entertainment, and housing costs. By 2010, the family spending had increased to $359,000. This is a 187% increase or almost tripling in spending over 20 years.

The spending is not a problem by itself as the family may have a very large income (taxes for the government). Our "family" had an income of $103,000 in 1990, and did pretty well growing it. By 2010, income had increased to $216,000. This is a 109% increase or more than doubling.

The problem is that, while the family now makes $216,000, it is spending $359,000. No family can do that for long without ending up in bankruptcy. By 2010 the family had a total accumulated debt of $1,415,000. Over $1.4 million dollars of debt with no savings! This family is in danger of bankruptcy as it owes almost 7 times what it takes in each year.

The first thing the family needs to do is only spend what it takes in. It cannot afford to keep adding to the debt. This means some unpleasant choices must be made. The family really likes spending $359,000 a year! They buy lots of really great stuff. But the family must cut up its credit cards and prioritize its spending if it is to survive. The federal government must do the same as the family and stop borrowing. It should prioritize spending and spend only what it takes in.

D. How Did the Nation get here? An Example
In March 2011, there was a federal budget spending debate in Washington in conjunction with efforts to raise the US debt ceiling (the amount of debt the Treasury can issue). Republicans proposed cutting spending by $61 billion. Democrats considered this cut too extreme and counter-proposed a cut of only $5 billion.

Sidebar: Going back to our household analogy, the family is

spending $359,000 a year. The proposals were to cut spending by either $6000 or $500. So the family will still be spending $351,000 or $358,500. Does either proposal now seem sufficient, much less extreme?

It is illustrative to the ways of government in Washington to examine the budget legislation that resulted from the debate. The US debt ceiling was increased from $14,300 billion to $16,700 billion. The politicians agreed to "cut" future spending by $1,700 billion. The legislation was named the Budget Control Act of 2011.

The top two chart lines are the proposed federal government spending before and after the Budget Control Act "cuts".

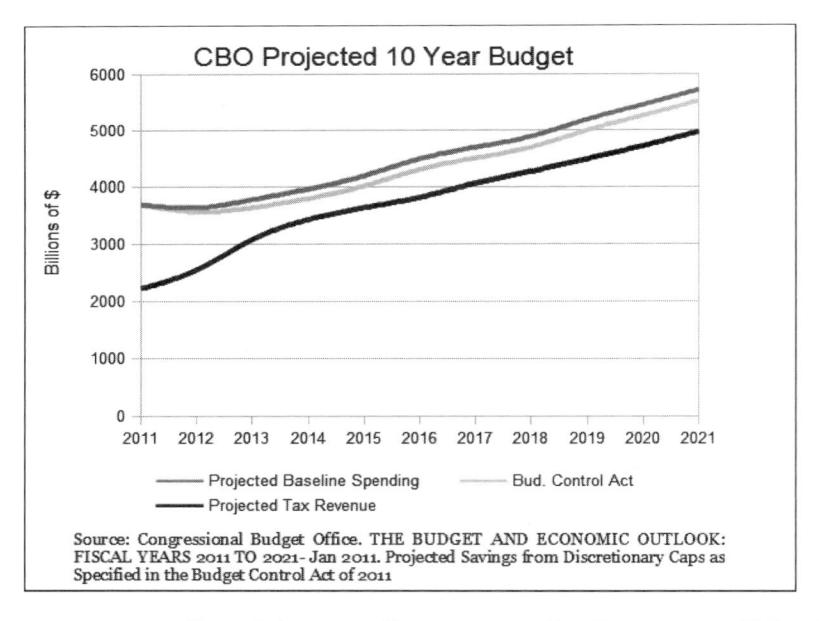

CBO Projected 10 Year Budget

— Projected Baseline Spending   — Bud. Control Act
— Projected Tax Revenue

Source: Congressional Budget Office. THE BUDGET AND ECONOMIC OUTLOOK: FISCAL YEARS 2011 TO 2021- Jan 2011. Projected Savings from Discretionary Caps as Specified in the Budget Control Act of 2011

Do you see any "cuts" in spending or any "budget control" in the chart?

The "spending cuts" in the Budget Control Act were over 10 years and subtracted from an assumed baseline budget that already had large spending increases built in. So even with a "spending cut" the actual amount spent rises every year. Also note that the tax revenue is never enough to cover the proposed spending. So much for budget control. Only the government could budget its spending with no regard as to whether the revenue will cover it.

When the average American hears $1,700 billion in "cuts" from a politician, he or she will assume the $3,600 billion budget was being reduced to $1,900 billion. Obviously this was not the case. The government projects it will continue to spend more than it takes in every year. The massive borrowing will cause the debt to approach $20,000 billion by the end of the 10 year period.

The "cuts" were "government-speak", not "household budget-speak" that American families or businesses use. In household budgeting, an $8000 cut means if the household spent $40,000, it will now only spend $32,000. **With government-speak, an $8000 cut comes from the *proposed* family budget of $50,000, which means the family will still spend $42,000 (a $2000 increase).**

Another fallacy with government budgeting is the huge focus on a 10 year cycle. The only budget numbers that really matter are the numbers for the current budget year because Congress always does a new budget and determines spending every new fiscal year. The great landmark Budget Control Act of 2011 made it a whole 2 years before Congress changed the law.

> Budget Bill Passes, Is Headed to President's Desk
> The measure, which sets spending levels at just over $1 trillion through 2015, ends a years-long budget stalemate in Congress,...
> [Some] Republican opposition to the bill centered on the measure's *increase of spending caps originally set through the 2011 Budget Control Act.*
> - www.realclearpolitics.com. Caitlin Huey-Burns. December 18, 2013.

The government should do 10 year budget projections, but the projections are mere estimates of what what the budget will look like *if* future Congresses do not change the law. Congress almost always changes the budget law from year to year. Also it is impossible to predict future economic events. The 10 year budget forecasts of 2006 did not predict the economic turmoil of 2008 – so were soon worthless.

II. Size of Federal Government Continues to Grow Despite Debt

The number of federal employees has also increased significantly over recent years despite the massive federal debt. There were over 2.6 million federal government employees in 2011. Over half of these were in the numerous federal agencies outside of the Defense Department and the Post Office.

Total Federal Government Employees

Total Federal Employees	2,681,000
Defense Department	757,000
US Post Office	574,000
Other Federal Civilian Agencies	1,350,000

US Postal Service Facts-2011; The Washington Times, February 2, 2010

There is no doubt that both the Defense Department and Post Office could become more efficient and reduce the personnel required to carry out their tasks. But both of these are constitutionally specified responsibilities for the federal government. Many agencies have no such constitutional authority.

When a business is deeply in debt as the federal government is, it often is forced close non-core areas of its business. Not so with the federal government. It just keeps borrowing and hiring more workers that it cannot afford to pay. Many are working in areas that the federal government shouldn't even be involved in.

III. Federal Workers Overpaid and Hard to Fire

When a business is deeply in debt, it will reduce salaries or layoff workers. Not so with the federal government. The US Government continues to hire more employees and pay them more than competing businesses pay-- yet another example of federal government mismanagement. The following suggest that federal workers are much better off than their private sector counterparts.

> Federal workers earning double their private counterparts
> At a time when workers' pay and benefits have stagnated, federal employees' average compensation has grown to more than double what private sector workers earn. Federal civil

servants earned **average pay and benefits of $123,049** in 2009 while **private workers made $61,051** in total compensation, according to the Bureau of Economic Analysis.   - USA TODAY. Dennis Cauchon. 8/13/2010.

Federal workers starting at much higher pay than in past
Newly hired federal workers are starting at much higher salaries than those who did the same jobs in the past, a lift that has elevated the salaries of scientists and custodians alike....The portion of federal workers earning **$100,000 or more** grew from 12% in 2006 to **22% in 2011**.
   - USA TODAY. Dennis Cauchon. 12/27/2011

Doctors, lawyers, dentists tops in fed jobs that pay $180K+
At least **17,828 federal employees whose annualized salaries totaled $180,000 or more** in September 2010.
   - USA TODAY. Kevin McCoy. 5/3/2011.

18,000 Federal workers making $180,000+ a year? 22% of the federal work force making over $100,000 a year? Federal pay doubling private sector pay when the lucrative federal pensions and healthcare benefits are included? With these facts it becomes pretty easy to say that indeed, federal workers are overpaid.

Every single federal worker is paid by taxpayers. Shouldn't taxpayers ask: "What are all of these workers doing?" and "Are the high salaries worth the cost?" as they pay their taxes every year? Couldn't many of the functions be done more efficiently by private businesses? Those functions needing government action can most assuredly by done more efficiently at the state or local level. The truly sad fact is, with the enormous amount of spending and size of the federal government, taxpayers are not getting good value for their money.

It's also very hard, if not impossible, to fire federal government workers. The "fired" employee enjoys a lengthy appeals process that takes over a year. The reviews are done by boards consisting of fellow government workers. The boards have no economic incentive to fire the worker, because there is no downside to any of the employees if the federal government loses money – it just borrows or prints more. Don't ignore the possibility of the boards containing government union members who would be willing to give a pass to a poorly performing employee who happens to also be active in the union.

> Under federal rules, a fired government worker has the right to appeal to the Merit Systems Protection Board. He or she can challenge the decision, argue that their actions don't meet the threshold for termination and ask to be reinstated — especially if there was no warning of trouble in past performance reviews.
>
> The board is set up so fired employees appealing their termination get two chances to prove they should stay..... The initial appeals take an average of 93 days to process, said William Spencer, a spokesman for the board.
>
> If the regional board rules against the [fired employee], they could appeal to the national Washington, D.C.-based board, which takes on average another 245 days.
>
> The [fired employee] wouldn't collect a paycheck during the appeals process. They would get back pay only if they are ultimately reinstated.
>
> Max Stier, who heads Partnership for Public Service, a nonprofit that recommends ways to improve the federal workforce, says it's "not impossible" to get rid of federal workers. In 2012, he says, 8,755 federal workers were fired, and others likely resigned to avoid the ax — although there are no estimates of how many because it's hard to track those kinds of departures.
>
> - freerepublic.com. David Nather and Rachael Bade. 5/22/2013.

Firing 8700 workers may seem like a lot until it is compared with the 2,681,000 federal employees. This works out to a rate of approximately 0.3% of workers fired per year.

For all the high pay and benefits they receive, the federal government was not able to prevent a financial crisis In fact many reports have shown the policies of the federal government contributed mightily to the crisis which cost almost every American, either in direct job loss, home loss due to foreclosure, or a substantial decrease in their retirement savings.

IV. The 2008 Mortgage Meltdown: Government Incompetence

How many liberal-Democrat politicians have blamed George W. Bush for the terrible economy largely caused by the mortgage/housing crisis? Too numerous to count. The most famous being Barack Obama as he ran for re-election in 2012. Bush can be blamed in small part – only because he did nothing to remove the federal government from interference in the mortgage system that his predecessor put in place. Bill Clinton was the person most responsible for creating the crisis.

> ### Housing Arsonist Bill Clinton Now Portrayed As Heroic Firefighter
>
> Truth is, it was his own reckless housing policies that wrecked the economy. ...under his National Homeownership Strategy, Clinton took more than 100 executive actions to pry bank lending windows wide open.
>
> First, using his executive order powers, he marshaled 10 federal agencies under the little-known Interagency Task Force on Fair Lending to enforce new "flexible" mortgage underwriting guidelines to combat "lending discrimination in any form." **For the first time, banks were ordered to qualify low-income minorities with spotty credit.** The 1994 policy planted the seeds of the mortgage crisis, as lenders abandoned prudent underwriting standards altogether.
>
> The next year, **Clinton set numerical targets for lending in predominantly minority census tracts under a revised Community Reinvestment Act**, and added several hundred bank examiners to enforce the tougher CRA rules. Banks that failed had their expansion plans put on hold, a slow death sentence in an era of bank mergers and acquisitions.
>
> For the first time, CRA ratings were made public, egging on Acorn and other radical inner-city groups, who used the reports to extort banks for more than $6 trillion in subprime and other loan set-asides by 2008. When bankers resisted being saddled with so many additional risky loans, Clinton tapped Fannie Mae and Freddie Mac to take them off their

books, while freeing bankers to originate more of the political loans. He directed HUD to hike Fannie's and Freddie's goals for underwriting affordable loans, which remained in force throughout the 2000s.

He also **authorized Fannie and Freddie for the first time to buy subprime securities** to earn credits against the HUD goals. The mortgage giants jumped at the chance, since it allowed them to meet the onerous new goals.
- Investors Business Daily (online). 9-7-2012.

Rather than blaming Presidents Clinton, Bush, or Obama, let's place the blame on the massive federal government and its intrusion into the American mortgage and housing market which operated perfectly well under free-market principles before the government intervened.

The federal government bureaucrats followed their directives and the two government backed agencies, Fannie Mae and Freddie Mac, played a significant role in the economic meltdown in America in 2008 by encouraging sub-prime loans to unqualified borrowers and assuming the responsibility if the loans went bad.

Government Mostly Responsible for 2008 Housing Bubble
Was the great financial crisis caused by....government housing policies that brought on the housing bubble and mismanaged the risks?

[Peter J. Wallison, a former general counsel of the U.S. Treasury and now a fellow at the American Enterprise Institute] argues that the housing bubble, driven by U.S. government policy to increase homeownership, is the primary cause of the financial crisis. He notes: "The most recent bubble involved increases in real [not nominal] home prices of 80 percent over 10 years, while the earlier ones involved increases of about 10 percent before they deflated."

Starting in the late 1990s, the government, as a social policy to boost homeownership, required Fannie Mae and Freddie Mac to acquire increasing numbers of "affordable" housing loans. (An "affordable loan" is made to people who normally would not qualify.) By 2007, 55 percent of all loans made by Fannie and Freddie had to be "affordable."

By June 2008, there were 27 million subprime housing loans outstanding (19.2 million of them directly owed by government or government-sponsored agencies), with an unpaid principal amount of $4.6 trillion.

By the middle of [2010], foreclosure starts jumped to a record 5 percent, four times higher than any previous housing bubble.

Wallison concludes his argument: "What we know is that almost 50 percent of all mortgages outstanding in the United States in 2008 were subprime or otherwise deficient and high-risk loans. The fact that two-thirds of these mortgages were on the balance sheets of government agencies, or firms required to buy them by government regulations, is irrefutable evidence that the **government's housing policies were responsible for most of the weak mortgages that became delinquent and defaulted in unprecedented numbers when the housing bubble collapsed**."

- Tuesday, 16 Nov 2010. The Washington Times, LLC

John Carney also detailed the government's role in the 2008 economic turmoil in a lengthy article for the businessinsider.com on June 27, 2009. To summarize the article: Government involvement began with *The Community Reinvestment Act passed in 1977*. The CRA was not a static piece of legislation and as with most government agencies, regulators continued to write new regulations and standards evolving the law. **Regulators encouraged low-to-no document mortgages and the elimination of downpayments.** Banks failing to follow the new regulations would be considered guilty of "unfair lending practices". Banks responded by increasing the CRA loans they made and relaxing their lending standards. The government (Fannie Mae and Freddie Mac) pushed for greater mortgage securitization in an effort to increase CRA lending, buying trillions of dollars of "affordable" mortgages. The government intentionally decreased the risks to the banks in order to increase loans to low-income borrowers and minorities, in particular.

So, governmental actions caused an unintended consequence. The goal was to increase minority home ownership, but the government failed to take into account the financial ability of the mortgage recipients to repay the loans. Thus the government succeeded in one goal, but unexpectedly (at least to bureaucrats) caused the entire home mortgage system to melt down. There are sound economic reasons that mortgage standards had been put in place and used by lenders for generations.

- Requiring a 20% downpayment insures that the borrower has equity in the home or "skin in the game". If the house loses 10% in value in a tough economy, the borrower still has equity. A borrower won't "walk away" from the mortgage and lose his downpayment.
- Requiring a borrower's monthly income to be well above the mortgage payment insures the borrower will be able to make payments, even if a tough economy causes their income to drop. Removing the requirement allows borrowers to buy more house than they can afford.

Both of these requirements also prevent housing prices from surging upward. They limit the pool of buyers and cause prices to stay lower. Removing them contributed to a bubble. Once the economy turned south, the housing bubble burst. By pushing the banks to lower lending standards, the government greatly contributed to housing prices rising to an artificially high level, then crashing back down to earth.

No document loans also distorted the housing market. Any bank loaning money with no documentation (taking the word of the borrower) is asking for fraudsters to take advantage of the situation. And they did. A self-employed person applies for a mortgage and claims he has $150,000 a year in income. No documentation means the bank doesn't check the applicant; they assume he's telling the truth and provide a loan accordingly. Is it any wonder that many of these people exaggerated their income and became unable to pay their mortgage?

Were greedy bankers partly to blame? Yes. But in a free market, greedy bankers lose everything if their risks don't pay off. It was government action to assume the risk in the loans that allowed bankers to make the risky loans with no personal consequences. When Fannie Mae and Freddie Mac bought mortgages from the banks, they assumed the risk. These two agencies were independent of government, yet their loan portfolios were guaranteed by taxpayers.

> ### Fannie, Freddie At Heart Of Financial Crisis
>
> The SEC is suing top officers at Fannie Mae and Freddie Mac for not disclosing their true exposure to subprime loans.
>
> To date, taxpayers have spent $169 billion on Fannie and Freddie's mistakes. But some analysts believe the losses could ultimately reach as much as $1 trillion.
>
> Now, the government's own market watchdog, the Securities and Exchange Commission... [is], going after former Fannie CEO Daniel Mudd and former Freddie CEO Richard Syron.
>
> From 2007 to 2008, according to SEC documents, executives at Freddie and Fannie together estimated their total exposure to subprime loans at about $10 billion.
>
> The real amount? Nearly $300 billion total.
>
> In short, Fannie and Freddie are frauds. They systematically hid their exposure to potential losses from investors, taxpayers and regulators.
> - Investors Business Daily. 12/16/2011.

Despite being under investigation by the SEC, the government has no qualms rewarding Fannie and Freddie executives who lose money with bonuses. Afterall it's only taxpayer dollars that are being lost – not their own money or shareholders' money.

> The Federal Housing Finance Agency, the government regulator for Fannie and Freddie, approved **$12.79 million in bonus pay** after 10 executives from the two government-sponsored corporations last year met modest performance targets.... The executives got the bonuses about two years after the federally backed mortgage giants received nearly **$170 billion in taxpayer bailouts** — and despite pledges by FHFA, the office tasked with keeping them solvent, that it would adjust the level of CEO-level pay after critics slammed

huge compensation packages paid out to former Fannie Mae CEO Franklin Raines and others.
- Politico. JOSH BOAK & JOSEPH WILLIAMS. 10/31/11.

A company being run incompetently like this would soon find itself bankrupt. That is how the free market punishes poor performance. Federal government workers don't have to worry if they lose money, though. Congress will just raise taxes or borrow more money.

Fannie Mae and Freddie Mac used to be semi-private, but after 2008 were taken over by the federal-government in another bailout action, meaning the executives are now government employees. Why are government employees being paid these huge bonuses – in addition to their regular pay???

After creating the housing problem, politicians tried to solve it with yet another federal government program: the Preforeclosue Sale Program. It's debatable how effective programs like this are, but they are usually very expensive and wasteful.

> <u>Audit: HUD Paid More than $1 Billion in Bogus Foreclosure Claims</u>
> The government's Preforeclosue Sale Program was supposed to save struggling homeowners from foreclosure, but the government might have paid more than $1 billion to homeowners who didn't qualify for it. Out of 80 randomly selected claims audited by the Office of the Inspector General of the Department of Housing and Urban Development (HUD), 61 did not meet the program's criteria [*That is 76% of payments made in error!*]. The audit showed that HUD paid $1.06 billion in claims for 11,693 preforeclosure sales that did not meet requirements of the Federal Housing Authority (FHA), which runs the program.
> - www.moneynews.com. Michael Kling. Friday, 21 Sep 2012

Surely the federal government learned the lesson that it isn't good policy to push banks to lend money to prospective homeowners with shaky credit. But, sadly, it appears many federal bureaucrats learned nothing and are repeating their same mistakes.

> Obama administration pushes banks to make home loans to people with weaker credit
> The Obama administration is engaged in a broad push to make more home loans available to people with weaker credit, an effort that officials say will help power the economic recovery but that skeptics say could open the door to the risky lending that caused the housing crash in the first place.   - The Washington Post. Zachary A. Goldfarb. Apr 03, 2013.

The federal government needs to be removed from the housing market. Their meddling only distorts the market, causes problems, and wastes tax dollars. Is there any better example of why the federal government needs to be restricted to its constitutional duties than the incredible mess it made in the housing market?

V. Federal Government: Waste, Excess and Incompetence
Chapter 8 detailed the abysmal failure of the national government's "War on Poverty". The federal government has proven it cannot win a war on poverty. How much longer will we allow it to continue wasting money on this fight?

Sidebar: Some wish to blame the recipients of government aid for taking it. This is a ridiculous argument. If there is a Crazy Uncle Sam who likes to stand on a street corner and give out $100 bills, is it the fault of those people taking the bills? No. It is the fault of the crazy uncle. Why would you blame those who accept a free gift? It is up to the family to keep the crazy uncle from giving away the family wealth (or borrowing money from a bank to give away). So do not blame the recipients for taking full advantage of mis-guided government programs.

A. Redundancy and Duplicate Programs
The other federal government agencies are also full of waste and redundant spending. Fox News reported on the Government Accountability Office (GAO) study released in February of 2011. The study provides numerous examples of the massive waste and inefficiency present in the federal government and its budget and appropriation process. The study found 33 areas with "overlap and fragmentation". The federal government doesn't do anything "small". Why have one program when you can have 75 or 80? Some

areas with multiple overlapping programs are listed below.

The Government Accountability Office (GAO) Study
- 80 different economic development programs.
- 47 job-training programs, 44 of which overlap. Only 5 could provide an "impact study" since 2004 looking at "outcomes." About half of them provided no performance review at all since 2004.
- 80 programs for the "transportation disadvantaged."
- 82 teacher quality programs spread across 10 separate agencies -- something hundreds of local school districts are already focused on.
- 56 programs across 20 agencies dealing with financial literacy.
- 20 programs across 7 agencies dealing with homelessness.
- 15 agencies administering 30 food-related laws. "Some of the oversight doesn't make any sense," the report stated bluntly.
- 18 food assistance programs administered by the U.S. Department of Agriculture, the Department of Homeland Security and the Department of Health and Human Services -- with GAO estimating $62.5 billion spent on them. "Little is known about the effectiveness" of 11 of those programs, the report states.
- More than 2,100 data centers -- up from 432 a little more than a decade ago -- across 24 federal agencies. GAO estimated the government could save up to $200 billion over the next decade by consolidating them.

Sen. Tom Coburn R-OK said in a statement: "This report confirms what most Americans assume about their government. We are spending trillions of dollars every year and nobody knows what we are doing. The executive branch doesn't know. The congressional branch doesn't know. Nobody knows. This report also shows we could save taxpayers hundreds of billions of dollars every year without cutting services."

Congress, consisting of 435 independent members, has proven it cannot be trusted to effectively manage multi-trillion dollar federal budgets.

B. Paying the Dead, Illegal and Fictitious

Another example of federal government incompetence: it routinely sends checks to people long after they have died. Why not? It's not the bureaucrats' money. The federal government simply is not a good steward of taxpayer dollars. Whether the programs are too big and complex to manage, or whether the government employees simply do not care, the government wasting money is a frequent occurrence. Two examples show agencies sending checks to dead people and illegals.

> #### Paying the Dead
> There isn't much about dysfunctional government that shocks me anymore, but this story did.
> According to a report by the Office of Personnel Management and reported in Ed O'Keefe's "Federal Eye" column in the Washington Post, our government has been sending checks to dead people. "In the last five years," O'Keefe writes, "the Office of Personnel Management has made more than $601 million in payments to dead federal retirees, according to the agency's inspector general. Total annual payouts range between $100 million and $150 million."
> This isn't new. Inspector General Patrick McFarland had urged OPM in 2005 and again in 2008 to more closely monitor such payments. It appears his advice has gone unheeded.
>   - Cal Thomas. 09/26/11 Column

> #### IRS Sent $7,319,518 in Refunds to One Bank Account Used by 2,706 Aliens
> The Internal Revenue Service sent $7,319,518 in tax refunds in 2011 to what theoretically were 2,706 aliens who were not authorized to work inside the United States and who all used the same bank account, according to an audit report by the Treasury Inspector General for Tax Administration.
>
> The 2,706 tax refunds worth a combined $7,319,518 that the IRS sent to a single bank account in 2011 were all paid on tax returns that used Individual Taxpayer Identification

Numbers.

The inspector general's audit report revealing this remarkable payout was spurred by two IRS employees who went to members of Congress "alleging that IRS management was requiring employees to assign Individual Taxpayer Identification Numbers (ITIN) even when the applications were fraudulent."
      - CNSnews.com. Terence P. Jeffrey. June 24, 2013

Sending 2700 checks to one address obviously indicates fraud and a scam. Most private companies would notice and stop payment, but the IRS just gave away $7 million dollars to crooks. In addition to the obvious fraudulent account, there were plenty of other checks sent to illegal aliens at other addresses. Which brings up the point: Why is the federal government sending checks to lawbreakers?

Remember these two stories next time you read a story on how federal government budgets are 'cut to the bone'.

Feds give millions in contracts to firms owned by fictitious people

... at least 15 false businesses in six states ...received government contracts despite ... being registered to people who did not exist. The businesses subcontracted all the work to other companies, then took the federal dollars without paying the companies doing the work.

The case illustrates how little federal officials know about where goods and services they purchase come from, with one Whitehead firm selling ammunition to the Army, according to government contracting records, thus raising questions about whether bullets of dubious quality wound up in soldiers' hands.

The Department of Homeland Security, with seemingly little investigation of the company's background, gave it a government credit card "to use for payment for goods provided pursuant to a government contract," on which Whitehead racked up $40,000 in charges.

It also highlights the lack of scrutiny of those receiving contracts under set-asides for small businesses and minorities, who simply self-certify, and who the government is pressured to source goods through over established vendors, even for goods like ammunition, which few fly-by-night firms are legitimately equipped to manufacture or supply.

The fake companies included the Encompass Group, which is registered to a ramshackle house in Maryland, touted its status as a black-owned firm and got contracts to do work for everything from teaching English to selling furniture, the Washington Examiner found.

- Washingtonexaminer.com. LUKE ROSIAK.| AUGUST 8, 2013.

Companies winning a bid through a set-aside are not supposed to be able to subcontract the work, but with so little information available, federal officials have no way of enforcing this.

C. The Fed: An Example of Congressional Oversight Failure
In 1913, Congress created The Federal Reserve (The Fed) to manage the money supply and currency for the Unites States. The Constitution gives the power to manage the nation's currency to Congress, so it is perfectly constitutional for Congress to delegate the responsibility to an agency that it creates. However, Congress then should assume the responsibility for managing and overseeing the agency. Unfortunately, Congress has abdicated their oversight responsibility. While finally authorizing an audit, Congress has still taken no action to curb the Fed's abuse(?) of power a year after the audit was completed.

The Fed Audit
The first top-to-bottom audit of the Federal Reserve [conducted by the Government Accountability Office] uncovered eye-popping new details about how the U.S. provided a whopping $16 trillion in secret loans to bail out American and foreign banks and businesses during the worst economic crisis since the Great Depression.

"As a result of this audit, we now know that the Federal Reserve provided more than $16 trillion in total financial assistance to some of the largest financial institutions and corporations in the United States and throughout the world," said Sanders.

> Among the investigation's key findings is that the Fed unilaterally provided trillions of dollars in financial assistance to foreign banks and corporations from South Korea to Scotland, according to the GAO report. "No agency of the United States government should be allowed to bailout a foreign bank or corporation without the direct approval of Congress and the president," Sanders said.
> - www.sanders.senate.gov July 21, 2011 (Sen. Bernie Sanders website)

$16 trillion was more that the entire US national debt at the time. That's the equivalent of a family owing $200,000 on its own mortgages and credit cards loaning an additional $220,000 to a family across town. The difference is, in the US, the Fed can create as many dollars as it wants and evidently give or loan the created dollars to whatever entities they want.

This is another horrific example of government incompetence. The Fed should not be lending US dollars to any foreign entity. Only Congress has the power to authorize that type of action, and it is high questionable if Congress should be doing that.

Congress has created so many agencies that it is no longer capable of overseeing and managing the functions that it is constitutionally required to do.

D. DEA Almost Kills Man Through Neglect
The Drug Enforcement Agency offers a cruel example of the federal government overstepping its authority and harming a person in the process. The DEA, arrested a man, then forgot about him, leaving him with no food, water, or toilet for 5 days in San Diego, California.

> ### Man Left in Cell 5 Days Without Food Will Sue
> A San Diego college student filed a legal claim Wednesday for damages suffered when he was left handcuffed and without food or water in a Drug Enforcement Administration holding cell for five days last month. After two days of being handcuffed in a tiny holding cell and desperate for food and water, Daniel Chong said he realized he had to stop wondering when he'd be let out and start thinking about how to stay alive. Entering what he called "survival mode," and

already drinking his own urine, he futilely tried to trigger an overhead fire sprinkler for some water, stacking clothes and a blanket and swinging his cuffed arms in an attempt to set it off.

Chong, 23, a student at the University of California, San Diego, had been picked up in a drug sweep but was never arrested or charged. He spent five days forgotten in the windowless cell before Drug Enforcement Administration agents opened the door.

The DEA has said he was "accidentally" left in the cell and has apologized to Chong.

After his release, he spent five days in the hospital for dehydration, kidney failure, cramps and a perforated esophagus. He had lost 15 pounds (6.8 kilograms).
- Newsmax Wires. 03 May 2012

Assuming the agents had a warrant, it is still highly questionable whether there is constitutional authority for a federal agency like the DEA, to enter a citizen's home. Drug laws and enforcement belong at the state level per the 10th Amendment. The federal government should stop the illegal import of goods across the border, but that was not the case here. Maybe if the federal government focused only on the the responsibilities given to it in the Constitution, it could do a better job.

E. US Post Office: Inefficient Government Management
Managing the US Post Office is a constitutional responsibility authorized to Congress. It is somewhat unique in that it operates on a business-type model: It provides a service that customers pay for. The Post Office delivers mail, and its customers pay it to do so. There is no forced taxation in its funding model. Unfortunately, the Post Office is a perfect example of how government bureaucrats cannot run a business efficiently.

Postal Service 'at the brink of default'
The United States Postal Service is "at the brink of default" and turned to Congress on Tuesday seeking billions in funding and legislation to help it restructure to remain in business.

> Facing a $10 billion loss in revenue this year, the Postal Service could be forced to shut down by August 2012 if drastic steps are not immediately taken to save it, USPS officials said.
>
> - Washington Examiner. Susan Ferrechio. 09/06/11

Of course Congress bailed out the Post Office. A lot of the USPS problem is the very high pay and benefits typical of federal workers. Only in this case there is not an unlimited amount of borrowed money to fund it. The USPS must earn its revenue by selling its services (mail delivery) to customers. Surprise! When given a choice, customers are choosing not to subsidize high federal salaries and benefits.

Most private companies have abandoned pensions (company guaranteed payments in retirement) for 401K plans (companies contribute to workers' retirement plans upfront). Companies did this because the cost of pensions was simply too high. They couldn't afford the premium worker retirement plans. The USPS has not done so. Funding pensions is a key expense driving the USPS into default.

With the decline in overall use of mail delivery (due to: e-mail, e-greeting cards, Facebook....) a wise business would have altered its business model to adapt. One logical plan would be to go to every-other-day delivery. Half of the customers get mail delivery on Monday-Wednesday-Friday. The other half get mail delivery on Tuesday-Thursday-Saturday. 50% of the postal carriers could be eliminated, and the overall delivery costs could be greatly reduced.
Some will say this is harsh! Workers should not be laid off. Well the alternative is to continue to raise the 1st class stamp price to ~ $.85, then $1, then $2. With each increase mail volume will further decline. This is the brutality of free markets. If there is not consumer demand for the service, the service cannot be continued. Customers are simply not willing to pay for it.

The fact is government does not respond well to market forces. Government is always inefficient and overpriced in the services it provides when compared to private companies.

F. Federal Income Tax Code : More Incompetence

Very little shows the bumbling federal government more than the tax code they have created (displayed in the chart).

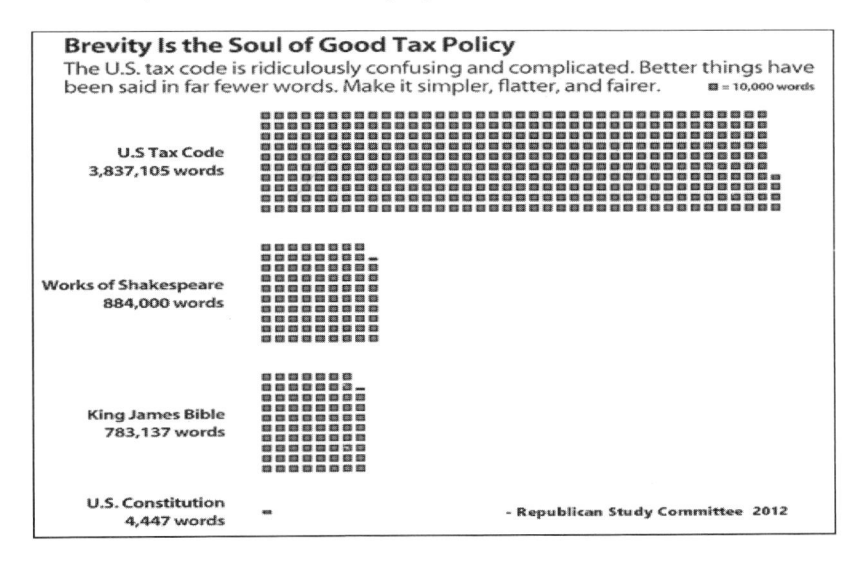

Brevity Is the Soul of Good Tax Policy
The U.S. tax code is ridiculously confusing and complicated. Better things have been said in far fewer words. Make it simpler, flatter, and fairer.   ■ = 10,000 words

- U.S Tax Code — 3,837,105 words
- Works of Shakespeare — 884,000 words
- King James Bible — 783,137 words
- U.S. Constitution — 4,447 words

- Republican Study Committee 2012

The US tax code has over 3.8 million words! Almost 5 times the number of words in the entire Bible! The founding fathers wrote the entire Constitution with only 4400 words.

A code this complex cannot be used by taxpayers to accurately compute the taxes they owe. The US tax code is an excellent example of why we should consider repealing the income tax at the federal level and junk the IRS.

The IRS and Congress's complex tax code causes people to waste time and effort complying with it as they try to pay their taxes.

> Our complex tax code is ruinous on so many levels it's hard to know where to start. Every page of this magazine could cite the code's follies and distortions. Here's one: Tax preparation for individuals and corporations is a $300 billion industry. This is good for CPAs, bad for the country's productivity.
> - Forbes. The 4% Solution. Rich Karlgaard. May 7, 2012.

Think about it. **$300 billion dollars a year** spent to calculate the tax burdens companies and citizens owe to the federal government. Consider the opportunity cost: What could citizens and companies buy with this $300 billion if not wasting it on tax preparation?

G. Silly Federal Regulations – Bad for Business
If Congress wishes to create all manner of ridiculous regulations for federal agencies and offices, that is fine. But they are wreaking havoc with numerous small businesses across the nation. Can you imagine a small restaurant being forced to admit a miniature horse into the establishment? Would the other patrons leave if forced to sit next to a horse during their meal?

> New Disability Regs Limit Slope of Mini Golf Holes, Require Businesses to Admit Mini Horses as Guide Animals.
> New Americans with Disabilities Act (ADA) guidelines are already being applied at miniature golf courses, driving ranges, amusement parks, shooting ranges and saunas. Among the provisions in the "Revised ADA Standards for Accessible Design," which went into effect on March 15, is one requiring businesses to allow miniature horses on their premises as guide animals for the disabled. Another limits the height of slopes on miniature golf holes.
>
> "Miniature horses were suggested by some commenters as viable alternatives to dogs for individuals with allergies, or for those whose religious beliefs preclude the use of dogs," the rules state.
> - CNSNews.com. Elizabeth Harrington. June 26, 2012

Obviously complying with this law imposes costs on business owners. They have to bear the costs of modifying their businesses to meet the regulators' wishes. How many small business owners simply fold rather than try to comply? Or cannot hire more workers because of the money spent complying? It is not good for the economy.

The ADA is a great example of Congress writing a vague law and unleashing the regulatory bureaucrats to fill in the details. However, in addition to being ludicrous, there is no constitutional authority for Congress to act so capriciously.   The federal government simply cannot tell a private businesses what kind of animals (if any) it must allow into its establishment. The business owner OWNS the property and should have the right to make that determination. Any applicable laws should be left to the states.

H. Government Creates New Agency With No Oversight
The Consumer Financial Protection Bureau (CFPB), was created under the massive Dodd-Frank financial legislation. Like many other government agencies, the CFFB has an unclear function and purpose, and of course pays its employees a salary and benefits that most taxpaying workers can only dream of. But this agency violates a clear constitutional principle – direct budget funding by Congress, the Peoples' House. The CFFB was set up to be funded entirely by the Federal Reserve, with no direct input or oversight by Congress.

> Answerable to No One
> The CFPB nullifies Congress's power to use the power of the purse to control bureaucracies because its funding — "determined by the director" — comes not from congressional appropriations but from the Federal Reserve. Untethered from all three branches of government, unlike anything created since 1789, the CFPB is uniquely sovereign: The president appoints the director for a five-year term — he can stay indefinitely, if no successor is confirmed — and the director can be removed, but not for policy reasons.
>
> One CFPB request for $94 million in Federal Reserve funds was made on a single sheet of paper. Its 2012 budget estimated $130 million for — this is the full explanation — "other services." So it has been hiring promiscuously and paying its hires lavishly: As of three months ago, approximately 60 percent of its then 958 employees were making more than $100,000 a year. Five percent were making $200,000 or more. (A Cabinet secretary makes $199,700.)
>
> The CFPB's mission is to prevent practices it is empowered to "declare" are "unfair, deceptive, or abusive." Law is supposed to give people due notice of what is proscribed or prescribed, and developed law does so concerning "unfair" and "deceptive" practices. Not so, "abusive."
>
> - The Washington Post. George F. Will. November 16, 2012

Not surprisingly the CFFB was created by a Democrat-controlled Congress and signed into law by a Democrat President. It is one more big government agency of dubious value that is busy spending taxpayer dollars.

I. ObamaCare Website Fails to Work

The federal government has a history of having computer systems that are out-of-date and cannot work with each other across agencies. Therefore, it is no surprise that it would not do a really professional job of establishing a website. Even if the website must be used by millions of Americans as their only way to get healthcare insurance, which ObamaCare mandates they purchase or pay a fine/tax.

> We paid $634 million for the ObamaCare sites and all we got was this lousy 404
>
> It's been one full week since the flagship technology portion of the Affordable Care Act (ObamaCare) went live. And since that time, the befuddled beast that is Healthcare.gov has shutdown, crapped out, stalled, and mis-loaded so consistently that its track record for failure is challenged only by Congress.
>
> The site itself, which apparently underwent major code renovations over the weekend, still rejects user logins, fails to load drop-down menus and other crucial components for users that successfully gain entrance, and otherwise prevents uninsured Americans in the 36 states it serves from purchasing healthcare at competitive rates – Healthcare.gov's primary purpose. The site is so busted that, as of a couple days ago, the number of people that successfully purchased healthcare through it was in the "single digits," according to the Washington Post.
>
> The exact cost to build Healthcare.gov, according to U.S. government records, appears to have been $634,320,919, which we paid to a company you probably never heard of: CGI Federal. The company originally won the contract back in 2011, but at that time, the cost was expected to run "up to" $93.7 million – still a chunk of change, but nothing near where it ended up.
>
> - Digitaltrends.com. Andrew Couts. October 8, 2013.

The Federal Government's Financial Crisis

It is truly incompetent for the government not to have a fully functioning working website after having 3 years to develop it from the time the ObamaCare law was passed. It is also typical of government that the cost was almost 7 times (680%) more than originally projected. And the cost will continue to rise as the site must still be made to work.

VI. Federal Government and Crony Capitalism
Crony capitalism refers to private companies being given special favors from the government that gives then an unearned competitive advantage. This can take many forms, including:

- A Congressman inserting a special provision benefiting a company into a law to reward a donor.
- A company seeking a bailout from the government after running the business poorly.
- The government "investing" in a company by giving it taxpayer dollars in the form of grants or low-cost loans.

Crony capitalism should outrage those Americans not receiving the largess. America was built on companies and entrepreneurs competing to deliver the best product and service to the buyer. Crony capitalism rewards those companies not able to compete in the marketplace.

Lobbying is the practice of trying to obtain these favors from politicians. It is not surprising that as the federal government has exceeded its specified roles, lobbying has also dramatically increased. It has led to the capitol city becoming home to a large number of the super-rich, the 1 percenters.

> Washington, D.C. Surpasses New York, L.A. as Fastest Growing Region of Wealth
> Washington, D.C. is booming. That's in large part because of a massive growth in lobbying expenditures and federal contracts.
>
> "The winners in the new Washington are not just the former senators, party consiglieri and four-star generals who have always profited from their connections. Now they are also

> the former bureaucrats, accountants and staff officers for whom unimagined riches are suddenly possible. They are the entrepreneurs attracted to the capital by its aura of prosperity and its super-educated workforce. They are the lawyers, lobbyists and executives who work for companies that barely had a presence in Washington before the boom," reports the Washington Post.
>
> "During the past decade, the region added 21,000 households in the nation's top 1 percent. No other metro area came close."
>
> - WeeklyStandard.com. Daniel Halper. Nov. 18, 2013

Not every federal contract is a result of crony capitalism. It is legitimate for companies to compete to offer the best product and service for those items the federal government needs to purchase to fulfill its constitutionally mandated duties. But should lobbying the federal government really be such a source of wealth that it is creating a class of super-rich in D.C., prospering from tax dollars?

A. <u>Auto Manufacturers: Bailing-Out Failing Companies</u>
An example of government crony capitalism is bailouts of the auto companies in 2008. The federal government spent $85 billion dollars bailing out General Motors and Chrysler. The politicians said the companies could not be allowed to fail because of the jobs they provided and the impact on the overall economy. Some politicians prattled on like every single auto worker for these companies would be out of a job, and the auto plants would cease to exist.

> The administration and President Barack Obama have argued that any losses on the auto bailout were worth the hundreds of thousands of jobs saved.
> "The investment paid off. The hundreds of thousands of jobs that have been saved made it worth it," he said at an appearance last month at GM's Orion Assembly plant.
>
> - Detroit News. U.S. boosts estimate of auto bailout losses to $23.6B. Nov. 14, 2011.

This shows the economic ignorance of the politicians. Had GM and Chrysler not been bailed out, they likely would have declared bankruptcy. Bankruptcy allows a company to restructure and renegotiate contracts with its creditors, bondholders, union workers, and suppliers. Usually the restructured company emerges post-bankruptcy and continues to operate. This has happened frequently in the airline industry. Bankruptcy allowed changes would have been made in the way the company operates. These changes were obviously needed since the company was failing if it needed to declare bankruptcy in the first place. Many workers would have been working and many plants would have been producing after the bankruptcy process concluded. Even if the companies were in bad enough shape that they needed to be liquidated, the plants would have been sold to other companies and some workers would still have had jobs – although with a new company.

This is the way free-market capitalism works. Poorly run companies eventually fail, and are replaced with better run companies. The government has no business or authority to interfere with this process. The government gets its money from successful companies and citizens through taxation. By spending these tax dollars on failing companies, the government is rewarding failure and punishing success. That leads to more failure and less success. Not a good scenario when the US needs strong companies to compete worldwide with companies in other nations.

B. Solyndra: Another example of the Failure of Government
Solyndra was a solar energy company that some politicians praised as a "green" energy company that would solve America's energy needs. Nothing wrong with politicians talking up companies. There is something very wrong when politicians use federal tax dollars to subsidize their favorite companies. This is unconstitutional. There is simply no authorization for the federal government to subsidize one company over another. Government loans to these favored companies often lead to a loss of taxpayer dollars.

> $528 billion Solyndra solar loan deal has White House scrambling.
>
> Solyndra, which received **$528 million in federal loans** under the stimulus law, declared bankruptcy late last month and laid off 1,100 workers.
>
> The Silicon Valley company was the first renewable-energy company to receive a loan guarantee under the 2009

stimulus law, and the Obama administration frequently touted Solyndra as a model for its clean energy program.
- Chicago Sun-Times. MATTHEW DALY. September 15, 2011.

Government should not be making investments in private companies. Too often, the government "investment" will go bad and the bureaucrat will simply walk away with no personal loss for his mistake. Leave investing to investors who will watch their money much more closely than a government bureaucrat will watch taxpayer money. When companies fail in a free-market economy, investors lose their investment – their own money. When government invests, it is taxpayers' money that is lost.

Once politicians start "investing" taxpayer money, it is an easy transition into crony capitalism where the politicians' friends are rewarded whether they provide the best option or not. The charge of crony capitalism has been levied against the Obama Administration because a number of company owners donated to the President, then received government loans or grants for their companies.

C. Many More Solyndras (Failed Government Investments)
Solyndra is far from the only failed government energy investment. There are many, many others.

President Obama's Taxpayer-Backed Green Energy Failures
It is no secret that President Obama's and green energy supporters' (from both parties) foray into venture capitalism has not gone well. But the extent of its failure has been largely ignored by the press. Sure, single instances garner attention as they happen, but they ignore past failures in order to make it seem like a rare case.

The truth is that the problem is widespread. The government's picking winners and losers in the energy market has cost taxpayers billions of dollars, and the rate of failure, cronyism, and corruption at the companies receiving the subsidies is substantial. The fact that some companies are not under financial duress does not make the policy a success. It simply means that our taxpayer dollars subsidized companies that would've found the financial support in the

The Federal Government's Financial Crisis

private market.

So far, 30 companies that were offered federal support from taxpayers are faltering — either having gone bankrupt or laying off workers or heading for bankruptcy.

Partial list of faltering or bankrupt green-energy companies that received federal money:

SpectraWatt ($500,000)*
Solyndra ($535 million)*
Nevada Geothermal ($98.5 million)
SunPower ($1.2 billion)
First Solar ($1.46 billion)
Babcock and Brown ($178 million)
EnerDel's subsidiary Ener1 ($118.5 million)*
Fisker Automotive ($529 million)
Abound Solar ($400 million)*
A123 Systems ($279 million)*
Johnson Controls ($299 million)
Brightsource ($1.6 billion)
ECOtality ($126.2 million)
Range Fuels ($80 million)*
Vestas ($50 million)
LG Chem's subsidiary Compact Power ($151 million)
Mascoma Corp. ($100 million)
*Denotes companies that have filed for bankruptcy.

The problem begins with the issue of government picking winners and losers in the first place. Venture capitalist firms exist for this very reason, and they choose what to invest in by looking at companies' business models and deciding if they are worthy. When the government plays venture capitalist, it tends to reward companies that are connected to the policymakers themselves or because it sounds nice to "invest" in green energy.

The 2009 stimulus set aside $80 billion to subsidize politically preferred energy projects. Since that time, 1,900 investigations have been opened to look into stimulus waste, fraud, and abuse (although not all are linked to the green-energy funds), and nearly 600 convictions have been made. Of that $80 billion in clean energy loans, grants, and tax

credits, at least 10 percent has gone to companies that have since either gone bankrupt or are circling the drain.
- The Foundry (Heritage.org). Ashe Schow. October 18, 2012.

Others also realize the problems with crony capitalism / government green energy investment projects:

> These projects don't make any economic sense, so they can't attract enough willing investors. Therefore, high-powered politicians and lobbyists force the rest of us to "invest" in them, so we can Win The Future. Meanwhile, these phony politically-invented "opportunities" attract investors who like the idea of government using compulsive force to make taxpayers cover any losses that might be incurred. Capital is thus diverted away from truly viable and useful opportunities.
> - Human Events.com. John Hayward. 01/13/2012.

Whether there was a donation-loan/grant causal relationship between the Obama Administration and the green energy companies may never be proven. What is certain is that government agencies wasted billions of taxpayer money when they "invested" in companies. **An incompetent investor loses his own money. An incompetent government loses your money.**

VII. A Final Example of Federal Government Excess: Transportation and the Federal Gas Tax

Another example of the federal government doing a job (poorly) that would better be done at the state level is road maintenance. The federal government did a good thing in the 1950s. The American generals returned from Germany after World War II after seeing first hand how a high speed highway system was useful for the defense (troop transport) as well as the commerce (goods transport) of a nation. So the government acted to build a US Interstate highway system. Designing and construction of the interstate highways definitely falls under the original understanding of the Constitution as practiced by the early Congresses. It served a national purpose that benefited all, and it was something that individual states could not effectively do. A national highway system required planning at the national level.

However, once the interstates were built, the federal government would have been wise to back out and let the states maintain the highways. How can those sitting in the nation's capitol efficiently determine whether a road needs repair in a state possibly thousands of miles away? The states have economic incentive to maintain the roads as they bring goods and services into the state. The federal role should have been finished.

Instead the federal government grew and expanded on the program, as the federal government always has since the 1930s. The federal government uses a gasoline tax to pay for the roads. As drivers purchase gas they pay a tax on a per-gallon basis that funds the road construction and maintenance. This is actually a smart tax as those who use the roads end up paying the tax. But the tax grew to its current $0.184 per gallon. Most drivers are not even aware of this as the price is built in to the gas price shown on the pump. But if you have a large vehicle and buy 20 gallons of fuel, you are paying $3.68 to the federal government. States also add their own gas tax on top of the federal charge. See Appendix 7 for a comparison of state gas taxes that range from $.47 in California to $.08 in Alaska.

Interstate highways were deemed necessary in Alaska and Hawaii even though since those states do not border on another state it was impossible for them to have an *inter*state highway (a highway between states). It's not hard to follow the logic however flawed: Residents in those states pay the gas tax too why shouldn't they get federal dollars for roads and construction jobs.

Of course Congressman and Senators who became powerful specialized in bringing home the "bacon" of federal highway dollars into their states or districts. Two of the best at this game were Republicans from Alaska: Senator Ted Stevens and House Transportation and Infrastructure Committee Chairman Don Young. An infamous example of questionable road spending was the Bridge to Nowhere.

> Dubbed the "Bridge to Nowhere," the bridge in Alaska would connect the town of Ketchikan (population 8,900) with its

airport on the Island of Gravina (population 50) at a cost to federal taxpayers of $320 million, by way of three separate earmarks in the recent highway bill. At present, a ferry service runs to the island, but some in the town complain about its wait (15 to 30 minutes) and fee ($6 per car).
- The Bridge to Nowhere: A National Embarrassment. The Heritage Foundation. 2005.

If the state of Alaska, or the local citizens choose to build this bridge, that is fine, but it clearly serves no national interest, and therefore should not be payed for with federal dollars. Having a large amount of money collected by the federal government via the gas tax allows powerful politicians to use it to buy votes for their re-election rather than spend it where it is most needed.

It would be bad enough if the politicians only bought roads that were of questionable need. But 1/3 of the gasoline tax collected by the federal government is not even spent on roads! Recall that building and maintaining roads is the purpose of the gasoline tax.

As The Heritage Foundation has noted in earlier reports, **about one-third of federal surface transportation spending from the highway trust fund** goes to purposes other than cost-effective modes that enhance mobility. These include costly and underused transit investments (transit receives 20 percent of the funds but serves less than 2 percent of passengers), bike and hiking paths, metropolitan planning organizations, covered bridge restoration, historic train station conversions, cityscapes and flower plantings, earmarks, U.S. Department of Transportation (USDOT) overhead, questionable research projects, livability schemes, and low-valued university transportation research centers.
- Setting Priorities for Transportation Spending in FY 2011 and FY 2012. Heritage Foundation.

Once again the federal government has shown it is not to be trusted to spend money for a desired purpose efficiently. Why are drivers paying gas taxes to the federal government to subsidize bicycle paths and mass transit systems? If a city wants to build a light rail or subway system, that is the city's prerogative. But the federal government should not be involved – there is no national interest.

It is also unfair to ask a city's drivers to pay a gasoline tax to subsidize a subway rider, but a city has the right to put that tax in place. Of course drivers may choose to purchase gas outside of the city limits to avoid the tax.

On August 1, 2007, the I35 Bridge spanning the Mississippi River in Minneapolis collapsed. A design flaw in the gusset plates (sized too thin) joining steel beams was determined by the National Transportation Safety Board to have been the cause of the collapse. The rush hour traffic, plus the weight of the construction equipment and materials (the bridge was under renovation) overloaded the bridge. Thirteen people were killed. In many ways it was a miracle that more people did not die considering the bridge collapsed during rush hour.

Many a liberal blogger or politician blamed the I35 Bridge collapse on taxes being too low. When a liberal says "taxes are too low" they usually mean taxes on the rich. In this case though, they would have been advocating for higher gas taxes (assuming they realized how road maintenance is funded). Middle class drivers foot the bill. It also shows the liberal response to every crisis – raise taxes and spend more money. There was no mention of the fact that the federal government mis-allocated one-third of the gas tax currently collected into non-road-maintenance projects. Maybe states will do a better job of actually using the gas tax to maintain the roads instead of building trains lines and bicycle paths.

VIII. Summary and the Solution
This chapter began with the prediction of a coming national crisis based on actions taken by the federal government. The crisis is likely to occur in the next decade if history is a guide. It is not hard to see that at least part of the crisis will be the huge amount of debt the federal government has created. There is time to avert the financial crisis - a window to take action. But the nation must act soon or it will be forced to act on terms that no citizen wants. The federal government has also assumed power in ways that have taken away freedom and free will from the citizens.

This chapter details numerous incompetencies of the federal government in trying to manage things that the founding fathers never imagined, and the Constitution prohibits. The solution is to shrink the federal government back to its constitutional role by transferring its extra-constitutional programs back to the states and letting the states manage them. This is detailed in the next chapter.

The Solution: Return to the Constitution

America's political leaders have strayed far from the Constitution, the rules made to govern the nation. This is not the only time in history that people and leaders have forgotten or ignored national rules. There is an interesting parallel in the Bible about 600 years before Christ arrived. The rulers of the nation had ignored their constitution, given to them by God. They had even lost the document!

> 2 Kings 22:3-13 In the eighteenth year of his reign, King Josiah sent the secretary... to the temple of the Lord.... Hilkiah the high priest said to Shaphan the secretary, "I have found the Book of the Law in the temple of the Lord." .... Then Shaphan the secretary informed the king, "Hilkiah the priest has given me a book." And Shaphan read from it in the presence of the king. When the king heard the words of the Book of the Law, he tore his robes. He gave these orders .... "Go and inquire of the Lord for me and for the people and for all Judah about what is written in this book that has been found. Great is the Lord's anger that burns against us because those who have gone before us have not obeyed the words of this book; they have not acted in accordance with all that is written there concerning us."

The Book of the Law was probably Deuteronomy which contained most of the national laws. It must be realized that more than 700 years had passed since Moses wrote the Torah, the first five books of the Bible. The people of Israel had used their free will to ignore God's Law, with the consequence of possibly triggering God's covenant sanctions which were spelled out in the law. There are always consequences with any free will action taken by people. In America, there are no sanctions from God if the people ignore the law. The consequence is the loss of freedom, as the government ignores constitutional rights put in place to protect those freedoms. If the citizens of America want to protect their freedom, they must educate their neighbors and hold their political representatives accountable.

America's founding fathers rebelled against a king who sought to rule over them with authoritarian powers. Today liberals favor a hugely powerful central government much more authoritarian than the King of England in 1776. The previous chapter detailed the federal government's poor track record of wasting money and incompetent management.

> Most of the energy of political work is devoted to correcting the effects of mismanagement of government.
> - Milton Friedman, Recipient of the Nobel Prize in Economic Sciences

Three political scenarios or pathways are possible for the nation.

1) The federal government continues as is (status quo). Spending continues with no changes to Washington's budgeting process or major programs. The government agencies continue to grow in power using their power to regulate and control the citizens. This leads to the economy weakening due to high taxes and regulations. Eventually the dollar will dramatically lower in value as the government creates too many dollars. A crisis occurs if too many lose faith in the dollar (and the American government). This is the approach followed by Democrats. (Although they probably do not believe a crisis will come).
2) Tweak the government budgeting process and reform the insolvent benefit programs. This will leave a massive federal government bureaucracy in place, along with its harmful regulations and high tax requirements. This is the approach favored by Establishment Republicans.
3) Return to the Constitution and its defined roles for federal and state government. This is the solution outlined in the next chapter. It will again allow maximum freedom for the citizens of America and return to the size of government that created our nation to begin with and allowed it to flourish.

This chapter deals with the third and best option: returning government functions to the states as prescribed in the Constitution. When the federal government began, it was assumed that it would only perform key duties that it could better accomplish than the states (Chapter 12). States were known to be more efficient at meeting the needs of their citizens.

States more efficient in Domestic Matters
The extent of our country was so great, and its former division into distinct states so established, that we thought it

The Solution: Return to the Constitution

> better to [nationalize] as to foreign affairs only. **Every state retained its self-government in domestic matters, as better qualified to direct them to the good and satisfaction of their citizens**, than a general government so distant from its remoter citizens, and so little familiar with the local peculiarities of the different parts.
> - Thomas Jefferson. 1823. TRTJ. P633.

If only liberals placed nearly as much importance on this Jeffersonian quote as they do behind his 'wall between church and state' quote! Jefferson wrote that state governments were much more efficient at handling the domestic needs of its people than the national government. He wrote this at the founding, when there were only 13 states along the eastern seaboard of the nation--not 50 states stretching from the Atlantic to the Pacific, up to Alaska, and out to the islands of Hawaii.

It is also key to note that Jefferson knew the Constitution left domestic government to the states with the 9th and 10th Amendments. This is the solution to the financial crisis America now faces. Return to the Constitution, and return domestic government to the state level.

> What's the common thread between Europe's financial mess, particularly among the PIIGS (Portugal, Ireland, Italy, Greece and Spain), and the financial mess in the U.S.? That question could be more easily answered if we asked instead: What's necessary to cure the financial mess in Europe and the U.S.? If European governments and the U.S. Congress ceased the practice of giving people what they have not earned, budgets would be more than balanced. For government to guarantee a person a right to goods and services he has not earned, it must diminish someone else's right to what he has earned, simply because governments have no resources of their very own.
> - Dr. Walter Williams. Column. 09/26/11

America, because of the federal government's infringements into state matters, is approaching a crisis. The nation can no longer ignore the leviathan in the room that is the out-of-control spending of the federal government. Past efforts to curb government spending growth (Reagan in 1980, Gingrich in 1994) were modestly successful in the short term, but failed longer term.

Why the failure? Bureaucracy is like a weed. If not pulled out at the root it grows back bigger than ever. Pruning doesn't work. Slowing growth in funding for an agency, or even cutting funding, still leaves the agency alive and ready for a growth spurt as soon as the political winds change. Congress must eliminate entire agencies and programs at the federal level and let the state take over the responsibility. Federal workers will become state workers (or private sector workers).

A better approach is to return the federal government to the role given it by the Constitution, by removing those agencies that are not authorized and transferring them to the states.

To review, the role of the federal government was limited in scope by the Constitutional Amendment soon after ratification by the states.

> Amendment 9: The enumeration in the Constitution, of certain rights, shall not be construed to deny or disparage others retained by the people. (Restated: If there is any doubt as to where the rights belong, they go to the people)
>
> Amendment 10: The powers not delegated to the United States by the Constitution, nor prohibited by it to the States, are reserved to the States respectively, or to the people.

The first ten amendments, also known as The Bill of Rights, were added to the Constitution specifically to restrict the role and power of the federal government. 65-70% of the federal budget disappears if the federal government follows these two amendments. All functions not specifically given to the federal government by the Constitution shall be the responsibility of the states or the people. The federal government should therefore transfer those programs and responsibilities to the states.

The Solution: Return to the Constitution

Look at the areas of the agencies covered by the GAO study in the previous chapter: economic development programs, job-training programs, transportation programs, teacher quality programs, financial literacy programs, homelessness programs, and food assistance programs. None of these areas are a constitutional responsibility of the federal government. Therefore, if the programs are needed, they should be carried out either by state or local governments or by private charities. All of these programs can be transferred to the states. Each state can then decide whether to use charity or government to meet these societal needs.

For example, take the $62.5 billion spent on federal government food assistance programs. This area is selected as the example because it will be the easiest to demonize by big-government lovers. Here is a three step procedure to transition a program from the federal government to the state governments.

1. The program is targeted to be transferred from the federal level to the state level (Year 1).
    - During a 6 month transition period, the states create a state program to take over *if the state chooses*.
    - Workers administering the federal programs will be laid off at the close of the transition period.
    - States may choose to hire former federal workers from the old agency.
2. During the next 6 months the states receive the money that would have been spent at the federal level in a one-time grant.
    - No federal restrictions as to how the money is spent.
    - The grant should be distributed via state population - 1 share per congressional representative.
3. In the next year (Year 2), there is no more federal expenditure for the program.
    - Federal taxes are correspondingly cut or the revenue is used to balance the budget.
    - States either raise state taxes to continue with the program or the state could drop the program - it is up

to the state.
- The state will run the program more efficiently, so will have lower costs than the federal-government.

It is well known that a number of federal politicians make a practice of spending federal dollars to "buy" votes. The bureaucrats in the federal government love their high-salaried jobs and top-notch pensions. The media is biased towards a big powerful central government (chapter 23). There will be much resistance to returning the federal government to its constitutional duties. The previous chapter showed where the US government is heading if it keeps on its current path. The longer it continues on this path, the more difficult and painful the transition to change course will be.

In general, here are five discussion points that can be used to effectively position the transfer of programs to the states.

1. No elimination. The programs are NOT being eliminated. They are being transferred to the states.
2. Constitutional. The functions are the responsibility of the states or the people as specified in the Constitution.
3. Efficiency. It is more efficient and simpler to administer to citizens at the state level rather than than 300+ million across all 50 states at federal level. How similar are Alaska and Hawaii?
4. Responsiveness. Moving the program to the state level will make it more responsive to the needs of the citizens.
5. State governments can tax citizens as well as the federal government can, so funding the programs is no more difficult at the state level than the federal level.

Sidebar: Assume that some say there exists an agency so important that it should cover multiple states even though it is not a constitutionally defined role of the federal government. Take the EPA (Environmental Protection Agency) for example. There is no reason that this agency, once its federal budget has been transferred to the states, cannot make its case to the states that the states should fund it as it exists. There is no reason why some or all of the states cannot fund a multi-state agency that they believe is better able to perform than a single agency in their state.

The Solution: Return to the Constitution

Going back to the easily demonized food programs, there is a typical attack that big government politicians and their sympathizers in the media will trumpet: The people will starve! This attack took the form of "The Republicans want grandma to eat dog food" in the 1980s, and "The Republicans want to starve the children" in the 1990s. (Refer back to the spending charts in Chapter 19: Do you see any cuts in federal government spending???) In addition to spouting ridiculous rhetoric, notice how the Democrats seldom if ever propose any programs they want to cut?

A simple question should be the response to attacks. It can take many forms.

> Would the Governor of "XYZ State" let his citizens starve?
>
> Which state governor will sit by and let his citizens starve?
>
> Which city mayor will let his citizens starve?
>
> Would the citizens of "XYZ State" let their fellow citizens starve?
>
> Would residents of "City XYZ" just sit by while their neighbors were starving?
>
> Would the journalists covering the story do nothing while watching someone starve?
>
> Would charities not step up? After all, millions of dollars were sent to Haiti by charities after a recent disaster there. Wouldn't even more money come forth to help fellow Americans?

Let's also look at healthcare as an example. How many times have liberals or Democrats stated 'There should be a right to healthcare in America' (often followed by something like 'other civilized nations have this'). When discussing healthcare, liberals will often use an emotional example like: 'are you going to let a child with cancer die in the street?' The unspoken implication is that anyone opposing their view is cold and heartless.

As was discussed in Chapter 12, there cannot be a 'right' to any good or service that others must provide. So fulfilling the 'right' of healthcare involves either slavery (forcing a person to work without wages) or the government paying the provider. Slavery *is* unconstitutional and therefore outlawed, so they are really advocating for government to provide the healthcare.

The emotional argument of children dying assumes that the federal government is the primary solution. Big-government supporters never address the massive amounts of fraud and waste present in federal healthcare programs (Chapter 21). Common sense dictates that a better solution is needed. The Constitution provides the solution: Let the states deal with the problem. In fact, the Constitution mandates the solution. The 10th Amendment prevents the federal government from running healthcare programs – unless there is enough support to pass an amendment making healthcare the responsibility of the federal government. The amendment *does not* prevent states from running healthcare programs. So states are free to experiment with devising healthcare systems as they choose to do so.

States can deal with healthcare as they see fit. A state may question the premise that only government can make sure a poor cancer-ridden child receives treatment. Or the state may decide this is a false premise. It is almost guaranteed that a doctor or hospital will *voluntarily* choose to treat the child out of charitable concern. If no doctor steps up, an existing charity probably will. And if that fails, the family can often raise funds with their own charity drive. Most media will cover and promote such events. Chapter 21 also explores low cost catastrophic health insurance, the free market solution to this problem. A state may even decide to offer this insurance to its citizens. Or a state may try to be the provider of healthcare.

A note of caution: What usually happens with government is that no matter how well intentioned, the program will soon become bogged down with many cumbersome rules and regulations and numerous bureaucrats who make their living by administering the program. Maybe some state will be able to overcome this obstacle and create a program that will deliver superior healthcare, but the author doubts it. If a great program is implemented and shown to be successful, other states can copy it.

The Solution: Return to the Constitution

So again, how to counter to the emotion-driven plea to not let children die in the streets from sickness? **There are numerous options to help the child: state government, county government, city government, pro-bono work by doctors and hospitals, and charities.**

Going back to the problem of feeding the poor, once the federal government and its rules and bureaucracy are out of the way, wise states, cities or churches can focus on solving the problem of feeding America's poor. No person in America should be allowed to starve, no matter how lazy (author's opinion). But taking advice from Benjamin Franklin, it is possible to make the "lazy poor" uncomfortable in their poverty. One way to do this is to implement a model developed by a charity to feed poor children outside America.

Feed My Starving Children (FMSC, www.fmsc.org) is a non-profit Christian organization committed to feeding God's children in poor countries around the world.. From its beginnings, FMSC has worked to develop a food mixture that would be easy and safe to transport, simple to make with only boiling water, and culturally acceptable worldwide.

> With the input of scientists from major food companies in the Twin Cities area—including Cargill and General Mills—FMSC developed MannaPack Rice, a formula consisting of:
>
> 1. Rice, the most widely accepted grain around the world.
>
> 2. Extruded soy nuggets, providing maximum protein at lowest cost.
>
> 3. Vitamins, minerals and a vegetarian flavoring to give growing children the critical nutritional elements they need.
>
> 4. Dehydrated vegetables for flavor and nutrition.
>
> Packaged in small pouches, this easy-to-prepare food blend has won rave reviews all over the world. While the formula was designed to save the lives of severely malnourished and starving children, the ingredients also improve the health, growth and physical well-being of children who are no longer in immediate danger of starvation. A team of food scientists continues to monitor the FMSC formula to ensure that it

meets nutritional needs of the world's hungry children.

A single bag of food—which provides highly nutritious meals for six children—costs around $1.44 to produce.

The meals are a little bland, but are nutritious – and they fill empty bellies. So it is possible to feed citizens for $0.75 a day should these meals be produced for America's poor. A state could therefore insure no citizen would starve by providing these meals. Of course able-bodied poor would soon tire of a diet of rice meals. They would probably be tempted to find a job to earn some spending money so they could buy some hamburgers or other favorite foods. That's the point. The chronic able-bodied poor need incentive to help themselves.

One problem in America today is that the federal government has created an entire class of dependent citizens. They have told these citizens that they are entitled to food, shelter and numerous other things that the federal government will provide them. Of course there is nothing in the Constitution allowing the federal government to take on this role. Politicians did it, either to buy votes or because they truly believed they were helping the poor. Get the federal government completely out of the "providing for the poor" business. If any government is to take on a role here, it should be done at the city or state level. This is where the Constitution places it.

A state government sustenance program combined with charities to further help the truly needy may be the best way to go. Of course, a state could decide to do whatever it wishes, including running their own "food stamp" type of program similar to the program the federal government presently runs. Each state will have the freedom and ability to make their own choice. Citizens will be free to move to the state that best suites them.

Sidebar: It must also be noted that a state, county, or city can put whatever requirements or restrictions on the programs it wishes. Those citizens accepting the free food will have to follow the requirements the provider establishes. Or they can choose to not take the food. When a citizen is a dependent, they can be treated like a dependent. Much like when a parent makes their children eat their vegetables before getting dessert.

The Solution: Return to the Constitution

What are some of the positive effects of moving federal programs to the states? One-size fits all federal programs are eliminated. Does anyone really think the needs of citizens in Hawaii and Alaska are similar? How about Montana and Rhode Island? Why force them into a single program administered in Washington DC?

<u>Positive Effects of State Programs</u>
1. 50 state laboratories. We can observe the social and economic policies of the different states. Effective policies or programs can be modified and copied into other states.
2. Competition between states will act as a check on poor government. Let a state tax at high rates and citizens may flee if the corresponding services aren't worth the taxes.
3. Liberty is enhanced. Citizens are free to move to a state that suits them. What Texas does doesn't affect California and vice-versa.

<u>How to Implement the Solution</u>
The easiest way to transfer federal government programs back to the states is to have a conservative president and a conservative-majority House and Senate. They can simply enact the transfer legislation described earlier as part of the budget process. Note that it must be conservative, not just Republican. The nation had a Republican President and Congress for much of the early 2000s but the federal government continued to grow. That is because the President (George W. Bush) and Congressional leaders (John Boehner and Mitch McConnell) during this time were establishment Republicans, not small-government constitutional-conservative Republicans. Therefore it is imperative to have small-government conservatives in Republican Party leadership positions for any reduction in the federal government to occur. See Chapter 25: Voting Strategy, for organizations that track representatives' voting records, so citizens can learn how conservative their representatives are.

It is also possible, but more difficult, to enact this transfer legislation with just a conservative Speaker and House of Representatives, because the House of Representatives is the ultimate authority on funding the federal government. The

Constitution mandates all spending bills originate in the House. The House can pick an agency or program and transfer the funding to the states. If the Senate refuses to go along, or the President vetoes the bill, the House can refuse to fund the agency/program at all. See Appendix 11: Defunding Agencies and Government Shutdowns. This approach usually works only when the bulk of the federal spending bills have been passed and signed.

As an additional benefit, notice how there are no secret negotiations with this approach? Everything is straightforward and aboveboard. The House will be following the constitutionally designed system. The founders never envisioned a massive federal government with so many different agencies that 10-15 massive comprehensive spending bills were needed to fund the government, largely because with the Constitution they wrote, most of these agencies are not allowed at the federal level.

While food and healthcare programs were used as examples because they will likely be the most difficult to transfer, it would be politically smart to begin the transfer process with some of the multitude of federal agencies listed in the following section. Many of these agencies and programs are meaningless to the voters, mattering only to the bureaucrats they employ.

Streamlining the Federal Government According to the Constitution
The previous chapter listed over 2.6 million federal employees in 2011with over 50% in the numerous federal agencies outside of the Defense Department and the Post Office (both of which are constitutionally specified responsibilities for the federal government). Many of these federal-government agencies have no such constitutional authority.

There are 15 Cabinet Level positions in the Executive Branch reporting to the President. 14 of these if you exclude the Department of Defense. These 14 Departments have 178 Key Agencies. (See Appendix 10 for a full list.) 178 Key Agencies? Of course there are multiple overlapping and redundant agencies. It's the federal government. It is to be expected. There are an additional 68 Independent Agencies that have been created by Congress. Does the Constitution grant the federal government the

The Solution: Return to the Constitution

power for 248 Key Agencies? The answer of course is: No.

Most Americans understand the attitude present in a government department. Those in it seek to constantly increase its power, authority, personnel and budget. Once a department or agency is created it will continue to seek to grow itself. Full employment is the top priority. And there is no free market power to serve as a check or balance. If a company adds too many redundant departments or overhead costs, it will have to raise its prices to cover the costs. Then its customers may choose to buy from a competitor. An inefficient company will soon price itself out of the market. With the federal government, there are no other options for the customer-taxpayer. There is no alternative. No competition to keep the government in check. That is one of the beauties of the Constitution – it leaves most of the power to the states where there is competition to check government power. Citizens can move to a new state if they decide their current state is too oppressive for their liking.

The federal government needs to be greatly streamlined, using the Constitution as a guide. Following is a blueprint that could be used:

First, reduce the number of Executive Cabinet Departments: Create a Department of Homeland Management (DHM) by merging nine existing departments. Many of the duties currently performed by these nine departments will be transferred to the states or private industry. The nine current departments to be merged are listed below along with their mission statements (as currently assigned by the federal government). Duties to be transferred to the state level or private companies are lined out.

Agriculture: ~~Promotes U.S. agriculture domestically and internationally,~~ (Better done by private companies.) manages forests, ~~researches new ways to grow crops and conserve natural resources,~~ ensures safe meat and poultry products, ~~and leads the Federal anti-hunger programs, such as the Supplemental Nutrition Assistance Program (formerly known as the Food Stamp program) and the National School Lunch Program.~~ (Transferred to states)

Health and Human Services: ~~Performs health and social science research,~~ assures the safety of drugs and foods other than meat and poultry, ~~and administers Medicare, Medicaid, and numerous other social service programs~~. (Transferred to states)

Interior: Manages federal lands, including the national parks, ~~runs hydroelectric power systems, and promotes conservation of natural resources.~~ (Sell utilities to private companies.)

Transportation: Sets national transportation policy, plans and funds the construction of highways and ~~mass transit systems~~, (Mass transit is a local issue.) and regulates railroad, aviation, and maritime operations.

Commerce: Forecasts the weather, charts the oceans, regulates patents and trademarks, conducts the census, compiles economic statistics, ~~and promotes U.S. economic growth by encouraging international trade.~~ (Better left to companies to promote their products)

Energy: ~~Coordinates the national use and provision of energy,~~ oversees the production and disposal of nuclear weapons, ~~and plans for future energy needs.~~ (Department has failed its objective to make America energy independent)

Labor: ~~Enforces laws guaranteeing fair pay, workplace safety, and equal job opportunity, administers unemployment insurance (UI) to State UI agencies, regulates pension funds; and collects and analyzes economic data.~~ (Sent to state level.)

Housing and Urban Development: ~~Funds public housing projects, enforces equal housing laws, and insures and finances mortgages.~~ (Housing falls to state level. Mortgage financing to private industry.)

Education: ~~Monitors and distributes financial aid to schools and students, collects and disseminates data on schools and other education matters, and prohibits discrimination in education.~~ (Education is a state or local responsibility)

Sidebar: In a disturbing trend, many of these unconstitutional federal agencies have created agency SWAT teams and have used them against non-violent "offenders". See Appendix 12 for examples.

The Solution: Return to the Constitution

The Streamlined Cabinet Level Departments of the Executive Branch are as follows:
Department of Homeland Management (DHM): Manages federal lands including the national parks and forests; sets national transportation policy; assures the safety of drugs and foods; plans and funds the construction of highways; regulates interstate railroad, aviation, and maritime operations; forecasts the weather; charts the oceans; regulates patents and trademarks; conducts the census; compiles economic statistics; oversees the production and disposal of nuclear weapons, regulates nuclear power.

Department of Defense (DoD): Manages the military forces that protect our country and its interests, including the Departments of the Army, Navy, and Air Force and a number of smaller agencies.

Department of Veterans Affairs (DVA) : Administers programs to aid U.S. veterans and their families, runs the veterans' hospital system, and operates our national cemeteries.

Department of Homeland Security (DHS): Works to prevent terrorist attacks within the United States, reduce vulnerability to terrorism, and minimize the damage from potential attacks and natural disasters. It also administers the country's immigration policies and oversees the Coast Guard.

Department of Treasury (DoT): Regulates banks and other financial institutions, administers the public debt, prints currency, and collects federal income taxes.

Department of Justice (DoJ): Works with state and local governments and other agencies to prevent and control crime and ensure public safety against threats, both domestic and foreign. It also enforces federal laws, prosecutes cases in federal courts, and runs federal prisons.

Department of State (DoS): Oversees the nation's embassies and consulates, issues passports, monitors U.S. interests abroad, and represents the United States before international organizations.

There are **68 other major agencies** also listed on the usa.gov website. The list can be narrowed to 25 that serve a national interest where a large majority of citizens are served, or where there is a constitutionally authorized power, such as regulating interstate commerce. See Appendix 10 for those agencies recommended to be kept, transferred, or eliminated.

The author is not an expert on all of these agencies. (Is anyone??) This is only a proposal to generate discussion and point out how government could be reduced, streamlined and made more efficient, as well as reducing the scope of the federal government back to its constitutionally allowed responsibilities. Congress and the President need to examine each agency and justify its right to exist in the federal government, applying the limited powers prescribed by the Constitution.

End Baseline Budgeting for the remaining Federal Agencies
Chapter 19 discussed baseline budgeting used in the federal government as part of the 2011 Budget Control Act. Under baseline budgeting, a percentage increase is built in to increase the agency budget every year. An example if a household budget worked this way:

> Family budget of $50,000
> Baseline increase of 10% = $5000 increase for next year
> Next year's budget = $55,000

Using this example if $52,000 is actually spent by the family, it would be called a *cut* of $3000, even though the family spent $2000 more than the previous year.

Obviously baseline budgeting plays into the dreams of those politicians desiring a perpetually growing government. Of course this practice was begun by Democrats, the party of big government. But it is sad that Republicans did not alter the process when they had power. Baseline budgeting skews the debate toward *how much* to increase budgets rather than *whether* to increase (or even decrease) budgets.

It is also extremely misleading to citizens. When news organizations or politicians talk about cuts, the average citizen will think of their own budget experiences where a *cut* means you spend *less*. With baseline budgeting, this is not the case at all. This kind of Washington double-speak prevents an honest discussion from even

The Solution: Return to the Constitution

occurring. **Americans should all agree that a cut is a cut, and an increase is an increase.**

There will be consequences if government spending is reduced and government jobs eliminated. The Washington D.C. area will be hit especially hard. But then again, the area has reaped disproportional success at the expense of taxpayers in the rest of the nation.

> Times Are Booming for Washington's Governing Class
> While much of the nation has been struggling through stormy economic times, one locale has been weathering that storm just fine — Washington, D.C.
>
> The reason, of course: the huge population of government workers and contractors in the nation's capital living on the taxpayers' dime.
>
> A Money magazine analysis of the 3,033 counties in the United States found that of the 15 counties with the highest median household incomes, 10 are in the Washington area, and "they have an average income almost double that of the nation as a whole," according to John H. Fund, a senior editor of The American Spectator.
>
> "Four of the remaining five surround New York City, and are populated by many Wall Streeters who benefited from TARP and other federal bailouts."
>
> The Politico website noted in 2010 that "the massive expansion of government under Obama has basically guaranteed a robust job market for policy professionals, regulators and contractors for years to come."
>
> The Cato Institute disclosed that in 2008, the average compensation in pay and benefits for federal civilian employees was $119,900 a year, compared to $59,900 in private industry.
> - Newsmax.com. Sunday, 29 Jul 2012.

Federal Tax System
It is also critical to correspondingly reduce the federal tax burden as the size of the federal government is reduced. It may be appropriate to cap the top federal tax rate at 10%. This was the level thought to be onerously high in the days of the biblical kings of Israel (1 Samuel

8 from Chapter 6). It should suffice for a streamlined federal government.

Perhaps nothing demonstrates the incompetence and inefficiency of the federal government as well as the tax system it has created. The complexity either costs the taxpayer time as he or she struggles to fill out the blizzard of forms, or money as the taxpayer pays an accountant to fill out the forms.

> According to the National Taxpayers Union, we each waste about 12 hours a year, every year, filling out this crazy stuff [IRS Tax Forms]. Schedule B. Schedule C. Above the line. Below the line. Deductions, exemptions, non-refundable credits. Medical bills over 7.5% of adjusted gross income.
>
> It's like we're being mugged and held hostage. Every year.
>
> The instruction booklet for the 1040 now runs to 189 pages. No kidding. Seventy-five years ago, says the NTU, it was two pages.
>
> The U.S. tax code is insane and out of control. It's tripled in a decade. It now runs to 3.8 million words. To put that in context, William Shakespeare only needed 900,000 words to say everything he had to say. Hamlet. Othello. The history plays. The sonnets. The whole shebang. But the IRS needs four times as many words? Really?
>
> - SmartMoney.com. 10 Things I Hate About Tax Day. APRIL 11, 2012.

IRS rules and regulations are so complex that rarely do *tax lawyers* agree on the proper tax owed. Financial magazines have for years created a fictional family and submitted the family's tax information to tax preparers. Almost always, 50 preparers will give 50 different tax bills for the family. The IRS code is simply too complex to accurately calculate the correct amount owed.

If the Constitution is followed, the primary tax collection will shift from the federal government to the state governments (because states will now be running the bulk of the government programs). States usually have much simpler tax forms to complete.

The states will need to raise their taxes as they absorb the duties

The Solution: Return to the Constitution

formerly done by the federal government. Each state will need to decide which duties to assume and how to fund them.

Lets look at California as an example. Assume the California state government takes on all of the responsibilities from the federal government. California would then raise its taxes to cover the responsibilities. But, it is a safe assumption that at least 30% of the federal government spending is wasted with excess bureaucracy and redundant, competing agencies. So California will only need 70% of the revenue Let's take the top tax rates as an example:

- Federal Top Income Tax Rate goes from 35% to 10%
 (A 25 point reduction.)
- But only 18 points need to be added to California's top rate.
 (25 points x 70%)
- California raises their Top Income Tax Rate from 11% to 29%
 (Lower tier rates would similarly adjust)

So the new top tier tax rates are 10% for the federal government and 29% for California. Of course, California could decide to raise the top rate on the rich even more if they choose.

Looking at Texas, the state has no income tax. Should Texas assume all of the responsibilities being transferred from the federal government, Texas would need to adopt an 18% top tier income tax rate, or Texas would have to significantly raise their state sales tax. Of course Texas may very well opt to not do all of the tasks the federal government had been doing. In that case Texas would not need to raise their taxes as much. Remember, it is up to each state to decide how much government to have. States could shift the government work and tax collection to the county or city level.

As the nation returns to federalism, states will be free to diverge and follow conservative or liberal paths. Some counties may not agree with the direction their state goes and opt for change. Appendix 1: County and State Re-Alignment, lists a process where counties could decide to change states, if their current state government no longer represents them adequately.

With the states now doing the bulk of the tax collection, it may even be possible to eliminate the IRS and have the states collect the money for the federal government as well. This would to restore a check on the federal government that the states lost with passage of the 16th Amendment on federal income tax.

This was the way the US was supposed to work. The Constitution limits the power and responsibilities of the federal government, but gives the states much greater power to assume responsibilities. It makes no sense for the federal government to offer one-size-fits-all programs. California, Alaska, North Dakota, Delaware, Florida and Hawaii are all very different. Let the citizens design the government they want for their respective states.

This Plan has Worked Before
A similar approach to the above plan (transferring all non-constitutional federal spending to the states, while correspondingly cutting federal tax rates) occurred in America after World War I in 1918. The US had massive increases in federal spending to fight the war which also led to massive national debt. After the war federal spending was slashed. This caused a short depression, followed by a long term boom, the decade referred to as "The Roaring '20s" in history books because of the economic prosperity brought about under policies of slashing federal government spending and federal tax rates.

The Depression You've Never Heard Of: 1920-1921
At the conclusion of World War I, U.S. officials found themselves in a bleak position. The federal debt had exploded because of wartime expenditures, and annual consumer price inflation rates had jumped well above 20 percent by the end of the war.

To restore fiscal and price sanity, the authorities implemented what today strikes us as incredibly "merciless" policies. From FY 1919 to 1920, federal spending was slashed from $18.5 billion to $6.4 billion—a 65 percent reduction in one year [entirely from the defense budget as the war ended]. The budget was pushed down the next two years as well, to $3.3 billion in FY 1922. On the monetary side, the New York Fed raised its discount rate to a record high 7 percent by June 1920. ... From its peak in June 1920 the

The Solution: Return to the Constitution

Consumer Price Index fell 15.8 percent over the next 12 months. Whether we look at nominal interest rates or "real" (inflation-adjusted) interest rates, the Fed was very "tight" during the 1920–1921 depression... [Necessary to eliminate inflation and achieve sound stable money].

To be sure, the 1920–1921 depression was painful. The unemployment rate peaked at 11.7 percent in 1921. But it had dropped to 6.7 percent by the following year, and was down to 2.4 percent by 1923. After the depression the United States proceeded to enjoy the "Roaring Twenties," arguably the most prosperous decade in the country's history.

- www.fee.org/the_freeman. ROBERT P. MURPHY. NOVEMBER 18, 2009

Reductions in federal government spending can be expected to have a negative short term impact on the economy, but cause a long term boom. While painful at the time, the economic correction will soon be over and rapid economic growth can follow. Notice how history books do not discuss the "Depression of 1920", just the Great Depression of the 1930s, where big government attempted to solve the problem with more government.

Calvin Coolidge Cut It Big Time As President
Coolidge administration accomplishments:
- Top [federal] income tax rates were lowered from 73% to 24%.
- By the end of his term, 98% of the population paid no income tax at all.
- The federal budget was reduced by 35%.
- Per capita income increased more than 30%.
- Unemployment averaged 3.3%.
- GNP grew at the fastest compound rate of any eight-year period in U.S. history.

- INVESTOR'S BUSINESS DAILY. BUCKY FOX. 07/24/2012.

This plan was carried out by Warren Harding and Calvin Coolidge (small government Republicans and conservatives), who were elected as the President and Vice-President in 1920. Coolidge became President after Warren Harding died in 1923 and was reelected in 1924. Coolidge did not seek re-election in 1928, even though he would have been a prohibitive favorite given his successful economic track record.

President Ronald Reagan used similar policies (reductions in government regulation, tax rate cuts and high interest rates to eliminate inflation) in the early 1980s to create another boom. (Cuts in federal spending did not happen as the Democrat Congress would not reduce non-defense spending, and Reagan also increased defense spending to fight the USSR in the Cold War.) Reagan's boom in the 80s was also preceded by a severe recession early in his term. It takes time for the economy to correct and recover.

The difference between this plan and the 1920s and 1980s is that by transferring large portions of the taxing and spending from the federal government to state governments, the economic downturn can be minimized.

Social Issues
The transferring of authority to the states approach should be used for social issues as well. While the author believes abortion to be as abhorrent today as slavery was in earlier times, until there is a constitutional amendment banning abortion, it should be regulated at the state level. Drug-use laws, marriage laws, divorce laws, prostitution laws, adultery laws, food safety laws, should all be decided and enforced at the state level. A benefit of this is citizens will be able to examine individual states and see the results of different approaches. For example, a state may find it is better to legalize marijuana and tax it like cigarettes, or it may discover that too many citizens become addicts with the drug legally available.

Those who claim a return of these regulatory powers to the states (states rights) will allow some states to return to slavery are idiotic. There are three separate constitutional amendments (see Chapter 15) that give the federal government constitutional power and authority to stop any state attempting to do this. No state will be allowed to violate the constitutional rights of any citizen.

A National Debate: Should Two Amendments be Repealed?
Two amendments greatly changed the way in which the federal

The Solution: Return to the Constitution

government worked and allowed it to become much bigger and more powerful. They are Amendments 16 and 17, the Federal Income Tax and Direct Election of Senators by the people.

> AMENDMENT 16: Income Tax
> (Ratified February 3, 1913, modifying
> Article I, section 9, of the Constitution)
> The Congress shall have power to lay and collect taxes on incomes, from whatever source derived, without apportionment among the several States, and without regard to any census or enumeration.
>
> (The 16th Amendment has done more to destroy an American citizen's privacy than any other. Citizens are now required to tell the IRS every aspect of their financial lives. Every dollar a citizen makes, every savings account, every investment account, must be reported to the IRS.)
>
> AMENDMENT 17: Direct Election of Senators
> (Ratified April 8, 1913, modifying
> Article I, section 3, of the Constitution)
> The Senate of the United States shall be composed of two Senators from each State, elected by the people thereof, for six years; and each Senator shall have one vote. ....

Both of these amendments went into effect in 1913 and marked a dramatic shift in power from states to Washington DC.

Before the Income Tax and the IRS became law, the federal government collected its money by issuing tariffs and fees on imported goods. If the government needed more money, it taxed the states on a per-person basis. States with larger populations paid more, smaller population states paid less. The share paid was in proportion to the citizens in each state. But the states collected the tax from the state's citizens and passed it on to the federal government. The federal government had no means of directly taxing citizens incomes. (See Heritage Guide to the Constitution : Amendment XVI.)

For example, Congress needed $1Billion in revenue. California has

20% of the population, so California was billed $200 million – their fair share. Idaho with 1.5% of the nations population would be billed $15 million – their fair share.

If the 16th Amendment were repealed, this is how taxes would be collected again. A great side benefit: The IRS and its piles of paperwork disappear. Plus citizens once again have financial privacy from the federal government. They are no longer required to submit every financial detail of their lives to an IRS agent.

Sidebar: Politicians haven't changed in the last 100 years. The income tax was sold as a "small percentage" tax on just the "very rich". Within seven years, the few percent was increased to 90% on "the rich" under Democrat Woodrow Wilson. Not surprisingly, the economy didn't do well and the voters changed leadership. Top tax rates were cut to 25%, and the "roaring '20s resulted. The economy will always do better with lower taxes if all other factors are equal. Also with a 90% tax rate, can anyone really say that a citizen still has freedom and liberty? When basically all of their income above an arbitrary threshold is seized by the government?

On the surface direct election of Senators by citizens seemed like a good thing. But it removed a key check that the states had on the federal government. With Senators appointed by the State Legislatures, the Senators represented the State Governments in Washington DC (citizens still had a voice in the process as they elected the state legislature). So if the tax being imposed by the federal government on the states got too high, the Senate, representing the states, would reduce it. Likewise, federal unfunded mandates, directing states how to spend state money, would seldom make it through the Senate. A Senator voting for either of these might soon find himself replaced by the state legislature.

The founders designed the government this way in the Constitution for these very reasons.

> Federalist Papers. No. 62. Section III.
> In this spirit it may be remarked, that the equal vote allowed to each State is at once a constitutional recognition of the

The Solution: Return to the Constitution

>portion of sovereignty remaining in the individual States, and an instrument for preserving that residuary sovereignty.... to guard, by every possible expedient, against an improper consolidation of the States into one simple republic.
>
>Another advantage accruing from this ingredient in the constitution of the Senate is, the additional impediment it must prove against improper acts of legislation. No law or resolution can now be passed without the concurrence, first, of a majority of the people, and then, of a majority of the States....

Note the specific references to each state remaining individual and sovereign within the republic, and the US Senate was to be the branch of government controlled by the states. Repeating a key point for emphasis: **No federal law could be passed without: "first, of a majority of the people, and then, of a majority of the States."** The 17th Amendment removed the states check on the power of the federal government.

In combination, these twin amendments gave the federal government huge amounts of new power.

There should be a national debate on repealing these two amendments. To amend the Constitution, there has to be overwhelming public support. But there is no reason these amendments could not be repealed as the amendment on prohibition of alcohol was repealed.

In any case, it will be a long debate, and the solution to America's crisis is not dependent on repealing these two amendments. By recognizing and following the 10th Amendment, the federal government will be forced to transfer both spending and responsibility to the states. But it will take many citizens demanding the changes. There is much power and wealth to be had by Congressmen and Senators under the current system, when they get to spend trillions of tax dollars and can make rules affecting every American – even down to which light bulbs citizens can buy. They will not want to give up their power and will not unless the citizens demand it.

Amending the Constitution

Long debates are nice academic exercises, but sometimes accomplish little in the real world. In the case of the federal government, the author has doubts that a majority of the Senators and Representatives will willingly cede the power they have worked so hard to obtain, back to the people or the state governments. But there is a way to force their hand, so to speak:

State Legislatures can bypass the Congress and amend the Constitution by themselves.

Method Two to Amend the Constitution
1) 2/3 of the State Legislatures (34 States) call a convention to propose amendments.
2) 3/4 of the State Legislatures (38 States) ratify the amendment (or 38 state delegations at the convention ratify).

The Convention of States (www.conventionofstates.com), has already begun such a process. The organization is working with state legislatures in 40 states to reach the 34 needed to call a convention to propose amendments.

The author believes the convention could also be an open-ended one. There are no rules stating conventions must be in one location or conclude in a certain number of days. Therefore a convention could be created in conjunction with amendments. A state legislature could vote to place itself in "convention". Then it could ratify any amendments to the Constitution that it wishes to.

This isn't wild or "out of control". The purpose of the convention is to agree on common amendment language before ratification. This requirement is still there. Amendment language must be the same, and ratified by 38 states for any amendment to be valid and to take effect. This is still a huge hurdle to overcome.

Any proposed amendment origination from the states should begin with language similar to "The state of XYZ hereby authorizes and approves a Constitutional Convention *with the sole purpose* to propose and ratify the following amendment. The convention shall

The Solution: Return to the Constitution

consist of the legislatures of the 50 states. The Convention shall remain open until 38 state legislatures have ratified the Amendment, thereby making it part of the Constitution and the Law of the Nation."

Amendments could include:

- **Repeal Amendment 16 on federal income tax**
  (or at least cap it at 15-20% maximum rate)

- **Repeal Amendment 17 on senatorial elections**

- **Term Limits for Congress Amendment.** No person may run for election for Congress after serving more than 7 terms (14 years) as a US Representative, or more than 3 terms (18 years) as a US Senator. Or more than 18 years of total service.

  Sidebar: The author favors longer term limits for Congress. others favor shorter terms: 6 years for the House, and 2 terms (12 years) for the Senate. For an amendment to be ratified there must be agreement on the number of years/terms by the states.

  Consideration could also be given to an old-age limit. Should those over 70 or 80 be allowed on the ballot? Some corporations restrict their officers to being under age 65. There is already a young-age restriction in the Constitution.

- **Attorney General Appointment/Election by Governors**
  One of the problems exposed in the federal government has been holding the president and his advisers accountable for real or alleged lawbreaking. President Nixon (Watergate) is a Republican example. President Clinton (perjury in court) and Obama (IRS used for political purposes) are Democrat examples. The issue is the Attorney General is the top federal law enforcement official, but is appointed by the President. Will the Attorney General honestly investigate his boss, especially if the AG is a political appointment? In the examples mentioned, the answer was "No", at least from the opposing political party. It may be better to have the state

governors select/nominate the Attorney General, then have Senate confirmation.

Getting 38 state legislatures to pass an identically worded amendment will be a difficult process, as it should be. The Constitution should not be amended lightly. There will have to be a large amount of public support for an amendment to pass.

Whether Congress or the state legislatures propose an amendment, the ratification process often takes years. The longest ratification period was the 27th Amendment, which took over 200 years for the states to ratify!

Other resources:
Mark Levin has authored a book called *The Liberty Amendments* as his suggestions for returning the federal government to its original charter. The author especially likes his suggested amendment to also term limit federal judges.

Sound Money: A US Dollar Good as Gold
The previous chapter listed one of the failings of the federal government is the failure to protect the money its citizens use. One way to avoid inflation is to tie the currency to gold. This was done in the past by many nations, including the early United States. There is a problem with this, though, since the world's supply of gold can and does change. There was inflation during the California gold rush in the 1800s as new gold was found and mined. More money means higher prices.

Rather than returning to gold alone, a better way may be to tie the dollar to an index or basket of currencies and commodities. For example the index could use the following:

Currencies	Commodities
Swiss Franc	Oz of Gold
Euro	Oz of Silver
Japanese Yen	Barrel of Oil
Canadian Dollar	Ton of Coal
	Bushel of Wheat
	Bushel of Corn

The Solution: Return to the Constitution

The basket can and should be flexible in that it changes as the world changes. For example in the 1800s whale oil would have definitely been in the basket as it was a primary source of energy. Today it would make no sense to be in the basket as it is no longer widely used. In the future, uranium may become part of the basket if nuclear power becomes the nation's main source of energy. The basket would be adjusted much as the Dow Jones Index of 30 stocks changes as some companies become more important and others become less important.

The Fed's sole purpose should be to manage the supply of US Dollars to keep this basket index within a specified range. This fixes the value of the dollar, achieving price stability and sound money. And delivers a US dollar that is worthy of being the world reserve currency that will benefit the world-wide economy.

Health Care Cost Crisis and Solution

WASHINGTON — The U.S. health care system squanders $750 billion a year — **roughly 30 cents of every medical dollar** — through unneeded care, byzantine paperwork, fraud and other waste, the influential Institute of Medicine said... - Associated Press. RICARDO ALONSO-ZALDIVAR. 9/6/2012

Healthcare vs Food
America has a Food Crisis! Citizens are beginning to question whether the food insurance bill the government signed into law was such a good idea. At first it worked great. Pay $100 a month to the food insurance company. Shop at any grocery store, put whatever you want in your cart, and show your insurance card to the check-out clerk. Soon, the prices on the food items are no longer posted, because shoppers no longer pay cash. Shoppers just use their food insurance card and with a small co-pay, the food is yours! Everyone signed up. Of course, the prices soon begin to rise on food items, but the insurance card still covers it, so who cares? Except the food insurance premiums soon begin rising to $300 a month, then $400 a month, and there are rumors it may go to $500 a month next year. It's a Food Crisis! Many cannot afford to pay that much! Some politicians are proposing a single-payer food plan run by the federal government to control food costs.

The above paragraph, of course, is not happening, unless one substitutes "Healthcare" for "Food", then it fairly accurately describes America's current healthcare problem. When consumers "shop" for healthcare services, they usually do not know what the prices are because they do not pay for each service item. Therefore healthcare service prices are high because there is no consumer incentive to shop for the best price. Free markets, using human nature, have proven continually to provide the best possible goods and services for consumers at the lowest prices.

This chapter has four main sections.
  I. History of the Federal Government Intrusion into Healthcare
     A) Tying Health Insurance to Companies
     B) Medicare and Medicaid
     C) ObamaCare
     D) Federal Government as Sole Payer?
  II. Federal Government Healthcare Waste and Fraud
  III. Health-care Laws Violating the Constitution and Freedom of Citizens

IV. Healthcare Solutions
   A) Transfer Responsibility to State or Local Governments
   B) Healthcare Choices at the State Level

I. History of the Federal Government Intrusion into Healthcare

When people criticize the flaws in the American healthcare system, they usually attribute the failures to a "free-market system". They ignore or do not understand the effects that continuous federal government intervention has had on the system, beginning in the 1940s.

A. Tying Health Insurance to Companies

America's healthcare cost problem is happening because the federal government has interfered with free market forces. The same ones that allow grocery store shelves to be filled with an abundance of food at low prices. The first intrusion of the federal government into healthcare came during World War II. It was an unintended consequence, as is often the result of government action. With many men serving as soldiers and out of the labor force, the federal government tried to control wages with regulation. Their rationale was rising wages would lead to inflation. Companies needing to pay workers more, causes the cost of the produced goods to rise, so companies will raise their prices on goods to compensate. The government was determined to prevent inflation, and also regulated good prices on many items in addition to wages.

> Employer-Sponsored Health Insurance and Health Reform
> ...the link between employment and private health insurance was strengthened by three key government decisions in the 1940s and 1950s. First, during World War II the War Labor Board ruled that wage and price controls did not apply to fringe benefits such as health insurance, leading many employers to institute [employer-sponsored insurance]. Second, in the late 1940s the National Labor Relations Board ruled that health insurance and other employee benefit plans were subject to collective bargaining. Third, in 1954 the Internal Revenue Service decreed that health insurance premiums paid by employers were exempt from income taxation.
> - National Bureau of Economic Research. (www.nber.org)

Health Care Cost Crisis and Solution

Price controls have never worked. The price controls led to rationing of key goods like metals and gasoline. Employers still needed to compete with other companies to attract workers. Unable to use higher wages, they substituted health insurance benefits in lieu of the wages the government restricted them from paying. The federal wage controls just changed employee compensation from paycheck to benefits. After the war ended, the government followed with the declaration that health benefits paid by employers were not taxable, making them attractive to both employer and employee. Employer healthcare became an entrenched benefit. This created several problems.

Insurance Non-portability: A downside is health insurance became tied to companies. When a worker loses his or her job, health insurance is now lost too. This is not an issue if people buy their insurance directly. Imagine if food was primarily purchased through company food stores. Lose the job and the food source is lost too. It's a poor model and it was initiated by short-sighted federal government policy.

Payment Model: Previous to the government (and employer) intervention, most healthcare was purchased directly by the user. Patients paid their doctors or hospitals directly for the care they received. (the free market model). Now healthcare evolved into a premium model with a third party insurance company. With patients now paying premiums and not paying their doctors directly, the free market excellence in controlling prices was lost. See the example in the beginning of the chapter where food insurance became the mechanism for buying food.

A key reason that healthcare is so expensive and food is not, even though food is more critical to human survival than healthcare, is the government intervention that removed free market principles from the healthcare system. American consumers have been trained to pay a single premium and expect the rest of their healthcare to be free (as in paid for by the insurance company, not them). Any good or service bought that way will see dramatic cost increases or shortages. It's Economics 101.

Government involvement did not end after the 1940s. In the 1960s, the federal government initiated a program that would become the largest healthcare insurance business in the nation: Medicare and Medicaid.

B. Medicare and Medicaid
July 30, 1965: President Lyndon B. Johnson signs the bill creating Medicare and Medicaid.

Thus entered the federal government directly into the healthcare / health insurance business. As a result, the country now has a crisis in escalating and out-of-control healthcare costs. Take a large, bloated, inefficient organization like the federal government and put it in charge of an insurance-model business already geared to drive prices upward, and it is not surprising to see skyrocketing healthcare costs and 30% levels of waste. Federal government involvement makes everything more expensive. The bureaucrats who administer the program must be paid. The demographics of the program allowed politicians to make awesome promises that could not be delivered on in the long term. As with Social Security in the next chapter, the federal government used a large number of workers and a small number of retiree users, to give benefits to the retirees. The system begins to collapse when the number of retirees grows and the number of contributing workers shrinks. **But the program did allow politicians to use the benefits to persuade recipients to vote for them during elections.**

C. ObamaCare
The largest government intrusion into healthcare occurred in 2009 with the passage of the Affordable Care Act, better known as ObamaCare. ObamaCare isn't targeted to small groups like the retired or the poor. It targets everyone's healthcare and insurance with massive new rules, regulations and taxes.

> ObamaCare has become emblematic of **big government's arrogant incompetence**. It's a 2,700-page monstrosity whose rules are still being written more than a year after its passage. Its supporters could not be bothered to read it before forcing it upon us, even as one of their own called it "a Ponzi scheme of the first order, the kind of thing Bernie Madoff would have been proud of." The landscape is littered with ObamaCare's broken promises: Keep your doctor. Keep

your insurance. Cut the deficit. Reduce premiums. Create 4 million new jobs. All lies. Instead, connected friends got ObamaCare waivers while the rest of America has seen an increase in premiums and the roles of the uninsured actually have increased. This is ObamaCare.

- Dr. Milton R. Wolf. The Washington Times. September 21, 2011

ObamaCare will not fully reveal its ineptness until 2014 when it goes into effect. So disruptive and unpopular was the law that the politician leading the charge, Barack Obama, made sure key provisions of the law did not take effect until after the 2012 presidential election – an election he won without voters seeing the law in action. There are two main issues with ObamaCare:

1) ObamaCare, like most liberal inspired programs is income-based (purchaser's costs will depend on their income level). So the state exchanges where people now will need to buy their health insurance, will need quick access to income data on the purchaser. Where does the data come from? The IRS of course. Except the IRS, like most federal government agencies, is hopelessly behind and outdated with respect to modern computer technology. The IRS was not designed and does not work in real-time. It often takes them months to process tax data and issue audits. When the state agencies cannot get data from the IRS, how will they be able to set the price for the health policy?

2) Health insurance premiums will soar as ObamaCare takes effect. Why? Simple economics. ObamaCare mandates everyone buy insurance or pay a fine, except the fine is only $95 per year to begin with. A young healthy person, when faced with either a health premium of $120-$300 per month or a fine of $95 per year, will choose the fine. When healthy people pay the fine rather than buying insurance, the health insurance companies must raise premiums on their remaining sicker customers to cover their costs. Remember, a healthy person without insurance doesn't need to buy it until they get sick, since ObamaCare mandates people with pre-existing illnesses cannot be refused insurance.

ObamaCare was bad law as passed and signed. It will not work and is an unconstitutional abuse of power by the federal government.

Just because a few Justices ignore two amendments in the Bill of Rights, and declare it "legal" does not make it so. But Democrats have acknowledged ObamaCare's design faults. The problem is Obama is changing the law on his own without Congress. That IS illegal. It sets a terrible precedent for future Presidents to change laws to suit themselves, which leads to lawlessness.

> ### Democrats Constitutionally Ignorant In ObamaCare Feud
> The president is illegally picking and choosing what parts to keep. Gone is the employer mandate, the cap on out-of-pocket expenses, income verification for subsidy recipients, and over half the deadlines in the law.
>
> These changes are not just illegal. They also shift billions of dollars in costs on to taxpayers, cheat seriously ill patients, leave employees in the lurch, all in a devious attempt to patch up an unworkable law.
>
> Madison anticipated this threat to freedom. In Federalist 62, he warned that it will be pointless for Americans to elect a Congress, if it in turn enacts laws "too voluminous to be read," or if these laws then " undergo such incessant changes that no man who knows what the law is today can guess what it will be tomorrow." That's ObamaCare.
>   - Investor's Business Daily. Betsy McCaughey. September 26, 2013

D. Federal Government as the Sole Payer?
Many on the conservative side have stated they believe the long term result or even goal of ObamaCare will be the bankruptcy of private health-insurance companies, leaving the government as the only option. If/when ObamaCare collapses, America will face a choice: Single payer government run healthcare or free market-driven healthcare. The author hopes America will choose wisely and return to a free market health insurance healthcare system. Conservatives must lead the way in convincing the public to follow the Constitution and send healthcare law to the states.

Single payer describes a system most American's have never seen. Every doctor payment, surgeon payment, or prescription drug payment will be made by the federal government. Liberals believe that this will be a wonderful, caring system. The government will pay all of the bills and everyone will get all the healthcare they want for free! Conservatives point out that nothing is free. Government must first take money from someone before it can use it to pay healthcare costs of others. Also government has a track record of managing things very poorly and inefficiently (See Chapter 19). This means a government run healthcare system will be much more costly than a privately run one. Government will have to control costs. Government will then decide which patients get treatment and which do not. President Obama acknowledges this when he says that some will not get the surgeries they want but will just be given a pain pill (ABC video available on YouTube, search Obama, pill). Realize that with government in control, there is always the potential for abuse of power: a government bureaucrat denying healthcare payments for political opponents.

Sidebar: Veterans have seen government as the sole provider. The federal government operates healthcare for them under the Department of Veteran's Affairs. The treatment for veterans is usually very good, *if* they can see doctors and specialists. The VA is notorious for long waiting lists to see doctors – sometimes months, even if the patient has a serious illness.

II. Federal Government Healthcare Waste and Fraud
Federal government involvement in healthcare drives up costs. This is true not just with healthcare, but almost every area the federal government is involved in. Most will remember reports of the Defense Department buying $900 hammers or other media-reported examples of government waste. Government is seldom efficient or frugal with tax dollars it spends. Healthcare is no different.

When the federal government pays a bill, it often mismanages it. A study shows 10% waste and fraud is present in the government programs. This is an unacceptably high level for such a large program. A business operating at this efficiency would soon be bankrupt, but of course the federal government cannot go bankrupt. It just raises taxes to cover its inefficiency.

> GAO: Medicare losing $48 billion
> Nearly **10 percent of all Medicare payments are fraudulent or otherwise improper,** and the government

isn't doing enough to stop them.

That's the conclusion of a Government Accountability Office report released Wednesday. The report, issued at the request of a House subcommittee investigating Medicare and Medicaid fraud, estimates that the federal government is losing $48 billion on the improper payments – a significant amount for a program that "is fiscally unsustainable in the long term" unless action is taken.
- Politico, BRETT COUGHLIN. 3/2/11

Medicare is a program for the retired. Medicaid is for the poor. Neither program is well run by any standard. Evidence has been uncovered of rampant fraud with little effort by the programs front-line workers to prevent it.

Medicaid Fraud with Government Workers to Assist You
Investigative journalist James O'Keefe has uncovered several unbelievable stories where government workers actually assisted in Medicare fraud. The report is impossible to dispute because the workers are video taped in the act. The videos, taken in 2011, are available on YouTube or on O'Keefe's Project Veritas website.

> "In this time of economic uncertainty, the American people deserve to know how their tax dollars are being wasted. This is hardly an isolated incident. Government workers willing to aid people with criminal backgrounds and great wealth, should be an outrage to every American."
> - James O'Keefe. TheProjectVeritas.com.

Project Veritas recorded five videos capturing federal workers abusing the system:

1) In one video, undercover reporters pose as wealthy drug dealers while visiting four different Medicaid offices in Ohio. The case workers were eager to assist filling out the Medicaid paperwork, and made no attempt to contact authorities even though criminal behavior was asserted by the applicants.

2) In the another video, filmed in several Medicaid offices in South Carolina, an applicant driving an expensive sports car, poses as part of a terrorist organization. The Medicaid case worker does not

probe into the nature of the applicant's work and helps him fill out a form.

3) In a third video, an undercover reporter attempts to apply for benefits at Medicaid offices in Maine. The reporter says his family has a pharmaceutical and fishing business and talks about his Corvette. He also says that his assets are in cash and precious metals which are less traceable. The Medicaid case worker coaches him by saying, "If you can't prove income, you don't have income." She also says "Don't say anything about your Corvette."

4) In the Gary, Indiana video, an undercover reporter applies for Medicaid benefits. The reporter indicates that he is a drug dealer who has "50 people who work for us." The Medicaid case worker says "We don't want to know that." In spite of hearing about Rolex watches and McLaren sports cars, a Medicaid worker counsels the applicant on how to transfer the title of a mansion from father to son, so that the father is eligible for Medicaid.

5) A video in Richmond, VA shows a worker telling a drug dealer with an $800,000 car, "just leave that off your application."

All five videos are available on YouTube or on Project Veritas (www.projectveritas.com).

Is it any wonder medical costs are soaring for this government program, with the program's workers actively participating in fraudulent applications?

These are multiple examples of the federal government being simply incapable of managing these programs. The federal government cannot manage healthcare programs any more efficiently that it manages its other bloated agencies discussed in the previous chapter.

III. Health-care Laws Violating the Constitution and Freedom of Citizens

Politicians usually imply citizens are not receiving the healthcare they require or are being turned away by providers. In actuality, there has been a federal law since 1986 that requires hospitals to treat patients regardless of whether they can pay or even whether they are citizens. Unfortunately, this law must be considered a violation of the constitutional rights and freedoms of healthcare providers.

EMTALA: The Emergency Medical Treatment and Active Labor Act (TITLE 42 > CHAPTER 7 > SUBCHAPTER XVIII > Part E) requires hospitals and ambulance services to provide care to anyone seeking emergency healthcare treatment regardless of citizenship, legal status or ability to pay. The government does not reimburse the provider. Patients can be discharged only under their own informed consent or when their condition requires transfer to a hospital better equipped to administer the treatment.

> EMTALA: what it is and what it means for physicians
> The Emergency Medical Treatment and Active Labor Act (EMTALA) was passed by the US Congress in 1986 as part of the Consolidated Omnibus Reconciliation Act (COBRA), much of which dealt with Medicare issues..... Although only 4 pages in length and barely noticed at the time, EMTALA has created a storm of controversy... it is now considered one of the most comprehensive laws guaranteeing nondiscriminatory access to... the health care system. Even though its initial language covered the care of emergency medical conditions, through interpretations by [federal government agencies], as well as various court decisions, the statute now potentially applies to virtually all aspects of patient care in the hospital setting.
> - Baylor University Medical Center Proceedings. October. 2001.

The EMTALA law is also another example of government action increasing healthcare costs. If a clinic cannot collect payment from someone they are forced to treat, they will either pass the cost along to paying customers or simply go out of business. In the first case, the cost of care increases for paying patients or their insurance companies (resulting in higher premiums for the patients). In the second case, there becomes less (or no) choice for the healthcare patients as facilities go out of business.

The law was passed to prevent private hospitals from transferring uninsured patients to public hospitals. Public hospitals receive funding from government, so the government can direct them to treat patients unable to pay, if the government wishes to. However, with private hospitals, the government should have made arrangements to pay the bills if it wanted uninsured patients treated. Instead the government just used brute force of law to push its obligations onto private hospitals and doctors. (Note: The federal government should not be funding local hospitals according to the Constitution. States, counties or cities may choose to do so.)

EMTALA must be considered unconstitutional. Under what authority can the federal government demand a doctor or nurse treat a patient? This is their skill, their job. The mandate requires them to perform it without compensation. This approaches slavery, where blacks were told they must work for their master, without compensation, against their will. The US Constitution bans slavery.

EMTALA types laws for everyone?
Where else should this government force be applied? College education is important. Let's mandate that professors must teach any student who shows up. If the students cannot pay, well too bad. That's the professors' problem. Food is of critical importance. So anyone walking into a grocery store should be able to take what they please and if they cannot pay, well that's the store owner's problem. Only a tyrannical government would dictate that a worker provide a product or service and get no compensation for it.

Many journalists advocate for laws that force the treatment of sick people who cannot pay. Well, information is very important to our society. Would these journalists also be OK with laws mandating their work must be provided for free to anyone who can't pay? The information is too important to corrupt with advertising. Journalists should work for free with no pay. It's their civic duty. Isn't that an absurd argument? Well, it's equally absurd to mandate healthcare workers provide their work for free.

To those favoring mandate laws such as EMTALA: Would you be OK if your city or county of residence passed a law stating that you had to provide shelter to anyone needing it? Requiring you to open up your house to any homeless person needing a place to stay? After all, you have plenty of rooms – and only sleep in one at a time. Anyone in favor of mandates on another's resources should be fine with a mandate on their own personal resources.

Now if a journalist, doctor, nurse, grocer, or professor chooses to give their services to a poor person of their own free will, they should be commended by society for doing a good deed. They have practiced Christian charity and good works described as pleasing to God in the Bible. Refer to the Good Samaritan parable taught by Jesus (Luke 10, Ch.8). The Samaritan uses his *own* resources to care for the beaten man. Christians should do likewise, not expect the government to force someone else to do the good deed.

Legal Healthcare Assistance
But what if the The Emergency Medical Treatment and Active Labor Act was removed? Wouldn't greedy hospitals let people die of illness? Wouldn't that cause a crisis where people would be denied healthcare? The author does not think doctors would let patients die. They would treat those patients who truly needed care with their charitable spirit. Or a charitable rich person may pick up the bill. Or the state/county government could pay the bill. **But, the government cannot force doctors or hospitals to treat patients in a free society.**

Hypocrisy Alert: Liberals, like those living in Berkeley, CA, who preach healthcare is a "right" should begin by focusing on unionized healthcare workers. Because if healthcare is a "right" then healthcare workers are obligated to provide it. This means healthcare worker strikes are not allowed, as strikes prevent patients from receiving their "rights".

> Nurses at Alta Bates, other Bay Area hospitals, on strike
> Nurses at Alta Bates Summit Hospital on Ashby Avenue in Berkeley went out on strike today and will do so again tomorrow, the seventh walk-out since September 2011.
> - berkeleyside.com. Tracey Taylor. November 20, 2012.

If a state or local government wants to assist with healthcare, there are three options that do not violate a doctor's right to own his or her labor:

1) Pay the doctor's fee for treatment of the poor.

2) Form a government-run clinic where the government hires the doctors and runs the care for the poor. This is the Veteran's Affairs (VA) model.

3) Group the poor and negotiate an advance fee with doctors for treatment. This is the Medicaid model.

IV. Healthcare Solutions

As stated in Chapter 20, the primary solution to fixing America's healthcare system begins with returning to the Constitution and transferring the responsibility of these programs to the states.

A terrific side benefit is the nation can end the debate as to the type of healthcare system that works best. There are four main system types:

1) Free Market Healthcare using private companies.

2) Quasi-free market with heavy government regulation.

3) Single Payer where the government pays all citizens health bills.

4) Full Socialization, where the government owns the doctors, hospitals and other providers.

States will be free to design their systems using the principles of any of these four types and will show in the real world the strengths and weaknesses of each system type.

A. Transfer Responsibility to State or Local Governments

A potential approach to transferring responsibility for healthcare is the HealthCare Compact. It proposes transferring management of the Medicare and Medicaid programs to the states, but leaves the taxation at the federal level.

> Health Care Compact (www.healthcarecompact.org)
> The Health Care Compact moves the responsibility and authority for regulating healthcare from the federal government to the states. Is this a good idea?
> Yes, for two primary reasons:
> 1. Healthcare is simply too large and complex to manage at the federal level.
> 2. States have generally been shown to be more effective

regulators than the federal government.

To demonstrate the challenge of regulating healthcare at the federal level, consider the following facts:

- A federal system impacts 300+ million people
- Healthcare spending exceeds $2.3 trillion annually
- More than 14 million people work in the healthcare industry
- There are 2,688 pages of regulations for Medicare and Medicaid

Centralized planning of an industry that is this large and complex is not possible, and has never been successful in the history of mankind.

Proposed Compact Elements:

Pledge: Member states agree to work together to pass this Compact, and to improve the health care in their respective states.

State Control: In member states, states can suspend federal health care regulations. Federal and state health care laws remain in force in a state until states enact superseding regulations.

Funding: *Member states get an amount of money from the federal government each year to pay for health care.* The funding is mandatory spending, and not subject to annual appropriations. Each state's funding is based on the federal funds spent in their state on health care in 2010. Each state will confirm their funding before joining this Compact. This funding level will be adjusted annually for changes in population and inflation.

The HealthCare Compact is on the right track. States will be more efficient managers than the federal government. States have the constitutional authority and responsibility to regulate healthcare to the extent that it is regulated. But the funding mechanism is flawed. With the federal government collecting the taxes, it is only a matter of time before federal agencies begin attaching strings to the money it distributes. It is the nature of bureaucrats to regulate, and they will soon be telling the states how to run the program.

Why let the federal government collect taxes with the sole purpose of passing out money to the states? **Let the states collect their own money from their own citizens to pay for their own healthcare programs.** States should provide their own funding for any program they implement. The Medicare/Medicaid taxes now collected by the federal government, should be transferred to the states. The states can then adjust the tax levels and benefit levels as they deem best.

Transfer Medicaid, Medicare and ObamaCare to the States
Medicare and Medicaid should be transferred to the states under the process described in Chapter 20. The states can adopt all, or part of, or none of the federal regulations for their own use. The paycheck taxes that fund these programs will become state taxes.

An issue will be inter-state insurance portability. For example, a resident of New York pays state taxes while working, but retires in Florida. Florida just added a retiree that didn't pay taxes while working. This is a major flaw in the current federal Medicare program – it just transfers money from current workers to current retirees. States will have to take this into account as they design their systems.

ObamaCare should be repealed as soon as possible. Part of the repeal bill could send the entire law to the states, giving them the option to codify all or parts of ObamaCare into their law. Unfortunately, ObamaCare is so poorly written, it is doubtful any state would want any section of it. The key is to remove the federal government from the healthcare system. The federal government has shown it cannot manage these programs or develop effective solutions. Let states take over - with their own solutions.

B. Healthcare Choices at the State Level
There will be 50 state laboratories to study which healthcare systems work best, and which fail. America's Constitution offers states a great deal of independence with respect to their domestic matters. States will demonstrate how well different systems work.

If one state's citizens feel government run healthcare is a great system, show the nation. It is perfectly constitutional to implement it at the state level. California, New Jersey, or New York are all fine candidates for this demonstration. Just get the state government to go to single payer. Let the state become the only payer and decider for healthcare needs of the citizens of the state. Or take it a step further and fully socialize the system. Let California, for example, buy the doctors, hospitals, and pharmacies in the state. All the doctors, surgeons and pharmacists will then be state government employees. If government healthcare care is a smashing success, other states will surely copy it.

> Sidebar on human nature: There is a misconception by many that government workers are driven by altruism and an angelic desire to help others, while private insurance company workers are driven by a desire to hurt their customers and abuse them as much as possible. In reality, both of these types of workers are going to be found in government or private systems. The difference is that customers can leave a poorly run private insurance company. Not so with a poorly run government system. The Bible teaches, and America's founders realized, that humans are capable of great good as well as great evil. That is why checks and limitations were placed on federal government power.

Massachusetts has already implemented a program that mandates all citizens buy health insurance or pay a fine to the government. This is similar to the system President Obama pushed through Congress at a national level. Massachusetts Care will likely fail over time if an earlier attempt in Tennessee is any indication.

HillaryCare in Tennessee
In 1994, Tennessee passed what was then a very hot new Democrat idea -- call it government managed care -- a version of the reform [Hillary Clinton] was also pitching nationwide. TennCare promised the impossible dream of politicians everywhere: Lower health-care costs while covering more of the "uninsured." They got the impossible, all right. After 10 years of mismanagement and lawsuits, TennCare now eats up one-third of the state's entire budget and is growing fast. Governor Phil Bredesen, a Democrat, is

preparing to pull the plug...
- Wall Street Journal. wsj.com. Dec. 6, 2004

Before Tennessee pulled the plug on TennCare, they **rationed** healthcare by limiting participants and limiting benefits.

> The total annual budget for TennCare increased from $2.64 billion in 1994 to more than $8.5 billion in fiscal year 2005, with essentially no change in the number of participants enrolled. .... The McKinsey report, issued in late 2003, concluded that TennCare was not financially viable.... In response to these reports and to stem the growth in costs, in 2005 the state implemented several program changes, including removing about 190,000 participants, imposing limits on the number of prescription medications each participant could receive, and reducing other benefits.
> - Wikipedia. TennCare. 2012.

It is the author's belief that the laws of economics will doom the Massachusetts approach to contain healthcare costs, just as they doomed Tennessee's. The best way to lower costs is to let the free markets work. These principles have made America an economic superpower, and they will lower healthcare costs if given the chance to work. But, nobody has to take the word of a conservative. Any state is free to lead the way in proving these free-market principles wrong. The beauty of 50 different state programs, is citizens will not have to take the liberal or conservative view on faith alone. There will be ample data provided by the states.

Sidebar: The Massachusetts program and any other similar state programs must be ruled legal by the state courts for the state to mandate citizens purchase health insurance; and federal courts must determine whether the mandated insurance purchase violates the gray area of the 14th Amendment (Do states violate a citizen's US Constitutional rights by forcing them to buy a product?). It is definitely against the free will of citizens to force them to purchase health insurance, or any other product.

Conservative states can implement market-driven options in states to lower costs. For example:

The Bible and Constitution Made America Great

1) Post all healthcare prices in on-line marketplaces. If a patient needs a medical test or procedure done, they can price-shop just like they shop for groceries or automobiles. This will lower prices. Free market forces always drive down prices.
2) Same for prescription drugs. If Canada or European countries subsidize drugs to lower prices, let American citizens, insurance companies, or pharmacies buy and import those drugs.
3) Move insurance to individual policies rather than corporate group policies. Citizens buy auto insurance this way. This prevents loss of insurance when switching jobs or being unemployed. Since most Americans no longer work their entire careers for the same company, the model of company-provided health insurance no longer works well. (Remember, company provided health insurance is an anomaly going back to WWII, when the government imposed wage controls. Companies responded by offering health insurance in lieu of the wages they were not allowed to raise.)
4) Remove state mandates on insurance coverage. Politicians love to mandate policies cover items like drug abuse, mental health, and birth control; but these drive up the cost of premiums for those who do not need those coverages. Give the consumer the choice of a catastrophic care policy (covering only major events like heart attacks, cancer...) with much lower premiums. Imagine how expensive auto insurance would be if oil changes and gasoline purchases were mandated to be covered.

> Note: Every item added to insurance costs something, much like when buying a car, power windows cost extra. Say the cost of power windows is $600. The government could mandate all cars have these, but that just results in the $600 being built into the car cost. Customers lose the option of saving $600 by not selecting the power window option. So a government mandating drug abuse coverage makes for a great soundbite for politicians, but results in loss of choice and higher insurance premiums for everyone.

5) Medical Savings Accounts. Rather than the government taxing workers and giving benefits to retirees, let workers put money into accounts that are used only for their medical needs. These accounts will grow tax-free over time. People are always more frugal with their own money then when spending someone else's money.

Economic principles and free markets will lower costs, but they must be allowed to work. If a person chooses not to buy health insurance and gets a serious disease with expensive treatment costs, the person must either pay the costs of treatment or rely on charity. If a state government intervenes and pays for these health treatments, there is no reason for others to buy health insurance – and they will not. The market will breakdown. This is exactly what is happening with our current healthcare system. The mandate to purchase health insurance in Massachusetts is a government solution to the problem government itself is creating by interfering with the markets.

Going back to the auto example, if the government told citizens that auto travel was essential, therefore the government would pay for repairs from auto accidents, why would anyone buy collision insurance? Nobody would as the government will repair your car.

In Conclusion:
As the federal healthcare programs (ObamaCare, Medicare, and Medicaid) fail due to their size, complexity, and fraud, the constitutional answer is to send the entire government responsibility in healthcare to the states. If the Constitution had been followed, the federal government would not have become involved in healthcare to begin with. The 10th Amendment leaves this to the states or the people. This unfortunately did not stop federal politicians from grabbing unauthorized power. Government involvement or solutions should be at the local level, not the federal level.

America's Founders assumed that the citizens were a moral people who would follow the biblical principles of charity for those truly in need (Ch. 8). When the founders spoke of a moral citizenry being required for America to succeed, they meant the need for a nation of

Good Samaritans (parable, Luke 10) rather than a nation of Rich men (Rich Man and Lazarus parable, Luke 16). Charity, along with free markets, is the best way for a society to provide itself with healthcare.

Social Security

Social Security is the crowning achievement of big-government advocates. Liberal politicians point to it as a spectacular success. If the program is so successful and popular, why does the federal government force citizens to participate? The federal government could have made the program optional. Citizens could have been free to evaluate the program on its merits and decide whether or not they wanted to participate in it. But, the federal government gave citizens no such choice. It forced them to pay Social Security taxes (FICA from every paycheck), then gave itself the power to decide how much to pay back to retirees in benefits. It is a gross violation of citizens free will and their constitutional rights. Not to mention it stole the opportunity from citizens to invest that money and a have a much richer retirement.

Social Security is not constitutional and never has been. Per the 10th Amendment the federal government is not allowed to create and run a massive retirement – wealth redistribution (from workers to retirees) program. Yes, the Supreme Court, under political pressure, did rule that the program was constitutional in the 1930s (see Chapter 12 on the Constitution). Likewise, in Chapter 13 on Freedom of Religion, it was shown how judges have often ruled exactly opposite of what the constitutional language states. The nation has seen many judges in the last 100 years who believe "the Constitution is what the judges say it is."

Despite Social Security not belonging at the federal level of government, it simply cannot and should NOT be eliminated or transferred to the states at the current time. Retired people have been taxed their entire working lives, promised benefits, and planned their lives according to Social Security. It is not fair to suddenly cancel these promises. In addition the program no longer generates excess cash, but is barely able to cover the benefits with current tax receipts. Social Security has huge liabilities (promises to retirees), and it is not fair to send these liabilities to the states.

Many retirees think that the FICA taxes they paid into Social Security have been put into an account and they are now getting their benefits from that account. That is not true and never has been true. Social Security has always collected FICA taxes from workers and immediately spent those tax dollars on retiree benefits (and other non-related federal programs).

IOU's and False Promises

Retirees can be excused for not knowing the truth. They have been lied to by the government since Social Security's inception.

> Here's what the 1936 government pamphlet on Social Security said: "After the first 3 years -- that is to say, beginning in 1940 -- you will pay, and your employer will pay, 1.5 cents for each dollar you earn, up to $3,000 a year. ... Beginning in 1943, you will pay 2 cents, and so will your employer, for every dollar you earn for the next 3 years. ... And finally, beginning in 1949, twelve years from now, you and your employer will each pay 3 cents on each dollar you earn, up to $3,000 a year." Here's Congress' lying promise: "That is the most you will ever pay."
>
> Another lie in the Social Security pamphlet is: "Beginning November 24, 1936, the United States government will set up a Social Security account for you. ... The checks will come to you as a right." Therefore, Americans were sold on the belief that Social Security is like a retirement account and money placed in it is our property. The fact of the matter is you have no property right whatsoever to your Social Security "contributions."
>
>   - Dr. Walter E. Williams. Professor of Economics. 9/21/2011

Examining a history of Social Security confirms the lies Dr. Williams refers to in the "propaganda" pamphlet. Some background information:

Social Security taxes workers (FICA tax) and distributes the money to retirees (benefit checks). If the Social Security Administration (SSA) collects more in taxes than it pays out, it sends the money to the Treasury and it becomes part of the general fund. SSA receives an IOU note from the Treasury. For it's entire history, SSA has been sending excess money to the Treasury each year. SSA is now reaching the point where it is no longer generating revenue, but paying out more than it takes in. SSA will make up the difference by redeeming the IOUs it has collected. Except the Treasury is already in debt (Chapter 19)!

In any year in which the FICA Taxes do not cover benefit payments,

SSA will go to the Treasury and turn in its IOUs. Congress then must account for the expenditure in the budget to redeem the IOUs. IF SSA needs $100 million to cover benefits, Congress must do one of the following:

1) Borrow $100 million and send it to the SSA
2) Increase taxes by $100 million to fund SSA
3) Cut spending by $100 million in another program to fund SSA

But can't the SSA simply sell the IOUs? No. They are not legal bonds owed to a creditor. The IOUs are internal government instruments. A real world example: A man wishes to have an emergency fund. So he keeps $100 in a side compartment of his wallet. The compartment is separate from the main compartment where he conducts his cash transactions. One day the man sees a great new power tool that he really wants to buy, but is short of cash. So he takes the $100 from his emergency compartment. Not wanting to be without his emergency fund, he writes an IOU note for $100 and puts that in his emergency compartment. The man now feels much better with his emergency account fully funded. Silly isn't it? The man cannot use the IOU to buy anything at a store. It's worthless. But, this is what the government has done. Placed a bunch of IOUs in an account inside the government and called it "the Social Security Trust Fund". The government must replace the IOUs with cash before it can send out a check.

Pay-as-you-go with Poor Demographics
Prudential has a good historical summary of Social Security (www.prudential.com/Social-Security)

> President Franklin D. Roosevelt signed the Social Security Act in 1935 as a direct result of the economic depression of the 1930s. Originally, only retirement benefits were paid to the primary worker. The law was amended in 1939 to add survivors' benefits and benefits for the retiree's spouse and children. Disability benefits were added in 1956.
>
> Social Security is a "pay-as-you-go" program, which means that today's workers are paying for the benefits to today's

beneficiaries through their payroll taxes. <u>In 1940, there were 42 workers per retiree</u>. In <u>1950, the ratio was 16-to-1</u>. <u>Today, there are 3.3 workers per retiree</u>, and within 40 years, it's projected that there will be just <u>2 workers per retiree</u>. At the present rate, as the population ages and life expectancies continue to rise, the system will not be able to sustain itself into the future without major reform.

Currently, you and your employer <u>each pay 6.2 percent</u> of a predetermined portion of your salary into the system.

Your retirement benefits are calculated on a complex formula based on the "best" 35 years of your earnings..... Social Security was intended to be one source of your income after retirement, but not the sole source.

When Social Security was initially set up, the full retirement age was 65, and it still is for people born before 1938. But as life expectancies have increased, the age for receiving full retirement benefits has crept up as well. If you were born between 1938 and 1960, your full retirement age is somewhere on a sliding scale between 65 and 67. Anyone born in 1960 or later will now have to wait until age 67 for full benefits.

The impact on Social Security of the average lifespan of Americans cannot be understated.. In 1940 the average age at death was 63. By 2010 Americans were living to 78 years on average. So the original Social Security program paid benefits beginning at age 65, above the average age of death. As medical technology enabled Americans to live longer, Social Security continued to pay benefits at age 65, and politicians even lowered the benefit age to 62 for early retirees.

<u>History of Expansion into Insolvency and Fraud</u>
If the demographics for Social Security were not bad enough, politicians made it worse by expanding the program and spending its tax dollars on more than retiree benefits. Some key historical dates from *the Social Security Administration Online*:

> **1935:** The Social Security Act becomes law.

Social Security

1937: The first Social Security benefits are paid (one-time payment only).

1939: The Social Security Act Amendments of 1939 broadens the program to include benefits for dependents and survivors.

1956: The Social Security Act is amended to provide monthly benefits to permanently and totally disabled workers ages 50 to 64 and for adult children of deceased or retired workers, if disabled before age 18.

> Sidebar: Because the program was bringing in much more money that it paid out, it offered greedy politicians "free money" to spend on other areas. Never mind the promises of a "trust fund".

1961: The Social Security Amendments of 1961 are signed permitting all workers to elect reduced retirement at age 62.

1972: P.L. 92-336 becomes law, which authorizes a 20 percent cost-of-living adjustment (COLA) effective September 1972 and establishes the procedures for issuing automatic annual COLAs beginning in 1975.

1956 is a key date. Expanding the program to cover disability is one of the reasons the program is facing funding issues today, especially once it was further expanded to include non-verifiable conditions like depression and back pain as disabilities. Social Security expansions have added costly obligations to compete with retiree benefits that were once the sole purpose of the program.

<u>Social Security Disability Insolvent Unless Congress Votes</u>

The [Social Security] disability program, which has been spending more than it receives in revenue for four consecutive years, is projected to exhaust its trust fund in 2016, according to a Social Security trustees report.

The disability program currently pays benefits averaging $1,111 a month, with the money coming from the Social Security payroll tax taken out of workers' paychecks.

The program cost $132 billion last year, more than the combined annual budgets of the departments of Agriculture,

Homeland Security, Commerce, Labor, Interior and Justice.

.... One reason is that the program, which once focused largely on people who suffered from strokes, cancer and heart attacks, increasingly supports those with depression, back pain, chronic fatigue syndrome and other comparatively subjective conditions.

... the last time the disability program faced insolvency. Congress voted in 1994 to increase the share of the Social Security payroll tax that supports disabled workers, which shored up disability payments at the expense of the retirees' program.
- Newsmax.com. May29, 2012

Social Security Disability needed more funding because the number of people making claims on the program has skyrocketed in recent years.

10,962,532: U.S. Disability Beneficiaries Exceed Population of Greece

The total number of people in the United States now receiving federal disability benefits hit a record 10,962,532 million in April, which exceeds the 10,815,197 people who live in the nation of Greece.

According to newly released data from the Social Security Administration, the record 10,962,532 total disability beneficiaries in April, included a record 8,865,586 disabled workers (up from 8,853,614 in March), 1,936,236 children of disabled workers, and 160,710 spouses of disabled workers.
- CNSNews.com. Terence P. Jeffrey. May 7, 2013

It can be guaranteed that there is a massive amount of fraud in the disability component of Social Security. Back pain and depression are covered. These are horrible illnesses to those afflicted with them. But, they are also easily faked by fraudsters. There is no way to medically prove whether someone actually has these illnesses or is faking them to get benefits. Plus there are some doctors or social workers who will intentionally abuse the program by declaring healthy people to be "disabled" for the purpose of receiving benefits. See the Project Veritas report on Medicaid fraud in Chapter 21.

Able-Bodied People Defrauding Social Security Disability Program

An 18-month investigation by a Senate subcommittee reports that in more than 25 percent of cases reviewed, evidence confirming disabilities was "insufficient, contradictory, or incomplete." The staff reviewed 300 decisions in which individuals were awarded disability benefits by administrative law judges. A 2011 internal Social Security Administration report echoed the findings, showing a national error rate of 22 percent.

[Senator Tom] Coburn, a medical doctor, personally reviewed the application and evidence in 100 individual cases. His summation was even more startling: "In about 75% of the cases I went through, people were not truly disabled."

- Heritage.org: The Foundry. Laura Trueman. October 12, 2012.

Amazing: 25% to 75% of the nearly 11 million people receiving SSI Disability payments are not really disabled and should not be receiving benefits.

So senior citizens, how does it feel to know the taxes you paid to Social Security are being given to fraudulent "disabled" workers rather than as benefits to you? It is no wonder that Social Security's money originally intended for retirees is falling short earlier than projected. Once again a federal government program has its scope expanded, and Congress fails to effectively manage it.

Social Security Taxes

Social Security taxes were, of course, very small to begin with: a maximum of $60 in 1937. So the burden on workers was small. By 2010, the maximum tax had grown to $13,243: a substantial burden on workers. Historical taxes and rates are shown on the following page.

Social Security Taxes			
Year	Maximum taxable earnings	OASDI tax rate	Maximum Tax per person
1937	$3,000	2%	$60
1954	$3,600	4%	$144
1960	$4,800	6%	$288
1966	$6,600	7.7%	$508
1969	$7,800	8.4%	$655
1971	$7,800	9.2%	$718
1974	$13,200	9.9%	$1,307
1978	$17,700	10.1%	$1,788
1981	$29,700	10.7%	$3,178
1990	$51,300	12.4%	$6,361
2010	$106,800	12.4%	$13,243

- The tax rate refers to the combined rate for employers and employees.
- OASDI is the "Old-Age, Survivors, and Disability Insurance" program.
- Max. earning limit automatically increase annually after 1971.

Source: Social Security Administration Online

Remember the original Social Security pamphlet? "And finally, beginning in 1949, twelve years from now, you and your employer will each pay 3 cents on each dollar you earn, up to $3,000 a year." Here's Congress' lying promise: "That is the most you will ever pay." $13,243 seems a little bit more than $3000!

It is *not fair* to change the retirement age, alter benefits, or change payroll tax rates. Yet all of these have been done repeatedly during the roughly 75-year lifespan of Social Security.

Politicians have been expanding Social Security for years. The taxes used to fund the program have dramatically increased. Benefits for dependents and survivors were added, then disability payments. Allowing early retirement at age 62 was added. COLA automatically increased benefit levels. This was easy to do because there were many more workers than retirees. Unfortunately, the expansions depleted resources from the program's intent, which was to *supplement* income for the oldest Americans.

It was very easy for a politician to increase benefit checks when there were many workers per retiree. It made them very popular with the seniors receiving the checks. The politicians also used the massive Social Security FICA taxes to pay for other programs they wanted to implement. Well, the time of plenty is over. FICA taxes no longer produce huge excess streams of cash for the politicians to spend.

The Result: A Failing Program
In 2010, the Social Security trustees released their annual report. The Heritage Foundation summarized some key findings from this report.

- Social Security is predicted to run cash-flow deficits in both 2010 and 2011 due to the effects of the recession. [FICA taxes collected do not cover benefit payments, so money must be spent from the general treasury to make-up the difference.]
- The 2010 report shows that over the next 75 years, **Social Security owes $7.9 trillion more in benefits than it will receive in tax revenues.**
- In net present value terms, assuming the program runs forever, the projected unfunded liability is $16.1 trillion, including money necessary to repay bonds in the trust fund. [That is over $53,000 for every citizen assuming 300 million citizens – including children.]
- In 2037— the Social Security trust funds run out of special issue bonds [IOUs]. This has little importance, as Congress would already have been paying about $250 billion a year to repay those bonds for about seven years.

Also in the report was a reminder that all Social Security benefits come from taxes, There is no trust fund of securities to sell.

- The President's Office of Management and Budget (OMB) explained that the Social Security "trust funds" do not contain stocks, bonds, or other assets that could be sold directly for cash. Unlike private-sector trust funds, the Social Security trust funds contain only IOUs that will have to be paid back with future taxes. As OMB noted (in 2000):

    "These balances are available to finance future benefit payments...only in a bookkeeping sense. They do not consist of real economic assets that can be drawn down in the future to fund benefits. Instead, they are claims on the Treasury that, when redeemed, will have to be financed by raising taxes, borrowing from the public, or reducing benefits, or other expenditures."

Although Congress has to this point been extremely generous in handing out benefits to recipients, this is likely to change as the massive debt makes it impossible to maintain current spending levels. Also, *Congress has no legal obligation to pay any benefits*, according to the law it passed.

> Social Security Online - History (www.socialsecurity.gov)
> There has been a temptation throughout the program's history for some people to suppose that their FICA payroll taxes entitle them to a benefit in a legal, contractual sense. That is to say, if a person makes FICA contributions over a number of years, Congress cannot, according to this reasoning, change the rules in such a way that deprives a contributor of a promised future benefit.... Congress clearly had no such limitation in mind when crafting the law. Section 1104 of the 1935 Act, entitled "RESERVATION OF POWER," specifically said: "The right to alter, amend, or repeal any provision of this Act is hereby reserved to the Congress."
>
> In a 1960 ruling, the [Supreme] Court... established the principle that entitlement to Social Security benefits is not a contractual right.

There is a lesson for every citizen here: Don't listen to what the politicians say, read the laws they pass. Congress set up Social Security as a system that they could change at their whim. Citizens having paid large amounts of their savings into Social Security are only entitled to the amount of benefits that Congress decides to give them. Citizens have *no right* to receive benefits according to the law Congress passed. This should change!

Poor Social Security Returns
In addition to not having the right to receive benefits, every FICA-

taxpaying citizen has been harmed by Social Security's poor returns. Most retirees receiving Social Security benefits never calculate how much they paid in taxes during their working years, and how large a lump sum they could have had in their own personal retirement account with those taxes. Try it. It will be eye-opener.

Private plans reward workers with much better benefits. An example is Galveston County employees who left the Social Security System in favor of a private plan. They have been greatly rewarded for "opting out" of Social Security.

Galveston County: A Model for Social Security Reform
by Ray Holbrook and Alcestis "Cooky" Oberg, 2005

The initial Social Security Act permitted municipal governments to opt out of the system - a loophole that Congress closed in 1983. In 1981, employees of Galveston County, Texas, chose by a vote of 78 percent to 22 percent to leave Social Security for a private alternative. Brazoria and Matagorda counties soon followed, swelling the private plan to more than 5,000 participants today. In the private plan, contributions are similar to those for Social Security but returns are quite different.

The benefits, like a savings account, could be passed on to family members upon death.

The Galveston Plan, put together by financial experts, was a "banking model" rather than an "investment model." To eliminate the risks of the up-and-down stock market, workers' contributions were put into <u>conservative fixed-rate guaranteed annuities</u>, rather than fluctuating stocks, bonds or mutual funds. Our results have been impressive: We've averaged an annual rate of return of about 6.5 percent over 24 years. And we've provided substantially better benefits in all three Social Security categories: retirement, survivorship and disability.

Galveston vs. Social Security. Upon retirement after 30 years, and assuming a 5 percent rate of return - more conservative than Galveston workers have earned - all workers would do better for the same contribution as Social Security:

Data Comparing Social Security to a Private Plan
- Workers making $17,000 a year are expected to receive about 50 percent more per month than on Social Security - **$1,036 instead of $683.**
- Workers making $26,000 a year will make **$1,500 instead of $853**.
- Workers making $51,000 a year will get **$3,103 instead of $1,368.**
- Workers making $75,000 or more will nearly triple Social Security - **$4,540 instead of $1,645.**

Another example of a private plan running circles around Social Security is evident in Chile. Some Americans may belie Chile to be a third world country, but their retirement system is fully modern, while it is America's Social Security that is old-fashioned and antiquated.

The Proof's in the Pension

[Both America's and Chile's] pension systems were going broke. Chile responded by pioneering a system of private accounts in 1981. America rescued its traditional system in the early 1980's by cutting benefits and raising taxes, with the promise that the extra money would go into a trust to finance the baby boomers' retirement. As it happened, our countries have required our employers to set aside roughly the same portion of our income, a little over 12 percent...

After comparing our relative payments to our pension systems, we extrapolated what would have happened if I'd put my money into [the Chile] mutual fund instead of the Social Security trust fund. We came up with three projections for my old age, each one offering a pension that, like Social Security's, would be indexed to compensate for inflation:

> (1) Retire in 10 years, at age 62, with an annual pension of $55,000. That would be **more than triple the $18,000** I can expect from Social Security at that age.
>
> (2) Retire at age 65 with an annual pension of $70,000. That would be **almost triple the**

Social Security

$25,000 pension promised by Social Security starting a year later, at age 66.

(3)Retire at age 65 with an annual pension of $53,000 and a one-time cash payment of $223,000.
- www.nytimes.com. JOHN TIERNEY. April 26, 2005.

When comparing the performance numbers of Social Security and other plans, it is easily seen just how badly **the federal government bureaucrats and politicians have ripped off the American people with Social Security.** Another example of federal government incompetence.

In the 1980s Chilean leaders recognized the faults of government social retirement systems and they corrected them. US leaders so far have not done so, to the detriment of the American citizens. The problems Chile saw were identical to the ones America saw, and still sees today.

<u>Chile's Privatized Social Security Program is 30 Years Old, and Prospering</u>
As a quiet example of how privatizing Social Security works in the real world, Chile's 30-year experiment is succeeding beyond expectations. Instead of running huge deficits to fund the old "PayGo" system, private savings now exceed 50 percent of the country's Gross Domestic Product.

Prior to May 1, 1981, the Chilean system required contributions from workers and was clearly in grave financial trouble. Instead of nibbling around the edges to shore up the program for another few years, José Piñera, Secretary of Labor and Pensions under Augusto Pinochet, decided to do a major overhaul of the system:

We knew that cosmetic changes — increasing the retirement age, increasing taxes — would not be enough. We understood that the pay-as-you-go system had a fundamental flaw, one rooted in a false conception of how human beings behave. That flaw was lack of a link between what people put into their pension program and what they take out....

So we decided to go in the other direction, to link benefits to contributions. The money that a worker pays into the system goes into an account that is owned by the worker.

The system still required contributions of 10 percent of salary, but the money was deposited in any one of an array of private investment companies. Upon retirement, the worker had a number of options, including purchasing an annuity for life. Along the way he could track the performance of his account, and increase his contribution (up to 20 percent) if he wanted to retire earlier, or increase his payout at retirement.
- www.thenewamerican.com. Bob Adelmann. May 3, 2011.

It would have been wonderful if every citizen could have had the ability to opt out of Social Security as Galveston County workers did, or if the federal government had modernized Social Security as Chile did. But as they say, it is water under the bridge. We must move forward from where we find ourselves today, not where we could have been had we acted 30 years ago.

Social Security Reform Plan
There is little doubt that given the freedom to leave the Social Security program, most young workers would do so immediately. The program simply does not serve their needs or best interests. Yet previous politicians have promised current retirees benefits based on the taxes from those young workers. This benefit money has to come from somewhere. So the author suggests a compromise plan that accomplishes both goals, while eventually removing politicians' ability to over-promise benefits. The plan has three phases:

Phase I: Use all FICA taxes for Retirement Benefits

- Transfer all Social Security Disability responsibility to the states per the Chapter 20 model.

The states will have to define who qualifies for state disability payments. The reports listed earlier have shown Congress and the federal government are not able to manage this. The tax revenue to fund the program should be raised by the states (after the initial federal transfer funding) as the states see fit. FICA taxes that were going to disability can then be *used to pay retirement benefits*.

Social Security

Phase II: Optional Personal Accounts

- Citizens *may choose* to place their Social Security taxes (FICA) into personal accounts. The SSA will take the cash from these accounts and replace it with <u>US Government Social Security (SS) bonds.</u>
    - SS bonds are a new idea to replace the IOUs with real bonds (fully backed by the Treasury) that are tradeable on the open market. The SS bonds (30-year, no-coupon) return will mirror those on equivalent Treasury bonds when issued. The government promises to pay the principle and interest on the bond at maturity.
- The citizen account owners may then choose to keep the SS bonds, or sell them and reinvest the proceeds into state or municipal bond funds, US corporate bond funds, or corporate stock funds. There are numerous ETF options trading on the major US stock exchanges that could be used for the accounts.

The Social Security Administration will still collect the same income as under the present system. There is no change. But now instead of IOUs, the federal government promises will be on the books in real world bonds. Corporations must honestly report their liabilities, the government should too.

Social Security has been one of the most politicized programs ever in existence. Politicians routinely run scare ads accusing opponents of cutting seniors' benefits. Any proposals to move to a system similar to Chile or Galveston is met with cries of "they want to kill Social Security" or they want to "force you into the risky stock market". This plan takes great effort to NOT force any citizen to leave Social Security. Some key points of this reform:

- It doesn't touch current benefits.
- No one is forced into the new system. The default option is status quo Social Security.
- Citizens will have the opportunity to get personal accounts *if they choose*.

- Citizens will have the opportunity to sell the government SS bonds in their accounts and make other investments *if they choose.*
- Those opposing this reform *ARE forcing* citizens to remain in a system against their will.

Citizens choose whether to stay in the retirement system designed by politicians. Of course, historical examples (Galveston County, Chile) show huge rewards possible by choosing to manage their own accounts, but it is up to each citizen to decide.

Phase III: Managing the Current Social Security System
Most retirees will choose to stay in Social Security as is. Their working years are over and it would not make sense for them to give up their promised benefits. Their current benefit checks WILL NOT BE CUT. However, reforms will be needed to make the current system sustainable. The Congressional Budget Office projects full Social Security benefit payments will stop in 2033.

> The 2013 Long-Term Projections for Social Security: Additional Information
> In calendar year 2010, for the first time since the enactment of the Social Security Amendments of 1983, *annual outlays* for the program exceeded *annual tax revenues*. In 2012, outlays exceeded noninterest income by about 7 percent, and CBO projects that the gap will average about 12 percent of tax revenues over the next decade. ....the gap will grow larger in the 2020s and will exceed 30 percent of revenues by 2030.
>
> CBO projects that under current law, the OASI trust fund will be exhausted in 2033. If a trust fund's balance fell to zero and current revenues were insufficient to cover the benefits specified in law, the Social Security Administration would no longer have legal authority to pay full benefits when they were due.   - CBO. December 17, 2013.

Social Security, as currently designed by previous Congresses, is paying out more than it takes in. Removing disability payments will help correct this, but more changes will be needed to prevent a sudden slashing of benefit checks in 2033. As was noted earlier, Social Security has seen multiple changes regarding tax rates, benefits, eligibility, and retirement age over the years. For those staying in the current Social Security system, Congress will need to balance benefit payments with the FICA tax revenue and borrowing. Again, there should be *no reduction in current Social Security checks for current retirees.* Some changes that could be implemented to achieve balance:

- Congress could raise the FICA taxes. After Phase II becomes law, this will mean issuing more SS Bonds that immediately show up on the government's balance sheets.
- COLA, created in 1972, could be suspended or reduced.
- The early retirement age could be raised to 70 and the regular retirement age raised to 75 to reflect the much longer lifespans of Americans. The change could be done gradually.
- Illegal aliens and other non-citizens could be prevented from collecting benefits.

It is important to realize that Social Security must not hinder a healthy economy. Retirees should not ask workers to bear a heavy tax burden, that they themselves did not bear while they worked. America needs a retirement system that is fair to both retirees and workers.

Putting Social Security Returns in Context:
- Those citizens who retired years ago received a great deal with Social Security. Much like those who invested in Bernie Madoff's ponzi scheme, and cashed out early, received great returns.
- Those citizens who retired more recently will likely get their money back, but have much less than had they been allowed to invest their contributions in a retirement plan like Chile or Galveston County.
- Those citizens still working today, with the large number of retirees being supported by a small number of workers, will get a terrible return on their contribution: just like those who try to cash out after the ponzi scheme goes broke.

- Ponzi scheme may be a harsh term, but the government itself is giving a "go broke" date of 2033 when it flatly states it will not be able to pay the benefits it promised.

This proposal could become a critical step toward returning financial liberty to the American people and removing the federal government from running a retirement program (which it has botched horribly) that is clearly not prescribed by the Constitution.

Political Bias in the News Media

During the 2004 Presidential Election where Democratic Senator John Kerry challenged President George W. Bush, campaign journalists based in Washington, D.C. **favored Kerry's election by a 12-to-1 ratio.**
- John Tierney Survey-NY Times. www.mrc.org. Media Bias. Exhibit 1-14.

One of the reasons America has veered away from its Christian conservative roots towards liberal secularism in recent decades is the biased news coverage that American citizens receive. Bias is one's way of looking at things, a worldview, that influences one's thoughts and conclusions. The above survey indicated that journalists covering the presidential campaign of 2004 favored the Democrat by a 12-1 margin. Voters meanwhile elected the Republican by a narrow margin: 50% - 48%. It is easy to conclude that the journalists' views are therefore much more liberal than the general public, and favor the policies of the Democrats. This by itself does not prove bias. A good, honest journalist would be able to filter out their personal beliefs and report facts without letting their views be known. But often this has not happened, and the media's views have slanted news coverage to favor Democrats, secularism, and liberalism. This slanted coverage can influence citizens who only follow news/politics casually. For example, in the 2004 election, those only listening to the occasional news story may become more likely to vote for Kerry if the stories they hear about him are positive, while the stories about Bush are negative.

This chapter will focus on numerous examples of political bias in the media. It is this bias that has given an advantage to liberal politicians and their policies. Policies which are often not biblical or constitutional.

The survey of campaign journalists showed an overwhelming preference for John Kerry over George W. Bush. It is not surprising that their reporting reflects their worldview. Most journalists are politically liberal and identify with the Democrat Party, the home of liberalism.

Media Bias 101: What Journalists Really Think
Surveys over the past 30 years have consistently found that journalists — especially those at the highest ranks of their profession — are much more liberal than rest of America.

They are more likely to vote liberal, more likely to describe themselves as liberal, and more likely to agree with the liberal position on policy matters than members of the general public.   - www.mrc.org. 1/23/2014.

Just because journalists have a set of beliefs does not mean their reporting is biased. They, like all people, are capable of separating facts from opinions if they choose to do so. But often they choose not to make this separation. The author believes that the bias has become much more pronounced in the last decade or so as journalists attempt to counter the rise of talk radio, which is heavily conservative commentary. So journalism has become more liberal commentary than solid reporting of facts.

One example does not make the case for bias. It takes many examples. The bulk of this chapter is dedicated to illustrating the biased reporting of journalists at major media centers (ABC, NBC, CBS, NY Times...). It begins with numerous examples of bias and ends with a study done by a UCLA professor that quantifies the bias and its effects.

There are numerous examples of establishment journalists inducing bias into news stories. The media tends to spend a lot of time on violent stories, likely because the audience ratings make it good for business. But the media shows its anti-conservative bias when it injects commentary into a story that doesn't agree with the facts.

Media Incorrectly Blames Conservatives for Acts of Violence
Often when a senseless act of violence occurs, like a shooting or bombing, reporters in the media immediately speculate as to why the perpetrator acted. This in itself is poor journalism as news reporting should consist of facts, not speculation. But it becomes an easy to spot example of media bias when time after time, the media attempt to blame portions of society they disagree with. Usually the targets are the TEA Party or conservative talk radio hosts.

>Here are 6 Moments Where the Media has Wrongly Blamed Conservatives (and the Tea Party) for Violence.
>After James "The Joker" Holmes committed unspeakable acts of violence at a midnight screening of "The Dark Knight

Rises" last Friday [July 20], ABC's Brian Ross — in what can only be described as a sloppy act of journalism — practically jumped at the chance to tie the shooter to the Tea Party.

"There is a Jim Holmes of Aurora, CO, uh Paige, on the Colorado Tea Party site as well, talking about him joining the Tea Party last summer. We don't know if this is the same Jim Holmes, but it is Jim Holmes of Aurora, Colorado," Ross said.

Problem: Ross and ABC never investigated the connection. Had they checked their facts, they would've discovered that the 52-year-old Tea Partier was not, in fact, the same man arrested by Aurora police that morning. But that didn't stop Ross. He went on national television and casually tossed out the idea that the Tea Party might somehow be connected to the "Batman" massacre.

Of course, ABC and Ross have apologized for their sloppy reporting, but the speculation remains: Somebody, whether it was Ross or his producers, wanted to tie the conservative grassroots movement to the nightmarish events that took place that night.

- The Blaze. Becket Adams. July 24, 2012.

The Blaze article goes on to list 6 other tragic violent events where liberals or the media immediately and incorrectly blamed conservatives before the facts were known.

• Jared Loughner on January 8, 2011, took a taxi to a Safeway supermarket in Casas Adobes, AZ, and opened fire on a crowd gathered to meet Rep. Gabby Giffords (D-AZ). The shooting left six people dead and injured thirteen more, including the congresswoman who, miraculously, survived a bullet to the head. The media accused former Alaska Gov. Sarah Palin, and conservative radio talk show hosts of being partly responsible for the massacre. Actual investigation showed that Loughner didn't listen to talk radio, but instead studied "The Communist Manifesto" and Adolf Hitler's "Mein Kampf." He was also registered as an independent voter.

• On May 1, 2010, two street vendors in New York City

noticed smoke pouring out of an SUV and alerted a police officer. Authorities discovered a car bomb that had failed to detonate and removed it without any further incident. Mayor Michael Bloomberg told Katie Couric that the person was probably "a mentally deranged person or somebody with a political agenda that doesn't like the health-care bill or something." Other media blamed the TEA Party. The bomber ended up being Faisal Shahza who was trained in a Pakistani terrorist camp.

• University of Alabama professor Dr. Amy Bishop on February 12, 2010, opened fire on 12 of her colleagues with 9-millimeter handgun, killing three and wounding three more.

• Reuters Foundation Fellow Jonathan Curiel blamed the shooting on "racism" and "the tea party movement". Except Bisop had a long history of violence and "was a far-left political extremist who was obsessed with President Obama," according to her family.

• Armed with two starter pistols and an explosive device, 43-year-old eco-terrorist James Lee entered the Discovery Communications headquarters in Silver Spring, Md., on September 1, 2010, and took three people hostage. After a tense four-hour standoff, authorities shot Lee dead and freed the hostages. Liberal media rushed to claim that Lee's manifesto was similar to conservative immigration reform groups. Except Lee's manifesto could have been taken from the website of Green Peace or a number of other liberal environmental groups.

• US Census Bureau worker Bill Sparkman's nude body was found tied to a tree with the word "fed" scribbled across his chest on September 12, 2009, in Clay County, Kentucky. His government ID was taped his neck and his feet and hands were bound with duct tape. The media suggested he was murdered by anti-government conservatives. As it turns out, Sparkman killed himself and staged it to look like a murder so his family could collect the insurance money.

• Software consultant Andrew Stack flew a plane into an IRS building in Austin, TX on February 18, 2010, killing himself and IRS manager Vernon Hunter and injuring thirteen others. The media template again kicked into gear again, reporting that Stack was part of the extreme conservative TEA Party movement. Of course Stack's suicide note includes "The communist creed: From each according to his ability, to each according to his need." Another case where the perpetrator's beliefs were much more closely tied to liberal views that conservative views.

It is entirely possible that liberals truly believe that conservatives are evil and therefore find it natural to assume evil-doers must be conservative. Or maybe the liberals in the media are just trying to tarnish conservatives in order to help their fellow liberal politicians. Regardless, everyone should be aware that the next time a violent tragedy occurs, it will likely be reported that the perpetrator was a conservative or had conservative beliefs – whether true or not. Several of these examples go beyond media bias and enter into the realm of false, erroneous reporting.

> Sidebar: Most conservatives believe there is a God, just like the nation's founders did. Belief in a God that both loves you and judges you at your death discourages random violent behavior that harms others. However, the belief that there is no God and nothing after your earthly life takes away a powerful dis-incentive to not sin. When the belief in God is removed from many in a society, it is not surprising to the author that senseless violent acts increase in that society.

Party Responsible for Government Shutdown

Another example of the major media reporting opinion and bias rather than facts, is the government shutdown that occurred in October, 2013. Here are the facts: Government spending bills are passed by the House, then by the Senate, then signed by the President in order to become law, which authorizes the spending. In this case, the House (controlled by Republicans) passed a bill that funded the federal government, except for ObamaCare. They removed any funding for that program. The Senate (controlled by Democrats), voted down this bill, and passed a bill funding the government including ObamaCare. Usually, when the House and Senate pass differing bills, they form a joint committee to negotiate the differences and create a single bill, which both sides then vote on. In this case, the Senate refused to form a committee for negotiation purposes.

So how was this reported in the major media?

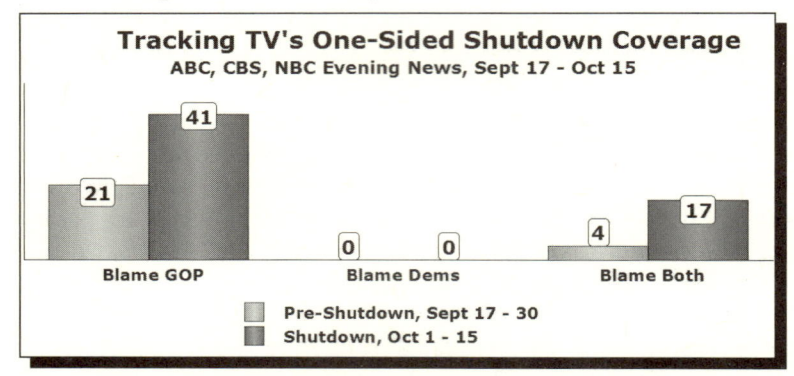

Tracking TV's One-Sided Shutdown Coverage
ABC, CBS, NBC Evening News, Sept 17 - Oct 15

Blame GOP	Blame Dems	Blame Both
21 / 41	0 / 0	4 / 17

Pre-Shutdown, Sept 17 - 30
Shutdown, Oct 1 - 15

For millions of Americans, big political contests such as presidential elections and pivotal congressional hearings are still largely witnessed through the lens of ABC's, CBS's and NBC's evening newscasts. According to Nielsen Research, more than 20 million viewers tuned in over the past two weeks for the Big Three's take on the shutdown drama.

What those viewers heard... was a version of the shutdown story that could easily have emanated from Barack Obama's own White House. The broadcast networks invariably blamed Republicans for the impasse; spotlighted dozens of examples of how Americans were being victimized; and ran scores of soundbites from furloughed federal workers and others harmed by the shutdown...
- www.mrc.org. Rich Noyes. 10/17/2013.

Truly unbiased reporting would have stated that the government funding bill failed to pass because the House and Senate could not agree on a major provision: the funding of ObamaCare. Instead the House received the lion's share of the blame. Of the 83 stories, 75% blamed the GOP House. That is biased reporting.

Sidebar: Is your Republican representative a politician first or a conservative first? A politician wants to be liked, so will usually try to please everyone, including major media. They abhor negative press coverage. A conservative first representative will stand on principle, and promote conservative positions even when the media is attacking those positions.

Media Labels Republicans During Scandals, Not Democrats

Politicians sometimes do stupid or illegal activities and get caught. It becomes a scandal. There are two non-biased ways to report this: 1) Name the politician without labeling their party. 2) Name the politician and state their party. It is biased reporting when party affiliation is only given for politicians from one of the parties.

Networks Rush to Label Former Governor Bob McDonnell a Republican

Less than 24-hours after former Governor Bob McDonnell (R-VA) was indicted on 14 charges including conspiracy and fraud, all three network morning shows immediately identified McDonnell as a Republican. While McDonnell's potential crimes are serious, the media failed to uphold the same party ID standard when it involved a scandal plagued Democratic governor.

NBC led their January 22 coverage of the McDonnell scandal with Today host Savannah Guthrie introducing the segment by saying, "And now to that bombshell indictment of the former governor of Virginia, Bob McDonnell, a one-time rising star in the Republican Party." ABC provided an on-screen graphic identifying McDonnell as a Republican and CBS This Morning's Nancy Cordes said that "McDonnell was once considered a possible presidential contender for the GOP."

In contrast, in March 2008 Democratic Governor Elliot Spitzer of New York was identified as "Client Number 9" in a prostitution ring, but for two straight days ABC and NBC failed to label Spitzer as a Democrat. At the time, my colleague Brent Baker noted how "in lead stories Monday night about New York Governor Eliot Spitzer being linked to a prostitution ring, neither ABC's World News nor the NBC Nightly News verbally identified Spitzer's political party."

At the time, NewsBusters noted how:

On ABC, the only hints as to Spitzer's party were a

few seconds of video of Spitzer beside Hillary Clinton as they walked down some steps and a (D) on screen by Spitzer's name over part of one soundbite. NBC didn't even do that.

In total, NBC and CBS referenced McDonnell's Republican affiliation three times by name, whereas it took ABC three days to identify Spitzer as a Democrat in 2008 and even longer for NBC to do so. In fact, in 2008, both ABC and NBC found time to "applaud his [Elliott Spitzer] reputation and effectiveness as the Empire State's Attorney General before becoming Governor." In contrast, both CBS and NBC noted how McDonnell is "the first Virginia governor ever to be charged with a crime and the charges he's facing carry the possibility of decades behind bars."

CBS's Nancy Cordes hyped how, "It wasn't that long ago that McDonnell was considered a rising Republican star and possible presidential candidate in 2016" and ABC's Josh Elliott said McDonnell was "once considered a possible presidential candidate." In contrast, in the first two days following the Spitzer scandal, NBC's Today ran seven Spitzer-related segments and one interview with then-candidate Barack Obama, without once mentioning Spitzer's Democratic affiliation.

While both governors were embroiled in highly politicized scandals, the networks have made a concerted effort to let their viewers know when a Republican is in trouble but punt when it comes to identifying a Democrat. Unsurprisingly, this practice by ABC, NBC, and CBS is nothing new and they will likely continue to rush to identify Republicans plagued in scandal while giving Democrats a pass.

- newsbusters.org. Jeffrey Meyer. January 22, 2014.

The media alternated reporting standards for the scandals, choosing the one that helped Democrats and hurt Republicans. This is often done. Another example is Mayor Nagin of New Orleans.

The Man With No Party
Networks don't mention Nagin is a Democrat
CBS Evening News, NBC Nightly News and ABC World News

broadcasts gave brief mention to the conviction of former New Orleans mayor Ray Nagin Wednesday on 20 federal counts, including bribery and conspiracy, but all three omitted the fact that he was a Democrat....He became a household name after Hurricane Katrina devastated New Orleans in 2005, during his first term.
- Washington Free Beacon. Staff. February 12, 2014.

The media reporting tarnishes the name Republican, but not Democrat. This is bias.

Anecdotes of Biased Media Reporting Helping/Harming Politicians
These next examples focus on the media using biased reporting to promote politicians they like or harm politicians they disagree with. Sometimes phony information is used, but most often the bias is a double standard that is only seen when comparing the coverage of two politicians.

Media Airs Falsified Bush Vietnam Documents
Occasionally the media bias leads to nonfactual reporting, as when CBS News and 60 Minutes ran major stories during the 2000 presidential election alleging that George W. Bush 'pulled strings' to avoid duty in Vietnam when he was in the Texas Air National Guard. The stories were based on documents that were proven to be falsified. The documents were created using word processor fonts – not available on typewriters when authentic documents would have been created. CBS News has a liberal bias and was anxious to "break" a story that would harm the Republican Presidential candidate and help the more liberal Democratic candidate – Al Gore. In this case the source documents were not fully vetted and nonfactual reports were made.

Media Coverage of Gaffes: Obama-Quayle-Bachmann
More often, the media reporting contains accurate facts, but the bias shows itself in what stories are covered and how much print or airtime the story receives. This is very obviously seen in how gaffes are covered. A gaffe occurs when a politician misspeaks. The gaffe can be reported differently for different candidates though.

- In 2008, candidate Barack Obama declared on the campaign trail that he had been in 57 states and had one more to go. Conservative talk radio played the comment extensively and questioned the candidate's intelligence. Liberal media like the national network news ignored the story or excused the gaffe as Obama just being jet-lagged.
- Dan Quayle misspelled potato in 1992 (The card he read from had "potatoe") as he moderated a school spelling bee. Quayle was widely criticized for being ignorant and stupid in the liberal, slanted national news media of the day. There wasn't any national conservative media then.
- In 2011, during a trip to London's Westminster Abbey, President Obama signed the guest book and dated it 24 May 2008 - off by three years. Again, no to little coverage in the liberal-biased network news media, and definitely no suggestion of stupidity or incompetence.
- Michele Bachmann, a Republican candidate for President in 2011, officially launched her presidential campaign in Waterloo, Iowa, where she was born, and claimed to share the hometown with John Wayne. In fact, John Wayne's parents did live in Waterloo, but Wayne himself was born in Winterset, Iowa. John Wayne Gacy, Jr., an infamous serial killer had lived in Waterloo. The liberally-slanted media immediately ran with the story and, of course, the accusations that Bachmann was stupid and could not keep her facts straight.

Note the double standard. Depending on the candidate's party and views, the media reports a gaffe as a sign of stupidity or just a simple misstatement. This is bias.

Media Templates: Bush Stupid, Gore & Kerry Smart
Viewers or readers also need to be aware of templates in the media. A template is a particular viewpoint that is promoted as factual, sometimes without any evidence. One liberal-media template is that Republican presidential candidates are stupid. We've seen that already with the portrayals of gaffes by Michele Bachmann and Dan Quayle. George W. Bush was the most famous example. Bush tended to misspeak and stumble over words from time to time. So

the template became Bush was a dim-bulb at best or an illiterate boob at worst. Jay Leno who usually parrots the media template ran skit after skit of "Bush" riding a tricycle; reading a picture book; or doing other pre-school activities. Or "Bush" was portrayed in a Jeopardy game show skit giving ridiculously dumb answers to the questions. Meanwhile, Democrat Party candidates are always portrayed as smart. That was the case with Al Gore, John Kerry, and Barack Obama. Now Gore and Kerry's grades and school performance have been reported by more conservative media and are slightly less impressive than Bush's. Obama has never released his grades. Obama (57 states?) has made more misstatements than Bush. On what basis is one group of candidates smart and the other group dumb? Both groups have members with mediocre-to-average school grades. Both groups have members making gaffes. Media templates like the smartness or dumbness of candidates are another sign of bias.

Media Double Standard: Clinton & Cain & Thomas
There is also a double standard used in reporting acts of certain politicians. Sexual harassment is a serious matter. But is it only serious when a politician from one of the parties commits it? There is no greater example of bias than the liberal media coverage of Bill Clinton and Herman Cain. Bill Clinton was a sitting President when three women came forward with allegations of sexual impropriety. One accused Clinton of dropping his pants and asking for a sexual favor, one of being groped, and the third of being raped by Clinton.

These charges against Clinton were questioned by the media, as they should have been. The accusers came forth years after the events were supposed to have occurred. But in 2011, several women came forward anonymously and accused conservative presidential candidate Herman Cain of sexual harassment – again years after the acts supposedly happened. The charges in the early days had no specifics – just inappropriate behavior. That did not stop the media from running heavily with the story. It is an outlandish example of biased reporting when compared to the reporting done with the Clinton allegations (three specific women with specific allegations).

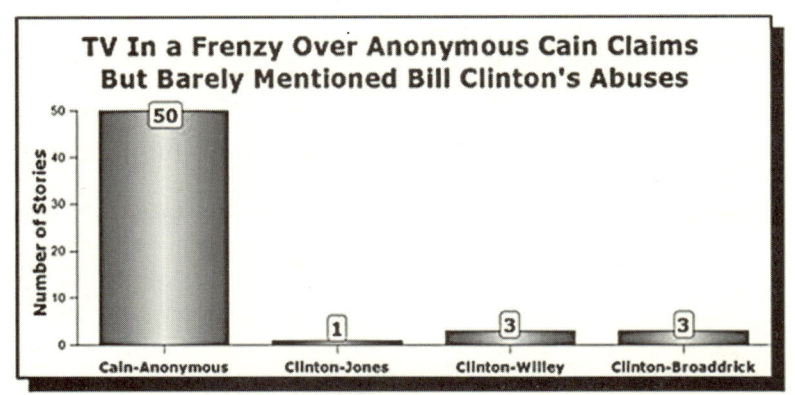

TV In a Frenzy Over Anonymous Cain Claims But Barely Mentioned Bill Clinton's Abuses

Cain-Anonymous	Clinton-Jones	Clinton-Willey	Clinton-Broaddrick
50	1	3	3

Stories on the ABC, CBS and NBC morning and evening news programs in the first 3 days after each scandal first broke.

Over a period of just three and a half days, NBC, CBS and ABC have developed an insatiable hunger for the Herman Cain sexual harassment story, devoting an incredible 50 stories to the allegations. In contrast, over a similar period these networks mostly ignored far more substantial and serious scandals relating to Bill Clinton.

After Paula Jones held a public press conference in February of 1994, there was only one report on her allegations. Following Kathleen Willey's July 1997 claims of being groped by the President, there were a mere three reports. For Juanita Broaddrick, who came forward in February 1999 to say Clinton raped her, only three stories followed charges appearing in the Wall Street Journal.

- Media Research Center

The media coverage was sufficient to make Herman Cain drop his candidacy for president, so the nation will never know if there was any hard proof to support the allegations against Cain. Meanwhile there was hard evidence to support Clinton being unfaithful to his wife and being a womanizer. Gennifer Flowers had taped phone messages of her and Bill Clinton that she made public during his initial presidential campaign. Paula Jones claimed there was a distinguishing feature regarding Clinton's penis. Something that is verifiable. Monica Lewinsky had a dress with a semen stain. Bill Clinton was convicted of perjury because of this hard, verifiable evidence. Paula Jones won a settlement from Clinton. Yet the media focused on these Clinton stories much less than the Cain stories. This is bias.

> Broaddrick case now just another scandal
> WASHINGTON -- The press is doing a little hand-wringing over the Juanita Broaddrick story. But not much.
> We seem to have reached the point at which someone accusing the president of the United States of rape qualifies as just the latest news story to be absorbed and forgotten. And that reality speaks volumes about how the presidency and Bill Clinton have been devalued by the Monica Lewinsky episode.
> - Baltimore Sun. Jack W. Germond and Jules Witcover. March 01, 1999

The Bill Clinton scandals peaked with the president being accused of RAPE. That that's right: rape. Yet the media, because Clinton was aligned with them politically, had little interest in covering or further exposing this potential blockbuster scandal story. The media take of Clinton's being accused of rape is summarized above: "just the latest news story to be absorbed and forgotten."
Note the difference in standards applied to Bill Clinton and Herman Cain. Surely anonymous accusations of harmless (compared to rape) sexual harassment would also be just another "news story to be absorbed and forgotten." No, because Herman Cain was a conservative, the media covered the story to the point of driving Cain from the GOP presidential primary race.

Maybe standards changed with time? Nope. But they do change with respect to the party and views of the accused candidate. Clarence Thomas, another conservative, was pilloried in the media in the 1980s for being accused of sexual harassment well before the media gave Clinton a pass for being accused of rape. Thomas' "alleged act": Telling a joke to Anita Hill about a pubic hair on a can of coke. Thomas denied the claim and there was no physical evidence the joke was ever told. But even if was true, the act was poor taste, not harassment. How does it relate to a governor lowering his pants and asking for sexual favors from a lower level government employee? If it's Bill Clinton, and the liberal network news media, it's evidently much much worse to tell a bad joke. It's biased reporting.

Sidebar 1: Both Cain and Thomas happen to be black. Liberals would normally claim such biased coverage is racist, harming the black candidates, while helping the white one. Except liberals only claim racism when it affects a liberal black candidate. Search NAACP - Cain - Thomas online and see if these men received any support from the civil rights organization.

Sidebar 2: How should Harassment be covered?
Sexual harassment is a very difficult crime to prosecute if there is no hard evidence. Let the courts decide rather than public opinion and media. It often comes down to a man and a woman alone with only their testimony. It's he-said / she-said. It could be that the man has acted in a totally offensive and inappropriate manner. It could also be the woman is making the whole thing up to try to get a settlement or get back at the man. That is why the media, whether liberal or conservative, should use extreme caution when reporting on cases having no hard proof. It becomes more likely that the accusations are true if multiple victims come forward.

Justifiable Double Standard Argument
Some in the media will say there should be a double standard on sex activities of candidates in the two parties. After all, Republicans are viewed as the party of morality and family values, while the Democrats are viewed as the party of openness and acceptance of various sexual practices. Let's assume that is fair – and there should be a double standard here. Logically, that would mean there should be a double standard in other areas of party differences as well. Take taxes for example. The Democrat party is viewed as the party of higher taxes; the Republican party is viewed as being for tax cuts and lower taxes. So applying the double standard argument: Republicans should be given a pass if ever found in violation of tax laws – they are for lower taxes. Any politician in the Democrat party should be forced to resign if ever found cheating on their taxes. Democrats want high taxes so their standard should be high. Yet when long-time Democrat Representative Charlie Rangel was found to have significantly underpaid his taxes for years, there was no media outrage or calls for his resignation. He did not resign. Likewise when Obama Treasury Secretary Timothy Geitner was found to have underpaid his taxes over a multi-year period, there was no high standard applied. Geitner did not resign, and there was

no media pressure applied to Obama to remove him. The media "issue-specific double standard" argument falls apart pretty quickly.

<u>Media Smear Campaigns: Gingrich – Palin – Clinton (not)</u>
There is a very dangerous trend happening in American politics. It's called smear campaigns or "the politics of personal destruction." When a politician becomes successful and cannot be defeated with facts, opposing politicians attempt to destroy the successful politician by manufacturing scandals. To be clear, there should be a high standard applied to political leaders. But the standard must be equally applied to all political leaders consistently. In America, it has not been. Of course, the media has taken sides rather than reporting facts and proper context. Let's examine Speaker Newt Gingrich, VP nominee Sarah Palin, and President Bill Clinton to illustrate the problem.

The case of Speaker Newt Gingrich occurred in the mid 1990s, after Gingrich had led the GOP to its first House majority in 40 years. Byron York summarized the case for the Washington Examiner:

> • Stunned by their loss of control of the House -- a loss engineered by Gingrich -- House Democrats began pushing a variety of ethics complaints against the new Speaker
>
> • With the charges against Gingrich megaphoned in the press, Gingrich and Republicans were under intense pressure to end the ordeal. In January, 1997, Gingrich agreed to make a limited confession of wrongdoing in which he pleaded guilty to the previously unknown offense of failing to seek sufficiently detailed advice from a tax lawyer before proceeding with the course. (Gingrich had in fact sought advice from two such lawyers in relation to the course.) Gingrich also admitted that he had provided "inaccurate, incomplete, and unreliable" information to Ethics Committee investigators. That "inaccurate" information was Gingrich's contention that the course was not political -- a claim Cole and the committee did not accept, but the IRS later would.
>
> • In return for those admissions, the House reprimanded Gingrich and levied an unprecedented $300,000 fine. The size of the penalty was not so much about the misdeed itself

but the fact that the Speaker was involved in it.

• It was a huge victory for Democrats. They had deeply wounded the Speaker. But they hadn't brought him down. So, as Bonior suggested, they sought to push law enforcement to begin a criminal investigation of Gingrich. [Leading to an IRS investigation]

• The bottom line: Gingrich acted properly and violated no laws. There was no tax fraud scheme. Of course, by that time, Gingrich was out of office, widely presumed to be guilty of something, and his career in politics was (seemingly) over.
- What really happened in the Gingrich ethics case? 1/24/2012

A key point is "megaphoned in the press". This tactic won't really work without a biased media. This is the same establishment media that after the 1994 election declared the nation "threw a tantrum" (why else would their preferred Democrats lose the election?) and ran magazine cover stories "The Gingrich who stole Christmas". The media was more than happy to help manufacture a scandal to help bring down their enemy.

Sarah Palin, Governor of Alaska, became a political rock star when John McCain picked her to become his VP. Many conservatives claimed they voted for Palin, not McCain in the 2008 election. There is no doubt that Palin drew large crowds and became a favorite in the conservative movement. She had the ability to connect with crowds, and had a successful record in Alaska as a small-government, non-establishment governor. Palin was so successful as a candidate that her opponents began to fear her.

McCain-Palin lost the race for president, but Palin was still governor of Alaska, and a favorite of conservatives to run for president in 2012. So her hard-left political opponents acted following the "smear" model used against Gingrich a decade earlier. They brought numerous lawsuits of dubious nature. Alaska law prohibited the use of state funds for legal defense of officials, so Palin had to defend herself with her own money.

Sarah Palin in her own words:

In early 2009... we were faced with attorney's bills that would grow to more than $500,000 – a lot more than my total salary for all the time I served as governor.... As the number of [frivolous ethics] complaints mounted, I remembered the observations of the left-wing-radical-turned-conservative-activist David Horowitz in his treatise *The Art of Political War*.... His book explained the stark difference between the left's expert use of the weapon's of political warfare and the right's high-minded but ineffective approach. One of the left's favorite weapons is frivolous ethics complaints.... Back in the 1990's Democrats had Newt in their sights. And strangely enough, the more influential he became, the more "unethical" he became – at least if you counted the number of complaints filed against him. Horowitz wrote "Eventually Democrats lodged 74 separate charges against Gingrich, 65 of which were summarily laughed out of committee."...

In my case, one by one, every ethics charge filed against me and my staff was tossed out. But there was one that was settled with a finding of no wrongdoing... I signed a settlement that stated clearly I had not violated any law,... I knew how the media would spin it.

And spin it they did. The result is that instead of reporting that an independent board of review found me not guilty of any wrongdoing and that all ethics charges filed against me have been dismissed, the media made statements like: "Gov. Palin has been dogged by ethics complaints, most of which have been dismissed."...

In the end, Newt Gingrich lost his battle on one complaint and was assessed a $300,000 fine. Three years later, the IRS exonerated him. But it was too late: the image of Newt as ethically challenged had become part of the media record. Democrats had neutered their nemesis and pushed him to the back-burner...

Now they were trying to consign us to the same fate.....
    - Going Rogue. P363-367

In the case of Palin, she was faced with no real choice. Palin was not a multimillionaire. If she remained as governor, the legal defense bills from fighting the frivolous charges were much larger than her salary and would have bankrupted her and her family. So she resigned. Would anybody else do differently? Many politicians and commentators criticized her decision to resign. The author would like to see how long those commentators remained in their jobs *if* it was costing them money every day they worked. *If* they had to borrow money just to keep doing their job; every day going deeper into debt.

This is a travesty in America. Something has to be done to stop it. The nation must be able to distinguish between frivolous charges and real charges of corruption. The nation should be able to depend on media reporting to do this. But a biased media won't prevent injustice from occurring to those they do not like.

Many Democrats will say that Bill Clinton was unfairly damaged by "false charges" in the effort to impeach him in the late 1990s. Clinton was famous for claiming he was a victim of "right wing conspiracy theories" and the "politics of personal destruction." The only problem is, Bill Clinton was found to be guilty.

Most of the media tried to spin the Bill Clinton impeachment as being about prudish conservatives fixating on "consensual sex" between two adults. That conveniently ignores the reason Bill Clinton was in court. Monica Lewinsky did not sue Bill Clinton. Paula Jones did: on the grounds of sexual harassment while Jones was an employee under then governor Clinton. Democrats and liberals, especially feminists, had been huge proponents of strict sexual harassment laws. As stated earlier this is a very difficult crime to prove as it often happens in private, and comes down to two competing claims of what took place – with no corroboration. But largely because of the laws put in place by Clinton's fellow Democrats, Paula Jones had every right to take her case to court and she did.

Once in court, to prove the claim, most plaintiffs will seek to prove there is a pattern of harassment. Jones did this against Clinton. Hence, Monica Lewinsky was uncovered as part of the Clinton-Jones case. In court, Bill Clinton was forced to testify about his actions both with Jones and Lewinsky, standard protocol for sexual harassment cases.

Once the case had been filed, Clinton unleashed an attack machine smearing Jones as "trailer park trash". He also held an infamous press conference in which he declared "I did not have sex with that woman, Ms Lewinsky." Nothing illegal with either of those actions. The sex with the intern Lewinsky was embarrassing, unethical, and politically damaging, but not illegal.

However, in court, when Clinton claimed to never have had sex with Lewinsky, he was under oath. Like all witnesses Clinton placed his hand on a Bible and swore to God to tell the truth. This is a foundation of the American legal system. It requires a "moral" people to function. If a witness is found to have not told the truth, it becomes perjury, a serious crime. Especially for the President, who is the head of the Executive Branch of government responsible for law enforcement. The president oversees both the Justice Department and the FBI. Unfortunately, for Clinton, his testimony turned out to contain lies. Monica Lewinsky had a dress stained with Clinton's semen. Jones testified that Clinton's penis had distinguishing features that were not publicly known. So Clinton was caught in two lies under oath. He had committed double perjury. Perjury was the main crime used in the impeachment trial held by the Senate.

> Sidebar: Another double standard. Is perjury a serious crime or not? It evidently depends on who you are and which political party you are in. "Scooter" Libby was an aide to VP Dick Cheney under President G.W. Bush. He was convicted of perjury and given jail time and a fine.
>
>> Former White House aide Lewis "Scooter" Libby was found guilty Tuesday of four of five counts of perjury, lying to the FBI and obstructing an investigation....
>>
>> Libby left a federal courtroom with his wife Tuesday after being sentenced to 30 months in prison and a $250,000 fine....   - FoxNews.com. March 7, 2007. June 5, 2007
>
> So why wasn't President Clinton brought to trial in a criminal court? The Senate decided not to remove Clinton from

office. That is no reason not to pursue criminal charges in a criminal court, as was done with Libby. The president should be held to a higher standard than a presidential aide. Yet Clinton never faced a jury for his crimes and was never given jail time. A crime should be a crime. The standard should be the same for every politician.

So in conclusion, Bill Clinton was not harassed with frivolous charges. He was actually given a pass on perjury, a crime for which others have served jail time.

In each of these cases, the establishment media took sides rather than reporting clear facts based on a common standard. The media opposed Newt Gingrich, Sarah Palin, and Scooter Libby, while being a proponent of Bill Clinton. These actions almost go beyond bias, venturing into the arena of propaganda. What else can it be called, when networks alter standards to build up politicians they like, and destroy politicians they disagree with?

Putting smear campaigns aside, the media is capable of reporting facts while adding in commentary that is loaded with bias. The bias is only seen when coverages are compared. Employment numbers are a measure of the nation's economic strength, which in turn, usually correlate with presidential approval ratings. Biased reporting will attempt to influence the approval rating depending on which party is in office.

Media Reporting Bias with Unemployment Numbers
Let's examine one example using the New York Times, which is liberally-biased. The following table lists the unemployment facts for each year (note the much lower unemployment rate in 2004):

Facts/ Year	President	Unemployment Rate	Jobs Added	New Jobs Desired
2004	Bush	5.40%	96,000	> 150,000
2012	Obama	7.80%	114,000	> 150,000

Compare the coverage between 2004 and 2012, both election years with an incumbent President seeking re-election. The bias is easily seen when the raw statistics and story slant are compared. In 2004, the incumbent President was George W. Bush, who the Times did not like; in 2012, the incumbent was Barack Obama, who the Times did like.

Here are the headlines and first few story paragraphs that ran in the New York Times about the respective election year employment data:

> Bush faces slowing job growth
> Employment growth in the United States slowed last month, falling far short of expectations, the U.S. government reported Friday.
> The new jobs report cast doubts on the strength of the U.S. economic expansion and appeared to bolster Senator John Kerry's case against President George W. Bush's handling of the economy just hours before the second presidential debate.
> The Labor Department reported that the U.S. economy added just 96,000 jobs in September, substantially less than the roughly 150,000 needed to keep pace with the expansion in the labor force and start absorbing the slack in the job market. - New York Times. Eduardo Porter. October 9, 2004

> Drop in Jobless Figure Gives Jolt to Race for President
> The jobless rate abruptly dropped in September to its lowest level since the month President Obama took office, indicating a steadier recovery than previously thought and delivering another jolt to the presidential campaign.
> The improvement lent ballast to Mr. Obama's case that the economy is on the mend and threatened the central argument of Mitt Romney's candidacy, that Mr. Obama's failed stewardship is reason enough to replace him.
> Employers added a modest 114,000 jobs last month, the Labor Department reported on Friday.....
> - New York Times. NSHAILA DEWAN and MARK LANDLER. October 5, 2012.

Isn't 114,000 jobs also "substantially less than the roughly 150,000 needed to keep pace with the expansion in the labor force" that the

NYT reported in 2004? Of course it is. The NYT is spinning the storyline in both cases. In 2004, they spin the story in a negative light (short of expectations, less than needed, cast doubts on the economy) to harm Bush. In 2012 they spin the story in a positive manner (steadier recovery, economy on mend, jolt, improvement) to help Obama.

Here's how a conservative biased news source could spin the stories:

> In 2004: The September jobless numbers are in and the economy remains healthy. Although slightly fewer new jobs were created than desired, the unemployment rate remains low at 5.4%.

> In 2012: The unemployment rate inched lower to 7.8%, but remains stubbornly high as it has through-out Obama's entire 4 year term in office. While 114,000 jobs were added, this is significantly less than the 150,000 needed to keep pace with the growing labor force. The tiny rate drop may have been largely caused by disgruntled workers giving up their job search due to the tough economic times.

It really is amazing the amount of bias that comes with the news Americans receive. In all four of these stories (two real, two author-created) the facts are identical, but the spin is dramatically different, depending on the candidate the writer wishes to support.

Sometimes the media create an entire storyline when it suite their purposes. They did this with homelessness.

Homelessness: Only a story when a Republican is President
Bernard Goldberg, an award winning journalist at CBS News, has written a number of books documenting media bias and inaccurate reporting of the major networks and newspapers. His first book, *Bias*, has 15 chapters documenting bias and shoddy reporting by the major establishment media. One chapter deals with homelessness and how the media change reporting based on their political agenda.

> No one knows how many homeless there were in America in the 1980's and early 1990's, but there were researched

educated guesses. For example, the US Census Bureau figured it was about 230,000. The General Accounting Office put the number between 300,000 and 600,000....
(Bias. P66)

The book then quotes news reports at CNN, CBS and NBC, claiming 3 million homeless, 5 million homeless, with the potential to grow to 19 million homeless. Obviously the size and scope of the homeless problem was exaggerated by the media. Why? Because a Republican was president.

> But on the evening newscasts, the drumbeat went on and on. It was Reagan who was to blame.... There was The Other America, where the homeless lived on the street and ate in soup kitchens, innocent victims of a conservative president's insensitivity.
> It was a great story even if it wasn't quite true...
> In the end it didn't matter, because in the early 1990's a miracle descended upon the land. Homelessness disappeared. It was over. It no longer existed in the entire United States of America! ...
> ... I think homelessness ended the day Bill Clinton was sworn in as president. Which is one of those incredible coincidences, since it pretty much began the day Ronald Reagan was sworn in as president. (Bias p71-72)

The actual number of homeless people changed very little if at all under Clinton and Reagan. But many media news organizations drastically changed their coverage of the issue. They used the homelessness storyline to attack a Republican president they did not like, then ignored the story when a Democrat president they did like was in office. What can one say except these media sources chose sides and are selecting their stories to help the political party they favor.

Further proof is the total absence of homelessness reporting during Barack Obama's presidency. Most statistics say the economy has been relatively weak under Obama. The number of people dropping out of the labor force have been especially high, a statistic that should correlate with homelessness. The establishment media have no interest in trying to find and report on the homeless, with a president they like in office.

2008 Election Bias
A film documentary, **Media Malpractice**, records the media bias in the 2008 election where Barack Obama went largely unvetted, while Sarah Palin was relentlessly targeted and even smeared. Sarah Palin was only a VP candidate, but she was much more popular than the GOP nominee, John McCain.

> Filmmaker John Ziegler examines the role of the media during America's 2008 presidential election, using clips from TV news and other sources to argue that Barack Obama received preferential treatment over his political rivals. Declaring that media bias all but swept Obama to victory, the film also features an interview with Sarah Palin, who alleges that journalists unfairly maligned her throughout the campaign. - Media Malpractice. 2009. 115 minutes

2012 Election Bias
Brent Bozell tirelessly documents the bias of the establishment media on his website, Newsbusters.org. He also has a book documenting the biased reporting of the 2012 presidential election between Mitt Romney and Barack Obama.

> Collusion: How the Media Stole the 2012 Election
> Never before has the so-called mainstream media shown such naked political bias as in the 2012 presidential election.
>
> In 2012 Barack Obama was narrowly reelected, with naked support from a liberal media desperate to hide his failures, trumpet his accomplishments, and discredit his GOP rivals. Bachmann, Perry, Cain, Gingrich, Santorum: one by one the media took them apart using hidden-camera exposés, innuendo from anonymous accusers, repetition of harmful sound bites, and irrelevant—even untrue—storytelling.
>
> As soon as Mitt Romney emerged as the Republican Party's nominee, the liberal media went to work in earnest. They repeated Obama's campaign caricatures that Romney terrified his family dog, enjoyed firing people, and was

nothing more than a willing tool of wealthy radical-right extremists. The Washington Post published a 5,400-word "exposé" on the allegation that in 1965 he may have pinned down a boy and cut his hair. Those same Post readers were then treated to 5,500 words on Barack Obama's lifelong love of basketball.

Unquestionably, 2012 was the year when the liberal news media did all in their power to steal the presidential election —and they arguably succeeded.
- L. Brent Bozell, Tim Graham. 2013.

At the beginning of this section, the author stated that it would take numerous examples to prove political bias existed in the establishment media. To recap, here they are:

- The tilting of the 2008 and 2012 elections in favor of Barack Obama.
- Homelessness being a story when a Republican is president, but not when a Democrat is.
- Media spinning economic reports positively with Democrats in office, but negatively with Republicans in office.
- The media orchestrating smear campaigns against conservative politicians Newt Gingrich and Sarah Palin, while downplaying stories that could hurt Bill Clinton.
- A clear media double standard with respect to sexual harassment accusations: Democrat Bill Clinton is given a pass, while every attempt is made to drive conservatives Clarence Thomas and Herman Cain from the public.
- A recurring establishment media template that Republican President George W. Bush was stupid, while Democrat candidates Al Gore and John Kerry were smart.
- The media coverage of gaffes by politicians: Obama just misspeaks, but conservatives like Dan Quayle or Michele Bachmann are stupid.
- The media airing a major negative story on George W. Bush's Vietnam military record during the 2000

presidential election – with documents that were obvious forgeries.
- The establishment media routinely jumping to unfounded conclusions that violent acts of bombings or shootings are likely committed by conservatives.
- Blaming the GOP for a government shutdown that factually was the fault of both parties.

One must conclude there is a clear effort by journalists to turn the public opinion toward their liberal worldview and against conservatism and Republicans. This effort has not gone unnoticed. Some in the public have realized it.

> Scoring the Bias – Rating the News Agencies
> A full 68 percent of voters consider the news media biased, the poll found. Most, 46 percent, believe the media generally favor Democrats, while 22 percent said they believe Republicans are favored, with 28 percent saying the media is reasonably balanced.
> - The Hill Poll: Most voters see media as biased and unethical. 07/25/11

Quantifying the Political Bias in the News Media

There has now been work performed to quantify the media bias rather than only relying on anecdotes. The following study was conducted by the University of Missouri, home to a leading school of journalism, and UCLA.

> Research Exposes Liberal Bias in Mainstream Media
> Pundits have long argued about the liberal bias of mainstream mass media outlets, presenting cases on both sides of the issue. Applying a novel approach based on frequently used ratings of the liberal or conservative leaning of politicians, a researcher at the University of Missouri-Columbia discovered that **most mainstream media outlets do exhibit a strong liberal bias.**
>
> "We found that most of the mainstream media view events through a 'lens' that is very similar to that used by Democrats in Congress," said Jeff Milyo, MU associate professor of economics and public affairs. "That is, most major media outlets and Democrats cite similar sources of expertise, such

as particular think tanks and advocacy groups. This suggests that popular complaints about a liberal bias in the media are well-founded."

To determine the bias of media outlets, Milyo and colleague Tim Groseclose, a political scientist at UCLA, applied the (ADA) scoring system. ADA scores are used widely in political science to describe the placement of an individual member of Congress on an ideological scale, from conservative to liberal. The researchers examined the patterns by which media outlets cited particular think tanks and policy groups, and then compared these to the citation patterns of legislators with known ADA scores. This research is unique from previous studies because it does not rely upon subjective classifications, Milyo said.

"Up to this time, evidence has consisted mainly of anecdotes, or relied upon highly subjective analyses of news reports," Milyo said. "Ours is a systematic and objective test of the liberal media hypothesis."

The results demonstrate a strong liberal bias. All news outlets examined, except for Fox News' Special Report and the Washington Times, *received a score to the left of, or more liberal than, the estimated position of the average U.S. voter*. The scores for CBS Evening News and the New York Times were among the most liberal, while outlets such as USA Today, NPR's Morning Edition, NBC's Nightly News and ABC's World News Tonight were moderately liberal. The most neutral outlets were the Newshour with Jim Lehrer, CNN's NewsNight with Aaron Brown and ABC's Good Morning America. Fox News' Special Report, while more conservative, was closer to the center than any of the three major networks' evening news broadcasts.

The study referred strictly to the news stories of the outlets, omitting editorials, book reviews and letters to the editor, Milyo said.

- Mizzou News. Jeremy Diener. February. 2005.

Tim Groseclose, a partner in the study with the University of Missouri, has published a book further documenting media bias: *Left Turn: How Liberal Media Bias Distorts the American Mind*

(Tim Groseclose. 2011) If *Left Turn* is accurate in its ratings, Fox News Channel and Drudge Report are both more centrist that conservative biased. They may be conservative only in the relative when compared to the much more liberal left leaning news sources. Paul Bedard describes the book and some key insights.

> Describing the Book on media bias, *Left Turn:*
>
> The liberal bias of the mainstream media tilts so far left that any outlets not in that political lane, like the Drudge Report and Fox News Channel, look far more conservative than they really are, according to a UCLA professor's new book out next month.
>
> In a crushing body blow to the pushers of the so-called "Fox Effect," which claims the conservative media is dragging the left into the center, UCLA political science professor Tim Groseclose in Left Turn claims that **"all" mainstream news outlets have a liberal bias in their reporting** that makes even moderate organizations appear out of the mainstream and decidedly right-wing to news consumers who are influenced by the slant.
>
> "Fox News is clearly more conservative than ABC, CBS, CNN, NBC and National Public Radio. Some will conclude that 'therefore, this means that Fox News has a conservative bias,'" he writes in an advance copy provided to Washington Whispers. "Instead, maybe it is centrist, and possibly even left-leaning, while all the others are far left. It's like concluding that six-three is short just because it is short compared to professional basketball players."
>
> What's more, he says, "this point illustrates a common misconception about the Drudge Report. According to my analysis, the Drudge Report is approximately the most fair, balanced, and centrist news outlet in the United States. Yet, the overwhelming majority of media commentators claim that it has a conservative bias. The problem, I believe, is that such commentators mistake relative bias for absolute bias. Yes, the Drudge Report is more conservative than the average U.S. news outlet. But it is a logic mistake to use that to infer that it is based on an absolute scale."
>
> And in further analysis sure to enrage critics of conservative

media, Groseclose determines that Drudge, on a conservative to liberal scale of 0-100, with 50 being centrist, actually leans a bit left of center with a score of 60.4. The reason: Drudge mostly links to the sites of the mainstream media, with just a few written by Matt Drudge himself. "Since these links come from a broad mix of media outlets, and since the news in general is left-leaning, it should not be surprising that the slant quotient of the Drudge Report leans left," he writes.

The author developed a calculation to figure out the "political quotient" to find the bias of media outlets and the average slant of an organization.

Groseclose opens his book quoting a well-known poll in which Washington correspondents declared that they vote Democratic 93 percent to 7 percent, while the nation is split about 50-50. As a result, he says, most reporters write with a liberal filter. "Using objective, social-scientific methods, the filtering prevents us from seeing the world as it actually is. Instead, we see only a distorted version of it. It is as if we see the world through a glass—a glass that magnifies the facts that liberals want us to see and shrinks the facts that conservatives want us to see."

He adds: "That bias makes us more liberal, which makes us less able to detect the bias, which allows the media to get away with more bias, which makes us even more liberal."

Some key points:

"Every mainstream national news outlet in the United States has a liberal bias."

"Supposedly conservative news outlets are not far right. For instance, the conservative bias of [Fox's] Special Report is significantly less than the liberal bias of CBS Evening News."

"Media bias aids Democratic candidates by about 8 to 10 percentage points in a typical election. I find, for instance, that if media bias didn't exist, John McCain would have defeated Barack Obama 56 percent to 42 percent, instead of losing 53-46."

Perhaps the most useful part of his book is the slant ratings of the media. The numbers are based on a conservative-to-

liberal 0-100 rating, with 50 being centrist:
New York Times-73.7.
CBS Evening News-73.7.
NPR Morning Edition-66.3.
U.S. News & World Report-65.8.
Drudge Report-60.4.
ABC Good Morning America-56.1.
Washington Times-35.4.
- Washington Examiner. Paul Bedard. Washington Whispers. June 16, 2011

It is important to stay informed on current events so that you are an educated voter. It is also important to realize the bias present in the news sources where information is gathered. Most news sources have a built in bias. The following table lists a number of media outlets and which side of the bias divide they reside on. The most unbiased: **Fox News Channel** for Cable News as defined by the metrics in *Left Turn*.

It is not surprising that the media in America has become partisan and actively seeks to promote the political party it favors. This was the case in early America. The newspapers of that day were filled with stories attacking candidates the owner of the paper did not like. Some of these reports contained "made-up" facts with little-to-no evidence to back them up. This evolved into most big cities having two main newspapers – one favoring the views of each of the major parties (for example, in St Louis, MO, the papers were the Globe-Democrat and the Post-Dispatch; In Washington DC, the papers were the Times and the Post). But newspapers offered readers many things besides political commentary and reporting--things such as classified ads, store ads, and sports team coverage. Most cities ended up with one dominant paper, as these items were subject to economies of scale where a single paper is more efficient.

For much of America's history, the news sources have been partisan. In the authors view, here is the media bias partisan divide in present times (following table next page):

Political Bias in the News Media

Media	Liberal Biased	Conservative Biased
Network News	ABC CBS NBC	None.
Cable News	MSNBC CNN	Fox Business The Blaze TV Newsmax TV
National Newspapers	New York Times Washington Post USA Today	Wall Street Journal Investors Business Daily Washington Times
News Magazines	Time Newsweek US News and World Report	National Review Weekly Standard Human Events Reason
National Talk Radio Shows	NPR (National Public Radio) Alan Combs Ed Schultz	Rush Limbaugh Sean Hannity Mark Levin Steve Deace Laura Ingraham Glenn Beck
Political News and Commentary Internet Sites	AOL-Huffington Post Politico.com TalkLeft.com Slate.com Salon.com	Breitbart.com RedState.com Newsmax.com TheBlaze.com Townhall.com CNSNews.com

Sidebar: News Corp. Political Contributions

Most liberals will insist that Fox News and its parent company News Corp. is a stringent right wing ideologically-driven company. An examination of the political donations of NewsCorp reveals a dramatically different story however. NewsCorp donates more money to Democrat political groups than Republican ones. In fact in 2012 it was 2:1 in favor of Democrats in general, and almost 5:1 in favor of Barack Obama.

News Corp: All Federal Campaign Donations 2012 Cycle (from opensecrets.org):

Total Donations: $529,362 to Democrat groups   (66%)
                  $277,704 to Republican groups (34%)

For President: Obama, Barack (D) $147,464 (83%)
                Romney, Mitt (R) $29,950 (17%)

The truly conservative news channels have limited distribution on cable and satellite providers. Several have recently launched:

The Blaze TV launching on cable and satellite providers nationwide
The Blaze TV will be carried on cable and satellite providers nationwide, beginning today with DISH Network.
- www.glennbeck.com. Sep. 12, 2012.

The Blaze TV is a conservative/libertarian/independent news channel founded by Glenn Beck, an entrepreneur and talk radio show host.

NewsmaxTV
Newsmax TV will provide independent news with a mainstream conservative tilt, while offering a balanced perspective and open to all points of view. More than just a politically focused channel, Newsmax TV will provide a full range of informational programming and lifestyle content for boomers in the areas of health, finance, and personal well-being.   - www.Newsmax.com

The Washington Times extending reach with cable network
One America News Network will provide Americans a new, credible source for national and international news and investigative reporting as well as talk shows designed to foster an independent, cutting-edge debate about the policies, issues and solutions facing the country.

The intent is to provide credible news and thoughtful analysis for viewers with self-described independent, conservative and libertarian values. Fox News has done a great job serving the center-right and independent audiences. But those who consider themselves liberal have a half dozen or more choices on TV each day from which to get their news.
- The Washington Times. Jennifer Harper. March 13, 2013

These channels offer a solid conservative alternative to the liberal news channels CNN and MSNBC and Fox News which often is centrist rather than straight conservative.

Once these new channels obtain sufficient distribution, they are almost assured of getting ratings. The nation has at least as many conservative viewers as liberal ones, but most news channels are liberally biased. Presidential elections show that 40% of the country consistently votes Republican, 40% consistently votes Democrat, and 20% is independent, swinging between the parties. So shouldn't there be at least 40% of the news channels with a Republican/conservative focus?

The media continues to be left-liberal biased even when it costs them profits. It is a matter of record that Fox News Channel became very successful (most watched cable news channel) and profitable as a centrist news channel. It stood out from its left leaning competitors. So with 40+% of the nation being conservative, wouldn't it be logical that one of the network news agencies (ABC, CBS, NBC) would be conservative? But all are liberal-biased. There is a simple business plan for one of these networks to become the ratings leader and profitable: Become a truly conservative news source, and advertise the fact on conservative talk radio shows. Within 6 months, the ratings and profits would soar for this news network as it fills an unmet need with the population. But this hasn't happened. The network news departments prefer their liberal-bias to profits.

The author will close this chapter with an example of factual reporting by CNS News that holds a politician to past statements. Politicians should never be allowed to speak in a vacuum. Their statements on a given topic should be taken in context with previous statements made. Too often, politicians such as former Speaker Nancy Pelosi end up speaking out of both sides of their mouths, and the media lets them get away with it.

> Flashback - Pelosi '07: Blames Bush for $3.07 Gas, In '12 Blames 'Speculators'
>
> In **May of 2007** then-House Speaker Rep. Nancy Pelosi (D-Calif.) was critical of the nationwide price of gas reaching a $3.07 average and squarely **placed the blame on the Bush administration.**
>
> "Drivers are paying a heavy price for the Bush administration's failure to enact a comprehensive energy

strategy," Pelosi said.

"Years of Bush Administration's policies that have favored big oil over the consumers have resulted in record dependence on foreign oil, leaving American families and businesses to pay even higher prices."

Pelsoi continued, "This Congress, under the Democratic leadership, is working to make up for years of inaction, taking America in a new direction that helps bring down the cost of gas and promotes energy independence. Energy independence is essential, essential to reducing the price at the pump."

As of **March 2012** the average nationwide price of gas is $3.79, but Pelosi does not blame the Obama administration or the president's plan for energy independence. **Instead she focuses her criticism on speculators.**

"Supply is up. Demand is down, you would think the price would come down. Enter the speculators," Pelosi said on March 1, 2012.

"Not the healthy speculation that is normal to the marketplace, but a speculation that can add 20 percent to the cost of a barrel of oil. The American people have to know that, because this has happened before."

- CNSNews.com. March 6, 2012.

When her statements on gas prices are compared, it becomes obvious that Nancy Pelosi is acting like a political hack – simply saying what is politically beneficial to her and her party at a given point in time. This is often seen with politicians today. In part, because most are lawyers who are trained to argue both sides of a case depending whether they are assigned to the defense or the plaintiff. All news media should ferret out this behavior from politicians in all parties. But it is seldom done.

Informed citizens should be aware of the biases present in the news received from various sources, and the impact the bias has on political issues. Only by hearing both the liberal and conservative viewpoint can one be informed and decide for themselves. Conservatives, especially need to seek out media outlets that counter the dominant liberal bias found in most major media.

Christians No Longer Welcome in Democrat Party

Acts 2:18-20 Then [the Jewish rulers in the Sanhedrin] called them in again and commanded them not to speak or teach at all in the name of Jesus. But Peter and John replied, "Which is right in God's eyes: to listen to you, or to him? You be the judges! As for us, we cannot help speaking about what we have seen and heard."

The above passage occurs shortly after Jesus' resurrection and ascension into Heaven. The Apostles, led by Peter and John, were preaching the Gospel of Jesus to the people. The Jewish government jailed the two Apostles overnight, then ordered them to cease and desist from their teaching. The Apostles refused! In an act of civil disobedience, they followed God rather than government leaders. This was very courageous of the Apostles. The Sanhedrin had killed Jesus, and therefore could kill them too.

In America, citizens should never have to make a hard, life threatening choice such as the one that the Apostles faced. Our Constitution was written by Christians and protects freedom of worship by expressly preventing the federal government from interfering with citizens' religious activities. But as detailed in Chapter 13, the federal government has been using its power to remove Christianity from the public. American Christians have an alternative to civil disobedience. We can vow to support only those politicians who will follow the Constitution's words, including religious protections, and shun those politicians who want to use government force to violate citizens' rights and freedoms.

A political party is free to shun or disavow God. Members of a party are free to do likewise. Remember, there is God given free will to do so. But going back to the Apostles, should a Christian be a member of such a party or vote for the party's candidates? The Apostles risked their lives to be able to talk about Jesus in public. All Christians in America have to do is *not* support, or vote for, politicians who shun God or make laws counter to a biblical way of life. Chapter 14 showed that many times these politicians are deceptive, in that they say what conservative or Christian voters want to hear, but then place judges on federal courts who unconstitutionally make laws the politicians claim to oppose.

To be clear, it is not the politicians' personal faith that is important from a political standpoint. Atheists, Jews or even Muslims can be good representatives - IF they understand the Constitution and use their offices to limit the power of the federal government according to the Constitution.

America has a relatively unique system where throughout her history there have been two major political parties, composed of different factions or components. The parties have platforms which state the unifying beliefs of the members. Platforms have always included a recognition of God, much like America's founding documents, and the state constitutions. Sadly, this is beginning to change.

Those who follow the teachings of the Bible and use them as a life-guide, no longer seem welcome in the Democrat Party. Now it is very true that some factions in the Republican Party would also prefer Christians be seen but not heard. Some establishment Republicans and some libertarian Republicans also think God should be out of the public, and abortion and homosexual marriage are acceptable "freedoms". But the Republican Party platform still follows a pro-biblical theme on these issues.

Sidebar: Republican representatives who vote against these issues after pretending to be in favor of them should be shunned as well. Likewise, if they vote to confirm judges making law on these issues. Chapters 14 and 25 call out a few of these representatives.

In a way, the Democrat Party has abandoned biblical teaching going back to the 1940s where its politicians used federal judges to attack the 1st Amendment. Chapter 14 detailed ruling by ruling how activist judges removed religious courses, prayer, and Bibles from public venues – all in violation of 1st Amendment rights of citizens. The divide has increased with the party's adoption of abortion in the 1970s and its recent embrace of homosexual marriage.

The positions of the Democrat Party and the Roman Catholic Church (plus many Protestant denominations) in America have been in conflict for years. The Catholic Church teaches there are "four non-negotiables: abortion, embryonic stem-cell research, euthanasia and same-sex marriage" that Catholics should oppose on moral grounds. Yet Democrat Party leaders in Washington DC, who claim to be Catholic, must support these to remain in good standing with their party. They are forced to choose between their church and their party, and they choose party.

New Pope: No Communion for Pro-Abortion Politicians

New Pope Francis I is a conservative in the mold of his predecessor, Pope Benedict XVI and Pope John Paul II. That's especially true on the issue of abortion, which he called a "death sentence" for the unborn in 2007.

"we should commit ourselves to 'eucharistic coherence,' that is, we should be conscious that people cannot receive holy communion and at the same time act or speak against the commandments, in particular when abortions, euthanasia, and other serious crimes against life and family are facilitated. **This responsibility applies particularly to legislators,** governors, and health professionals."

- Breitbart.com. Breitbart News. 13 Mar 2013.

Bishop Sheridan on Catholics, the Pope and Politicians

[Michael Sheridan, Bishop of the Catholic Diocese of Colorado Springs]: "It's clear to me that the Code of Canon Law, Canon 915, says that **a Catholic politician who publicly espouses positions that are contrary, not just to any teachings of the Church, but to serious moral teachings, should not receive Holy Communion until they recant those positions publicly**. Voters needs a little bit more nuance, because there the question is, are we voting for those politicians precisely because of their positions on those non-negotiable issues? Here is what I would say: It would be very difficult for me to understand how, if there are two candidates quite far apart in their positions on these matters, I could vote for the one who consistently opposes these Church teachings, simply because he might be in favor of a few good things."

- The Colorado Springs Gazette. DANIEL COLE. October 09, 2012.

Sidebar: How could a church be so harsh as to deny Communion to a member? Because it is also church teaching that to receive Communion, one must have repented of their sins. When a member openly supports and promotes an activity that the church considers sinful, that member has not recognized the sin nor repented.

Sidebar 2: **Nationally elected Democrats (and their voters) who call themselves Catholic, have a serious contradiction: their faith does not align with their political views.** For those who do not like the biblical teachings of the Catholic Church, there are a few denominations that ignore entire sections of the Bible and openly embrace these non-biblical teachings. For example, the Episcopal Church's leadership has been taken over by homosexual activists. This Church now takes positions very similar to the Democrat Party. The author wonders why Democrat politicians do not just join the Episcopal Church so their political and religious beliefs are in alignment. Of course, just because a church proclaims an activity is not sinful does not mean God does not consider it sinful.

In addition to opposing biblical teachings on prayer, abortion, and marriage, the leaders of the Democrat Party have become openly hostile to Christianity. (Biblical Christianity that is. Social justice "Christianity", which is more about government force than faith, is still welcome.) Two events highlight this trend: The Democrat Party Convention's 'Booing' of God and the attempt to ban Chick-Fil-A restaurants solely because the owner expressed support for a biblical teaching.

The Democrat Party Convention of 2012
At their convention, the Democrats continued to support the right of a woman to abort her baby at any time, as long as the head remains within her womb. But this convention marked the first time the Democrats adopted homosexual or same-sex marriage, redefining marriage from one man and one woman, to now include two men or two women.

>Democratic Party Platform
>Abortion:
>"Democrats will continue to stand up to Republican efforts to defund Planned Parenthood health centers."
>"We oppose any and all efforts to weaken or undermine that right [to abortion]."

Gay Marriage:
"We support marriage equality and support the movement to secure equal treatment under law for same-sex couples. "
- www.huffingtonpost.com/2012/09/03/democratic-party-platform

This marked the first time a major party adopted homosexual marriage which is solidly against biblical teaching (See Chapter 17). So the Democrat Party is now at odds with the Bible on two major societal issues: Abortion and redefining marriage to include same-sex. Various pastors and priests are coming to realize this incompatibility.

Pastor John MacArthur: Democrats 'Adopted The Sins of Romans 1 As Their Platform'

"And as you know," MacArthur told his Southern California congregation on Sept. 30, "I'm not one to talk about politics as such, but I was essentially amazed that one of the historic parties here in the United States adopted the sins of Romans 1 as their platform. This is a new day in our country. Parties which used to differ on economics now differ dramatically on issues that invade the realm of God's law and morality."

"In an ideal situation, their platform would mean that the government passes out condoms so people can fornicate at will," said MacArthur. "For those who happen to get pregnant in the process, the platform advocates that you kill the baby at the will of the mother, up and including the ninth month."

"At the same time," he said, "it advocates homosexual marriage, which is an oxymoron, an utter impossibility, and a gross violation of the law of God. And then, to add to that, the murder of abortion and then the platform originally leaving God out. All of that is Romans 1...."

"And then Romans 1 also says God will judge those nations that advocate homosexual behavior, men with men, women with women, doing what is unnatural," said Pastor MacArthur. "They are also haters of God, haters of God."

MacArthur is an author, pastor of Grace Community Church in Sun Valley, Calif., president of The Master's College and

Seminary, and a teacher at Grace to You media ministry.
- CNSNews.com. Jon Street. December 10, 2012.

Given the discrepancy between the Democrat Party and God's teachings, perhaps it was an afterthought to drop God altogether from the platform and convention. Both parties have referred to God in their platforms, mimicking the nation's founding documents. The Declaration of Independence reads: "We hold these truths to be self-evident, that all men are created equal, that they are **endowed by their Creator** with certain unalienable Rights...." The political parties routinely included similar language recognizing God. (Note: every State Constitution does this as well. See Chap. 10.) 2012 marked the year that the Democrats chose to omit God from their party platform.

> Democrats Drop "God" From Party Platform
> God's name has been removed from the Democratic National Committee platform. This is the paragraph that was in the 2008 platform:
> "We need a government that stands up for the hopes, values, and interests of working people, and gives everyone willing to work hard the chance to make the most of their God-given potential."
> Now the words "God-given" have been removed.
> - The Brody File. CBN News. 9-4-2012.

Maybe this was really no big deal, as party platforms tend to be long and are pretty much ignored after the convention closes. Except CBN picked up on the fact and reported it. Other internet and talk radio media also reported on it. (This wasn't considered newsworthy to the TV network news media, who did not report on it.) As a result, the news got out, and the Obama Campaign (sitting presidents control their conventions) did not want to be seen by the public as "omitting God". They obviously considered it damaging to their political prospects.

So the party decided to re-insert God into the platform. Since the platform had already been voted on and approved by the convention, it was necessary to amend the platform. The convention rules stated a 2/3 majority was required to pass amendments. But at conventions it is common practice to use voice votes whenever possible. It is much quicker than voting which requires the distribution of ballots, then collecting them and tabulating them. The convention chair has the power to deem whether the measure passes based on the sound of the "ayes" or "nays".

So the Democrats did a voice vote, except there was loud opposition to the amendment to insert God into the platform, instead of the acceptance the chair desired.

> Democrats' Efforts To Reinsert 'God' And 'Jerusalem' Into Platform Met With Loud Opposition
> After they took heat for omitting any reference to "God" in their platform, and for eliminating language from the 2008 platform that identified Jerusalem as the capital of Israel, Democrats tried to add the language back into their party platform with a voice vote.
>
> But when Los Angeles Mayor Antonio Villaraigosa, the convention chairman, came to the podium to ask for the approval of the delegates, those who shouted opposition to the language change were as loud, if not louder, than those who voiced their support.
>
> Villaraigosa, in what quickly became an awkward moment, asked for the voice vote three times in all. After the second time, he paused for several seconds and looked behind him for guidance from a convention staffer -- possibly a parliamentarian -- before turning back and asking for a third vote.
>
> Even though the no's were again as loud if not louder than the aye's on the third vote, Villaraigosa said he had determined that two thirds of those present had voted in favor. Boos filled the arena in response.
>   - HuffingtonPost.com/2012/09/05

It is unfortunate that the members of the convention opposing the amendment did not know the rules. Robert's Rules of Order state: "When the vote is taken by voice or show of hands any member has a right to require a division of the assembly by having the affirmative rise and then the negative, so that all may see how members vote." If the Huffington Post report is accurate, and the author believes it to be so after listening to the video, then the amendment would not have passed, and God could have been left out, as the majority of convention attendees desired. In the author's opinion, omitting God is very sad indeed, but it would have made clear to the public where the Democrat delegates stood on God.

A Godless Party Expels the Creator
For the first time — and in the longest Democratic platform in history, 26,000 words — there was not a single mention of God, the Creator, whom Thomas Jefferson himself, father of the party, proclaimed to be the author of our right to life and liberty.

The convention had approved the new platform, but when a firestorm erupted [in the conservative and centrist media; liberal media largely failed to report], a panicked Barack Obama hastily ordered "God" reinstated.

But when the amendment was offered to the convention by its chairman, Antonio Villaraigosa, the idea of restoring the name of God to the platform was hooted, jeered and booed by half the delegates on the floor, who three times howled, "No!"

The omission of God is being called an oversight. But the viral reaction to returning God, even when Obama asked that it be done, testifies that this was no accident. God was deleted deliberately.
- CNSNews.com. Patrick J. Buchanan. September 7, 2012

Anyone familiar with the Bible cannot help but notice the similarity between the Democrat Party's three time denial to include God at the convention and the Apostle Peter, who denied Christ three times shortly before Jesus' crucifixion.

Attempts by Democrats to Ban Chick-Fil-A
2012 also marked the year that a number of Democrat politicians called for the banning of a business, the sole reason being it is owned by a Christian who supported a biblical teaching.

Christians No Longer Welcome in Democrat Party

Chick-Fil-A is a restaurant specializing in chicken sandwiches that also tries to run its business on Christian principles. They are not open on Sundays, to respect the day of rest described in the Bible. Chick-Fil-A provides numerous scholarships for their employees, and actively supports several charities, described on the Chick-Fil-A website:

> WinShape Foundation was founded more than 20 years ago by Truett and Jeannette Cathy [founders of Chick-Fil-A]. Under the WinShape Foundation umbrella, there are several programs, including WinShape Homes®, which currently operates 11 foster care homes in Georgia, Tennessee and Alabama. The WinShape College Program℠ at Berry College in Rome, Georgia, is a co-op program offering joint four-year scholarship funding to incoming freshmen of up to $32,000. WinShape Camps℠ offers boys and girls summer programs at the college, which will be attended by more than 15,000 campers in 2012.
>
> Additionally, WinShape also operates the WinShape Retreat℠, which offers a sequestered setting for marriage support and counseling and other gatherings on the Mountain Campus of Berry College. Held at WinShape Retreat, WinShape Marriage℠ aims to help married couples by offering intervention for couples in crisis, preparation for engaged couples and enrichment for those interested in growing their marriage.

But Chick-Fil-A doesn't cater to a Christian-only clientele. It serves anyone and everyone. Its business is selling chicken sandwiches, not religion.

So why would a number of Democrat politicians want to ban Chick-Fil-A from their communities? Because of an interview by current CEO Dan Cathy. Cathy responded to a question during an interview about the company supporting traditional, biblical, man-woman marriage. The interview was with the Biblical Recorder in North Carolina (which was circulated by Baptist Press). Here are the direct quotes from Cathy:

"We don't claim to be a Christian business," Cathy told the Biblical Recorder in a recent visit to North Carolina. He attended a business leadership conference many years ago where he heard Christian businessman Fred Roach say, "There is no such thing as a Christian business."

"That got my attention," Cathy said. "Roach went on to say, 'Christ never died for a corporation. He died for you and me.' "

"In that spirit ... [Christianity] is about a personal relationship. Companies are not lost or saved, but certainly individuals are," Cathy added. "But as an organization we can operate on biblical principles. So that is what we claim to be. [We are] based on biblical principles, asking God and pleading with God to give us wisdom on decisions we make about people and the programs and partnerships we have. And He has blessed us."

[Interviewer Allan Blume:] Some have opposed the company's support of the traditional family.

"Well, guilty as charged," said Cathy when asked about the company's position. "We are very much supportive of the family — the biblical definition of the family unit. ...

"We are very much committed to that," Cathy emphasized. "We intend to stay the course," he said. "We know that it might not be popular with everyone, but thank the Lord, we live in a country where we can share our values and operate on biblical principles."

- Quotes taken from www.getreligion.org. July 20, 2012.

Dan Cathy may have been incorrect about being able to share his values and principles, at least in a number of cities controlled by Democrats. The leaders of the attempt to "punish" the business were lead by typical liberal cities like Boston, San Francisco, and Chicago. Chicago is especially telling, as the effort there is lead by President Obama's former Chief of Staff, Rahm Emanuel.

Mayor Rahm Emanuel said Monday he has no regrets about saying that "Chick-Fil-A's values are not Chicago's values" because the company president opposes gay marriage.

"No. I don't regret it", the mayor said under questioning at an unrelated jobs announcement. "And the simple reason is, when it comes to values, there's a policy as it relates to gay marriage. The values of our city are ones that welcome and recognize that, and I will continue to fight for that."

- suntimes.com. FRAN SPIELMAN. July 30, 2012.

Note that Chick-Fil-A serves homosexual people as well as heterosexual people. The company doesn't discriminate. The company serves all manner of sinners. In fact it's entire clientele consists of sinful human beings. That is a base tenet of Christianity – humans have fallen into sin with acts and deeds and therefore require their Savior to redeem them.

Any homosexual or liberal person who doesn't like the views of Chick-Fil-A's owners is free to go to another restaurant. That is one of the great things about freedom in America – Its citizens can patronize or not patronize a business for any reason they choose.

But Rahm Emanuel isn't content to disagree with a business owner who happens to follow the Bible. Emanuel takes action and tries to ban the business for its owners beliefs. Emanuel takes away freedom for both the restaurant and the citizens of his city.

The larger picture isn't about a single business or mayor, it is about how Christian-biblical beliefs are no longer tolerated in the Democrat Party. If Emanuel gets his way, Chick-Fil-A will be banned from Chicago, simply because its owners expressed a support for a biblical teaching. Likewise, those Christian beliefs are no longer welcome in the political party where Emanuel remains a powerful leader.

But Rahm Emanuel's anger and outrage against those supporting traditional marriage appears to be quite selective. The Nation of Islam, also opposed to homosexual marriage, is welcomed into Chicago with Emanuel's open arms. He even partners with them. **Seemingly, Emanuel's hostility is only directed against Bible-following Christians, not to followers of Islam.**

Crime-Fighting Makes For Strange Friends: Rahm Emanuel, Louis Farrakhan Working Together In Chicago

Chicago's first Jewish mayor, Rahm Emanuel, has formed a team (of sorts) with the help of Nation of Islam leader Louis Farrakhan, a man many view as an aggressive anti-Semite, to help cut the 40 percent surge in homicides in the city's neighborhoods.

"People of faith have a role to play, and community leaders have a role to play in helping to protect our neighborhoods and our citizens," Emanuel told the paper. "You cannot get there on just one piece of an anti-crime strategy."
- International Business Times. Laura Matthews. July 26, 2012.

Here is Louis Farrakhan's view of homosexual marriage:

Louis Farrakhan Critiques Obama's Gay Marriage Endorsement

Minister Louis Farrakhan recently responded to President Obama's endorsement of gay marriage calling him "the first president that sanctioned what the scriptures forbid."

"Males coming to males with lust in their hearts as they should to a female," he said. "Now don't you dare say Farrakhan was preaching hate; he's homophobic. I'm not afraid of my brothers and sisters or others who may be practicing what God condemned in the days of Lot. That's not our job to be hateful of our people. Our job is to call us to sanity."

Farrakhan goes on to call out clergy who support gay marriage, saying they are placing society's needs over God's.
- The Huffington Post. Danielle Cadet. 05/29/2012

Louis Farrakhan is considered by many to be a racist based on his long history of controversial statements such as these:

"White people are potential humans - they haven't evolved yet." -*Philadelphia Inquirer*, March 2000

"It seems like being gay or whatever sin you wish to be a part of is okay ... but I have the duty to lift that gay person up to the standard to ask if they want to live the life that God wants them to or live the lifestyle that they want to live." - Boston speech, August 1997

"Do you mean to tell me that Jews have never done any evil to black people? ... Were they not involved in the slave trade? Yes, they were ... and to the extent that they were involved, somebody has to bring them to account. And I believe that has fallen on me." - Interview with *New York Amsterdam News*, January 1994
   - guardian.co.uk. Derek Brown. July 31, 2001.

So why does Mayor Emanuel welcome Louis Farrakhan into Chicago, but try to ban Chick-Fil-A restaurants? Farrakhan's statements are much stronger than Dan Cathy's. Plus Farrakhan is known for making anti-Jewish statements, which one would think, would offend Rahm Emanuel who claims to be Jewish. An explanation is Emanuel is driven by politics rather than faith, and he views Christians as political enemies. But these actions are perfect examples of anti-Christian, anti-Bible bigotry by Rahm Emanuel and other key leaders of the Democrat Party.

<u>Democrat Party controlled State Governments teach the Homosexual Lifestyle in Schools</u>
State governments controlled by Democrats are also beginning to teach homosexuality in schools. Chapter 11 details examples of California and Minnesota developing and implementing pro-homosexual school curricula for young children in grade schools. Schools taught biblical principles in early America, but now Democrat Party leaders (or their interest-group backers) are teaching children behavior that God describes as "detestable" is good.

In fairness, both the teaching of the Bible and the teaching of the homosexual lifestyle are indoctrination. But it is interesting that powerful elements of a major political party now seem fully invested in teaching non-Christian behavior.

<u>Homosexual Marriage</u>
In Chapter 16, Michele Obama was quoted as saying the courts would be used to advance homosexual marriage. This effort is now

in full swing with Obama's Attorney General leading the charge.

> Holder Invites State AGs to Do As He Did: Refuse to Defend Laws Banning Same-Sex Marriage
> State attorneys-general who refuse to defend state laws banning same-sex marriage won't face any objection from the nation's top law enforcement official. In fact, Attorney General Eric Holder will applaud them.
>
> According to Holder, "decisions at any level not to defend individual laws must be exceedingly rare. They must be reserved only for exceptional – truly exceptional – circumstances.' ... state laws banning same-sex marriage rise to that...standard -- because they do not "advance the values that once led our forebears to declare unequivocally that all are created equal and entitled to equal opportunity."
>
> Holder said he and Obama were "motivated by the strong belief that all measures that distinguish among people based on their sexual orientation must be subjected to a heightened standard of scrutiny...and therefore this measure (DOMA) was unconstitutional discrimination."
>   - www.cnsnews.com. Susan Jones. February 25, 2014

First, remember that marriage has always been defined as a man and a woman. So a man having a relationship with a man, a dog, a horse, or any other pet cannot be called a marriage. Unless one changes the definition in such a way as to make the word meaningless. Since every person can still marry one of the opposite sex, as marriage means, there is no discrimination or denial of rights.

Secondly, Holder is blatantly breaking the law with his decision to not enforce nor defend DOMA, a law passed by a Republican Congress and signed by Democrat President Bill Clinton. Holder and Obama want a federal court to undo the law and make new law. This is not the constitutionally defined process for making or changing law. In addition to breaking the law himself, Holder is cheering on top law enforcers in states to follow his lead and also break the law.

Thirdly, the actions of Clinton and Obama reflect what the activist base of the Democrat Party wants. In the 1990s it was traditional marriage. Now it is homosexual marriage. The question for Christians remains: Do the views of the activists reflect your views? Each Christian must answer for themselves.

Pastors and priests were quoted earlier in this chapter answering that question. The party positions were not compatible with their biblical faith views. A group of black pastors is coming to the same conclusion. They are taking it a step further and calling for the impeachment of Eric Holder for his failure to uphold constitutionally made law.

CAAP Press Release 2-25-2014

Washington, DC— A coalition of African American civil rights leaders and pastors today said they will launch a grassroots effort seeking to secure the signatures of one million people calling for Attorney General Eric Holder to be impeached. The Coalition of African American Pastors (CAAP) cited numerous instances of Holder attempting to impose same-sex 'marriage' throughout the nation despite federal law, rulings by the US Supreme Court, and state constitutional amendments to the contrary.

"The Attorney General of the United States should be impeached over his repeated lawlessness in attempting to impose same-sex marriage throughout the nation," said Reverend Bill Owens, CAAP Founder and President. "It's one thing to make a political argument that gay marriage should be the law, but it's quite another to take actions that ignore federal law, Supreme Court rulings, and the constitutions of dozens of states that have specifically rejected the redefinition of marriage which the administration is trying to impose."

"As much as President Obama and Attorney General Holder would like it to be otherwise, we live in a democracy—with government of, by, and for the people—not a monarchy ruled by a king issuing decrees from on high," Reverend Owens continued. "The citizens of several states who have voted overwhelmingly to preserve marriage have had their votes voided and thrown out by radical federal judges; and the Obama administration—in particular the Justice Department

—has been shamefully complicit in this attack on the rights of those voters."

States have historically defined marriage as the union of one man and one woman, and the majority of states continue to do so. Thirty states have in fact enacted constitutional amendments to this effect. Furthermore, still binding federal law contained in Section II of the Defense of Marriage Act (DOMA) provides that no state shall be required to recognize same-sex 'marriages' performed in other states. The U.S Supreme Court ruled last year in Windsor v. United States that the federal government must respect the role of states to define marriage.

Despite all this, Attorney General Holder has announced that the federal government will treat any 'married' same-sex couple as legally married even in states that define marriage as solely the union of a man and a woman. Holder has directed the government to extend provisions providing same-sex couples immunity from testifying against a 'spouse,' treatment as 'married' persons in bankruptcy court, 'spousal' visitation rights and compassionate release in the case of federal prison inmates, and federal death benefits.

Previously, Holder supported the Obama Administration's efforts to allow foreign gay 'spouses' immigration rights, attempts to pressure military chaplains to perform same-sex ceremonies, and extension of federal benefits to same-sex partners of federal employees.

"What we have in Attorney General Holder is a man so political in his zeal to redefine marriage that he is willing to run roughshod over the rulings of the Supreme Court, binding federal law, and the United States Constitution along with the constitutions of a majority of states," Reverend Owens said. "Yet our leaders in Washington are letting him get away with his illegal conduct and doing nothing meaningful to hold him accountable. Our campaign to gather one million signatures of citizens calling for Holder's impeachment is intended to create a groundswell of support, giving Congressional leadership the encouragement necessary to remove this dangerous ideologue from public office."

Owens stressed that the petition is meant for all citizens regardless of race or creed: "Marriage is an institution that benefits all of society; therefore every citizen has an interest in protecting marriage from these brazen attacks," Owens said. Citizens can sign the open letter to Congress at www.HolderImpeachment.com.
- caapus.org.

The petition may be a worthwhile effort. The author firmly believes in impeaching those politicians and judges who do not uphold the Constitution. Another effective way to get the attention of politicians is to withhold votes from them. As Chapter 14 clearly showed, when Democrat Presidents and Senators win elections, the federal courts are often used to force policies like homosexual marriage onto the nation. These black pastors should encourage their parishioners and others in their community to withhold votes from politicians who oppose their faith values.

Another minister makes a strong case for Christians to leave the Democrat Party. Bishop E.W. Jackson is President of STAND (Staying True to America's National Destiny), founder of Exodus Faith Ministries, and has run for office as a Republican.

> <u>Bishop Calls on All Christians to Leave Democratic Party.</u>
> Bishop E.W. Jackson is making a war cry: "Let God's people go!"
>
> Jackson, a Marine Corps veteran, graduate of Harvard Law School and adjunct professor of law, is echoing the words of Moses in a campaign to persuade Christians of all races that the time has come for a wholesale exodus of Christians from the Democrat Party.
>
> The former candidate for U.S. Senate in Virginia points to what he calls the Democrat party's "cult-like devotion" to abortion; the rejection of the traditional biblical model of family; the hostility hurled at those who express a Christian viewpoint such as Chick-Fil-A president and Chief Operating Officer Dan Cathy; the actions of organizations such as the ACLU and the Foundation For Freedom From Religion in

suing cities and towns for displaying crosses at memorials or mentioning the name Jesus in prayer at official events.

Later this month when Democrats make same-sex marriage part of their official Party Platform, the former practicing attorney says they will be spitting in the face of every Bible-believing Christian in America: "They will be saying, 'We don't care what you think, what you believe, or what the Bible or the God of the Bible says. We know better than God.'"

Jackson's message to Christians is, "The Democrat Party has turned its back on Christians. It is time to turn our backs on the Democrat Party."
- Charisma News Staff. 8/8/2012.

It is well known that the Democrat Party is the party of big-government. What is now becoming increasingly clear is that the big government they run is committed to secularism and promoting non-biblical policies. An example of this is ObamaCare – a program passed exclusively by Democrats, without a single Republican vote. This quintessential big government program promised health insurance for everyone. While failing on that promise, it is trying to force religious institutions to pay for abortion on demand through the guise of "health insurance". This forces religious organizations to violate their core beliefs.

Twenty-four religious leaders from different religious organizations signed the following letter objecting to the federal government violating their 1st Amendment Rights with ObamaCare.

FREE EXERCISE OF RELIGION: Putting Beliefs into Practice - An Open Letter from Religious Leaders in the United States to All Americans

June 21, 2012

Dear Friends,

Religious institutions are established because of religious beliefs and convictions. Such institutions include not only churches, synagogues, mosques, and other places of worship, but also schools and colleges, shelters and community kitchens, adoption agencies and hospitals, organizations that provide care and services during natural disasters, and countless other organizations that exist to put specific religious beliefs into practice. Many such organizations have provided services and care to both members and non-members of their religious communities since before the Revolutionary War, saving and improving the lives of countless American citizens.

As religious leaders from a variety of perspectives and communities, we are compelled to make known our protest against the incursion of the United States Department of Health and Human Services (HHS) into the realm of religious liberty. HHS has mandated that religious institutions, with only a narrow religious exception, must provide access to certain contraceptive benefits, even if the covered medications or procedures are contradictory to their beliefs. We who oppose the application of this mandate to religious institutions include not only the leaders of religious groups morally opposed to contraception, but also leaders of other religious groups that do not share that particular moral conviction.

That we share an opposition to the mandate to religious institutions while disagreeing about specific moral teachings is a crucial fact. Religious freedom is the principle on which we stand. Because of differing understandings of moral and religious authority, people of good will can and often do come to different conclusions about moral questions. Yet, even we who hold differing convictions on specific moral issues are united in the conviction that no religious institution should be penalized for refusing to go against its beliefs. The issue is the First Amendment, not specific moral teachings or specific products or services.

The HHS mandate implicitly acknowledged that an incursion into religion is involved in the mandate. However, the narrowness of the proposed exemption is revealing for it applies only to religious organizations that serve or support their own members. In so doing, the government is establishing favored and disfavored religious organizations: a privatized religious organization that serves only itself is exempted from regulation, while one that believes it should also serve the public beyond its membership is denied a religious exemption. The so-called accommodation and the subsequent Advance Notice of Proposed Rulemaking (ANPRM) do little or nothing to alleviate the problem.

No government should tell religious organizations either what to believe or how to put their beliefs into practice. We indeed hold this to be an unalienable, constitutional right. If freedom of religion is a constitutional value to be protected, then institutions developed by religious groups to implement their core beliefs in education, in care for the sick or suffering, and in other tasks must also be protected. Only by doing so can the free exercise of religion have any meaning. The HHS mandate prevents this free exercise. For the well-being of our country, we oppose the application of the contraceptive mandate to religious institutions and plead for its retraction.

The Rev. Dr. Matthew C. Harrison, president of The Lutheran Church—Missouri Synod (LCMS), authored and issued this open letter to all Americans voicing opposition to the U.S. Department of Health and Human Services' (HHS) contraceptive mandate found in ObamaCare. The complete list of signers can be found at: www.lcms.org/hhsmandate. It includes Catholic, Protestant and Muslim institutions.

Lutheran pastors in the LCMS had bulletin inserts containing this letter. Many Catholic churches had similar messages.

> ObamaCare vs. the Catholics
> On the last weekend of January, priests in Catholic churches across America read extraordinary letters to their congregations. The missives informed the laity that President Obama and his administration had launched an assault on the church......
>
> But what made the moment even more remarkable is that the bishops were not exaggerating. It is now a requirement of ObamaCare that every Catholic institution larger than a single church —and even including some single churches — must pay for contraceptives, sterilization, and morning-after

abortifacients for its employees. Each of these is directly contrary to the Catholic faith. But the Obama administration does not care. They have said, in effect, Do what we tell you—or else.
- The Weekly Standard. JONATHAN V. LAST. Feb 13, 2012, Vol. 17, No. 21

The Reverend Billy Graham, perhaps the world's best know evangelist of our era, has also recognized the dramatic shift in the Democrat Party and the federal government with respect to biblical values.

Obama's unprecedented attacks on life, freedom, faith and family have prompted the Rev. Billy Graham, for instance, to run full-page advertisements in newspapers across the country, urging voters to choose candidates who support biblical values of life, natural marriage, and religious liberty.

"This is unprecedented for the world's best-known evangelist," said Mat Staver, Founder and Chairman of Liberty Counsel. "Billy Graham has always steered clear of politics. In reality, Billy Graham has merely raised his prophetic voice like any preacher should when biblical and moral values are placed in jeopardy by politicians."
- IRS Surrenders: 'Holding Any Potential Church Audits In Abeyance'. CNSNews.com. J. Matt Barber. November 5, 2012.

The author is greatly saddened that the Democrat Party has abandoned Christians and become hostile to them. The author believes the nation is better off when both major political parties honor God and follow biblical teachings. But at least at this moment in time, the party has solidly staked out its anti-biblical positions.

Christian - Biblical views and beliefs are no longer welcome or tolerated within the Democrat Party.

So Democrats who are Christian have several options:

1. Abandon the Democrat Party at the national level. Refuse to vote for any Democrat candidate who is openly hostile to biblical teaching or for any candidate who nominates/confirms judges that force non-constitutional, non-biblical teaching onto the citizenry.

2. Abandon your faith. Place the Democrat party above your religious faith. If this is the option chosen, then why not leave the Catholic Church and major Protestant denominations, and join a fringe church that no longer follows the Bible? This is the logical, consistent thing to do.

3. Try to change the Democrat Party and restore it, so it once again follows constitutional biblical values. Realize that there a number of activists in the party who will fight to block this effort.

In conclusion, The Democrat Party has:

- Used government force via federal judges to ban the Bible, prayer, and religious symbols across the nation.

- Used government force via federal judges to force the legalization of abortion in every state in the nation.

- Used ObamaCare to force Christian institutions to pay for abortions.

- Become a champion for homosexual marriage and attempts to force it on every state.

- Attempted to use government force to ban Christian businesses for practicing their 1st Amendment free speech rights.

Every citizen has the free will to choose the politicians and parties they support. But citizens should align their faith with their politics. Following God is not meant to be a "only-in-church" lifestyle.

How many Americans realize that conservative hero, President Ronald Reagan, was once a Democrat? He commented that he did not leave the Democrat Party, it left him. The Democrat Party has been undergoing steady liberal, secular change for years. President John F. Kennedy, a Democrat hero, had more in common politically (anti-abortion, speeches calling for tax cuts and economic growth) with Reagan, than with Democrat Ted Kennedy. This chapter documents how Christians have been left by the Democrat Party. Will they now leave it?

Federal Elections: Return to the Constitution

When asked what kind of government the Constitutional Convention had created, Benjamin Franklin answered: "A republic, if you can keep it." (TRBF. P263) How to keep America's Constitutional Republic and the maximum freedom it offers? The first way is by educating citizens about the historical meaning of the Constitution. This book is a tool for that process. Please use it as a reference and share it with others. The second is by identifying and voting for national leaders who share the desire to follow the actual meanings of the Constitution.

To review, some key topics covered in previous chapters are:

- The Bible is a life-guide for followers of God. God offers free will to all, but expects His followers to worship Him and voluntarily (using our free will) help those in need.
- The Founders were Christians and created a constitutional government with defined federal powers. State governments were given much broader powers, as they were closer to the citizens. Both levels of government were supposed to maximize freedom for the citizens.
- A number of politicians of both major political parties have either abandoned many of these principles or ignored them while governing.

The previous chapter discussed how the Democrat Party, at least the national portion of it, has become hostile to the Christian religion as taught in the Bible. It has also become the party that most ignores those portions of the Constitution that limit federal government power and authority to specific defined areas.

The Republican Party at the national level is made up of two main wings: conservatives and establishment/moderates. Conservatives tend to follow the Constitution's plan of a smaller federal government. The establishment Republicans tend to have held office for a number years in Washington and are perfectly happy with the political power and prestige that comes from managing a large federal government. Of course, at election time, EVERY Republican will claim to be a conservative, as conservatives form a large majority of Republican voters. That is why it is so important to examine the politicians' voting records, rather than listening to campaign commercials. Some excellent research sites are listed later in the chapter.

To summarize, the current federal government is made up of three main factions:
1) Democrats – These politicians seek for ever increasing federal government power. Their preference is for the federal government to control both businesses and individuals. The example of this is ObamaCare or HillaryCare from the 1990s. The political philosophy resembles fascism, where the party in power has significant ability to control businesses without owning them. Note, fascism is *not* Nazism and death camps. There isn't an American political party favoring the extermination of citizens.
2) Establishment Republicans - As stated earlier, these politicians enjoy the power and privileges that come with managing a large government. They usually are in favor of the status quo. But, the status quo is a gradual increase in federal government power every year - caused by both the federal budget process and the numerous federal agencies writing new regulations. When in power, they usually do not offer large increases in government. But neither do they offer any reductions in government power.

   (These two factions currently form a large majority of our elected representatives which is the best argument for term limits. Power seeking people gravitate to Washington and don't leave once there. Term limits remove them.)
3) Constitutional Conservative / TEA Party Republicans – These politicians seek to reduce the size and power of the federal government. Not eliminate the federal government, as some Democrats charge, but return it to the level authorized by the Constitution. That is the level that was present in America for the first 150 years of the nation's life.

It is not hard to see why big-government politicians of the first two factions attack and demonize this faction. Their source of power and privilege is being threatened.

Federal Elections: Return to the Constitution

The ultimate solution, both for solving America's debt crisis and returning maximum freedom to the citizenry, is to return to the rules for government spelled out in our Constitution. Chapter 20 lays out the plan to transfer those federal agencies not allowed by the Constitution's 9th and 10th Amendments back to the states. The states will always administer government more efficiently than the federal government. The author firmly believes the only way to avert the federal government's looming fiscal crisis is to identify and support politicians who will follow this plan. **A constitutional conservative candidate will have a list of federal programs/agencies they wish to transfer to the states.**

At the national level both Democrats and establishment Republicans will likely reject the plan outlined in this book to return the federal government to its limited responsibilities. Those politicians must be convinced to adopt these positions or be defeated in the voting booth. It will be up to the American citizens to decide if they will make their representatives honor the constitutional rights of citizens.

Outline
- I. Defining a Constitutional Conservative
- II. Conservatism Wins When Tried
- III. Republican Party Is the Home of Conservatives
- IV. Voting Strategy in Primaries
  - A) Choose the Team
    1. Conservative Candidate Qualities
    2. Ability to Win Criteria
- V. Presidential General Elections
  - A) Vote for the most conservative candidate (Republican or Democrat)
    1. The Danger of Third Parties
       - Thank Ross Perot for ObamaCare
       - The Cost of Replacing the Republican Party
       - Danger of Protest Voting for President: 2012 Election
- VI. Congressional Elections
  - A) Protest/Third Party Voting
  - B) Research Sites for Congressional Incumbents
- VII. Maximize Influence: Organize into Political Groups

I. Defining a Constitutional Conservative

For the purposes of this chapter, a Constitutional Conservative is defined as:

- Supporting a return to the role of the federal government defined by the Constitution.
- Supporting only originalist judges (and opposing/voting down activist judges).
- Favoring immigration policy that creates citizens who will value, respect, and follow the US Constitution.
- Supporting economic growth by reducing the federal government taxes and regulations.
- Supporting a strong national defense (security for the nation).
- Being pro-religious freedom and anti-abortion (social conservatives).
  - Note: The Constitution places abortion law at the state rather than national level. This will be the case until a constitutional amendment addressing abortion is ratified.

Closely related, if not identical, to constitutional conservatism is the TEA Party movement. Tea Party Patriots list their core principles on their website:

> Tea Party Patriots stands for every American,... At its root the American Dream is about freedom. Freedom to work hard and the freedom to keep the fruits of your labor to use as you see fit without harming others and without hindering their freedom. Very simply, three guiding principles give rise to the freedom necessary to pursue and live the American Dream:
>
> - Constitutionally Limited Government or your personal freedom and your rights
> - Free Market Economics or economic freedom to grow jobs and your opportunities
> - Fiscal Responsibility or very simply, a debt free future for you and generations to come

The US Constitution brought together a number of states with very different political positions on certain issues into a nation. Only a libertarian federal government could have been approved, a government that left divisive political issues to the states as much as possible, giving them the freedom to choose their positions. The Constitution is a way to bring together Americans today as well, if Americans agree to let states decide today's divisive issues for themselves.

A true libertarian will want to ignore the social issues that are important to a social conservative. Constitutional conservatism attempts to bring those groups together at the national level by shifting most decisions to the states. Barring constitutional amendment, states should regulate marriage, abortion, and drugs, run welfare and healthcare programs, and determine education spending/ curriculum. National defense and foreign relations should be the prime focus of the national government.

Sidebar: Constitutional Conservatives and War
Article 1 section 8 of the Constitution gives Congress the power to declare war. There are some constitutional conservatives who feel American military actions like Korea (1950s), Vietnam (1970s), or Iraq (2010s) are not constitutional because Congress did not declare war. The Constitution *does not state* Congress must declare war before the military is used. Congress was consulted and authorized each of these military actions, making them constitutional. Congress chose to authorize each without a declaration of war. Citizens are free to debate whether these campaigns were wise, or unwise, uses of the American military. The author prefers using the American military only when there is a strong national benefit and the objective is total victory.

With to respect to the isolationist or non-interventionist foreign policy some in America prefer, America has often intervened in matters outside her borders to protect her interests. The earliest example is The Monroe Doctrine formed in the 1820s. This US policy prevented European nations from colonizing or interfering with lands in North or South America.

II. Nationally: Conservatism Wins When Tried
President Ronald Reagan is the most recent politician to illustrate this type of conservatism at the national level. He united fiscal-

economic conservatives, strong national defense conservatives, and social conservatives into a powerful coalition that carried him to two landslide electoral wins. Reagan's unapologetic conservative positions won over many who hadn't previously considered voting Republican, so much so that an entire class of voters were created: Reagan Democrats.

Contrast Reagan's huge electoral successes with the much less successful, more moderate-establishment candidates that followed him:

GOP Candidate	Electoral Votes Won	Electoral Votes Lost
Reagan (1980)	**489**	49
Reagan (1984)	**525**	13
Bush (1992)	168	**370**
Dole (1996)	159	**379**
Bush (2000)	**271**	266
Bush (2004)	**286**	251
McCain (2008)	173	**365**
Romney (2012)	206	**332**

George W. Bush did win two elections running on a platform of "compassionate conservatism". When a politician uses the word "compassion", they mean giving away money belonging to one group, collected by government taxation, to people in a different group. Some will argue that this is not conservatism at all, but there is no doubt it is not constitutional conservatism. In essence Bush and his team tried to compete with the Democrats by playing on their field – using the federal government to take care of people (or buy votes, if one is cynical). This strategy allowed Bush to barely squeak out two victories, compared to Reagan's landslide wins.

Bush's policies also failed to help his party. Part of Bush's "compassion" was creating a new prescription drug benefit in Medicare, thus further involving the federal government in a function that according to the Constitution should be left to the states.

> Bush's costly Medicare legacy
> Saying that Medicare Part D is a "fiscally sober entitlement plan" is sort of like saying that somebody is quite temperate — for a heroine addict. In 2011, according to the Medicare Trustees, the federal government spent $53 billion on prescription drug subsidies through the program. None of that is paid for either through a revenue stream or cuts to existing government programs.... With Medicare Part D, Bush didn't even pretend that the law paid for itself on paper...
>
> [Bush's] legacy on entitlements will be the largest (pre-ObamaCare) expansion of them since Lyndon B. Johnson created Medicare and Medicaid in 1965. This, of course, is only a part of Bush's disastrous fiscal record, which saw the federal budget spike from $1.86 trillion in 2001 to $2.98 trillion in 2008.
>
> Bush's legacy isn't something for conservatives to celebrate. It's something for them to mourn.
> - WashingtonExaminer.com. Philip Klein. April 24, 2013.

Medicare part D was sold by Bush's team as a winning political strategy that would win over seniors. So what happened in 2006? The Republican Party lost control of the House of Representatives. If some seniors were "won over", the number was smaller than the number of conservatives that chose not to vote. They no longer saw a difference between a big-spending Republican Congress and a Democrat-controlled Congress. A strong case can be made that Bush's big government policies contributed greatly to the Republican Congressional defeat of 2006.

> Sidebar: George W. Bush had a Republican Congress that offered him an opportunity to remake government that Reagan could only dream about. However, instead of reducing the scope of the federal government, Bush increased it. He added to federal spending and the national debt. For example: Reagan campaigned on eliminating the federal Department of Education; Bush passed No Child Left

Behind, which greatly increased spending at the Department of Education.

After Bush had disheartened many conservatives with his complete lack of any advancement of the conservative agenda, the next two national presidential elections also offered little promise. McCain and Romney ran campaigns de-emphasizing conservative themes. That, plus their records as being big-government politicians, ended up dooming their campaigns to failure. Many conservatives simply had had enough and stayed home. The case will be made later why this is a very poor choice for conservative voters in a presidential election. The Republican Party would be wise to select stronger conservative nominees in the future.

The plan outlined in Chapter 20 of transferring spending and taxation responsibilities back to the states will win at the national level if tried. Rush Limbaugh summarized the 2012 election results as : "It's hard to beat Santa Claus". Meaning its difficult to beat a politician/party that promises to give voters things. **The Constitutional Conservative plan doesn't take away "goodies". It just makes the states responsible for their distribution. So federal politicians can run on transferring programs to the more efficient states rather than eliminating them.**

III. Republican Party Is the Home of Conservatives
Constitutional conservatives need to pick a single party and work within that party to maximize their political influence. There may come a time when the Republican Party declines and disappears, yielding to a new conservative party. But that time is not yet here. A legitimate third party will have at least ten representatives in Congress. Until that time, a third party is only a means of protest voting and defeating the Republican candidate. A few examples will be discussed later in the chapter.

Despite the presence of some establishment, big-government politicians, the Republican Party is still the vehicle best used for promoting conservatism at the federal level. There are few if any Democrats in national office who favor any policies close to constitutional conservatism. (The author hopes this changes and the Democrat Party will offer candidates that respect limited government and religious freedom at the national level.) Third parties are discussed below.

This is not just the author's opinion. It is backed up by voting records of the parties at the national level.

- In Chapter 14, the Senate's record of supporting originalist judges was examined. It is critical to vote for originalist judges who follow the Constitution's meaning and against activist judges who rule for their political beliefs. On the last four Supreme Court confirmation votes Republicans voted in an originalist constitutional manner 90% of the time; Democrats just 35% of the time.

Originalist justices will prevent the government from banning religion in public (Chapter 14), as well as, mandating what products a citizen must buy, or what and how much a citizen can produce in the name of regulating commerce (Chapter 12).

As stated in Chapter 14: Unless a Democrat Senator specifically promises not to confirm activist judges, a vote for them is a vote to use the power of the federal government to remove crosses and war memorials from public land and continue the unconstitutional banning of prayer and other religious activity by the federal government.

Chapter 21 contains a section on **ObamaCare,** a huge federal government program that intervenes in the healthcare for every American. The Constitution clearly does not give the federal government power to do this. It was passed **exclusively by Democrats in the Congress** and signed by a Democrat President.

Chapter 24 details how the Democrat Party delegates booed the inclusion of God in their 2012 party platform as just one example of an increase in hostility to Christianity and biblical teachings. God is present in the Declaration of Independence, the Constitution, and the 50 State Constitutions. So the "rejection of God" by these party leaders is a clear break from America's religious heritage (Chapter 10).

America has traditionally had two dominant political parties. There are a large number of conservatives already in the Republican Party. In addition a constitutional conservative is closer politically to moderate Republicans than Democrats. The Republican Party is the natural home for conservatives. It is a worthwhile goal to make the party even more conservative.

IV. Voting Strategy in Primaries
A concerned conservative citizen should vote in every federal election possible: both primary and general; even year and odd year; every time there is a representative, senator, or president on the ballot.

ALWAYS VOTE. Politicians fight to win VOTERS; they do not care about non-voters. Not voting makes you irrelevant to a politician. Conversely, voting in primaries makes you even more relevant. Primary elections allow voters to shape their party by selecting the politicians who get to represent the party on the ballot.

A. Choose the Team
A party is analogous to a sports team. Those who root for a favorite team know how frustrating it can be when the team is losing and often making dumb mistakes. Teams draft or trade players poorly, the coaches call plays that even the announcers question, and the team seems to lack any kind of strategy. Fans usually call for the coach to be fired. In politics, conservatives' favorite team is the Republican Party. But what if the team seems to lose much more than it wins, and it doesn't follow a strategy that makes sense? While sports teams reward fans with making the playoffs, political teams determine the future of the nation. They are much more important. The primary elections are the place where voters have input to choosing their political team members.

Some (usually establishment types) say that incumbent Republicans should never be challenged as this weakens the party for the general election. As a voter, are you happy with the way your Republican team is playing? If the answer is "No", maybe a new team member should be chosen in the primary elections. This is especially true if voters are represented by a politician in a leadership position. There are a number of websites listed later in the chapter where

Federal Elections: Return to the Constitution

voters can evaluate their incumbents' voting records. Republicans vary with scores ranging from the 90s to the 40s.

Vote in a manner to make your party more conservative and for politicians that will more closely follow the rules of the Constitution. Primary elections are the most effective way to do this. Each vote is more valuable in determining the outcome, as fewer citizens bother to vote in them. This is another reason why it is important for conservatives to gather in a single party to maximize their influence over the party.

William F. Buckley Jr., founder of *National Review,* one of the first conservative magazines, had a rule he followed when voting in primaries: "The wisest choice would be the one who would win...... I'd be for the most [conservative], viable candidate who could win."

1. Conservative Candidate Qualities
    - Does the candidate support the plan to return the federal government to its constitutional responsibilities? Do they understand constitutional limits on federal government power?
    (If a candidate does not propose eliminating at least one government agency from the hundreds listed in Chapter 20 – they are NOT a limited-government conservative.)
    - Is the candidate committed to controlling immigration to America and preventing amnesty?
    - Does the candidate have a conservative record? Has he or she previously governed in a conservative manor?
    - Is the candidate trustworthy? Will he or she keep campaign promises made?

2. Able to win Criteria
    - Does the candidate have money or is able to raise money to run a successful campaign in the general election? Candidates must be able to get their message out and refute attacks from their opponent. This requires money.
    - Does the candidate have name recognition? Is he or she liked by the populace? Does the candidate have charisma?
    - Able to communicate the conservative message effectively?

- Able to handle questions from a hostile, liberal-leaning media?
- No skeletons in closet (extra-marital affairs, racist comments or statements, illegal business activities, ...)

Ultimately it is up to the individual voter to use their intellect and free will to determine the candidate they believe best. Just remember that no candidate will match the voter's views perfectly. The goal is to select a solid conservative candidate that will appeal to enough voters to be able to win the general election.

Specific general election voting strategies should be determined by the office. A different voting strategy should be used for presidential, senatorial, and congressional elections.

V. Presidential General Elections

The President is the most important office in the nation. The President has tremendous power to shape policy and policy debates. The President can veto any budget, spending bill, or legislation. The president nominates all federal judges to lifetime appointments to the federal courts, including the Supreme Court. The President appoints/hires (or his appointees hire) the employees of the entire Executive Branch (see Appendix 10 for a listing of the hundreds of agencies).

Because of this tremendous power it is always important to have someone holding the office who shares at least some conservative beliefs. It is a priority to NOT let the Presidency go to a big-government Democrat, who will fill the agency with fellow big-government liberals. It is no coincidence that the last two Democrat presidencies saw attempts to nationalize healthcare under control of the federal government. HillaryCare was defeated in the 1990s. ObamaCare became law. Even moderate Republicans do not produce these types of horrendous government programs.

A. Rule: Vote for the most conservative candidate between the Republican and the Democrat, never for a third party.

Federal Elections: Return to the Constitution

Hint: This candidate hasn't been a Democrat for decades. It can be argued that John F. Kennedy was the last conservative Democrat to run for President. That was in 1960. Both Clinton and Obama ran their initial campaigns based on a considerable dose of conservative statements. Once in office they governed like big-government liberals.

1. The Danger of Third Parties

In modern times a third party has never won a presidential election. The third parties in recent history are shells, in that they often only run a presidential candidate. To be considered a true national party, it should first win a few House or Senate races and field candidates in most House districts. There are 435 Congressional races that occur every 2 years. If a third party cannot attract enough votes to win a few Congressional races; why would anyone think that party could ever win a national race for President?

> "Is it a third party we need, or is it a new and revitalized second party, raising a banner of no pale pastels, but bold colors which make it unmistakably clear where we stand on all of the issues troubling the people?"
> - Ronald Reagan. 1975 CPAC Speech.

Reagan went on to show what a revitalized Republican Party could accomplish under his leadership in the 1980s. Today, some misguided conservatives also seek a third party solution to achieve their goals. A vote for a third party often has the opposite effect to what the voter intends, especially for national offices like President. Two examples where a conservative-majority bloc split between the Republican party and a third party with unintended consequence:.

> The Presidential Election of 1912
> 23% of vote - Incumbent President William Howard Taft -
>   Republican (conservative wing)
> 27% of vote - Former President Theodore Roosevelt -
>   Republican (progressive wing)
> **42% of vote** - Woodrow Wilson - Democrat
>   (6% went to a Socialist Party Candidate)

Had there been not been a third party, headed by a former Republican president, the Republicans win the popular vote 50-42, and coast to an easy election victory. Eliminating the Socialist candidate likely would have given Wilson another 6%, but not enough to prevail.

> The Presidential Election of 1992
> 37% of vote - Incumbent President George H. W. Bush - Republican
> **43% of vote** - Bill Clinton - Democrat
> 19% of vote - Ross Perot - Independent

In 1992 many Republicans were deeply dissatisfied with the moderate incumbent President Bush. Many abandoned him and voted for Ross Perot, a more conservative third party candidate. Combined, Perot and Bush captured 56% of the vote. But with the conservative vote divided, Bill Clinton was able to become President despite receiving only 43% support.

In both cases, a large number of Republican voters voted for the candidate they most preferred, but by failing to coalesce around a single candidate they divided their vote and gave the election to the opposing party – the candidate they preferred least.

Thank Ross Perot (in part) for ObamaCare
Think it didn't matter that Bill Clinton won the presidency? Refer back to Chapter 14: Judges and Senators. Bill Clinton placed two diehard liberal activist judges on the Supreme Court, Stephen Breyer and Ruth Bader Ginsburg. These judges routinely voted to increase the power of the federal government beyond what is authorized by the Constitution, taking away religious liberty and economic freedoms. These judges both voted to declare ObamaCare constitutional. Had these judges been appointed by Republican presidents, there is an 80% chance that ObamaCare dies at the Supreme Court. **4 of 5 Republican appointees ruled against ObamaCare – 4 of 4 Democrat appointees ruled for it.**

The Cost of Replacing the Republican Party
It can be very tempting for a conservative to look at the moderate, ineffective Republican leaders of late and think a third party would be a better option. But there is a cost to this strategy. The last time a true third party came to power was when the Republican Party replaced the Whig Party. This culminated in the election of 1860. The Whig Party steadily declined from 1852 through 1860, while the

new Republican Party ascended. In 1860, The Republican Party, running Abraham Lincoln, was able to win the presidency ONLY because the Democrat Party also split into two separate parties: Northern Democrats and Southern Democrats. The election of 1860 was the last election before the Civil War and a time of national turmoil as the country dealt with the moral-political issue of human slavery.

It takes Time to Replace a Party

Percent Popular Vote

Party/Election Year	1852	1856	1860
Democrat	50.8%	45.3%	
Southern Democratic			18.1%
Northern Democratic			29.5%
Whig	43.9%	21.6%	12.6%
Republican		33.1%	39.8%

It took eight years for the Republican party to replace the Whig party. A united Democrat party can be expected to sweep presidential and congressional elections during this span. A high cost to pay for conservatives.

Fast forward to today. What will happen to the country if the Democrat Party controls Congress and the presidency for eight years, as the new conservative party replaces the Republican Party? Conservatives have seen a preview. After 2008 the nation saw Barack Obama, Harry Reid, and Nancy Pelosi, all very liberal Democrats, have national control for two years. Imagine it for eight years as the new conservative party battles and defeats the old Republican Party.

There is a better way. Work within the Republican Party. Vote in Republican primaries. Use third party or protest votes to target *specific* Republican representatives who have non-conservative voting records or are outspoken against other constitutional conservatives / Tea party Republicans. There is no need to blow up the entire party if the "problem" politicians can be removed over time.

Danger of Protest Voting for President: 2012 Election

There were a number of reasons for conservatives to be unhappy with Republican candidate Mitt Romney in 2012. He came from a heavily Democrat state, Massachusetts, so had a moderate political track record. In addition, Romney often made statements at different times in which he took both sides on a number of issues. In sum, Romney was far from a principled constitutional conservative. But none-the-less, Romney ended up winning the primary race and was the Republican nominee.

A perfect example of smart, principled people making unwise "protest vote" decisions is Judge Andrew Napolitano. The author is a fan of the judge. He is a constitutional expert and an originalist. He has hosted his own TV show on Fox Business. Judge Napolitano gave a radio interview on Sean Hannity's show shortly after the 2012 re-election of Barack Obama. In the interview the judge bemoaned the fact that so many parts of the Constitution are ignored by the federal government. He was hopeful that conservative originalist judges might one day reign in the non-constitutional programs the federal government now runs.

The problem is the judge's pre-election actions helped Barack Obama win – and *guaranteed* that an originalist judge would not make it on the Supreme Court for the next four years. But wait, surely Judge Napolitano didn't endorse Obama? No, his actions were indirect in nature. The judge clearly supported two candidates in the 2012 primaries: Ron Paul and Gary Johnson. Ron Paul could never have won the election because of past skeletons (racial comments in his newsletters) in his closet. Gary Johnson, a former Governor of New Mexico, had no such issues and had a better chance of winning. But the libertarian minded voters in the GOP rallied to Paul, leaving Johnson with no support. Johnson was soon out of the race for the GOP presidential nomination. But Johnson, rather than accept defeat, decided to run as a 3rd party protest candidate. He became the Libertarian Party nominee for President.

> Sidebar: Presidential candidates, need to pick a party and stay there. If they want to be a Republican, be a Republican. If they want to be a Libertarian, be a Libertarian. It's sour grapes to run for one party nomination, then abandon the

party if you lose.

This is where Judge Napolitano exercised poor political judgment (in the author's opinion). The judge actively encouraged his followers to not vote for Romney. Both on Facebook and Twitter, the judge repeatedly told his followers that a vote for 3rd party candidate Johnson was not a "wasted" vote. There is no question that Gov. Johnson would have made a much more constitutional-minded president than Romney. But Johnson had no chance to win. Either Obama or Romney was going to be the next president.

Judge Napolitano and his followers won their "protest". A moderate Republican candidate for president lost. But Romney's loss also ended any hope of putting originalist judges on the federal courts for four more years. Instead Barack Obama will put liberal-activist judges on the courts at every opportunity. Those judges will change the Constitution as they see fit with their rulings.

With the current make-up of the national Democrat Party, any Democrat president will nominate liberal-activist judges to all levels of federal courts. Judicial appointments are one of the most important and longest lasting of the presidential powers. The record is clear what Democrats do with this power.

VI. Congressional General Elections
In congressional races, the primary elections are the place to select true constitutional conservative candidates for the Republican team. By the time the November general election arrives the usual choice is between the Democrat and the Republican. In most cases the Republican is the best choice.

The Heritage Action scorecard is one tool that measures how conservative (supporting a smaller limited federal government) members of Congress are. There is a dramatic difference between the parties:
- In the House of Representatives, **Republicans averaged 66%; Democrats 15%;**
- In the Senate, **Republicans averaged 73%; Democrats 6%**
    - The scored voting records cover the 2011-12 Sessions of Congress.

It seldom makes political sense to replace a representative voting conservatively 60-70% of the time with one voting that way only 10-15% of the time. But what if your representative scores in the 50s or even 40s? It may be time to send the representative a message by voting protest or third party in the general election. This could result in the Republican losing the election. However, a single member of Congress has much less power than a president, and usually will not change the direction of the nation. So losing the race is not nearly as damaging to the conservative cause as losing the presidency.

A. Protest/Third Party Voting
Protest voting in the general election should be done rarely and only when the individual candidate earns it. In cases such as:

- The candidate insists on outspokenly promoting an issue counter to one of the defining traits of a constitutional conservative.
- The candidate has often spoken out publicly against tea party or constitutional conservative candidates or worked against their positions/objectives. If the candidate enjoys "sticking it" to conservatives, why should conservatives vote for them?
- The candidate has aggressively worked to pass non-conservative pieces of legislation. For example, amnesty, new spending programs or agencies not constitutionally authorized, or federal gun restrictions. (Often bragging about working with Democrats to do so.)
- The candidate occupies a congressional leadership position but is so ineffective that their strategies and political compromises with Democrats never yield anything of value to conservatives.

In these cases it is possible to *increase* the conservativeness of the party by *subtracting* the candidate. In extreme cases a conservative could even vote for a Democrat candidate if they are seeking to do everything possible in order to "retire" the non-conservative Republican.

Even in these rare cases there are negatives to protest voting.

Especially in the Senate where a liberal will hold the seat for six years until the next election. Voters should use their freedom but use it wisely.

B. Research Sites for Congressional Incumbents:
Nothing is better than following your representative closely and tracking his or her voting record. Most people do not have time to do this. The best sites to help you with this (that the author has found) are following. Note that for most part these sites are focused on reducing spending at the federal level. The author firmly believes that, going forward, politicians will need to be evaluated on whether they vote for and support transferring programs and agencies back to the state level of government.

Heritage Action for America Scorecard.
www.heritageactionscorecard.com/scorecard
The Heritage Action Scorecard measures votes and other legislative activity to show how conservative Members of Congress are. The scorecard measures both Senators and Representatives and can be broken down by state.

Club for Growth Scorecard. www.clubforgrowth.org
Club for Growth publishes this scorecard so our members and the public can monitor the actions and the voting records of members of Congress on economic growth issues. The scorecard measures both Senators and Representatives.

The Madison Project. www.conservativevotingrecords.com
The Madison Performance Index (MPI) combines a Representative's voting record with the conservative rating in the district. It measures how closely a member of Congress is over-performing or under-performing the expected conservative score for his or her district. By understanding voting records within this context, we can better use the electoral map to push for stronger, more principled conservatives, especially in conservative districts. Sortable by state.

> This is a very useful site. A voter can click on their home state and see how their Republican representative's voting record compares to the district. If the district is strongly conservative, but the voting record is moderate, it is likely

time to replace the representative in a primary. Likewise if the district is more liberal, the representative might be excused for voting in a more moderate manner.

For America. www.foramerica.org
For America's mission is to reinvigorate the American people with the principles of American exceptionalism: personal freedom, personal responsibility, a commitment to **Judeo-Christian** values, and a strong national defense. We believe in limited government with Constitutionally-enumerated powers only. We believe that the size of the federal government should be dramatically reduced and that government's regulatory stranglehold on the free enterprise system should be lifted. We believe in freedom.

The website also scores members of Congress voting records and gives the results on a "FreedomMeter". The average party scores again indicate the home of Christians and conservatives is in the Republican party. Average party scores in 2012: Average Republican – House 86%, Senate 88%; Average Democrat – House 10%, Senate 9%. The site also allows the user to see the scores for their representatives and senators.

Numbers USA. www.numbersusa.com
Chapter 18 showed the danger of unlimited immigration (legal and illegal) with respect to the erosion of the nation's founding constitutional principles. They tabulate each action congressional representatives take into a report card.

Christian Coalition Congressional Scorecards.
www.cc.org/voter_education
Site focuses on social issues as well as spending. Scorecards can be downloaded in .pdf format from the website. Scorecards rank Senators and Congressmen based on the votes that were most important to the conservative and family agenda.

Senate Conservatives Fund www.senateconservatives.com
Mission is electing true conservatives to the U.S. Senate. Does not maintain a scorecard, but recommends conservative challengers and allows citizens to donate to those candidates.

Political TV Commercials
A voter needs to ignore the political commercials seen on TV and heard on the radio. They may be true, or they may be total lies. There is no truth in advertising law applicable, because of the free speech protections of the 1st Amendment. So the candidate may be lying, or not. A conservative voter should be especially aware of and ignore two types of ads:

1) A liberal Democrat runs an ad claiming the Republican wants to "slash" funding to a program, thereby "killing" someone. Refer to chapter 19. There have not been any true cuts in federal government spending since Coolidge in the 1920s. The ad is a total lie.
2) A moderate Republican incumbent will run ads in a primary race claiming they are a "true" conservative champion. Sometimes also claiming their opponent supports liberal policies. The ad may be true or not. That is why it is so important to use the scoring websites. They will tell the truth about the candidates record.

Wise voters choose to use their DVR to skip the glut of political TV ads before every election. They often offer little educational value.

VII. Maximize Influence: Organize into Political Groups
Another thing citizens can do to increase their influence at the congressional level is to join a group. For example, a congressman may listen to a single gun owner, but he will definitely listen to the National Rifle Association, which contains millions of gun owners. There are many national groups that could be joined that could speak for you. Examples include the NRA, multiple TEA Party organizations, or the Christian Coalition.

The author would suggest grouping by congressional district. The groups can spread information to cut through the often dubious political TV commercials. The goal of the group should be to network with grassroots and gather as many people as possible under the constitutional conservative political positions expressed earlier in the chapter. A group with 10s or 100s of thousands of members - voters living in their district - will be listened to. More members equals more influence. Leaders of the groups can also lobby the Congressman and Senators.

> Sidebar: Realize that conservatives living in a heavily Democrat district will likely have a Congressman who will not care about the group's minority views. (Think Nancy Pelosi in San Francisco.) Groups in these districts must reach out to Democrats (many who live their lives in a conservative manner) and convince them that their interests are served by joining the group. Visiting churches and reaching out to Christians using the messages contained in this book is an excellent starting point.

The district group can be structured to benefit those seeking a high level of activity and those seeking only to gather reliable information before they vote.

High Activity Group Members
- Organize and administer the group
- Build group membership
- Contact the Congressman and Senators to lobby them on important votes/issues
- Vet potential candidates. National groups cannot do this for every congressional race.
- Pass along detailed reliable information to other group members
- Remind members of primary and special elections.

Low Activity Group Members
- Join the group to maximize your influence
- Utilize the candidate information the group offers
- Vote in every federal election
- Spread the word about the group to friends and colleagues

A few helpful hints for those who decide to organize a group:
- ✗ Communicate via Website, Facebook, Email, Twitter, or whatever medium works best. The internet has created massive abilities for individuals to connect and organize with like-minded people.
- ✗ Don't get "hung-up" on fancy leadership titles. Make room

for all who want to be active.
- ✗ Keep the group focus on national issues, not state or local.
- ✗ Recognize the level of communication group members want. Some will want to be notified of key votes so they can call their representatives on issues. Some will just want an informative email with candidate information before primary and general elections.
- ✗ Focus on sharing information and voting, not fundraising. It can be a huge turn-off to be constantly asked for donations.
- ✗ NEVER give out the group contact list to a campaign or party. Respect member privacy.

In conclusion, for America to keep the constitutional republic that made it a great nation, it will be imperative for concerned citizens to become active, especially at the ballot box. Identifying and voting for those candidates who recognize and will work to reestablish the proper roles of federal and state government is the responsibility of every citizen. Christians need to play as large a role in American politics today as they did at the nation's founding. Pro-secular forces have succeeded in using the federal government and courts to diminish religious freedom. Voting for constitutional-respecting representatives can redeem those rights.

Summary

Most important theme: Human Free Will – God gives it; Government should protect it.

Freedom and liberty. God gives it to humans. Government can protect it or take it away from its citizens. A government can maximize freedom for citizens by using force only to prevent one citizen from interfering with another's freedom.

God through the Bible, tells people how to live their lives. However God gives people free-will whether to heed His advice or not. God does not *force* people to follow His advice. Why should a government then be able to *force* people to live their lives in a certain manner? Government force should only be used to defend the nation from attack, and punish those who do harm to another citizen.

America has succeeded largely because its government protected citizens from harm, while giving them freedom seldom seen in the previous governments in history. If America is truly to remain a great nation, it must return to the biblical and constitutional principles upon which it was founded. Citizens have a role to play. They must learn these principles, be able to discuss them with friends and neighbors, and require their representatives uphold them. This book offers a summary of those principles.

<u>America Faces a Freedom Crisis Caused by Its Government</u>
The current federal government is far from the one designed by the nation's founders. It has become massive with thousands of agencies and departments, many of which issue regulations restricting the freedom of the citizenry. These bureaucrats must be paid for with tax dollars, again reducing the freedom of citizens. In addition, the federal government has made promises in program after program that exceed its already large tax revenue. The borrowing restricts the freedom of future generations of citizens.

It has become obvious to almost everyone that the federal government has become inept and incompetent in trying to administer thousands upon thousands of programs and agencies affecting every aspect of its citizens lives. The nation has assumed debt levels in proportion to the size of the economy, that are higher at any time in the nations history except for immediately after World War II. The nation handled that debt, as the war ended and government spending dramatically decreased. There is NO SIGN of federal government spending decreasing today. Which means the federal debt can be expected to continue to increase. The national debt will eventually severely harm the economy. Just as a family cannot borrow indefinitely to live above its income level, without adverse consequences.

Federal spending and regulation is out of control because the politicians in the government do not follow the constitution's rules. They discard them to gain power or enrich themselves. These politicians gain their power by their ability to control the citizens, and direct their lives.

History shows that heavy-handed national government control leads to poor economic performance or even disaster. Look no further than the old communist Soviet Union, the ultimate in powerful government. The state collapsed onto itself. Instead of "burying" America as Premier Khrushchev claimed, the Soviet State buried itself and disintegrated. Japan was the wonder-nation of the 1980's. Many looked at their economy in awe and the success that government guidance and planning had achieved. Until their crash in 1989. Suddenly the government planners couldn't restart the Japanese economy, despite massive spending. The 1990s, 2000s and even 2010s are referred to as "lost decades" in Japan. China is now the new darling of the large government planning crowd. China hasn't fallen yet, but they will. The seeds are already there. Especially if you look at the disastrous one-child policy created by government planners. This policy was shortsighted even if it worked as planned: limiting each family to one child. The result will be a ratio of twice the number of elderly to working adults – not a very stable societal situation. The unintended side effect of the policy is many parents are *killing* daughters, because if limited to one child, they want a son. So there will be large numbers of men with no hope of finding a wife in China – there won't be enough women. China will be very lucky if these men just immigrate out (further worsening the ratio of elderly-to-working adults), and unlucky if the men decide to take out their plight on society at large (or the government planners who created the mess).

Government planning has not worked in America either when it has been attempted. Since 1900 there have been several Presidents with

Summary

central-planning-leaning policies. Woodrow Wilson (1913-1921) was the first. His policies led to large debt (despite the new income tax) and a slowed economy. The Great Depression was largely the result of Hoover (1929-1933) and FDR (1933-1945) unsuccessfully using government planning to attempt to stimulate the economy following the crash of 1929.

Following the crash of 2008 in America, Obama initiated the largest government spending and effort to control the economy the nation has ever seen. The results are predictable to anyone familiar with the economic history of the nation. Years into the government planning of Obama, the nation is looking at its own lost decade. Note the similarity to Japan's lost decades. Crashes and recessions are part of the economic reality just like booms. The business leaders and workers are better able to restart the economy after a crash-recession than a government worker is.

Government planning never works when it tries to manage something as large and complex as a modern economy. Why would anyone think it would? Government is made up of imperfect human beings. Government workers and politicians are no smarter than the citizens. (Many will claim much less smarter!) Therefore, who can manage a business better – those running the business and working in it, or a government worker who is paid regardless of whether the business succeeds or fails?

Fortunately, America has always had leaders come forward to scale back government when it became large enough to be harmful to the economy. Coolidge (1923-1929) fixed the policies of Wilson. Truman and Eisenhower scaled back government spending after WWII. Reagan undid the economic malaise of the Carter administration. Hopefully, a new president will emerge who restores America's freedom and her economy to robust growth by scaling back the federal government once again.

Rather than relying on big government which traces its history to the monarchs of Europe, Let America's citizens return the country to the ideal upon which she was founded as expressed in her Constitution. Here are some of the key points covered on the Constitution.

The Constitution
In America, the government, and its authority is determined by the Constitution.

- The Constitution formed a federal government offering maximum freedom, both to states, and the citizens of those states.
  - The Constitution is the ultimate law of the nation. The rules the federal government must follow.
  - The Constitution is a contract, not a living document. It contains the process for amending/changing it any time a large majority of the states wish to do so.
    (The process does not allow judges to arbitrarily "change" the Constitution by rulings from the bench.)
- The 1st Amendment to the Constitution protects religious liberty. It forbids the federal government from banning any religious activity of the citizens.
  - This includes public prayer or reading the Bible in public, and banning the teaching of creation in schools.
- The 10th Amendment expressly states any government action not given to the federal government should be placed at the state level.
  - This gives states and their citizens the maximum freedom to choose the level of government they want.

Key Point: The best and most responsive government is located closely to the people. Programs should be located first at city level, then county, then state, then federal.

The 10th Amendment should be the section of the Constitution most quoted by citizens today. It shifts big-government back to the states. **At the state level it will be obvious to all whether government programs and policies truly benefit the citizens.** Whether they they create economic panaceas, slums, or something in between.

To return to the freedoms offered by the Constitution, many programs and agencies must be transferred back to the states using the 10th Amendment as a guide.

Summary

Returning to the Constitution and the Freedoms it Offers
- America has run up a debt of trillions of dollars. Mostly caused by the **federal government running programs and agencies that should have been left to the states** according to the Constitution.
- The federal government has proven itself to be woefully inefficient at administering these programs.
- The solution to the debt crisis is to return the federal government to its constitutionally defined responsibilities. **Areas that are the responsibility of states should be transferred to states.**
    - There are hundreds of federal agencies administering hundreds of programs that should be transferred to the states. There are likely a number of programs that mean little to a majority of citizens that states will allow to disappear.
    - The federal government meddling has distorted the housing market, caused bubbles, and wasted tax dollars. It is a good example of why the federal government needs to be restricted to its constitutional duties which do not include housing. States can administer housing programs for the poor if needed.
    - Healthcare programs are a prime examples of programs that the federal government has mismanaged. Returning these to states can potentially save millions of dollars now wasted by the federal government's inefficiency. Citizens will benefit.
    - Welfare programs have also been grossly mismanaged by the federal government. The proper constitutional place for these programs is at the state or local level.
- Social Security has also been mismanaged by Congress. It cannot easily be returned to the states because of its poor demographics.
    - Citizens should have the option of placing their social security taxes into an account that they own and manage.
    - The federal government can use special bonds to replace the taxes so no revenue is lost for those still in the program.

- Citizens should be free to choose the best option for their retirement. Not forced by the federal government into a one-size fits all system.
  - Millions of people residing in America were not born here, and do not respect the Constitution. **If America does not manage immigration and her borders, the time will likely arrive when a majority no longer want the Constitution and its limits on government power.**
    - This will harm the freedom of every citizen as the freedoms originate in the Constitution.
  - The only way to return America to the Constitution is for a majority of citizens to elect representatives that pledge to follow the its rules.
    - **Federal judges, including Supreme Court justices, are placed onto their positions by our federal representatives. The representatives need to be held responsible for judges' rulings.**

The Constitution is a powerful document, but no document will grant a citizen freedom - only action can. The current federal government in America has many in it that wish to take that freedom away. This includes economic freedom, as well as religious freedom. **In America, citizens can keep their freedoms simply by voting for constitution-minded representatives**. And by educating their fellow citizens to do likewise.

Several changes to the Constitution will greatly assist in returning the appropriate power and responsibility to the states. Two of these changes are simply reversing earlier amendments which federal representatives used to bolster their power. The third limits the time a federal representative may govern over the citizens. The states can ratify these amendments *without* federal involvement or approval.

<u>Amending the Constitution</u>
- Repealing Amendment 16 can restore a great deal of privacy and freedom to citizens. This amendment created the IRS and the federal income tax. Citizens are required to report every financial detail of their lives, and are assumed guilty if

Summary

  the IRS takes them to federal tax court.
  - The federal government is constitutionally authorized to collect money from states to run the government. States are capable of having their own income tax if needed to satisfy their federal obligations.
- Repealing Amendment 17 will allow states a seat inside the federal government. Senators were intended to represent the states' interests, and be a check on federal government power. Direct elections of senators removed this important check.
  - The citizens will still determine senators, but indirectly through their state legislature elections.
- Term Limits. A new amendment on term limits for elected federal representatives and judges should be added.
  - This will do more than anything else to counter a career political class that believe they can perpetually rule over the nation for their entire lives.
- **The Constitution contains a procedure where states may propose and ratify these amendments if they choose to do so – without consulting Congress.**

The founders of America were predominantly Christian, and they strove to form a God-pleasing government. There is a rich Christian heritage in America obvious to any who look for it. However, the same people who want to ignore the Constitution, also tend to want to ignore the religious heritage of America. Big federal government advocates tend to be secular.

America's Christian Heritage
- There is indisputable evidence of America's Christian heritage, including her founding documents which reverently refer to God.
  - The Declaration of Independence
  - The US Constitution, written in the "Year of our Lord" 1787.
    (People submit to their lord, the Founders acknowledged submission to God with this phrase)

- The state constitutions, each of which refer to God
- Numerous national monuments with inscriptions praising God
- Presidents are sworn into office using the Bible
- Many states taught Christian religion in public schools, some used the Bible to teach reading

Given where America was with respect to religion at her founding, and where she is now, where have the churches and Christians been as the government forced societal movement away from God?

> *Matthew 13: 3-8 The Parable of the Sower*
> *Then he told them many things in parables, saying: "A farmer went out to sow his seed. As he was scattering the seed, some fell along the path, and the birds came and ate it up. Some fell on rocky places, where it did not have much soil. It sprang up quickly, because the soil was shallow. But when the sun came up, the plants were scorched, and they withered because they had no root. Other seed fell among thorns, which grew up and choked the plants. Still other seed fell on good soil, where it produced a crop—a hundred, sixty or thirty times what was sown.*

Jesus explains this parable: The seeds are the word of God and the ground is the people hearing the message of the kingdom of heaven. First, this parable illustrates the free will for those hearing the word. Note how some choose to ignore it, while others accept and follow it. Second, the sowers are the churches and Christians in the world. The more good soil that exists, the more effective the sowing will be.

The founders believed in promoting Christianity. Refer to Chapter 11 and the schools that the federal government ran in new territories. God was a key element in the curriculum. In other words, the government helped create good soil for each church to sow seed. Now the government works to create poor rocky soil or sows thorns. How? By opposing God and removing Him from the public at every opportunity.

During the first 150 years or so the federal government was pro-

Summary

church and pro-Christian. However, over the last 80 years, the federal government has become an enemy of the church. Look at the weeds the federal government has sown. It took the American school system, which was predominantly Christian-focused, and made it illegal to have prayers in public, or teach creationism. Meanwhile, it promotes the teaching of god-less evolution as scientific fact. (Chapter 3 demonstrates the theory has not been proven. Science classes should focus more on the scientific method, and less on theories.) The federal government has distorted the US Constitution to the point where it is now even being used to remove Christian crosses from war memorials (Chapter 13). Lately the federal government has become focused on forcing homosexuality and homosexual marriage to be accepted by the population as normal healthy behavior, rather than sinful behavior as the Bible defines it. Referring back to the parable, how can one not conclude that the federal government is actively working against the growing of grain that is God's crop?

While the church's main focus should be preaching the Gospel and saving as many souls as possible, why has it ignored the federal government taking actions hostile to Christianity? American Christians do not cower in fear for their safety as in tyrannical regimes like China or Iran. **Church members are also citizens who have a say and a vote in how the federal government behaves.** Representatives are selected by Americans, most of whom consider themselves Christian. Why shouldn't Christians analyze representative's voting records and support only those who respect their religion? With US Senators, shouldn't the support of originalist judges be a key litmus test? Said another way, why would a Christian vote for a Senator who allows federal government judges to work against God and violate the Constitution with their rulings?

America's citizens, including Christians, get to choose the type of nation we live in. Every two years we elect federal Representatives and Senators; every four years a president. These politicians pass the national laws and place federal judges on courts. While every American has free will to vote for whomever they please, elections have consequences. Some national politicians (most Democrats, some Republicans) have placed liberal-activist judges on the federal courts that ignore the restraints the Constitution places on government power. This has harmed religious liberty.

A significant number of churches/pastors in America today follow the two kingdoms philosophy. They concern themselves only with the eternal spiritual kingdom, and stay away from earthly political kingdoms. This was not the case at other times in American history. A number of the signers of the Declaration of Independence had theological degrees. During the 1850s pastors came out against slavery, a societal evil at the time. In the 1960s large numbers of pastors came out for civil rights for black Americans. The leader being Dr. Martin Luther King Jr., himself a pastor.

If America is to keep her religious heritage alive, and refrain from becoming a secular dominated society, churches will have to play an active role. Shouldn't pastors and churches inform their members when a politician or political party follows policies that violate God's Word or work to ban God from society? The author believes so, although pastors have free will to make their own choices and decisions.

If churches continue to be ambivalent about America's future expect the nation to continue the march toward secularism. Pastors may be prevented from teaching parts of the Bible *by the government*. It has already happened in other western nations, where homosexuality cannot be labeled sinful. The secular federal government forces believe abortion is not the death of a human baby, but a health procedure to be covered by insurance policies – including those of church organizations. Do not be surprised if the tax exempt status is removed for churches as well. Why would a secular government not make churches pay taxes? It was a religious government and nation that created the tax exemption.

The Bible would never have been removed from schools by the federal government, if churches and Christians had understood their constitutional rights and voted only for those representatives who honored those rights.

Finally, back to the Bible. The author firmly hopes every American will adopt its principles into their lives, but recognizes each person's freedom to reject God's Word. Following are key bullet points

Summary

summarizing the Bible as discussed in the book.

<u>The Bible</u>
- The Bible begins with the story of God creating the heavens, the earth, and man.
  - These are supernatural events that cannot be explained by science.
  - Creation can be viewed as a scientific theory, but cannot be proven.
  - An alternative theory of evolution has been proposed by man. It also cannot be proven.
    - Chaos theory, or the second law of thermodynamics, state that in nature things move toward dis-order. This contradicts evolution, which calls for things moving toward order.
- The Bible teaches EVERY human is related by common ancestry. Evolution teaches that some humans may be "less developed" than other humans.
- The biblical narrative shows man using his free will to disobey God's directive. This results in punishment including earthly death. **God as Creator is justified in ruling His creation**.
- The Bible tells of several more instances of God punishing people for massive amounts of sin. The largest being a worldwide flood that killed most living things.
- A focus of the Bible is God's plan to redeem man from sin through a Savior, Jesus Christ.
  - Jesus offers eternal life for those who choose to follow Him.
  - The Bible clearly teaches individuals are judged by God for their behavior, and saved through their faith in Jesus.
- Jesus tells his followers to spread the gospel message through peaceful teaching.
  - Jesus differs from Muhammad, who often spread his religion of Islam by force.
- God's Law has changed over time from a few initial commands in Genesis, to the laws for Israel given to Moses,

to the current law implemented by Jesus and Paul in the New Testament.
- God, as Creator, can change the Law. Man has no standing with God to do so.
- Certain behaviors have always been declared sinful. These include murder, abortion, forced slavery, theft, and homosexual acts.

Additional Biblical Teachings with Respect to the Poor
- The Bible teaches that there will always be poor people. It is pleasing to God when His followers, of their own free will, choose to help those in need. The Bible lists caring for the poor as a responsibility of individuals, family, and the church.
- Jesus emphasized the rich helping the poor in several parables. **None of these parables recommend a government tax the rich or otherwise force them to care for the poor.**
- The Bible consistently states that loving and worshiping God is more important than loving or helping a neighbor.
  - If government force can be used to make people care for the poor, as some Americans advocate, why not use it to make people worship God? Both violate God-given free will.

<u>The Society Established by God</u>
God established the society of ancient Israel to prepare the way for the Messiah to redeem the world. This society can offer insights to a God-pleasing society.
- God was the Leader of the nation
  - Initially there was no king (powerful national government). God filled that role.
- Laws were enforced at the local level through town elders who functioned as judges and courts.
- Property belonged to God, but was controlled by individual citizens.
- Taxes and tithing (giving) were important elements of the society.

Summary

- The overall societal burden was about 25% of income (flat-rate that applied to all)
  - The king collected a 10% national income tax to support the king and pay for national defense. (The people went against God's local-only government and requested a king.)
  - Individuals were expected to give 10% (tithe) to support the priests (church).
  - Individuals were expected to give another 3-4% annually to priests to support the poor.
- There were a number of serious crimes including: blaspheming God, murdering another human; murdering a baby in the womb, committing adultery and homosexual acts.

  (The New Testament still lists these actions as sins, but leaves penalties up to governing authorities.)

Churches should use the Bible to instruct and teach all who will listen about God, lifestyles that please Him, and God's kingdom in heaven. With respect to their faith, Christians need to balance evangelism with respect for non-believers freedom. Trying to force biblical views or faith on non-Christians is a waste of time and violates God given free will. God didn't make humans automatons; humans are free thinkers. Likewise, churches should respect the rights of citizens by never advocating for government to force a citizen to behave in a certain way, as long as the citizen isn't harming another human. For example, a church respecting human free will shouldn't advocate their government *force people* to worship God in church, care for the poor, or outlaw homosexual practices. A society cannot be truly free with a government force being used in such a manner.

Appendix 1: County and State Re-Alignment

Over the last several decades there has been an interesting division in America. It can best be seen by looking at a color-coded map showing the results of a presidential vote by county. There are dots of blue (Democrat) that represent large cities and metropolitan areas which are more liberal. Then there is a surrounding sea of red (Republican) representing rural counties which are more conservative.

Often cities and urban areas, with their higher populations, dominate state governments by electing a majority of the state legislators. There is nothing wrong with this, except there can be conflict when a majority imposes its view on the minority. In this case it is liberal cities imposing their political beliefs and agendas on conservative counties.

What are the issues? A few are:
- Gun control laws that restrict ownership of guns or ammunition.
- Green energy laws that mandate certain percentages of energy be produced from wind power or solar power.
- Restrictions on oil or natural gas exploration and production.
- Laws forcing homosexual marriages to be performed.
- Laws requiring homosexuality be taught in schools.
- High income tax rates (that may be used to pay for programs primarily benefiting residents of cities).
- Restrictions on agricultural activities on farm land.

In America today, there are major cultural and economic differences between liberals and conservatives. A number of conservative counties are growing tired of having liberal city politicians dictate and mandate their government policy. They feel they are being denied their right to self-government.

America has had settled state boundaries for well over a century. But as the power of state government has grown and become more invasive in the lives of citizens, there are some who resent it. Sometimes those resenting the state government intrusion form a

Appendix 1: County and State Re-Alignment

majority vote of a county. What options do residents of the county have if their concerns are being ignored by their state government? They cannot easily secede to form a new state; the Constitution makes that difficult.

> U.S. Constitution. Article IV. Section. 3.
> New States may be admitted by the Congress into this Union; but no new State shall be formed or erected within the Jurisdiction of any other State; nor any State be formed by the Junction of two or more States, or Parts of States, without the Consent of the Legislatures of the States concerned as well as of the Congress.
>
> The Congress shall have Power to dispose of and make all needful Rules and Regulations respecting the Territory or other Property belonging to the United States; and nothing in this Constitution shall be so construed as to Prejudice any Claims of the United States, or of any particular State.

There may be another alternative for these counties. The key wording is: "no new State shall be formed... without the Consent of the Legislatures of the States concerned as well as of the Congress." That language imposes a significant barrier, requiring both states and Congress to agree. This is most likely impossible, as the politicians of states like power and their power is greater with more constituents living under their jurisdiction. However, there has been an interesting observation in a Wall Street Journal law blog post:

> How to Secede from a State Without Really Trying
> There might be an easier way, says Eugene Kontorovich, a law professor at Northwestern University, ... Rather than forming a new "51st" state, how about seceding to join an existing state?
>
> "The Constitution's requirement of home-state and congressional consent only clearly applies to the creation of a 'new state,' " Mr. Kontorovich writes.
>
> Mr. Kontorovich concedes that it's not totally clear what it means to "form" a new state. But he thinks one can make a more compelling case that merely shrinking or enlarging boundaries isn't the same thing as creating a new state.

Appendix 1: County and State Re-Alignment

> "If western Maryland secedes to join West Virginia, would one say West Virginia has been 'formed' by the merger of West Virginia and parts of Maryland? I would say 'West Virginia' has already been formed," he writes.
>
> He says the historical context also jibes with his reading of it. The Founders, he says, inserted that provision to deal with carving up the western territories and the incorporation of the Republic of Vermont.
>
> - JACOB GERSHMAN. WSJ.com. Law Blog. 10-11-13.

In essence, since a new state will not be formed, groups of counties switching states have a much lower hurdle to clear. If a group of counties leaves state A to join state B, all that is required is an affirmative secession vote by the counties and acceptance by state B to let them join the state.

There is no question state A will sue to prevent the counties from leaving its jurisdiction, and the case will go to the Supreme Court, as it should. New law is being made. The author's guess is that if the Court has a majority of originalist justices (Chapter 14), who interpret the Constitution as it was written, the ruling will confirm "a new state is not being formed" and the counties will be allowed to leave.

Shouldn't counties have the right to choose the type of government that they desire? Isn't this consistent with freedom?

As the article postulates, the most natural test case is the counties of western Maryland leaving to join the state of West Virginia. Looking at a map, this re-alignment makes geographical sense as western Maryland is a little spit of land extending between West Virginia and Pennsylvania.

But there are plenty of other cases that could arise. For Example:

- Central California counties could leave to join Nevada or Arizona. California state government is dominated by the liberal coastal cities of Los Angeles and San Francisco.

Appendix 1: County and State Re-Alignment

- Illinois counties could join Indiana. The state government of Illinois is dominated by the cities of Chicago and East St. Louis.
- Conservative counties in northern Colorado could join the states of Wyoming or Nebraska. Colorado state government has become dominated by Denver.
- Western New York counties might seek to escape to Pennsylvania to avoid domination by New York City.

In all likelihood, there will not be mass numbers of counties changing states. But the threat of being able to leave will enable conservative counties to be heard in state governments and bargain for state laws more to their liking. It is healthy when politicians need to compete to attract citizens. The citizens benefit.

What is a logical solution to this problem? Shift more government decisions to local jurisdictions, allowing counties and cities to establish their preferred governmental policies and tax rates.

Appendix 2: Kings of Judah

Four hundred thirty-three years are recorded beginning with King Solomon. Solomon ruled over a united Israel as had King David and King Saul. Israel divided into a North and South Kingdoms upon Solomon's death. Solomon is first in the chronology because he built the Temple and this event is a milestone in biblical history. Zedekiah ruled until Jerusalem and Judea fell to the Babylonians. Scripture records both the reigns of kings in Judah (the Southern Kingdom of Ancient Israel) and the kings of the Northern Kingdom. Only the rulers of Judah in Jerusalem are listed here.

Timeline: Kings of Judah from Solomon to Zedekiah (the Temple to the Fall): 433 Years

Judah Falls.....

2 Kings 24:18 Zedekiah was twenty-one years old when he became king, and he reigned in Jerusalem **11 years.**

2 Kings 24:8 Jehoiachin was eighteen years old when he became king, and he reigned in Jerusalem three months

2 Kings 23:36 Jehoiakim was twenty-five years old when he became king, and he reigned in Jerusalem **11 years.**

2 Kings 23:31 Jehoahaz was twenty-three years old when he became king, and he reigned in Jerusalem three months.

2 Kings 22:1 Josiah was eight years old when he became king, and he reigned in Jerusalem **31 years.**

2 Kings 21:19 Amon was twenty-two years old when he became king, and he reigned in Jerusalem **2 years.**

2 Kings 21:1 Manasseh was twelve years old when he became king, and he reigned in Jerusalem **55 years.**

2 Kings 18:1-2 Hezekiah son of Ahaz king of Judah began to reign. He was twenty-five years old when he became king, and he reigned in Jerusalem **29 years**

2 Kings 16:1-2 Ahaz son of Jotham king of Judah began to reign. Ahaz was twenty years old when he became king, and he reigned in Jerusalem **16 years.**

2 Kings 15:32-33 Jotham son of [Azariah] king of Judah began to reign. He was twenty-five years old when he became king, and he

Appendix 2: Kings of Judah

reigned in Jerusalem **16 years.**

2 Kings 15:1-2 Azariah son of Amaziah king of Judah began to reign. He was sixteen years old when he became king, and he reigned in Jerusalem **52 years.**

2 Kings 14:1-2 Amaziah son of Joash king of Judah began to reign. He was twenty-five years old when he became king, and he reigned in Jerusalem **29 years.**

2 Kings 12:1 Joash became king, and he reigned in Jerusalem **40 years.**

2 Kings 11:1-3 When Athaliah the mother of Ahaziah saw that her son was dead......, for **6 years** *while Athaliah ruled the land.*

2 Kings 8:25-26 Ahaziah son of Jehoram king of Judah began to reign. Ahaziah was twenty-two years old when he became king, and he reigned in Jerusalem **1 year.**

2 Kings 8:16-17 Jehoram son of Jehoshaphat began his reign as king of Judah. He was thirty-two years old when he became king, and he reigned in Jerusalem **8 years.**

1 Kings 22:41-42 Jehoshaphat son of Asa became king of Judah in the fourth year of Ahab king of Israel. Jehoshaphat was thirty-five years old when he became king, and he reigned in Jerusalem **25 years**.

1 Kings 15:9-10 Asa became king of Judah, and he reigned in Jerusalem **41 years.**

1 Kings 15:1-2 Abijah became king of Judah, and he reigned in Jerusalem **3 years**.

1 Kings 14:21 Rehoboam son of Solomon was king in Judah. He was forty-one years old when he became king, and he reigned **17 years** *in Jerusalem.*

1 Kings 11:42 Solomon reigned in Jerusalem over all Israel **40 years**.

..... King Solomon constructed the Temple during his reign.

Appendix 3: Biblical Genealogies from Shem to Abram

The time that passed from Shem to Abraham can be determined by summing the ages of the fathers when the next son in the ancestral line is born. For example, when Shem fathered Arphaxad, 100 years had passed. When Arphaxad fathered Enosh, 35 years had passed; or 135 years had passed in total. So 390 years passed from Shem's birth until Abraham (Abram) was born.

Genesis 11:10–32 **From Shem to Abram (Abraham)**

This is the account of Shem's family line.

*Two years after the flood, when Shem was **100 years** old, he became the father of Arphaxad. And after he became the father of Arphaxad, Shem lived 500 years and had other sons and daughters.*

*When Arphaxad had lived **35 years**, he became the father of Shelah. And after he became the father of Shelah, Arphaxad lived 403 years and had other sons and daughters.*

*When Shelah had lived **30 years**, he became the father of Eber. And after he became the father of Eber, Shelah lived 403 years and had other sons and daughters.*

*When Eber had lived **34 years**, he became the father of Peleg. And after he became the father of Peleg, Eber lived 430 years and had other sons and daughters.*

*When Peleg had lived **30 years**, he became the father of Reu. And after he became the father of Reu, Peleg lived 209 years and had other sons and daughters.*

*When Reu had lived **32 years**, he became the father of Serug. And after he became the father of Serug, Reu lived 207 years and had other sons and daughters.*

*When Serug had lived **30 years**, he became the father of Nahor. And after he became the father of Nahor, Serug lived 200 years and had other sons and daughters.*

*When Nahor had lived **29 years**, he became the father of Terah. And after he became the father of Terah, Nahor lived 119 years and*

Appendix 3: Biblical Genealogies from Shem to Abram

had other sons and daughters.

*After Terah had lived **70 years**, he became the father of **Abram**, Nahor and Haran.*

Abram's Family

This is the account of Terah's family line.

Terah became the father of Abram, Nahor and Haran. And Haran became the father of Lot. While his father Terah was still alive, Haran died in Ur of the Chaldeans, in the land of his birth. Abram and Nahor both married. The name of Abram's wife was Sarai, and the name of Nahor's wife was Milkah; she was the daughter of Haran, the father of both Milkah and Iskah. Now Sarai was childless because she was not able to conceive.

Terah took his son Abram, his grandson Lot son of Haran, and his daughter-in-law Sarai, the wife of his son Abram, and together they set out from Ur of the Chaldeans to go to Canaan. But when they came to Harran, they settled there.

Terah lived 205 years, and he died in Harran.

Appendix 4: Biblical Genealogies from Noah to Adam

This is Noah's family tree going back to Adam. It's very likely that other families of that era also recorded their ancestral histories, just as some families do today. This explains why only one son in each generation is listed. Noah recorded only his father, grandfather, great-grandfather and so on. Scripture records the key genealogical record from Adam to Christ.

The time that passed from Adam to Noah can be determined by summing the ages of the fathers when the next son in the ancestral line is born. For example, when Adam fathered Seth, 130 years had passed. When Seth fathered Enosh, 105 years had passed; or 235 years had passed from Creation. So 1556 years passed from Creation until Shem was born.

Genesis 5 *From Adam to Noah (1556 Years)*

This is the written account of Adam's family line.

When God created mankind, he made them in the likeness of God. He created them male and female and blessed them. And he named them "Mankind" when they were created.

*When Adam had lived **130 years**, he had a son in his own likeness, in his own image; and he named him Seth. After Seth was born, Adam lived 800 years and had other sons and daughters. Altogether, Adam lived a total of 930 years, and then he died.*

*When Seth had lived **105 years**, he became the father of Enosh. After he became the father of Enosh, Seth lived 807 years and had other sons and daughters. Altogether, Seth lived a total of 912 years, and then he died.*

*When Enosh had lived **90 years**, he became the father of Kenan. After he became the father of Kenan, Enosh lived 815 years and had other sons and daughters. Altogether, Enosh lived a total of 905 years, and then he died.*

*When Kenan had lived **70 years**, he became the father of Mahalalel. After he became the father of Mahalalel, Kenan lived 840 years and had other sons and daughters. Altogether, Kenan lived a total of 910 years, and then he died.*

*When Mahalalel had lived **65 years**, he became the father of*

Appendix 4: Biblical Genealogies from Noah to Adam

Jared. After he became the father of Jared, Mahalalel lived 830 years and had other sons and daughters. Altogether, Mahalalel lived a total of 895 years, and then he died.

When Jared had lived **162 years**, he became the father of Enoch. After he became the father of Enoch, Jared lived 800 years and had other sons and daughters. Altogether, Jared lived a total of 962 years, and then he died.

When Enoch had lived **65 years**, he became the father of Methuselah. After he became the father of Methuselah, Enoch walked faithfully with God 300 years and had other sons and daughters. Altogether, Enoch lived a total of 365 years. Enoch walked faithfully with God; then he was no more, because God took him away.

When Methuselah had lived **187 years**, he became the father of Lamech. After he became the father of Lamech, Methuselah lived 782 years and had other sons and daughters. Altogether, Methuselah lived a total of 969 years, and then he died.

When Lamech had lived **182 years**, he had a son. He named him Noah and said, "He will comfort us in the labor and painful toil of our hands caused by the ground the LORD has cursed." After Noah was born, Lamech lived 595 years and had other sons and daughters. Altogether, Lamech lived a total of 777 years, and then he died.

After Noah was **500 years** old, he became the father of Shem, Ham and Japheth.

Appendix 5: Education Spending Per Student by State in 2011

State	Amount	State	Amount
Alabama	$8,813	Montana	$10,639
Alaska	$16,674	Nebraska	$10,825
Arizona	$7,666	Nevada	$8,527
Arkansas	$9,353	New Hampshire	$13,224
California	$9,139	New Jersey	$15,968
Colorado	$8,724	New Mexico	$9,070
Connecticut	$15,600	New York	$19,076
Delaware	$12,685	North Carolina	$8,312
District of Columbia	$18,475	North Dakota	$11,420
Florida	$8,887	Ohio	$11,223
Georgia	$9,253	Oklahoma	$7,587
Hawaii	$12,004	Oregon	$9,682
Idaho	$6,824	Pennsylvania	$13,467
Illinois	$10,774	Rhode Island	$13,815
Indiana	$9,370	South Carolina	$8,986
Iowa	$9,807	South Dakota	$8,805
Kansas	$9,498	Tennessee	$8,242
Kentucky	$9,309	Texas	$8,671
Louisiana	$10,723	Utah	$6,212
Maine	$11,438	Vermont	$15,925
Maryland	$13,871	Virginia	$10,364
Massachusetts	$13,941	Washington	$9,483
Michigan	$10,823	West Virginia	$11,846
Minnesota	$10,712	Wisconsin	$11,774
Mississippi	$7,928	Wyoming	$15,849
Missouri	$9,410		

- www.governing.com

Appendix 6: Senate Vote to Confirm Justice Kagan to Supreme Court

For Kagan		**Against Kagan**	
Akaka, Daniel [D]	HI	Alexander, Lamar [R]	TN
Baucus, Max [D]	MT	Barrasso, John [R]	WY
Bayh, Evan [D]	IN	Bennett, Robert [R]	UT
Begich, Mark [D]	AK	Bond, Christopher [R]	MO
Bennet, Michael [D]	CO	Brown, Scott [R]	MA
Bingaman, Jeff [D]	NM	Brownback, Samuel [R]	KS
Boxer, Barbara [D]	CA	Bunning, Jim [R]	KY
Brown, Sherrod [D]	OH	Burr, Richard [R]	NC
Burris, Roland [D]	IL	Chambliss, Saxby [R]	GA
Cantwell, Maria [D]	WA	Coburn, Thomas [R]	OK
Cardin, Benjamin [D]	MD	Cochran, Thad [R]	MS
Carper, Thomas [D]	DE	Corker, Bob [R]	TN
Casey, Robert [D]	PA	Cornyn, John [R]	TX
Conrad, Kent [D]	ND	Crapo, Michael [R]	ID
Dodd, Christopher [D]	CT	DeMint, Jim [R]	SC
Dorgan, Byron [D]	ND	Ensign, John [R]	NV
Durbin, Richard [D]	IL	Enzi, Michael [R]	WY
Feingold, Russell [D]	WI	Grassley, Charles [R]	IA
Feinstein, Dianne [D]	CA	Hatch, Orrin [R]	UT
Franken, Al [D]	MN	Hutchison, Kay [R]	TX
Gillibrand, Kirsten [D]	NY	Inhofe, James [R]	OK
Goodwin, Carte [D]	WV	Isakson, John [R]	GA
Hagan, Kay [D]	NC	Johanns, Mike [R]	NE
Harkin, Thomas [D]	IA	Kyl, Jon [R]	AZ
Inouye, Daniel [D]	HI	LeMieux, George [R]	FL
Johnson, Tim [D]	SD	McCain, John [R]	AZ
Kaufman, Edward [D]	DE	McConnell, Mitch [R]	KY
Kerry, John [D]	MA	Murkowski, Lisa [R]	AK
Klobuchar, Amy [D]	MN	Risch, James [R]	ID
Kohl, Herbert [D]	WI	Roberts, Pat [R]	KS
Landrieu, Mary [D]	LA	Sessions, Jefferson [R]	AL
Lautenberg, Frank [D]	NJ	Shelby, Richard [R]	AL
Leahy, Patrick [D]	VT	Thune, John [R]	SD
Levin, Carl [D]	MI	Vitter, David [R]	LA
Lincoln, Blanche [D]	AR	Voinovich, George [R]	OH

Appendix 6: Senate Vote to Confirm Justice Kagan to Supreme Court

For Kagan

McCaskill, Claire [D]	MO
Menendez, Robert [D]	NJ
Merkley, Jeff [D]	OR
Mikulski, Barbara [D]	MD
Murray, Patty [D]	WA
Nelson, Bill [D]	FL
Pryor, Mark [D]	AR
Reed, John [D]	RI
Reid, Harry [D]	NV
Rockefeller, John [D]	WV
Schumer, Charles [D]	NY
Shaheen, Jeanne [D]	NH
Specter, Arlen [D]	PA
Stabenow, Debbie [D]	MI
Tester, Jon [D]	MT
Udall, Mark [D]	CO
Udall, Tom [D]	NM
Warner, Mark [D]	VA
Webb, Jim [D]	VA
Whitehouse, Sheldon [D]	RI
Wyden, Ron [D]	OR
Lieberman, Joseph [I]	CT
Sanders, Bernard [I]	VT
Collins, Susan [R]	ME
Snowe, Olympia [R]	ME
Lugar, Richard [R]	IN
Gregg, Judd [R]	NH
Graham, Lindsey [R]	SC

Against Kagan

Wicker, Roger [R]	MS
Nelson, Ben [D]	NE

Appendix 7: US Census Data on Immigrants

During the last 50 years, the foreign-born population of the U.S. has undergone dramatic changes in size, origins, and geographic distributions. In **1960**, this population represented about 1 in 20 residents, **mostly from countries in Europe** who settled in the Northeast and Midwest. Today's foreign-born population makes up about 1 in 8 residents, **mostly immigrants from Latin America and Asia** who have settled in the West and South. The decennial census and the annual American Community Survey allow us to trace the changes in the foreign-born population over time in this infographic.

Long-term trends

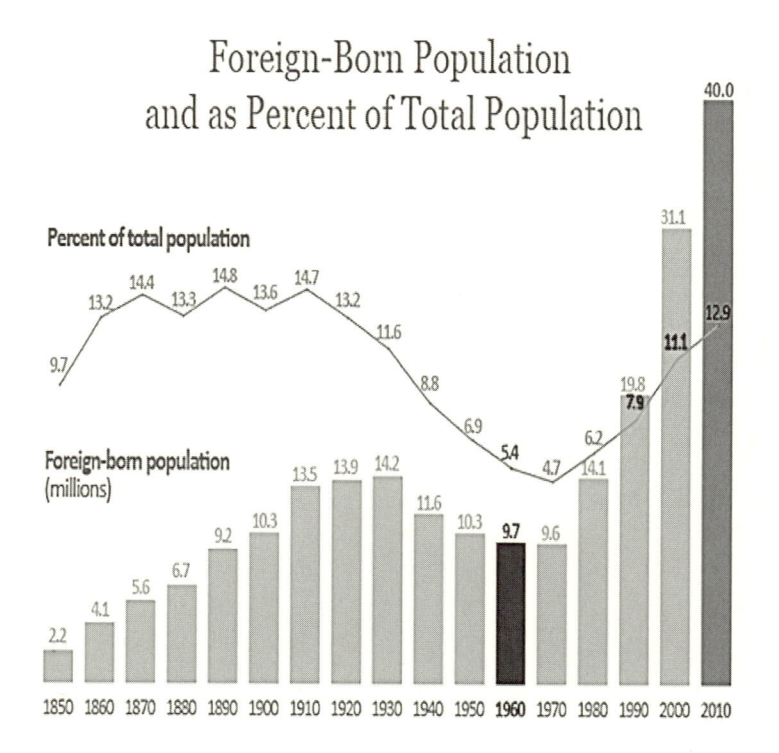

Foreign-Born Population and as Percent of Total Population

Percent of total population: 9.7 (1850), 13.2 (1860), 14.4 (1870), 13.3 (1880), 14.8 (1890), 13.6 (1900), 14.7 (1910), 13.2 (1920), 11.6 (1930), 8.8 (1940), 6.9 (1950), 5.4 (1960), 4.7 (1970), 6.2 (1980), 7.9 (1990), 11.1 (2000), 12.9 (2010)

Foreign-born population (millions): 2.2 (1850), 4.1 (1860), 5.6 (1870), 6.7 (1880), 9.2 (1890), 10.3 (1900), 13.5 (1910), 13.9 (1920), 14.2 (1930), 11.6 (1940), 10.3 (1950), 9.7 (1960), 9.6 (1970), 14.1 (1980), 19.8 (1990), 31.1 (2000), 40.0 (2010)

Source: U.S. Census Bureau, 1850–2000 Decennial Census; 2010 American Community Survey.

Appendix 7: US Census Data on Immigrants

Where they come from

Change in Foreign-Born Population by Region of Birth

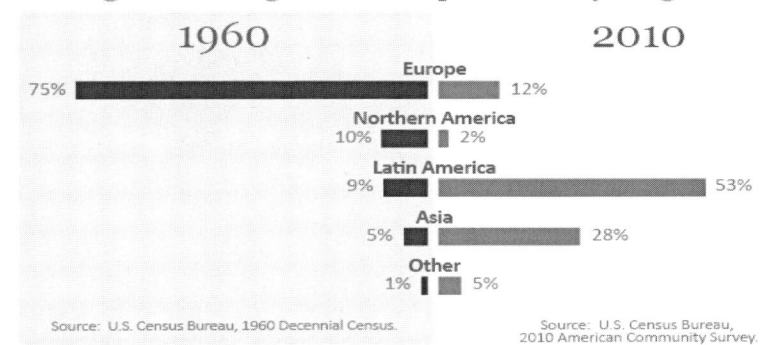

1960 | **2010**

- Europe: 75% | 12%
- Northern America: 10% | 2%
- Latin America: 9% | 53%
- Asia: 5% | 28%
- Other: 1% | 5%

Source: U.S. Census Bureau, 1960 Decennial Census.
Source: U.S. Census Bureau, 2010 American Community Survey.

Top 10 Countries of Birth

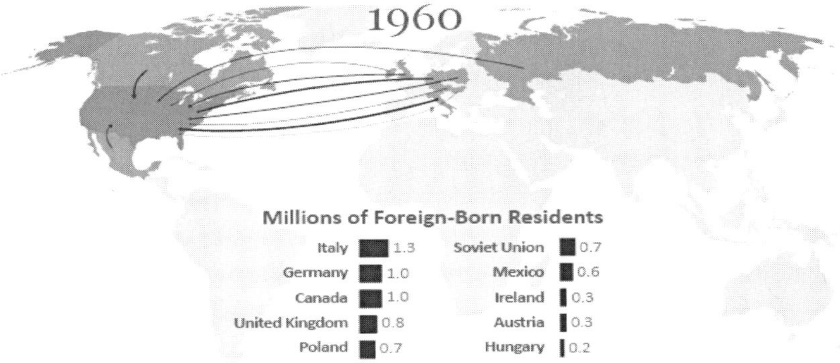

1960

Millions of Foreign-Born Residents

Italy	1.3	Soviet Union	0.7
Germany	1.0	Mexico	0.6
Canada	1.0	Ireland	0.3
United Kingdom	0.8	Austria	0.3
Poland	0.7	Hungary	0.2

Source: U.S. Census Bureau, 1960 Decennial Census.

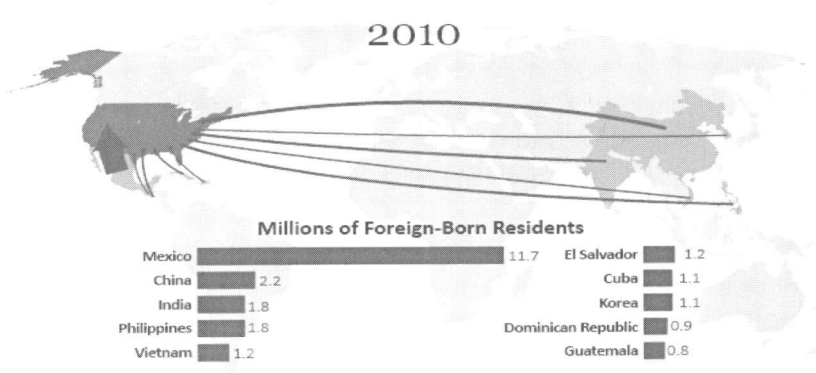

2010

Millions of Foreign-Born Residents

Mexico	11.7	El Salvador	1.2
China	2.2	Cuba	1.1
India	1.8	Korea	1.1
Philippines	1.8	Dominican Republic	0.9
Vietnam	1.2	Guatemala	0.8

Source: U.S. Census Bureau, 2010 American Community Survey.

Appendix 8: Immigration Made California a Big Government Democrat Party State

Destroying the GOP: How Immigration Turned California Blue
Republicans won California in every presidential election of the '50s, '60s, '70s, and '80s, except for the '64 Goldwater loss. Now California has a third-world economy with one-party dominance.

The pro-amnesty Republicans should think clearly about what happened to the Golden State.

Today, California's GOP has withered to a small fraction of the state's registered voters. Since the state began tracking party affiliation in 1922, Republicans have never had such a low share. Republicans are now 29 percent of voters; Democrats are 44 percent.

But California did not go quietly. In 1994, California voters, and governor Pete Wilson, tried to eliminate the incentives for illegal immigration with Proposition 187. Prop 187 sought to prevent people from receiving social services or public education until they were verified as U.S. citizens. Law enforcement agencies were to report illegals to state and federal authorities.

The proposition passed by a stunning 59%-to-41% margin in 1994. However, by 1999, Prop 187 was invalidated by court rulings pushed by liberal organizations. California is now known as Mexifornia.

How could the state that passed Prop 187 and had been a stalwart for Republican presidents have fallen so far?

California was a red state, but as the Hispanic population increased, it became a blue state, and it has remained so since. There is no sign of going back; the mainstream press gloats that California is "a one-party state."

As the graphs [show], demography was electoral destiny for California.... The state's Electoral College votes went blue in tandem with the rising Hispanic population.

Appendix 8: Immigration Made California a Big Government Democrat Party State

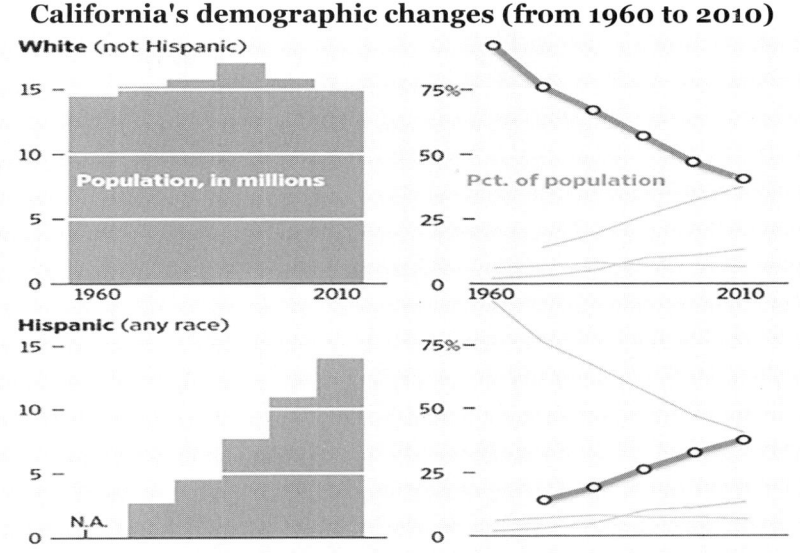

California's demographic changes (from 1960 to 2010)

Note that in 2010 hispanics now equal whites in the population.

The state Republicans died out not because of inevitable demographic changes; the outcome could have been different. Nor did they die out because they were not "sensitive" enough to Hispanics, as former national GOP Chairman Marc Racicot said with reference to Prop 187.

California was faced with a choice: stop the influx of welfare-state constituents, or be washed away by the growing welfare state. The problems stemming from illegal immigration were so great that even the liberal Urban Institute acknowledged, in a 1994 report, that one in five inmates in California state prisons were deportable aliens. Bill Clinton, in a 1994 speech in California, told his audience, "[I]t is not wrong for you to want to reduce illegal immigration."

Prop 187 was an attempt to address a set of challenges tied to illegal immigration. By 2002, the state was "struggling to balance a budget saddled with costs for illegal immigrants' education and health care," as the Wall Street Journal reported. Wilson and the 59% of voters who supported Prop 187 were vindicated on the merits. However, given the gradually changing population, the statists sidestepped the merits and won through superior numbers.

Appendix 8: Immigration Made California a Big Government Democrat Party State

Now, a decade later, there is no struggle to balance the state's budget. There is only a Democratic supermajority, more spending, more debt, and what the Associated Press calls a Hispanic population that increasingly lives in "racial isolation." All the while, this population is "[a]ssimilating into the welfare system," according to Harvard economist George Borjas.

California's Shift to a Third-World Economy
There is a common notion that immigrants come to America to escape their home governments. Given that immigrants often maintain significant aspects of the culture from their country of origin, it would also make sense if many immigrants actually maintained the style of governance found in their country of origin.

State control has swept over California, together with sustained high levels of immigration from Latin America. The resulting crisis is summed up by Stanford professors Michael Boskin and John Cogan:

> From the mid-1980s to 2005, California's population grew by 10 million, while Medicaid recipients soared by seven million; tax filers paying income taxes rose by just 150,000; and the prison population swelled by 115,000.

The Golden State has 12% of the country's population and one third of its welfare recipients. California's middle class is decimated. The growth of government services and regulation, together with downward pressure on wages, had the predictable outcome.

As the chart shows, there was not a sudden population shift in California. The number of whites, who provided the bulk of the GOP vote, didn't drop enough to explain the political outcome. Instead, there was a steady and significant increase in the legal and illegal immigrant population over several decades, a population which no amount of GOP outreach or sensitivity was going to turn into Burkeans.

That is how the Republican Party was destroyed in California, how the state plunged towards a third-world economic model, and why overall immigration needs to be reconsidered.
- www.americanthinker.com. John Bennett. February 25, 2014.

Appendix 9: State Gasoline Taxes

State Gasoline Tax Rates

as of January 1, 2011
Does not include the federal tax on gasoline of 18.4 cents per gallon.

State	Total State Gas Tax (cents / gal.)	Rank	State	Total State Gas Tax (cents / gal.)	Rank
Ala.	20.9	36	Nebr.	27.3	20
Alaska	8	50	Nev.	33.1	10
Ariz.	19	42	N.H.	19.6	41
Ark.	21.8	34	N.J.	14.5	48
Calif.	47.7	1	N.M.	18.8	43
Colo.	22	32	N.Y.	47.3	2
Conn.	45.2	4	N.C.	32.8	13
Del.	23	29	N.D.	23	29
Fla.	34.4	9	Ohio	28	18
Ga.	20.8	37	Okla.	17	46
Hawaii	45.8	3	Ore.	31	16
Idaho	25	22	Pa.	32.3	14
Ill.	42.8	5	R.I.	33	11
Ind.	37.2	8	S.C.	16.8	47
Iowa	22	32	S.D.	24	26
Kans.	25	22	Tenn.	21.4	35
Ky.	22.5	31	Tex.	20	38
La.	20	38	Utah	24.5	25
Maine	31	16	Vt.	25	22
Md.	23.5	27	Va.	19.7	40
Mass.	23.5	27	Wash.	37.5	7
Mich.	37.7	6	W.Va.	32.2	15
Minn.	27.2	21	Wis.	32.9	12
Miss.	18.8	43	Wyo.	14	49
Mo.	17.3	45	DC	23.5	-
Mont.	27.8	19	Average	26.65	-

Source: American Petroleum Institute and The Tax Foundation

Appendix 10: US Government Agencies

Taken from **USA.gov** in 2011.

Cabinet Departments
Each of the **15 executive cabinet departments** administers programs that oversee an aspect of life in the United States. The highest departmental official of each Cabinet department, called the Secretary, is a member of the President's Cabinet.

Defense: Manages the military forces that protect our country and its interests, including the Departments of the Army, Navy, and Air Force and a number of smaller agencies. The civilian workforce employed by the Department of Defense performs various support activities, such as payroll and public relations.

Veterans Affairs: Administers programs to aid U.S. veterans and their families, runs the veterans' hospital system, and operates our national cemeteries.

Homeland Security: Works to prevent terrorist attacks within the United States, reduce vulnerability to terrorism, and minimize the damage from potential attacks and natural disasters. It also administers the country's immigration policies and oversees the Coast Guard.

Treasury: Regulates banks and other financial institutions, administers the public debt, prints currency, and collects Federal income taxes.

Justice: Works with State and local governments and other agencies to prevent and control crime and ensure public safety against threats, both domestic and foreign. It also enforces Federal laws, prosecutes cases in Federal courts, and runs Federal prisons.

Agriculture: Promotes U.S. agriculture domestically and internationally, manages forests, researches new ways to grow crops and conserve natural resources, ensures safe meat and poultry products, and leads the Federal anti-hunger programs, such as the Supplemental Nutrition Assistance Program (formerly known as the Food Stamp program) and the National School Lunch Program.

Health and Human Services: Performs health and social science research, assures the safety of drugs and foods other than meat and poultry, and administers Medicare, Medicaid, and numerous other social service programs.

Interior: Manages Federal lands, including the national parks, runs hydroelectric power systems, and promotes conservation of natural resources.

Transportation: Sets national transportation policy, plans and funds the construction of highways and mass transit systems, and regulates railroad, aviation, and maritime operations.

Commerce: Forecasts the weather, charts the oceans, regulates patents and trademarks, conducts the census, compiles economic statistics, and promotes U.S. economic growth by encouraging international trade.

Energy: Coordinates the national use and provision of energy, oversees the

Appendix 10: US Government Agencies

production and disposal of nuclear weapons, and plans for future energy needs.

Labor: Enforces laws guaranteeing fair pay, workplace safety, and equal job opportunity, administers unemployment insurance (UI) to State UI agencies, regulates pension funds; and collects and analyzes economic data.

State: Oversees the Nation's embassies and consulates, issues passports, monitors U.S. interests abroad, and represents the United States before international organizations.

Housing and Urban Development: Funds public housing projects, enforces equal housing laws, and insures and finances mortgages.

Education: Monitors and distributes financial aid to schools and students, collects and disseminates data on schools and other education matters, and prohibits discrimination in education.

Key Federal Agencies within Cabinets
Department of Agriculture (USDA) – 24 Key Agencies
    Agricultural Marketing Service
    Agricultural Research Service
    Animal and Plant Health Inspection Service
    Center for Nutrition Policy and Promotion
    Commodity Credit Corporation
    Economic Research Service
    Farm Service Agency
    Food and Nutrition Service
    Food Safety and Inspection Service
    Foreign Agricultural Service
    Forest Service
    Graduate School
    Grain Inspection, Packers and Stockyards Administration
    Marketing and Regulatory Programs
    National Agricultural Statistics Service
    National Institute of Food and Agriculture
    Natural Resources and Environment
    Natural Resources Conservation Service
    Research, Education and Economics
    Risk Management Agency
    Rural Business and Cooperative Programs
    Rural Development
    Rural Housing Service
    Rural Utilities Service

Department of Commerce (DOC) - 23 Key Agencies
    Bureau of Economic Analysis (BEA)

Appendix 10: US Government Agencies

Bureau of Industry and Security
Bureau of the Census
Economic Development Administration
Economics & Statistics Administration
Export Enforcement
Import Administration
International Trade Administration (ITA)
Manufacturing and Services
Marine and Aviation Operations
Market Access and Compliance
Minority Business Development Agency
National Environmental Satellite, Data, and Information Service
National Institute of Standards & Technology (NIST)
National Marine Fisheries Service
National Oceanic & Atmospheric Administration (NOAA)
National Ocean Service
National Technical Information Service
National Telecommunications & Information Administration
National Weather Service (NOAA)
Oceanic and Atmospheric Research
Patent & Trademark Office
Trade Promotion and U.S. and Foreign Commercial Service

Department of Defense (DOD)– 36 Key Agencies
Office of the Secretary of Defense (OSD)
Air Force
Army
Marines
Navy
Joint Chiefs of Staff
Inspector General
Defense Agencies:
    Defense Advanced Research Projects Agency (DARPA)
    Defense Commissary Agency
    Defense Contract Audit Agency (DCAA)
    Defense Contract Management Agency
    Defense Finance and Accounting Service (DFAS)
    Defense Information Systems Agency (DISA)
    Defense Intelligence Agency (DIA)
    Defense Legal Services Agency
    Defense Logistics Agency (DLA)
    Defense Security Cooperation Agency (DSCA)
    Defense Security Service (DSS)
    Defense Threat Reduction Agency (DTRA)

Appendix 10: US Government Agencies

        Missile Defense Agency (MDA)
        National Geospatial-Intelligence Agency
        National Security Agency (NSA)
        Pentagon Force Protection Agency
    Defense Technical Information Center
    Economic Adjustment Office
    Education
    Human Resources
    Prisoner of War/Missing Personnel Office
    TRICARE Management
    Washington Headquarters Services
    Joint Service Schools:
        Defense Acquisition University
        Defense Language Institute Foreign Language Center
        Defense Resources Management Institute
        Joint Military Intelligence College
        National Defense University
        Uniformed Services University of the Health Sciences

Department of Education (ED) – 12 Key Agencies
    Federal Student Aid (FSA)
    Institute of Education Sciences (IES)
    National Assessment Governing Board (NAGB)
    National Center for Education Statistics (NCES)
    Office for Civil Rights (OCR)
    Office of Elementary and Secondary Education (OESE)
    Office of English Language Acquisition (OELA)
    Office of Innovation and Improvement (OII)
    Office of Postsecondary Education (OPE)
    Office of Safe and Drug-Free Schools (OSDFS)
    Office of Special Education and Rehabilitative Services (OSERS)
    Office of Vocational and Adult Education (OVAE)

Department of Energy (DOE) – 16 Key Agencies
    Bonneville Power Administration
    Civilian Radioactive Waste Management
    Energy Efficiency and Renewable Energy
    Energy Information
    Environmental Management
    Federal Energy Regulatory Commission
    Fossil Energy
    National Laboratories
    National Nuclear Security Administration
    Nuclear Energy, Science and Technology

Appendix 10: US Government Agencies

Office of Administration
Office of Science
Office of Scientific and Technical Information
Southeastern Power Administration
Southwestern Power Administration
Western Area Power Administration

Department of Health and Human Services (HHS) – 15 Key Agencies
Administration for Children and Families (ACF)
Administration for Native Americans
Administration on Aging (AoA)
Administration on Developmental Disabilities
Agency for Healthcare Research and Quality (AHRQ)
Agency for Toxic Substances and Disease Registry
Centers for Disease Control and Prevention (CDC)
Centers for Medicare & Medicaid Services (formerly the Health Care Financing Administration)
Food and Drug Administration (FDA)
Health Resources and Services Administration (HRSA)
Indian Health Service (IHS)
National Institutes of Health (NIH)
Office of Refugee Resettlement
Program Support Center
Substance Abuse and Mental Health Services Administration (SAMHSA)

Department of Homeland Security (DHS) – 15 Key Agencies
Computer Emergency Readiness Team (US CERT)
Domestic Nuclear Detection Office
Federal Emergency Management Agency (FEMA)
Federal Law Enforcement Training Center
Management Under Secretary
Operations Coordination Office
Policy Office
Preparedness Directorate
Science and Technology Directorate
Transportation Security Administration
U.S. Citizenship and Immigration Services
U.S. Coast Guard
U.S. Customs and Border Protection
U.S. Immigration and Customs Enforcement
U.S. Secret Service

Department of Housing and Urban Development (HUD) – 9 Key Agencies
Community Planning and Development

Appendix 10: US Government Agencies

   Government National Mortgage Association (Ginnie Mae)
   Multifamily Housing
   Office of Fair Housing and Equal Opportunity
   Office of Federal Housing Enterprise Oversight
   Office of Healthy Homes and Lead Hazard Control
   Office of Housing
   Office of Public and Indian Housing
   Policy Development and Research

Department of Justice (DOJ) – 15 Key Agencies
   Alcohol, Tobacco, Firearms, and Explosives
   Community Oriented Policing Services (COPS)
   Drug Enforcement Administration (DEA)
   Executive Office for Immigration Review
   Executive Office for U.S. Attorneys
   Federal Bureau of Investigation (FBI)
   Federal Bureau of Prisons
   Foreign Claims Settlement Commission
   National Drug Intelligence Center
   Office of Justice Programs (Juvenile Justice, Victims of Crime, Violence Against Women and more)
   Office of the Pardon Attorney
   U.S. Marshals Service
   U.S. National Central Bureau of Interpol
   U.S. Parole Commission
   U.S. Trustee Program

Department of Labor (DOL) – 9 Key Agencies
   Bureau of International Labor Affairs
   Bureau of Labor Statistics (BLS)
   Employee Benefits Security Administration (formerly Pension and Welfare Benefits Administration)
   Employment and Training Administration (ETA)
   Mine Safety and Health Administration
   Occupational Safety & Health Administration (OSHA)
   Office of Disability Employment Policy
   Veterans' Employment and Training Service (VETS)
   Women's Bureau

Department of State (DOS) – 7 Key Agencies
   Arms Control and International Security
   Economic, Business, and Agricultural Affairs
   Global Affairs
   Management

Appendix 10: US Government Agencies

   Political Affairs
   Public Diplomacy and Public Affairs
   U.S. Mission to the United Nations

Department of the Interior (DOI) – 9 Key Agencies
   Bureau of Indian Affairs (BIA)
   Bureau of Land Management (BLM)
   Bureau of Reclamation
   Fish & Wildlife Service
   Geological Survey (USGS)
   Mineral Management Service
   National Interagency Fire Center
   National Park Service
   Office of Surface Mining, Reclamation & Enforcement

Department of the Treasury – 9 Key Agencies
   Alcohol and Tobacco Tax and Trade Bureau
   Bureau of Consumer Financial Protection
   Bureau of Engraving and Printing
   Bureau of Public Debt
   Financial Management Service (FMS)
   Internal Revenue Service (IRS)
   Office of the Comptroller of the Currency
   Office of Thrift Supervision (OTS)
   U.S. Mint

Department of Transportation (DOT) – 12 Key Agencies
   Bureau of Transportation Statistics
   Federal Aviation Administration (FAA)
   Federal Highway Administration
   Federal Motor Carrier Safety Administration
   Federal Railroad Administration
   Federal Transit Administration
   Maritime Administration
   National Highway Traffic Safety Administration
   Pipeline and Hazardous Materials Safety Administration
   Research and Innovative Technology Administration
   Saint Lawrence Seaway Development Corporation
   Surface Transportation Board

Department of Veterans Affairs (VA) – 3 Key Agencies
   National Cemetery Administration
   Veterans Benefits Administration
   Veterans Health Administration

Appendix 10: US Government Agencies

Independent Agencies and Government Corporations – 68 Agencies

25 Agencies to Keep in the Federal Government
1. Central Intelligence Agency (CIA)
2. Court Services and Offender Supervision Agency for the District of Columbia
3. Export-Import Bank of the United States
4. Federal Communications Commission (FCC)
5. Federal Deposit Insurance Corporation (FDIC)
6. Federal Election Commission (FEC)
7. Federal Reserve System
8. Federal Retirement Thrift Investment Board
9. Federal Trade Commission (FTC)
10. General Services Administration (GSA)
11. Institute of Museum and Library Services
12. International Broadcasting Bureau (IBB)
13. National Credit Union Administration (NCUA)
14. National Aeronautics and Space Administration (NASA)
15. National Archives and Records Administration (NARA)
16. National Capital Planning Commission
17. Pension Benefit Guaranty Corporation
18. Postal Regulatory Commission
19. Securities and Exchange Commission (SEC)
20. Selective Service System
21. Social Security Administration (SSA)
22. U.S. Trade and Development Agency
23. United States Agency for International Development
24. United States International Trade Commission
25. United States Postal Service (USPS)

Those recommended for elimination, reassignment, or transferral
(authors comments in italics)
Administrative Conference of the United States *(What does it do?)*
African Development Foundation *(Why is the US developing Africa?)*
AMTRAK *(Why is the government in the passenger railroad business?)*
Commission on Civil Rights *(Can't Congress pass the necessary laws?)*
Commodity Futures Trading Commission *(Shouldn't this be under the SEC?)*
Consumer Product Safety Commission *(Shouldn't this be done at the state level?)*
Corporation for National and Community Service *(Shouldn't this be a charity?)*
Defense Nuclear Facilities Safety Board *(Put this under DHM)*
Election Assistance Commission *(States should manage their own elections)*
Environmental Protection Agency (EPA) *(Shouldn't the states regulate their*

Appendix 10: US Government Agencies

environments?)

Equal Employment Opportunity Commission (EEOC) *(Where is the authority for this to apply to private business?)*

Farm Credit Administration *(Can't private companies provide credit for farms?)*

Federal Energy Regulatory Commission *(Shouldn't this be under DHM?)*

Federal Housing Finance Board *(Can't private companies finance homes?)*

Federal Labor Relations Authority *(Why is government involved in labor relations?)*

Federal Maritime Commission *(Isn't this redundant with DHM duties?)*

Federal Mediation and Conciliation Service *(Aren't there private industry mediators?)*

Federal Mine Safety and Health Review Commission *(Can't states regulate their mines?)*

Inter-American Foundation *(What does this do?)*

Millennium Challenge Corporation *(What does this do and is it needed?)*

National Council on Disability *(Why can't states or charities do this?)*

National Endowment for the Arts *(Why is the government funding art?)*

National Endowment for the Humanities *(Why is the government funding humanities?)*

National Labor Relations Board (NLRB) *(Where in the Constitution is the federal government given power to intervene in business-labor relations?)*

National Mediation Board *(Can't this be privatized?)*

National Science Foundation (NSF) *(Shouldn't universities or companies be doing science research?)*

National Transportation Safety Board *(Already under DHM)*

Nuclear Regulatory Commission (NRC) *(Place under DHM)*

Occupational Safety and Health Review Commission *(Isn't this better left to the states?)*

(Shouldn't these next 4 be combined into HR Departments at the various agencies?)

Merit Systems Protection Board

Office of Compliance

Office of Government Ethics

Office of Personnel Management

Office of Special Counsel *(Isn't this better handled by the DoJ and Congress?)*

Office of the Director of National Intelligence *(Shouldn't this be under the CIA or NSA?)*

Appendix 10: US Government Agencies

Office of the National Counterintelligence Executive *(Shouldn't this be under the CIA or NSA?)*

Overseas Private Investment Corporation *(Isn't this corporate welfare?)*

Panama Canal Commission *(Didn't the US sell the Canal?)*

Peace Corps *(Shouldn't this be a charity?)*

Railroad Retirement Board *(Why do railroad workers have their own retirement board?)*

Small Business Administration (SBA) *(Small business can do fine without government help)*

Tennessee Valley Authority *(Why is the government running an electric utility company?)*

Appendix 11: Defunding Agencies and Government Shutdowns

Often when there are disputes on agency funding levels between the branches of government a short government shutdown can occur. This happened when President Reagan and Speaker Tip O'Neill disagreed in the 1980's, and again when President Clinton and Speaker Gingrich disagreed in the 1990's.

This strategy could be be used to return the federal government to its constitutional limitations by defunding agencies or programs not authorized under the 10th Amendment. As discussed in Chapter 20, defunding alone equals elimination which is easily demonized. Defunding is best used in conjunction with 'transferring to the states where the program belongs constitutionally'.

House Speaker John Boehner half-heartedly tried defunding in 2013 with ObamaCare. The Democrats in the Senate responded by not passing any spending bills, thus shutting down the entire federal government. (President Clinton also did this with vetoes in the 1990s.) Of course, the biased media blamed the Republicans for shutting down the government, mimicking the Democrat talking points. Speaker Boehner caved within a week. The ultimate in foolishness is starting the defund strategy without being willing to finish it. Boehner appeared weak for caving, and Republicans received negative press without gaining anything with their efforts.

The House did not set up their strategy properly. Usually, there are twelve major appropriations bills that are used to fund the federal government. The House should have passed all bills except the one containing ObamaCare funding, localizing the fight to one bill rather than all of the bills. Done strategically correctly, Boehner could have forced the president and Senate to either pass the Health and Human Services funding bill with no ObamaCare funding, or shut down those agencies.

To be successful, defunding must be carried through to its end. Democrats *are* the party of big federal government. They and their supporters *depend* on the government. So if the shutdown lasts a week or so the only damage will be to the Republicans. If the shutdown lasts multiple weeks or months, *Democrats and their*

Appendix 11: Defunding Agencies and Government Shutdowns

supporters feel the pain. So conservatives must stand firm. Democrats will eventually cave; their supporters will demand it to stop a prolonged shutdown.

There should be a strategy to deal with the media, which can be counted on to begin running horror stories about poor people who are starving or dying because the federal government program XYZ has stopped – because of the government shutdown. It's what the media always does. In this case, the House defunded ObamaCare, while funding everything else. So every media story should have been blamed on the Senate. The House needed a rapid response team. Within 24 hours of a media story, they could have passed a spending bill funding program XYZ described in the story at the same level as the previous year. Then called on the Senate to pass the bill, as is, immediately to prevent suffering caused by lack of funding. The House could have kept a running tally of the spending bills sent to the Senate, those that passed the Senate, and those not voted on by the Senate. The House could have continued to ask reporters why the Senate was not passing bills. Be especially sure to focus on funding for the troops and Social Security recipients. Scold the Senate for playing politics if they do not immediately pass these crucial bills.

Sidebar: In reality, during this episode, there were a number of establishment Republicans in both the House and Senate who went to microphones and touted the Democrat line – blaming conservatives for the shutdown. Representatives like this in the GOP will prevent defunding from ever working. Of course, these Republicans do not want a return to constitutional limits on government either.

Appendix 12: Federal Government Abuse of Freedoms

This appendix will examine government abuse with respect to harassment of political enemies, and excessive para-military force by agencies.

Harassment of Political Enemies
The American citizens cannot be free if their government abuses its power to take away freedoms. One of the trademarks of authoritarian regimes is their use of government power to control the population. This practice has never been the norm in the US, where political free speech is embedded in the [First] Amendment. However is speech free if a government agency attacks a citizen for their speech?

Under the Obama Administration, the IRS and other agencies have begun using their power to intimidate political opponents who speak out. There are numerous examples since Obama's election of citizens who "suddenly" are subject to audits after speaking out against Obama or big government. Did the White House issue orders? Probably not. But government force is obviously being used by some high level political appointees to intimidate the president's political foes. The following account is by Wayne Root, a classmate of Obama and a vocal critic. He and a number of others have been audited by the IRS.

> Is this the IRS scandal's smoking gun?
>
> This scandal is much bigger than Tea Party groups. It is a widespread criminal conspiracy to attack, punish and silence Obama's critics and political opposition.
>
> The second of Nixon's Articles of Impeachment was for the crime of using the IRS to punish his political opponents. Don't look now, but we've got another Nixon in the White House. The difference is that Barack Obama's IRS scandal makes Richard Nixon look like a minor league rookie.
>
> This scandal is much bigger than Tea Party groups. It is a widespread criminal conspiracy to attack, punish and silence Obama's critics and political opposition.
>
> Tea Parties are just one part of this widespread conspiracy. I was personally targeted along with many others including

Appendix 12: Federal Government Abuse of Freedoms

Dr. Benjamin Carson; former GOP Senate candidate Christine O'Donnell; a stage 4 terminal cancer victim (after appearing on Fox News); conservative filmmakers like Jerry Mullen (Dinesh D'Souza's partner) and Joel Gilbert; Christian minister, Billy Graham; Catherine Engelbrecht, who was targeted over 15 times by the IRS and other government agencies after founding her Tea Party; and numerous prominent GOP donors.

There is a clear pattern of a criminal conspiracy to use the IRS to intimidate and punish critics of the current administration. The only question is: can Obama be connected? If he can, this becomes the biggest scandal in modern U.S. political history....
- FoxNews.com. Wayne Allyn Root. March 04, 2014.

Sidebar: This is a perfect example of media bias explored in Chapter 24. When Republican Richard Nixon was thought to have looked into using the IRS to intimidate his opponents, it became significant news on the major networks (ABC, CBS, NBC) of the day. It was listed as an Article of Impeachment against Nixon. When Obama appears to have used the IRS there is little if any coverage. The networks would likely be outraged if Articles of Impeachment were brought up against Obama.

Catherine Engelbrecht has perhaps been the most targeted "enemy". She is guilty of a double whammy: founding both a TEA Party group and a voter integrity group. Is it a coincidence that a group dedicated to election integrity might be greatly disliked by Chicago-trained politicians? Chicago has long been viewed as the vote fraud capital of America.

How Chicago and Obama Globalized Voter Fraud
Chicago has a long tradition of padding its vote totals by placing homeless and deceased persons on its voter registration list. Jim Laski, who once served as the City Clerk of Chicago, second in power only to the mayor, noted in his book My Fall From Grace that fraudulent voters were registered to addresses that included cemeteries, municipal buildings, and taverns.
- www.americanthinker.com. Michael Bargo Jr. December 30, 2012.

Appendix 12: Federal Government Abuse of Freedoms

Back to Engelbrecht. She became the target of audits and visits by numerous federal agencies. It is hard to imagine that so many agencies taking interest in her and her husband, in such a short time, was not somehow coordinated.

> True Scandal
> A tea-party group targeted by Democrats gets attention from the IRS—and the FBI, OSHA, and the ATF.
>
> Yet as news emerges that the Internal Revenue Service wielded its power to obstruct conservative groups, [Catherine Engelbrecht's] story... raises questions about whether other federal agencies have used their executive powers to target those deemed political enemies.
>
> [Catherine founded] two organizations: King Street Patriots, a local community group that hosts weekly discussions on personal and economic freedoms; and True the Vote, which seeks to prevent voter fraud and trains volunteers to work as election monitors. It also registers voters, attempts to validate voter-registration lists, and pursues fraud reports to push for prosecution if illegal activity has occurred.
>
> Cleta Mitchell, a lawyer who specializes in representing conservative organizations, says that the Engelbrecht family's experience is "just the tip of the iceberg. . . . I think there's definitely a Chicago-politics-style enemies list in this administration, and I think it permeates this branch of the federal government."
>
> - www.nationalreview.com. Jillian Kay Melchior. May 20, 2013.

The article goes on to document the federal government harassing Engelbrecht's business and family.

- The Federal Bureau of Investigation came several times with questions.
- The IRS visited the Engelbrechts' shop and conducted an on-site audit of both their business and their personal returns.
- The Bureau of Alcohol, Tobacco, Firearms and Explosives (ATF) launched an unscheduled audit of their business.
- The IRS initiated multiple rounds of "approval" questions for both Catherine's groups.

Appendix 12: Federal Government Abuse of Freedoms

- The Occupational Safety and Health Administration audited to Engelbrecht's business and levied $25,000 in fines.

While likely the most extreme example of harassment, Catherine Engelbrecht was not alone. Over 40 other conservative groups were also harassed: mostly by the IRS as they attempted to receive tax-exempt status.

The American Center for Law and Justice has filed a lawsuit in federal court on behalf of these groups. The suit alleges the IRS violated constitutional law and 1st Amendment rights of these groups.

> ACLJ suit against IRS grows to 41 groups
> The ACLJ's amended complaint states: IRS agents "working in offices from California to Washington, D.C., pulled applications from conservative organizations, delaying processing those applications for sometimes well over a year, then made probing and unconstitutional requests for additional information that often required applicants to disclose, among other things, donor lists, direct and indirect communications with members of legislative bodies, Internet passwords and user names, copies of social media and other Internet postings, and even the political and charitable activities of family members."
> - www.washingtontimes.com. Cheryl K. Chumley June 26, 2013.

Para-Military Units in Federal Agencies
As if using federal agencies to harass political opponents wasn't enough. The federal government has begun to arm agents in multiple agencies. The Wall Street Journal has reported on large numbers of agents now carrying weapons. Do the Departments of Housing and Urban Development, and Health and Human Services really need hundreds of armed enforcement agents?

> The Government's Growing Police Force
> Government agencies of all stripes have become the front-line enforcers for many of the laws Congress has written the past four decades. Currently, there are believed to be around 25,000 sworn law enforcement officers in federal agencies not traditionally associated with crime-fighting. Among

Appendix 12: Federal Government Abuse of Freedoms

them are 3,812 criminal investigators working for departments other than Treasury, Justice, Defense and what is now Homeland Security.

Federal Agency	1973	1998	2008	2011
Department of Agriculture	225	378	292	291
Department of Commerce	16	118	256	253
Department of Education	0	78	89	95
Department of Energy	0	42	69	77
Department of Health and Human Services	1	398	577	686
Department of Housing and Urban Development	66	171	228	264
Department of Interior	77	235	495	547
Department of Labor	2	127	239	225
Department of State	1	46	91	109
Department of Transportation	0	96	99	101
Department of Veterans Affairs	5	103	181	207
Environmental Protection Agency	0	258	239	265
Federal Deposit Insurance Corporation	0	37	35	45
Federal Housing Finance Agency	0	0	0	14
General Services Administration	62	116	65	69
National Aeronautics and Space Administration	0	50	52	62
Nuclear Regulatory Commission	0	53	46	44
Office of Personnel Management	0	10	26	30
Railroad Retirement Board	0	17	16	19
Small Business Administration	0	38	34	38
Social Security Administration	7	228	283	289
U.S. Agency for International Development	39	19	27	30
Other	6	34	40	52
TOTAL criminal investigators in non-traditional civilian agencies	507	2652	3479	3812

- www.online.wsj.com. December 17, 2011.

The multitude of federal agencies are buying large amounts of ammunition too, either for training purposes, or for possible future use.

US Postal Service Joins in Federal Ammo Purchases
Add the U.S. Postal Service to the list of federal agencies seeking to purchase what some Second Amendment activists say are alarmingly large quantities of ammunition.... It's not just the USPS that is stocking up on ammo.

A little more than a year ago, the Social Security Administration put in a request for 174,000 rounds of ".357 Sig 125 grain bonded jacketed hollow-point" bullets.

Appendix 12: Federal Government Abuse of Freedoms

Before that, it was the Department of Agriculture requesting 320,000 rounds. More recently, the Department of Homeland Security raised eyebrows with its request for 450 million rounds — at about the same time the FBI separately sought 100 million hollow-point rounds.

The National Oceanic and Atmospheric Administration also requested 46,000 rounds.

Philip Van Cleave, president of the Virginia Citizens Defense League, asked: why exactly does a weather service need ammunition?

"NOAA — really? They have a need? One just doesn't know why they're doing this," he said. "The problem is, all these agencies have their own SWAT teams, their own police departments, which is crazy. In theory, it was supposed to be the U.S. marshals that was the armed branch for the federal government."

- Newsmax.com. Cheryl K. Chumley. 15 April 15, 2014.

The federal agents aren't just carrying sidearms either. It appears a number of the armed agents are part of agency SWAT teams with para-military training.

<u>The United States of SWAT?</u>
Military-style units from government agencies are wreaking havoc on non-violent citizens.

Dozens of federal agencies now have Special Weapons and Tactics (SWAT) teams to further an expanding definition of their missions. It's not controversial that the Secret Service and the Bureau of Prisons have them. But what about the Department of Agriculture, the Railroad Retirement Board, the Tennessee Valley Authority, the Office of Personnel Management, the Consumer Product Safety Commission, and the U.S. Fish and Wildlife Service? All of these have their own SWAT units and are part of a worrying trend towards the militarization of federal agencies — not to mention local police forces.

"Law-enforcement agencies across the U.S., at every level of government, have been blurring the line between police officer and soldier," journalist Radley Balko writes in his

Appendix 12: Federal Government Abuse of Freedoms

2013 book Rise of the Warrior Cop

The proliferation of paramilitary federal SWAT teams inevitably brings abuses that have nothing to do with either drugs or terrorism. Many of the raids they conduct are against harmless, often innocent, Americans who typically are accused of non-violent civil or administrative violations.

Brian Walsh, a senior legal analyst with the Heritage Foundation, says it is inexplicable why so many federal agencies need to be battle-ready: "If these agencies occasionally have a legitimate need for force to execute a warrant, they should be required to call a real law-enforcement agency, one that has a better sense of perspective. The FBI, for example, can draw upon its vast experience to determine whether there is an actual need for a dozen SWAT agents."

- www.nationalreview.com. John Fund. April 18, 2014.

The article mentions two cases of SWAT style tactics used against nonviolent offenders: by the Department of Education, and the Food and Drug Administration.

- Kenneth Wright of Stockton, Calif. was "visited" by a SWAT team from the U.S. Department of Education in June 2011. Agents battered down the door of his home at 6 a.m., dragged him outside in his boxer shorts, and handcuffed him as they put his three children (ages 3, 7, and 11) in a police car for two hours while they searched his home. The raid was to gather information on Wright's estranged wife, Michelle, who hadn't been living with him and was suspected of college financial-aid fraud.

- A SWAT team from the Food and Drug Administration raided the farm of Dan Allgyer of Lancaster, Pa. His crime was shipping unpasteurized milk across state lines to a cooperative of young women with children in Washington, D.C., called Grass Fed on the Hill. Raw milk can be sold in Pennsylvania, but it is illegal to transport it across state lines. The raid forced Allgyer to close down his business.

There have been other instances of these agency "SWAT forces" in action. An Environmental Protection Agency team led an armed raid in Alaska, where it appeared no show of force was needed.

> ### Alaska governor calls for investigation of armed, EPA-led task force
> Alaska Gov. Sean Parnell has called for a special counsel to investigate the actions of the EPA-led, Alaska Environmental Crimes Task Force that caused fear and consternation among small-scale gold miners... Between Aug. 18 and 24, eight armed agents -- all wearing body armor and jackets with the word POLICE emblazoned on them -- descended on 30 placer gold mining operations... Most are small, family-run mines that use nearby streams and rivers to separate gold from mud, rock, and dirt.
> - alaskadispatch.com. Sean Doogan. September 5, 2013.

The Bureau of Land Management demonstrated it has a significant SWAT style force at its disposal as well. It used the quasi-military force to surround a ranch and intimidate the rancher and his family.

> ### Last Man Standing
> A two-decades-old battle between a Nevada rancher and the Bureau of Land Management (BLM) has resulted in officials armed with machine guns surrounding the ranch and forcibly removing the owner's cattle, according to the rancher's family...
>
> "The battle's been going on for 20 years," Bundy told the Washington Free Beacon. "What's happened the last two weeks, the United States government, the bureaus are getting this army together and they're going to get their job done and they're going to prove two things. They're going to prove they can do it, and they're gonna prove that they have unlimited power, and that they control the policing power over this public land. That's what they're trying to prove."
>
> Bundy said the government has brought everything but tanks and rocket launchers. "They're carrying the same things a soldier would," he said. "Automatic weapons, sniper rifles, top communication, top surveillance equipment, lots of vehicles. It's heavy soldier type equipment."
>
> His wife, Carol Bundy, said that roughly 200 armed agents

Appendix 12: Federal Government Abuse of Freedoms

from the BLM and FBI are stationed around their land, located about 75 miles outside of Las Vegas. Helicopters circle the premises, and the airspace and nearby roads remain blocked.

"The story is a lot about the cattle, but the bigger story is about our loss of freedom," Carol Bundy added. "They have come and taken over this whole corner of the county. They've taken over policing power, they've taken over our freedom, and they're stealing cattle."

"And our sheriff says he just doesn't have authority, our governor says he doesn't have authority, and we're saying, why are we a state?".... "This is just about power of the government," Carol Bundy said.

Nevada Gov. Brian Sandoval (R.) voiced his concern about so-called "First Amendment Areas," designated locations set up by the BLM where citizens can protest the removal..... "Most disturbing to me is the BLM's establishment of a 'First Amendment Area' that tramples upon Nevadans' fundamental rights under the U.S. Constitution," he said in a statement Tuesday.

"To that end, I have advised the BLM that such conduct is offensive to me and countless others and that the 'First Amendment Area' should be dismantled immediately," he said. "No cow justifies the atmosphere of intimidation which currently exists nor the limitation of constitutional rights that are sacred to all Nevadans. The BLM needs to reconsider its approach to this matter and act accordingly."

Sandoval also said his office has received numerous complaints about the BLM's conduct, including road closures and "other disturbances."

    - Washington Free Beacon. Elizabeth Harrington. April 8, 2014

In both of these cases the state governors spoke out that the federal government agents abused constitutional rights of the citizens. The federal government didn't need heavily armed agents. It could have worked through county sheriffs and avoided the drama. Fortunately, no one was killed in these instances. **The federal government using this kind of firepower to intimidate citizens is a gross violation of freedom of the citizenry.** The

Appendix 12: Federal Government Abuse of Freedoms

federal agency SWAT teams need to be disbanded. The federal government cannot not have the power to terrorize citizens, *if* the citizens are to have freedom.

Referring to Chapter 20, many of these federal agencies are not constitutionally authorized. Their responsibilities are left to the states according to our national law.

Bibliography – Resources - References

American History
Five Thousand Year Leap. 28 Great Ideas that Changed the World. W. Cleon Skousen

Founding Father Quotes www.foundingfatherquotes.com

Fourth Turning, The. An American Prophecy. William Strauss and Neil Howe. 1997.

George Washington, Thomas Jefferson & Slavery in Virginia. David Barton. 1/2000 www.wallbuilders.com

Manumission Takes Careful Planning and Plenty of Savvy After 1723. Linda Rowe. Colonial Williamsburg Website – Historical Research.

New Deal or Raw Deal?: How FDR's Economic Legacy Has Damaged America. Burton W. Folsom Jr. 2009.

One Nation Under Man? The Worldview War Between Christians and the Secular Left. Brannon Howse.

Procon.org www.procon.org

Real Benjamin Franklin, The. (TRBF) Andrew Allison, Richard Maxfield, W. Cleon Skousen. 2008

Real George Washington, The. (TRGW) Jay A. Parry, Andrew M. Allison, W. Cleon Skousen. 2008

Real Thomas Jefferson, The. (TRTJ) Andrew Allison, Richard Maxfield, Delynn Cook, W. Cleon Skousen. 2008

Rediscovering God in America. Reflections on the Role of Faith in Our Nation's History and Future. Newt Gingrich.

ReligiousLiberty.Com www.religiousliberty.com

Bible
Bible Passages: NIV Translation. www.biblica.com/bible
NIV Translation. www.biblegateway.com

Concordia Self Study Bible. NIV. 1986.

How to Read the Bible for All Its Worth. Douglas Stuart and Gordon D. Fee. 2003.

Bibliography – Resources - References

Biblical Support
90 Minutes in Heaven: A True Story of Death and Life. Don Piper with Cecil Murphey. 2004.
Eusebius - The Church History: A New Translation with Commentary. Dr. Paul L. Maier. 1999..
More Than A Carpenter. Josh McDowell. 1977, 2005.

Constitution
Commentaries on the Constitution of the United States. Vols. 1, 2, 3. 1833. Supreme Court Justice Joseph Story. Google.com/books.
Heritage Guide to the Constitution, The. The Heritage Foundation. 2005.

Creation/Evolution
All About the Journey. Theory of Evolution. www.allaboutthejourney.org
Center for Scientific Creation, The. www.creationscience.com
Creation Revolution .com : www.creationrevolution.com
Defense of Literal Days in the Creation Week. A. Detroit Baptist Seminary Journal 5:97–123. Fall 2000. McCabe, Robert.
Dinosaur Protein Is Primordial. http://crev.info/content/ 110726-dinosaur_protein_is_primordial July 26, 2011
Expelled: No Intelligence Allowed. Ben Stein Documentary. 2008.
First Cell's Survival Odds Not in Evolution's Favor. Institute for Creation Research. Brian Thomas, M.S. September 8, 2011
History of the World from a Biblical Perspective. Critical Path for Biblical Chronology. www.bibleworldhistory.com
In the Beginning: Compelling Evidence for Creation and the Flood. Dr. Walt Brown. 2008
In Six Days. Why 50 Scientists Choose to Believe in Creation. Dr. John Ashton. 2001
Refuting Evolution. Jonathan Sarfati. 2008
Theologian: Genesis Means What it Says! Jonathan Sarfati. Posted on August 30, 2011. creationrevolution.com

Bibliography – Resources - References

Media Bias

Bias: A CBS Insider Exposes How the Media Distorts the News. Bernard Goldberg. 2003.

Left Turn: How Liberal Media Bias Distorts the American Mind. Timothy Groseclose. 2011

Media Malpractice. John Zeigler. Documentary, 115 minutes. 2009.

Sarah Palin: Going Rogue, an American life. Sarah Palin. 2009

Poverty

"Air Conditioning, Cable TV, and an Xbox: What Is Poverty in the United States Today?" Executive Summary. Heritage Foundation. Robert Rector and Rachel Sheffield

Welfare the False and the True: Part II. June 13, 2011. disciplenations.wordpress.com

Ratings for Congress

Christian Coalition Congressional Scorecards.
www.cc.org/voter_education

Club for Growth Congressional Scorecard:
www.clubforgrowth.org//projects/

For America. www.foramerica.org/home/

Heritage Action for America Scorecard.
heritageactionscorecard.com/scorecard/index.html

Madison Project Congressional Performance Index.
www.conservativevotingrecords.com

Other

Project Veritas. www.theprojectveritas.com James O'Keefe's investigative journalist website.

Real Crash: America's Coming Bankruptcy, The – How to Save Yourself and Your Country. Peter Schiff. 2012.

STAND (Staying True to America's National Destiny). www.standamerica.us